CW00764848

# THE HELEN FORRESTER OMNIBUS

*by the same author*

THREE WOMEN OF LIVERPOOL
LIVERPOOL DAISY
THURSDAY'S CHILD
THE MONEYLENDERS OF SHAHPUR
THE LATCHKEY KID
YES, MAMA
THE LEMON TREE

# THE HELEN FORRESTER OMNIBUS

*Twopence to Cross
the Mersey*

*Liverpool Miss*

*By the Waters
of Liverpool*

*Lime Street at Two*

**THE BODLEY HEAD**
LONDON

This edition first published 1990
Reprinted 1990
The Bodley Head Ltd, 20 Vauxhall Bridge Road, London SW1V 2SA

*Twopence to Cross the Mersey*
© Jamunadevi Bhatia 1974

*Liverpool Miss*
(first published under the title *Minerva's Stepchild*)
© Jamunadevi Bhatia 1979

*By the Waters of Liverpool*
© Jamunadevi Bhatia 1981

*Lime Street at Two*
© Jamunadevi Bhatia 1985

A CIP catalogue record for this book
is available from the British Library

ISBN 0-370-31503-0

Printed in Great Britain by
Mackays of Chatham PLC

# Contents

*Twopence to Cross
the Mersey*

*To the Liverpool City Police*

# Chapter one

Liverpool is a city through which visitors pass on their way to other places. It is to them a dull world of shipping and commerce which sprawls untidily along the north bank of the River Mersey. Many of them will not know that it has a sister port, Birkenhead, on the opposite bank, which is linked to it by ferry-boats, a railway tunnel and a road tunnel. Beyond Birkenhead lie the small seaside towns of the Wirral peninsula and behind them is pleasant countryside. My widowed grandmother lived in the Wirral, and here, while visiting her, I spent the happiest days of my childhood, on sandy beaches or in wind-swept gardens. I remember with love the rain-soaked hills looking out on to stormy seas and the turbulent estuary of the Mersey.

It used to cost twopence to cross the river on the ferry-boat from Liverpool to Birkenhead. Twopence is not a very large sum, but if one has no money, the river is a real barrier, and, during the Depression years, was an impassable one to many of the poverty-stricken people of Liverpool.

Not so many years ago, I took my little Canadian-born son to see Liverpool and the places of my childhood.

'Did you live here when you were small, Ma?' he asked incredulously, his strong North American accent sounding strange amid the thick, nasal speech around him.

'Yes, I was in Liverpool for part of my life.'

'My, it's dirty! Do you mind it being dirty?'

I smiled, seeing it all through his stranger's eyes, eyes accustomed to new buildings, miles of neon signs, miles of prairie golden with wheat or diamond-white with snow.

I laughed down at him a little ruefully.

'Yes, at first I did mind. Not now, though. I soon learned that people and cities which do the hard, unpleasant work of the world can't help getting dirty. Liverpool's a wonderful place when you get to know it.'

He looked at me derisively and said, with all the cold logic of a five-year-old, 'They should use more soap and wash the streets.'

My smile faded, as cold shadows of winters past crept over me. That was how I had felt, when first I had really looked at the city and not passed through it as a traveller. God, how I had minded the dirt! How terrified I had been! How menacingly grotesque the people had looked; children of the industrial revolution, nurtured for generations on poor food in smoke-laden air, grim and twisted, foul-mouthed and coarse, shaped in this strange gloomy world to serve the trade to the Americas. And I, a middle-class girl of the gentler south-west of England who had been shielded from the rougher side of life by a private school system and obedient servants, had nearly gone mad with panic when, with little warning, I had been thrown amongst them. Gone was the protection of money and privilege; I had to make what I could of this grimy city and its bitterly humorous inhabitants and share with them their suffering during the Depression years.

I clutched my son's confiding little hand in mine, as, for a second, I felt again the fear which had enveloped me that January day in 1931, when, at the age of eleven and a half, I arrived in Liverpool, not to pass through it as I had done before, but to live in it.

It seemed to me that it was not my son's hand which I held so tightly but the hand of my youngest sister, Avril, and that I could hear her snivelling, as we looked out from the entrance of Lime Street Station and saw, through icy, driving rain, a city which seemed to be slowly dying, unloved and unsung, in the Depression of the nineteen-thirties.

# Chapter two

'Shut up, Avril,' I said sternly, between chattering teeth. 'Everything is going to be all right.'

'I'm cold and I'm hungry.' The wail threatened to become one of three-year-old Avril's howling tantrums, as she started to kick off her patent-leather shoes and tear at her blue satin bonnet-strings.

I loosened the wet elastic of my black school hat from under my chin. The hat, as usual, had been crammed down on top of a large ribbon bow, which held my front hair ruthlessly scraped back from a too high forehead. My spectacles were sprayed with rain and I could not see very well as I peered short-sightedly down Lime Street.

I lifted Avril up and hugged her to my damp school uniform.

'Behave yourself,' I ordered sharply. 'We are all hungry. You must be brave until Daddy comes back to collect us.'

Fortunately, I did not know that my father, at that moment walking the streets of Liverpool in search of shelter for his sick wife and seven children, had no real idea of what to do to mitigate the catastrophe which had struck him. I presumed that adults always knew what they were doing and the likely outcome of their actions. I did not know that my mother, lying on a stretcher in the ladies' waiting-room, her six-week-old son beside her, was sweating with pain after a major abdominal operation and was bordering on a nervous breakdown. I could not understand why we could not go to stay with my grandmother, who lived only a few miles away in the Wirral peninsula. No one had told me she had quarrelled violently with her son and his wife, whom she condemned jointly as worthless spendthrifts, and would have no more to do with us.

Busy with childish affairs of school and girl friends, I had noticed only that during the last few weeks my parents' friends were not dropping in for a drink as frequently as usual; in fact the house had been almost free of visitors for a couple of months.

Alan, who was a year younger than I, had pointed out to me a few months earlier that Mother's wonderful collection of Georgian silver had vanished from the antique sideboard on which it was normally displayed, and I had asked my mother where it had gone.

11

'Girls should not poke their noses into the business of grown-ups,' I had been told tartly, and I had retreated to Alan for consolation.

'Perhaps it has been sold,' he had whispered uneasily, as he ran his fingers through his corn-coloured hair.

'Why?' I asked, my eyes goggled in surprise.

He stared at me reflectively, his wide, blue eyes troubled. 'I don't know. There is something wrong. Mary Ann packed her suitcase and left on Saturday.'

Mary Ann was our housemaid, a jolly, outspoken girl.

'I thought she had gone home to visit her mother for a few days – that's what she told me.'

'I don't think so. She seems to have taken everything with her. She even asked Cook for her curling-tongs back – Cook was always borrowing them.'

Our uneasiness grew while Mother was in hospital, until an idle word from a schoolfriend gave us a clue.

Father had done a mysterious thing called 'going bankrupt', a not uncommon occurrence in the world of 1930, but strange to me. I had heard vaguely that going bankrupt was an American disease which had struck Wall Street in New York, and that Americans committed suicide when this happened to them; mentally, I saw dozens of them hurling themselves off the tops of skyscrapers, and I wondered where Father would find a skyscraper.

Father was a public school man who had been sent to boarding school by his widowed mother when he was only six years old; he had left it at nineteen to join the army in 1914. My mother, an orphan, had been brought up by nuns. Neither had had any training in the management of a family or a domestic budget, and they had enjoyed a high standard of living by being permanently in debt. Further, they had had seven children. Bankruptcy was inevitable, once the Depression set in and dividends dried up.

The remainder of our servants left in a body, while Mother was still in hospital, and I was left to manage the home as best I could, until we moved to Liverpool. One of our unpaid domestics took the opportunity, while my parents were absent, to take away my mother's entire wardrobe, leaving her only the outfit she had been wearing when she was whisked into hospital.

Father had no knowledge of the legal rights of a bankrupt to clothing and bedding, so he sent the key of our house to his main creditor, a moneylender, with instructions to sell the house and its contents, and to reimburse himself from the proceeds. From a misguided sense of honour, he left everything we possessed, except the clothing in which he and his family were dressed, taking only a pair of blankets in which to wrap my mother and the new baby, Edward. Then, with his last ten pounds in cash, he bought tickets on the train to Liverpool, which was his birthplace.

He remembered Liverpool as a bustling, wealthy city and hoped to find employment there, perhaps as an accountant, in a shipping company. Having lived for years in prosperous, southern market-towns, he could not visualise what the Depression was doing to the north of England. He could not imagine that a man who desired work would not be able to find it.

Liverpool looked a dreadfully dismal place to my untutored eyes. Water swirled along the gutters, carrying a horrid collection of garbage. Across the road, the fine Corinthian pillars of St George's Hall looked like a row of rotting teeth, and to my right, down William Brown Street, marched a series of equally large, black buildings. When I peeked further out of the station I could see the entrance of a big theatre, the Empire, and further along at the corner was a public house, the Legs o' Man, near which a number of seamen stood laughing and joking, oblivious of the rain. Much later on, a sailor told me that sooner or later everybody in the world passed the Legs o' Man and if you waited long enough you could meet there anybody you cared to look for; certainly, it was a great meeting-place.

Along the pavement men in shabby cloth caps shuffled from litter-bin to litter-bin to sift through the garbage for food and cigarette-ends. In the gutter stood four unemployed Welsh miners, caps held hopefully out while they sang over and over again in sad tenor voices 'Land of our Fathers' and 'All through the Night'.

'Are you lost?'

I jumped and Avril stopped wailing. A policeman, water running down his cape and helmet, was bending over us, his red face concerned.

'No, thank you,' I said primly, and, since he continued to look down at us doubtfully, I added, 'Mummy is in the waiting-room.' He smiled in a friendly fashion. 'Better go back to her, luv,' he said, 'Lime Street is no place for a nice young lady – and ye'll get wet.'

Reluctantly, I retraced my steps to the waiting-room.

Father had been away four hours or more. Baby Edward had not been fed and was crying lustily. Brian and Tony, aged six and five respectively, were playing tag round and round the high, varnished benches. Despite his determined effort at playing, I could see that Brian was afraid. Taut and dark as an Indian, so highly strung that he suffered constantly from nightmares, his little hands were clenched tight and his heart-shaped face was grim. Tony was playing the game with his usual cool care, watching his elder brother closely so as to anticipate every move he made. His mind seemed to work with such intelligence that it was as if he had been born with a brain already mature and furnished with knowledge. Sometimes when I stroked his silky, flaxen head I was almost unnerved by the idea of the latent power beneath my hand.

Fiona, aged nine, was still sitting silently by my mother, nursing her favourite doll, her huge, pale-blue eyes wide with dumb fear. We all loved Fiona with unquestioning devotion. She never had tantrums as Avril and

I did; she never seemed to get dirty or forget her table manners. I always had a book in my hand, hated to miss school and loved an argument; Fiona adored her large doll family, accepted school but learned little. She was our placid refuge when we had been spanked, which was not infrequently, but now *she* needed asylum.

Mother lay on the stretcher, her eyes closed, her face ethereally white. An empty teacup on the bench beside her spoke of the kindness of the lavatory attendant, who stood leaning against her cupboard door, smoking a cigarette and regarding us curiously. There was no one else in the waiting-room.

None of us had eaten since breakfast, a meal of toast hastily consumed, and now it was after four o'clock. I knew that my mother had no money in her handbag, so it was no good offering to go and buy something to eat from the station restaurant.

I went up to my mother. A tear lay on her cheek. 'Are you all right, Mummy?'

'Yes, dear. I got up and walked for a few moments a little while ago.'

'You'll soon be better, Mummy?'

'Yes – yes, I have to be.'

I picked Edward up from beside her and, holding him against my shoulder, tried to stop his healthy bellows for food by walking up and down with him and patting his tiny back.

Alan had been kneeling on a bench by the window, watching the horses and drays in the station yard. Now he came and walked with me. We did not talk; both our hearts were too heavy.

I knew that Mother had been ill after Edward was born and had been in hospital until Christmas Eve, a scant eight days ago. I realised, with a sense of shock, that Christmas and New Year had passed uncelebrated, lost in a foggy nightmare of quarrels, recrimination and general disorder in the house. Mother had discharged herself from hospital, before the doctors thought she should, so that we could come to Liverpool.

As I clucked sympathetically at Edward, it seemed madness to me to embark on such a journey. I could not understand why the moneylender could not wait a few days more before taking legal action, so that Mother could get a little stronger before she moved. I had no conception of the panic gripping my parents, a panic which had made them lose completely any sense of proportion. They had been brought up in a little world of moneyed people, insulated by their private means from any real difficulties or hardships. When there was no money, they had no idea what to do, beyond trying to obtain a 'suitable' position. A moneylender was, to them, a ruthless Scrooge, and I do not think that it occurred to them that if he had been apprised of Mother's illness he might have had a little compassion. And so they compounded their troubles to an unnecessary degree.

My relief was overwhelming when my father, soaking wet, came into the waiting-room, with a muttered apology to the attendant. He went straight to my mother. She opened her eyes and surveyed him sullenly.

'I have obtained two rooms. Not very good. Just for a week.' He sounded breathless and on edge. 'Had to pay in advance. Walked back. I'm going to get a cab.'

My mother closed her eyes, and my heart sank. They were trying not to talk to one another again.

Father vanished again into the vast cavern of the station, and Mother told me to help the boys get their overcoats on.

A few minutes later, Mother was carried on the stretcher with the aid of a porter to a taxi-cab, the children trailing behind and the baby and Avril still crying. The procession caused some interest in the station, and I remember my face burning with embarrassment under the shadow of my velour school hat. Well-bred people, I had had it drummed into me, did not draw attention to themselves.

Mother crawled into the cab, and the porter folded up the stretcher, which belonged to the railway company. Somehow we all squeezed into the taxi, a hungry, forlorn group too tired to talk.

# Chapter three

A stout, untidy blonde opened the door to us. A suffocating odour of unwashed bodies, old cooking and cats rolled over us. The woman beamed at us, however, and welcomed Father like an old friend. She helped him assist Mother into a room so shabby and so dirty that I could honestly say that I had never seen anything like it before. Next to it was a bedroom with two double beds crammed into it. There were no sheets or pillow-cases, just greasy pillows and grey blankets.

Mother sank on to a broken settee, while our landlady looked us over.

'You can keep coal out back and use t' kitchen and bathroom. There's eight other tenants upstairs and me and me sons on the top floor, so keep as quiet as yer can.' Her battered face showed pity. 'Ah'll give yer enough coal to start a fire. Coalman'll be along the street this afternoon and you can get some then.'

The room was very cold and Mother looked round it disdainfully, but she said 'Thank you' in response to this offer of fuel.

'Come on, luv,' the landlady addressed me. 'There's a booket in that cupboard. We'll fill it and you can bring it back.'

After a trip through linoleumed passages and a littered, stinking kitchen to a coal-house by the back door, I staggered back with a bucket of coal, some wood chips and a newspaper. After much anxious effort, Father got a fire going. It was the first time he had ever made a fire.

Tony and Brian, usually the best of friends, had been bickering irritably for some time, and they now turned on Alan, who was himself fretful with hunger. Furiously, he cuffed the younger boys and made them cry.

Father snapped at him to stop.

Alan, usually so cheerful, stopped, and said heavily, 'When shall we be able to have something to eat?'

'How much money have you?'asked Mother. She had sat silently staring into space, while we had divested ourselves of our coats and Father had lit the fire.

Father went through his pockets, and laid the results of his search on the settee, so that we could see the small pile of coins in the light of the bare electric bulb hanging from the ceiling.

'Two and ninepence,' he announced helplessly.

16

Thirty-three precious pennies would buy quite a lot in those days, though they would not last long in a family the size of ours.

In a dull monotone, Mother upbraided him bitterly about the mess he had got us all into, and Father snarled back that she had never been any help to him. Finally, Edward's wailing drew his attention to more immediate concerns, and he said, 'There is a little corner shop down the road. We could at least get some milk for Edward.'

'And for me,' said Avril, thrusting her small chin aggressively forward.

'Be quiet, Avril,' I hissed, afraid that my parents would start to quarrel again.

'Won't,' replied Avril defiantly, but she did keep quiet thereafter.

Finally, it was decided that since Father was already wet through he might as well get a bit more wet by going out to the shop and buying all the food he could for the money he had.

When he had departed, the children crouched around the miserable fire, and Mother managed to change Edward's nappy. We had only three nappies with us, and the baby had not been changed since we had set out that morning. He was, therefore, in a disgusting condition. Mother gave me the nappy she had removed, told me to find the bathroom, wash the dirty garment and bring it back to dry by the fire. I wandered off, sick and dejected, and did the best I could with cold water and no soap in a Victorian bathroom which stank of half a century of neglect.

Afterwards, Alan and I went to the kitchen, where a few dust-covered dishes were strewn along open shelves. We collected them and washed them under the only tap and, with frozen fingers, carried them back to our room. With nervous and uncertain gestures, we laid them on the table, which was covered with torn, stained oilcloth. We also had hopefully brought with us a saucepan and a frying-pan, since there was no stove in the kitchen on which to cook.

Our spirits rose when Father returned with milk, two loaves of bread, margarine, tea, sugar and a small packet of sausages. He had also brought a twopenny packet of Woodbines. With cigarettes in their mouths, our parents became a little more civil to each other.

Under Mother's instructions, I made a feed for Edward and then fed him: he was ravenous and took the whole small bottle full. Father cooked sausages on the smoking fire, found a knife in the kitchen and cut the bread and spread it with margarine. We sat around on whatever we could find and ate a sausage apiece in our fingers. He managed to boil a pan of water and make tea in it. Mother drank much and ate little, refusing a sausage which was happily snatched up by Avril. Father finally ate, and only afterwards I realised that he had not had a sausage, and I felt a crushing sense of guilt about it.

Our landlady called down the stairs to say that she could hear the coalman coming, and my father looked aghast. The coal donated by our landlady was already nearly consumed and we had exactly a penny left. We could do nothing, and sat hopelessly silent, as the shout of 'Coal, coal, one and nine a hundredweight' faded down the street.

That was the first of many years of nights I spent tossing restlessly, napping, waking, unable to settle because of cold or gnawing hunger. Four of us, still dressed in our underwear, were packed somehow into one bed, and Father, Alan and Brian were to manage in the other bed. Mother stayed on the settee with the baby. For a long time I lay and listened to my parents quarrelling with each other, while the baby whimpered and Fiona, her head against my shoulder, chattered inconsequently in her own uneasy sleep, her doll clasped tightly to her. I fell into a doze, from which I was awakened by Mother calling me in the early morning. I was glad to leave the bed, which smelled of urine, put on my gym slip and blouse and go to her.

It had been decided, she said, that Father should enrol Alan, Fiona, Brian and Tony at an elementary school he had noticed on his way to the corner shop the previous night. I was to stay at home and help with the baby. My loud protest that I would get behind with my schooling was sharply hushed. I was to see the children washed and tidied for school and was to divide the remaining bread and margarine between them for breakfast. All this I did, whilst shivering with cold. Brian and Tony were also shivering and were scared of going to school; Fiona and Alan were frankly relieved at the thought of something normal creeping back into their lives.

A breakfastless Father was gone with them for an hour and came back to report the children safely ensconced. He had put into his pocket, when leaving home, an old-fashioned cut-throat razor, and he now did his best to shave with it, in cold water, without soap. The result was not very good, and his clothing, still wet from yesterday's soaking, looked crumpled and old. He then departed for the employment exchange, a three-mile walk.

Mother, Avril and I sat almost silent in the icy room. Occasionally, we would feed the baby a little of the remaining milk. We warmed it slightly by putting the bottle next to Mother's skin down the front of her dress, and we wrapped the baby in Mother's coat, which had not got much wetted the previous day. I then tucked our two precious blankets round both mother and child. I longed to get out of the fetid room, even if it was only to stand at the front door, but I was too afraid of my mother in her present state to ask permission to do so.

The other children cane home for lunch, but there was no lunch, and they departed again for school, cold, hungry and in tears, even brave Alan's lips quivering. Mother, Avril and I, like Father, had neither eaten nor drunk.

The afternoon dragged on and the children returned, except for Fiona.

18

'Fiona's ill,' explained Alan anxiously. 'A teacher is going to bring her home in a little while, when she feels better.'

I suppose my mother was past caring, for she said nothing, but, to the griping hunger pains in my stomach, was added a tightening pain of apprehension for Fiona, the frailest of us all. I tried, however, to be cheerful while I helped the boys off with their coats and then put them on again immediately, because they said they were so cold.

The front door bell clanged sonorously through the house. I expected to hear the clatter of our landlady coming down the stairs to open it, but there was no sound from the upper regions of the house, so very diffidently I rose and answered it.

At the door, stood an enormously tall man in long, black skirts. In his arms he carried Fiona.

# Chapter four

I quailed before the apparition on the doorstep – it reminded me of an outsize bat and my over-stimulated imagination suggested that it might be a vampire; in the chaotic mess that our world had become, anything was possible. The voice that issued from the apparition's bearded face was, however, gentle and melodious, and asked to see my mother.

Nervously, I invited him (it was obviously male, despite the long, black dress) into the hall, and he slid a whey-faced Fiona to the floor, while I went to see Mother. She told me to bring the gentleman into our room, and, for the first time since our arrival, a slight animation was apparent in her face.

He entered, leading Fiona by the hand, and immediately my mother assumed the gracious manner which had, in the past, contributed to her reputation as an accomplished hostess.

'Father!' Her voice was bell-like. 'This is a pleasure! Come in. Do sit down.' She ignored poor Fiona, who came and stood by me, and stared dumbly at our new-found friend.

'Father'? It was beyond me. I had never seen an Anglican priest in high church robes, nor yet a Roman Catholic one, in the small towns in which we had previously lived. I stood, with fingers pressed against my mouth, and wondered what further troubles this visit portended.

He was explaining to Mother that the school was an Anglican Church school. After Fiona had come out of her faint, the headmistress had wormed out of her something of what was happening to us, and had then telephoned him. The advent of four well-dressed, well-behaved children entering a slum school had already caused some stir among the teachers and considerable jeering and cat-calling among the other pupils, so the headmistress had asked him to call upon us. Here he was, he announced gravely, and could he be of help?

As I examined the beautiful, serene face of the young priest, Mother poured out a condensed version of the story of Father's losses. He was a Liverpool man originally, she said, and had come back to his native city in the hope of earning his living there. To me, the well-edited tale still presented a picture of foolishness, extravagance and carelessness.

Now, at last, I knew why we were in Liverpool and what the word 'bankruptcy' really meant to our family. I knew, with terrible clarity, that I would never see my bosom friend, Joan, again, never play with my doll's house, never be the captain of the hockey team or be in the Easter pageant. My little world was swept away.

I looked at Alan, who was standing equally silently by the window. His eyes met mine and we shared the same sense of desolation. Then his golden eyelashes covered his eyes and shone with tears, half-hidden.

'Have you no relations who would help you?' asked the priest.

'I have no relations,' said Mother coldly, 'and my husband's refused to know us at present.'

The priest combed his beard with his fingers, and smiled when Avril tried to reach up to touch it. He took her hand gently and held it, and within thirty seconds she had established herself triumphantly on his knee, from which safe throne she surveyed the rest of the family gleefully.

'There is a great deal of unemployment in Liverpool,' he said. 'I fear your husband may find difficulty in finding work.'

Mother just stared disconsolately at him.

At that moment Father entered, dragging his feet slowly and looking almost as hopeless as Mother. The children ignored him, the exhausted baby slept.

Desperate to fill the silence, I cried gladly, 'Daddy!'

He managed to smile faintly.

Mother introduced him formally to the priest, and he sat down and waited politely to hear why the priest was there. This was explained to him, while he shivered with cold and rubbed his blue hands together to restore the circulation.

Finally, the priest said to him, 'First things first. You must have a fire or your youngest child will die. Probably I can persuade old Wright to bring up a hundredweight of coal. I have some small funds and I will bring some food. After you have eaten perhaps I can advise you a little.'

He put his hand out over the children's heads in a gesture of blessing, said goodbye, strode out of the room and let himself out of the house.

The boys immediately broke into jubilant conversation with each other at the idea of food, and gradually Father began to relax a little for the same reason, though his face looked pinched and white. He had spent hour upon hour in the employment exchange, being chivvied from one huge queue to another, until he had finally got himself registered for work as a clerk. He was not eligible for unemployment insurance as he had never contributed to that fund, and the employment exchange clerk just laughed when he asked when he might hope to be sent to apply for a job. There were, he said, a hundred men for every job, and my father's age was a grave difficulty – at thirty-eight he was too old to hope seriously for employment.

He had hardly finished telling us of his adventures, when the doorbell rang again. I answered it quickly this time.

A surly voice from beneath a large hump inquired where it should put t' coal, and not to keep 'im waiting cos 'e 'adn't all night to run after folks as 'adn't enough sense to get it in the daytime.

The landlady had shown me where our coal could be stored, and the coalman clomped through the house behind me, scattering slack liberally around him, and heaved the coal expertly over his head, out of the sack and into a broken-down box in an outhouse. Then, still muttering about improvident folks, he stomped back through the passage and departed into the darkness.

I flew in to Mother, and it seemed no time at all before we had a huge fire glowing, with Father's coat and jacket and Edward's nappy steaming in front of it. The already heavy atmosphere of the room was intensified by the cloying stench of these garments drying, but we did not care. We learned then that, when one has to choose between warmth and being half-fed, except in the last extremities of starvation, warmth is the better choice.

An hour later the priest presented himself again, carrying two large boxes and accompanied by a boy carrying two more. The boy dropped his burdens on the step and trotted away. The priest came in, at my shy invitation. He smiled at the sight of the comforted children kneeling by the fire between the drying clothes, and, with Father's aid, he unpacked the boxes.

The table was soon loaded with six loaves of bread, oatmeal, potatoes, sugar, margarine, a tin of baby milk, two bottles of milk, salt, bacon, some tea, a bar of common soap, a pile of torn-up old sheeting (for cleaning, and for the baby, he explained apologetically) and, wonder of wonders, a towel, a big one.

The priest sat down, and called the boys to him, while Father and I made baby formula and porridge, and Alan collected all the dishes he could find. It felt oddly like a Christmas celebration, and even Mother seemed to come a little out of her apathy as she sipped the tea and ate the porridge Father eventually brought to her. I fed the baby while the children stuffed themselves with porridge, bread and margarine and chattered excitedly, Avril's shrill falsetto and Brian's contralto occasionally emerging from the general hubbub. At the priest's insistence, Father and I finally ate, and Father became more his old, lively self.

We boiled another panful of water, and I took Fiona, Brian, Tony and Avril to the bathroom, and washed their hands, faces and knees. They had not had their underclothes off for thirty-six hours and did not smell very sweet, even after my washing efforts, but a quart of water does not go very far in washing four people, and I reasoned that the beds stank so much that they were bound to smell by morning no matter what I did.

Afterwards I took them into the bedroom, tucked their overcoats over them, covered these with a greasy blanket, heard their prayers, and returned to Alan and my parents.

# Chapter five

Unemployment was so rampant in Liverpool that the young priest felt it necessary to warn Father that getting work would be a very slow process – he was too kind to say that it would be virtually impossible. He suggested that Father should apply for parish relief.

'What is that?' asked Father.

'Well, it is really the old poor-law relief for the destitute, but it is now administered by the city through the public assistance committee. More help is given by way of allowances rather than by committal to the workhouse.'

Father went white at the mention of the workhouse. I stared in shocked horror at the priest. I had read all of Charles Dickens's books – I knew about workhouses.

'I see,' said Father, his voice not much more than a whisper. 'I suppose I have no alternative.'

The priest asked about our accommodation, and sat, drumming his fingertips upon his skirt-clad knee, when he was told that our landlady wanted her rooms back for another tenant, at the end of the week.

At last he spoke.

'There are a lot of older houses in the south end of the city. You might find a couple of rooms in one of those. Some of them are still quite respectable. There is also a high church school in that area, which is a little better than an ordinary board school. However, you might have to pay twopence a week for each child at the school – and that might pose a problem.'

Father said optimistically that he could not imagine such a small amount being a problem, once we got settled.

The priest smiled at him pityingly, opened his mouth to speak and then decided otherwise. We would soon learn.

'Would you like to ask me about anything else?' he inquired.

'No, thank you,' said Mother suddenly. 'You have been most kind.'

I was surprised at her firmness, and then remembered that neither she nor Father had ever had any great respect for the Church. In addition, the priest represented to her the class of people who, she must have felt, had left her in the lurch when she most needed friends. She had accepted this

23

stranger's help because she had to, but her grey eyes were steely when she politely held out her hand to indicate dismissal.

I could see Father beginning to dither, like Bertie Wooster. He was obviously loath to let the priest go and yet was afraid that, if he said anything, Mother might start another bitter family row.

The priest settled the question by getting up abruptly. There was a hurt expression in the mild eyes. He ignored Mother's hand but inclined his head slightly towards her, as he moved through the crowded room to the door. Alan, Father and I hastened to see him out, with many protestations of gratitude. He bowed gravely, blessed us and, with slow, dignified tread, went down the steps into the darkness.

I closed the door, and stood leaning against the inside of it, while the others went back to the family. I had hoped so much that the young priest would have noticed that there were five children of school age in the family and realised that only four had been enrolled in his school. I had envisaged him instructing Father to send me with the others for lessons the following morning. But he had not noticed. I fought back my disappointment and told myself that I would probably go to school as soon as we were settled in a more permanent home, and then I would be able to play in the fresh air with new friends and perhaps even be top of the class in English once more.

The untold amount of anguish that I could have been saved if the good priest had only counted his little flock is hard to imagine. Undoubtedly, the education committee and its army of attendance officers and inspectors would have enforced my right to schooling had he but observed and reported this discrepancy.

I slunk back into the room.

'A capable man,' Mother was saying to Father, with a look which added 'unlike you'.

Before this subtle barb could be plucked out and shot back, she announced that she would go up to the bathroom. She had, hitherto, managed to use an ancient, cracked chamberpot found under one of the beds.

Refusing Father's help with a lofty air, but using me and anything else she could to hold on to, she slowly eased her way into the hall and halfway up the narrow staircase. We sat down and rested on the stairs, and then continued. This was her first real effort to walk since her return from hospital, and she came down the stairs by going from step to step on her bottom. In spite of all the calamities she was undergoing, her strong body was healing and all that was required to return her to reasonable physical health was the will to try and strengthen her muscles. Her pretty, pink wool dress was already spoiled where the baby had wetted it, and the journey down the dusty stairs did not improve it.

The following day, she pottered round the room quite a lot, while Father went in search of that mysterious personage, 'The Parish'. The children, including Fiona, went to school and I again stayed at home. Father had made the fire and I managed to heat some water and wash Edward. When the sun came out about mid-morning, on Mother's instructions I gingerly wrapped the baby in one of the blankets.

'Take him outside and walk up and down in the sun with him,' she said.

I was gone in a flash, the startled child whimpering at my sudden movements.

The bliss of being out of the fetid room overwhelmed me, though the street was not much better. The wind, sweeping in from the estuary, was, however, invigorating despite the gas fumes carried on it. A blank brick wall shielded one side of the street, and from behind it came the shuddering sounds of shunting trains.

The house in which we were staying was one of a row of shabby, jerry-built Edwardian houses, with a grocery store at one end of the block and a public house at the other end. Toddlers with runny noses and sores on their faces scrabbled around in the gutter. An older boy, a piece of jammy bread in one hand, flitted barefoot up the road and called something insolent after me. At the door of the public house, droopy men in shabby raincoats waited for opening time. They stared at me, and I wondered why, but I must have been an unusual sight in my private school uniform, ugly velour hat rammed neatly down on to my forehead, and carrying an almost new baby up and down the pavement. School uniforms would not, in those days, have been seen in such a slummy area. I endured the silent observation with embarrassment.

A sudden diversion brought a number of women to their doors, and in some houses ragged blinds and curtains were hastily drawn.

A funeral procession came slowly down the street, led by a gaunt man in deep black. He was followed by the hearse, a wonderful creation of black and silver, with glass side panels and small, black curtains drawn back to expose the fine wooden coffin. The coffin itself was almost covered by wreath after wreath of gorgeous flowers, including many arum lilies. The four horses which drew the hearse were well-matched black carriage-horses and as they paced slowly along they tossed their heads as if to show off the long black plumes fastened to their bridles. They were driven by a coachman draped in a black cloak and wearing a top hat which shone in the sun; his face beneath the shadow of the hat looked suitably lugubrious.

The men outside the public house, with one accord, removed their caps, and the toddlers scampered out of the gutter and took refuge behind me.

The hearse was followed by a carriage in which sat a woman dressed in heavy widow's weeds. She sat well forward, so that all could see her, and dabbed her purple face from time to time with a white handkerchief edged with black. Occasionally, she would bow, in a fair imitation of royalty, to one of the onlookers and then put her handkerchief again to her dry eyes. Opposite her, sat two pale, acne-pocked young men in black suits too large for them, looking thoroughly uncomfortable.

The widow's carriage was followed by five other carriages, each filled with black-clad mourners.

'Smith always does 'is funerals very nice,' said a voice behind me, rich with approval.

I glanced back quickly.

Two fat women, garbed in grubby, flowered cotton frocks, their arms tucked into their equally grubby pinafores to keep them a little warm, had come out to see the procession.

''e does. Better'n old Johnson. 'e did her daughter's wedding, too.'

There was a faint chuckle from the first woman. 'She's got more money to spend on 'er 'usband's funeral than she 'ad on the wedding, what with 'is insurance and all.' There was silence for a moment, then the voice continued, 'Ah wonder if 'er Joe will keep on the rag-and-bone business?'

Her companion murmured some reply, but I was too intrigued at the idea of a rag-and-bone man having such a large funeral procession to be interested in them further. Everybody I had seen that morning had looked so poor, and yet one of their number was being laid to rest like a prince. Surely the money such a thing would cost was needed for food.

The sun went in and my spirits drooped as the cortège turned round the corner grocery store and disappeared. Like most children, I was afraid of death and the funeral seemed an ill omen to me.

I turned, and went indoors.

Alan came home at lunchtime with a black eye. A boy had asked him if he carried a marble in his mouth, because he spoke so queerly. Alan had replied that he spoke properly, not like a half-baked savage. The half-baked savage had then blacked his eye for him.

'He's got a black eye, too,' said Alan with some satisfaction as I put a wet piece of cloth over the injured part. 'You're lucky not to have to go to this school – even the girls fight.'

'I'd like to go, just to get out of this horrid house,' I said vehemently. 'And, oh, Alan, I'm so afraid Father won't bother about sending me. You know he has always said that all a woman needed was to be able to read and write, and I can do that.'

'He'll have to send you. Isn't there a law about it?'

'Yes there is.'

'Well, the school inspector will tell him he must.'

I removed the wet cloth from his eye and cooled it again under the tap. 'If he knew I existed, I expect he would,' I agreed. 'But, Alan, I was thinking about it all night and if Father never tells them about me they will never know I am here.'

He looked at me uneasily before closing his eyes again so that I could replace the cloth over the blackened one. After wincing at my ministrations, he said doubtfully, 'Probably when we get a proper house, he'll arrange for you to go.'

'I hope so,' I responded earnestly; but I remembered the funeral and my stomach muscles were clenched with apprehension.

# Chapter six

Father returned at lunchtime with food vouchers to last us for two days, while 'The Parish' made inquiries as to the rates of relief paid in the small town from which we came. Apparently, this town would have to reimburse the Liverpool public assistance committee for any relief given to us. It was expected that we would be granted forty-three shillings per week. This sum must cover everything for nine people – rent, food, clothing, heating, lighting, washing, doctor, medicines, haircuts and the thousand and one needs of a growing family.

Mother looked at him disbelievingly.

'It's impossible,' she said, her unpainted face puckered up with surprise. She was used to spending more than that on a hat.

'I can't help it,' Father said helplessly. 'That is what they told me.'

He sat, rubbing his cold hands gently together to restore the circulation, anxiety apparent in every line of him.

'I must obtain a position. But I don't even know anybody whom I could ask about a post. I have never lived in Liverpool long enough to make close friends, as you know.'

I remembered that when Mother wanted a servant she used sometimes to advertise in the newspaper, and I suggested that perhaps other posts were advertised also.

This idea was a revelation to Father and he hailed it with delight.

'By Jove, the girl is right. Look in the newspapers.'

We succeeded in borrowing the landlady's newspaper, after promising faithfully to return it intact.

And so began an endless writing of replies to advertisements on pennyworths of notepaper. Father did not know that firms frequently got seventy to eighty replies to an advertisement for a clerk, and that they just picked a few envelopes at random from the mighty pile, knowing that almost every applicant would be qualified for the post advertised.

That afternoon, Father undertook another long, cold walk, this time to the south end of the city, to look for accommodation. He had no success and returned hungry and dispirited.

Two days later 'The Parish' presented him with thirty-eight shillings, which represented forty-three shillings less five shillings for the food vouchers already supplied.

Only two more days were left of our tenancy of the rooms and our landlady had already reminded us, quite civilly, that she would require the rooms at the end of the week. Mother said, therefore, that she would take the money from 'The Parish' and, with the aid of a taxi, go to the south end of the town to see if she could find us a home.

Father protested that she was not fit for the journey, but she insisted coldly that she could manage and, after instructing me to look after Baby Edward and Avril, she sent him to arrange for a taxi.

I was truly relieved to see Mother beginning to take an interest in what was to become of us, but I did not dare to tell her that my throat was ominously sore and I feared that I was getting tonsillitis again, a disease which had always plagued me.

On the advice of the taxi-driver, she alighted in an area of tall, narrow, Victorian houses surrounding a series of squares. In the middle of each square was a communal garden which seemed to be permanently locked.

From house to house, up and down the imposing front steps, she dragged herself, knocking on doors which were cautiously opened by black, white, brown and yellow hands. Nobody would consider a family of seven children.

When she had come almost to the point of giving up, she came to a house where the doorbell actually worked. She could hear the old-fashioned clapper bell pealing in the basement. The door was answered by a tiny old lady in a long black-and-white-striped dress and a black apron. Her white hair was brushed up in Edwardian poufs and she looked very clean.

In reply to Mother's query regarding accommodation, she lifted a finger heavenward and announced piously, 'The Lord will provide!'

Mother blinked and prepared to turn away.

'Wait!' exclaimed the old lady imperiously. 'I will call Mrs Foster. Please step into the hall.'

Mother stepped in, as requested. The house was not nearly as clean as the old lady, and the lofty hall, with its peeling, olive-green wallpaper, its threadbare, dusty rug and strong smell of cooking, did not inspire confidence. An old-fashioned hatrack and an umbrella-stand made from an elephant's foot stood near the door, and behind them, set rigidly against the wall, were three Edwardian dining chairs, their woodwork lustreless and their upholstery torn.

The old lady toddled to the back of the hall and shrieked up the stairs in a strong, Liverpool accent, 'Bissis Fostaire!'

A door upstairs squeaked open and a deeper shriek replied, followed by a heavy tread on the stairs.

'God bless you, my child,' said the old lady to Mother, and vanished into what must once have been the dining-room of the house.

There was the sound of steady panting coming closer down the stairs, and Mrs Foster emerged from the gloom of the staircase.

She probably measured nearly as much round as she did in height, a veritable ball of a woman, clad in folds of black chiffon. Her neck was draped in a series of long bead necklaces, such as were worn in the nineteen-twenties, and as she moved they swayed across her bosom making rhythmical tiny clicks as they hit each other. Her pale-blue eyes had a hard, myopic stare and her double chin wobbled, as she continued to pant after reaching the hall.

Mother repeated her inquiry regarding rooms, then sat down suddenly on one of the hall chairs, and fainted.

She was aroused by the strong odour of smelling salts proffered by an old gentleman with a tobacco-stained handlebar moustache. She was vaguely aware that she was leaning against the ample bulk of Mrs Foster who was sitting in the next chair, still panting softly, like a lap-dog.

With the aid of the old gentleman and encouragement from Mrs Foster plodding up behind her, she managed to climb a double flight of stairs into what had been the drawing-room of the house, on the first floor.

The room was furnished as a bed-sitting-room. Two Cairn terriers frolicked under the high double bed; in the window stood a large cage occupied by two dismal grey parrots, and near it a cat lay on the linoleum and watched the birds with narrow, lazy eyes. The unmade bed was piled high with old clothes, and a basket table held a perilous pile of dirty dishes, while the shelf underneath it was filled with dusty ladies' magazines. A strong aroma of cats and birds permeated everything.

Mother was assisted to a chair by the cheerfully blazing fire and after a moment's hesitation the old gentleman retired, closing the door quietly after him. Mrs Foster pushed a kettle already standing on the hob round on to the fire.

'You'll feel better when you've had a cup o' tea, luv. Would you like to take off yer hat?'

Mother thankfully took off her hat and leaned back in her chair.

'That was me brother,' remarked Mrs Foster, gesturing towards the closed door. 'He has the old breakfast-room and does for himself. Me grandfather built this house.' She looked round the room proudly. 'Left it to me father, and he left it to me brother and me. We must be almost the only people left round here as owns their own house.'

She turned round and surveyed Mother, weighing her up quite accurately, as it transpired. She observed the fashionable hat, the dirty dress, the beautifully cut tweed coat, the white hands and, finally, the dead, grey face.

'Been real ill, haven't yer, luv?'

'I have, rather.'

'And you want a place for you 'n' the kids?'

'And my husband.'

'Oh, I thought mebbe he'd left you.'

'No.'

Mrs Foster silently considered this information while she assembled a tray of fine, rose-patterned crockery from a corner cupboard and made the tea.

She poured Mother a cup of tea, ladling a generous amount of sugar into it, and then sat down herself, stirring her own tea with slow, thoughtful turning of the battered spoon.

'I've got two rooms and an attic at the top of the house,' she said. 'I hadn't had in mind to have kids in them.' She paused and ran her tongue round her ill-fitting, artificial teeth. 'I had three kids there before, but they was little horrors, if you know what I mean. I don't suppose yours will be that bad.'

'They are fairly well-mannered,' Mother assured her hopefully. She sipped her over-sweet tea and its scalding heat began to revive her.

'I got two married couples and two single ladies in the rooms underneath. The married ones is at work all day, so they won't hear the noise, and the ladies – well, there's plenty like them, if they don't like it.' She put her spoon into the saucer with a decisive smack, her mind made up. 'You can have the rooms for twenty-seven shillings a week – in advance, mind you. There's a gas meter and gaslight in the kitchen-living-room.'

Mother was too thankful at having found a place for us to live in to realise that the rent was exorbitant for such accommodation.

'Is it furnished?' Mother asked.

'Yes. There's enough furniture – and you can add a bit of your own, no doubt.'

Mother put down her cup.

'I wonder if I may see it?'

'Certainly, if you feel O.K. now.'

Laboriously, Mother climbed thirty-two more stairs; they were covered in ancient linoleum in which the holes threatened to trip her up from time to time.

There was a kitchen-living-room with a small bedroom fireplace. It contained a wooden table, two straight chairs, a cupboard with odds and ends of crockery and a couple of saucepans in it, a rickety bamboo bookcase filled with dusty books and a horsehair sofa exhibiting its intestines.

The bedroom held a black metal double bed, covered with a lumpy, stained mattress, and an ancient wardrobe with a broken door and no mirror. A further small staircase led to an attic which held another double bed. This bed lacked a leg and one corner was held up by a pile of bricks. Two trunks lay in a corner, and an old door was propped against one wall. A forgotten candlestick lay on the floor by the bed. All the floors had some linoleum on them, with dirty, wooden floor showing through in places, and all the windows were shrouded in lace curtains, grey and ragged with age.

Mother looked around her in despair.

'Nobody'd take seven children nowadays,' puffed Mrs Foster, as they descended the stairs once more.

Mother knew this to be true and, since the accommodation represented at least a roof under which to shelter, she said, 'I appreciate that, and I will take the rooms.'

They went back to Mrs Foster's room, a rent book was carefully made out and Mother paid over a week's rent. She was informed that she could hang clothes out to dry in the tiny, overgrown back garden, but the children could not play there because, to quote Mrs Foster: 'Me brother faces out back and he can't stand noise – he's a professional pianist. He used to play reelly well in a cinema.'

Mother sighed. She must have been sickened by the squalor of the place. She asked how to reach our present rooms by bus and found that a tram went from a nearby corner.

The trams were open at the front and back and the driver in a shabby uniform augmented by a huge scarf round his neck stood exposed to wind and rain, his foot forever on his clanging bell. The conductor, not quite so well armoured against the elements, heaved young and old on and off, crammed the vehicle with loud admonitions to 'Move farther daan t' back there and make some room for them as comes atter yer', and collected the fares into his leather pouch with jingling efficiency, as he shoved and pushed his way between his close-packed passengers.

As she sat swaying in the noisy vehicle, Mother watched them work and realised that Mrs Foster had not asked if Father was employed or not; we discovered later that she had taken it for granted that he was not.

Darkness had long since fallen when Mother at last staggered into our living-room and collapsed on to the settee.

# Chapter seven

Half an hour after moving into our new abode on the following Monday, we began to appreciate some of the difficulties of living there.

Our coal was to be kept in a cupboard by the back door of the basement, where a series of old pantries had been converted for this purpose. This meant that every bucketful had to be carried up sixty-four stairs. We were to share the bathroom on the first floor with eleven other residents, and this meant innumerable trips for me up and down thirty-two stairs, since Brian, Tony and Avril were far too scared of the dark staircase and cryptlike, filthy bathroom to go down alone, and they needed help to manage in such a dirty place. I was getting resigned to disgusting bathrooms – they seemed to be part of the way of life in Liverpool, as I saw it.

The gas for the light in the living-room, and for a gas stove if we had had one to put in, came through a slot meter which ate pennies at an alarming rate. We did not know that such subsidiary meters were installed and set by landlords at the highest rate they thought they could squeeze out of their tenants. The landlords emptied these meters. They had only to pay the gas company the amount calculated on the reading of the main house meter in the basement, and they pocketed quite a substantial profit on this transaction, in addition to their rent. A more worldly-wise person than my mother would have inserted a penny and run the gas, to see how long a penny lasted, before accepting the tenancy.

Father went out and stopped a passing coal-cart, and the man brought in a sack of coal. He then went to buy cigarettes at a tiny corner store. Both he and Mother had been heavy smokers and found their enforced abstinence hard to bear.

We had brought with us on our tram journey a little oatmeal, a few potatoes, sugar and tea. There was still some baby food for Edward, and, since it was late afternoon by the time we arrived and Edward was whimpering, I made a bottle of formula and then some porridge for the other children. Alan had managed to get a smoky fire going, having lugged a handleless bucket full of coal upstairs by hugging it to his chest. His shirt, already dirty from a week's wear, was now streaked with coal dust.

Although my head was throbbing and my throat was very sore, I ate some porridge gratefully.

As there was no hot water in the bathroom, I afterwards heated pans of water on our fire, and, starting with Avril, washed all the children, except Alan, who washed himself. Little Tony, fair and silent like Fiona, felt very hot, tóo, and I sat him on my knee and got him back into his grubby clothes as fast as possible.

I tucked Alan, Brian and Tony up in the bed in the attic, spreading over them their three overcoats, and left them squabbling with each other regarding the fair distribution of room in the bed.

My weary mother had been resting on the bed in the bedroom, and we now held a hasty debate about where Fiona, Avril and I should sleep, it being tacitly agreed that Mother, still in pain, had to have a bed. After a long argument, Father and I brought down into the bedroom the old door which had been left in the attic. We propped this up at each corner with a pile of long-forgotten Victorian books taken from the bamboo bookcase, and then covered it with crumpled newspaper found in the wardrobe. Avril had a wonderful time chasing the spiders we dislodged from the bookcase when we took the books out. She was delighted that Fiona, she and I were going to share this improbable bed. Father and Edward would share Mother's bed.

Mother got up and went into the living-room, while I put Avril to bed, and when I joined my parents later, they were quietly muttering reproaches at each other through clouds of cigarette smoke. The problem was that we had only three shillings left from our parish relief, and we had to live, somehow, nearly three more days until Thursday afternoon when the benevolent parish would disgorge another forty-three shillings.

As I entered they broke off their recriminations and Father told me to go to bed. I went, thankfully, clinging to Fiona because I felt so dizzy. Fiona, as she took off her shoes preparatory to crawling in beside a soundly sleeping Avril, was crying silently as if her heart was already broken. Avril refused to make room for us when we pushed her gently, and grumbled drowsily that it was her bed. Desperate with the need to lie down, I slapped her legs and, with a howl and an occasional kick at her not-too-loving sisters, she made way.

With nothing over us except our overcoats, and only newspaper under us, it was unbearably cold, and yet at times I felt dreadfully hot.

After a broken night of bad dreams, through which I could hear Edward crying steadily most of the time, I staggered out of bed when Mother called me. I could hardly speak and my throat was swollen from ear to chin.

With eyes still closed she told me in a whisper to call the others, get them ready for school, cut them some bread to eat and make some milkless tea to drink.

Obediently, I built a fire and when I had fanned it with a newspaper into some semblance of heat, I put a pan of water on to it for the tea. Fiona got up from her rustling couch, leaving Avril still slumbering, and without being bidden, went downstairs to wash in the bathroom.

'The minister's soap is nearly finished,' she reported as she brought the remains of the tablet back to me.

I went upstairs to call the boys and clung to the rickety banister because of the dizziness that enveloped me. The boys were not making their usual rumpus, and I found Alan anxiously surveying a tearful Tony, whose neck was as swollen as mine, while Brian, his small brown face looking wizened and old, was lying miserably on the mattress and saying that he didn't feel well and he wanted to go home.

'I'll tell Mother,' I said, through nearly closed lips. I noticed, in terror, that we all seemed to have very large red spots on us – mine itched abominably.

Mother looked so utterly defeated when I told her about the boys and when she had really looked at me that my heart went out to her. She woke Father, who had been sleeping the deep sleep of exhaustion.

He sat up quickly, looking very quaint in his rumpled outer clothes, and put on his spectacles.

He peered at me in an effort to persuade his slumber-ridden eyes to focus.

'I think it's mumps,' he said incredulously.

'It's my old tonsillitis,' I said in a whisper. 'My ear hurts like it always does when tonsillitis is coming.'

My voice and the room seemed to be receding from me and I burned with heat.

'I think you have mumps as well.'

'Does mumps bring you out in spots?' I asked.

He was scratching absent-mindedly at himself, as I spoke.

'Oh my God!'

He looked at his own arms, and then at my bright red tummy, which I obligingly bared for his inspection.

'Bug bites, I think,' he said slowly. 'Saw them in the army.'

Slow tears welled into Mother's eyes.

'I can't bear it!' she cried out suddenly. 'I can't bear it!' She hammered the mattress with closed fists. 'I can't bear it!' she screamed, her pretty face distorted. 'I can't stand any more.'

She continued to shriek hysterically as we gaped at her in terrified silence. For me the scene was almost totally unreal, as fever gained on me; yet I knew that one of my parents had nearly reached the end of the amount of suffering she could accept, and it was difficult for me to contain my own screams of sheer fright.

There was the sound of heavy feet on the stairs and a coarse male voice shouted up, 'For Christ's sake, shut up up there!'

In spite of the pain it gave my throat, I began to cry.

'Don't cry, Mummy,' I begged, 'we'll get through somehow.'

Father, ever optimistic like Mr Micawber that something would turn up, bestirred himself and scrambled out of bed.

'Yes, don't cry,' he said kindly. 'I'll tell Mrs Foster about the bugs – she'll probably do something about them.'

Having seen Mrs Foster I doubted this, but I heartily agreed. Anything, I thought, to get that desperate look off Mother's face and stop her screaming.

Slowly, as Father pottered round trying to bring some order to his distraught family, her cries gave way to sobs and she laid her head down on the mattress. She continued to weep, sobbing quietly to herself for hours.

Father trailed down to the basement to fetch some more coal and coaxed the fire into a more cheerful blaze than I had been able to create. Then we all went and stood by it while he took us one by one and looked us over.

Mother wept on, Edward and Avril slept.

In his opinion, Father said with a sigh, Tony and I had mumps. In addition, I undoubtedly had tonsillitis. Everybody was so used to my sporadic bouts of tonsillitis that this latter pronouncement did not bring me any particular sympathy. Rather, it was taken as an example of my usual awkwardness and waywardness of character. As Father said, 'You would! Just at this time.'

It was presumed that Brian was also sickening with mumps.

We three sick children were piled into the attic bed. I hardly knew, by this time, what was happening around me. Apparently, Mother was persuaded to feed Edward, when he woke, and Father fed Fiona and Alan. He then took them to their new school, where he had to part with fourpence for a week's fees.

I am not sure how my parents managed during the next few days, except that, according to Alan, they pawned my overcoat for two shillings in order to be able to buy coal. I remember, between bouts of delirium, seeing my mother crawling about, sometimes literally on her hands and knees, tears streaming down her face, as she struggled to look after Edward; and Fiona bringing me drinks of hot water with a tiny piece of Oxo cube dissolved in it.

The pain in my ears was intolerable, but there was no doctor to paint my throat with glycerine and tannin, no hot-water bottle or aspirin to ease the searing pain, no drops in my ears to encourage a discharge. The mumps soon decreased, but it was several days before the agony in my ears suddenly diminished. There was a heavy discharge from them on to the bare mattress and my temperature began to go down. I became aware that Brian and Tony were no longer with me, and I called out, my voice seeming muffled and far away to me.

They both came clattering up the attic stairs.

Their faces seemed to have shrunk far more than the vanquished mumps justified. Brian looked more monkey-like than ever, and Tony's blue eyes and the bones of his head seemed grotesquely prominent. They both had large, scarlet spots about their faces and necks.

'It's very quiet,' I whispered. 'Where is everyone?'

'Alan and Fiona are at school. Mummy's in the living-room with the baby. We have to be quiet so she can rest.'

'That is right,' I said, trying to sit up and finding that the room swam around me, so that I was glad to lie down again. I looked imploringly at Brian. 'I'm so cold, Brian. Could you find something more to cover me with?'

He immediately went and fetched his overcoat and put it over my shoulders.

'Where is Daddy?'

'He's gone to see Mr Parish,' volunteered Tony.

I smiled at his name for the public assistance committee.

'Be a darling and bring me my specs,' I commanded him. 'I think I have to stay here a little longer. I still feel a bit hot between the shivers. Gosh, I do smell!'

The sides of my head were sticky with the discharge from my ears, but for the moment I had neither the strength nor the will to do anything about it.

'Tell Daddy I'm better, when he comes,' I said. 'You can play in here if you like.' And I closed my eyes, thankful to be free of pain at last, and fell into a deep sleep while the boys played tag up and down the room. I awoke much later to find Father bending over me, trying to see me by the light of a candle-stub. He felt my head. It was cool.

'Feel better?' he asked.

'Yes.'

'That's my girl.'

'How is Mummy?'

'Much better. She is walking quite well now.'

'Has she stopped crying?' I could not keep a hint of fear out of my voice.

Father looked old and very tired, as he said quietly, 'Yes, she is better now.'

'Can I get up?'

'Yes, I think it would be a good idea. We've got a fire today, so it's warmer in the other room.'

I craved a hot cup of tea and I hoped that if we had a fire to boil the water we might also have a little tea in the cupboard. My legs almost refused to obey me and I clung to Father's arm as I shuffled across the floor, down the attic stairs and into the living-room, where I was greeted rapturously by Fiona and Alan and with a wan smile by my exhausted mother. Avril was sitting on the floor in a corner, her face red and tear-stained, getting over a tantrum.

# Chapter eight

Brian and Tony went back to school, two subdued ghosts walking hand in hand for fear of being bullied by the heavily booted older boys in the street.

Mrs Foster, declaring that she had never had a complaint before, produced half a tin of Keating's powder to repel the bugs. It did have some temporary effect, but the pests were coming in from the house next door and only a thorough stoving of both houses would ever have cleared them. We had to learn to live with them, just as we soon had to learn to live with head-lice which the children picked up in school.

I went through each child's clothing before it set off for school, hoping to save them the humiliation of being labelled verminous; they were already cowed enough.

The days dragged by and both Mother and I became stronger, despite our poor diet of white bread, potatoes and tea. Though Mother's physical health was improving, she seemed to withdraw further and further away from us. It was as if she could not bear to face the miserable existence which was our lot. She tried very hard to appear normal and calm, but attacks of hopeless hysteria descended on her without warning and she would rage and weep over some trifle, while whichever child happened to be the cause of the explosion made matters worse by trying to defend himself verbally. We were all still at the age when we believed that grown-ups knew what they were about and had sensible reasons for all that they did, and in consequence we were thrown into real fright each time one of these distressing scenes occurred. The idea that a person's life could be so shattered that they were unable to build anything new was unknown to us. We were young – we hoped for better times in the early future.

I learned to do practically everything for the baby, and when my legs were steady enough I borrowed Mother's overcoat, which though too wide was not too long for me, and took Edward and Avril down to the street for fresh air.

In Victorian times the street had been quite a fashionable one and each house had a flight of steps up to its front door. The steps had heavy iron railings running up either side and round the area bordering the basement

39

of the building, so that no one should fall into these tiny front yards below the level of the street.

Avril, like a squirrel released from a cage, skipped joyfully up and down the pavement, stopping occasionally to peek through the railings and catch a glimpse of someone's basement home. Her pretty blue satin bonnet, though by now rather battered, caused quite a number of favourable comments from women sitting on the steps or standing in groups gossiping. The women were mostly of the labouring class, dressing in dull greys and blacks, some with flowered pinafores and most of them wearing black shawls as protection against the cold wind. Their hair either hung in greasy confusion to their shoulders or was braided and pinned up in fashions I had seen in early Victorian photographs. Their teeth, when they smiled at Edward, were uniformly bad or non-existent. I passed them without speaking as I shyly walked up and down with Edward in my arms.

A Spanish woman was seated on the steps of the next-door house. Her greying hair was done high on her head and held at the back by a fine tortoiseshell comb and she watched my promenade with merry black eyes. Finally, she called me to her.

'Can I see your baby?' she asked in a throaty voice.

Obediently I brought Edward to her and lowered him so that she could see his sleepy face. She made delighted clucking sounds at him.

'You not have pram?' she asked.

'No.'

She looked at me carefully, weighing me up.

'Not your baby?'

'Of course he's my baby. He's my brother.'

My innocence nonplussed her for a moment. Then she laughed and pinched my cheek.

'So! He is little brother.'

'Yes. Mummy's ill,' I volunteered, warmed by her cheerfulness.

'I know. Mrs Foster tell me.'

She put her finger into Edward's hand. He promptly clutched it, and she sighed gustily.

'I got old pram. You have it. My baby big boy now. No more babies for me. You wait.'

She got up and tripped down the area steps and into the basement door under the main front steps, and I waited quietly, rocking Edward in my arms under the approving glances of her neighbours.

The best that could be said about that pram was that it had four wheels. Its lining was torn and grey with dirt; its wheels had no tyres; the ribs of its hood stood out as if it was hungry and its cover had so many cracks in it that it looked like a map of Europe. When it was moved it squeaked steadily in protest. It was, however, to be my constant companion for years and the cover had the virtue that it was firm enough to support an open book, so that I could read as I trudged along.

I was immensely grateful to my new friend and I happily laid the swaddled Edward into his new carriage. Cautiously I pulled it up the front steps of Mrs Foster's house, then up the three double flights of stairs to our room. Bumpety-bump it went on each stair and bumpety-bump went the patient Edward inside it. Mrs Foster's brother, Mr Ferris, infuriated by the regular pounding on the stairs, burst out of his room.

'For God Almighty's sake be quiet!' he shouted up. 'I can't concentrate.'

I did not answer him. I did not care about his practising on his piano. I was triumphant at having found something for Edward to sleep in and to wheel him out in.

Mother was lying down on the bed but, at the sound of the pram's appalling squeak in the room, she sat up.

'Good heavens!' she exclaimed. 'Where did you get that ghastly chariot?'

I explained, as I took Edward out of it.

'We can't put him in a thing like that,' Mother said.

'Why not?' I asked. 'It gives him a place to sleep – you might be able to sleep better, if he wasn't in the same bed as you.'

Mother nodded acceptance, her face mirroring the hopelessness which recent events had made part of her character.

So the Chariot became part of Edward's and my life and squeaked its way painfully through miles and miles of black Liverpool streets. Sometimes I think there must still be two little ghosts and a squeak floating gently through Princes Park because we went there so often.

# Chapter nine

Mother still had in the stitches from the major operation which had been performed upon her soon after Edward's birth. I had seen the scarifying gash which ran from above her waist to her pelvis; it was now healed and should really have been examined by a surgeon some time back. We considered getting the stitches out ourselves, but we had no scissors and Father was afraid to risk cutting them with his blunt razor. It was decided, therefore, that next time Father drew our allowance from the public assistance committee, Mother would have to see a doctor, no matter what we had to go without as a result of having to pay his fee.

Two mysterious middle-aged ladies, who went out only in the evening, and two married couples lived on the floor below us. With strict instructions from Father not to speak to either of the single ladies, who were, I was assured, not 'nice', I was dispatched to inquire from one of the married couples the name of a doctor.

A man in mechanic's overalls answered my knock. He was undersized and very thin, his hair slicked back from a long, narrow face. Tired, hazel eyes regarded me kindly.

'What do you want, luv?'

'My father sent me down to ask if you know where we could find a doctor round here.'

'Soombody took ill, luv?' His voice was much more alert.

'No, thank you. Mummy was very ill before we came here and now she must see a doctor – to have her stitches removed.'

'Oh, aye. Just a minute, ducks, I'll ask the wife.'

He left me standing at the open door, while he retreated into the room. I caught a glimpse of a stoutish blonde girl ladling stew out of a saucepan on to plates at a table by the window. The room was crowded with a bed, a stove and living-room furniture, but the general effect was of cosy friendliness. The smell of the stew was unbelievably good and I sniffed appreciatively as I waited.

The girl put down the saucepan and they both came to the door. She wiped her hands on a grubby apron as she looked down at me.

'There's the parish doctor,' she said doubtfully. 'But none of us goes to 'im unless we're dying. Tell yer dad that Dr Dent around the corner by the grocery shop is proper kind. He wouldn't charge you much – but you'd better take half a crown, in case.'

I thanked her and was just about to turn and run back upstairs, when she put her hand in her pocket and brought out a toffee. ''Ere yer are, luv. Have a toffee.'

I had not tasted a sweet since I had arrived in Liverpool and I accepted the gift delightedly and rushed up the stairs with unseemly exuberance.

''is surgery hours are seven to nine,' she called up after me.

Father normally went to the library in the evening to read the *Liverpool Echo* and write replies to any advertisements which offered office jobs, so I was told to accompany Mother to the doctor's surgery. Alan would take care of the rest of the family while we were away.

Mother washed herself as best she could with a piece of rag dipped into cold water, and made sure she had no vermin on her. I did the same and also combed my hair; we had only one small pocket comb between us and were always afraid of breaking it, as we could not afford to replace it; consequently, I hardly ever combed my straggling locks. Since my overcoat was still in pawn, I borrowed Fiona's.

For the first time since she had arrived, Mother made the long trip downstairs. The night was clear and frosty and she paused at the top of the front steps to take a big breath of fresh air; it smelled good after the foul atmosphere of the house. Slowly we proceeded down the steps and down the street, to a cross street of smaller houses and shops. We found the doctor's front door, which led straight off the street, except for two small steps. A notice on the door invited us to enter. I turned the well-polished brass handle, it gave, and we went in.

We found ourselves in a narrow hall in which ancient brown linoleum gleamed with much polishing under a low-watt light. To our right was a door slightly ajar, marked 'Waiting-Room'. This proved to be packed with people, many of them Negroes, sitting on chairs ranged round the walls of the room; the centre was occupied by a large Victorian dining-table on which a number of tattered magazines lay in disarray. A gas fire, turned low, stood in front of a black, iron fireplace. On the varnished mantelpiece a marble clock ticked despondently, while on either side of it two cast-iron Greek warriors kept guard.

A whisper of conversation ceased as we entered and all eyes regarded us. I suppose that Mother's pale pink hat caused the interest. While we hesitated, a huge man in an old macintosh got up off his chair and offered it to Mother, who, by this time, was looking very white.

'Thank you,' she said and sat down gratefully.

The man grinned sheepishly, his great red face breaking into a thousand wrinkles, as he stood near us fingering a greasy cap. I stood close to Mother, feeling a little frightened. This was all so different from the chintz-clad sitting-room of our old doctor and the ready welcome of his smart little wife.

Neither of us had any idea how one communicated the fact of one's presence to the doctor. But we soon saw that at the other end of the room was another door and that at the sound of a buzzer people went in and out of it. Presumably the doctor was in the next room. We could not guess how people established when they could go in so we sat and sat until we were the last people in the waiting-room, and the front door was closed and locked by an elderly woman. When the buzzer rang again, Mother rose and went in to see the doctor, and I was left alone.

I got up and went to stand by the gas fire. The unaccustomed warmth was delicious and wrapped itself around me in a comfortable blanket of heat. I gazed at the iron Greek soldiers on the mantelpiece and smiled at them. My grandmother had such a pair on her kitchen mantelpiece in her beautiful little house on the other side of the Mersey. The tears sprang to my eyes as I remembered it. How long would it be, I wondered, before I had twopence so that I could take the ferry across the Mersey and visit her. My parents never mentioned her and she did not write to me. Probably she did not even know where I was. I wondered if I dare write to her without my parents' permission. Impatiently I wiped away the tears. Paper and stamps cost money, too, you stupid, I told myself.

The doctor was taking a long time over Mother's stitches. Perhaps he would make her quite well. Then she could look after the children and I could go back to school. Perhaps in school there would be a schoolteacher who would tell me what steps one had to take to get work when one had finished school.

I had always wanted to be a ballet dancer and my father had indulged me in this by sending me to a very good teacher when I was about five years old. Just before my seventh birthday, however, a very heavy, old-fashioned wardrobe had unexpectedly fallen over while I was in my parents' bedroom, catching my legs under it. This had resulted in one of my feet being permanently slightly twisted. It was not an unsightly crippling but was sufficient to make any dancing career impossible. During the months I had had to lie with the foot up I had discovered a natural ability for drawing, and this had led to an ambition to design clothes for the theatre.

I gazed into the doctor's miserable gas fire and saw gorgeous imaginary figures in clothes designed by me tripping and leaping across an imaginary stage. I wished I had a pencil and paper to catch and record permanently my pretty dream. If only the doctor would make Mother well, I would study and draw and practise and fill the stage of the Liverpool Empire with such glamour as its old walls had never seen before.

There was a click as the doctor opened his surgery door for Mother and bowed her out, and she smiled her delicate, beguiling smile at him.

He was a dark, intense-looking young man; he was, I later discovered, an ardent Communist who tried his best to practise his beliefs in the stinking slum in which we lived. He grinned cheerfully at me and said good night to us both.

'What did he say?' I asked anxiously as I held Mother's arm to steady her, after the doctor's housekeeper had locked the front door behind us.

We walked slowly down the empty street for a little way before Mother answered.

'He said I should have gone to the outpatients department of a hospital.'

'Did he take the stitches out? Did it hurt?'

'Yes, he took them out – it didn't hurt much – he's a surgeon as well as a physician.'

In a trembling voice I asked another question, one with selfish intent. Behind it was my despair at the drudgery I was facing and my hopes that if I was allowed to go to school I might find a way out from being for ever the unpaid, unthanked housekeeper for our poverty-stricken family.

'Will you be all right?' I asked. 'Will you get better?'

'He thinks I will, if I go to work – in the open air.'

'Work?' I was truly astonished.

At my query she looked down at me, but there was no affection, no real interest in her gaze or in her voice as she answered, 'Yes. Work.'

The idea that work could cure someone who had been ill was too difficult for me to understand. I knew nothing of mental illness, except that lunatics were shut up in lunatic asylums, and I had no comprehension of the mental stress under which my poor mother laboured and which the doctor had diagnosed.

'You can't,' I said desperately. 'There is Edward – and Avril – and me – I haven't got my matric yet – I have to go back to school.'

'We shall see,' she said thoughtfully.

My stomach clenched in a deadly nervous pain. In a perceptive flash I saw myself for ever at home, the uneducated daughter retained to help in the house – and there were still some of these when I was a child – grey, uninteresting, the butt of everyone's ill-temper, without money of my own and consequently entirely dependent upon the goodwill of the rest of the family. I saw myself forever struggling with the care of Edward, with Avril's tantrums and the boys' fights, with Mr Parish's miserable pittance, and I realised that the daughter who did not have to go to school or to work would be the one to be clothed and fed last.

I burst into tears, my hopes shattered.

'Oh no, Mummy!' I wailed. 'I want to go to school! I want to be like other girls!'

'Be quiet,' said Mother sharply. 'You are making an exhibition of yourself.'

I continued to weep – but quietly. Little ladies did not make exhibitions of themselves in public.

'You have to learn that you cannot have everything you want. The family must come first.'

# Chapter ten

Immediately we arrived home, I threw a tantrum which left even Avril awed. I stamped, I cried, I shouted that I would go to school. Eleven and a half was too young an age to have to leave. I would not stay at home and look after babies.

My bewildered father, who did not know what the cause of my rage was, shouted at me above the storm to be quiet. Mother shouted back at him. Fiona and Tony, terrified by the noise, wept steadily in a corner, while Alan did his best to placate the various contestants by telling everyone to shut up. Brian took refuge halfway up the attic stairs and watched through the banister. Baby Edward cried for his forgotten bottle. A voice from below yelled up to us, 'Shut that bloody racket, can't yer!'

As my anger gave way to hopeless tears Father gradually picked up the story and said he thought the doctor's idea of Mother's going to work was an excellent one and that it would probably be for only a little while. When I continued to weep passionately, he slapped me across the buttocks and told me to go into the bedroom until I could behave in a civilised manner.

I lay face down on the bed until I could not stand the stench of it any more. The nervous strain under which the children laboured in their cold, hungry, new world was so great that Brian, Tony and Avril had become incontinent at night and Edward had no rubber undersheet to help him, so that the already disgusting beds had become even more so and were invariably wet somewhere on their surface.

Emerging finally in sulky silence and with bloodshot eyes, I found Edward still whimpering disconsolately, but the children were silently getting themselves ready for bed, by taking off their outer clothes. My parents were arguing heatedly about what kind of occupation my mother could undertake.

Still sniffing, I made a bottle for Edward with the last of the baby food, and, since I was still filled with resentment at my parents, I took him outside and sat down on the top stair of the long flights of gloomy staircase and fed him.

The smell of the overcrowded, verminous house, its filthy, over-used bathroom and the efforts of nine different cooks combined with Edward's rancid odour was almost overpowering, and I put my cheek against his scurfy little head and wept again.

During the next few days my mother went out each afternoon for a walk to strengthen her legs, and then one day she sponged her dress and pressed it with an iron borrowed from Miss Sinford, the benevolent, crazy old lady on the ground floor, wiped her shoes over with a wet cloth, and washed herself down with a rag and cold water. She then made up her face with the last of her make-up and the aid of her handbag mirror, and went out without saying where she was going.

As she went down the stairs, I realised for the first time how much my mother had changed. She had been considered beautiful and extremely vivacious and had always had a court of young men who called upon her – there were still some gentlemen who lived on private incomes in those days and who had time to call and take tea with a pretty woman and her friends – but now her dress hung loosely on her, her face was haggard and lined, her shining black hair, which had been exquisitely kept by her hairdresser, had grown long and straggling; she had pushed it up under her hat before going out. The polished ovals of her nails were ruined by her having to bite them to shorten them, as we all had to do, because we had no scissors. How much had Father changed? I wondered. And the children? And me?

Avril was howling because she could not go out too, and I decided that I might create a diversion by washing her and washing Edward.

We had a fire that day, a luxury we frequently had to forgo despite the icy February weather, so I went down to the bathroom with our kettle and only saucepan, filled them with water, brought them upstairs and set them on the fire. Carrying Edward on my hip, I took the handleless coal bucket down to the basement area, a stone-lined yard from which steps led up to the back garden. I laid Edward on a counter which must have been part of a butler's pantry in the more palmy days of the house, and washed the coal dust out of the bucket as thoroughly as I could under a tap in the yard.

Watched by a fascinated Avril, who had by now forgotten her desire to go out and had tripped up and downstairs behind me puffing excitedly, I set the bucket in front of the fire, put the warm water in it, stripped a protesting Edward and washed him from head to heel, holding him on my knee as I had seen my nanny hold Avril when she was a baby. This was the first time he had had a complete bath since we had left home and I found that he had numerous bug bites and his little back was sore where the urine had not been properly washed off him; his head was covered with scurf.

I had no change of clothing for him, but I pinned a piece of the rag the priest had given us on him as a rough diaper and laid his blanket over him to keep him warm in the Chariot while I dealt with Avril.

Fortunately, Avril thought it was a wonderful game and submitted to being rubbed all over with a wet cloth. I could not wash her head because I could not think how to do it in a bucket. Dirt was ingrained in her skin and I could not get her completely clean without soap. I had an uneasy feeling that her fine golden hair was verminous and certainly she had scurf around her forehead and along the line of the parting. It seemed, too, as if the hair on the crown of her head was thinner than before. I told her cheerfully, however, that I would wash her vest and knickers after she was in bed.

I sighed as I slicked the water off her in front of the fire, so that she would dry quickly. She, like Mother, had changed. She had been a pudgy child with rosy cheeks; now she looked wan, her ribs showed and her stomach stuck out too much.

While I scrubbed the children, Father was stuck in one of his everlasting queues.

He worked very hard at being unemployed. He spent most of two days a week walking to the employment exchange, standing in a long queue, signing on as being available for work and walking back up the hill which was Leece Street, pausing outside the old Philharmonic Hall to read the concert notices with wistful attention, then on past the black-faced ear, nose and throat hospital and then through an endless maze of decaying Victorian houses to our comfortless eyrie at the top of one of them. He was not so badly off as dock labourers, he told us. They had to sign on for work twice a day.

Another day was spent walking to the offices of the public assistance committee, where could be found Tony's 'Mr Parish'. Here he stood in a long queue again, soaked by rain or frozen in the winter wind, and received his precious forty-three shillings a week. He then walked home. On the other three mornings a week he went to the public library, scanned the advertisements in the newspapers in the reading-room, and wrote replies to those offering work he felt he could do. Then he walked all the way into the centre of the town to deliver his replies to the offices of the *Liverpool Echo* in Victoria Street, because we had no money for stamps – the postage for a letter in those days was three-halfpence.

His shoes wore through at the soles and he stuffed them with cardboard begged from the corner grocery shop, until the holes were so big that the cardboard would not stay in place. Without tools he could not hope to mend them himself, so one week we very nearly starved completely while we paid the shoemaker. He had not had a haircut or a clean shirt for a month, though he had managed to wash himself quite thoroughly. His socks had very little left from the ankle down, and I remember his blue, frozen feet sticking out of them when he removed his soaking wet shoes on his return in the evenings. I think it was rubbing his feet with my hands which truly brought home to me our desperate position and made me accept the fact that I had to stay at home. I would rub until I had the circulation going again and he would whistle under his breath with the pain of it, and each time it happened my heart broke anew.

For a month or more, he never spoke to anyone outside the family, except the city and government clerks who dealt with him and to whom he was just another statistic. One morning, however, the wait at the employment exchange was particularly long and chilly, and the ragged queue of weary men began to mutter rebelliously, and Father was drawn into sympathetic conversation with his fellow sufferers. They were, for the most part, respectable working men many of whose jobs were dependent upon the ships which went in and out of the port of Liverpool in normal times. They were curious about my father, because he spoke like an educated man. They could not imagine that anyone highly educated could be unemployed; they assumed, and Father did not disillusion them, that he had been a senior clerk in one of the shipping companies which had been dispensing with its office staff. They were friendly and, as Father met them again and again, they began to fill him in on how to stay alive under almost impossible circumstances.

He discovered that many of them had wives who went out cleaning private homes or worked in stores to augment their parish relief; though these earnings should have been declared to the public assistance committee, they were not, and they made all the difference between starvation and dying more slowly of malnutrition.

'If you can live long enough, there just might be a job for you one morning,' a leather-faced old warehouseman told him jokingly.

There were agencies in the town, he was told, which would provide the odd pair of shoes or an old blanket for a child. There were regimental funds willing to provide a little help to old soldiers. He gathered other scraps of information, which were revelations to a man who had never had to think twice about the basic necessities of life. An open fire, he was assured, could be kept going almost all day from the refuse of the streets, old shoes, scraps of paper, twigs, wooden boxes, potato peelings; if one was very ill or had a broken bone, the outpatients departments of most of the local hospitals would give some medical care. Pawnbrokers would take almost anything saleable, and one could buy second-hand clothing from them. Junkyards would sometimes yield a much needed pram wheel or a piece for an old bike. One could travel from Liverpool to London by tramcar, if one knew the route, and it was much cheaper than going by train. Some of the men had done it several times in an effort to find work in the more prosperous south-east of the country.

Father thanked them gratefully and came home very thoughtful, marvelling at their sheer resilience and good nature in such adversity.

All of us had colds, including the baby, and lacked even handkerchiefs, though we did our best by using newspaper culled from the greengrocer, who wrapped our small purchases of potatoes in it. Father began to realise that unless help came quickly the younger children would probably die from the first germ that infected them. The death rate in Liverpool, at that time, was one of the highest in the country and the infant mortality rate was correspondingly horrifying. He knew that we were worse off than most of the people who stood in the endless queues with him, since we did not draw the Liverpool level of relief, nor were we eligible for help with clothing which 'Mr Parish' sometimes gave out. No one, in all his conversations, happened to tell him that he was paying three times the rent that most people paid and that this was largely what was crippling us.

By far the greatest proportion of the Liverpool workforce was casual labour, dependent upon the erratic comings and goings of ships in the river, and most men were accustomed to being unemployed from time to time, particularly dock labourers. Their pattern of life reflected this in that they could never make a proper domestic budget, because they never knew from one week to the next what their earnings would be. They spent their earnings and 'made do' in between jobs. My father, being an educated man trained to study economic trends, could never manage to be as philosophical and optimistic as they were. He feared not only for himself but for his children's future.

In those days there were no midday meals or drinks of milk at school to help children along. One good lady who suggested that the skimmed milk thrown down the drain by one of the city's bigger dairies might be given free to children in the elementary schools was soundly snubbed for her socialistic ideas.

Father swallowed what little pride he had left. He sat down at our greasy table and wrote to the headquarters of his old regiment.

Mother came home white with weariness and irritable with frustration, having tried unsuccessfully against about thirty other applicants for a job as a saleswoman.

'They looked like a flock of crows,' she remarked of the applicants. 'They all wore black dresses, stockings and shoes – just little white collars to relieve the dreariness.'

'I thought that was what shop-girls always wore,' replied Father.

'I suppose so,' Mother said. She added, 'And the hours one was expected to work – nine until nine on Saturdays!'

'What wages were they offering?'

'Fifteen shillings a week.'

Father whistled. 'That's not a living wage,' he said.

'They don't care,' replied Mother wearily. 'All the women there were anxious to get the job.'

# Chapter eleven

Each day my mother went out to try to get work and spent most of the morning and afternoon in a fruitless round of offices and shops. Before leaving, she would give me a shilling to buy the day's food. This I laid out to the best of my ability on bread, potatoes, rice, tea, sugar, pennyworths of bacon scraps or margarine and, that dire necessity, a pint of milk for Edward, which cost twopence.

At first, Edward used to cry with hunger, but as he grew a little older, he would lie lethargically in the Chariot, making no sound most of the time. The other children also grew apathetic and the smaller ones tried to take bits of bread when I was not looking. We never heard from the school about their progress nor did my father inquire.

One morning my parents went out quite early, before Edward had been fed. After the children had been given a meagre bowl of porridge each and had been sent to school, there was no food left in the house. I was desperate with hunger. And the usual pint of milk would, I knew, not be enough to last Edward for twenty-four hours. However, clutching the shilling, I wrapped Edward up in his stinking blanket, put on my woollen cardigan, my coat being still in pawn, and went downstairs to buy milk from the first passing milkman.

Standing on the doorstep were two pint bottles of milk, presumably delivered for Miss Sinford, the lady with religious mania, and Mrs Hicks, who lived with her unemployed husband in the bowels of the basement. The other tenants patronised a milkman who came later.

I looked at the bottles and then up and down the apparently empty street, hoping that the milkman might still be nearby. There was no sign of him, however, and I turned back into the house with the idea of getting out the Chariot and wheeling it round to the dairy to purchase Edward's precious pint.

Edward began to whimper. I looked down longingly at the milk bottles. Then, like a fleeing cat, I tore up the stairs, Edward bobbing up and down in my arms. I laid him down gently in the Chariot, took our two cracked cups, ran down to the bathroom and filled one with water, then ran silently down the rest of the stairs to the front door.

I glanced quickly up and down the street. Everyone was apparently sleeping the long hopeless sleep of the unemployed.

Quickly I took the lids off the bottles, filled the empty cup with a little milk from each bottle, topped the bottles up with water, carefully replaced the lids, shook the bottles gently, and then crept upstairs again with my precious prize.

I managed to make a feed for Edward before the little fire I made from paper flickered out, and I fed him contentedly, knowing that I could make the pint of milk I would buy stretch further for him. I had no qualms of conscience about my theft – I thought only of Edward – and I was mercifully unaware that the policeman on the beat had quietly watched the whole operation.

It was late February, with days of pouring rain interspersed with weak sunshine. The trees and bushes in the locked gardens in the squares were beginning to show a faint swelling of their buds, and, as I wheeled Edward to the tiny local grocery shop and to the greengrocer's each day, I would wonder why the children running in and out of the traffic or playing with cigarette cards on the pavement could not be allowed to play in the gardens. I would stand watching them dully as they cursed and tumbled each other about, their white or black skins equally grey with dirt and dust, their noses dribbling, their bare legs chapped and with septic sores on their knees. Little girls would play endless games of skipping and hopscotch, each with its appropriate song, learned from their elder sisters and passed down from generation to generation.

> 'I am a girl guide dressed i' blue,
> These are the actions I must do.
> Salute to the King, bow to the Queen
> And turn my back to the people.
> Pepper!'

And at the word 'pepper' they would turn the skipping-rope with feverish speed to see how many fast skips they could do before being tripped up. Sometimes, I would wish wistfully that I might be able to join in, but I had always to watch Avril and Edward and I was mortally afraid of something happening to them in this strange world which I did not understand.

Another pleasure was to stand in front of the greengrocer's and contemplate the neat pyramids of oranges, apples, lemons and toma-toes. Mentally, I ate my way through the piles from top to bottom. I lacked the courage and initiative of the little street arabs, who would sometimes snatch a piece of fruit and fly like jets down the narrow back alleys, there to consume it with much ribaldry at the expense of the outraged greengrocer. A cry of 'Bobby' or 'Cop' or

'Flattie' would, however, send them speeding off again, old gym shoes or bare feet thudding over the flagstones like rapidly bouncing rubber balls.

With Edward replete with Miss Sinford's and Mrs Hicks's milk and sleeping quietly in the Chariot, Avril and I went on the usual shopping round. At the greengrocer's I stood and dithered. If I bought rice, I argued with myself, Mother would say that I should have bought potatoes; if potatoes, then she would say rice. I knew I could not win. Mother was getting better and her increasing irritability at my sins was a sign of it.

The policeman on his beat stopped and chucked Edward under his chin. Edward opened his eyes and managed a small smile. I looked up and smiled too, my morning peccadillo completely forgotten.

'Nice baby you've got,' he said, putting his hands behind his back and rocking gently on his heels. He beamed at me from under his helmet. 'What's his name?'

'Edward,' I said. He was a nice-looking young man, neat and clean, despite the acne spots all over his face.

'And what's your name?'

'Helen,' I replied promptly.

He looked down at the baby again, while the greengrocer peered through the glass of his window, which he had been polishing.

'No mummy?'

'Yes, she's looking for work. So's Daddy.'

He looked surprised, apparently at my clear English, so different from that of the other children round about. It was better English than he spoke himself.

'Having a hard time? Got any other brothers and sisters?'

'Yes,' I said simply, in answer to the first question. 'We are seven. The others are all at school.'

The wind was getting up and it was beginning to rain. My teeth started to chatter and I wrapped my cardigan closer round me.

The policeman stared at me with calm blue eyes and said, 'Humph.' He adjusted the collar of his cape. I became aware of the interested gaze of the greengrocer, and decided on rice for supper.

'Goodbye,' I said to the policeman and pushed the pram a bit farther along the street and parked it outside the grocery shop, where Avril watched it while I went inside. The policeman, after a moment's hesitation, went into the greengrocer's shop.

The following morning a pint of milk was delivered to the top landing of our staircase. When I ran downstairs to catch the milkman and return the bottle to him, he insisted that it was for Edward and was sent by a friend, and not even Father could make him say any more. For two long intolerable years the milkman stolidly climbed the stairs and deposited a pint of milk on our top step. It probably saved Edward's life.

Many years later, the greengrocer told my mother about the young policeman who had inquired about us from him, and had then gone round to the dairy and ordered a daily pint of milk to be delivered for Edward, and had paid for it out of his own meagre wages.

# Chapter twelve

One of the advantages of being very poor is that one has time. Since we had no clothes except those on our backs, there was no pile of washing to be dealt with each Monday. When there is little food, there is little cooking, and since we possessed no bed linen, towels, cleaning materials or tools, most other domestic jobs either were non-existent or could not be carried out. As the weather improved, therefore, I began to take a walk each day, pushing Edward and Avril in the Chariot.

These were, for me, voyages of discovery into a world I had never dreamed of before. I meandered along narrow streets, where the soot-blackened early Victorian houses opened directly upon the pavement. Some of the houses had the flagstone across their front door scrubbed and neatly whitened, with a strip of well-shone brass covering the sill; their painted windowsills were carefully polished and their garish chintz curtains were starched as stiff as the sentries outside Buckingham Palace. Others were like our house: dull windows veiled in grey webs of lace, windowpanes missing and filled in with cardboard, old orange peel and cigarette ends littering their frontage.

The local pawnbroker's shop, with its dusty sign of three golden balls hanging outside over a wooden table piled high with second-hand clothing, made for me a fascinating treat. I loved to gaze in the windows at the rows of Victorian and Edwardian rings for sale, the war medals, violins, blankets, china ornaments and sailors' lucky gold charms.

The pawnbroker himself was part of the scene, as he stood in his doorway puffing at a cigarette, shirtsleeves rolled up to show olive-coloured arms, tight black curls receding from his forehead, a magnificent watch-chain with dangling seals swathed across a wrinkled, blue serge waistcoat over a comfortable paunch.

'Come on, me little blue-eyed duck!' he would call to Avril when he saw her, and occasionally he would feel around in his waistcoat pocket with his tobacco-stained fingers to dig out a grubby sweet for her. She loved him and would howl dismally on the days when we did not walk that way. For me, he would have a polite nod and a brief 'Afternoon. Nice day', regardless of whether it rained or shone.

One mild March afternoon, I circled the cathedral and listened to the ring of the stonemasons' tools on its great sandstone walls. It rose like a graceful queen above slums which put Christianity to shame. I stared up the beautiful sweep of steps leading to its entrance, wondering if I dare go in, but I was too afraid. I had not seen myself in a mirror since coming to Liverpool, but I knew I was both dirty and shabby. My hat and shoes had been passed to Fiona, who was obliged to go out to school, whereas I could stay indoors. The shoes had been replaced by a pair of second-hand running shoes with holes in the toes; my head was bare and my hair straggled in an unruly mass down my neck; it was rarely combed and never washed.

Still pushing aimlessly, I wandered along Rodney Street, a lovely street of well-kept Georgian houses, the homes and surgeries of Liverpool's more eminent doctors. A brass plaque on No. 62 informed me that Gladstone was born there. Mr Gladstone was not one of my heroes, so I continued onward enjoying the peace and orderliness of the quiet road.

I turned down Leece Street, past the employment exchange where Father spent so many unhappy hours, past tall, black St Luke's Church and into Bold Street, the most elegant shopping centre in Liverpool. Although there were at least a dozen empty shops up for rent, the atmosphere was one of opulence. I pushed past women in fur coats and pretty hats, who stared at me in disgust, to look in windows which held a single dress or fur or a few discreet bottles of perfume. A delicious odour of roasting coffee permeated the place.

Onward I went, through the packed shopping area of Church Street, where trams, nose to tail, clanged their way amid horsedrawn drays, delivery vans and private cars, and newspaper men shouted to me to 'read all abaat it'. The cry of '*Echo, Echo, Liverpool Echo*, sir' comes wafting down the years, like the overwhelming scent of vanilla pods, the sound and smell of a great port.

'I know where we'll go,' I said to Avril, who was bouncing up and down in the Chariot pretending it was a horse.

'Where?'

'We'll go down to the Pier Head!'

I knew this part of the town, because I had been shopping in it on many occasions with my grandmother. I pushed the Chariot purposefully up Lord Street to the top of the hill, where Queen Victoria in pigeon-dropped grey stone presided, down the hill, through a district of shipping offices with noble names upon their doors: Cunard, White Star, Union Castle, Pacific & Orient, the fine strands which tied Liverpool to the whole world. Past the end of the Goree Piazzas, an arcade of tiny shops and offices, where out-of-work sailors lounged and spat tobacco and called hopefully after me, under the overhead railway which served to take the dockers to work, and a last wild run across the Pier Head, dodging trams and taxis, to the entrance to the floating dock.

At last I had found it!

The river scintillated in the sunshine; a row of ships was coming in on the tide; a ferry-boat and a pilot-boat tethered to the landing-stage rocked rhythmically; screeching gulls circled overhead and swooped occasionally to snatch food from the river. A cold wind from the sea tore at my cardigan, jostling and buffeting my skinny frame. I put the hood of the Chariot up to shield Avril and Edward from it.

The shore hands were casting off the ferry-boat, and I looked wistfully out across the water at the empty Cammell Laird shipyards in Birkenhead. My eyes followed the shore along to the spires of Wallasey, and mentally I followed the railway with all its dear familiar station names along the coast to West Kirby. On that railway line lived Grandma, who was so angry with Father that she never wrote to us. There was a middle-class world, where people could still wash every day in clean bathrooms. The slump had reached some of them, I guessed; but once past Birkenhead, I thought sadly, it could not be half as miserable as Liverpool was. Perhaps, if I could see Grandma and describe to her my mother's terrible suffering and my father's despair, she would forgive them and help them.

I longed to push the Chariot up the ramp of the ferry-boat and escape, run away from our smelly rooms, from hunger and cold, the cold which was raking through me mercilessly now, and from people who looked like the gargoyles on the old cathedrals I had attended in the past.

'The ferry costs twopence,' I reminded myself, as I wrapped Avril and Edward closer in their inadequate piece of blanket, 'and you haven't got twopence.' Furthermore, Grandma, though long since widowed, had been married to a businessman who never failed, and who had come from a long line of ironmasters and merchants who always seemed to have done very well for themselves – she just would not understand.

The way home seemed incredibly long, and I paused at the bottom of Bold Street, to stand for a moment in the warmth of a shop doorway before continuing. A shopwalker behind the glass door frowned at me as I hauled the Chariot close in. The shoppers were thinning out rapidly and I watched them hurrying to their cars, parked at the kerb, or into Central Station. And there she was!

Joan! My own best friend!

She was sauntering down the pavement in her neat school uniform, her mother beside her, presumably here on one of her visits to her grand-mother. I had not seen her since leaving my old home and, presumably, she knew nothing of my recent adventures – one day I had attended school with her; the next day I had been whisked away to Liverpool.

I started forward.

'Joan!' I cried, my heart so full of gladness I thought that I would burst with sheer joy. 'Oh, Joan!'

The mother stopped, as did Joan. The smiles which had begun to curve on their lips died half born. Without a word, they both wheeled towards the road, crossed it and disappeared into Central Station.

I stared after them dumbly. They *had* recognised me. I knew they had. Then why had they not stopped and spoken to me?

A gentleman told me irritably to get out of the way and I became aware that the Chariot and I were blocking the pavement. Still dumbfounded, I turned the pram homeward and slowly pushed it up the hill, gazing vacantly before me.

Coming towards me, amid the well-dressed shoppers, was an apparition. A very thin thing draped in an indescribably dirty woollen garment which flapped hopelessly, hair which hung in rat's tails over a wraithlike grey face, thin legs partially encased in black stockings torn at the knees and gaping at the thighs, flapping, broken canvas covering the feet. This thing was attached to another one which rolled drunkenly along on four bent wheels; it had a torn hood through which metal ribs poked rakishly.

I slowed down nervously, and then stared with dawning horror.

I was looking at myself in a dress-shop window.

It was a moment of terrifying revelation and I started to run away from myself, pushing the pram recklessly through groups of irate pedestrians, nearly running down a neatly gaitered bishop. Every instinct demanded that I run away and hide, and for a few minutes my feet were winged. Halfway up the hill, back in the shadow of St Luke's, however, undernourishment had its say, and I sank exhausted on the church steps, while Avril giggled contentedly in the pram after her rapid transit up the street.

I was disgusted with myself. I felt I could have done more. I was old enough to know that I should wash myself; at least cold water was available. And if I could wash garments through for the children, I could have put some of my own through the same water. I realised, with some astonishment, that I had always been told what to do. The lives of all the children had until recently been strictly regulated by a whole hierarchy of domestics, some of them very heavy-handed, and a father who had, at times, used a cane with sharp effect. I washed when told to wash, went to school when told to go, however irksome it seemed, got out my playthings when permission was given. Disobedience was a crime and to query or object to adult orders, which were given without any supporting explanation or reason for them, was quite unthinkable. I don't think that I had ever had an original thought until I had been plunged into this queer life in Liverpool, where I had been given the job of looking after my brothers and sisters.

Now, sitting on the blackened stone steps of the soaring Gothic church, I realised that neither Father nor Mother nor Grandmother nor servant was particularly interested in me. With all the bitterness and unreasonableness of a budding teenager, I saw myself as a convenient tool of my parents, my only reason for existence that I could take the care of the children off them.

I fastened the two remaining buttons of my cardigan, got up and wheeled the Chariot slowly up Upper Duke Street, skirting St James Cemetery with some trepidation in the gathering gloom. For the first time, I tried to think constructively, to devise ways in which the family might get out of the morass in which it was floundering; but my experience was too limited and my mind too dulled by lack of use, my body by lack of food, for me to be able to come up with a possible solution. Greater minds than mine were having trouble with the same problem. We were but one family amid millions of others.

I cried openly as I trudged along, my glasses sliding slowly down my nose, the tears making white rivers in my grey face.

When my parents came in that evening, I again brought up the question of my going to school. I was always very nervous when trying to communicate with them and probably I mentioned the subject too diffidently, because when I suggested that I would have to complete my education before I could hope to go to work in the future, Mother simply dismissed me by saying, 'Don't be absurd. Go and put Avril to bed.' Father laughed and added, 'I hope no daughter of mine will ever have to go to work.'

Father's kindly meant remark startled me. Even a young girl like myself knew that times were changing and more and more women were entering the labour force. Lancashire had, in addition, a long tradition of women working, and the only future I could visualise as holding an iota of happiness for myself was one which contained a career.

'But . . .' I began.

'That is enough, Helen. Do as you are told.'

And Helen, being a coward, did as she was told.

# Chapter thirteen

With the exception of a weekly visit from an officer of the public assistance committee, which consisted of a quick counting of heads and a few questions snapped at my parents, we had no visitors. I was, therefore, surprised when I arrived home from one of my visits to the Pier Head to find a well-dressed gentleman standing at the door, asking Miss Sinford where he could find my father.

I waved at Alan, who was shepherding the other children along the road, and went up the steps backwards pulling the Chariot up with me. The gentleman retreated a couple of feet from me.

Miss Sinford noted the movement and said promptly, 'Suffer the little children to come unto me and forbid them not. Child, take this gentleman to your father,' and did her usual vanishing trick into her room next to the front door.

The gentleman regarded me with obvious repulsion, but insisted on helping me up the stairs with the Chariot, which meant that Edward sailed up still sleeping and Avril had a wonderful ride.

Father was at home, reading one of the books from the small battered bookcase which formed part of the furniture of the apartment. He immediately offered his chair to the strange gentleman, who sat down reluctantly as he surveyed the smelly room. His rubicund face, plump figure and well-tailored clothes suggested a successful businessman of some kind.

He cleared his throat, rubbed his well-shaven chin, and said hesitantly, 'I – er – we served in the same regiment – you wrote to our commanding officer. I was asked to call on you.'

Hope lit up my father's face.

The gentleman again cleared his throat, as we stood, tense and silent round him.

'I am authorised to make you a grant of five pounds from our regimental fund, if conditions seem to warrant it.'

He looked round again at the empty fireplace and the ragged, gaunt children watching him breathlessly, and sighed heavily.

Father nodded.

'Could you show me your discharge papers?'

'Yes, indeed I can.'

He took an old business envelope from the top of the bookcase and, from among a pile of birth certificates, finally extracted the precious papers, and handed them to our visitor.

The gentleman examined them.

'You were a private?'

'Yes.'

'I thought you were a lieutenant.'

'I was. I got tired of guarding the East Coast, so I resigned my commission and remustered as a private – and was sent to Russia.'

The gentleman looked very impressed. 'Were you? That was no picnic.'

They went on to discuss the Russian campaign for a few minutes, while the children continued to watch in rapt attention. Alan's hands were clenched together as if in supplication.

Five whole pounds! Would he give it?

He smiled and drew out his wallet, and the sound of a tremendous sigh of relief went through the children. Brian shouted 'Hooray' and went bounding round the room, his little monkey face alight as it had not been for weeks. We all laughed hysterically and escorted our bountiful visitor affectionately down the stairs.

Mother came home and was told the good news and it was wonderful to me to see her expression relax and some of the tenseness go out of her.

Alan and I were immediately dispatched to buy a vast quantity of fish and chips and peas and milk, and we spent a blissful ten minutes of anticipation, standing in the steam of the fish-and-chip shop among a shabby, hungry crowd, while the fish sizzled in a great vat of boiling fat.

A fat, sharp-eyed little man, who kept a newspaper and tobacco shop nearby, heard me give a big order to the shopkeeper.

'Ain't you the kids from Number Twelve?' he asked.

'Yes,' replied Alan.

'Got a lot of money to throw around tonight, ain't yer?'

'A man from Daddy's regiment gave us five pounds,' said Alan frankly.

The man's eyes gleamed malevolently.

'Eeee! 'e did, did 'e. Well, yer can tell yer dad fra' me that I'll be coming over ternight. Yea, ternight!'

The last word came out like a small explosion and was obviously a threat.

Alan whitened visibly, though he answered quite steadily, 'I'll tell Daddy.'

We picked up the two big newspaper parcels handed us by the fish-and-chip merchant, paid for them with a pound note, grabbed our change, and ran down the steps and through the gloomy, gas-lit streets as if pursued by ghosts. We knew instinctively what the newspaper-shop man was. He was a Creditor! Creditors had crowded round Daddy before and caused all our troubles.

'Do you think he'll take our five pounds?' I panted to Alan.

'Not all of it,' said Alan defiantly. 'We'll have finished the fish and chips before he gets to our house. Let's get the milk quickly.'

Not even the colossal row which immediately broke out between my parents when we told them about the Creditor could dim the pleasure of eating, really eating, once more. My fish and chips and peas were cold by the time I had fed Edward and got the children settled at their meal, but they still tasted like a meal fit for a king.

'Well, where did you think I got the cigarettes from?' asked Father, his teeth deep in fish.

'I never considered the matter,' said Mother haughtily.

I had been so used to seeing my parents smoke that it had never struck me to question the source of the supply of cigarettes which I had sometimes seen them consume lately.

'How did you imagine you would pay for them?' she inquired.

'I didn't know. I *had* to have a smoke. You smoked them, too!'

Mother began to cry, while Father phlegmatically started to gnaw at another piece of fish.

'I don't know how you persuaded him to trust you,' she sniffed unhappily.

I knew how he had obtained credit. I had already discovered that a good Oxford accent was a much respected asset. A man who spoke as Father did would be trusted by working-class people; they would be sure in their minds that a man who was so well spoken and refined would have the means to pay, no matter how shabby he was.

At that moment there was a knock on the door of the room, and a fearful silence fell upon us all.

Trying not to tremble, I opened the door to reveal an irate member of the working class, our Creditor.

'I want me money,' he said grimly.

'How much?' asked Father, licking his fingers as he got up.

'You know! Thirty-seven and sixpence – and I want it all. Pack o' bloody liars, the lot o' ye,' and he glared around the room.

'Here,' said Father, counting out the money, 'and get out before I throw you out for swearing in front of a lady.'

Quite undaunted, the little man carefully pocketed the money before he moved.

'Lady!' he sneered. 'Ha.'

Father was very neatly made, though by no means tall. His face went red, and he charged straight at the offender, who shot down the first flight of stairs with a nimbleness which would have done credit to a ballet dancer, from which comparatively safe refuge he shook his fist, and then continued downward.

Mother had sat silently through the exchange. Alan and I looked at each other. I could see his visions of plenty to eat for days mixed up with hopes of a new pair of socks slowly fading away. Thirty-seven and sixpence was more than a quarter of the regiment's grant. My own dreams of a broom to sweep with and piles and piles of soap lay shattered.

Fiona, who had not understood anything except the threat of a fight, whimpered and ran to me, and made me take a further step towards growing up.

I put my arms around her and said, with reassuring cheerfulness, 'Daddy still has lots of money left, haven't you, Daddy? We'll be able to have fish and chips again tomorrow, won't we?'

Father had come back into the room and was standing looking worn out in front of the fireplace, but he caught his cue.

'Of course, Fiona, of course we will. Don't worry, little girl. Fish and chips tomorrow.'

Brian suddenly vomited. It seemed to me the worst possible waste of good fish and chips.

# Chapter fourteen

Mother went to town on a shopping expedition the following morning, while Edward, Avril and I went to the pawnbroker's to redeem my overcoat.

The pawnbroker hailed his blue-eyed duck with pleasure, when, trembling with apprehension at my unaccustomed task, I entered the dark, back part of his shop, pawn-ticket in hand.

He smiled at us both, his dark face gleaming in the poor light like a portrait by Frans Hals.

'Sit the little girl up on the counter, while I deal with these ladies,' he told me cheerfully.

I lifted Avril on to the high counter.

The counter was divided up into three by means of partitions, so as to give people a little privacy in their transactions, and in the next cubicle were a couple of Irish women in black shawls and white aprons. They had each brought their husband's best suit to pawn, since both men had got ships and gone to sea.

The pawnbroker pulled down his waistcoat over his bursting waistline. 'Now, ladies?'

'Himself sailed last night, and a bloody good riddance to him, I say.'

A bundled-up suit was pushed over the counter.

'Will you get an allotment?' asked the pawnbroker, as he inspected the seams of the jacket for wear.

'Och, for sure. Not much though – himself will see to that.'

'I won't be seeing you for a while then, once that starts to come in.'

'And will it be breaking your heart?' She dug a stout elbow into her friend's ribs, and they both chortled.

'I don't think I'll be able to live without you.'

And so on, bickering about how much the suits were worth – worth more than shiftless husbands, I gathered – until finally they swayed out of the shop, their layers of black skirts giving out an unbelievable stench as they moved.

Mother had given me three shillings, which I handed to the pawnbroker with his receipt for the coat. He gave it to his gangling young assistant, who disappeared up a ladder into the loft. A bundle wrapped in a piece of cloth was tossed down and neatly caught by the pawn-broker.

'There you are. When you bring it back, wrap it in the cloth again,' he said kindly. 'Everything has to be wrapped up in a bundle.' He pushed the tightly wrapped package over the counter to me. 'You should undo it and check it.'

I did this and my hopelessly crushed coat was revealed.

'Would threepence buy an iron?' I asked, emboldened by his amiable manner.

His black eyebrows shot up and his sharp brown eyes looked at me shrewdly, when he heard me speak. He rubbed his chin thoughtfully.

'Not from me,' he replied. 'You might get one from the junkyard at the back.'

He turned, and shouted up the shute to the storeroom above, 'George! Mind shop! I'm going out back a minute.'

George came tumbling down the ladder, and I lifted Avril off the counter, where she had been contentedly kicking her heels and watching the proceedings.

We went out through the back door, and through the pawnbroker's yard. The yard was paved with brick, and neat flower-beds filled with daffodils lined the high walls. A hut next to the back gate presumably held a lavatory. He opened the gate and we crossed the narrow alley separating the two lines of business properties, and went into a yard piled high with rusting iron – all the domestic debris of the neighbourhood, from old bedsteads to hip baths.

'Hey, Joe! Where are ye? Got any old flat irons?'

An aged, hunchbacked gnome emerged from under a lean-to. He peered at us from under a greasy black cap, with the bright perky look of a blackbird. I had often heard him calling through the streets as he pushed his handcart along, 'Any rags, bottles or bones? Any old rags today?' His cry would bring the children rushing to him, armed with jam jars or rags to trade for a windmill or some other small toy.

'Humph,' he grunted. 'Ah might 'ave.'

He rooted through a collection of old kitchen pails, washboards and dollies lying under an ancient wooden mangle, and finally came up with a small, rusty iron, which he agreed to part with for threepence.

Back in the pawnbroker's shop, I was made to wait while George was instructed to find a piece of sandpaper and rub the iron clean for me.

Gold teeth flashing amid tobacco-stained white ones, the pawnbroker finally presented me with quite a respectable-looking iron.

'There ye are, luv,' he said.

'Thank you very, very much,' I said, and swept out, iron in hand, my coat with its attendant bit of cloth over my arm, and a protesting Avril held firmly by the other hand.

'I want to stay here,' she yelled. 'I like it here.'

I had not forgotten the awful scarecrow I had seen in the Bold Street shop window, however, and I took Edward and her straight home, because I was determined to make a fire with some of the coal the regimental grant had enabled us to buy, heat water and wash myself.

This I did, though I had no soap. I hoped Mother would buy plenty of washing soap, so that I could wash my clothes, too. I knew that our family looked far more neglected than many children did.

I had pressed my coat reasonably well by the time Mother came home. She was laden with socks, vests, a real towel, a wash bowl, some cups, saucers and plates, knives and forks, a saucepan, some aspirin, some cigarettes, and, best of all, some toilet soap and soap powder.

It was Friday, and, when the children came home, I stripped their clothes off them, put on their overcoats, which they considered a great joke, and washed everything. Soon the room was festooned with steaming garments.

Then I washed the children thoroughly, one by one. They were all emaciated, bug-bitten and shaky on their feet in spite of their two fish-and-chip dinners. Only years later, when I saw pictures of the prisoners released from Belsen, did I fully realise how close we were to dying of starvation, and also what an ordeal it must have been for those children at school to drag themselves there and back and try to pay attention while their bodies gradually wasted.

Nobody in the school seemed to notice the children's suffering. The school nurse found that their hair was verminous, and sent a note to say that we should buy a certain kind of ointment and rub it into their scalps. We had no money for ointment, however, so nothing was done.

No priest of any denomination ever came to see us, though the school was a Church school and a Church of England minister came once or twice to visit Miss Sinford. We knew that we were too dirty and shabby to be welcome in a church, and, except for any religious instruction the children might have received in school, God, like Santa Claus, went out of our lives.

For some time, our only entertainment was to walk the streets and look in shop windows, but gradually the younger ones found ways of amusing themselves. Better weather brought little urchins out to play cricket, with a piece of wood for a bat and a couple of beer bottles for wickets, and my brothers were tolerated in these games. Fiona and Avril learned from Fiona's schoolfriends how to skip and play hopscotch on the pavement in front of the house. They all quickly learned to scream and swear with an unlovely Liverpool accent, though they did not do so in their own home.

I read all the books in the small bookcase in our room. I often read while washing the dishes or feeding the baby and it was then that I discovered that a book laid on the cover of the Chariot could be read while pushing it along the street. I waded through a curious collection of reading matter, including *Hadji Baba of Isphahan, Ideal Marriage*, most of Walter Scott's works, a handbook for midwives and several copies of *Moore's Almanac.*

With the last few pennies from the grant from the regiment, Father enrolled himself and Mother in the local branch of the public library, and immediately life seemed filled with untold riches, because I, too, could obtain books on their tickets. The modest little building had a certain elegance – and it was warm. I could not sit in it for hours, as Father did, because I had Edward and Avril always with me and they could not keep quiet for long, but I eagerly snatched books from the shelves and read avidly and haphazardly.

In her shopping list, Mother had included a packet of needles and darning wool and black and white cotton. I now spent most of my evenings darning socks, since nylon socks were not yet on the market, and doing other mending, until the cotton and wool ran out.

The good effect of the regimental grant remained with us, in some degree, for several weeks, though we were still verminous, still had no change of clothing, and were desperate over the need for shoe repairs and, indeed, for new shoes, particularly in the spring rain. We searched the second-hand shops for old running shoes, anything to cover our feet. Even a few pence spent on such things, however, meant that we could not, at times, have even enough starches to eat. Mother and I found it ever more difficult to drag ourselves up and down the endless stairs; and Father looked like a scarecrow.

Would it ever end? I wondered; and then was seized with childish terror that it might end in death.

Then, in April Mother got a job. She had tried recently for domestic work, but well-to-do housewives did not want a refined woman to scrub their floors; it made them feel uncomfortable. She had also tried all the city shops. But many of them employed, as far as possible, girls under sixteen years of age, and dismissed them on their sixteenth birthday, because at that age they had to pay to the government heavier National Health and unemployment insurance contributions for them. The number of women seeking work was so great that some stores demanded and got girls of matriculation standard to run their lifts and clean their lavatories. Almost all of those who survived their sixteenth birthday in employment lost their jobs when they were eighteen because at that age, again, the employers' contributions to their insurance went up. Perhaps it was as well that my parents did not know that in Liverpool unemployment was rapidly reaching a peak of 31.5 per cent, one of the highest in the country; they were close enough to suicide as it was.

Mother's employer was a slippery eel of a man who lived nearby. In his kitchen, he mixed that old-fashioned spring remedy, brimstone and treacle, filled ice-cream cartons with it, and sold it door-to-door for threepence and sixpence a pot, according to size. He had done so well that he decided to employ Mother on a commission basis. She would receive a halfpenny on a small pot and a penny on any larger pot she sold.

Unaware of the need for a pedlar's licence, Mother set out hopefully to knock on the front doors of the better-class districts, her supply of brimstone and treacle carried in a paper bag.

Since she had a very dignified presence, not many doors were slammed in her face, and at the end of a six-day week she found she had made seven shillings and sixpence and her tram fares. The weather had mercifully been fine and the steady walking had strengthened her muscles. Moreover, a number of kindly housewives had helped her along with cups of tea and biscuits.

It was agreed that her wages must be spent on new shoes for her, so that she could continue to work. I tucked my bare feet under the rickety table. Mother looked really animated for the first time since we had arrived in Liverpool, and took a penny tram ride to town at our urging, to buy the precious shoes.

Mother's modest success at her first job dimmed considerably any hope I had of ever being able to go to school again; it was as if a jailer had clanged shut yet another prison door between me and freedom. I realised abruptly how deeply I had hoped she would prove a failure at work, so that she would be forced to stay at home and take over from me her normal duties as a mother. I felt wretched and could comfort myself only with the thought that when Father got work I might stand a chance of going to school, since possibly Mother would then feel there was no necessity for her to work.

After she had left for town, I bumped the Chariot slowly down the stairs. Edward who, by now, was trying to sit up, hit his head when I went over a stair more clumsily than usual and started to cry. Avril, who was hungry and tired, joined in.

At the bottom of the stairs, an infuriated Mr Ferris awaited me. His droopy yellow moustache was fluffed out as he blew through it with rage and his eyes bulged like a Pekinese dog's.

'What the hell are you doing, making such a noise?' he shouted.

I stared blankly at him, not knowing how to reply.

'I can't practise with such a racket. I won't stand for it! You'll have to go. Mrs Foster will have to put you out!'

Miss Sinford came through her door, like the old lady on a weather vane.

'Thou shalt not take the Name of the Lord in vain,' she said primly to Mr Ferris. 'I am preparing to go to Communion. Kindly be quiet.'

'I have not taken Him in vain,' roared Mr Ferris, his false teeth threatening to come out, as he nearly spat at her.

Miss Sinford shook a blue-veined fist at him.

'Go back to your piano, sir,' she squeaked. 'And pray for forgiveness for your bad temper.'

I stood between them as they ranted at each other, so filled with fear that I could not move.

He had said: 'You'll have to go! Mrs Foster will have to put you out!'

'Oh no, O Lord,' I prayed. 'Nobody else will ever take us in. We'll have to go to the workhouse. Don't, please don't, let Mrs Foster turn us out.'

Miss Sinford had dived past the Chariot and struck Mr Ferris a sharp blow on the nose, and, like a terrified rabbit, I was suddenly galvanised into trying to escape.

Hastily, I manœuvred the Chariot past the contestants, through the front door and down the worn steps to the street. Fear beat at me, and I ran as fast as the Chariot and its two wailing passengers would allow me to.

I ran blindly through the grey streets and did not stop until my sticklike legs began to fail me and I found myself on Princes Avenue.

The workhouse or Institution, as it had recently been renamed, loomed like a scarifying black shadow over all the destitute of England; even I knew that. And I was ready to die of fear.

# Chapter fifteen

Very slowly I trundled the Chariot down the avenue. The trees which lined it were in leaf, and each leaf of the privet hedges in the small town gardens in front of the houses looked as if it had been specially polished. On the stone-flagged pavement the puddles from recent rain were drying up under a mild sun. It was mid-afternoon and very quiet. My teeth gradually stopped chattering, and Avril ceased her lament and demanded to be lifted out so that she could walk.

When I picked her up out of the pram she felt remarkably light, even in my wasted arms, and my teeth again began to chatter like castanets, as I looked down at her. She began to toddle along contentedly, however, singing in a rasping little voice 'Little Bo Peep' which we had been practising together.

The warmth of the sun and the peace had its effect. Perhaps, I argued to myself, 'Mr Parish' or even Daddy's regiment would protect us from the ire of Mr Ferris. I stopped in the middle of the pavement and smiled to myself, as I visualised Father's regiment marching down the street, their putteed legs moving in purposeful unison, to rescue us from Mr Ferris.

'Frog's eyes! Frog's eyes!' shouted a rough voice in my ear, and a couple of big boys made playful snatches at my spectacles.

Avril screamed. I instinctively clutched at the precious spectacles. They laughed, and quickly kicked my shins with their heavy boots. Screaming wildly, they ran on down the avenue, leaving me quivering with pain and mortification.

'Beasts!' shouted Avril after them, with considerable spirit.

Crying quietly with pain, I walked on into Princes Park and into the rose garden which, though as yet bare of roses, was a pretty place, with a little lake much favoured by ducks and other small water birds.

My legs felt like jelly and I thought I was going to faint, so I sat down on the first bench we could find. At the other end of the seat was an old gentleman. He was shabbily, though respectably, dressed, with a stiff winged collar encircling a thin, turtle-like neck. A heavily moustached, sallow face was framed by a trilby hat set a little to the back of his head. His expression was benign and he had an air of quiet dignity. He was perusing a small, leatherbound book.

71

Avril came to sit on my knee, and I began to teach her the names of the various kinds of ducks swimming on the lake. The faintness receded and I forgot my bruised shins.

Our peace was soon broken.

'Hey, you there with the pram! Get out o' here! No children allowed in this here garden without an adult.' A uniformed park attendant was waving a stick at us from the rose-garden gate.

Because I did not immediately respond – I was still unaccustomed to my reduction to the ranks of the underprivileged – he started down the path towards us, his stick raised menacingly.

Without warning, a quiet commanding voice beside me said, 'The children are with me. I am responsible for them.'

The old gentleman had closed his book, and was staring coldly at the attendant.

The parkkeeper lowered his stick and looked disbelievingly at the old gentleman, who gazed back calmly at him, until finally the parkkeeper, his lips curled in a sneer, grunted, 'Humph!' and turned away, to continue his promenade through the park.

In a quiet voice, with an accent that might have been French, the old gentleman asked me, 'And where did you learn to speak English like that, child?'

I blushed guiltily. He must have been listening to Avril and me.

What was wrong with my English? And how does one learn one's own language? I asked myself. I was nonplussed.

Sharp brown eyes, with yellowed whites, appraised my bare feet, greasy gym slip, worn without a blouse, which I had had to lend to Fiona, and knitted cardigan with holes through which my elbows stuck.

Ashamed, I bowed my head so that my face was shielded by a mass of untended hair.

'I . . . er . . . I learned it at home,' I muttered.

'You speak it beautifully,' he said with a gentle smile. 'I have not heard better speech during my many years in Liverpool.' The intonation was definitely foreign.

The bent head shot up. This was the first compliment anyone had ever paid me.

'Do you really think so?' I asked incredulously.

'I do.'

I said impulsively, 'Mummy and Nanny thought it was important to speak well. Neither of them seemed to think that I spoke very well.'

'Nanny?'

I nodded confusedly.

'We don't have a nurse now.'

A watery sniff muffled the much admired accent.

He said dryly, 'I imagine not.'

Avril clambered down off my knee and went on one of her small perambulations. Edward slept. My acquaintance opened his book, as if to continue his reading. Instead, he sat tapping the page with a swollen, chilblained finger.

My eyes were carried to the page by the pointing finger, and I was astonished to see that the print in the book consisted of curly dashes with occasional dots.

He noticed my interest, and smiled at me.

'It is Arabic,' he said.

I was impressed.

'Can you speak it, sir?'

'Of course. My mother was an Arab.'

That accounted for the darker skin, I thought, and I wondered if I dare ask him what brought him to England. How romantic to have a real Arab for a mother! I wondered if she wore a yashmak and transparent trousers, like the princesses in my fairytale books.

His eyes were twinkling. Perhaps he was lonely, too, for he said suddenly, 'I speak seven languages and can read four more.'

'How wonderful!' I exclaimed in genuine admiration, remembering my own struggles with the French language.

'Tell me,' he said. 'How is it that – that – ' and he waved his hand in a comprehensive gesture, which took in the Chariot with its half-starved baby and Avril's and my deplorable condition.

Hesitating and seeking for words at first, I explained as best I could about bankruptcy and unemployment. Gradually I gained courage and confided in him my despair at not being able to continue at school and my fear of what would become of us.

He listened patiently, occasionally interjecting a question or nodding understandingly.

Finally I trailed to a hopeless stop.

He sat silent for a while, contemplating the lake, his book still open on his knee, his face full of the sad resignation of the very old.

At last, he sighed and said, 'You know, child, it is not what happens to you that matters – it is how you deal with it.'

This was a new idea to me and I pondered on it, as I shyly watched his face.

'You can read?'

'Yes.'

'You go to the library?'

'Yes.'

'Then read! Read everything you can. Read the great historians, the philosophers, especially the German ones, read autobiographies, read novels. One day, you will have the opportunity to make use of the knowledge you will accumulate, and you will be surprised to find that you know much more than those who have had a more formal education.'

He closed his book and put it in his pocket, and then said quite cheerfully, 'Your day will come, child. Your parents are having a difficult time at present and cannot help you.'

He got up from his seat slowly and stiffly and then bowed politely to me.

'I come here every sunny afternoon to commune with nature. Come one day and tell me what you have read.'

The faintness which had threatened me before was making his face dim to me, but I thanked him warmly and promised that I would come. I felt wonderfully comforted.

I sat down again after he had left, to allow my faintness to recede. Then I called Avril and hastened out of the rose garden before the keeper could find us without a guardian.

The way home seemed infinitely long and the momentary peace engendered by the conversation with the old man gradually left me, to be replaced with memories of Dickens's descriptions of workhouses.

# Chapter sixteen

When I arrived home, Alan and Fiona were sitting on the bottom step of the imposing flight of steps which led up to the front door of Mrs Foster's house. The evening was drawing on and the lamplighter was going on his rounds, pulling on the gaslights with his long rod as he paused, wobbling on his bicycle, at each lamp post.

Alan was talking cheerfully to Fiona, who looked white and woebegone, her blue eyes wide and her china-doll features crumpled with fear.

'What's the matter?' I asked in some alarm, as I stopped the Chariot beside them.

Alan peered up at me through his tousled mop of yellow hair.

'Fiona's scared, and I'm telling her that there is nothing to be scared about,' he said stoutly.

Trying not to show that I was frightened, I lifted Avril out of the Chariot with elaborate casualness and clucked encouragingly at Edward, who smiled at me angelically.

I sat down beside Alan.

'What *is* the matter?'

Fiona answered through trembling lips.

'Mrs Foster is shouting at Mother, and Mother is shouting at Father – and – and it's an awful noise.

'And I want to go home to Nanny!' And she began to cry.

'Be quiet!' I snapped at her, and she was immediately reduced to cowed silence.

I turned to Alan.

'Has Mr Ferris complained?'

Alan looked puzzled.

'Mr Ferris? You mean about the noise we make?'

'Yes.'

'Oh no.' Alan chuckled suddenly and began to play an imaginary piano with gusto. 'He makes too much noise himself. He just shouts at us because it makes him feel better.' He tossed back his hair, exactly as Mr Ferris did, and finished his piano piece with a mighty boom on the bottom notes, 'Boom-tiddly-boom – boo–om – boom!'

I wished that I had Alan's cool common sense. In one sentence he had calmed my fears. But not Fiona's apparently. Tears were running down her cheeks like raindrops.

'What has happened, then?'

Alan sobered.

'Daddy didn't pay the rent. He spent the money on cigarettes, and Mrs Foster is as cross as two sticks. And Mother is crossest of all, because she helped to smoke the cigarettes without thinking of where they came from. And – well, you know Mother.'

I did know Mother. Even in her most halcyon days, her temper had been something to avoid at all costs. Now, sick, bewildered, hungry and despairing, her bouts of temper bordered on insanity. She was terrifying in her rages, more terrifying in her subsequent withdrawn silences.

I licked my lips and voiced my dread in a whisper, so as not to frighten Avril, who was sitting on the pavement playing with two matchsticks and a piece of orange peel. Alan and Fiona bent their heads close to mine.

'Do you think she'll turn us out into the street – Mrs Foster, I mean?'

'No idea,' replied Alan phlegmatically. 'Fiona and I just opened the door when we came back from school, and understood what the trouble was inside a minute. So we just left them to it – and came down here.'

'Where are Brian and Tony?'

Alan sighed. 'They bounced right into the room. Now they'll be expected to take sides – and Brian will have nightmares – and probably be sick after tea.'

I nodded silent agreement. Poor Brian, sensitive to every nuance of every word spoken to him, would be reduced to incoherence by such an episode.

'Have we got bread for tea?' asked Fiona.

'A little,' I said.

'Shall we ever have butter again?'

'Of course,' said Alan.

Avril toddled up to us.

'I like jam as well as butter,' she announced. 'I want jam for tea.'

I suppressed an irrational desire to slap Avril, and we sat quietly watching seamen crowding into the hall of a house opposite to ours. In this house lived an assortment of middle-aged women, who were a great mystery to me. They were much better dressed than their neighbours, though they never seemed to go out to work. And they had lots of visitors – all men.

I watched the rolling gait of the men lounging up the steps. Many of them were already drunk. They shouted raucously to each other and laughed at remarks of which I did not get the import.

One of the single ladies who lived on the same floor as Mrs Foster came down our steps and paused by us. She looked across the road and then regarded us uneasily.

'Dawn't yer think ye'd better go in, luv?' she asked.

I looked up at her dully. She seemed magnificent to me with her veiled, flowered hat and flashing diamanté earrings. Her silver evening shoes and rayon stockings were close to me, however, and she did not smell very nice.

Uneasily, I turned my head away.

'We can't,' I said.

'Daddy and Mummy are cross,' announced Avril, rising from the pavement and dusting down her little backside.

The lady bit her scarlet lower lip, as she considered this, and then said in confidential tones to me, 'Eee, luv, ah think you had better get inside. Over there is going to be ruddy noisy – and rough to the likes o' you. There's four ships in.'

Though none of us knew what she meant, we rose reluctantly and Alan helped me pull the Chariot up the steps.

I appreciated that she had tried to be kind to us, and I thanked her, as she started to walk with swaying hips to the bus stop at the corner.

'That's all right, luv,' she said cheerfully, and she hitched her mangy fox fur up round her chin and called to Avril, 'Now, run along, luv.'

'She's pretty kind, isn't she?' I remarked to Alan, as we jointly heaved the Chariot up the stairs to the top of the house, from whence the sounds of battle still proceeded.

'Yes,' said Alan. But he did not sound convinced, though he added, 'She gave me a sweet the other day.'

Just as we were about to tackle the last flight of stairs, we heard Mrs Foster's heavy tread coming down. We cringed together on the landing as, without a word, she passed us, her black georgette draperies floating around her. Behind her she left a mixed odour of cats and birds.

Dead silence greeted us as we entered our room. My parents occupied the two kitchen chairs which the room boasted. Their mouths were clamped shut, and only my mother's fast breathing told of the earlier strife. Brian was biting his nails feverishly, as he stood watching them. Tony was calmly playing with a pebble on the table, pretending it was a train: he muttered 'chuff-chuff-chuff' to himself as he ran it into a station. He looked up as we entered, his large intelligent eyes sad with a sadness unnatural in one so young.

'Hello, Helen,' he said, his voice sounding loud in the prevailing quietness. 'What about some tea – it's late.'

I did not know what to do about my parents, so I ignored them and answered him.

'Yes, dear. Just let me unload.'

From around Edward's feet in the pram, I exhumed a mass of small pieces of rubbish, which I had gleaned during my walk, and laid them in the hearth. There were empty match-boxes, cigarette cartons – which did not usually burn very well – bits of stick, twigs and paper of every description, and a whole tattered copy of the *Liverpool Echo*.

I raked through the cold ashes in the grate and salvaged a few cinders. Would I have enough fuel to boil some water? I wondered anxiously.

Alan kindly volunteered to run down to the bathroom and fetch a pan of water, and Fiona, without being asked, took Edward on her knee. She gasped as his wet napkin damped her gym slip and bare legs, but she did not complain. And all the time my parents sat in silence, almost prostrated by their quarrels.

It was nearly dark by the time the water was persuaded to boil and the tea was made. I cut a dry, white loaf into eight pieces of roughly equal size, and gave each of my parents a piece of it with a cup of the smoky tea, which had, of course, no milk or sugar in it. I gave a little tea to each child in whatever receptacles I could muster, with a piece of bread.

'Can I dip?' asked Tony. 'The crust is too hard to bite.'

I looked at my mother, who ignored the question and stared moodily into her teacup.

My father picked up his cup, and said suddenly, 'You may.'

Thankfully, Tony and Brian plunged their bread into their tea.

'The bread is so stale it's second-hand,' remarked Tony.

Brian giggled and snorted helplessly into his jam jar of tea. 'I've got a second-hand teacup to match,' he gurgled, a note of hysteria in his voice.

'I want some jam,' shouted Avril.

'Be quiet, Avril,' said Fiona, who had given a little of her bread to Edward to suck on. 'You know there is no jam.'

'Not even any second-hand jam?' the younger girl demanded with mock indignation.

My father began to laugh, at first a small wry chuckle in his throat and, then, gaining momentum, one of his old hearty laughs. I joined in, and soon the whole family was laughing hysterically, the noise pealing along the cobwebbed ceiling and down the stairs to the floor below, where the other tenants, hearing us, must have believed us to be mad.

Only Mother, wrapped in pain, fatigue and semi-starvation, sat silently staring at her cup of tea, her piece of bread in her hand.

# Chapter seventeen

We crept through the spring and summer, cursing wet days, rejoicing in warm, dry ones, ignoring petty ailments and hunger, since we could do nothing about either.

Several of the children had sores which took a long time to heal. These were sometimes caused by normal cuts and abrasions, acquired while playing, going septic; and sometimes from their scratching at their vermin-ridden bodies. We nearly all suffered from toothache from time to time, and Mother's teeth began to loosen. Brian suffered torture from gumboils. His first teeth had been good but he had several large cavities in his second ones, caused, perhaps, by the large amount of white bread in his diet. His wizened face would swell up and he would cry hour after hour, until finally the abscess would burst and the pain would be reduced. On one occasion his weeping was heard as far away as the basement of the house; and Mrs Hicks, prodded by her out-of-work bricklayer husband, made the long journey up the stairs, to inquire what was the matter.

'He's got a bad tooth,' I explained. 'He can't go to school today, because it hurts too much.'

'Well, poor luv!' she exclaimed, her double chin, with its little crown of spiky hairs, wobbling sympathetically. 'Na, then, I got some oil of cloves. Come daanstairs with me, luv,' she called to Brian, who was hovering nervously in the background. 'Ah got somethin' as will help yer. Come on, na.'

Brian allowed himself to be beguiled downstairs, where he spent the afternoon lying on Mrs Hicks's horsehair sofa in front of her blazing fire, having hot cloths put on his cheeks and quantities of bitter oil of cloves dabbed into his cavities.

Nobody had ever made such a fuss of him, and, despite the pain and the foul taste of oil of cloves, he loved it. He loved also the warmth, the cosiness and the old tin teapot keeping its contents warm on the hob.

Mr Hicks called him a brave lad, and, when he was feeling better, and was ready to return to our cold, clammy apartment, Mrs Hicks invited him to come down again on a day when his teeth were not hurting, and have a cup of tea and a homemade scone with them.

79

He came back full of glee, in spite of his swollen face, and remained Mr and Mrs Hicks's devoted friend and message-runner for years.

The Hickses had so little, and yet they managed to make their dark basement so cosy. Mrs Hicks must have been an excellent housekeeper and, unlike many of her neighbours, she understood the nutritional value of many cheap foods like herrings and lentils, and she pointed out to me that brown bread was better than white. My mother, like many middle-class English people at that time, knew very little about the need for a well-balanced diet.

Another good cook was the Spanish lady who had given us the Chariot. I found she had a Spanish husband, who was a warehouseman in one of the fruit warehouses near the Fruit Exchange, and he kept her well supplied with oranges, apples and other delicacies in season. He was, she confided to me as we sat on the steps in the sun, a man of choleric temper and colossal jealousy. But, ah me, what a man!

I smiled sympathetically, and bounced Edward up and down on my knee, to his great delight.

She pulled her black knitted shawl tightly round her shoulders, and looked at me coquettishly.

'You not understand yet, I think. But you learn.'

'I expect so,' I replied guardedly, not at all sure what I would learn but sensing it would be something interesting.

She cooed in Spanish to Edward.

He could crawl a little now, but he was not a pretty baby. His head, which looked too big, was covered with scurf, and his stomach stuck out grotesquely. His smile, however, was sweet as he responded to the Spanish words.

'My last boy, Peter, he go to school with your Tony. Say your Tony very clever – can read well and do his arithmetic.'

This was news to me, there being no contact between home and school. My father, eternally busy at being unemployed, had given no consideration to his children's progress. My mother, after the brimstone and treacle season came to an end, about the end of May, kept trying unsuccessfully for other work, and long walks to see prospective employers took up much of her time. She was now well, in the sense that she had recovered from Edward's birth and her subsequent major operation, but she was nearly starving and was still walking the razor's edge between mental health and nervous breakdown. She was a mere wreckage of the lovely woman she had been a short eighteen months previously.

The Spanish lady was speaking again.

'What your dadda work at?'

'He is registered as a bookkeeper–clerk.'

I felt reticent. I did not want to tell our story to anyone who asked, and I parried all further questions.

Frequently, I walked down the avenue to Princes Park and, seated on the sun-warmed bench in the rose garden, had long conversations with the old gentleman who had defended us against the parkkeeper.

'I was never rich,' he once volunteered in his precise English. 'I have always worked as an interpreter – and I still do sometimes interpret for Arab and Chinese seamen in the magistrate's court.'

'Were you born in China, sir?' I ventured.

'No. I was born in Lebanon. My father was a German and, as I think I told you once, Mother was an Arab. So I had three languages – German, Arabic and French, which is widely spoken in Lebanon. Father was an engineer by profession and I had the chance to learn Chinese and English while he was working in Singapore, then Spanish in Mexico and Portuguese in Brazil. I taught myself Italian.' He paused for breath, and then went on, 'Now I study Greek and Hebrew, so that I can study the Scriptures in more detail.'

I was awed by such a catalogue of learning.

'You must have been able to live quite comfortably,' I hazarded.

'I had sufficient. But, you must know, child, that scholarship does not often bring one money – one can earn, yes – but it is the enrichment of the mind rather than of the pocket which it gives.' He laughed softly. 'I was rich in friends, a good wife, three sons . . .' His voice broke, and he stopped.

'Do your boys live with you?' I inquired, wondering that he had not mentioned them before.

He looked at me absently.

'My boys – my wonderful boys – all died in the war. My dear wife followed them three years ago. Soon I shall join them.' He snapped his little book shut as if to show how suddenly he would finish.

I was ashamed at having pried into his affairs. Adult suffering had a way of springing upon one from unexpected sources, and I had yet to learn how heavy a burden the adult world carried at times.

'I'm truly sorry to have been so impertinent,' I mumbled.

I hoped passionately that he would not die. He was the only clean, civilised person I knew in Liverpool; and he was as wise as my grandmother, who lived so far away, a whole twopence away, in the Wirral. That my parents were civilised did not occur to me. They always seemed to be so far away from me.

The old gentleman shook his depression away, realised I was distressed and comforted me.

'When you are eighty-one years old, you look forward to being once more with your loved ones,' he said.

We sat quietly together. I tended to agree with him that death was something to look forward to.

'Do you believe in God – and Heaven?' I asked timidly.

81

'Yes, indeed,' he said. 'My mother was a Mohammedan and my father was a Lutheran, and neither impressed a religion upon me. They both explained their beliefs to me, but they made me study and search for God.'

'We are Church of England,' I said. 'That is ...' I hesitated. 'That is, when we are clean and rich we are Church of England. I suppose at present we are nothing.' I laughed a little guiltily. 'I have never been inside a church in Liverpool. When we were at home, the minister called from time to time – but he does not do so here. I suppose we are too wicked.'

He sat contemplating the placid lake for a minute, and then asked, 'Has nobody from your church been to see you?'

'Yes. When we first came, a very kind priest in a long black robe brought us some food. He was very nice. I do not think our present house is in his parish.'

'You should go to your parish church.'

'We could not,' I replied emphatically. 'We are so dirty – we can't afford soap.'

He nodded understandingly.

I added, 'I do not know what we did to deserve it all.'

He smiled gently.

'God tries us all, child. pray to Him for help. He will hear you.'

I thanked him, and got up heavily from the bench. There was no hope in me.

All the way home, however, I prayed silently in the well-known words of the Anglican prayer-book, in the belief that there is no harm in trying.

# Chapter eighteen

One of the penalties frequently paid for being poor is that of being cut off from the rest of the world. The normal means of communication such as newspapers, radio and letters cost money. Some of our neighbours had radios, and they clung to them no matter what else they had to part with. It was their main source of both entertainment and news, as long as they had a penny to put into the electric meter or could afford to get the wet batteries recharged. These families could hear the first rumbling of the Nazi movement in Germany and Mussolini's fiery speeches, and of strikes and riots in Spain, the prelude to the Spanish Civil War. Nearer home, there was the crisis of the resignation of the Labour Government.

My father read several national newspapers and the *Liverpool Echo* whenever he went to the library. My mother, also, would skim through the *Echo* during a quick visit to the library, when she would jot down on a piece of paper details of jobs advertised. They were, however, the exception; most people around us found reading a laborious effort and there was a fair sprinkling among the older inhabitants who could neither read nor write.

The newspaper room in the library seemed to be the preserve of adults, who did not like a dirty ragamuffin with a baby on her hip, pushing in front of them. In consequence, I knew more about Walsingham and Lord Burghley, Queen Elizabeth I's ministers, than I did about George V's Ramsay MacDonald.

I knew nobody of my own age and was cut off from all forms of play. Some girls of about fourteen years of age lived in the vicinity. They were tough, brassy lasses, who regarded themselves as adults and worked all day in factories or shops. Each girl had a best friend who was known as her mate and together they went to the cinema or to dances, where they danced together; if a boy asked one of them for a dance she circled the floor with him in silence, her face exhibiting about as much expression as the back of a tram. Every Friday evening they solemnly washed and set each other's hair, and on Sundays, dressed in their best, they would walk together in the streets, regarding hopeful males with joint disdain. This was a matriarchal society where ferocious grandmothers and nagging mothers reigned supreme and men seemed to have hardly a toehold in the home, and these young girls were already aware of this.

They were cheap labour and at the age of sixteen they would often be unemployed, like their elder sisters, but in the meantime they were frequently the most affluent members of their household, with money to spend in Woolworth's on cosmetics and rhinestone jewellery. I envied them their neat black work dresses and, even more, their best Sunday coats and hats and high-heeled shoes. They never spoke to me, except sometimes to jeer at my rags. At such times my glasses would mist over with tears, and I would whisk Avril and the Chariot round a corner, before the children could realise what was happening.

The local boys bullied both Avril and me, just as they did a subnormal boy who lived in the next street and a little Negress, the daughter of a medical student, who lived round the corner. None of us was human by the standards of these lads – we looked different – and we ranked with dogs and cats, to be teased and mishandled if caught.

Our family received no letters. It was as if everybody we had known before that first day in Liverpool had dropped dead. My parents always hoped for letters in reply to the endless applications for work which they wrote, but nothing arrived. Occasionally, my mother would write to an old acquaintance to beg for financial help in our predicament; there was no response.

I longed passionately to go to school, to have some small communion with a more ordered world where I might find some spark of hope of a better life through learning. I continued to pray that, since my brothers and sisters attended a Church school, the priest would one day call upon us and would discover my existence; I was sure he could make my parents send me to his school. But the Church knew us not, and I was thrown back upon my library books and what I could remember from the past.

Unlike many children, I had always enjoyed going to church. The major festivals of the year were to me wonderful theatrical productions, and my introduction to the works of many great composers had been through hearing their music pouring forth from a well-played organ on such occasions. Some of the churches I had attended were hundreds of years old and had priceless paintings, tapestries, vestments, carvings in stone and wood, magnificent brasswork and gold ornaments, a wealth of beauty on which the myopic eyes of a small girl could feast when the sermon became boring.

The beauty of the language of King James's Version of the Bible and of the Church of England Prayer-Book and the rich poetry of the hymn-book were not lost upon me, and enriched my knowledge of the English tongue.

Now, when mental stimulus was most required and religious comfort desperately needed, these things were gone from us. I believed that God was not just angry with us – He was simply furious.

Apart from being exposed to the scholarship and intellectual wealth of the Church of England, I was fortunate in having well-educated parents. They were extremely modern in their day and surrounded themselves with friends who discussed at length ideas and concepts of the times as well as more mundane matters.

As the eldest child, I was sometimes allowed to leave the nursery and sit with my elders in the drawing-room. Bearing in mind the hissed instructions of Nanny to 'hold my hush', I would sit, like a sleepy owl, on a stool by the white marble fireplace, admiring Mother's collection of Georgian silver which winked at me in the firelight from an antique sideboard.

The drawing-room always seemed to be full of well-tailored gentlemen, some of them economists and bankers, others wealthy merchants; and a younger group clustered round my mother talking witty nonsense to her. I did not always understand what was discussed – I was too young. I soon became aware of the world and its problems, however, as seen through the eyes of the upper middle class. There was a place called the Stock Market inhabited by bulls and bears; and there were far-away countries, like India and China, where men made fortunes. There were terrifying food shortages called famines when men died in the streets; there were wonderful farms, full of sheep, in Australia, and others equally full of wheat in Canada. There were ships to be built, railways to sell and venturesome investments to be made in car, radio and electric-light-bulb firms.

The world was a wonderful, exciting place, and I longed to grow up and be part of it.

Nobody mentioned the kind of world in which I now lived. Perhaps my father's friends did not know of its existence, or, if they did, preferred to forget it. And where were my father's friends?

I kneeled on the floor by the window of our top-floor eyrie and looked down at the unemployed men playing one of their endless games of ollies, a form of marbles. I remembered how Joan had ignored me when I had met her. I supposed that Father's friends had done the same.

So much for friendship.

One form of communication which was very rare in such streets as I looked down upon was telephoning. The public telephone was beginning to make its appearance; but even that assumed that the public had friends or businesses with telephones, to whom they wished to speak. In my new world, families still sent one of the family with either a written or verbal message.

Father had always been interested in French history, particularly the reign of Louis XIV, and I had been with him on a number of interesting trips to museums to see new acquisitions of jewellery, clothing or furniture of this period. It occurred to me, one day, that Avril and I could go to the museum together, so I pushed the little girl and Edward in the Chariot all the way to the city and then across it to William Brown Street. I pulled the Chariot up and down three huge flights of steps until I found the right building, and was just struggling to get the pram through a recalcitrant door when a voice boomed, 'Where are you going with that thing?'

A very large commissionaire stood behind me.

'I'm going to the museum,' I replied nervously.

'Not with that you're not.'

His remark was clear enough, but there was a hint of puzzlement in the tone of his voice when he made it.

I looked sadly down at Avril. I was afraid to leave the Chariot outside, in case some urchin thought it was abandoned and took it to play with.

I looked up at the commissionaire and was prepared to do battle.

He must have seen the malignant gleam in my eye, because he said sharply, 'Now you just take that thing back to where you found it, and don't let me find you loitering round here again.'

Loitering was something one could be arrested for, I knew, so I swallowed the bitter words that came to mind, and silently turned and bounced the Chariot back down the steps so fast that I cannonaded into an elderly, distinguished-looking gentleman coming up.

'Oh, I beg your pardon, sir,' I said, horrified at having struck such a gentle, scholarly type of person. 'I hope I haven't hurt you badly.'

'Not at all. My briefcase took the blow,' he replied kindly, as he stared in surprise at Avril and me. His lips parted, as if to ask me something, but I had been so humiliated by the commissionaire that I felt I was going to cry, and I hastened onward across the street to St George's Hall. Once there, I looked back.

The gentleman was standing at the door of the museum still staring curiously at me.

I giggled suddenly through my tears. An Oxford accent coming from a bundle of rags and bones like me must have really puzzled him. It had not, however, impressed the commissionaire and gained me entry to the museum.

So much for public cultural emporia.

# Chapter nineteen

Summertime had always meant to me a period of waving green wheat slowly turning yellow, a time for walks along a meadow-bordered river where buttercups waited to be threaded into chains, a time to lie under a plum-tree and read to my heart's content, a time to play at theatres and dressing-up with my friend, Joan, while the walnuts ripened overhead.

Liverpool summers are not like that. In the nineteen-thirties not much was understood about pollution; and on days when it did not rain the acrid smoke was enough to obscure the sun until a harsh Atlantic wind temporarily lifted the veil. On hot days the alleyways and garbage cans stank, despite the ministrations of an army of dustmen who not only laboriously cleared the garbage but also washed down the alleys themselves. There were still a lot of horses in Liverpool and where there are horses there are always myriads of flies to carry dysentery. Our milkman kept his cows in a shippen at the back of his dairy, but fortunately in summer for part of the time they grazed outside the city, and took their quota of flies with them.

Hens and pigeons were common in back yards. Men kept fighting-cocks, though this was illegal, and many were the bloody battles in the long summer evenings on which men wagered a large portion of their public assistance money.

Much of this the younger children were able to accept as a way of life as they slowly forgot their earlier life, though Tony once said to me earnestly as I bathed a grazed knee he had acquired while playing rounders in the street, 'I don't like the kind of life we live, Helen, and when I grow big I shall change it.'

'I hope you will,' I replied equally gravely. 'You've got brains and you could get a scholarship to a better school – and that would get you out of it.'

'Why don't you go to school, Helen?'

The tears, never far from my myopic eyes, sprang up. I bent my head so that he could not see them. 'Mother needs me at home, dear.'

'How will you get out of it then?'

'I really don't know.' I made myself sound cheerful, as I carefully dried the small wound because wounds seemed to go septic so fast. 'When Daddy gets a job, things will change a lot.'

He stood up and stretched his thin little body. 'Perhaps you will marry a prince,' he suggested hopefully.

'Perhaps,' I agreed, though I knew that girls as ugly as I who also wore spectacles did not stand a chance of matrimony; my mother had always indicated that such was the case and I think I had already been written off as a future maiden aunt. This did not stop me, however, from dreaming for the rest of the afternoon that I married the beautiful, humane and exciting Edward, Prince of Wales.

Tony and Brian also had a dream world of their own. They rarely quarrelled and, with Fiona, they played highly imaginative games in which they sailed the world – Brian always fell overboard and was rescued by Tony – or drove trains and cars which had innumerable comic accidents.

Playing in the open, even if the air was polluted, made them more hungry and it was impossible to satisfy them. If we were to cook anything, we still had to buy coal, so that summer expenses were much the same as winter ones.

We approached our second winter in Liverpool with undisguised dread. We had commenced the first bitter January there with one set of good winter clothing apiece and two blankets. Now, not one of us had a whole garment or a pair of shoes without holes in them. Indeed, four of us were reduced to ragged running shoes or nothing at all on our feet.

My father was a pitiful sight even in comparison with the ragged crew who lined up with him for public assistance. His elbows stuck through the sleeves of what had once been a tweed jacket and his knees were equally naked. He had no socks and there was very little left of his shirt. He used to thread the remains of his old school tie through the torn collar and knot it, in the mistaken belief that nobody would notice the bare chest underneath it. His underwear had, like that of the rest of the family, worn out, its life shortened by inadequate laundering. His chest was red from being chapped by the wind; but he suffered most from pain in his hands.

Both hands had been badly frostbitten during his military service in Russia, and, on the hospital ship which brought him home, the surgeons had debated whether or not they should be amputated. The wonderful care he received, however, saved him from this; but intensely cold weather turned them white, and I used to sit and massage them to revive the circulation. It was then that they became most painful.

One freezing November day, urged on by two shipping clerks shivering with him in one of the endless queues in which he spent most of his life, he applied to the relieving officer of the public assistance committee for help to buy a pair of shoes and a pair of gloves.

Clothing, he was told tartly, was given in kind and stamped with the initials of the public assistance committee, so that it could not be sold or pawned.

'I don't mind what it is stamped with,' replied Father humbly, 'as long as it lessens the pain in my hands.'

His case file was sent for and examined.

'You are not eligible for help with clothing,' was the verdict. 'You do not come under the jurisdiction of Liverpool.'

The same old problem. We were not from Liverpool. Our rate of public assistance was that given in the small town from which we came, and the sum was collected from that town by Liverpool. We got none of the little extras such as money for winter coal or for Christmas which Liverpool struggled to give its less fortunate citizens, nor were we eligible for clothing.

'What shall I do?' my father cried, in despair.

'Try one of the voluntary agencies.'

So Father got the run-around as it was sometimes called. He was sent from agency to agency. And they all said they could not help, because he was drawing public assistance and could get boots from that committee. In vain, he explained that the town from which we had come did not give clothing and we were ineligible for help from Liverpool.

One agency offered second-hand boots at a very reduced price, but any price was too high for us to pay. We had once spent three shillings in a second-hand clothes shop in an effort to make my mother presentable again, feeling that she had the better chance of employment, and had had to reduce our meagre food intake to a dangerous level, in consequence. If it had not been for our kind policeman's pint of milk, Edward would have surely died that week.

Then Mother suddenly got a job 'on commission only'. She was to sell radios from door to door.

Up and down the better-class streets she tramped, knocking at each door and trying to beguile reluctant housewives into agreeing to a demonstration of the radio in their homes. On the third day, she did find a woman willing to listen to her, and it was agreed that the radio would be brought that night for her husband to see.

The demonstration radio, meanwhile, was delivered to the door of our house by a supervisor, and was taken in by Miss Sinford, the most presentable of all the inhabitants.

'Helen!' she shrieked up the stairs to me. 'Come and remove this wicked temptation from the hall!'

I ran down the stairs with Edward on my hip.

Miss Sinford pointed an accusing finger at a cardboard box and a wet battery beside it. The box was clearly marked that it contained a radio, and I guessed that it had been delivered in connection with Mother's new job.

'Thank you, Miss Sinford.'

I sat Edward down on the grubby hall runner, and Miss Sinford with-drew with one of her loudest sniffs of disapproval. Avril had followed me down, and I left her to mind Edward while I puffed my way upstairs again with the radio. I made a second journey for the wet battery and carried it up so fast that I splashed some of the acid on my bare legs, burning them painfully.

A third journey was made to retrieve Edward and Avril.

Still panting from the journeys up and down, I read the instructions on the outside of the box to Avril, and then very carefully unpacked the radio and put it on the table. I plugged in the wet and dry batteries and nervously turned one of the knobs. The shining newness of it awed us both.

Suddenly the room was filled with the sweet sound of violins.

Avril climbed up on to one of the chairs and put her head close to the speaker and Edward smiled and sucked his thumb. I stood in ecstasy while the music swept round me.

We spent a blissful afternoon listening to a far-away world where people spoke as we did and music was part of life.

My parents were extremely angry when they came home and found the radio unpacked and working.

'It does not belong to us,' said my mother furiously. 'You know quite well that you are not to touch anything which does not belong to you.'

'I haven't harmed it,' I said defiantly.

'No, she has not,' interrupted Avril aggressively. 'And I heard a nice lady say "happy birthday" and "hello, twins" on Children's Hour and I liked it.'

'Well,' said Father, turning it off firmly. 'Don't touch it again.'

Mother said, 'I have to demonstrate it tonight, to Mr and Mrs Smithers, and I don't know how to do it.'

'You just put these plugs in here, like Helen did, and you turn that knob there,' instructed Avril, stabbing the appropriate plugs and knob with a grubby finger. 'And it goes.'

She looked up at my mother with hard blue eyes, as if daring her to say she was not right.

Father smiled.

'She is right, you know. That is all you have to do.' He looked worried. 'I suppose the supervisor will move the thing to the Smithers' house for you in his car?'

'Heavens, no. I have to take it myself.'

'But you can't carry that weight,' we said in chorus.

'Besides,' I added, sadly surveying the burning marks on my grey legs, 'the acid from the wet battery can splash and burn your stockings.'

We all knew that without stockings Mother was not suitably dressed for work, and we had all observed that even if she was not much interested in us, she was more alive, more aware of things going on around her, when looking for work.

Silence fell upon the family. The radio and its batteries were really too awkward for anyone to carry any distance.

Tony, who had been playing one of his endless games of puffer-trains with a dead cinder from the fireplace, looked up, as he shunted his imaginary train into an imaginary siding, and said quietly, 'Put it in the Chariot and wheel it round to the lady's house.'

We all burst out laughing, and I snatched Edward out of the pram. 'Try it for size,' I invited.

Very carefully, the radio was put back into its box and lowered into the stinking pram. The batteries followed. It all fitted in.

A gentle sigh of relief went through the family.

We ate a hasty meal of boiled potatoes, which tasted strongly of the smoke from an old shoe I had picked up in the street and brought home for fuel. Then, since it was dark, the whole family went in procession behind Father, who carefully wheeled the Chariot with its unusual contents. I clutched Edward to me and brought up the rear.

Down the street under the light of the gas lamps we marched, past the brothels, past the garish lights and conversational roar of the local pub, past the boys lounging at the street corners, who watched the weird procession speculatively, out of the slum which was our world, into quieter streets of neat terrace housing.

At a corner, out of sight of the home of Mother's customer, we unloaded the radio and set it down on the pavement. We whispered conspiratorially together, trying to decide how to get it to the house concerned, without the customer seeing any of us except Mother.

Father finally decided that he would make the first sortie and carry the batteries to the front step of the customer's house which led straight on to the pavement; there was no front yard or garden to be negotiated.

We watched with excited anticipation as he glided ghostlike down the empty street, quickly deposited the batteries, and continued on down the street, round the block and back to us, so that he actually passed the house only once. Then Alan and Mother together carried the radio itself to the house, and put it down on the step. Mother stood by it, while Alan fled down the street, taking the same course as Father had.

Mother was out of sight of all of us, but we heard the peal of the old-fashioned front door bell when she rang it; and the sounds of the door opening and shutting and of strong Lancashire voices came to us clearly through the frosty air.

Brian and Tony started an excited conversation. Father hushed them immediately. He was standing tense, listening like a hound.

My arms were aching with Edward's weight, so I put him into the pram. Avril complained that she was cold and I put her in with him and rubbed her legs which were mottled like an old woman's from exposure.

Coatless, hatless and hungry, we were all shivering by the time we heard the sound of the door opening again and cheerful voices bidding Mother 'good night'.

She was coming slowly towards us. In the gaslight, her face had a look of stupefied wonderment, as if she had just experienced a religious revelation of some kind.

The policeman on the beat was coming slowly towards us, trying the doors of each shop which faced the road on which we stood; and Father, ever fearful of being arrested for vagrancy, moved us slowly to meet Mother.

'I sold it – that very one – they wanted the demonstration model. They signed the hire purchase agreement and gave me the deposit there and then. And they gave me tea and cake.' Her voice quivered, as she mentioned the last item.

'Really?' exclaimed Father, unable to believe that in Depression-bound Liverpool anybody could afford to buy anything. 'Are you sure?'

'Yes,' she whispered, sudden pride in her voice.

'What will you get for it? Your commission?'

'Thirty shillings.'

'We shall have to tell the public assistance committee. The little bit you earned selling treacle was not worth worrying about. We shall have to declare thirty shillings – and they will just cut it off our allowance.' Father's voice was tired and old.

'Are you mad?' cried Mother with an unexpected burst of spirit.

'No, of course not. But it is not honest not to tell them.'

'We will not tell them,' said Mother savagely. 'They'd let us die. They don't care. Why should we bother about what is honest and what is not?' The bitter question sounded all the more so because it was expressed in her beautiful contralto voice, a voice almost identical to Brian's.

Father had his arms crossed over his chest and his hands tucked into his armpits to keep them warm. He said in a broken voice, 'I must have some gloves. I can't bear the pain in my hands any more.'

'And I must have lots of fish and chips,' shouted Avril unexpectedly. 'Lots of lovely fish and chips.'

Fiona clutched my arm.

'Helen, I feel awfully odd.' Her face was ashen.

I caught her as she fainted. She was the quietest, most uncomplaining of us all and, as I held her frail little frame in my arms and looked down at her closed eyes with lashes like Michaelmas daisies, it seemed as if Death was breathing down the back of my neck.

'Fish and chips,' roared Avril again, quite unperturbed by her sister's collapse.

# Chapter twenty

Mother never sold another radio. It did teach her, however, that she might be able to sell things. Even her dismissal a week later because of her lack of sales did not deter her, and a little while later she got a temporary job in a store demonstrating baby baths. The store was gloriously warm, and she spent her days bathing a doll and extolling the virtues of rubber baths to expectant mothers who came to buy layettes in the baby-wear department. An arduous week's bathing netted her ten shillings in commission, which she spent on shoes and stockings for herself, necessities if she was to continue to try for work.

Christmas loomed near. I did not mention it to Avril or Edward. The other children whispered to each other about it. None of them was in the Christmas play the school was producing and it was clear that none of them had any hope of our being able to celebrate the birth of Christ.

On Christmas Eve, we were all seated in our living-room. The only light was a shaft of moonlight across the floor. We had a small stub of candle and a couple of matches to be used in emergency and these lay ready on the mantelpiece. Outside the church bells were ringing for Christmas services, and across the road in the mysterious house doors slammed occasionally and rowdy voices rose and fell upon the still air.

I had just decided that Edward, Avril and Tony should go to bed, when Mrs Foster's genteel bass could be heard in the lower hall.

'A parcel has come for the top floor. Please come and collect it!'

We were all immediately galvanised into action, except Mother, who continued to sit with her head leaning against the window-frame staring out of the window. We clattered like an army down the myriad of stairs into the hallway, which was dimly lit by a single gas jet.

'Wow!' exclaimed Tony.

It was a very large parcel, addressed to Father, and it took the combined strength of Father, Alan and me to carry it up to our top-floor rooms.

We placed it reverently on the dirty table, and, with shaking hands, Father fumbled with the knots of twine, trying to open it. Finally, he gave up, and we tore at the brown paper and the corrugated cardboard box underneath, frantically trying to find the contents.

We clawed at straw and the infuriating string, and suddenly a golden orange rolled out, sailed slowly across the table and fell with a juicy plonk on to the floor.

An *orange!* An exquisitely perfumed, golden fruit was sitting right in the middle of our floor.

We all gaped at it, and then renewed our frenzied opening up of the package, while Edward crawled across to look at the strange object which had fallen off the table.

We disinterred a turkey of proportions generous enough to have pleased a king, a large plum pudding in a bowl, a bag of potatoes, more oranges, and a box of sweets. Sweets! We were nearly hysterical with excitement.

We had heard of these Christmas parcels, though we had not expected to be the recipients of one; there had been considerable controversy about them in the columns of the *Liverpool Echo.* Many people held that it was ridiculous to help the poor only at Christmas, that the money spent could be put to better uses throughout the year. Whoever made up the parcel for us, however, would have been amply rewarded by the ecstasy with which we received it. It was too much for me, and I burst into tears.

All this time, Mother had continued to sit with her head against the window-frame, though she had shown some interest at first. Suddenly she began to laugh in a high-pitched, wild fashion.

We were silenced immediately. My father was trembling visibly, as he looked at her. Was this the breakdown he had been fearing?

'How are we going to cook it?' she screamed between gusts of laughter. 'With no fire, no oven, no nothing!'

'Be quiet!' Father said firmly, trying to keep a grip on the situation.

Edward and Avril began to cry. Brian stood, an orange in his hand, as if turned to stone. Fiona, clutching the tattered remains of her doll, moved closer to Alan, who put his arm protectively round her shoulder. The darkness of the room made the whole scene macabre and unreal.

Tony, who had been about to open the box of sweets, said, 'Listen!'

Through Mother's wild laughter could be heard the sound of a heavy tread on the top staircase leading to our landing.

'Mrs Foster,' muttered Brian, his voice full of dread. 'Have we paid our rent?'

Avril stopped crying and listened: 'Mr Parish,' she suggested.

The thought of the public assistance committee's visitor discovering that we had a secret hoard of turkey and oranges and deducting its value from our miserable weekly pittance made me frantic, and I ran to the door with the idea of stopping his entering.

I was too late.

A knock sounded on our door.

Mother was still giggling to herself and Father seemed unable to move.

I will be brave. I will be polite, I told myself, and opened the door.

A huge, joint sigh of relief nearly blew the visitor back down the stairs.

'Ah come,' said the visitor, peering round in the gloom, 'to wish yer all a Happy Christmas from Mr Hicks and meself.'

'Mrs Hicks!' exclaimed Brian, and flew to his dear friend from the basement. She caught him in her one free arm.

'Well, now, me little peacock! How's our Brian?'

Father came out of his trance and led her through the darkness to our second chair. She sat down and carefully arranged her skirts over it like Queen Victoria about to be photographed.

Mother was quietened by this unexpected visitor and regarded her with silent dislike. Mother, as far as possible, never spoke to anyone in the house, except Mrs Foster, and regarded all our neighbours with abhorrence. Her chilling stare did nothing to cool Mrs Hicks's exuberance. She carefully laid a paper shopping bag on the floor in front of her, and one by one she brought out a little package for each child and for Father. Lastly, she brought one out for Mother.

'Here yer are, luv. Happy Christmas to yez.'

Mother just stared.

'Come on, luv. It won't always be like this. Maybe the New Year'll bring some luck to yez.'

I could see my mother fighting to make a tremendous effort, and, at last, in a little, panting voice, she said, 'Thank you, Mrs Hicks. You are very kind. I heartily reciprocate your good wishes.' She took the parcel and laid it in her lap.

Mrs Hicks was obviously nonplussed by the word 'reciprocate' but she beamed at Mother in a maternally approving way, and said, 'Na, that's better. You'll soon be well, luv.'

'Helen, can we open them? Please!' Fiona had forgotten her earlier fright and was entranced at having a present.

I looked at Father and he said, 'Yes, of course.'

We all tore at the crumpled old tissue paper of our parcels.

Mrs Hicks had knitted each of us a pair of gloves and each pair had a distinguishing Fair Isle pattern in a contrasting colour worked into it.

'So as you will know whose is which,' she explained. 'Ah made 'em outta a couple of old pullovers ah bought at Maurrie's.'

I looked at her with wonderment. Such an enterprising idea had never occurred to me. The idea was better than the Christmas present itself, for I could knit. Grandma had taught me. Mrs Hicks was brilliant! Bits of old hand-knitted sweaters and cardigans, too holey to be sold as complete garments, could be bought from old Maurrie at the second-hand clothing store for as little as two for a penny. I could buy some, unravel them and knit, just as old Mrs Hicks had done. Edward could have a warm sweater. I forgot my earlier tears in the splendour of this new idea.

95

Mrs Hicks meantime had grown accustomed to the darkness and spotted the turkey on the table.

'Got a Christmas parcel, have yer? Proper nice, ain't it?'

Father agreed that it was proper nice. Mother stared emptily at the naked bird.

'There is one difficulty,' said Father.

Mrs Hicks looked puzzled.

'We haven't got an oven to cook it in,' and he added rather apologetically, 'or a knife to cut it up small enough to stew on our fireplace.'

'We haven't even got a fire,' said Alan.

'Oh aye,' responded Mrs Hicks. 'Now that's a bit of a difficulty, ain't it?' She ran her red hands up and down her ample thighs while she considered the matter.

'Tell yer what. Ah'll be cooking me own turkey on the morning, but there's a good fire going downstairs now. If I turn it to the oven you could cook yours now. It would be cooked afore midnight, when we goes to bed.'

'Oh, Mrs Hicks!' I burst out. 'That would be marvellous.'

Father looked dimly hopeful.

'Would you mind?' he asked.

She laughed at him. 'Not a bit. You could put some potatoes round it, to bake, and you'd have a reet good meal.' She looked at our dead fireplace, and added, 'You can put the pudding at the back o' me fire at the same time. Most o' the heat's only going up t' chimney right now.'

Mother said suddenly, 'Thank you, Mrs Hicks.' I thought for a horrid minute that she was going to follow it with 'But we do not require your assistance'. She controlled herself, however, when the whole family, sensing this, turned on her in frozen, silent rage.

While the children sucked the oranges, Father and I took the bird, the pudding and the potatoes downstairs.

Mrs Hicks put it into a baking-tin which was thick with the encrustations of twenty-five years of cooking, and larded it with a bit of bacon fat. Then, guided by her instructions, Father laid it in the ancient oven to the side of the kitchen fire. Some potatoes followed and the heavy, iron door was swung shut, Mrs Hicks having carefully checked that the cat, who apparently slept there normally, was not inside behind the turkey. Mr Hicks grinned all over his little, ferrety face and promised to sit and watch that it did not burn and to add water as needed to the blackened saucepan into which the pudding was subsequently lowered.

'One of yez come down in three hours' time,' commanded Mrs Hicks, poking up the fire with a large iron poker. 'Ah reckon it'll be done by then. You could wrap it in a blanket and it'll keep a bit warm till tomorrer.'

Joy gave strength to our weakened legs and we ran all the way up the stairs, to sink, half fainting, upon the floor when we got to the top.

Nobody could bear to be put to bed, so we sat around in the dim light from the moon and the street, until the closing of the nearby public house told us it was ten o'clock. After that we took it in turns to count up to sixty, so as to make a rough estimate of thirty minutes more, at the end of which Alan and I bolted down to the basement.

We knocked and entered the vast cavern which had been the kitchen when the house was built. Our bare feet pattered on the old brick tiles as we crossed to the fireplace in response to Mr Hicks's invitation to come and get warm. He was just lifting the pudding saucepan from the hob. His wife took it from him and carried it across to the sandstone sink in the corner. With a skilful twist she got the pudding out without scalding herself, and set it on the bare wooden table, which I noticed with surprise was scrubbed almost pure white. She spread a newspaper on another corner and went to the oven to get the turkey.

Immediately she unlatched the heavy door a heavenly aroma flooded the room, drowning out the usual odours of damp pine disinfectant and unwashed winter clothes. Saliva ran from my mouth and I hastily brushed it away.

'Ah think it's cooked,' she said, twisting one of the bird's legs with expert fingers. 'Are yer goin' to carry it oop like it is?'

We had few plates and none big enough to hold a turkey, so I said that we would carry it up in the meat-tin and bring the receptacle back in the morning, early enough for her to cook her own Christmas dinner in it. I did not tell her that I could not bear, in any case, to part with a single drop of the fat in the pan.

She agreed to this cheerfully, wrapped up the baked potatoes in a newspaper, then told us to wait a moment, while she rummaged in the back of her dusty kitchen dresser.

'Here yer are,' she said triumphantly. 'Here's a bit o' candle to light you up them stairs.'

She lit the small candle stub she had found and presented it to Alan, gave me two crumpled sheets of newspaper so that I would not burn my hands while carrying the hot meat-tin, and sent us upstairs again.

'Gosh, the pudding feels lovely and hot,' exclaimed Alan, as he staggered up with the paper parcels of pudding and potatoes.

The family, except for Mother, was gathered to greet us on the top landing, and a great oooh sounded at the sight of the turkey, as we mounted the last flight.

'I'll wrap it in the newspaper I carried it with,' I said firmly. 'Perhaps it will keep it a little warm till tomorrow.'

I could see Father's Adam's apple bob in the candlelight, as he swallowed; and hope died on the children's faces.

Avril kicked my shin to draw my attention to her.

'I want to eat mine now,' she said determinedly.

Tony's eyes looked enormous in his death's-head face.

Again the saliva gathered in my mouth, but I said, 'It's not Christmas until tomorrow.'

'To hell with Christmas,' said Alan bitterly.

An hour later, there was only a white skeleton left, scraped clean by small clawing hands and teeth. Even Mother came alive, after devouring nearly a whole leg with the gulping enthusiasm of an ex-prisoner of war. We ate the baked potatoes, skin and all, we ate the sweets and pudding, every scrap.

We slept.

# Chapter twenty-one

Malnutrition, when much prolonged, causes a terrible apathy, an inability to concentrate or think constructively, and that winter was so grim that my mind was closed to the intense suffering of my parents. A child's world is a small one and, given a reasonable round of home and school, his life is fairly full. Our little ones suffered unbelievably, however, as they dragged themselves to and from school through snow and rain. Even brave Alan cried when the great chilblains on his heels burst and went septic, and it seemed as if the clothes of all of them were permanently wet; good fires are a necessity in a climate as rainy as Lancashire's. In my parents' case, however, they suffered not only all that we did but also from social deprivation; they starved mentally as well as physically.

To me, the suffering of Fiona and Baby Edward was the more scarifying, because it was silent. Fiona never complained as the others did; she sat quiet and terrified in a kind of mental burrow like a fox that has been savaged by hounds and must be quiet lest they find him again; only when she was playing with Brian and Tony did a happier little girl emerge. And I loved her so much that it filled me with grief to be unable to comfort her – she was past comforting. Edward, who could now crawl rapidly and occasionally stood up, was making valiant efforts to speak. He seemed to have a natural serenity, but when he cried (which he rarely did), it was with terrible deep sobs that came slowly, not at all like Avril's ferocious bellows when she was thwarted in any way.

Until hunger made him fall into lethargy, my father tried to pick the brains of other men who stood with him in the endless queues. He tried to find out how they stayed alive and how they hoped to get a job. But, finally, it took all his strength to get to the labour exchange or to the offices of the public assistance committee and stand, without fainting, until he received a curt 'nothing today' from the former and forty-three shillings each Thursday from the latter.

We always had colds. Old copies of the *Liverpool Echo* were collected from anywhere we could find them and torn up for use as handkerchiefs. The paper was then used to make a fire in the tiny bedroom fireplace in our living-room.

The acid which I had spilled on my leg from the battery of the radio caused a burn which went septic, and the sore showed signs of spreading. Old Miss Sinford noticed the mark on my leg as I went upstairs one day and commanded that I come into her room to have it examined. She sat me down on a wooden chair placed on a piece of newspaper and, having put on a pair of gold-rimmed spectacles, she took a good look at it.

'I'll poultice it for you,' she decided. 'You should have kept it cleaner.'

The fact that I was seated in the middle of a newspaper indicated that she knew how dirty our family was, so I just smiled weakly.

She found a clean piece of white cloth, put it in an old sugar basin and poured over it boiling water from the kettle on the hob. She then wrung it out and slapped it on to the sore, scalding the surrounding flesh until I clutched Edward too hard and he cried out. She hurled texts about Good Samaritans at me, as she worked with trembly ancient fingers, and then ordered me down to her room the next morning for a repeat performance.

Her room was spotless, filled with crochet work which she had done herself. In the window on a wickerwork table stood a large aspidistra in a plum-coloured china pot, and I gathered that an aspidistra was a lot of work, as she felt the need to dust it daily. She cooked at the fireplace, which was larger than ours, her room having been the dining-room of the original home.

It was from her that I learned that the house opposite, which was visited by so many seamen, was a House of Sin and that the women who lived in it were harlots. 'Harlot' was a word which occurred in the Bible, so I ventured to ask her what it meant.

She blinked at me through her spectacles, as if realising for the first time how young and innocent I was. Then she pointed a bony finger at me and said sharply, 'Girls should not ask such questions.' Her voice became shrill. 'It is not a word I should have used. It is a word you must not use. Out! I must pray!'

She seized me by the shoulder, turned me about and pushed me into the hall.

Bewildered, I took myself back upstairs and left my leg to heal by itself, which it eventually did.

Next time I went to the library, I looked up the offending word. It really sounded very wicked indeed, and I was most impressed.

Fiona came home from school one day, in tears. She said she had a pain in her back and chest. I felt her forehead. It was burning with heat. Helplessly, I looked at her and we were both terribly afraid.

When Father came home from the library, I told him about Fiona. I had laid her on the bed and, to keep her warm, had covered her with what few odds and ends of blanket and garments I could find.

We went to look at her and found that she had tossed aside her wrappings and was muttering feverishly, her mouselike hands clenching and unclenching.

Father clamped his mouth tight. His breath came in small gasps and perspiration glistened on his forehead.

Alan came softly up to us.

'Don't you think we had better send for the doctor, Daddy?' he asked.

'I haven't any money to pay him,' was the despairing response.

'We could tell him that.' Alan's lips trembled. Like all of us, he loved Fiona. 'He might come anyway.'

I said, 'We have nothing to lose by asking. Is Fiona very ill, Daddy?'

'Yes,' he replied. 'I can see that she is very ill indeed – I am not sure what it is, though.'

I leaned over Fiona and whispered that we would get a doctor for her and she would soon be better.

'I'll go and ask,' said Alan in his bravest voice, sticking his chest out and trying to look strong.

'Yes, do so. I think Helen and I had better stay here. I haven't any paper on which to write a letter. You will have to explain to him yourself. Tell him about the pain and the temperature.'

Tony, Brian and Avril tiptoed into the room and went silently out again.

Alan plunged out into the February wind once more. Terrified of facing whoever would answer the doctor's door but even more terrified about Fiona's illness, he seized the doctor's brass knocker and banged it.

The door was answered by a neatly dressed older woman.

'The doctor's out,' she said before Alan could open his mouth.

'It's my sister,' said Alan. 'She's awfully ill and we haven't any money to pay the doctor. But, please, will he come?'

The boy's evident fear made the woman soften her tone.

'Well,' she said, 'step in, lad. I am not sure that the doctor can come. He's very busy.'

Alan, shivering, stepped into the linoleumed hall. Under the faint light of a very low-wattage electric light bulb, the lady surveyed him.

She sighed at what she saw, and took down a notebook from beside a telephone on the hall wall. 'Tell me your name and address and I'll ask him. Now then.'

Alan told her, and explained the symptoms of the illness as best he could.

'Now mind,' said his questioner as she shut the notebook. 'I don't know whether the doctor can come. I'll have to ask him. If he does come, it will be after surgery, about half past nine.'

The hours dragged by. We took it in turns to sit by Fiona. She would not take the tea we offered her. I wetted our only towel which was, as usual, very dirty, and wiped her face and hands with cold water.

This seemed to console her a little. Occasionally, she was racked by coughing.

Mother came home and stared dumbly at her second daughter. It was as if she could not let any more troubles in upon herself; she seemed numbed, unable to accept any more. Her unkempt hair had escaped from her hat and hung in straggling oily tails down to her shoulders. Her hands were swollen with chilblains, in spite of Mrs Hicks's gloves, and she stood awkwardly, because the heels of her shoes were worn down so badly that she walked almost as if she was bandy-legged.

'We must keep her covered,' she said at last.

It was difficult to see in the reflected light from the street lamp, and Father said worriedly, 'I don't know how the doctor is going to be able to see to examine her – if he comes.'

'Couldn't we borrow a shilling to put in the electric meter?' I asked.

'Brian went down and tried the couple below; they didn't have one. I can't ask Mrs Foster – we still owe her a week's rent – and I can't ask Mrs Hicks because I haven't yet paid her back the last shilling I borrowed.'

This was the first intimation I had had of his borrowing from the other tenants; it accounted for a general coldness towards us recently.

Without a watch it was difficult to tell the time, but both house and street were quiet when the front door bell rang. Hopefully, Brian pounded down the stairs to open the door.

A firm voice said, 'We can't afford to fall down this black pit – I'll put my flashlight on.'

Brian laughed shrilly and called, 'Daddy, Daddy, Helen! The doctor has come!'

The bedroom door opened and the light of a torch blinded me momentarily. The doctor must have had long experience of the straits of poverty to carry such a powerful torch.

'Come in, come in,' said Father, his voice filled with relief.

I stood up respectfully as the doctor put down his bag.

'Now, what have we here?' he asked as he got out his stethoscope, and then took Fiona's wrist in long, capable fingers.

Father explained the symptoms and I nearly stopped breathing as the doctor listened to his patient's labouring lungs and frequent coughing.

'Pleurisy, I think,' he said. 'She must have hospital treatment immediately. I will go and telephone the Children's Sanatorium, and arrange for an ambulance.'

Father whispered, 'It isn't tuberculosis, is it?' In those days, tuberculosis was still a major killer.

'I doubt it. The hospital will take X-rays.' He stood looking down at Fiona's face by the light of the torch. 'Does she have a mother?'

'Yes,' Father replied. 'You kindly took some stitches out for her after an abdominal operation some time ago.'

'Oh, did I?' he said absently, and then rather more alertly, 'Yes, I remember. How is she?'

Father looked uneasily at me, and then plunged in. 'Her physical health has improved – as far as it can in our circumstances.' He paused, and then added, 'She isn't herself, though.'

The doctor nodded understandingly. He did not offer any more help. He would deal with our emergency; he could not do more. He had to treat first those patients who could pay. In the torchlight I could see the frayed cuffs of his overcoat and I guessed that he had very little himself.

The doctor asked to see Mother, who had been up in the attic room dealing with Tony. Tony had had a nightmare and had woken up screaming.

When she came, he instructed her to get Fiona ready for hospital.

Mother said in a flat tone of voice, 'There is nothing to do. She must go as she is. She has no other garments than those she has on – and I cannot wash her in cold water in her present state.'

So Fiona went to a huge hospital on the farther outskirts of the city, without benefit of bath, toothbrush or nightgown, and my poor, crushed mother suffered the indignity of seeing her almost unconscious child stripped of her clothes and plunged into a disinfecting bath, her head rolling on her neck as the probationers washed her crawling hair. The tattered clothes were rolled into a bundle and handed to Mother, with the curt information that she could wait.

Mother was used to waiting – she spent her days in office and shop waiting-rooms as she applied for job after job with hordes of other applicants. Finally, about three in the morning a night nurse remembered that she was still there and told her she could go.

'I want to know what is the matter with the child and I want to see her, now she is in bed.'

'You will have to come on visiting days. Your doctor will be informed regarding her illness, and he will tell you.'

My mother lifted her hand to slap this inhuman automaton, but she was afraid of what might happen to Fiona if she made a fuss of any kind, so she turned slowly into the long, brown corridor to the front door.

She had come to the hospital with Fiona in the ambulance. Nobody had considered how she was to get home again. Outside was the dark and bitter cold of a February night.

She paused on the step, shaken by the knowledge that the only way to get home was to walk the seven miles to our part of the city. She was not even sure of the route.

The city was completely quiet and, emboldened by this, she set out, following the tram lines which glimmered in the gaslight. The freezing wind cut into her and, after a couple of miles, she was so cold that she was staggering in a ragged line along the pavement.

A dim light at a corner attracted her attention. It was a telephone box, and she quickened her step and sought refuge inside it.

Paralysed with cold, she stood there looking dully at the receiver on its hook, the telephone book hanging below it, and at two buttons marked 'A' and 'B'. Idly, she read the instructions for making a call.

'Insert two pennies. When the telephone is answered press Button A. If no reply, press Button B for the return of the twopence.'

Return of the twopence!

She hopefully pressed Button B.

Nothing happened, so, after a few minutes, she started again on her long hike homewards. An early tram rumbled past her, its lights flashing as it pitched and tossed its way along the lines.

When she reached the next public telephone box, she entered it and, without much hope, pressed Button B, and was immediately rewarded by the happy rattle of two falling pennies. She snatched them up and took the next tram home.

Father and I had waited up for her and were frantic with anxiety. Our anxiety turned to fury when we heard of the discourteous treatment she had received, and we did our best to comfort her before managing to get her to go to bed.

Our visits to the sanatorium were strictly regulated by whether we could find a telephone box where someone had forgotten to press Button B for the return of their twopence – and it was remarkable how many we found.

Though Fiona's illness was long and our public assistance was reduced by the amount given for her maintenance, we were not altogether sorry. She was at least fed in hospital – great hunks of bread and margarine, bowls of sugarless porridge, meat stews, boiled puddings and steamed fish. Patients were expected to augment the hospital's food by supplying their own sugar, jam, cake and fruit. We had nothing to bring Fiona. The diet was, however, so much better than she had received for many a month that, once the pleurisy was drained, she began to look much stronger.

She was sorely troubled by bugs in the hospital bed. Father complained, and was told roughly that she must have brought them in with her.

'She was stripped and bathed when she came in,' he said. 'Perhaps the bed could be stoved.'

A ferocious female, who looked as if she had been put through a starch solution with her uniform, said cruelly, 'Of course it will be stoved – after your child is discharged.'

Father's expression, after that remark, was like that in the painting of Christ crucified which hung over my grandmother's bed. He bowed his head and turned silently away.

A slightly plumper waif of a child was returned to us six weeks later. There was no ambulance this time and she found the long tram ride a sore trial. She came home to again face hunger and cold with us.

'The spring is coming,' we comforted her.

The studied rudeness with which every member of the family was faced whenever dealing with officialdom, as personified by the public assistance committee, by the labour exchanges, by the voluntary agencies working in the city, was a revelation to us. We began to understand, as never before, the great gulf between rich and poor, between middle class and labour. It considerably improved our manners towards our less fortunate neighbours.

When I grew up, I told myself, I would do some kind of work which would improve this situation and make it possible for people to be helped without at the same time humiliating them.

When I grew up!

But I was growing up. Even in my pinched body, changes were taking place which indicated that soon I would be a young woman. A ghastly, ugly, uneducated wreck of a young woman but still a woman.

As I sat on the doorstep in the weak April sunshine, Edward on my knee, I wondered what would become of me. Other girls went to school and then to work, but for me life had stopped in one place on my first day in Liverpool. The other children were getting at least a basic education; Alan talked hopefully of Tony and Brian being able to win scholarships to grammar school; he himself was too old to sit the examination, but he worked hard at school and read a lot afterwards. At fourteen, he could leave school and he hoped to get a job 'with a future'. Fiona, I thought, would sooner or later marry well – she was so pretty; I did not consider how, in this wilderness of slum, she would manage to do that.

Avril, throwing her weight about both physically and verbally, amongst a number of small girls from neighbouring houses, was tough enough to take care of herself, and Edward, watching the world go by from the safe refuge of my lap, was young enough not to have to worry.

Without an education, I saw myself being kept at home until my parents died and then becoming some bad-tempered old lady's companion-help, subject always to the whims and fancies of others. I knew I was far too plain ever to hope for marriage.

I laid my cheek on little Edward's scurfy head and decided that such a life was not worth living.

# Chapter twenty-two

Encouraged by the friendly old gentleman on the park bench, I continued to read. When I explained to him that I ought to be in school, he said firmly and wisely that it was my parents' responsibility. He pointed out that, in studying by myself, I was following in the footsteps of many great Lancastrians, who, though doomed to poverty because they were weavers and caught up in the industrial revolution, found means to study and outshine their better-educated contemporaries. He cited the examples of John Butterworth, the mathematician from Haggate, who never earned more than fifteen shillings a week and learned to read and write at the age of twenty. Such was his love of learning that he became one of the finest geometricians of his day; and James Crowther and Richard Buxton, the Manchester botanists, both self-taught, both always poor, both famous.

I sighed. There was no help there. I wanted to eat and be warm every day of my life.

Avril and I had discovered one beautifully warm spot in Liverpool, although it was rather a long way from home. Sefton Park had a fine glass palmhouse, which was kept at tropical temperatures to encourage the growth of the palms and similar plants inside. Avril, Edward and I used to go into it often and crawl under the great creepers to get warm, emerging later with our bottoms covered with earth, damper but warmer.

Once we were discovered by two earnest young men carrying notebooks and pencils. They were wreathed around with long scarves in the colours of the university, and when they found us they were at first puzzled and then amused.

Avril and I stared at them like a pair of scared rabbits.

'Hide and seek?' one young man inquired.

I nodded assent, and, like fellow conspirators, they rearranged the foliage over us and tiptoed away. A gardener on another occasion was not so kind.

'We don't want no dirty ragamuffins in here,' he shouted, and sent us packing.

Crestfallen, we stalked out of the glass-house with what dignity we could muster, and I pushed the Chariot homeward, passing through a working-class shopping street on the way.

Halfway up the street, I came to a large, red brick building surrounded by a matching brick wall. It was an elementary school, silent and deserted because it was Saturday. I was about to pass it without much interest, when the remains of a poster flapping in the wind caught my attention. It announced the opening of evening school the previous September. Courses in commercial arithmetic, bookkeeping, English, shorthand and several other subjects were offered.

I stopped.

I had never heard of evening school and I could hardly believe that one could go to school outside the normal hours. I could have skipped for joy.

I wondered if one could enrol at times other than September. Perhaps there would be someone on the premises who could tell me about it. I wheeled the Chariot through the gate leading to the school yard and was hesitantly moving round the building searching for a door, when a hoarse voice shouted, 'What the hell do you think you're doing?'

The voice came from an upper window, where a bald man in shirt-sleeves, holding a duster he had apparently been shaking, was looking down at me. His expression was hostile, and I wilted.

'I – I was looking for someone to ask about evening school,' I stuttered.

My questioner looked pained.

'There's not likely to be night school on Saturday afternoon, now is there? You'll have to come on Monday night.' And he started to lower the window.

I did not move. I wanted to ask what time I should come.

He threw the window up again impatiently.

'Now get outta here! We don't want the likes of you hanging around. Get out!'

I got out, and stood in the street quivering with mortification.

Avril, looking like a pocket-sized thundercloud, stamped her foot and said, 'Nasty old man! I don't like him.'

I laughed a little weakly, and looked again at the poster. It said the classes were from 7.30 p.m. to 9.30 p.m.

My mind made up, I went home determined not to be put off by nasty old men.

Father was sitting by the empty fireplace, reading *War and Peace*. Without preamble, I mentioned the evening school to him.

He hardly seemed to hear me, and I busied myself making a bit of fire to boil a panful of water for tea.

'Daddy?' I queried again.

At last he said, 'You cannot go to evening school.'

'But, Daddy, why not?' I protested. 'Fiona and you could watch Avril, and I could put Edward to bed before I went. Tony and Brian will go to bed whenever you or Mother tell them.'

His face was wooden, though at the same time sad.

'If you go to evening school, my dear, it will be necessary to state your age and other details. You are not yet fourteen and the school inspectors would order you back to day school.'

'Well, I can't see why I can't go to either day school or evening school,' I said with all the irritating belligerence of a thirteen-year-old. 'Why can't Mother look after Edward and Avril, while I go to school? She's much better now.'

'Mother still isn't fit, you know that. She is doing her very best.' He stopped. The marriage had been far from happy; yet they had stayed together and his anxiety about Mother was based on genuine respect for her. 'Your mother is just able to manage if she goes out into the fresh air or works among adults,' he continued. 'I don't know what might happen to her if she was confined with a whining baby.'

'He doesn't whine,' I exclaimed angrily. 'And I nearly go mad trying to make this beastly fire and buy us enough to eat, and ... and ...' I burst into loud crying.

That was the beginning of a tremendous family row, in which everyone joined.

Alan tried to soothe me. 'You could go back to school when Edward's bigger,' he said hopefully.

'Once I am fourteen the school won't take me back,' I screamed in an abandonment of rage.

'Stop making an exhibition of yourself,' said Father. 'When I get a job, you will be able to go to finishing school.'

I looked at him scornfully. French finishing schools were expensive and seemed far removed from the realities of life in Liverpool.

Fiona began to cry. 'Don't be cross with Helen, Daddy.'

'Oh, shut up, Fiona,' I snarled.

'I want my tea,' demanded Avril.

I slapped her.

She immediately began to bellow like a lovesick moose.

This brought Tony hotly to her defence and a smart rebuke to me from Father.

Into the uproar came Mother, weary and hungry.

'What *is* the matter?' she asked, putting down her battered handbag.

'Helen wants to go to evening school and I have told her that it is impractical, because the school inspectors would pick her up as being young enough for day school.'

'Well, why can't I go to day school?'

Mother's lips began to tremble. 'You are needed at home, dear.'

'No, I am not. You can very well look after the children.'

'I have to go to work. The doctor recommended it. And I am the most likely one to get work.'

'I don't believe it,' I said. Thirteen-year-olds can be very cruel.

'The general welfare of the family demands that you stay home.'

'I won't!'

Mother suddenly started to cry hysterically, shrieking that it was too much and I was a hard-hearted, thankless daughter.

'I have nothing to be thankful for,' I retorted bitterly.

'Helen, Helen, don't!' Fiona whispered, her eyes wide and terrified, as she clutched my arm. Alan, from across the room, implored me silently.

The fight went out of me. I turned to Fiona and let her lead me back to our newspaper bed. There, crouched together with my head on her shoulder, I wept myself to exhaustion. I had lost my Waterloo.

By mid-May, Fiona seemed well enough to go back to school. She was by nature placid to the point of apathy, and her gentle pliability made her popular at school. At home, she received no attention and, without playthings, she began to get bored and to ask to be allowed to return to the more lively world of school. My parents had not mentioned school to her. They went out on their various rounds of employment agencies, libraries, etc., and seemed to have forgotten her. I, therefore, prepared her for school one morning as best I could.

At the last moment she balked.

'I feel shy,' she said, standing uneasily in the dark hall and rubbing one foot against the other. 'And I haven't got twopence for the fee. Alan should have waited for me.'

Impatiently I thrust twopence into her hand from the daily shilling I received to buy food. But still she would not move and stood biting her nails and staring anxiously through the glass door at the busy street.

'Come with me,' she demanded.

In a home as empty as ours, there was little for me to do, so I put Edward and Avril into the Chariot and together we walked the four blocks to school.

The school was a fine stone building, matching architecturally the adjoining church and presbytery. A high iron railing surrounded the playground, and we paused by the gate to see if we could find one of Fiona's playmates, so that she would not feel so lonely when going into school.

A pretty lady teacher came hurrying towards the gate. When she saw Fiona she smiled at her through the veil of her smart little hat.

'Good morning, Fiona. I am glad to see you back. Are you feeling quite well again now? Alan told me that you were in hospital.'

She ran her eyes over Fiona's thin, underclothed body and returned Fiona's angelic, worshipping smile. Then she looked at me in a puzzled fashion. A question trembled on her lips.

Fiona had been brought up properly and she immediately said politely,

'Miss Brough, may I introduce my elder sister, Helen, and this is Avril and this is my baby brother, Edward.'

Miss Brough's brow cleared.

She said, 'How do you do?'

I murmured, 'Very well, thank you.'

'I don't remember you going through our school, my dear,' she remarked to me. 'You must have left before I came – I have only been here three years.' She chucked Edward under the chin with a finger clothed in good brown leather. Then she looked at me again, more sharply. 'But that is not possible – you are quite young.' She laughed. 'You must have gone to school somewhere else.'

My tongue clove to the roof of my mouth and I could not answer.

Fiona said brightly, 'She used to go to our old school. She has never been to school in Liverpool.'

'Haven't you, my dear?'

'No, Miss Brough.'

I was nearly tongue-tied with fear of what my parents would say if they found out about this conversation.

She was looking at me keenly now, and must have seen the stark fright in my eyes. She pursed her delicately painted lips, and said, 'Well, never mind. Fiona, hurry up or you will be late.'

The school bell began to ring and she smiled reassuringly at me and said, 'Goodbye. Goodbye, Avril and Edward.'

'Goodbye,' I muttered through clenched teeth.

My legs were shaking so much that I could not start the pram. I watched her disappear through the school's ornately carved doorway before, at last, I could make my feet move.

I said nothing to my parents.

A week later a school attendance officer called upon my parents while I was out. How they evaded being prosecuted and sent to prison for my long truancy I will never know. Perhaps their calm authoritative manners made even school attendance officers quail. My immediate attendance was, however, ordered.

I faced two outraged parents every day for the next six weeks until my fourteenth birthday. The day after that, I was back home again looking after Edward.

I had never been to an elementary school, and I found myself far ahead of the other children in the class in everything except mathematics. It was, however, bliss to hold a pencil in my unaccustomed fingers and to try my wits against the work put before me.

This school had a new and enthusiastic drawing-master. He had to teach children who, for the most part, hardly knew that artists created pictures, and he had only pencils, paper and pastel crayons with which to work, but at my first lesson he did his utmost to explain perspective to the disinterested class.

'Any questions?' he asked.

While the rest of the class stared at him glumly, I put up my hand.

'Could you explain why medieval pictures often look so alive and real though they have no perspective?' I asked hopefully.

The class turned round in a body and stared at me open-mouthed. The teacher's Adam's apple bobbed up and down as he sought to reply to me.

Finally, he answered me briefly and then set the class the task of drawing a picture of mountains and roads.

He came and sat on the bench beside me and examined my work. He looked carefully at the little picture and suggested a technical method of improving the texture of the shading in it, while I sat in frozen silence beside him afraid that I would smell abominable to him.

'I should like you to draw me one or two more, as homework,' he said at last. 'You can sketch anything which takes your fancy. I want to see what you can do.'

Breathless with excitement, I said I would like to do the drawings but I had neither paper nor pencils.

He smiled and said calmly, 'I can provide you with them.'

I sat on the steps for several evenings, Edward crawling at my feet, while I sketched the life of the street and a picture of Avril, who was hugely flattered at having a drawing made of her.

A week or two later, the drawing-master expressed his approval of my work and produced a small examination paper for me to work my way through. The paper, with my drawings, vanished into officialdom.

'There is a scholarship available at the City School of Art,' he explained kindly to me, 'and I have put you in for it.'

I was happy. For the first time in two years I played with other girls, and I was being taught, though in a rough-and-ready manner. Nobody wanted to sit by me because I was so disgustingly dirty, even by the low standards prevalent in the neighbourhood, but in the open school yard I played tag and skipped until my limited strength gave out.

My fourteenth birthday passed, and my parents put an end to my little holiday. I wept and raged, but to no purpose. I was wanted at home, and Father thankfully turned over Avril and Edward to me again.

Although I had played with other girls at school, I had found nothing in common with them. They had a hearty vulgarity of speech and manner which made me recoil from them and, to them, a girl who spoke as if she had ollies in her mouth was very suspect. A small group of girls who were better behaved and came from better homes regarded me with undisguised horror.

I was back where I had started from, pushing Edward's Chariot to and from the shops or the park, and without any hope of bettering myself.

During the summer holidays, I took all the children to the parks to play, and sat wistfully amongst stout mothers in black shawls, watching my little charges play just as they did. The children accepted me as just another 'mum' and I was too shy to ask if I could play too.

September saw the children back at school again. I watched them go with envy. Now I was over fourteen I could not hope for further education.

# Chapter twenty-three

Alan and I sat huddled together on the front step. The October evening was cold and clammy; yet we were reluctant to go into the stuffy house. The gas lamps' light gleamed softly on the damp pavement and women hurried by, their black shawls held tightly round them, their children whining at their heels. Three young men lolled against the iron railings of the corner house; their noisy laughter mingled with that from the public house on the corner opposite to them. Maurrie, the second-hand-clothes man, shuffled by with a sack on his back.

An Irish woman plodded stolidly up the street. Near us, she stepped out into the middle of the street and turned, to take up a belligerent stance facing the front steps of the house opposite.

She was a scarifying-looking person, hugely fat with legs like wool-clad pillars. Her hair was parted across her head from ear to ear and the back parting had been plaited and made into a neat bun; the front hair had been parted again down the middle and plaited forwards, the resulting braids being draped down either side of her face and under her ears, to be fastened at the back. The result was outlandishly fierce-looking to anyone unaccustomed to the Victorian hairstyles of some Liverpool Irish women. She smoothed down her white apron over her black skirt, wrapped her black, crocheted shawl around her and folded her enormous arms. Then, gathering her breath until her purple cheeks stood out like balloons, she opened her mouth and screamed.

'Yer pack o' bloody whores!' she yelled at the house Miss Sinford called the House of Sin. 'I'll show yer! Taking a decent woman's hoosband.'

A crowd materialised from nowhere.

'Go it, Ma!' shouted one of the young men from the corner.

There was a flutter of sniggering laughter from the crowd and a murmur of encouragement.

A frail-looking, middle-aged woman, her bare legs thick with varicose veins and her feet shoved into ancient carpet slippers, was unwise enough to open the door and appear on the steps before her.

'You'd better stop that,' she shouted, 'or I'll call a copper.'

This produced such a description of the moral habits of the local constabulary that even the young men in the crowd were impressed. The

Irish have a vivid way of expressing themselves, and the shawl woman was no exception. She lifted a fist as stout as a leg of mutton and shook it at the prostitute.

'Yer harlot, yer!' She finished up, and spat accurately at the feet of the Lady of Sin.

Alan giggled behind his hand and whispered, 'Has the lady on the steps taken the other lady's husband from her?'

'Yes,' I said under my breath.

'I'm not surprised. I imagine he ran away from her – she looks as fierce as a tiger.'

I looked at the woman on the steps. She was quite old, her face haggard under its paint. Her hair was dyed a startling red, and diamanté earrings hung from each ear. I was mystified as to where her charm lay. I had read most of Emile Zola's works and now understood the occupation of the ladies opposite. But Zola's heroines were beautiful, and I had always gathered from the conversation of grown-ups that, unless one was beautiful, one did not stand a chance of even a husband, never mind a queue of men such as these ladies commanded.

The woman on the steps drew back towards her front door. She glanced uneasily up and down the street. Several possible clients, hands in pockets, were wandering a trifle unsteadily towards the crowd.

She became anxious to placate, and whined, 'Ah dawn't know who yer hoosband is. Ah dawn't even knaw who yer mean. Na go home,' she wheedled, 'and stop making an exhibition of yerself.'

This infuriated the Irish woman so much that she went up the steps like a tank and punched the small woman in the face.

In a moment, clutched together, they were rolling down the steps and on to the pavement, clawing at each other's eyes, using teeth and knees to inflict as much damage as possible.

The crowd surged forward, roaring approval, and shouting encouragement to whichever participant they favoured.

Three very large dock labourers, who had been standing uneasily watching the exchange, raised their voices against the general hubbub.

'Na, Ma, come on,' they cajoled the Irish woman. 'This is too much. Come on, na. Break it oop!'

But Ma, shawlless and nearly blouseless by now, was too busy holding off the red-haired cat she had provoked to take anybody's advice. Alan and I watched, open-mouthed, through the shifting legs of the crowd.

Suddenly, a little spurt of blood showed on the shawl woman's face, and the crowd hushed.

A male voice said sharply, 'Ee, that's not fair. Get off, you.'

A boot was sharply applied to the prostitute's bottom and she let go immediately, whipped to her feet and whirled on her new assailant.

He backed away from her warily.

'Na, you just take that blade out from under yer thumbnail, yer lousy bitch.'

The shawl woman heaved herself to her feet, panting. She wiped her face with the back of her hand. When she saw blood on it, she screamed in mixed rage and terror.

'I'll get yer for this!' she shrieked, at the same time putting a little distance between herself and her opponent.

Two of the dockers jumped the prostitute suddenly from behind, caught her arm and twisted it behind her back. While one held her, the other extracted a piece of razor blade from under one of her long nails and held it up for the crowd to see.

There was a threatening murmur.

'Let me go,' she shouted, her voice full of fear.

The men released her and she ran up the steps, her carpet slippers, still on her feet, flapping as they hit the stone.

We became aware of another heated altercation on the edge of the crowd. The pub had closed and its patrons were coming home, among them a huge, bull-necked man who was bellowing, 'Ah'll teach 'er to make a row in t' street, ah will!'

His friends pulled anxiously at his shabby jacket sleeve and murmured, 'Na, then, Bill. Na, then.'

With a sigh of delightful anticipation, the crowd opened to make way for the bull-necked man, while the prostitute vanished into the House of Sin and the sound of a bolt being shot on the inside of the door came clearly across the street.

The bull-necked man charged through the expectant crowd, undoing his trouser belt as he came. His seamed face was red with rage and the muscles and veins of his neck bulged above the neckband of his union shirt. With a smart pull, he whipped his belt out and, swinging it by its buckle, he advanced on the shawl woman, who came towards him, her shawl again draped across her back, but her huge bosom almost bare. She threw back her shoulders to exhibit her ample charm and swayed her hips seductively. Blood still trickled down her cheek but she smiled slyly at the newcomer.

'Na, then, our Mary Ann. What yer think yer doing? I won't stand for it, d' yer hear me!'

She stuck her chin in the air and spat an epithet at him.

Infuriated, he shot out a huge red fist, tore at her bun, took a firm hold on the tumbling plaits and twisted her by her hair till her back was towards him. Then, lifting his belt he brought it down hard on her buttocks. She screamed, and her shawl fell off again, revealing her fat, naked shoulders already scratched in the fight. A second time the belt whistled through the air and a red welt appeared across the buxom shoulders.

I started up with a cry of horror, but one of the women who lived in our house pushed me sharply down on to the step again.

'Let him be,' she hissed. 'She loves it.'

'Loves it?' I hissed back. 'But she's being hurt!' And I winced as the belt cracked down again, and the woman screamed.

The crowd was silent now, tense with the same tenseness of dogs sitting in front of a house where there is a bitch in heat. I felt sick.

The woman from our house said kindly, 'You go inside and leave the likes of them to themselves.'

Alan and I, both frightened, ran into the hall of our house, from which vantage point we continued to watch.

Beating her steadily, while the shawl woman alternately screamed and cursed, the man was gradually dragging the woman through the crowd and over the cross-road to a smaller house than ours farther down the street, where apparently they lived. He flung her against the closed door and she stood with her back against it, sobbing wildly. The man threw himself against her, and the crowd whooped.

'Go it, Bill,' they shouted.

Bill reached behind his wife and turned the door knob of his home, put his hand on the woman's naked breast and pushed her, so that she seemed to fly backwards into the narrow hall. He followed, and slammed the door after him.

Regretfully, the crowd slowly broke up and departed. Alan and I, both shaking with nervous tension, went slowly up to our apartment.

Fiona was sitting by the window having watched the same scene from a better vantage point. She had evidently been much impressed by the prostitute.

'Wasn't it exciting, Helen? Wasn't the little woman opposite brave to fight that big fat shawl woman? What were they fighting about?'

'I am not sure,' I said untruthfully.

Fiona said, 'You should draw a picture of it, Helen.'

I laughed.

'I don't think Mummy or Daddy would like me to draw pictures of things like that. Come along, I think you had better go to bed.'

Alan was wandering about the dark room and he came, finally, and stood by us, hands in pockets, looking down at the street which was now practically empty, except for one or two jolly-looking sailors rolling unsteadily up the steps of the House of Sin.

'Why didn't you go to art school, Helen?' Alan asked unexpectedly.

I turned and asked in surprise, 'Art school? What do you mean?'

The response was truly brotherly.

'Art school, stupid. What do you think I meant? You know, when you got the scholarship. I always meant to ask you, but there never seems to be much peace for conversations.'

'Scholarship? I have never won a scholarship, you know that.'

'Heavens, you are dumb! Don't you remember – you sat for it when you got caught and had to go back to school.'

Alan looked at me as if I had lost my reason.

'Oh, that. I didn't get it. I never heard anything about it, after Mr Piper entered my name for it.'

'But – but – ' stammered Alan, 'Mr Browning – the headmaster – asked me only the other day how you were getting on, and I meant to ask you what happened. If you got it, why didn't you go to art school? It would have been wonderful for you.'

The episode in the street had left me rather trembly and I sat down suddenly as a horrible suspicion went through my head.

Had I indeed won the scholarship? If I had, my parents would have been informed of it. Had they refused it on my behalf? They were perfectly entitled to do so – schooling was not compulsory after the age of fourteen.

This idea was so repulsive to me that at first I could not accept it. Surely, my parents would realise that it was a wonderful opportunity for me. Surely, they would have my interests at heart. It must be a mistake – I could not have won.

Yet if Alan's headmaster said I had won, won I had. He would not forget that one of the few scholarships available at that time had been awarded to his school.

'If I won,' I said through clenched teeth, 'I was never told about it.'

'How queer,' said Alan, and Fiona's enormous eyes widened even further as she, too, considered the matter. 'You'd better ask Mummy or Daddy.'

Such a rush of pain went through my skimpy body that I wrapped my arms around myself and leaned my head nearly down to my knees. In little gasps, I said, 'I don't think I want to ask them. I don't think I can bear to.'

'I'll ask,' said Alan stoutly. 'I'm not afraid.'

'Oh no, Alan,' I said. 'You will only be told that it's none of your business – and the whole family will be upset.'

He knew I was right and was silent.

I was almost certain in my mind that my parents had just not told me because my attendance at school for a prolonged period would have compounded their difficulties; they would have lost their baby-sitter and housekeeper – and they would have had to pay a substitute.

I rocked myself backwards and forwards, as my touching belief that my parents, even if they had not much love for me, would do their best for me, and that they had always done so, died. I was in agony. The research into the ruthless exploitation of the eldest child was still far in the future, and there was no explanation to console my childish despair.

Two bony pairs of arms were quietly wrapped around me, and two young heads came close to mine.

'Never mind, Helen. Please don't cry. What's a silly old scholarship, anyway? You got it. You're clever. You'll get another one some day.'

I did not cry. I could not.

Gently, I told Alan to go to bed.

I pushed Fiona quietly towards our pile of newspapers laid on top of the old door; the papers had an irritating habit of spreading themselves on to the floor as well. I laid myself down on them, facing the wall, and pulled my knees up tight like a baby in the womb. If I took little breaths and lay perfectly still, perhaps the pain inside me would go away.

I slept little, but felt calmer in the morning. The children were dispatched to school. Mother went out. Father hurriedly prepared to go down to the labour exchange. As he struggled to neaten himself, I asked him diffidently, 'Did you ever hear anything about the art scholarship I sat for?'

He looked at me abstractedly. 'Art scholarship?'

'Yes. You remember – the one I sat for while I was at school – just before my birthday.'

He was quiet for a moment and sat staring at his shoelace which had broken.

'Yes,' he said at last. 'We did hear something about it. It couldn't be awarded to you.'

'But did I win?' I asked in a whisper.

'You did. However, when we said that you were born in Cheshire, we were told that you were ineligible and should never have been entered for it. Cheshire comes under a different education committee.'

'Why didn't you tell me about it?'

'There seemed no point – children get upset about these things.'

I nodded. I could not speak because my teeth were chattering so much from the nervous effort I had made to ask about the scholarship.

I hugged Edward to me, while he seized his battered trilby hat and departed. I could hear the loose sole on one of his shoes flipping on each step.

All that morning, I thought about the scholarship. Pressed against the glass-topped biscuit tins in the tiny grocery store, the rancid smell of the bacon-cutting machine enveloping me, I had a long wait in the tiny shop while the grocery woman measured out single ounces of tea, sugar and margarine, climbed her ladder to reach down tins of condensed milk and had long arguments with several desperate women trying to extend their credit with her.

By the time it was my turn to be served with the twopennyworth of rice I wanted, I had come to the conclusion that I must accept my father's explanation, despite the fact that the school had known my place of birth.

# Chapter twenty-four

Dully, sulkily, I continued to look after the children through the winter, trying to dry their rags when they came in rain-soaked, trying to buy with pennies enough food for nine, living in a world where handkerchiefs, toilet-paper, hot water and soap ranked as unobtainable luxuries. Fortunately, the stomach can become accustomed to very little food, and the children did not now cry very often that they were hungry, as long as they had bread and potatoes.

In an effort to make sales and increase their profits, even the more reputable local shopkeepers now cut margarine into quarter pounds, though it cost only fourpence to buy a whole pound, and opened pots of jam to sell at a penny a tablespoonful – bring your own cup. One tiny corner shop, presided over by a skinny harridan whose hands never seemed to have been washed, would make up a pennyworth of almost anything that could be divided up. This resulted in a very high price per pound – but if one has only a penny one has little choice in the matter.

A learned professor published a detailed menu showing that a full-grown man could eat well on four shillings a week but it was of no help to me. Four shillings per week per head to spend on food would have represented to us an unattainable height of luxurious living.

In the city council, a stout, outspoken Labour couple tore into the mayor, aldermen and councillors with bitter tongues on behalf of the unemployed, the homeless and the aged. Mr and Mrs Braddock – our Bessie, as Mrs Braddock was known to many – started a lifelong battle on behalf of the poor of Liverpool. On the docks, the Communists made inroads among the despised and ill-treated dock labourers, the results of which are still apparent in the labour unrest rampant in the docks of Liverpool forty years later.

City health officials looked in despair at horrifying infant mortality rates and at a general death rate nearly the highest in the country. Nobody, of course, died of starvation – only of malnutrition.

The Roman Catholic Church and the Church of England continued to build themselves a cathedral apiece and solicited donations.

My parents at about this time seemed to have given up all hope of any real future and struggled on from one day to the next, too dulled by hunger and privation to plan how they might get out of the morass they were in.

My father tended to sit silently indoors now, only going to the labour exchange and the public assistance committee, because he was more ragged than the most poverty-stricken tramp I ever encountered. My mother still made valiant efforts to keep her appearance reasonable so that she could apply to shops and offices for work.

One sunny Sunday in March, however, Father decided he could stand the rank atmosphere of the house no more and he and Brian went for a walk in the town, which was fairly deserted on Sundays. Father always feared being arrested for vagrancy, but he hoped police would be few and far between on this day of rest.

Two hours later, a petrified Brian came rushing up the stairs and into our living-room, where I was rocking Edward to sleep in his Chariot. He buried his face in my shoulder.

'Daddy's been arrested,' he cried.

I jumped up in alarm and Edward cried out as the rocking ceased.

'Oh, heavens! Whatever did he do?'

Brian continued to sob in my arms in sheer fright.

'Tell me, Brian. What did he do? Did he steal some cigarettes?'

I felt Brian nod negatively.

'Well, he must have done *something!*'

'He didn't do anything.'

I knelt down and hugged Brian close.

'Well, tell me what happened. Come on, love, tell me.'

Brian's sobs reduced to sniffs and with all the maddening long-windedness of children, he said, 'Well, we walked down into the town and we looked in Cooper's and MacSymon's windows at all the lovely food – they had peaches in brandy in Cooper's. And then we looked in the furniture stores and Daddy showed me a jade idol in Bunney's, at the corner of Whitechapel. Then we walked up Lord Street – opposite Frisby Dykes – and looked at the tailors' shops in North John Street.'

'Yes, yes,' I said impatiently.

'Well, then Daddy wanted to look at the gentlemen's shops in the arcade in Cook Street – and it was at the corner of Cook Street that we saw this strange man.'

'What kind of a strange man?'

'Well, he was big and nicely dressed with lovely polished boots. Daddy said he was a plain-clothes policeman – and we were both a bit scared – but Daddy said to keep on walking as if there was nothing wrong.' Brian wiped his nose on the cuff of his jersey. 'So we did – and we looked at all the pipes and tobacco and suits and things and this man started to walk up behind us.'

'What did you do?'

'We started to walk faster and faster and when we got to Castle Street and turned the corner, we ran like anything and the man ran after us. Daddy pushed me into a doorway by a pillar and told me to stay there, and he went on running. When the policeman had passed me by, I peeped out – and the policeman had his hand on Daddy's shoulder like they do in books.' Brian burst into tears again. 'So I doubled back down Cook Street and came home,' he wailed.

'Never mind, Brian. I am sure Daddy will be all right. It is probably a mistake. We'll tell Mummy about it. You just wait here a minute.'

Mother was taking a little nap in the bedroom and I was very afraid that if I woke her with Brian's story she would have one of her periodic outbursts of temper, or perhaps have hysterics; but she sat on the edge of the old mattress while she considered it, and then said quite sensibly, 'I don't think we can do anything except wait. We don't know which police station he is in. I expect they will let us know what he is charged with.'

Her calmness calmed Brian and me, and he went off to play with Tony, while I went back to my book. I could not read, however. I realised suddenly how much officialdom Father coped with on our behalf. Without him, we were defenceless against those who would put us in the workhouse.

I began to shake with fear, fear for my father and terror at the inhumanity of the workhouse.

# Chapter twenty-five

Edward had been put to bed and Mother and I sat on our two chairs staring out of the window, united by our worry over Father. Occasionally, there was a steady clang-clang and flashes of electricity from behind the houses opposite as tram cars a couple of streets away swayed around a corner. The irate 'whip-whip-whip' of a naval vessel making its way upriver competed with the noise of the trams, and, in the far distance, the shunting yard at Edge Hill lent a background of clanking to the other sounds. No cars passed – the district was too poor for anything more ambitious than a horsedrawn milk cart. A boy came by on a bicycle and two giggling girls paused to gossip under the gaslight outside.

A car drew up outside our house so quietly that we were at first unaware of its presence. Someone got out.

'Good night, and – thank you very much.'

It was Father. His voice was unmistakable.

We jumped up as the front door slammed in the distance. We could hear Father's laborious step on the stairs. He was whistling 'It's a Long Way to Tipperary'.

Never had the old tune sounded so welcome. If he could whistle, things were not that bad. We ran to the top of the stairs, six small grey ghosts and one adult, and peered over the banisters.

'Hello, children. Is Brian safely home?'

'Yes,' we chorused. 'What happened to you?'

Father emerged from the darkness of the stairwell. He was smiling broadly and his step was jaunty.

'It's a long story. Come in and I'll tell you.'

He even smiled at his wife, I noticed, and I could see in the small light from the street the sudden, unreasoned hope spring in Mother's eyes when she saw Father's cheerful expression.

'Come in. I have lots to tell you, and you are all old enough to hear it.'

He led us, like the Pied Piper, into the living-room.

'Tell us,' we implored, hunger, filth, misery forgotten.

Father made the most of his moment. He settled himself in a chair and took Avril on his knee. He was still beaming.

He cleared his throat.

'I expect Brian told you about our walk.'

'Yes,' we said impatiently.

'What happened when the policeman caught you?' asked Brian.

'He wanted to see my tie.'

'Your tie?' exclaimed Mother.

'Yes, my old All Saints tie. I thought he was mad, but I was afraid to do anything else but pull it out and show it to him.'

Avril shoved herself around on Father's lap and pulled out the sad remains of his old school tie. It looked the same as usual.

'When he saw it, he opened his own overcoat at the neck, and he was wearing the same tie – I mean a nice new version of it.'

Alan whistled.

'He asked me how I came to be down and out.

'"It is a long story," I told him. Suddenly, my legs began to give under me – we had walked a very long way, you know, and I get faint very easily these days. He saw that I was feeling ill, and said it didn't matter.

'"Come and sit in the car for a few minutes," he said. "I have to wait for a colleague who has business in this building here."

'I was thankful to get into the car and sit down. Almost immediately his colleague came and was surprised to find me in the car – I suppose he thought the man on the beat would normally deal with vagrants like me. However, my friend of the tie put the car into gear and said that we were going to go to the police canteen.

'"Don't get the wind up," he said to me. "I think you can do with a meal."

'I felt too weak to care what happened to me, but a meal sounded a wonderful idea. So away we went to the police station and through to the canteen.' He paused reminiscently, and then went on, 'He stood me a full meal – stew and steamed pudding.'

'Delicious,' we murmured enviously.

'And when I had finished, he gave me a cigarette, and he seemed such a decent sort that I told him about everything that happened to us.

'He did not interrupt me once – and his friend sat and watched me. At the end they looked at each other – and mulled over what I had said.

'He asked me quite a lot about our school, and then said he remembered me. He left All Saints the year after I was sent there, but he recollected that blow on the head I got from a cricket ball; it caused a good deal of consternation because I took a long time to come round and they were not able to get a doctor for some time.'

'Childhood episodes do stick in one's mind,' said Mother.

I looked at her in surprise. It had never occurred to me that she understood the world of children or that she had been a child herself. Nanny was the person who understood children.

Father continued, 'He said he thought he could get me a job with the City.'

'Really?' queried Mother, frank disbelief in her voice.

'Yes. I told him that I had made every endeavour to obtain employment – but now I was so shabby it was impossible. I said frankly that the rags he saw me in were all I had, that I had not even soap to wash myself with.

'And do you know what he said then? It was most unexpected.'

'No?' we breathed.

'He said the school would undoubtedly outfit me from their benevolent fund – I used to subscribe to that, you know, but I never thought of it in connection with myself. He is going to write tonight to ask for immediate help. Meantime, he is going to talk to the City about me.'

'How wonderful,' Alan cried.

'Yes, it is,' said Mother.

Fiona began to cry slowly; they were tears of relief. Her illness had left her with practically no stamina, but she rarely complained and, I believe, most of the family hardly realised she existed.

She was a great contrast to her lively, noisy younger sister, who now said unsympathetically, 'Oh, shut up, Fiona. You're supposed to be glad, not sad!' And cuddling up to Father, she inquired, 'Shall we be able to have a roast joint?'

We all laughed, and afterwards we sat up late while we discussed every detail of this miraculous encounter. Even Mother was quite excited and animated about it.

The days dragged by, however, and nothing happened. Father stood in his queues; Mother got two days' work, looking after a special photography display in a store which found that cameras were a slow-moving item amid the general penury in the city. We ate fish and chips one night as a result of this windfall, and Mother was able to buy some stockings, make-up, etc., so that she could look more respectable and, therefore, more employable. We always despaired about our lack of simple articles, like scissors, combs, hair grips, things one takes for granted in a normal home.

At last, when we had given up standing on the front steps waiting for the postman and the spring had again gone out of Father's step, the plain-clothes man called in person. He was let in by Miss Sinford, who fortunately did not connect him with the police, and he clumped up to our evil-smelling den.

Father was out.

Mother received him with her usual grace and sat down on one chair, while he, in response to her invitation, lowered himself cautiously on to the other. Most of the children were at school; Avril, Edward and I, however, stood in a group and stared goggle-eyed at our saviour.

All Saints School, the visitor said with a friendly grin, had made a grant sufficient to outfit Father completely, provided he shopped carefully. He stopped, his beefy face showing some concern. 'Er – the school has asked me to administer the grant – and – er – I hate to say this – they want me to go with your husband to shop. Now, I don't mind in the least – but I hope he won't be offended.'

'I am sure he won't,' said Mother with unusual briskness. 'However, you will appreciate that he is in no state to go out with you – or enter a decent shop.' Her voice broke, and she looked as if she was going to weep. She recovered herself, however, and said as she studied her chapped, unmanicured hands, 'Do you think the grant committee would mind giving enough money first to buy some soap for a bath – and a haircut?'

The plain-clothes man leaned forward and patted her hand.

'I am sure that would be all right. I do understand – you know, in my job I see a lot of things.' He thought for a moment, and then added, 'The public swimming-baths have also places where you can take a full bath – I think it costs sixpence – and they provide soap and towels, as well.'

I marvelled that a man whose life had obviously been comfortable should understand that it was likely we had no towels.

'Oh, how lovely,' I said impetuously, only to be silenced by an icy look from Mother.

I could hear Father dragging himself slowly up our endless staircase, and, picking up Edward, I ran to meet him and whispered about the visitor.

When Father entered, the man rose courteously and held out his hand. Father clasped it. I doubt if anyone had felt that his hand was worth shaking since our arrival in Liverpool.

Father's fatigue fell away from him. It was arranged that the policeman would buy some underwear and bring it to us. He also said gently that, if Father would accept them, he could bring a pair of flannels and an old tweed jacket from his own home, so that Father could go into a store without embarrassment to choose a suit and raincoat.

It was obvious that Father felt his humiliation very deeply. His face was sadder than I had ever seen it. He appreciated, however, the great kindness of this police officer on whom he had no other call than that they had attended the same public school, and he thanked him gratefully for his thoughtfulness.

'I have tentatively arranged for you to see this man in the Municipal Buildings at ten o'clock next Friday morning,' said our friend, standing up and handing Father a slip of paper.

Father nodded, took the slip of paper and carefully laid it on the dusty mantelpiece.

'I don't know how I am going to repay you for all this,' he said.

'Don't mention it,' said the plain-clothes man cheerfully. 'Very glad to be able to help – put it down to the old school tie!'

The underwear, trousers, jacket and a shirt arrived in a brown paper parcel, addressed to Father and left on our landing. When I asked our incorrigible old lookout, Miss Sinford, who had delivered the parcel, she insisted that nobody had called at the house that day. I can only imagine that someone like the milkman, who still brought Edward his pint of milk, must have been asked to bring them in, so as to avoid a police car being yet again stationed outside the house. Miss Sinford would not have counted the milkman as being a person; like the postman, the public assistance visitor and the poor, he was always with us.

Armed with five shillings given him for the purpose, Father went to the public baths and found that, indeed, a spotlessly clean bath, towels and soap, not to speak of hot water, were all his for the sum of sixpence. Apparently, he spent so much time in the bath that the attendant threatened to charge him another sixpence or empty the bath if Father did not come out.

He dressed himself in his clean clothes, rolled up his rags into a bundle, except for his broken-down shoes, which he had, perforce, to retain, dumped the bundle into a litter-bin outside the baths, and went for a shave and a haircut.

When he came home, I hardly knew him. Although the jacket and pants were too large for him and his shoes were a mess, he had an aura of respectability about him that did more for our spirits than anything heretofore.

There was still some money left from the five shillings, and Father sent Alan and Fiona to buy fish and chips and peas and a packet of cigarettes. I hoped that All Saints School did not learn, by some extraordinary means, that we had spent two and sixpence of their money on food instead of on outfitting Father, and, even worse, sixpence on cigarettes.

The detective picked Father up two days later, and they went together to buy a good ready-made suit, another shirt, a raincoat and a pair of shoes.

It seemed to Alan and me that we had got our father back from the dead, because he now looked to us as he had done before we came to Liverpool, except that he had shrunk considerably.

Without any difficulty, Father got the clerical post for which he was interviewed – the detective was apparently sufficient reference. He was infinitely better educated and more widely experienced in the business world than the type of clerk the City was normally able to command, and, except when it came to running his own affairs, had a clear and analytical mind.

Though the post was a temporary one, he soon discovered that many of his colleagues had been 'temporary' for ten years or more – it saved the impoverished City from having to provide pensions for them.

He served the city of his birth faithfully and well. Later, he became part of its permanent staff, and, when his department was taken over by the government as part of the new National Health scheme, he became a civil servant and gradually worked his way upwards. He was never very well-to-do again; on the other hand, he was never again reduced to penury, and he managed to enjoy the latter part of his life in a modest way.

# Chapter twenty-six

It seemed reasonable to assume that Father's going to work would make a considerable difference to our standard of living and, consequently, to my own life. The hope that had sustained me through all our bad times had been pinned on this one point. Now, at last, perhaps I would be allowed to go to evening school or take some kind of work and Mother would take her rightful place at home. Life, however, went on exactly as before as far as Edward and I were concerned.

There was no more money to spend on food than there had been before. Wages were so low in Liverpool that Father did not earn much more than he had received when unemployed; the difference was swallowed up in tram fares, lunches and cigarettes – and, of course, the need to keep himself clean and tidy.

Childish hopes waxed again when Mother began to get more regular employment; she was proving to be an excellent saleswoman and was recommended by one employer to another for moving specially difficult merchandise. If she must work, I argued, she might soon earn enough to employ a girl to look after Edward and so release me. In her case also, however, she had first to meet her expenses and then extend her wardrobe so that she looked decent enough to continue work.

Father's being employed sparked a desire in my parents to find a better place in which to live. It had been hopeless even to consider this while he was unemployed – no landlord was prepared to rent a house to an unemployed man with seven children. A city clerk was a different matter, and they finally obtained a neat-looking terrace house with three bedrooms, a sitting-room and a living-room. It had no bathroom, and the water-closet was at the far end of a soot-begrimed back yard. Cooking was done on an old-fashioned coal range in the living-room. It was unfurnished and the rent was seventeen shillings a week. It was a great improvement upon our present accommodation, though not to be compared with the home we had abandoned to our creditors. The relief from climbing stairs was tremendous and, of course, we would save ten shillings a week in rent.

Moving was not difficult as we had almost nothing to move, and suddenly it seemed as if we needed everything much more than we had done before – I suppose it was because we had a whole house to ourselves.

There are always sharks willing to oblige the foolish. In their eagerness to become once more established, my parents bought a set of drawing-room furniture and curtains for the whole house on hire purchase. A hint that we needed beds met with a sharp rebuke. An iniquitous system of 'cheques' enabled them to purchase bedding, crockery and kitchen tools, all of which we badly needed. The cheques, however, were peddled by finance companies and consisted of a permit to buy a given amount of goods from a limited list of stores at greatly inflated prices. Repayment and interest were collected in weekly instalments by the companies' agents. The goods rarely lasted until they were paid for and the rate of interest was high. This type of indebtedness was very prevalent in Liverpool.

This plunge into debt meant that Mother had to work, whether she wished to or not, and I had to care for the children. My little faint hope which had lighted my way through so much was doused, and dark clouds of melancholy gathered round me and were made worse by indifferent health. I watched as the heavy weekly payments drained away money urgently needed for clothing and food. Sufficient did trickle down to buy new running shoes for the older children; but Edward and Avril had the Chariot to ride in and I did not have to go anywhere except to the shops.

Avril started school in September and Alan would be leaving it at Christmas, a poignant reminder that everybody was making a little progress except me. Would Edward and I always be chained together? Would our needs always be at the bottom of the family's list? Would I always be hungry?

My despair was abysmal. I felt I had no one to turn to for comfort or help. Even hours of weeping as I went about my household tasks failed to relieve the depression which engulfed me.

My father had spent some time talking with Alan about what he would do when he finished school, and it had been agreed that he would try for a job as office boy in a firm where there was a certain amount of training given and where he might sit professionally set examinations. Amongst other openings, this gave him a choice of estate agencies, banking and shipping firms. A bright fourteen-year-old could do better than his forty-year-old father, as far as choice of jobs was concerned.

Nobody asked me what I would like to do. My role in life had been silently decided for me. It was obvious that my parents had no intention of allowing me to be anything but an unpaid, unrespected housekeeper. With all the passion of a fifteen-year-old, I decided that such a life was not worth living.

A foggy September day saw Edward being pushed in the Chariot along the gently heaving Georges Landing-Stage. The Birkenhead ferry was slowly leaving the stage and vanishing into the misty river. The shore hands were coiling up their ropes ready for the next ferry-boat. Upon the invisible river invisible ferries clanged their bells and were answered by freighters sounding their foghorns. Behind me, the lights of the Royal Liver and Cunard buildings barely penetrated the unseasonable gloom. At one end of the landing-stage a pilot-boat had just returned from beyond the bar, after collecting the pilot from an outgoing ship. At the other end a group of customs officers chatted, their raincoats gleaming with moisture. No passengers were waiting for the ferries.

Carefully, I tucked the cover round the sleeping Edward and made sure that the hood protected him from the slight wind which occasionally lifted the fog. I hoped someone kind would find him and take him home and love him. I propped the pram against a post so that it could not roll into the water, and left it.

Very slowly, I approached the chain fence that stopped pedestrians from falling off the edge of the landing-stage. When I felt its cold links against my shins, I paused. Some three feet still separated me from the swirling water, invisible for the moment because of the mist.

I stepped over the fence and took a couple of paces more. I could see the water now. Everyone in Liverpool knew that if anybody fell into the water at the end of the landing-stage the tremendous undertow would suck them right under the stage to certain death. It would not take long.

I was shivering violently, nauseated by the thought of the oily water and the choking death which seemed to be the only available way of committing suicide. At the same time I could not bear the thought of turning back into a life which was unendurable to me.

I took a large breath preparatory to jumping.

A huge paw clamped suddenly down on my shoulders and a voice behind me said, 'And phwhat in the Name o' God do you think you're doing?'

The sudden interruption was so terrifying that my knees buckled under me, and another huge hand grasped the back of my dress, and I was yanked bodily back over the fence.

Supported only by the iron grip on my shoulder, I found myself looking at the middle fastenings of a sailor's waterproofs. I followed the line of the fastenings upwards with my eyes and found myself looking into the rubicund face of the pilot who had just landed. The water dripping off the peak of his cap did not obscure the concern in his eyes.

I could not answer. I was fainting.

'Mother of Heaven, you gave me a fright,' he said sharply.

I must have fainted completely, because the next thing I remember was being in a little canteen and having hot tea forced between my lips by a careworn woman in grubby white.

'Och, you'll be all right now,' she said in a rich Irish voice. 'Sure, and you frightened the Captain out of his wits.'

I put my head down on the tea-stained table by me until the world ceased whirling round me. I felt dreadfully cold and so tired that all I could think about was sleep.

After a minute or two, I straightened up. My rescuer said heartily, 'Well, now, you'll be all right. And don't you step over that chain again, young lady, or you'll fall right in.' He turned to the hovering waitress, put his hand in his trouser pocket, took out a coin and gave it to her. 'Here's for the tea. I've no doubt the gel will be all right in a minute or two. I have to report to the office.'

He looked down at me, his face beaming.

'Goodbye, young lady.'

'Goodbye,' I said, 'and thank you.'

I drank the rest of the tea gratefully and, at the urging of the waitress, sat for about ten minutes to rest. Gradually, my numbed brain began to work once more. I knew I could not screw up enough courage to go out into the fog and try to jump again; yet I could not stay long where I was.

I suddenly remembered Edward.

It seemed that I would have to go home, because there was nowhere else to go.

Slowly I got up, thanked the waitress and, with many protestations that I was now quite well, I went to collect the Chariot. Edward was sitting up and whimpering.

The children were home when I arrived, slowly dragging the Chariot after me.

'You haven't got tea ready,' said Avril indignantly, 'and Alan can't find a knife to cut the bread.'

# Chapter twenty-seven

Very few people who try to commit suicide really want to kill themselves; their attempt is a last hysterical cry for help. When willing hands are outstretched to aid them and some effort is made to alter the circumstances that drove them to such despair, they will try again to cope with life. I was no exception; two people had been very kind to me and I was extremely touched by the fact. On my return home, the necessity of dealing with the children's needs steadied me and Fiona's loving help with these tasks comforted me. I clung to her when we went to bed and drew some strength from the touch of her frail body and from her gentle spirit. By morning, something of my normal common sense had returned.

The day was as bright and clear as its predecessor had been foggy and damp. The family dispersed to school and to work, Avril going proudly to school holding Fiona's hand. Edward and I were left to contemplate a bare house, except for our shiny new drawing-room, which I dusted very carefully from time to time. The few dishes were soon washed, what beds and substitutes for beds we had were soon tidied and the fire allowed to go out until evening. Though still very exhausted, my spirits rose a little as Edward and I went out to buy food.

Outside the elementary school a fresh poster announced the opening of evening schools that day for the winter session. I contemplated it with a feeling of hopelessness. It would certainly be inconvenient to my parents if I was out in the evening – they would almost certainly veto any such idea.

The hopelessness gave way to a slow burning anger, and then to determination. I would try once more to go to school. Perhaps if Father and Mother were faced with a *fait accompli*, they would give in. I therefore took Fiona and Alan into my confidence at teatime, and they agreed to help with Edward and Avril while I was away and to cover up for me if my parents noticed my absence.

When both parents went out to the library, I slipped away to the school and joined a crowd of youngsters moving slowly through the entrance.

A young teacher asked me, as I stood uncertainly in the hall, what courses I wanted to take.

I was aghast. I had no idea what courses to take. All I wanted was to continue my education from where I had left off over three years earlier.

'I am not sure,' I managed to mutter. 'I know I need to learn arithmetic.'

She pointed to an open doorway farther down the hall.

'Try bookkeeping,' she said kindly, as she turned to attend to another lost youngster.

I did not know what bookkeeping was, but I was so scared of the shifting, staring young people crowding round me, some of whom sniggered when they looked at me, that I bolted down the corridor and turned thankfully into a classroom holding about a dozen boys and girls and a young lady teacher.

The classroom, with its walls of frosted glass and varnished wood, had enough desks, made to accommodate two pupils each, to swallow about fifty children; four electric lights hanging from the ceiling failed to illuminate it adequately; the bare wooden floor was grey from years of tramping boots. Facing the pupils' desks was a high, single desk for the teacher and near it stood a blackboard on an easel. The air smelled of chalk dust and damp woollens. A dingy, uninspiring room it was, but it was made more lively by the buzz of conversation among the pupils.

As I came through the door, the teacher looked up, and a pall of silence fell upon the gathering. The mouths of the neatly clad, well-scrubbed young people fell open. Then a well-curled blonde began to giggle. She hastily stuffed her handkerchief into her mouth, while a derisive grin spread through the class.

The dim electric lights became blurred, as tears of realisation welled up. I must have been a horrible sight, with hair draggling round my shoulders, its greasiness combed through with my fingers; septic acne sores all over my face; hands with dirty, broken nails, sticking out from an ancient cardigan with huge holes in its elbows, no blouse, and a gym slip shiny with accumulated grime. Red blotches of bug bites were clearly visible on my naked legs and thighs, our new house being equally as verminous as our old one, and my toes stuck out of the holes in the laceless gym shoes on my feet.

I fought back my tears. I was made of better stuff than the children before me. My family had been fighting England's battles while theirs were still serfs fit only to keep pigs. I would show them.

Lifting my ugly hooked nose into the air I stared calmly back at them. Gradually, the grins were replaced by uneasy looks and they began self-consciously to talk to each other again.

There ought to be a special medal for understanding teachers. I do not know what prompted the small, perfumed occupant of the teacher's podium to come down from her perch, put her arm around my shoulders, regardless of the fact that I was obviously verminous, and say sweetly, 'Do you want to take bookkeeping, too, my dear?'

She was taken aback visibly when I answered her in my clearest English – she must have expected a strong Liverpool accent.

'I had hoped to learn arithmetic, ma'am. Do you teach it?'

She recovered herself and guided me to an unoccupied double desk at the front of the class, as she replied.

'No. This school has only commercial courses – it is assumed that you will have done the necessary arithmetic already in day school.'

The other children were again staring at me, and she turned to them and said sharply, 'Please fill in the forms I have given to you. I will take them in in a few minutes.' She turned back to me. 'Now,' she said, 'what kind of arithmetic do you want to learn?'

I explained my lack of algebra, that my academic training had come to an end at a chapter called 'Compound Interest', and that was as much as I knew.

She sat casually on the desk in front of me and looked me over thoughtfully.

'When did you leave school?' she asked.

I explained about leaving school when I was eleven and the subsequent glorious six weeks I had enjoyed just before my fourteenth birthday, and about Edward and Avril and the family.

'I see,' she said, drawing her pale blue cardigan more tightly around her. 'Do you want to train for any particular occupation?'

An occupation seemed so far away, so unattainable, that I said hastily, 'I have not thought of anything special – except that I would like to be able to help the hungry, unemployed people round me.'

She smiled at this and suggested, after some consideration, that I should take the standard commercial course, in which she taught bookkeeping. In addition, she would guide me through a basic course in arithmetic and algebra, which I could do as part of my homework.

'If you take the commercial course, it will form a basis for several different ways of earning a living,' she said practically.

I agreed because it seemed that I had no choice and, at least, she had opened a tiny door of hope for me. Yesterday there had been no hope; today there was a faint gleam.

She lent me her pen and I filled in the form she gave me, while the other members of the class handed theirs in, had them checked and were told to report back two nights later to commence their instruction.

When the classroom had emptied, I went to the teacher's desk and handed in my form.

'Fine,' she said cheerfully. 'Now, that will be half a crown; and here is a list of books you will need. They will cost about ten and sixpence.'

I was stunned. My tiny hope door slammed shut. I managed to gasp out, 'I did not know there was a fee for evening school – I thought it was like elementary day school – provided by the city – so – so I haven't brought any money.'

The amounts were so small; but they might just as well have been hundreds of pounds, because I did not have them.

The teacher was collecting her papers, and she replied, without looking up, 'Well, never mind. Ask your mother to give you the fee for next time – and you can get the books from any bookshop some time during the week. Now, be here on Thursday at seven thirty, remember.'

'Yes, ma'am,' I said heavily. 'Good night – and thank you.'

I turned and marched out.

As soon as I was outside the school, I rushed to a corner behind a buttress of the building where the street lamps' rays did not penetrate, and, putting my face against the damp red bricks of the wall, I cried hopelessly and helplessly until not another tear would come. I cried from the frightful pent-up tension of yesterday and the disappointment and humiliation of today. I cried because I was drifting helplessly on a sea of life for which I had not been prepared and which I did not understand. I cried for the perfect peace and safe refuge of my grandmother's house by the sea. I cried because I could not cross the Mersey to reach the green fields and wild seashores I loved.

Frozen and exhausted, I stuffed my blue hands into my cardigan pockets and turned towards home.

I took two steps and stopped. In my pocket was a hard little card. Mother's library card!

Books! Perhaps the library had the books I needed. If they had, I could keep on reborrowing them, I argued. If it was not yet nine o'clock, I could run to the library and look.

I tore through the streets, taking shortcuts through every alleyway I could, regardless of danger. Dogs barked and cats and rats scampered away at the sound of my thudding feet.

I squeezed into the library's muggy warmth five minutes before closing-time, the list of books clutched in one hand.

Feverishly, I sought through the index. Had they got them? Had they? They had.

A few minutes later, I emerged, equipped with text-books.

At home I poured out my adventures to Alan and Fiona. It was a long time since I had had such a conversation with any of the family, and they were jubilant about the enrolment and the books. Alan offered to lend me his pen each evening.

'If you don't remind them, perhaps they'll forget that you owe them half a crown,' he said hopefully, in reference to the school fee.

'They will have to,' I said woodenly, 'because I am going to school, no matter what happens.'

Brave words, but I still needed at least one notebook, and, as I put the family to bed, I worried more about obtaining twopence to buy a notebook than I worried about the half-crown.

On Wednesday, I found a piece of comb in a gutter and painfully attacked my tangled mop of hair with it. Mother had a tiny pocket-comb, which of a necessity she had kept for herself, because she could not make herself neat for work if the precious object was broken. Father was fortunately almost bald. The children went uncombed and, mostly, unwashed, until more regular work enabled Mother to buy a strong comb for use by the family.

If ever I became rich, I told myself savagely, I would help to provide a basic kit for the more unfortunate of this world. It would consist of a large bar of kitchen soap, a pile of old white cloth, a pile of newspapers (newspapers can be made into beds, handkerchiefs, toilet-paper, warm padding under thin garments, draught excluders, makeshift window-pane replacements, firing, and a thousand other uses), some razor blades, for beards and nails, and a comb. One has to be without such small amenities to appreciate their worth.

My appearance was not much improved when I again presented myself at school, quailing at the thought of not being able to pay the fee.

The bookkeeping teacher was as kind as before and, after she had given the class some work to do, she brought over to me a small arithmetic text-book, told me to take it home, read the instructions in the first chapter and see if I could work my way through the problems based on them. She promised to mark the work for me.

Several children had no notebooks, so she provided some paper both for their work and mine. I soon became absorbed in the struggle to make my sluggish brain work, and forgot the silent distaste with which my fellow students were treating me.

Halfway through the evening, the class was taken over by a thin, energetic teacher who was to instruct us in English grammar. She proved equally as friendly and as helpful as the bookkeeping teacher.

Evening school has a long tradition in Lancashire and all over the city classrooms were crowded with young people desirous of improving their education. Again I was following in the footsteps of the humble weavers about whom my old gentleman in the park had told me.

It was Fiona who, accidentally, let fall one evening the information to my parents that I had gone to evening school.

They were rightly angry that I had taken such action without consulting them and both stormed at me about it.

It would have brought more wrath down upon my head if I had defended myself by saying that I had long since concluded that consultation was a waste of time, so I just stated firmly, 'I have been going to evening school and I'm going to continue going.' I had nothing to lose but my chains.

'Where did you get the money from?' asked Mother suddenly, her voice full of suspicion.

I had to own up that I owed the Liverpool education committee two shillings and sixpence – and, worse still, I needed two shillings more for bookkeeping books and other notebooks.

This led to further recrimination, and, with unusual impudence, I asked, 'Would you prefer that I stole it rather than owed it?'

Such insolence was so unlike me that it brought my parents up short.

Mother said quietly, in a tone more normal than anything she had used since we had arrived in Liverpool, 'No, we would not. Probably we shall manage to find the money somehow.'

This sudden reasonableness frightened me more than if she had had hysterics. I had become so used to her being ill and being unable to pay normal attention to us that I had forgotten that new hope had recently entered her life and was helping her to get better quite rapidly. Once I had got over the shock and stopped staring at her, round-eyed and fearful, I was piteously grateful.

The following Tuesday evening, hair neatly combed into a bun held with a piece of string, and wearing Fiona's cardigan, which was reasonably clean, I ran through the dank September evening to school. Hot in the palm of my hand was a half-crown, the most important coin I was ever to possess. I was to spend seven years in evening schools and I managed in each subsequent year to win a small scholarship, which covered the increasing fees and my books, as I advanced through the system; so that I did not cost my parents anything more.

The electric lights had already been turned on in the school and a great shaft of light blazed out across the pavement from the main doorway. It was early and no one else was entering. I looked up the stone steps, hollowed out by hundreds of feet, through the hall and up the staircase to the second floor.

The welcoming doorway was my hoping door; the worn stone steps my ladder to the stars. Kind hands, earnest people, were there to help me up them.

I bared my yellow teeth in a smile of pure happiness, charged across the threshold and galloped up the stairs.

# Liverpool Miss

*To my family and friends
who helped me to remember*

# Chapter one

It had begun to rain and I was shivering as I manœuvred the squeaking Chariot over the road to the corner of Castle Street. Avril was red in the face with rage. She stormed at me because I would not take her out of the pram and let her walk amid the busy lunchtime crowd. At the other end of the pram, beneath the leaking hood, Baby Edward grizzled miserably for the same reason.

Since the October day was too cold for us to walk in the park, I had brought them into the city, thinking that it would be more sheltered and that we could amuse ourselves looking in the shop windows. And now we had wandered into the business district.

Pretty secretaries, rushing back from lunch, and smart businessmen, carrying umbrellas and briefcases, glanced impatiently at the intruding pram with two grubby urchins in noisy protest. It belonged away in the slums, like the tatterdemalion who pushed it.

I did not care. I was resigned to people staring at my long, wind-chapped, bare legs, at my toes sticking through a pair of old plimsolls, at an outgrown gym slip worn without a blouse, a ragged cardigan covering part of my nakedness.

Through the increasing rain, I pushed the pram dreamily amongst them. In my mind I was not walking in black, depressing Liverpool; I was in the countryside and then in the fine old southern town from which I had been unceremoniously plucked two years before. It was market day, and Father and I were looking at the horses brought in for sale. As we moved about, the ploughmen, the shepherds and the farmers would touch their forelocks to the distinguished-looking gentleman, strolling around with a little daughter in the uniform of a good private school.

'*Echo! Liverpool Echo.* Read all about it!' shouted a man in a cloth cap, thrusting a paper towards the hurrying throng. I blinked, and hurriedly swerved to avoid him.

Would we always have to stay in Liverpool? I wondered depressedly. Would we always be cold and hungry?

'Oh, shut up, Avril,' I scolded crossly, and stopped the pram while I tucked an old overcoat round Baby Edward's knees and then pushed the edges of it up over her lap. 'Look, love. See up there – on the top of the Town Hall. There's Minerva. She's looking at you.'

Avril turned her woebegone face upwards towards the dome I had pointed out.

'See,' I said. 'She's smiling at you. Hasn't she got a lovely golden face? But I think she's got smuts on her nose, just like you.' I touched Avril's damp little nose with a playful finger, and she sniffed and stopped crying.

Baby Edward could not see what I had pointed out; but, when I touched his nose and laughed at him, he saw hope of a game and tried to reach forward to touch my hooked nose. Tiny fingers grasped at my horn-rimmed glasses. I backed away hastily before they fell off.

Laughing at each other, we continued along the street.

Many people thought it was Britannia who sat looking down at Liverpool, but Father had told me it was Minerva, the Goddess of Wisdom, Invention and Handicrafts. He assured me that she also took care of dramatic poets and actors.

There were plenty of craftsmen in Liverpool of whom she might have been proud, even some actors and a poet or two, but most of them queued at the Labour Exchanges, their abilities unused. They stood idly round the dock gates, where ships lay in every stage of decay. They hung around outside the gaily lit public houses. Her sailors, skilled men, sat hungry in their cold kitchens, while their despairing wives nagged and their children went barefoot.

Amongst the defeated men in the queues at the Labour Exchange, Father had stood for over two years. Ruined by the Depression and, in part, by his own extravagances, he had brought us back to his native city in the hope of finding work. But, in the Liverpool wet, he had seemed like a lost butterfly, with wings beaten useless by the rain. He had watched, helpless, as Mother struggled, without medical aid, to recuperate from a major operation and a mental breakdown. Though the wartime marriage had not been a happy one, her degeneration into a haggard virago must have broken his heart.

To look at his seven children was almost too much for him. We were a hungry, ragged and increasingly unruly crew, disoriented by our parents' disasters, seven small sparrows with our beaks open, loudly demanding to be fed.

Because Mother was at first so ill, I suddenly had thrust upon me, as the eldest child, the task of caring for her and for my brothers and sisters. The Public Assistance Committee gave Father forty-three shillings a week, out of which we paid twenty-seven shillings a week for three unheated attic rooms. The remaining sixteen shillings had to cover every need of nine people; and for a time it seemed certain that Baby Edward would die for lack of milk, and I often looked with terror at our empty food shelf.

Recently, a little hope had entered our lives. Father had obtained a small clerical job with the Liverpool Corporation. He earned only a few shillings more than the Public Assistance allowance and the extra money was swallowed up by his expenses. But it was a new beginning for him.

About the same time, we obtained a bug-ridden terrace house at a few shillings less rent than our rooms. I no longer had to face the irate complaints of the tenants in the rooms beneath us, about the noise the children made. The bugs bit unmercifully and they made a horrible smell, but the children did not complain.

I had high hopes, when Father started work, that I would be allowed to go to school and then to work, and that Mother would become the housekeeper. But Mother had obtained part-time employment as a demonstrator in various department stores, and she announced that she would be continuing this work.

'Why can't you stay at home, like other mothers do?' I implored.

'The doctor said I should work – remember?'

'Yes. But that was when you were convalescent. He wanted you to walk about in the fresh air to get strong again. But you are quite well now.'

'Oh, don't be stupid, Helen. Stop arguing. We need the money.'

'But must I always stay at home, Mummy? I'm over fourteen now. I should be at work like other girls are. Couldn't we find someone to help out at home?'

'Really, Helen. Be sensible. How could we afford to *pay* anyone?'

We did need the money, it was true, and we never paid anybody we could avoid paying but I had all the adolescent's doubts about my elders, and I distrusted Mother's motives. There had never been much love between us. I had always been taken care of by servants; in fact, Mother had never had to take complete care of any of her children. I sensed angrily that she found it easier to go out to work than to stay at home and face the care of seven noisy children. I found coping with six brothers and sisters, who daily became less disciplined, very hard indeed.

So, as I walked through the rain along Castle Street and absent-mindedly played with Baby Edward, and diverted Avril's attention to Minerva and then to a warehouse cat stalking solemnly across the street, I was bitterly unhappy.

We had to stop, while a desk was carried across the pavement from a furniture van into an office building; and I looked again up at Minerva.

She seemed almost to float in the misty rain, and I wondered suddenly if something more than a statue was really there, some hidden power of ancient gods that we do not understand, and I said impulsively, 'Hey, Minerva. Help *me* – please.'

The big man in a sacking apron, who was supervising the transfer of the desk, turned round and asked, not unkindly, 'Wot yer say, luv?'

I blushed with embarrassment. I must be going mad with all the strain. I'm crazy.

'Nothing,' I said hastily. 'I was just amusing the baby.'

'Oh, aye,' he replied, smiling down at Edward, while the desk disappeared through a fine oak doorway. 'You can get by now, luv.'

# Chapter two

I was eleven and a half when we first came to Liverpool, and my parents were able to keep me at home because the Liverpool Education Committee did not know of my existence. I had come from another town and did not appear in any of their records. Six weeks before my fourteenth birthday my presence in Liverpool was reported by my sister, Fiona's, schoolteacher. And much to my parents' annoyance, I had to attend school for those six weeks.

Now I was over fourteen, my parents had no further legal obligations in respect of my education. So, at home I stayed, simmering with all the fury of a caged cat.

I had had an aunt, a spinster, kept at home all her life to be company to my grandmother, who lived on the other side of the River Mersey. This aunt seemed to have no real life of her own, and I dreaded being like her, at the beck and call of my relations, a useful unpaid servant, without the rights of a servant. She was such a shadow of a person that I never ever thought that she might help me.

I raged to myself that I was always the last to be provided with food and clothing. I did not even think about the lack of pocket money or other small pleasures – they were beyond my ken.

In our hard-pressed family, shoes and clothing were given first to those who had to look neat for work, and then to those who went to school. I could always manage because I did not have to go out, I was told sharply.

As housekeeper, I had to apportion the food. I fed Baby Edward first, then Avril, who was nearly five, then the two little boys, Brian and Tony. After them, frail, lovely Fiona and cheery Alan. I would then serve Father, who never complained about the small amount on his plate. What was left was shared between Mother and me. Sometimes there were no vegetables left for us, and frequently no meat, so we had a slice of bread each, with margarine, washed down with tea lacking both sugar and milk.

Mother still looked so dreadfully haggard that I would sometimes say, with a lump in my throat, that I was not hungry and would press the last remaining bits of meat and vegetable upon her. All my life I had been afraid of her tremendous temper, but such fear had long been overridden by a greater fear that she might die.

145

In response to my frequent complaints at not being allowed to go to work, Mother often said absently, 'Later on, you will marry. Staying at home is good practice for it.'

But I had always been assured by Mother and the servants that Fiona had the necessary beauty to be married; and I – well, I did have brains.

'You can't help your looks,' our nanny, Edith, used to say, as she scrubbed my face. 'Maybe your yellow complexion is from being ill so much. It might improve as you get older.' She used to seize a brush and scrape back my straight, mousy hair into a confining ribbon bow on the top of my head; but she spent ages curling Fiona's soft waves into ringlets.

'Why do you have to be so disobedient? You're nothing but a little vixen, you are. Nobody's going to marry a faggot like you when you grow up,' she would shout exasperatedly. 'Get those muddy shoes off, before I clout you.'

In a desperate effort to save myself from spinsterhood, I learned to obey a raised voice like a circus dog. But it did not do me much good. I was still sallow and plain, sickly and irritable.

After Father found a job, I fought a great battle with my parents for permission to attend night school three evenings a week. It became the single joy of my life. There was order and purpose in the musty, badly lit classrooms with their double wooden desks in which, for most classes, sat more than forty pupils. The bare board floors, the faded green paint and chipped varnish were much more pleasant and clean than my home.

For the first two winters of my attendance, nobody would sit by me, because I was so blatantly dirty and I stank. Only the teachers spoke to me. In some subjects I was so behind that I needed dedicated helpers. And the teachers gave me that help.

The bookkeeping teacher taught me the simple arithmetic which I had forgotten through long absence from school. The English teachers gave me essays to write, in addition to the business letters they demanded from their other pupils. They drew my attention to poems and to essays I should read. Later, I took German and French, and again the teacher drummed additional grammar into me, and introduced me to the translated works of foreign authors. Shorthand, a possible gateway to employment, was largely a matter of practice, and I practised zealously.

I dreamed of becoming the treasured secretary of some great man of affairs, like Sir Montague Norman, the Governor of the Bank of England, to whom I had once been introduced. He had given the silent, small girl by Father's side a new shilling, and I had curled up in an agony of shyness and refused to say thank you, much to Father's embarrassment. But, of course, when I became a secretary, I would always be ready with the correct polite remark and flawlessly typed letters ready to be signed.

During the day, as I walked little Edward in the squeaky Chariot and, particularly after my more trying charge, Avril, had joined her brothers and sister at school, I read books balanced on the pram's raincover. I discovered Trevelyan's histories and read all those that the library had. The librarian suggested histories of other countries, so I read not only the histories of France and Germany, but those of China and Japan, of the United States and of the countries of South America.

The heroines of some of the Victorian novels I read studied philosophy in their spare time, so I plodded through the works of several German philosophers far too difficult for me.

'Don't know what they are talking about,' I told Edward crossly.

I found a book by Sigmund Freud and decided that he did not understand females at all. And what was it that people were supposed to be repressing all the time? Men behaved like men and women behaved like women. How could they behave any way other than by being natural?

I tied myself up in mental knots, considering Freud, and never associated his work with the strange spasms and longings in my own maturing body. To my mind, Freud did not seem to do so well at interpreting dreams as Joseph in the Bible did.

Beneath this rabid desire for an education, for knowledge, simmered a mixture of fear and rage: I felt my parents did not really care what happened to me, as long as I continued to serve them.

# Chapter three

Despite our big family, I suffered great loneliness. When Father was not too tired he would sometimes talk to me about his wartime experiences in Russia or we would discuss eighteenth-century France, of which he had a considerable knowledge. Mother ordered; she did not discuss. Without pen, ink, paper or stamps, I could not write to the schoolfriends I had left behind in my earlier life. In fact, at first my parents refused obdurately to allow me to write.

'Why not?' I demanded crossly.

'Because it costs money, and there may be some creditors who still want to trace your father.'

They also forbade me to write to my grandmother, Father's mother, with whom I had always spent several months of each year. Grandma, Father said, had been most unreasonable and he had quarrelled with her. I suspected that she had finally grown tired of the scandals of the gay life my parents had led before the Depression, and then of helping to pay their debts.

When I went to the local shops, I saw only older, married women, or children sent on messages, and, to me, some of the girls who lived in neighbouring streets seemed hardly human. On Saturdays and Sundays they went about in twos and threes, dressed in cheap finery. They gawked and giggled and shrieked at the gangling youths hanging uneasily about the street corners. Because their labour was very cheap, these girls had work in stores and factories. Once they were sixteen years old they usually joined their unemployed brothers.

Sometimes, when I passed a group of them as I pushed Edward along in the Chariot, they stared and laughed at me behind their hands. Garbed in the tattered remnants of my school uniform, occasionally with no knickers under the short skirt, I had to walk very uprightly lest a bare bottom be revealed to them. Once or twice they shouted at the idling boys to inquire which of them had 'caught' me. It was a long time before I realised that it was generally assumed that Edward was my illegitimate child. When I did discover it, I cried with mortification, because I knew that to have a baby out of wedlock was very wicked.

I was very vague about the origins of babies. I did not think about it very

much. Dimly, uncertainly, I imagined that they came from the same place
as foals and lambs and calves did. But I had never actually seen a birth
and how this could be was beyond my imagining. I never equated men
with stallions, rams or bulls. But, to be respectable, a child had to have a
visible father or a substitute, like a gravestone, to account for his absence
– that I knew. Once, when I was small, Mother dismissed our parlourmaid without a moment's notice, and I knew from the maids' gossip that
she was expecting a baby – and she was not married.

Occasionally, when Edith was angry she would hiss savage remarks about
my parents' lack of feeling, and quote this incident as an example of it. The
housemaid left us shortly afterwards, in protest, according to Edith. Edith
herself stayed with us until we left the district, because she was engaged
to a young farmer nearby; and I clung to her as a mother substitute. She
was a plump, comfortable country girl with rosy cheeks and fluffy, long
brown hair, and was downright in her speech. I never doubted anything
she said.

I had only two close contacts to assuage this sense of isolation. One was
a very old interpreter, who sometimes sat in Princes Park to sun himself.
We talked a lot about the Middle East and about other languages, as I
sat and supervised the children's play. One day he was missing from his
usual seat and never came again. I presumed he had died and had gone
to join his wife and three sons. The boys had been killed in the war and
he grieved for them.

The other friend was a Spanish woman named Cristina. She and her
husband, Alonzo, lived in the basement of the house next door to that in
which we had originally rented an attic. Her children were all grown up
and had left home. She was extraordinarily kind to Edward and me, and
it was she who had given us the Chariot in which I wheeled Edward and
Avril around.

In my position as surrogate mother, I had neither time nor opportunity
to play. As the children became rougher and, in order to survive, became
more like the other boys and girls in the district, the gulf widened between
us and there seemed to be no close communication. Even Alan, so close
to me in age, was to me a child; I did not worry him with details of our
empty pantry.

Because I did not have a shopping bag, the greengrocer used to wrap
up potatoes and other vegetables in newspaper for me, and when I arrived
home I used to read these papers. There were descriptions of local tennis
tournaments amongst young people, and stories of balls and receptions.
I would stand dreaming with the muddy paper in my hands, imagining
myself scampering about a tennis court delivering serves that raised cheers
from the onlookers; or I would think how lovely it would be to skim around
a ballroom in a billowing net dress. And how good it would be to go to
the theatre again. In me were the stirrings of womanhood, though I did

not understand them, and I had an instinctive desire to be clean, to be prettily dressed, to hide as much as possible the ugliness which I had been assured was mine.

When I thought about it, I became so afraid of the friendless, empty future that sometimes my legs would begin to give under me, and I would have to stop walking and cling to the pram handle until the sense of blind panic passed.

# Chapter four

Mother worked on short contracts in the bigger city department stores. She demonstrated new products, like kitchen gadgets, or was engaged specially to sell slow-moving goods that might deteriorate if kept in stock too long. She slowly gained a good reputation, and stores would pass her from one to another, to get rid of piles of baby baths in unpopular colours, baby clothes that threatened to harbour moths, cameras and photographic supplies left over from the summer season, and the newest wringer washers and gas stoves.

She became an excellent saleswoman, and it used to amuse me to carry Edward into a shop and watch her demonstrate the use of a gadget. It fascinated me to observe how she could beguile housewives into impulsive purchases.

One day, Avril and I stood at a discreet distance behind her in a baby-wear department. I held Edward in my arms and, though he must have known he was watching his mother, he placidly sucked his thumb and did not call out. She was selling violently pink rubber baths.

She tenderly picked up a rubber doll and plunged it into imaginary water, talking all the time, first to the doll as if it were a baby and then to her audience, who, quite amused, slowly gathered round her. She dried the doll and dusted it with baby powder and put on its nappy. Young mothers and obviously expectant mothers were her targets, and they soon found themselves hooked into friendly conversation. Mother seemed to be able to make them feel that their baby was her only interest in life; and if they already had a baby bath, she would skilfully pass them to one of the shop assistants, whose battle for a sale of baby clothes was, of course, already half won.

Before Father went bankrupt, she had for years been a member of operatic and dramatic societies, and she knew enough of stagecraft to use her voice and manner to the best effect. She was never paid enough for her ability.

She looked very attractive, despite her thinness, in a black dress and black shoes purchased from a second-hand shop. I used to cut her hair for her with Father's cut-throat razor and then curl it each morning with a pair of curling tongs, bought for a penny from the pawnbroker's oddments table set up outside his shop.

Of course, I never approached her while she was working; and Avril understood that she must be quiet and tiptoe away at an appropriate moment. I doubt if she noticed that we were there, because she never mentioned seeing us.

Avril's and my great enemies were the shopwalkers. Sometimes when we were cold, we would go into a big shop and skulk around the different departments until we became warm again. And then the shopwalker would pounce.

Shopwalkers always looked very imposing. They were usually elderly gentlemen dressed in stiff, white, Victorian wing collars and black suits. They perambulated stiffly up and down the aisles of the shops, hands clasped behind their backs. They glared ferociously at the young girls and boys who served behind the counters. Then, with a slight bow, they would lend a courteous ear to customer inquiries, the whispered remarks almost drowned by the loud rings of the containers, holding payments or change, shooting along wires above their heads on their way from the counter to the cash office.

I never argued with shopwalkers.

'What do you want?' they would snarl.

'I'm just looking,' I would say loftily, exactly as I had heard people round me say.

The usual reply was, 'You can look in the windows.'

Then they would stride crossly to the nearest door and fling it open, and Edward, Avril and I would slink out like lost puppies.

One October day, we went into a shop in which Mother was working, to get warm. Mother was selling photograph albums. Her voice penetrated clearly through the murmur of shoppers as she extolled the advantages of having an album for each particular type of photograph. Avril, Edward and I settled down to watch.

I had not been feeling well for two days. My back ached, as did my head. I had got very wet in a rain storm earlier in the week, and I shrugged off the low-level discomfort as being due to this. As I watched, however, the pain in my back began to feel as if an iron belt had been suddenly clasped round my waist. Pains shot down the sides of my stomach.

I gasped to Avril that we had to go home quickly, and dragged her back to the pram, parked in the shop doorway. She protested in a loud whine as I plunked her into the pram with Edward. Panting with pain, I began the long ascent up Renshaw Street, Hardman Street and Leece Street.

The pain came in ever-increasing waves. Sweat beaded my forehead and I leaned on the pram handle for support, as I almost ran for home.

In St Catherine's Street, opposite the Women's Hospital, I stopped to lean against a brick wall as a particularly agonising pain ripped down the side of my stomach. Though I stared at the hospital with glazed eyes, it did not occur to me to seek succour there. To a child, in those days, hospitals were usually where old people went to die. Fiona had once gone to hospital and her lurid tales of her experiences had been enough to frighten all of the children. So the hospital was just another impersonal red brick building to stumble past on my way home.

Avril was whining and snatching at the twig with which Edward was playing. Mercifully, they both seemed unaware that anything was wrong.

I ran the pram up to the front step of our house, and tugged at the string sticking through the letterbox. The string pulled back the lock, the door swung open and I almost threw first Edward and then Avril into the narrow hall.

The pain was again surging in my stomach.

Frightened to death, I slammed the front door, snatched up Edward and carried him through to our back yard, leaving an angry Avril howling in the hall. Perhaps if I went to the lavatory I would feel better.

I left the lavatory door ajar, so that I could watch Edward, while I snatched down my knickers.

The torn, grey garment was covered with blood.

I thought I would faint with sheer terror.

Was it appendicitis?

Again the waves of pain. I dropped down on to the seat, clasping my stomach. When the pain cased slightly, I hitched up the soaked knickers and took Edward back into the house. I had to lie down.

Avril was sitting on an upturned paint can, nursing a stray cat which had wandered in a day or two before. She had been crying and when she saw me, she let out a fresh bellow. Normally, I would have comforted her, but this time I dumped Edward unceremoniously down beside her.

'Watch Edward,' I ordered.

Where should I lie?

My bed upstairs was a door set on four bricks and I could lie on it. But Edward might follow me up the stairs and then fall down again.

Better to go into the nicely furnished front room, a place I normally did not enter because Edward was usually with me – and he always had grubby hands and was not yet reliably watertight.

Edward did follow me in, and I hastily gave him the new, unused bronze fire irons to play with. A resentful Avril stayed with the cat.

My parents, with their usual blithe inconsequence, had furnished the front room very well on the hire purchase system, regardless of the fact that the children still slept three to a bed under a motley collection of old coats and bits of blanket; and I did not even have a bed.

I was thankful enough that day, however, to curl up on the green leatherette settee. In the foetal position the pain lessened, though during the next surge I fainted.

I sobbed to myself and prayed that Mother would come home soon. Then the scarifying spasms retreated slightly and I fell into a doze.

Father shook me gently to awaken me and asked anxiously, 'Are you all right, dear? You look very white.'

My stomach and back were tight knots of pain, increasing and decreasing like waves on a seashore. I was also shivering with cold from the unheated room. I hardly dared to move, as I whimpered out the story of the torment I was enduring.

'My underneaths are bleeding, Daddy. Do you think I've got appendicitis?'

Bent over me, he listened. Then his eyes began to twinkle, his lips to twitch. A loud guffaw burst from him.

I was horrified at such a reaction to my story.

'Daddy!' I reproached him, and then broke into a moan as the pain increased.

Father straightened up and, still smiling, let out a slow sigh of relief.

'Didn't your mother explain this to you?'

'What?'

'This – this bleeding?'

'No. Was she expecting it?' I was totally bewildered, and I sobbed as the pain hit new heights.

'Well, of course. She must have been. You're a girl.'

'Of course I'm a girl,' I gasped. 'What difference does that make? Daddy, could you get the doctor? The pain's getting worse.' I was deeply upset at his laconic attitude.

He hesitated for a moment. Then he said, 'You just stay where you are for the moment, until Mother comes home. Fiona's making the tea. I'll ask her to bring you a cup. She peeked in here and thought you were sleeping, so she has laid the table for you and cut the bread and butter. I will make the fire in the kitchen for the children.' His voice was kind.

With eyes screwed tight to help me bear the raging pain, I put my head down again on the inhospitable green leatherette. I heard him open the door, pause a moment and then say, 'Don't be afraid, old lady. This is nothing to be frightened about. You don't need a doctor.'

I did not answer him, because I did not believe him. I could not understand how anyone could be in such pain and not need a doctor. 'Mummy, come soon,' I sobbed. Cold, indifferent Mother seemed to be the key to it all.

The door clicked again and I opened my eyes. Fiona entered, carefully balancing a coarse china cup on a saucer which did not match. Despite her care, the tea slopped as she put the cup and saucer into my hand. She looked at me anxiously from beneath a roughly cut fringe of nut-brown hair.

'Daddy said to drink the tea while it is very hot. What's the matter, Helen? You look awful.'

I was shaking so much that, as I raised myself a little, I slopped the tea on to the new settee. 'I don't know, Fi,' I answered, as I tried to sip the scalding liquid. 'Daddy says it's nothing – but, oh, Fi, I've got such a terrible pain in my back and tummy – and I'm bleeding underneath.'

Fiona's pink cheeks blenched. 'Bleeding?'

I nodded affirmatively. The tea was comforting and I drank it eagerly, though it was hot enough to burn my tongue.

'Oh, Helen!' she whispered.

'Daddy said to stay here till Mummy came. Can you manage?'

'Yes, of course. Daddy's making the fire and Alan is fetching the coal for him. You rest. Mummy will come soon.' She was trying hard not to panic herself.

'Where's Edward?' I asked.

'He's in the kitchen. He's fine.'

I could feel a warm trickle between my thighs and I took deep breaths to avoid screaming in fright.

'Go and have your own tea,' I told her in a strained whisper, and she went, stopping at the door to look back at me with fearful violet-blue eyes.

'Don't be afraid, Fi,' I panted and tried to muster a smile for her sake. 'I'll be all right.'

She smiled back with sudden relief and shut the door quietly after her.

I was sure, as I sank back on to the settee, that I was on my death bed. And Father did not care!

# Chapter five

Mother sat down on the green leatherette easy chair opposite to me, and took off her hat. She looked tired and irritable.

'Oh, Mummy,' I wailed. 'I've got such a terrible pain – and I'm bleeding.'

'Oh, stop crying, Helen,' Mother snapped wearily. 'There's nothing the matter with you. This is what I told you about years ago. All girls bleed every month.'

I looked at her with wide-eyed horror, while I pressed my hands into my raging stomach. 'I don't remember your telling me.'

'Of course I did – when you were about nine.'

If she had told me, the information must have been given so obliquely that it did not then register on my childish mind.

My teeth were chattering, as I asked incredulously, 'Every month – and pain like this?'

'Of course not. It doesn't hurt at all. You have just worked yourself into a panic, and that has caused the pain. It will go away quite soon. We'll try to get some aspirins, before it is due next time.'

Mother smoothed her hair, ruffled from her hat, and got up briskly. 'I'll put a kettle on and when it is boiled, you can come into the kitchen to wash yourself. I'll get a piece of cloth and show you how to keep yourself dry.'

'Will it be like this ever again?' I asked between dry sobs.

'I doubt it, if you don't have hysterics.'

Twenty minutes later, I was seated by the kitchen fire, washed and tidied, drinking another cup of hot tea. The heat from the fire helped and gradually the pain receded, as Mother had promised.

The boys stared at me because they had been told that I had had hysterics over a perfectly normal tummy ache; and they went away, Alan to night school, Brian and Tony to play bus on the stairs.

It had been a terrifying promotion to womanhood. I felt humiliated and stupid, and blamed myself for my pain. I had been aware of changes in my body, but I was so undernourished that the changes were slight and they had come slowly enough not to scare me.

Three weeks later, I collapsed with pain in night school. The English teacher made me swallow two aspirins, told me I would be all right in an hour and sent me home. Mother said the same thing and sent me up to bed, where I groaned and moaned my way through the next eight hours or so. In the early hours of the morning I fell asleep, exhausted.

From month to month the pain persisted, and Mother became more concerned. She bought dried mint and made a tea for me to drink at the onset of the first ache. It did not help. Cristina, my Spanish friend, recommended a thick paste made with ginger spice and hot water, to be licked off a spoon. Trustingly I downed this horrible concoction, but the pain continued. Cristina laughed, and said all the pain would cease either on marriage or after having a baby.

I knew I was too bad-tempered and too plain to hope for marriage; and I was certain in my mind that, however babies came, I was not going to have one outside marriage. So I smiled dimly at her and did not reply.

All the well-meaning adults in my life assured me that menstruation was just part of growing up and that some girls had more difficulty with it than others did. Nobody suggested that I should see a doctor. Since doctors cost money, and I rarely thought of acquiring anything that required payment, it did not occur to me either.

For a week or two, I would forget the pain in the bustle of caring for the children's endless needs, and running off to night school through misty streets, where strange, shadowy women lurked; and then apprehension would begin to creep over me. I would ask Mother for some of her aspirins and store them behind the alarm clock on the kitchen mantelpiece. I learned that heat was comforting and when I saw a pile of new bricks lying on a building site, I begged two cracked ones from the bricklayer and brought them home. I heated them in the oven beside the kitchen fire, and when the onslaught began I wrapped them in newspaper and lay on the green leatherette settee, clutching them close to me. Edward began to think it was a new game and wanted a brick for himself. He thought it was a great joke to cuddle up close with the bricks between us. Since he must often have been cold, the heat was probably comforting to him, too.

One freezing winter day, I fainted in the butcher's shop. When I came round I was in an easy chair beside a fire, in the living quarters behind his little shop. His wife was forcing brandy down my throat. She must have succeeded in getting me to swallow quite a lot, because the pain did dull slightly and I felt exhilarated and yet sleepy. Edward had been propped in a matching chair on the other side of the fireplace. White rivulets down either grubby cheek marked the passage of tears. He had, however, a cheering ring of red jam round his mouth and in one hand was holding the crumbling remains of a tart.

The tiny, stuffy room was packed with furniture, and the blaze in the hearth glanced off a gilded china shepherdess on a shining sideboard opposite to me. It danced off the glass dome covering a pair of stuffed birds and made the glasses of my hostess flash.

The butcher's wife was a tiny woman dressed in the greyish, washed-out skirt, blouse and cardigan which seemed to be the uniform of women in Liverpool. Wisps of hair had escaped from her bun and draggled round a careworn face.

'Are ye feeling better?' she asked.

'Yes, thank you,' I said. I blinked at her rather hazy face through spectacles that had slipped down my nose. 'In fact, I feel fine.'

'Aye, that's good brandy, that is. You gave me husband a real fright when you keeled over.'

'I am sorry. I get a pain each month,' I faltered shyly.

She smiled. 'Oh, that was it, was it? Oh, aye. Brandy was the best thing to give you then. Does a lot for a woman at such times.'

'It seems to,' I said blithely.

Then I remembered the children's lunch, yet to be made. 'I must go home,' I said hastily. 'My brothers and sisters will be coming from school.'

'Think you'll be all right? You only live down the road, don't you?'

'Yes.'

I got to my feet. They did not feel very certain as to where the floor was; but I managed to stagger over to Edward and to pick him up. He put his arms round my neck, and sent a shower of pastry crumbs over the threadbare carpet.

Reeling slightly, I again thanked the butcher's wife.

She laughed.

'It's nothing. Aye, brandy's gone to your head, hasn't it?'

'It has,' I giggled. 'But the pain is less.' I wanted to kiss her, but decided I could not aim straight. So I said effusively, 'Thank you very, very much,' and staggered, still giggling, through the lace-draped door to the shop, which she held open for me. She smiled broadly at me, as I passed.

Though sometimes the pain would rise above the effects of the brandy, and I had to stop walking and grip the handle of the old pram until the wave passed over, I hummed most of the way home. I was merrily drunk for the first time.

I rolled round the icy living-room and the kitchen as I boiled and thickened the minced meat I had bought; it was as well that it was ground, otherwise it would have been unchewable. I peeled the potatoes and boiled them to a mush, before the penny in the gas meter ran out and the gas stove refused to deliver any more heat. I spread clean newspaper on the table, and laid it. Seated on a wooden chair, I waited, at first happily, for the children to come in. But as the effects of the brandy began to seep out, the chill of the dirty, comfortless room began to invade – and the pain was once more paramount.

Edward, too, was chilled and hungry and began to whimper. I took him up on my knee and wrapped us both in the old coat I used to cover him in the pram. It smelled of urine and long use. We warmed each other a little. He sucked his thumb and dozed, while I wept silently on to his scurfy little head.

I wished I had some more brandy or anything else which would stop the grinding misery within me. As I waited, I saw suddenly the expression of pain which frequently lay on my father's face – and in a burst of warm understanding I realised why he needed to drink sometimes. The burden of bereavement from the loss of most of his friends, in a war which, though it seemed a long time ago to me, was probably still quite close to him. The terror of the long, threatening winters he had spent in tiny blockhouses or in peasants' huts during the Russian campaign, while the Revolution surged around the tiny force, so that one did not know who was friend and who was foe – what must it have done to a delicate, refined man unused to any hardship? And then to lose his fortune, his occupation, his home? He sometimes told us stories of his experiences both during the war and after it, and he made us laugh. But if one analysed those stories, they were filled with horrors.

Poor Father. I laid my head against Baby Edward's and wept not only for my own suffering, but for my father's distress as well.

Getting drunk can leave one very low afterwards, I discovered.

# Chapter six

There was a silent conspiracy between Father, Mother and me, to keep from the other children as many of our troubles as possible.

We had as many creditors in Liverpool as Father had had in wealthier days. Now, instead of the tailor, the dressmaker, the grocer and wine merchant, I faced the owner of the local tobacco and newspaper shop trying to collect for the cigarettes he had supplied, the club man demanding the weekly payment for cheques issued to my parents by finance companies, for purchase of clothing at specific shops; the agent of our aristocratic landlord threatening to throw us into the street; the heavy-jowled hire purchase man growling threats to repossess our well-chosen sitting-room furniture.

Ominous clouds of danger seemed to encompass me and sometimes, after getting rid of a desperate bullying man, I would lean against the inside of the front door and cry with pure fright.

In our other life in another world, I had often heard Mother say to the parlourmaid that she was not at home to anybody, and she thus evaded personal confrontation with creditors, whose bills and threatening letters lay in the wickerwork wastepaper basket.

Here in Liverpool I had to answer the door myself. No frilly-aproned, sniggering parlourmaid stood between me and outraged men whose own livelihood was precarious. Occasionally, when I felt defeated, I would prevail on Fiona to answer the heavy bangs on the front door. She looked much younger than her age and had an expression of angelic innocence. She would say with convincing firmness, 'Everybody is out except me.'

The creditor would leave, grumbling under his breath, to mount his bicycle parked at the pavement's edge. They never shouted at her, as they did at me.

I was never given a fixed sum from which to do the housekeeping. A shilling or two was slung on to the kitchen table with instructions to buy a list of groceries for which the money was almost invariably inadequate. Consequently, Edward and I tramped for miles to save a halfpenny on a loaf of bread, or to go to a shop which would cut a twopenny half-pound pack of margarine into quarter pounds, so that we could buy one. Stores which did this kind of splitting up of goods could, with patience, make a lot more than those which did not. A sixpenny one-pound pot of jam, sold by the ounce at a penny an ounce, assured an excellent profit. Such shops were filled with black-shawled, unwashed women and skinny, barefoot children.

We had two lots of wages coming into the house; yet no housekeeping priorities were ever established. Mother sometimes made long lists of proposed expenditures and debt repayments, but they always ended up being tossed into the fireplace. Creditors who shouted the loudest and threatened most got paid eventually; those that did not received nothing. Cajoling credit out of shopkeepers who respected an Oxford accent was reduced to a fine art by my parents.

I can remember one pay day Mother coming triumphantly home with a box of cream cakes, when we lacked meat, milk, shoes and soap. The children, of course, thought the cakes were wonderful, and I began dimly to understand why our rough, largely Irish, neighbours spent so outrageously on weddings and funerals, cinemas and drink, whenever they got the chance. Life seemed so hopeless that they snatched at any treat, as if they had only the present and there was no future.

There was, however, a number of families nearby with less money than we had, but whose kitchen grate always seemed to have a fire in it, though it might be of slowly collected driftwood rather than of coal. Their children, friends of Fiona, Brian and Tony, were neat and clean; they ate regularly, though I cannot remember a single fat child amongst them. Their mothers obviously mended and washed frequently and could often be seen sweeping the dust out of their front doors, across the pavement and into the gutter. I often heard the sharp snap of rugs being shaken in the back yards, and saw them kneeling on the front pavement as they scrubbed and donkey-stoned their single front step. Some of them even scrubbed the pavement itself as far as the street. The menfolk were usually craftsmen or seamen, skilled with their hands. Some of them, for a couple of shillings, rented a small allotment garden from the City. These gardens were often close to railway embankments or at the edge of the city, and good crops of fruit and vegetables were raised on them during the otherwise empty summer days.

Neither of my parents had been trained to manage money. Grandpa died when Father was six. Father was sent to an excellent public school when he was ten, a school famous for the Shakespearean plays its boys enacted. He acquired a deep understanding of French and English history, and his mathematical abilities were of university level. But nobody taught him how to keep a budget or to manage a family.

Mother was equally ill-prepared for life. She was an orphan, brought up in a convent. She learned how to embroider fine altar cloths and copes; she acquired a smattering of French and other social graces, and a great love of reading. She had a fine singing voice and she learned to sing very well, though not to professional level – that would have been vulgar. The nuns who taught her hammered in the need for virtue in women, but not the basic knowledge which would make a good housewife. Since all their charges were segregated from the opposite sex, except for the skirted priests, the girls appeared to have had a wild curiosity about men and to have forgotten their lessons on virtue. Some of the girls went home to a normal family life during their holidays. But Mother's guardian was a bachelor, so she stayed at school, to spend summer holidays taking walks with the nuns and other homeless girls, and Christmases and Easters largely in church.

Unlike most of her contemporaries, Mother had had some business experience. Her guardian was the owner of a string of libraries, and when Mother became fifteen he removed her from the convent and taught her his own business. A few years later, he married. Mother was jealous of the new wife and she ran away to North Wales, where she found a post as librarian. There, she met my father during the First World War and married him.

Now we were all suffering dreadfully as a result of their frivolous, irresponsible life after the war. Even hunger, cold, sickness and pain failed to teach them to manage any better.

Poor diet produces rotting teeth, and all of us at times had to endure severe toothache. To alleviate this, we painted the offending tooth with a pennyworth of oil of cloves. Though this did sometimes ease the pain, it did not stop the tooth from deteriorating further. Then abscesses formed. Brian and Avril often sat weeping, while I applied hot poultices to their faces until the abscesses swelled and burst. Father already had false teeth when we arrived in Liverpool. But Mother's excellent teeth began to loosen from gum disease. When one became too loose, she would wiggle it with her tongue until she could pull it out with her fingers. This must have hurt her and, of course, the gaps in her mouth did not improve her looks, which must have hurt even more. Mouths full of poor teeth were, however, very common in Liverpool, and it was not unusual, particularly in respect of women, to have lost all one's teeth by the age of twenty-five.

During the second winter of attendance at night school, I found I could not see very well. I had lost some sight and my glasses needed to be replaced. I had also grown, so that the frames were too small for me and my already plain face was made to look even more out of proportion.

A further affliction was an annoying disease called pink eye. At different times all the family caught it. It is an acute inflammation of the eye which causes a heavy discharge, so that the eyes are sealed tight during sleep and in the daytime are flushed a sickly pink. The chemist sold me tiny packets of boracic acid which we made into a solution with hot water, and it helped when we bathed our eyes with it.

But my eyes were always sore, from too much reading through wrong glasses in a bad light. Frequently we lacked pennies to push into the gas meter for the light in the living-room, so I read by candlelight or, if we had no candles, I would do my homework leaning against a lamp post, to take advantage of its dim rays. The streets were lit by gas in those days, and the lamplighter would dash on his bicycle from one cast-iron lamp post to the next to pull the chain that lit the lamp. In the early part of the night-school term, it was frequently warm enough for me to do my homework in the park, sitting on a bench watching the children, or there was sometimes sufficient daylight to enable me to do it at home. But the deep winter was a time to be dreaded.

I came to my studies hopelessly tired, and always hungry. The quiet order of the school, however, helped my mind to focus; and I made such a violent effort that at the end of the first year I was awarded a very small scholarship to cover the cost of books and fees for the following year. At the end of the second year, if I passed the examinations, I was to move on to a Senior Evening Institute. There the cost of books would be greater; and I had moments of panic while I waited for the results of the examinations, wondering what I would do if I did not win a scholarship this time. And even worse, what would be my fate if I failed the examination itself? My only hope would be gone.

With the exception of Baby Edward, who was still too young, the children had been sent to a local Church school as soon as they reached the proper age. They attended with reasonable regularity. If I was ill, Fiona was kept at home to help, but the boys never were. I resented this blatant discrimination. Why, I often argued, was so little attention given to Fiona's and my future? A lot of anxious talk went on about careers – never jobs – for the boys. Could not girls have careers? My parents thought such remarks were funny, and they laughed. Girls got married, they said.

At night school, the other girls were talking hopefully of getting jobs as shorthand typists or as bookkeepers, and some of them were already at work in shops and offices. They did not seem to be counting on having a husband to keep them, and yet they were all much prettier than me.

I used to watch them as they filed into class, usually dressed in hand-knitted jumpers and dark skirts, rayon stockings and high-heeled court shoes. Their hair was always neatly cut and sometimes marcel-waved. They used powder and lipstick generously and some of them, I noted wistfully, had necklaces, bracelets or rings.

I knew that unless a miracle occurred, I would never manage to look as nice as they did. What chance would I have of employment, even if my parents allowed me to apply for jobs? Just to get rid of the vermin on me would be a heavy task for a fairy godmother.

# Chapter seven

At best, the years between the ages of fourteen and seventeen are not very balanced ones. Children tend to query and test the prevailing social mores, even when they have been blessed with a stable, comfortable life. Like a windowpane through which a stone had been thrown, our family's life had splintered in every direction, leaving a gaping hole. Almost nothing that I had been taught as a child by Edith or by Grandma seemed to have any relevance in slums where fighting and drunkenness were everyday occurrences, where women stood in dark corners with men, fumbling with each other in a manner I was sure was wrong, though I had no inkling of what they were actually doing; a place where theft was considered smart and children openly showed the goods they had shoplifted; where hunchbacks and cripples of every kind got along as best they could with very little medical care; where language was so full of obscenity that for a long time I did not understand the meaning.

Even in my parents' light-hearted group, ideas had been discussed, theories of existence expounded, the war knowledgeably refought in the light of history. The availability of music, paintings and fine architecture had been taken for granted. Dress, deportment, manners, education, politics, were all taken seriously.

The comparison was so hopeless that I sometimes laughed. But beneath the laughter, I seethed with suppressed rage and apprehension that even if the rest of the family managed to crawl out of their present sorry state, I would be left behind.

Like water held behind a dam shaken by an earthquake, this anger burst through my natural diffidence, one wet February afternoon, when a plainly dressed lady called at our home. Her hair was hidden by a navy blue coif, such as our nanny used to wear; and her glasses were perched on a nose reddened by the chilly weather. She wore no make-up, and her navy blue mackintosh reached down to ankles covered in grey woollen stockings. Her black shoes, flat and frumpy, shone despite the rain. I did not recognise my fairy godmother.

When I opened the door a fraction, afraid of yet another creditor, she blinked at me in a friendly way and asked if Mother was at home.

'No,' I said cautiously, shifting Edward in my arm so that he could peep round the door, too, without my dropping him.

'And you are – ?'

'I'm Helen,' I said. 'Mother will be at home this evening, if you would like to call again then.'

The wind drove a patter of rain down the street and I heard the click of the front door of the next house as it was opened; the unemployed man next door liked to lean against his own door jamb and listen to my battles with creditors. He would stand and laugh as if he were watching a variety show, and then when it was over, would spit on to our doorstep and go indoors again.

Our visitor's eyes flickered towards the other door. Then she said, 'I wonder if I might come in for a moment? I am sure I can explain to you what I have come about.'

Reluctantly, I opened the door wider so that she could step into the muddy hallway. I heard the next door snap shut.

I ushered her into our front room. She paused on the threshold and looked round the room in obvious surprise, as she took off her gloves. The comparison between Edward's and my threadbare appearance and the pleasantly furnished room must have struck her immediately. The bugs in the walls gave it an unpleasant smell, but in the hope that they had not yet penetrated the pristine easy chairs, I invited her to sit down.

She sat down gingerly on the edge of one of the chairs, while I stood in front of her holding Edward. I did not want to put him down because his feet were bare and very cold.

She said she had come from the church to which the children's school was attached, and I nodded, though it seemed to me to be remarkable; during the two and a half years that the children had been attending the school no one from the church had called on us, and we, being so shabby, had never attempted to attend it. In fact, I had forgotten that the church existed.

Edward sucked his thumb and laid his head in the curve of my neck, so that throughout the conversation I could hear the placid slush-slush of his little tongue.

The visitor said in a bright, brittle voice that she had heard from Brian's and Tony's teachers that their singing voices were good enough for them to sing in the church choir. She had come to inquire if my parents and the boys would be agreeable to this. She knew that Mother worked part-time and she had hoped to catch her at home.

It was never possible for me to forecast what reaction my parents might have to any new situation, so I thanked her cautiously and said that Mother would be home at five o'clock.

She smiled gently up at me, but she did not get up to leave. Instead, she sighed and looked at Edward's blue bare feet.

There was an uneasy silence, and then she said in a much softer voice, 'Did you attend our school?'

'No.'

'Or the church? Have you been confirmed?'

I cleared my throat nervously and replied again, 'No.' Then, since my replies seemed abrupt, I added, 'I go to night school. I'm in Second Year Commerce.'

'Where did you go to school?'

Her face was so kind and her interest seemed genuine, so I told her about my four years in a variety of private schools up and down the country, and said rather sadly, 'I didn't learn very much. I think, if Grandma had not taught me to read and my aunt to write, I would be illiterate.'

Very slowly, while I rocked a sleepy Edward in my arms, she drew out of me the story of my struggle to go to night school, the fact that I had no clothing to speak of and the other children very little. And with a catch of self-pity in my voice, I finished up, 'There doesn't seem to be much hope for anything better for me, unless I can be free to go to work. But there is nobody to look after little Edward, if I do go.'

'But things seem to be getting better,' she comforted me. 'This room is very nicely furnished.'

'I'd rather Edward had some shoes and socks,' I retorted suddenly. 'And you should see the other rooms.'

The dam burst. 'Come and see,' I almost ordered her, and strode to the open door. 'Come and have a look.'

Without a word, her face very serious now, she got up and followed me.

Up the stairs she trudged after me, to the icy, fetid bedrooms, to inspect three iron beds with thin, old-fashioned felt mattresses on them, the urine stains uncovered by any sheet. I had tidied up the bits of blanket and old coats which we used to cover us, and some of the pillows had grubby, white pillow-cases on them.

She looked, aghast, at the door on which I slept. It was balanced on four bricks, one at each corner, and had wads of old newspaper piled on it, instead of a mattress, with a grey piece of sheeting to tuck over them. There was no other furniture, and, of course, there was no bathroom.

In a passion, I swept her downstairs again, to look at the living-room, with its bare deal table, assorted straight chairs and upturned paint cans helping out as seats. The only sign of comfort was an old wooden rocking chair and a very ancient, greasy-looking easy chair, in which was curled a stray cat which Brian had earlier brought in from the rain. On the tiled floor lay a piece of coconut matting, filled with dust. In the old-fashioned iron fireplace I had laid the fire, ready for the children's return home.

The kitchen looked quite large because there was so little in it. A small table flanked the gas stove, and there was a built-in soapstone sink in one corner. The opposite corner was taken up by a brick copper, with a tiny fireplace under it, for boiling washing. Our single bucket stood under the sink; our only wash basin caught the steady drip from the house's cold water tap.

Long lines of shelves ran down one side of the kitchen. They held a motley assortment of rough white dishes and cups, two saucepans and a dripping tin. A kettle sat on the gas stove beside a tin teapot. A small wooden table held our bits of food, a packet of tea and a blue-bagged pound of sugar, some margarine in a saucer and a new loaf.

I was shivering with cold and with emotion, and my visitor turned pitying, gentle eyes upon me. 'Don't you have a fire?' she asked. They were the first words she had spoken during our lightning tour.

'Edward and I manage during the day. I light the fire for the children coming home at lunchtime, and then I relight it for teatime.'

I realised, as I said this, that Edward and I were just as vulnerable to cold as the others were, but we remained in the frigid house while everyone else spent the day in warm buildings. No wonder my joints hurt when I moved. No wonder Edward sometimes cried because of the cold.

'Where do you keep your food?' she asked.

'On the table here,' I said. 'I buy it every day.'

She bit her lips, as she pondered over the bread and margarine, and I said a little defensively, 'Avril or Tony will fetch a pint of milk from the dairy when they come in.'

Edward had gone to sleep, so I led the way back into the living-room and laid him down in the easy chair, after pushing off the cat. He stirred, but slept on, his tiny legs spread-eagled. 'I'll get something to cover him,' I told the lady, and flashed up the stairs to get a coat.

When I came back she was still standing where I had left her, and I hastily tucked Edward up before I turned again to face her. My hysterical outburst had spent itself and I felt exhausted and ashamed.

'I'm sorry,' I said, 'I should not have bothered you with all this. And I'm sorry it is not very clean – but I have nothing but a broom and cold water with which to clean – it's just impossible.'

She seemed wrapped in thought, almost as if she had not heard me. Then she smiled at me very sweetly. 'I'm glad you did show me,' she said reassuringly. 'I can understand better the struggle you are having. Don't be discouraged – things have a way of getting better.'

I tried to smile back. I did not believe her.

'I'll come again this evening to see your mother,' she continued, a briskness in her voice.

As I let her out of the house, she turned again to me. 'Now remember. No getting discouraged.'

I nodded, then she smiled and went out into the rain; her coif was wet before I had closed the door.

She came, as promised, and then again and again. She was a deaconess, and Mother seemed to like her because she was a gentle, cultivated woman. First Brian and, later, Tony joined the choir, their white surplices saving them from the embarrassment of their shabby clothes. Later on, Tony became an altar boy, and the faith he acquired whilst kneeling in the richly decorated sanctuary never left him. He has always been an active member of the Church of England. The experience must also have helped mischievous, highly strung Brian because, if nothing else, he learned music by many of the great composers in a bright and beautiful church. Both boys were allowed to retain the one shilling and eightpence per month paid to them for their services.

Apparently, the deaconess did not tell Mother of her tour of our house. She did, however, become an earnest advocate on my behalf. Not all fairy godmothers carry wands.

# Chapter eight

Father sometimes bought a *Liverpool Echo* to read on the tram while coming home from work. A day or two later, before using the newspaper to start the fire, I would read it, as I knelt on the coconut matting in front of the big, black living-room fireplace.

I loved news of royalty. Love of the royal family is still quite strong, but in those days, particularly amongst women, it was close to a passion. All our princes were officially handsome, and the courtship of Princess Marina of Greece by Prince George, Duke of Kent, was a romance about which many a girl like myself dreamed wistfully. I followed developments from day to day with eager anticipation.

I also began to read the advertisements, including the ones offering jobs. Once or twice I stole a piece of Mother's notepaper and wrote replies. I was not a very good writer but I had been taught in night school how to formulate a letter of application, which was a help. I said I had been privately educated. This was true and absolved me from having to say how few years I had been in school. It also accounted for my not having matriculated, because some girls in private schools did not attempt matriculation; they went on to finishing schools in France or Switzerland. I imagined my childhood friend, Joan, was currently attending such a school.

I told the advertisers that my appearance was neat, which was far from true, and that I was honest and hardworking and was attending evening school. With the letters wrapped in a piece of newspaper to keep them clean, I then wheeled Edward down the long hill to Victoria Street in the centre of the town and hopefully slipped the letters in the box provided by the *Liverpool Echo* for replies.

Nothing happened.

Then one day I received a reply, in handwriting far worse than my own, from a sweetshop near St Luke's Church. They wanted an assistant and asked me to come to see them the following day, a Saturday. I was dazzled at the prospect.

I hummed all day, as I waited for the evening and the return of my parents. The children found me unusually cheerful at midday, as I gave them their main meal, a half-pound of stewed minced beef between the six of them, and mashed boiled potatoes. They had tea to drink. Because they had a little meat, the food was an improvement over their fare during the first two years of our sojourn in Liverpool. It was also easier for me to cook it. An old gas stove was already in the house when we rented it and it worked, as long as I had the necessary penny to put in the meter. In the apartment we had first rented, I had had to cook on a bedroom fireplace, on a fire frequently kept going with scraps of rubbish culled from the streets.

Mother and Father ate their lunches in cafés or took a sandwich with them. My lunch was boiled potato. This, with the occasional addition of carrots, onions or cabbage, was my staple meal for a number of years, and it is doubtful if my parents fared much better.

Lack of nourishing food added to my parents' irritation. Mother had always had an uncontrollable temper, terrifying to maids, children and shell-shocked husband alike, and these towering tantrums reached almost insane levels during the years in which we suffered so much poverty. So I approached my parents on the subject of the letter with the care of a cat stalking a mouse.

To no purpose.

Father, at times, seemed to live in a never-never land of illusion. He looked at me over his gold-rimmed spectacles, while he sipped a last cup of tea, and said firmly that I could not be spared to go to work at present. Who would look after Edward and the children's dinner if I were absent? Perhaps, later on, he added cheerfully, I could be sent to a teachers' training college and become a school mistress. But a shop assistant? Never! That would be absurd.

I almost laughed at him. 'Which training college would consider a girl with only four years of schooling?'

His reply was drowned out by Mother's musical contralto saying firmly, 'Your place is at home, Helen. It's the most sensible arrangement. In a few years you will marry and by then Edward will be old enough to look after himself.'

I was aghast. 'But you've always said – everybody's always said – that I am so plain. How can I get married if I'm so ugly? I'll be stuck here for ever.' I began to cry, with hot, angry sobs.

I knew I looked terrible. I had seen myself once in a shop mirror. There was no greater ragamuffin in all Liverpool than me. So when Father and Mother suddenly started to talk about my getting married, I became almost hysterical. I had read fairy tales where princes materialised from all kinds of unexpected places – but the princesses were always beautiful. No prince was going to come riding by to collect a sinful, ugly hoyden like me. I had shed many bitter tears already over this fact, so successfully hammered into me by a thoughtless mother and impatient servants. I classed myself with cripples who could hope only for attractive souls, appealing to God alone.

In a paroxysm of rage all the frustration came pouring out. I raved helplessly at them, and they raved back.

I was ungrateful, thoughtless, utterly selfish. Father and Mother worked all day to maintain the family. The least I could do was to keep house. And, anyway, no matter what happened, I could not become a shop assistant. It was beneath our station.

Beside myself with fury, I ranted that Mother was working in shops. Why could not I?

The boys, with long-suffering looks, went out to play with their friends. Avril burst into tears and howled nearly as loudly as me. At such times she would go so red that even her scalp under the fine golden hair and thick scurf would flush, and she would look as if she might at any moment drop dead from apoplexy.

Fiona snatched up her ancient doll and fled upstairs.

It was night school time, but still the argument raged. Finally, I could think of no more reasons why I should go to work and I sat on a paint can, buried my face in my hands and wept uncontrollably.

Mother angrily seized some of the dishes off the table and took them into the kitchen. Father folded up the newspaper into a neat small square, a habit he had. Suddenly the room was quiet, except for miserable sobs from Avril, sitting on the floor in a corner, sturdy small legs spread in front of her. Occasionally, she would kick the tiles with her heels, as if to emphasise her misery. My own sobs were almost silent; I had long ago learned to cry without drawing attention to myself.

Mother returned from the kitchen and Father said rather carefully to her, 'Perhaps if Helen went to this shop for the interview and saw how much work a place like that would expect from her, she might realise that she is better off at home. Small places like that usually squeeze the very life blood out of their people.' He ran one finger along the newspaper's folds to neaten it, while I looked up quickly at Mother.

I swallowed a sob. Here was a tiny opening. I was sure I could do any amount of work. I conveniently ignored the fact that my physical condition was so poor that quite small exertions could make me dizzy, and each month I had to face a day of almost unbearable pain.

Between sniffs, I begged Mother in watery, meek tones, to let me do as Father suggested.

Mother had wearied herself with her tirade. She sat down suddenly and was quiet. Then she said resignedly that she had no work for the next day, so she supposed she might as well take me to see the shop. Fiona could look after Edward, since the following day was Saturday.

I had not considered that Mother might accompany me, and I had expected to have to face the interview alone. This had worried me, because I had no idea how one should behave or what one should say in such a situation, particularly as I did not want to give any indication of the kind of life we led. I felt instinctively that I would stand a better chance of getting work if it appeared that I came from a stable working-class or lower-middle-class home, with less well-born parents than I had. What kind of an impact on a small businessman would Mother have, a lady who spoke 'with ollies in her mouth'?

I sighed, but made no objection to her coming. I said instead, 'I'd have to make myself look respectable, somehow.'

I looked at Mother hopefully. She was still dressed in her black business frock, though she had taken off her shoes and stockings and wore Father's old bedroom slippers on her feet. Her face looked haggard under her make-up and her hair, which I had waved the night before, was ruffled and untidy.

Mother returned my look. 'Yes, you would,' she replied, so sharply that it sounded like an implied threat and made me jump apprehensively.

I was as tall as Mother, though with a much slighter frame, and after surveying me for a moment, she said I could borrow the dress she was wearing. Since it would be Saturday the following day, I could also borrow Fiona's black woollen stockings and black flat-heeled shoes; Fiona was not consulted, and was very grumpy when she discovered what had been agreed. 'You'll tread them out,' she complained. 'Your feet are too big.'

'I'll be very careful,' I promised, as I recklessly washed my hair and then the rest of me in a quart of hot water in the tin basin, and used up the last sliver of soap we possessed. There would be a row with the boys in the morning about the lack of soap, but it could be endured.

I borrowed from Mother the only pair of scissors we had. She carried them in her handbag, so that they could not be misused, but even so, they were blunt and the nails on my right hand had to be finished off by biting them. Toenails were always left to grow until they broke off, and sometimes they looked like cruel yellow claws before they finally cracked off.

The scissors were too small to cut hair, so I combed my unkempt locks with the family comb, also normally carried in Mother's handbag, and hoped it would stay off my face until the interview was over. When I received some wages, I promised myself, I would ask Mother if I could buy some hair clips.

Even after these efforts, I must have looked very odd in a black dress too long and too loose for me and without an overcoat, though it was late February and the weather was damp and chilly.

Full of hope, though shivering with cold, I trotted along beside Mother through the misty morning, past the Rialto Cinema and Dance Hall with its tawdry posters, and the dim outline of the cathedral, to the sweetshop.

It was a very little shop, in a shabby block of other small shops and offices. Its window, however, sparkled with polishing despite the overcast day. Through the gleaming glass I could dimly see rows of large bottles of sweets and in front of them an arrangement of chocolate boxes, all of them free of dust. Beneath the window, a sign in faded gold lettering advertised Fry's Chocolate.

Mother, who had not spoken to me during the walk, paused in front of the shop and frowned. Then she swung open the glass-paned door and stalked in. I followed her, my heart going pit-a-pat, in unison with the click of Fiona's shoes on the highly polished, though worn, linoleum within.

An old-fashioned bell hung on a spring attached to the door was still tinkling softly when a stout, middle-aged woman with a beaming smile on her round face emerged through a lace-draped door leading to an inner room.

'Yes, luv?' she inquired cheerfully.

'I understand that you wrote to my daughter about a post in your shop?' Mother's voice was perfectly civil, but the word 'post' instead of 'job' sounded sarcastic.

The smile was swept from the woman's face. She looked us both up and down uncertainly, while I agonised over what Mother might say next.

'Helen?' the woman asked, running a stubby finger along her lower lip.

'Helen Forrester,' replied Mother icily.

'Ah did.' The voice had all the inflections of a born Liverpudlian. She looked past Mother, at me standing forlornly behind her. Her thoughtful expression cleared, and she smiled slightly at me. I smiled shyly back.

I felt her kindness like an aura round her and sensed that I would enjoy being with her, even if she did expect a lot of work from me.

'Have you ever worked before, luv?' she asked me, running fingers on which a wedding ring gleamed through hair which was improbably golden.

I nodded negatively. Then cleared my throat and said, 'Only at home.'

'What work would Helen be expected to do?' asked Mother, her clear voice cutting between the woman and me like a yacht in a fast wind. She had also the grace of a yacht in the wind; but the sweetshop owner was obviously finding her more trying than graceful and answered uncertainly, 'Well, now, I hadn't exactly thought. I need a bit o' help, that's all. 'Course she'd have to wash the floor and polish it, like, every day. And clean the window and dust the stock. And when I knowed her a bit she could probably help me with serving, like. I get proper busy at weekends – and in summer the ice cream trade brings in a lot o' kids, and you have to have eyes in the back o' your head or they'll steal the pants off you.'

Mother sniffed at this unseemly mention of underwear, and then nodded.

'And what would the salary be?'

I groaned inwardly. I was sure that in a little shop like this one earned wages not a salary.

The beginning of a smile twitched at the woman's lips, but she answered Mother gravely.

'Well, I'd start her on five shillings, and if she was any good I'd raise it.'

Even in those days, five shillings was not much. The woman seemed to realise this, because she added, 'And o' course, she can eat as many sweets as she likes. But no taking any out of the shop.'

I could imagine that this was not as generous as it sounded. After a week of eating too many sweets, the desire for them would be killed and few people would want them any more.

Mother inquired stiffly, 'And how many hours a week would she work for that?'

'Well, I open up at half past seven in the morning to catch the morning trade, you understand. And I close up at nine in the evening.' She paused a moment and then said, 'But I wouldn't need her after about seven o'clock. Me husband's home by then, and he helps me after he's had his tea. And I close Wednesday afternoons, so she'd have the afternoon off after she'd tidied up, like. Me husband helps me Sundays, too, so I wouldn't want her then either.'

I wanted the job so badly that I did not care how many hours I worked, how often I scrubbed the floor. The shop seemed so lovely and warm, after our house, and I sensed that in a rough way the woman would be kind to me. I tried to will the woman to agree to take me.

A little boy burst through the shop door, leaving the bell tinging madly after him. He pushed past us and leaned against the corner of the counter.

'Ah coom for me dad's ciggies,' he announced, turning a pinched, grubby face up towards the sweetshop owner.

'Have you got the money?'

'Oh, aye. He wants ten Woodbines.' A small hand was unclenched to show four large copper pennies.

The cigarettes were handed over and the pennies dropped into the wooden till.

'Now don't be smoking them yourself,' admonished the woman, with a laugh.

The boy grinned at her and bounced back to the door, his bare feet thudding. As he went through the door, he turned and gestured as if he were smoking.

'Aye, you little gint!' she said.

The interruption had given Mother time to make a rapid calculation. As the woman turned back to her, she said sharply, 'There is a law about how many hours a minor can work – and, incidentally, a law about selling cigarettes to minors. I am sure that over sixty hours a week – at less than a penny an hour – are far more hours than are allowed.'

The woman shrugged huffily; her eyes narrowed, giving her a cunning expression.

'I'm sure I don't know about that,' she replied tartly. 'If she doesn't want the job she doesn't have to take it. There's others as will be grateful for it.' She sniffed, and looked at me disparagingly. 'Anyway, I wouldn't take her. The sores on her face would put the customers off. I got to have a clean-looking girl.'

I looked at her appalled, hurt to the quick. In front of our broken piece of mirror, I had carefully squeezed each pimple on my face, so that the acne was temporarily reduced to raised red blotches with a fresh, golden scab on each. I had no make-up to cover the results. But I had hoped that I looked clean.

Mother's face flooded with angry colour. For a moment she looked like Avril in a tantrum. She cast a scornful glance at the shopkeeper, who stared back at her with her chin thrust upwards, quite unabashed.

'Good afternoon,' Mother snapped, as she swung round and opened the street door. The little bell tinkled crossly at being so forcibly disturbed.

'Helen, this way.'

It was an order, and I slouched out through the doorway, closely followed by my wrathful mother.

# Chapter nine

Mother scolded sibilantly all the way home, and blamed me for wasting her time. I was too crushed and disappointed to respond.

Back I went to the kitchen and little Edward, who trotted patiently by my side, while I fumed miserably. In saner moments, I acknowledged that Mother had saved me from savage exploitation. But her motives in doing so were, to me, suspect. And as the years went by I felt that my increasing efficiency at home was daily making more certain that I stay there. Probably a few pennies of pocket money or a modicum of praise would have done much to soothe me. But everything I did was taken for granted. Failures were bitingly criticised. There was no one to turn to for consolation, except, occasionally, to Fiona.

And yet I yearned to love my parents and be loved in return, to have with them the tender relationship I had had with Grandma during the long months I had frequently spent with her during my childhood. But Grandma had vanished with the rest of my friends. In my innocence, I did not understand that my parents' fast and extravagant life in the post World War years had alienated every relation they had. Father's widowed mother – the last to desert them – had left her son to learn the hard way the teachings she had failed to inculcate in him when young. She probably had no conception of the depth of our sufferings.

There is no doubt that Mother never forgave her friends for deserting her after Father went bankrupt; it was as if she declared a silent, ruthless war against her own class. The depth of her bitterness was immeasurable.

I remembered well the doll-like creatures who used to frequent our drawing-room and dining-room. In short beige georgette dresses, their marcel-waved hair covered by deep cloche hats, they teetered on high heels in and out of our old home in considerable numbers. Afternoon tea or dinner was served by a parlourmaid in black and white uniform. Sometimes well-tailored young men, who also had time to waste, came to drink a cocktail or have a cup of tea.

Several times, a man vanished from the usual circle. One of the ladies would say, between puffs on a cigarette held in a long holder, 'Gas, dahling – his lungs couldn't stand it,' or 'He was loaded with shrapnel – a piece moved round to his heart. Too utterly devastating.'

I was allowed to attend the tea parties. Edith would dress me in my best frock, usually shantung silk, long white socks and brown lace-up shoes, and I would sit and nibble a piece of cake and watch the prettily dressed visitors. I soon learned that most of the men were unemployed, ex-army officers; they usually had some private means left them by more enterprising forefathers, but as prices rose their money shrank. They had no special qualifications and sought jobs as car salesmen or vacuum cleaner salesmen. One of them regularly allowed me to reach up and touch the silver plate the doctors had implanted to replace the top of his skull; another had an artificial leg which creaked when he walked. Father himself had trouble with his hands, which had been frost-bitten during his service in Russia. He also got chest pains, forerunners of the heart attacks to come.

So, perhaps my parents' friends, bereaved, disillusioned, wounded in a war of frightful, unnecessary suffering, had so many troubles of their own that they were unable to help one of their number who had failed largely through his own inadequacies.

I was born after the war, so it was only history to me. Had I realised, when I got so cross with my parents' ineptitude, how close it still was to them, how they had already gone through the shock of seeing the kind of life they understood crumble, I would have been much more compassionate.

One windy March evening, when the children's need of clothing seemed particularly dire, Mother decided to write to some of her old acquaintances to ask for second-hand clothing. After all, she said bitterly to Father, the most she could lose was a three-halfpenny stamp, since she appeared to have lost any friendship there was.

When the children had gone to bed, she sat at one end of the living-room table and wrote three letters, while I sat at the other end and did my homework.

Three days later, a scented letter dropped through our letterbox. As far as I could remember, it was the first letter, other than a bill, which we had received since coming to Liverpool.

Opening it was a ceremony, carried out under the eager eyes of the entire family.

'It's from Katie,' said Mother, naming a gay, childless married friend as she slit the envelope with the kitchen knife.

It contained a single sheet of notepaper wrapped round a five-pound note. Katie was sorry about us and sent the enclosed with love. Mother had found a technique for adding to our income.

Until she had exhausted every possible person she could think of, Mother wrote at least one begging letter a week. She rarely got money out of the same person twice. But she had had an enormous circle of acquaintances, and when she ran out of these she wrote to the parents of the children's friends and also moving letters to their teachers. After that, she wrote to people whose names she had picked out of library reference books.

She learned to write eloquently of the children's woes and her own efforts to find work. She did not mention Father in letters to strangers, perhaps to give the impression, without actually saying so, that she was widowed. She frequently passed her efforts over to me to read – one of the few times when she took me into her confidence. I had never heard of confidence tricksters and I read them admiringly, believing them to be a perfectly honourable way of earning money. After all, Grandma had always said that charity was a great virtue, and we were certainly in need.

There were many professional begging letter writers in Liverpool at that time. Earnest gentlemen sat in their tiny bed-sitting rooms and wrote passionate appeals for help to any monied person who came to their attention. They invented whole families of starving children, aged parents in need of shoes, wives dying of tuberculosis, and so on. And they made a steady living at it. In contrast, Mother could say honestly that her children were in dreadful need, even if bad management was part of the cause of it.

Some well-to-do people, including royalty, who were bedevilled by begging letter writers, would send the letters to a charitable organisation in the city, with the request that they investigate the need; it was remarkable how generous people were when the need was found to be genuine. I do not recollect, however, anyone coming to investigate us as a result of one of Mother's letters.

Thanks to the kindness of many people unknown to me, a few comforts began to trickle into the house, amongst them a second-hand iron bed for me. The spring was hollowed out like a hammock and it was a number of years before I acquired a mattress. I shared it for a while with Edward, but it represented my first personal gain at home since we had arrived in Liverpool. It was at least another five years before I got proper blankets and sheets for it; and lying chilled to the marrow through endless winter nights was one of the greater hardships for all the children.

Sometimes parcels of clothing or bedding arrived in response to the letters. Clothing for the younger children was almost invariably given to them and it helped to keep them tidy for school. Sometimes there was clothing which fitted Mother; men's clothing was rarely sent, perhaps because of the difficulty of fitting. The bedding was usually bundled up with some of the clothing, ready for pawning.

Seared by disappointment, I would take the cloth-wrapped parcel to the crowded pawnbroker's shop with its three golden balls hanging in front of it, and, after much good-natured haggling with the pawnbroker, I would receive four or five shillings, and a ticket so that I could later redeem the parcel.

The parcel was whisked away from the high black counter and thrown up a chute to the pawnbroker's assistant in the storeroom above. After a year, if the goods had not been redeemed or interest paid on the loan, the parcel would be torn open and the contents sold. So many goods were for sale that the pawnbroker's was an excellent place to buy almost anything, from clothing and boots to an engagement ring or a bedspread or a concertina; and there were always women wrapped in shawls or in long, draggling men's overcoats, picking through the merchandise on the bargain tables set out in front of the store on fine days.

The money raised from the pawnbroker might be used for a little extra food or, more frequently, to pacify a creditor who had threatened court procedure. Cigarettes were almost always one of the first things bought with it, and sometimes Mother would go to the cinema. She often remarked angrily that if Father could afford a drink, she could afford a cinema seat.

The local newspaper-shop proprietor, after a fierce row with me because Father owed him a whole pound for cigarettes, obtained a court order against us. This meant that the bill had to be paid by regular instalments set by the court, on threat of the bailiffs selling us up if we failed to pay. This added enormously to my fears, because I had stood and watched while whole houses of furniture were sold by the bailiffs for a few shillings to settle a ridiculously small debt. Mother once bought for sixpence a superb hand-made rocking chair when there were no other bids for it.

I never knew where my parents might run up another bill or who might pounce on me, as the hapless housekeeper who had to answer the door. I had always been afraid of people who shouted, and I would stand shivering with my shoulder against the inside of the door, while someone hammered and shouted on the outside.

Once or twice I considered running away, but in those days there was no support from welfare organisations for such a runaway. And who would employ someone like me?

I once threatened to go to Grandma, but my Father said grimly that she would probably turn me away, that I should be thankful for what I had. Things would get better one of these days.

Grandma had become a loving, distant dream to me, and I was shocked beyond measure at the idea that she no longer cared. Yet I believed what Father said.

# Chapter ten

Spring had come at last. The trees lining Princes Avenue were stickily in bud; the privet hedges behind the low, confining front walls of the houses were already bursting into leaf, and the sparrows and pigeons were a-bustle with the need to mate.

I wheeled Edward down Parliament Street to the small Carnegie library in Windsor Street. A playful wind flipped dust and pieces of paper round its railings, against which women leaned, shopping bags on arm, to gossip in the pale sunshine. The soot-covered library was a handsome little building with high, arched windows which made it pleasantly light inside. Its battered books passed through my hands at the rate of about half a dozen a week and helped me to forget hunger, cold and humiliation. The librarians knew me and sometimes recommended a new book which had come in. In those days, librarians seemed to be great readers and both Father and I enjoyed discussions with them about books we had read.

I parked the Chariot close to the iron railings at the front. Edward was a patient child who would sit and watch the passers-by while I hastened to find something new to read.

As usual, I went directly to the section devoted to travel books. A new travel book was a great treat to me. I learned all I know of geography from them. I would carefully follow on the maps in the books journeys through countries as diverse as Tibet and Bermuda, examining myopically photographs which ranged from very fuzzy to very clear. I was always annoyed when there was no map in the book because I did not have an atlas, and poor photography was also a great disappointment. Later, more affluent generations would travel by hitchhiking the routes my fingers traced so longingly on maps.

I pushed my straggling hair back behind my ears and took off my faulty glasses to peer closer at the shelves; sometimes I could see better without the glasses than I could with them.

'Helen Forrester, isn't it?' inquired a voice from behind me.

I turned slowly, surprised that anyone should know me by name.

It was the deaconess from the church, to whom in a rage I had shown our house. It was no wonder that I had not recognised her voice. During our previous encounter, she had said so little while

I had said so much. I blushed at the memory of my unpardonable outburst.

I murmured shyly that I was Helen. She looked very sweet in her coif and frumpy clothes.

'I was about to come to see you,' she announced unexpectedly. Then she glanced round the book-lined room. 'Perhaps we could talk here, though. Let's go over there.' She took my elbow and guided me into a corner of the Fiction section.

'I wanted to ask you, my dear, if you would like a job as a telephonist. A charity I know of needs a girl, and I immediately thought of you, because you have such a pleasant voice.'

I gaped at her, struck dumb by the unexpectedness of the offer. Then I gasped, 'Oh, yes.'

She smiled at me, and continued, 'The salary is not much – about twelve and sixpence a week. Would you like me to arrange an interview for you?'

Twelve shillings and sixpence a week seemed a huge sum to me. All the wonderful things it would buy danced before me, mixed with a terrible apprehension that I would not get the job because I was so dirty and had no clothes except the grubby, ragged collection I was wearing.

The deaconess was talking. 'I thought I would ask you first, before speaking to your mother.'

At the mention of Mother, I remembered the sweetshop episode.

'My parents will never agree to it,' I said hopelessly. 'I have to look after Edward.'

'I've already thought of that,' she responded eagerly. 'Alice Davis lives a few doors away from you. She has an invalid mother who cannot be left alone and she badly needs to earn a few shillings. I am sure she would take care of Edward during the day – and she wouldn't charge much.'

A fairy godmother in a blue coif! A true fairy godmother. A wave of gratitude surged through me, but I did not know how to express it. 'Would she, really – would she do it?' I whispered.

'I'm sure she would, if I ask her.'

I was acquainted with Alice. She belonged to the Salvation Army. I said 'good morning' to her most Sundays, as she strode along the street pushing her mother's wheelchair down to the Citadel. Her mother would be bundled up in rough grey blankets, regardless of whether it was winter or summer; and Alice wore a navy blue uniform, with a matching Victorian bonnet trimmed with a red ribbon proclaiming 'Salvation Army' across the front. Her sturdy legs were clad in sensible black stockings and the shine on her black shoes equalled that on the shoes of our local police constable. Her cheerful face shone like her shoes. Occasionally, the Salvation Army band played at the end of our street, and Alice would rush down to them, clutching her cymbals, ready to join in while they were so close to her home. Alice was rough, but Edward would be safe with her.

Please, Lord, please let it happen, I prayed silently. Aloud, I said, 'Thank you very, very much. I would love the job if you think I can do it.'

She smiled. 'Of course you can do it. Shall I call on Mrs Forrester tonight? You might like to talk to both your father and your mother first.'

'I will,' I said, though I had no real hope. Perhaps, however, with an advocate like this respectable lady, just perhaps, they could be persuaded.

'I'll come this evening, then?'

'Yes, please,' I mumbled.

In a daze, I wheeled Edward home, pushing the pram unseeingly through the usual crowds of black, white and yellow men idling at the corners. Some of them murmured resentfully as the pram brushed carelessly past them.

How on earth was I to approach Mother and Father about this offer? I worried. A chance of freedom at last, a tiny flame of hope in a very bleak world.

The whole routine of the family would have to be altered. Alan and Fiona would have to shoulder some of my work. And Alice would have to be paid. Some clothes would have to be redeemed from the pawnbroker – or obtained from somewhere else. Where would Mother find the money?

At home, I poked up the fire and began to make toast for the children's tea, while I thought once again of running away. Could I live on twelve shillings and sixpence? Boys sometimes ran away to the south, where there was more work than in financially ruined Liverpool. Occasionally, girls did, too. I had, however, read in the newspaper about the flourishing white slave traffic into which girls were sold. I was not clear what happened to white slaves, except that they were kept in bondage and abused by ruthless men until they died. I imagined them being misused like American black slaves, and I had no wish to die a dramatic death like Uncle Tom in *Uncle Tom's Cabin*. I had wept over this tragedy as a small girl and did not wish for a similar fate.

I did some careful arithmetic. A small, unheated housekeeping room could be found for about seven shillings and sixpence a week; food, say, four shillings, firing in winter would take the other shilling, leaving nothing for clothing. I did not consider that I might need tram fares – I had been walking, now, for the past three years all over south Liverpool; make-up was beyond my experience, and pocket money an idle dream, anyway.

The children drifted in for tea and I dealt with their squabbles and their hunger as best I could.

Father and Mother returned from work soon after the children. Inside five minutes, they were quarrelling violently. I cannot remember what triggered the trouble. It did not matter, because the underlying animosity smouldered all the time and needed very little to make it flare up. As usual, they drew each child into the argument in an effort to make them take sides, and this frequently reduced Avril and Brian to hysterics as they agonised between the parents. Fiona and Alan were old enough to retreat to friends' homes if they got desperate enough, but poor Avril, Tony and Brian had no such refuges. Tony usually managed to stay a little calmer, though he was always upset, and Edward just stuck firmly in whichever lap he happened to be cradled when hostilities broke out.

Even when I was very small, I wondered why my parents stayed together. I knew a girl whose mother was divorced, and I quite envied her. But I had been fortunate in having Edith to take care of me and there were the long absences from home when I stayed with Grandma. In their conversations about the people they knew, they taught me that not all families were riven by warfare. Now, as the fight raged over the tea table, I wished passionately I could run to Grandma for help.

Alan had piled into the fight with some furious, rude remark and was sharply slapped by his father. He shot out of the kitchen door into the back yard, raging nearly as incoherently as Father was.

Fiona wept helplessly, her head on the table. Brian and Tony stonily munched their toast, their movements nervous and uncoordinated; they did not answer the passionate appeals of Mother and Father to take their side. Avril stood behind Mother's chair, holding on to it and shaking it, as she shouted hopelessly, 'Stop, everybody. Why can't you stop?'

Neither protagonist would give way.

I was silent with despair. I hardly heard the words hurled around me or addressed to me. What was I going to do when the church lady arrived? Mother seized a cup and saucer from the table and hurled them into a corner. Through her screams of rage, I heard a knock on the front door.

The other children had also heard the sharp rat-tat. When they instinctively turned their heads towards the front of the house, Mother stopped in mid-scream.

'What was that?' asked Father, his lips turned back in a snarl.

'Someone is at the door,' I said, too much in anguish to move.

'Well, get a move on, girl. Answer it. Say we are not at home.'

Reluctantly I obeyed, feet dragging. I shut the living-room door behind me.

As I turned the lock on the front door, I wished, for the first time, that it was only a creditor. The moment I swung back the door, she was in the muddy hall and pulling off her gloves, as the wind gusted behind her.

'It's quite cold this evening,' the deaconess said cheerfully. 'Well, have you asked them, my dear?'

'I haven't had an opportunity yet,' I apologised.

Her smile faded, and she sighed. 'Never mind. I'll ask for you.'

'They said they are not at home tonight.'

From behind the closed door came the sound of renewed strife, though the level seemed more subdued. The interruption had broken the continuity of the argument. The lady laughed and looked at me conspiratorially. The living-room was suddenly quiet. The feminine chuckle must have penetrated to the family.

The deaconess tucked her gloves into her handbag and said briskly, 'I imagine your mother would be at home to me. We know each other well enough to call occasionally without warning, don't we?'

I tried to smile at her as I heard the living-room door open behind me. 'Will you come into the front room?' I asked hastily. 'I'll inquire if they are at home.' These were phrases I had often heard May, our parlourmaid, use, and they came automatically to mind in such a difficult situation.

I opened the door to the front room and ushered the blue-clad lady into it, just as Avril stumped out of the other room, her eyes tearful, her mouth surrounded by black toast crumbs. She marched into the sitting-room after the visitor, and stood staring at her.

I heard the deaconess speaking softly to the frightened little girl, as nervously I announced our visitor to Mother and Father. Both parents were standing motionless, like alerted hares, as they tried to judge who the visitor was.

Mother, her face and neck still red from combat, pushed past me and went into the front room. Father gave a great sigh and flopped into a chair. His hands were trembling as they always did when he was upset.

Fiona had ceased to weep and gazed up at me with great pansy eyes still dewdropped. Brian and Tony asked Father's permission to leave the table.

'Yes,' he said peevishly.

They scrambled down from their chairs and I heard the back door slam, as they went out to play in the last of the evening light.

Father turned back to me. He gestured with his head towards the front room. 'What does she want?' he asked. I think he was always nervous that his wife had done something outrageous which he did not know about.

I knelt down on one knee and began to pick up the bits of cup and saucer that Mother had shattered. Through my draggling hair, I hesitantly answered him.

'She has come about me.'

He sat up straight and looked at me. 'About you? What have you done?'

I stood up and faced him. 'I haven't done anything. She's got a job for me. And she's keen that I should take it.'

'What nonsense!' He sniffed, and then added angrily, 'I wish she would mind her own business.'

'She means well, Daddy.'

'She should hie her back to her nunnery and stay there. She has no right to interfere with my family.' He thumped the arm of his chair. 'She has no right to put ideas into your head.'

I stood irresolutely before him, the broken dishes in my hand. I wanted to put my arms round him and beg him to intercede for me. When I was small and he was not too busy, we had been able to talk to each other. But this ease between us had got lost in the maelstrom of trouble which had engulfed us. So I hesitated, and the opportunity was lost.

'Where is the newspaper?' he demanded irritably.

I put down the broken china and picked up the paper from the floor, where it had been thrown down during the quarrel. He shook out the pages and vanished behind them.

# Chapter eleven

Washing greasy dishes in cold water without soap is not easy. The grease impregnates the hands and forms an oily ring round the basin. I had two saucepans left over from lunchtime to wash, and their exteriors were covered with soot from the fire. To save the gas, I had put the pans on the living-room fire to finish the cooking of the children's midday dinner. Now the soot floated revoltingly amid the grease. I did not dare to put a kettle of water on the fire as I was afraid of irritating Father further by pushing past him. I let the water from the single cold water tap cascade into our tin wash basin to sweep out some of the soot, and stood gazing at the backs of my hands in the light of the candle I had just lit.

My hands were small and well formed. The skin was ingrained with dirt and round the quicks the nails were almost black. The nail tips were long and uneven and filled with grime. Sometimes I tried to clean my nails with a sliver of wood, but without plenty of soap it was a hopeless task. I remembered the scathing remark of the sweetshop lady, and, with a stomach clenched with apprehension, I realised that to make myself thoroughly clean and neat for work would be very difficult.

In a painfully sweet voice, Mother suddenly called me from the front room, and I was jolted back from depressing contemplation to frightening reality.

I wiped my hands on the family's solitary towel which hung on a hook on the back door. The towel was nearly black from use by nine people and it invariably stank. I added a streak of soot to it.

Father had joined Mother and the deaconess, Miss Ferguson, in the front room, and was perched uncomfortably on the edge of one of the easy chairs. I could feel the blood draining from my face; and, as I gave Miss Ferguson a nervous smile, I wanted to faint.

'Miss Ferguson insists on hearing from you personally that you do not want to go to work,' announced Mother frigidly, and Miss Ferguson shifted uncomfortably around in her chair. 'I understand she spoke to you in the library this afternoon.'

'Yes, she did,' I whispered, in answer to the second statement.

Miss Ferguson took a large breath, as if the effort to speak was going to be too much for her. Then she turned her worried-looking face towards me, and said very carefully, 'I have been trying to persuade Mr and Mrs Forrester that it would be greatly to your advantage if you could go to work and be trained for some worthy occupation, and that it would be possible for them to spare you from the house to do this. I tentatively made an appointment for you for tomorrow afternoon at three o'clock.'

Father made a wry face, and I had the feeling he wished he was a hundred miles away.

Mother interjected, 'Helen will not be keeping the appointment, I am sure.'

Undeterred, Miss Ferguson pressed on. 'I have assured your mother that you will be working with nice women, all from good families, and I am sure you will be well trained.' She turned to Father and said very earnestly, 'She would be quite safe there,' as if any other place of work was probably a cesspool of immorality.

Father was embarrassed. 'I don't doubt it,' he muttered, and looked across at Mother.

I looked down at my hands resting on the back of the easy chair, and burst into tears. It was easy to see that my parents were boiling with suppressed anger at the intrepid little deaconess's foray into our affairs. They would raise hell when she was gone. I put my head down on my hands and cried until the tears ran through the fingers on to the shiny green leatherette of the chair.

Avril, who had been sitting on a matching pouf, sucking her thumb and watching the proceedings very quietly, suddenly started to cry as well, and was immediately whisked into the hall and the door shut on her. I could hear her wailing in the dark.

'Don't cry, Helen,' said Father ineffectually.

Mother turned to Miss Ferguson, as she shut the door after Avril.

'Helen is obviously very upset, Miss Ferguson. Perhaps we should discuss the matter with her and let you know in a day or two what has been decided.'

I was not just upset; I was nearly out of my mind with despair. But the tears came with such tremendous force that I could do nothing to stop Miss Ferguson being quickly, though politely, eased out of the house.

When I heard the latch on the front door click shut, I flung myself wildly on to the settee and continued to sob. What was the use of a day or two, when the appointment was for tomorrow?

It was fortunate that Father and Mother had already exhausted themselves with one quarrel that evening, and Mother, therefore, contented herself with ordering me to control myself, while Father asked how they could talk to me when I was making such a racket.

I made a violent effort, sat up and dried my face with the backs of my hands.

Mother looked so terribly exhausted, when finally I lifted my eyes to look at her, that I felt an overwhelming guilt and said, 'I'm sorry, I really am.'

Mother had been dreadfully ill just before we arrived in Liverpool. She had had no real care since then, so that she was soon drained of strength. I truly did not want to add to her hardships; yet I could not bear my present miseries much longer.

'Have you been talking to Miss Ferguson or to the Fathers at the church, behind our backs, Helen?' asked Mother. There was an implied threat in the question. Family affairs, we had been taught from infancy, were not discussed with servants or outsiders. Childish revelations, whenever discovered, had been dealt with by a sharp spanking or, sometimes, caning.

I was too upset to care or remember about Miss Ferguson's tour of our house, so I said indignantly that I had not. I took off my glasses and wiped them down the front of my gym slip, while I tried to think how my going to work could be managed.

'You know, Daddy,' I said, approaching the weaker partner, 'the salary offered is quite good. It would mean three salaries coming into the house.'

'Alice Davis wants ten shillings a week to look after Edward,' interrupted Mother. 'And there are still the other children's needs.'

'Surely if everybody helped, we could manage between us. It wouldn't hurt Fiona and Alan to help – they are quite big now.'

Mother dismissed Fiona and Alan with a gesture.

'On Sundays I could clean the house, and, if Fiona and Alan could make the tea, I could put Edward and Avril to bed when I came in.'

'It is not very practical,' Father said. 'Someone has to be at home to make the children's lunch.'

My temper was rising, that incorrigible devil which dwelt within me. I fought it by praying each night that I would manage to keep calm until prayers the following night, and so often I failed. I made tremendous efforts to control it, not realising that insufferable people and unbearable circumstances could make a saint angry.

I stood up and flounced towards the door.

'I am going for the interview, whether you like it or not. I may never get such a chance again. I must take it.'

'Helen, you forget yourself,' exploded Father.

'Oh, no, I do not. For once, I am remembering myself.'

'Helen!'

Mother's voice came in behind him. There was more than a little malice in her tone, as she said, 'You have no suitable clothing, anyway.'

'I'll borrow some,' I replied recklessly.

'Helen! That would not do at all.' Father sounded genuinely shocked.

'It's no worse than borrowing money,' I retorted, and his face whitened. I had hit home most cruelly. Savagely satisfied, I fled from the room and back to the sooty saucepans.

# Chapter twelve

I peeped over the railings surrounding the area. The curtains had not yet been drawn over the barred windows of my dear Spanish lady's basement living-room. In the soft light of her oil lamp, I could see her sitting in an easy chair on one side of the fireplace, with a pile of crochet work on her lap. Her handsome, black-eyed husband, Alonzo Gomez, sat opposite her on another easy chair. He was reading the newspaper, while a large black cat crouched on his shoulder, its lemon-shaped eyes glowing in the light. The remains of their evening meal still lay on a nearby table.

I opened the iron gate and ran down the winding iron steps of the area, knocked at the plank door under the main entrance steps of the house and, after waiting a moment, walked in.

I was engulfed by skinny brown arms and a flood of mixed Spanish and English words of welcome. Alonzo put down his paper as I entered their living-room.

'Come, come,' he said, gesturing towards the blazing fire with one hand, while he smoothed his handlebar moustache with the other. He got up and bowed me to his chair.

Suddenly, I was in a different world.

Despite the general squalor, there were many people like Cristina Gomez who created real homes out of attic crannies or damp basements in once fashionable houses. There was never much money, though Alonzo Gomez worked as a carter for a fruit merchant in the city and the couple's children were now grown up and had moved away; and yet the old kitchen had an air of cosiness, as if affection exuded from the walls with the damp. The few pieces of well-worn furniture, the primitive cooking utensils hanging by the fireplace, the stone floor covered in the centre by a piece of coconut matting, all were clean and well cared for. Alonzo was known to have an explosive temper, but the explosions seemed to be rare, and at other times there was a lot of good-natured banter and teasing, when they laughed like children.

Cristina Gomez had a good collection of clothing. She had once told me that whenever her husband earned overtime money or won on the horses, he would spend the money on clothes for one or the other of them. And now I needed to borrow a whole outfit.

All Cristina's clothes were black, even her petticoats, but that would not matter. Black was the uniform of work. It was usually worn by shop assistants and by many office workers.

After I had been cuddled and installed in Alonzo's chair, while he sat on a straight-backed one, an orange was sliced and put on a saucer and a cup of strong black coffee set before me on a brown-painted orange box. The health of all the family was inquired after by Cristina, and Mother's poor health sighed over with much rolling of eyes and shrugging of shoulders.

At the mention of Mother's health, my determination faltered. If I went to work, her load would inevitably be increased. Then, as Alonzo told a funny story about a cart horse which loved to steal apples from displays outside the Fruit Exchange, I realised that, on average, Mother did not earn much more than I would get, that if she stayed at home to look after the family, we would be very little poorer. And my resolve hardened.

Cristina asked me how I was faring at night school, and this gave me a chance to talk about my own troubles and the reason for my visit, to borrow a dress, shoes and stockings, if she would be kind enough to lend them to me.

'Certain, certain, you can have anything.' She paused and looked uneasily at her husband. 'I would not wish to anger your good mother, though.'

'She need never know where I got the clothes from,' I assured her. 'I only need them for one afternoon. I'll think of another way of getting clothes for the job itself.' I had already thought of a possible source from which to obtain at least a dress, but not quickly enough for the interview.

Though Cristina might have qualms about offending my parents, her swaggering gallant of a husband had none. I think he had always resented my parents' supercilious attitude towards their neighbours and his pride had been hurt.

'Give them to her,' he ordered his wife, with such a lordly gesture that the cat was disturbed from his shoulder and did a quick leap to the floor.

Cristina's eyebrows went up expressively and she shrugged. She got up from her chair, flicked her black shawl up round her shoulders, and said kindly to me, 'All right, my little one. Let us see what we can find.'

I bounced out of my chair, suddenly gay, and followed her. She had lent me old shoes on one or two earlier occasions, when she had observed that my running shoes were soaking wet; and long ago her gift of the Chariot had saved me the heavy task of carrying Edward everywhere when he was too young to walk.

Half an hour later, I glided through our back door, through the deserted kitchen and down the steps to the coal cellar, where I stowed away a brown paper bag containing shoes and stockings. On the inside of the cellar door, I hung a coat hanger which held a black dress with matching jacket shrouded in a piece of discarded curtaining.

'Who is there?' Father's voice came sharply from the living-room.

'It's only me, Daddy.'

I opened the door and went in. The gaslight had been lit. The mantle was broken and the flame hissed and flickered over the comfortless room. The fire was out. Upstairs, I could hear the boys fighting in their bedroom. Presumably, Fiona, Avril and little Edward were asleep, since there seemed no sound from them.

'Where have you been?' Father's voice was freezing.

'To see Mrs Gomez. Where's Mummy?'

'She has gone down to Granby Street to buy a pair of stockings.' He flicked over a page of his book impatiently. 'You know I don't like you mixing with local people.'

I hung my head, but did not reply.

'If you have no homework to do, you had better go to bed.'

'Yes, Daddy.' I wondered if I should give him his usual good-night kiss, but he did not look up from his book, so I crept by him and went forlornly up to bed. I knew I had hurt him beyond forgiveness, and perhaps he really did not know how to cope with me.

# Chapter thirteen

In the usual rush to get everybody off to school and themselves off to work, my parents had no time to discuss Miss Ferguson's visit with me. Mother gave me a shilling, as usual, to buy food, and two extra pennies to put in the gas meter. Father asked me to wash his second shirt ready for the next day, and suddenly Edward and I had the house to ourselves.

Greatly daring, I borrowed a large pair of scissors from a crippled Jewish lady who lived across the road. I was acquainted with her, because on cold winter Saturdays, Brian lit her fire for her and went over occasionally to make it up, since her religion demanded that she do no work on that day.

I stood in front of our piece of mirror in the kitchen window and hacked off the greasy rat's tails of hair until I was left with a short bob. I wished I had the family comb, but Mother had taken it to work with her. Then I attacked my nails, which were not very easy to cut with such big scissors, but finally they were snipped down to the flesh and that got rid of much of the dirt under them as well. Hair and body were then washed with a kettle of boiling water and a rag. I combed my hair with my fingers and smoothed it with the dirty towel.

My hands still looked awful. Then I remembered an old beauty trick of Grandma's. Feeling as if I was robbing Edward of a breakfast, I took a small pinch of oatmeal, damped the hands again and rubbed the oatmeal in hard. The hands emerged looking clean and much whiter than usual.

I put on the new pair of black woollen stockings which Cristina had lent me and found they would stay up fairly well if I twisted a piece of coal very tightly into the top of each.

How did one behave at an interview? I worried. What did one say? During the past three and a half years I had been practically cut off from all social contact. At an age when most middle-class girls would be being taught social graces by their school mistresses and their mothers, I had been walking the streets of Liverpool in rags, pushing a baby in a pram. Sometimes I was afraid I would forget how to speak properly. Only at night school did I ever get a chance to express myself. The lack of mental stimulation, the ever-present lack of food, and the lack of fun and young friends had played havoc with an already shy personality – and I knew it.

As I scuttled round the shops in Granby Street with Edward in tow, and bought bread and potatoes and margarine, I silently said the General Confession and then the Lord's Prayer, turning towards the only help I knew. God received a rather wild collection of prayers that morning.

This mental exercise reminded me of Father's question as to whether I had approached the Anglican Fathers at the church about a job. The pressure Miss Ferguson had put on my parents *was* more than might normally have been expected. Perhaps Miss Ferguson had, after her tour of our house, consulted the priests. None of them had come to see us; but they had hooked Brian and Tony into the choir, so they knew we were High Anglicans. The idea that they might be trying to help me filled my romantic teenage heart with a kind of joy and lifted me for a while out of my wretchedness.

I fed the children when they came in for dinner and then dragged Fiona into the kitchen and confided to her the story of the job. Would she look after Edward for me, while I went for the interview?

'What if Mummy finds out?' she quavered, her eyes wide with misgiving.

'Oh, Fi, just take Avril to school and then slip back here. I'll be back ages before the boys or Mummy and Daddy come. They'll never know.'

'I'm scared, Helen. Teacher may be cross, too.'

'Look, I'll take all the blame. You can say I bullied you into it. They'll believe that. They'll blame me anyway.'

'Helen!'

She was very frightened and yet I had to have a baby-sitter for a couple of hours.

'Please, Fi, darling. Please.'

She shifted around unhappily and finally agreed.

While she took Avril to school, I put on the dress and the little jacket and then, as I squeezed a large acne spot on my chin and anxiously examined two more at the side of my nose, I agonised that she might not return. I peered anxiously at myself in the broken mirror. Behind the outgrown glasses my eyes were red with strain or pink eye. A further black rim round them from lack of food and rest did not add to my looks. I sighed, and ran to the window of the sitting-room to see if Fiona was coming.

I had nearly given up hope when she suddenly rounded the corner and dawdled down the street towards our house.

The walk down the hill to town was more painful than I had expected. The borrowed shoes pressed on the ragingly painful chilblains on my heels and toes. The wind blew the carefully arranged hair all over the place, and emphasised the need of a hat and a comb. Some of the euphoria which had sustained me evaporated, and was replaced by plain fear of the unknown.

To add to that, I had defied Father and Mother and I feared that I might be punished by God for it. He had said, Honour thy Father and thy Mother, and I presumed He meant what He said.

The closer I got to the city centre the more I quailed. And yet some stubborn instinct kept me going.

Without a watch, I did not know whether I was late or early and I hurried into the office building, which I had passed many times with Edward in the pram. It was a tall, Victorian structure with high, narrow windows looking out on a very busy side street.

The main floor was occupied by a tea-blending firm, and this confused me for a moment. A jolly little woman with a steaming bowl of tea in her hand came to my rescue and directed me up the stone stairs.

I climbed and climbed. Halfway up I had to stop. Though I walked a lot in the fresh air, I was wasted from lack of food. A middle-aged lady in a green overall ran past me down the stairs without so much as a glance. A fat Irish woman in a black shawl and skirt panted her way upwards, muttering to herself. She gave me a sly grin as she passed.

Up I went again, and finally found the door mentioned by the lady with the tea bowl. I knocked and cautiously entered.

It was a big, ill-lit room with dusty yellow walls. There were several large tables, piled with files and papers, at which people sat engrossed in their work. In one corner stood a small table with a telephone on it. Behind the telephone stood a large wooden box with rows of knobs along its front. For a second, I imagined myself seated before the telephone transacting all kinds of important business.

At the back of the room stood rows of deep bookcases filled with files, and several girls in blue overalls were running about with stacks of brown folders in their arms. The only man in the room was a dark, saturnine person in a formal business suit, who sat at a large table writing in a big book. Two well-coiffured, smartly dressed ladies sat at the same table writing busily.

The gentleman looked up at my entrance.

'Yes?' he snapped.

Quivering with fright, I explained humbly over the bent heads of his lady helpers that I had come for an interview with the Secretary.

He sniffed, and gestured towards a young lady sitting before a typewriter. She smiled at me, took my name and made me sit down on a wooden chair with my back to the room.

While the typist knocked and went into an inner room, I thankfully regained my breath and tried surreptitiously to ease the agony of my feet inside the borrowed shoes.

When the typist returned to usher me into the inner room, I was sure I would faint with fright. However, she smiled very kindly at me, so I shuffled unhappily into the furnace.

At first I could not see anybody in the big, gloomy room. Then I realised that a woman, a tiny person, was seated at the desk by the window. I stood quaking just inside the door, after closing it silently behind me, until she looked up and took notice of me. She was plain to the point of ugliness, with greying hair combed neatly to her head. She had, however, a tremendous aura of authority, like all the ferocious headmistresses who had had me in their care rolled up into one powerful, scarifying personality.

While she examined me in the poor light from the overcast day, I stood with hands clenched together in front of me, awaiting the verdict.

Her voice when she spoke was cool and sibilant.

'You may sit down.'

Too scared to look at her again, I sat down on the edge of the chair by her desk. In answer to her questions, I said, 'Yes, madam,' or 'No, madam,' exactly as servants had done when addressed by Mother. I volunteered no information for which she did not explicitly ask. She had a file in front of her and occasionally she would flick over the papers in it with a long thin finger, It was apparent that she knew something of our family, and I presumed that Miss Ferguson had told her about us.

Finally, she said, without looking up, 'You may commence work next Monday. The hours are from nine to five thirty on week days and nine until twelve thirty on Saturdays. Two overalls will be provided for you to wear in the office and you will be expected to keep them clean. The salary is twelve shillings and sixpence a week.' She paused, and then said, after some consideration, 'The salary is payable monthly. However, in view of your family's circumstances I will arrange for you to be paid weekly.'

'Thank you, madam,' I said weakly. I'd got it! A real job!

'Report to Mr Ellis on Monday – in the outer office.'

'Yes, madam.'

I hesitated, uncertain whether I was dismissed or not. Part of me was mentally singing a Te Deum, part of me was so scared that for a moment or two I could not have moved.

'You may go now.' The voice was cold and disinterested, as if the mind behind it was already giving attention to other matters.

'Thank you very much, madam,' I said to a head already turned away from me.

But she had opened a Minute Book and was immersed in reading it, so I crept shakily to the door and went quietly out into the hustle of the general office.

I said, 'Thank you,' to the pretty typist, as I passed her and she nodded back cheerfully, her fingers keeping up a constant tattoo on the typewriter before her.

Nobody else took any notice of me, so I slipped away, down the long staircases, like a warehouse cat. For a moment I shivered in the great pseudo-Gothic doorway, and then plunged into the crowd which thronged the pavement.

A blister had formed on top of a chilblain on my heel and it hurt sharply as I climbed the long hill towards home. The wind was so strong that it pushed and tousled me as if it had human hands. Fear of what lay ahead at home stole through me and sapped the strength from me; fear also that I would not be able to please my new employer. She had such a fearsome presence that I quailed at the memory of her.

She had asked me a number of questions, but she had not asked me the most important one. Had I any experience of using a telephone?

I had never spoken on a telephone, never even held a receiver in my hand. What it sounded like, how it worked, were both mysteries to me. The closest I had ever been to a phone was when I had occasionally stepped into a public phone box to press the 'B' button, to see if I could retrieve twopence forgotten by a caller who had failed to get his connection.

# Chapter fourteen

It was nearly half past four when I hurried silently through the back door, slipping Cristina's jacket off as I ran.

The living-room door was slightly ajar, and I could hear the hurly-burly of the children at tea. Bless Fiona for making the tea!

In the cellar's cold blackness, smelling of coal and long-departed cats, I carefully removed the borrowed dress, shoes and stockings, and pushed the latter back into the brown paper bag I had left down there. Naked, except for a torn pair of knickers, I ran up the stone steps and hung the precious dress and jacket on the inside of the cellar door. I hoped frantically that there was no coal dust on them.

Standing on the top step I slipped on my hopelessly short gym slip and a grey cardigan long since abandoned by Mother. Back in the kitchen, I stuffed my tortured feet into battered gym shoes; and I was back in character.

In the living-room, Brian, Tony and Avril had left the table, and Brian was laying down the rules of a new game he had invented. The stairs would be a train, he would be the driver and the others the passengers. Without even looking at me, they ran into the hall, and I could hear them squabbling on the stairs about the details of the game and who would fall out first.

Edward was chewing a crust at the table, and I ruffled his hair playfully as I walked round him and sat down at the table opposite Fiona and Alan.

'How did you get on?' asked Alan. He nodded his blond head towards Fiona, and added, 'Fi told me.'

I told them of my success and they were jubilant. In spite of the family row the previous night Alan said he thought Mother and Father would relent. 'You've got to start some time,' he said firmly. 'It's only fair.'

It sounded as if he had given the matter some thought, and Fiona was equally enthusiastic, though it is doubtful if the poor, suppressed child ever really thought deeply about anything, other than what was happening to her at any given moment. Only when she unexpectedly burst into floods of tears did one know that deep inside the beautiful, doll-like creature was a human being who suffered dreadfully.

I had a misbegotten hope that my parents would be too tired to wage another battle. It was my mistake; they were never too tired to fight each other or lash out at me.

After they had eaten the scanty meal I had kept for them from the midday meal served to the children, and Mother was about to go upstairs to take off her work dress, I said in a carefully controlled voice that I would like to speak to them about Miss Ferguson's offer of a job.

They both looked at me with cold suspicion.

When I told them about the interview, they were outraged. I was standing quite close to Father and he was so furious that he jumped up and struck me across the head. This stalled the hysterics I could feel rising inside me. They seemed more incensed about my disobedience than by the actual interview, and they took turns ranting about my general insubordination and lack of respect for their wishes.

I was myself very fatigued and was therefore quieter than usual, so that, unfuelled, their fury began to trail off. Summoning up as much courage as I could muster, I announced that either I should be allowed to go to work or I would run away.

'What nonsense!' shouted Father. 'The police would bring you back, my girl. You are not even fifteen yet.'

I was frightened by his mention of the police, but I answered steadily, 'Not if I went to Grandma. If she lets my cousin work, she would let me go, too.'

Fortunately, they did not remember that I had no money for the ferry I would have to take to get to Grandma, and my threat sobered them.

Father laughed, and then said in a sad, dead voice, 'You would certainly not be welcome.'

Mother said savagely, 'The whole idea is absurd. You are needed at home.' She began to move towards the hall. 'Besides I could not possibly find the clothes for you. It's hard enough to keep myself dressed suitably.'

'I know, Mummy,' I replied quietly. 'And I've never ever asked you for clothes.' Then I added eagerly, 'But I have thought how I could get something to wear. If you would write to Mrs Fox, my friend Joan's mother, I think she would send me some. Joan and I were always much the same size – and she has wardrobes full of clothes.'

Mother tossed her head. 'I seem to remember your meeting Mrs Fox and her precious daughter in the town some time back, and that you told me they cut you dead.'

'They did, Mummy,' I agreed miserably. 'But when I thought about it some more, I think I understood how they felt. If they had stopped in Bold Street to speak to a ragamuffin like me, a crowd would have gathered. People would have thought I had stolen something off them or was begging.' I gave a shivery sigh. 'They did the right thing.'

'Humph,' said Mother, her hand on the knob of the hall door.

'I don't think you have ever written to Mrs Fox,' I went on persuasively. 'She's really very kind and generous.'

Father was looking me up and down, as if he had never seen my clothing before. He said suddenly, 'Helen needs clothes very badly by the look of her. That gym slip is hardly decent. It doesn't cover her properly.' He turned to Mother. 'Try to wheedle some clothes for her out of that Fox woman. She has more money than sense. It wouldn't hurt her to help her daughter's friend. I am sure Helen would feel much better if she had some decent garments.'

Perhaps he thought that, placated by some new clothes, I would be more amenable to being the family drudge.

'She might send some money, too,' I suggested.

Mother looked again at Father. He gave her the smallest affirmative nod.

'Very well,' said Mother coldly. 'I will write. We both need clothes.' Then in another burst of sudden anger, she turned to me. 'This doesn't mean that I have agreed to your going to work. I will not hear of it. You can't be spared.'

I ground my teeth, as I swallowed the angry retort I longed to make. Seething inwardly, I replied, 'Yes, Mother.'

The letter was written there and then, while Father watched; and the next few days were filled with anxiety. Creditors were visibly astonished when the front door was whipped open at their first knock, as I joyfully anticipated the coming of the postman. I listened sullenly to their upbraidings and then promised to tell Father all they threatened.

On the fourth day, the postal van arrived with two very large parcels. They were addressed to me, not to Mother.

I tore them open and went through the contents with wonderment. The dear woman had thought of everything: underwear, skirt, two blouses, shoes, gloves, overcoat, even a small, rather tired-looking handbag and a plain tam o'shanter for my head. There was a short letter wishing me well and mentioning that Joan was at a finishing school in Switzerland.

For a few moments, I touched and fondled the garments as if they were specially beloved possessions. I tried on the crumpled coat, a blouse and the skirt. They fitted reasonably well, though they were a little loose. I took them off reluctantly and folded everything into a pile. All the garments were so clean and sweet-smelling, a gift from a world of bathrooms with soap and hot water, efficient laundries, and houses kept sparkling clean by maids armed with the newly fashionable vacuum cleaner, tins of polish and bottles of disinfectant and liquid soap. As I stroked the little fur collar on the coat, I felt an overwhelming sadness, the sadness of someone bereaved who has come to terms with that bereavement but still at times mourns the loss.

I pulled myself together and picked up the string. Untangled, it would be strong enough to make a clothes-line across the kitchen on which to dry the children's clothes on wet days.

Gathering up the heap of clothes with the brown paper underneath them, I took them upstairs and laid them on Edward's and my bed. I hoped that the cleanliness of the clothing would deter the bugs from crawling on to them. When, later on, the fire would be lit for the children's homecoming I would heat our single flat iron and press the garments ready for Monday.

I dreaded the fighting yet before me; and I knew, from experience, that unless I was particularly adamant the parcel's contents would end up at the pawnbroker's.

# Chapter fifteen

Edward and I went for our afternoon walk. It was raining slightly, so he rode in the Chariot and I put the ancient pram's hood up to protect him from the wet. Though the frame protruded through the rents in the cover, it still sheltered him fairly well. The rain slowly soaked my cardigan. I was used to it and did not care.

Our street was a straight line of terrace houses, once respectable working-class homes. Now the inhabitants were very mixed; and my father and a fireman who lived further down the street were the only two men in regular employment. Many of the homes had more than one family in them and were dirty and neglected. A few were very well kept; mended curtains arranged neatly on either side of the front window, with an aspidistra in a pottery bowl filling up the middle space, the windowsill highly polished and the front step whitened.

Our beige curtains, as yet unpaid for, looked tidy behind windowpanes which I had washed with hot water and newspaper pads. Our front step, however, was littered with dried orange peel and cigarette ends flung there by our next-door neighbours, whose front door abutted ours. They also spat on our step, as they sat on their own doorstep and smoked and read comic books. We never spoke to the man and wife and toddler who lived there. They would stare at us when we passed them, as if we were beings from another planet, and I suspect that they made ribald jokes at our stuffiness.

We walked the length of the long street, crossed Kingsley Road, which still had some shabby gentility about it, and continued on to Lodge Lane, where we spent a little while shop-gazing, and I taught Edward the names of some of the household utensils exhibited in a chandlery shop.

The April clouds rolled away and the sun came out to make the rain-washed streets glitter with sudden cleanliness. When we neared home again, Edward said he wanted to walk. The pavement was no longer very wet, so I set him down on it and he ran ahead of me. I had made him a pair of bootees out of an old felt hat. They were stitched with wool from an unravelled sweater, and between two felt soles I had put a double layer of cardboard. I hoped the damp would not penetrate to his tiny feet.

Alice Davis was leaning against the door jamb of her home as we came near, and she called to the small boy. He stopped and gave her one of his winning smiles. She stepped into the street and squatted down in front of him to talk baby talk to him. Then she ran back into the house and returned with a plain biscuit for him, which he snatched gladly out of her hand.

Though Alice was only about twenty-five years old, her face was lined and her smile practically toothless. She wore her black hair screwed into an unbecoming bun at the back of her head. Her blue-grey eyes were merry as she gently teased Edward.

I stopped to thank her for the biscuit and made Edward say, 'Thank you.'

'That's nothing,' she replied. Then she went on, 'That Miss Ferguson come to see me about Edward. I said I'd take him. Did you get the job?' Her voice had the thick nasal accent of the born Liverpudlian.

'Yes,' I responded dully. 'I'm supposed to start on Monday.'

'Well, aren't you?' She looked me over disparagingly, and burst out, 'You're lucky, you are, to get a job.'

I nodded agreement. 'I know I am.' Then I thought suddenly that there is nothing like a *fait accompli*, so I said boldly, 'If you will look after Edward, I can start.'

'Oh, aye. I said I would. He's a little dear, he is.'

'I could pay you the ten shillings every Saturday afternoon when I come home from work. I think I would be paid on Fridays, but I am not certain. So I'll promise to bring it every Saturday.'

'Isn't that your mam's business?'

I hesitated. I could not say that I doubted if Mother would pay regularly, so I said, 'We'll settle it between us. I'll bring Edward down every morning before I go to work, and Fiona can collect him when she gets back from school.'

Alice threw back her head and laughed. 'First few days you could bring him. After that he'll run up and down by himself, won't you, luv?' She bent down and chucked Edward under the chin. He swallowed the last of the biscuit and giggled and twisted away from her. ''Tis only a few doors away,' she added.

'If you think he'll be all right,' I said anxiously.

'Sure, he will. I'll see our door is open for him. And he can have a bit to eat with us at dinner time.'

'Thank you, Alice. I'm very grateful to you. See you on Monday morning – about eight o'clock.'

Alice bent down again and picked up Edward and nuzzled her face into his, laughing all the time. 'Yes. We'll have a proper nice time together.'

And with great relief I felt that she was right.

*

Clean out the grate, make the fire, lay clean newspaper on the table, cut the bread, make the tea, all with a stomach tight with apprehension. Would I ever know what it was like not to be frightened?

It was worse than I had expected.

Firstly, I had opened the parcel. Did I not realise that letters and parcels were opened by parents, regardless of how they were addressed? Furthermore, I had ironed the garments, thus accepting them without parental permission.

I had no right to speak to Alice. I had no right to say that I would begin work on Monday. Parents decided such a thing and they had decided that I should stay at home. It seemed to me that I had no rights at all, only a formidable list of obligations.

Cornered, terrified rats turn and attack. Some human beings, however, have less courage, and I was ready to give in, when help came suddenly from an unexpected quarter.

Fiona said in a quivering voice, 'I can make the tea and take care of Edward and Avril till you come home, Mummy. And I can help to put them to bed. I could even do the shopping if you gave me a list.'

It must have cost her dearly to speak up on my behalf. It came as a surprise to me that she should love me enough to do so. I gave love but I did not expect anything in return. I had always protected her as much as I could from hunger and cold and jeering local boys and girls, helped her with her homework because she had great difficulty in learning, and frankly admired her because she had such a sweet temperament. And now, on my behalf, the gentle creature was laying herself open to our parents' bitter censure. I was moved beyond words and was still gaping at her when Alan put down his toast and said, 'I don't mind giving a hand as well.'

Alan and I had always got along very well, once I had recovered from the infant jealousy which his birth had engendered; and I was grateful for his intercession. Mother loved her sons and would listen to him.

Alan was saying stoutly that all girls went to work now. A lady from the Employment Exchange had come to the school to counsel them about work, and she had interviewed the girls as well as the boys. So it must be so.

Though Father was still trembling with rage, I could see he was listening to Alan's remarks. Mother started to cry and say that she could not manage, and I felt dreadful, because the ultimate responsibility for all of us rested on her shoulders. She was not idle after returning from work; she would rest for a little while and then spend some time with Edward and Avril. While I was at night school, she would check the children's clothes after they had gone to bed and sometimes did part of the washing and ironing. She was not in the best of health, and her tears racked me.

Fiona and Alan were, however, arguing in a soothing way that the family was big enough and each of them old enough to make it possible for me to be spared.

Father got up suddenly and swung out of the room. I saw him take his trilby hat off the hall peg and clap it down on his head. Without a word, he lifted the latch of the front door and went out into the ill-lit street. I knew from experience that when he came back he would smell of beer and would be amiably jocular with all of us.

As he went, Mother blew her nose quickly, and then shouted after him, 'You can't face anything, can you? Must you always waste money on drink?'

He did not reply. Shell-shocked, war-weary, he had been ill enough himself to draw a full army pension for several years after serving in Russia. Probably his nerves screamed for sedation, and his comfortless home and unruly family made the pain unbearable.

Fiona got up and put her arms round Mother's neck. 'Don't cry, Mummy. If Helen goes to work, she's so clever she'll soon earn lots and lots. And then you will be able to stay at home and not have to work any more.'

Fiona's and Alan's advocacy gave me a little courage again. I was so terribly unhappy myself that I felt I could not go on as I had been doing; something had to give. Unlike Fiona, I was quite sure that the last thing Mother wanted was to be at home with her family all day; yet my needs deserved consideration, too.

'Let us try, Mummy,' I begged. 'I should get more money after a little while and it would help.'

But Mother was still flaming with wrath. She pushed Fiona away, bounced out of her chair and shook her finger at me. 'You are talking rubbish. You are disobedient and ungrateful. You haven't even matriculated. You are unskilled in anything.'

I fired up immediately, 'And whose fault is that?'

Mother nearly choked. She slapped me across the face. 'I never heard such impudence,' she screamed.

I backed away from her, snatched up my night school books from the mantelpiece, and tried not to scream back, as I said, 'I don't care. I'm going to work on Monday. Otherwise, I am going to Granny's – so you won't have my help anyway.'

Mother had been a very beautiful woman. Convulsed with rage, she looked like an infuriated witch, and I was terrified.

'Go!' she yelled at me. 'All right. Go to work! You will soon discover that the world is a very cruel place and you will long to be at home again. Get out of my sight.'

By this time all the children were bellowing like frightened cows. Fiona and Avril clung to Mother, crying, 'Don't, Mummy, don't.' Brian, Tony and Edward were all in noisy tears. Only Alan sat tearless; he yelled, 'I don't know why everybody has to make such a row!'

I backed through the door. Then turned and followed Father into the night.

Mother did not need to tell me that the world outside was a cruel place. I knew that already. But faintly, faintly on the horizon it had its rays of hope.

# Chapter sixteen

'Mr Ellis,' I whispered shyly, 'I am the new telephone girl.'

Four other girls in the room paused in their work to stare at me, while Mr Ellis put down his pen carefully on his desk and looked up at me. He frowned at what he saw.

'Humph. You are?' He took out his handkerchief and held it to his nose. I heard a girl giggle.

I lowered my eyes. I knew I looked awful. Joan's skirt and blouse hung on me. My rough-cut hair could have served as a mop. Both feet throbbed with the pain of blisters rubbed on tender chilblains, and I was biting my lips as I endured the misery of it. Over me lay the smell of poverty, of a body poorly washed, clothes unaired, foul breath and fatigue.

The man before me was thin and dark-visaged, with the same air of nervous tension as Father had. He called to a girl sitting in front of the telephone switchboard.

'Miss Finch, show t' girl what to do.'

He gestured towards the switchboard with his pen, as he picked it up, so I silently went over to Miss Finch. While I stood awkwardly beside her, I could see out of the corner of my eye two other girls sniggering behind their hands as they watched.

Miss Finch answered the telephone in a thick Liverpool accent. In between calls, without preamble, she explained to me that people wishing to apply to the charity for help entered through the basement, where there was a waiting-room. A girl took their names and telephoned them up to the room we were in. The switchboard operator wrote them down and handed the slips of paper to the filing clerks. The applicant's file, if any, was then sent down to the Interviewing Floor directly below us, where there was another waiting-room.

The applicant was then sent upstairs, past the tea-blending company on the main floor, to be united with his file. At this point, a senior staff member inquired what he had come about, and he was then seated in the second waiting-room. He was finally interviewed in a side room. It was a long, slow process for the applicants.

Miss Finch was a black-haired, rosy-cheeked girl, who seemed to resent me very much. She told me she was the office girl and was filling in on the switchboard until I could take over. I presumed that she had not won promotion to the job of telephonist because of her bad accent.

'Names beginning A to J go to Dorothy Evans; K to Z to Phyllis over there.' She got up and handed me the phone. 'You take the next call from the basement.'

Gingerly, I lifted the receiver to my ear, while Miss Finch moved the appropriate switches. A garbled rattle came through the receiver. I could not interpret it. In a panic, I handed the instrument back to Miss Finch, who hastily jotted down a name on her pad.

'What's the matter?' she asked impatiently, as she handed me the slip. 'Give this to Phyllis Barker.' When I hesitated uncertainly, she hissed, 'Over there. Be quick.'

Phyllis snatched the slip out of my hand, quickly jumped up and vanished down her aisle of files. Her high-heeled patent-leather shoes flashed, as she moved.

'How do you answer the phone and deliver the names to the filing clerks at the same time?' I whispered to Miss Finch.

Miss Finch made a wry face. 'You run,' she whispered back. 'Everybody runs.'

She was right. The filing clerks, the telephonists, the disembodied voice in the basement, the whimpering nervous girl who served in the Cash Department next door, Miss Finch herself as she made tea and delivered letters, all ran. Like convicts, at the double, they scuttled upstairs and downstairs, scurrying in and out of offices to look for files or deliver messages, running, running, running. Sometimes, I almost expected them to take wing, like one does in nightmares. They were not allowed to use the lift, because the charity was short of money and it was necessary to keep the electricity bill to a minimum.

Miss Finch left me to manage the telephone alone for a few minutes. She had to sort some letters into a round for hand delivery and did this at another table. In seconds, the awesome Presence who had interviewed me and had given me the job shuffled out of her room, to inquire of Miss Danson, her secretary, why she had found herself speaking to her own basement when she wanted to speak to the Public Assistance Committee two miles away.

Miss Danson murmured about the new girl just starting and eased her back into her room, while Mr Ellis barked at both Miss Finch and me to be more careful.

It was a dreadful morning, during which I managed to create telephonic chaos. I could hardly hear what was said. I had no idea of the names of the other staff or where they were to be found. I had no list of commonly required outside numbers and had to look each of them up in the telephone book. And, quickly enough, I realised from Miss Finch's manner that she did not feel it was in her interest to help me to make a success of the job.

I was left alone, while Miss Finch went to make the office's morning tea, and I called almost tearfully to Phyllis to come to help me sort the switchboard out.

'Not Phyllis, Miss Forrester,' roared Mr Ellis, behind me, 'Miss Barker, if you please.' He paused, while I sat paralysed with fright, and then said, 'Can't you speak quieter? I can't stand that la-di-da accent.'

'Yes, sir,' I whispered, as Phyllis Barker kindly came to my aid.

I realised suddenly that, except for Mr Ellis, everyone in the room whispered. And nobody laughed. Not one girl, except Miss Barker, had even smiled at me yet. The constant tattoo of the typewriter of the Presence's secretary, the buzz of the telephone switchboard, the flutter of paper and the steady hiss of whispers made up the noises in the room.

Miss Finch told me my lunch hour would be from one thirty to two thirty, and the morning seemed endless. She dumped a cup of tea in front of me with a biscuit tucked in the saucer, and I ate and drank eagerly. In a quiet moment Miss Barker found me a list of commonly used telephone numbers and I tried to master it. The names and figures danced in front of me. I needed badly a list of the names of the staff and their numbers on the switchboard, so that I could connect incoming calls to the correct extension; and when Miss Finch returned to assist me, I asked her for this.

She shrugged and said I did not need a list. I would soon learn the names. In the meantime, outraged voices on every extension phone sibilantly rebuked me. It was a nightmare.

At twelve o'clock, the basement waiting-room closed and there were no more names to write down and deliver to the filing clerks. This gave me more time to deal with other calls and contemplate more quietly the hateful, buzzing board.

Just before lunchtime, a thin waif of a girl wearing large horn-rimmed glasses came out of a door on the other side of the room.

With an apprehensive glance at Mr Ellis, she crept over to me and said in an almost inaudible voice, 'The Cashier would like to see you during your lunch hour.' She sniffed, and I saw that she had been crying. Her nose was red and her eyes heavy with tears. It looked as if she had been in even more trouble than I had.

'The Cash Department is over there,' she added, pointing to the room from which she had come.

I smiled up at her. 'Thanks. I'll come.'

She managed a glimmer of a smile back and then fled across the room and through the door she had pointed out to me.

Fear of what lay in wait in the Cash Department was added to my fear of the telephone.

I knocked at the Cash Department door and a female voice snapped, 'Come in.'

I entered. The room was partly divided by a frosted glass screen and at first appeared to be empty. I paused.

'Well?' snapped the same voice again, from behind the glass screen.

I approached cautiously.

Behind the screen, at a littered desk, sat a small, grey-haired woman. She looked at me almost belligerently. 'What do you want?'

'You sent for me, madam. I am Helen Forrester.'

'Hmm.' She looked me up and down, and her nose wrinkled in distaste.

She turned round and took two folded blue garments from a shelf behind her. These she almost threw into my arms.

'Your overalls. You will wear them at all times in the office and will keep them clean.'

'Yes, madam.'

'You will be paid on Friday afternoons. Such a nuisance to have to pay a single member of the staff on a weekly basis. What is your full name and address? And age?'

I told her.

'Very well. You can go.' She turned back to her desk, and I tiptoed out, past two empty desks where presumably the weepy girl and another person worked.

The general office was empty, except for an elderly lady in a pretty grey dress who was manning the telephone. She nodded to me as I went out.

I went up to the cloakroom on the top floor of the building. This had been shown to me when I arrived, by a hurrying lady in a green overall whom I had met on the stairs. I laid the two blue overalls on the floor under the hook where I had hung my coat, and wondered what to do. There was nobody about and the silence seemed unearthly. I began to cry, my head pressed against my coat.

I had no money to buy lunch, and there had been no bread left after breakfast to bring with me. Both parents had left me severely alone, to get myself ready for work and Edward ready to go to Alice's. Feeling like a pariah, I had taken the cheerful little boy to his new friend's and he had stayed with her without a murmur, and then I had walked to work.

There was no doubt in my mind that my parents were united in their attitude that I should find going to work so difficult that I would eventually be thankful to return to housekeeping.

At the memory of their stony faces, I felt suddenly weak. I moved to the wash basin and clung to it, as my legs began to give under me. Wild colours flashed before my eyes and I felt myself sinking into oblivion. I knew from experience that I rarely passed out completely, so I clung to the wash basin until the world stopped swimming about.

I cupped my hand under the cold tap and drank some water, slurping it up and splashing my face. Greatly daring, I decided to have a wash. My face was soaped as it had never been soaped in the past three years. I rinsed and rinsed in gorgeous hot water, then dried myself on the spotlessly clean roller towel.

The light was poor, but in the mirror I could see green eyes with black rings round them, peering out of a face dead white, except where it was blotched with acne. Short eyelashes hardly showed on the reddened eyelids. Smooth eyebrows looked very black below a rough fringe of brown hair. I grinned ruefully at myself. The teeth thus exposed looked good – the cavities at the back did not show.

The wash had done me good and, as nobody disturbed me, I washed my glasses, dried them on the towel and put them on. The face in the mirror came into sharper focus, and I could see again how defeatingly plain I was. How I longed for a perfectly straight nose, like Fiona's, instead of the high-bridged, haughty-looking Forrester nose.

Without a watch I did not know the time. Meanwhile, I needed to sit down, and there was no chair in the cloakroom.

Hesitantly, I looked along the line of blue overalls hung neatly on their owners' hooks, and saw beyond them a door leading off the cloakroom.

Very quietly, I approached the door and opened it.

I was in a small passage. To my left, an open door revealed a neat kitchenette. It had a big window and was bright with light. Another closed door faced me. When I turned its handle, it gave a sharp click.

'Hello. Come in,' said a soft feminine voice very cheerfully.

# Chapter seventeen

Embarrassed that I had disturbed someone, I swung the door wide and stood dithering on the threshold of a small room that seemed packed with furniture bathed in dazzling sunlight. Light from a skylight poured down on to the burnished brown head of a thin woman, about twenty-five years of age, who was seated facing me behind one of the three typists' desks crowding the room. She had an open paperback in one hand and was eating a sandwich. As she looked up at me from her book, her long, narrow face radiated good humour. She had a beautiful pink and white skin, delicately accentuated by good make-up, and light, almost catlike brown eyes gazed at me through very large horn-rimmed glasses.

'Hello, come in,' she said, as she put her book down on top of her typewriter. 'What brings you here? You must be the new telephonist.'

'Yes,' I replied. 'I am sorry to intrude. I was looking for somewhere to sit down.'

'Oh, take Miss Short's chair for a while. She won't mind.' She pointed to a swivel chair by another typist's desk. 'Like a sandwich?'

'Thank you.'

I willed myself not to snatch from the proffered square of greaseproof paper. Carefully, I took the tiny triangle and made myself eat it in several delicate, polite bites, when I really longed to bolt it down. It was a cucumber sandwich and reminded me poignantly of long-ago afternoon teas. The other girl ate the two remaining sandwiches and tossed the empty wrapping into the wastepaper basket. She insisted on my sharing a small piece of fruit cake with her.

I smiled at her, as I ate the cake, and asked, 'Are you somebody's secretary?'

'No.' She laughed. 'I'm just one of the also-rans. I do any typing jobs they want.'

'Could I ask your name?' I queried. 'I don't know the names of any of the staff, except some of the filing clerks, and it is terribly difficult when answering the phone.'

'Well, I'm Miriam Enns. And Miss Short and Miss Brown work up here. Miss Short is the Head Typist. Then Miss Danson in the Filing

Department is the secretary to Miss MacAdam, who runs the place. You probably saw her when you applied for the job.'

'I did.' Then I added, without thinking, 'The Presence.'

'The what?' Miriam chuckled delightedly. 'That's lovely.'

I blushed, and smiled nervously. Then I said, 'Well, she seemed like a Presence.'

'You are right. She's a great lady and she works very hard, though she is so frail.' She swung round on her chair, took a piece of paper out of her stationery stand and put it into her typewriter. 'I'll make you a list of the staff – it won't take a minute. I don't know the numbers of their phones on the switchboard, but I can tell you which floor they are on.'

She rattled away on the machine, while I sat quietly watching her. She seemed to me the nicest person I had met for a very long time, and as I watched her long, slender fingers flash over the keyboard, a new emotion welled up in me, a great desire to give and receive friendship.

'That Ellis man should have seen that you got a list like this,' she said irritably, as she whipped the paper from the roller and handed it to me.

'Thanks,' I said happily, as I carefully folded the paper up. 'Is he the only man on the staff?'

'No, there is one more. But I think Ellis finds it hard in a sea of women.'

I did not venture a comment. I was a bit afraid of Mr Ellis, who did not approve of la-di-da accents.

'Have you got an overall yet?' asked Miriam. She took a packet of cigarettes out of her own blue overall pocket, struck a match from a box on her desk and lit up.

'Yes.'

'Better put it on. We lowly types wear blue ones. Senior staff – the social workers – wear green ones.'

I nodded agreement.

There was the sound of the cloakroom door being opened and slammed, and running feet.

Miriam glanced at her wrist watch. 'It's twenty-five past,' she said. 'Better put on your overall and go downstairs – or Ellis will be after your blood.'

I jumped up. I felt a lot better.

'Thank you for your help,' I said warmly, looking down at the pixie face of my new friend.

Miriam had the same type of wide, red-lipped mouth as Fiona had, and she smiled broadly up at me. 'When you get desperate, come up here,' she advised. Her smile became a yawn and she took off her glasses and rubbed her merry brown eyes with her knuckles.

'I'd love to,' I assured her enthusiastically.

'Shut the door as you go out. Miss Short doesn't like it left open.'

Obediently I closed the door after me. I paused in the passage outside, my hand still on the door knob, feeling again the warm friendliness of the girl in the typing room. For the first time since arriving in Liverpool, I had talked with someone fairly young, who spoke as I did and treated me as an equal.

# Chapter eighteen

The aim of the organisation in which I found myself was to make the poor aware of the many charities available to help them; to counsel; to provide a little legal aid given voluntarily by a few city lawyers; and to disburse, in the most constructive way, funds donated to the organisation itself. The senior staff provided a friendly ear for sorrows to be poured into, and sympathetic visitors to the sick and other housebound people; they tried also to aid the elderly and the many despairing mothers who, under impossible circumstances, struggled to make ends meet. Though they were not well paid, all the staff had shining, neatly combed hair, clear skins and well-fed bodies. Their clothes were fresh-looking and everything matched, as was the fashion. I was thankful to be shrouded in an overall.

Filled with dismay at my lack of knowledge, not only of the telephone, but of the myriad of social nuances, the courtesies, of this new world, I struggled on to the end of the day. The other girls, with a hasty 'good night' ran for their trams, and I trudged slowly home, head bent against a blustery wind. A cup of tea brought to me during the afternoon had reduced the pangs of hunger, but I felt very weak. Night school would begin at seven o'clock, and I wondered how I would manage to get there in time. I badly needed food, warmth, and a little comforting encouragement that tomorrow I would do better.

When I slowly opened the door of the living-room, I saw that Father was seated in the old easy chair, deep in a book. I wondered why he was not reading in the front room, but decided it was probably too cold for him in there. Alan, his blond cowlick swinging over his forehead, was seated on a small upturned oil drum by the fire. His head was bent over an exercise book while he did his homework.

Brian, Tony and Avril were sailing an imaginary ship across the floor. Brian was shouting to his bosun, Tony, 'Ahoy there, Bill. Belay there.' And then to Avril, he called, 'Hard astarboard, you lazy landlubber.' And Avril laboriously turned a huge, imaginary wheel. They were so absorbed in the game that they did not reply when I said, 'Hello, children.

'Hello, Daddy. Hello, Alan.'

They both looked up from their occupations and nodded acknowledgment in a vague, guarded way, then went back to their reading. Only Baby Edward, who was whining steadily, toddled towards me, to put his arms round my legs. I picked him up and hugged him, in an effort to assuage the terrible sense of emptiness within me, and carried him into the kitchen from which came the clatter of dishes.

Fiona was filling the sooty tin kettle from the tap, and she half-turned and smiled at me timorously in the flickering light of the candle on the draining board. Beside her, Mother was emptying teacups into the soapstone sink. She said, 'Oh, you've come, have you? You *are* late.'

I stroked the back of Edward's scurfy head, as I answered, 'It took a long time to walk home.'

I looked uneasily at both of them. I sensed that something had gone wrong. I could almost smell it. And it was my fault. I could see it in Mother's stiffened back and frozen look as she swung round to the back door, teapot in hand, to empty the leaves down the outside drain.

'Down?' requested Edward, and very slowly I slid him on to the worn tiles, my eyes on Fiona, in the hope that she would give me a hint while Mother's back was turned. Her eyebrows went up and she gave an almost imperceptible shrug. She seemed scared, and turned hastily back to the kettle, which was running over with water.

Mother clicked her tongue when she saw the overflow.

'Fiona, you stupid girl. Empty some of it out. Put the lid on and then put it on the fire.'

Obediently, Fiona did this and then slid past me into the living-room, to put the kettle on to heat. Edward toddled after her, and I could hear him saying to Brian, 'Me, too. I want to play.'

I was left to face Mother.

'You had better get yourself something to eat,' she said frigidly.

I had begun to tremble. It started in my legs and worked its way up, until all of me seemed to be shaking. Was nobody interested in what had happened to me? Surely, normal curiosity would have brought a question or two. Whatever had happened in my absence must indeed have been terrible to blot out all remembrance that this had been my first day at work. I waited for the blow to fall, as I whispered, 'Yes. I am very hungry.'

I turned to the deal kitchen table upon which lay half a loaf of bread and a very misused-looking pat of margarine sitting on its wrapping paper. 'Can I make some tea?'

'Yes,' replied Mother. 'The milk is still on the table. That's all the bread we've got.' She went swiftly into the living-room and I heard her go through to the front hall.

I closed my eyes, as if by shutting out the world I might persuade the trembling to cease. I wanted to seize the spongy piece of white bread, tear it apart and stuff it in my mouth and gobble it down. I could have eaten the margarine in big, revolting chunks. But Mother's words had gone into me like a sharp hatpin. What she had really said was, 'You should not eat anything. If you do, the children will not have any breakfast.'

But I had to eat. So I took up the knife and very carefully, because my hands were so unsteady, I cut a slice off the loaf and put some margarine on it. Despite a throat tight with misery, I ate it, standing there, staring down at the grey surface of the table.

When I went into the living-room to ask Fiona for some water from her kettle in order to make a cup of tea, she was standing aimlessly watching the game of ships. I touched her shoulder. She jumped and turned towards me, her expression unaccountably defensive as if she expected to be struck. I saw that she had been crying.

At my request, she took the singing kettle off the fire and brought it into the ill-lit kitchen.

I asked in a low voice, as I put a pinch of tea into a cup and poured water on to it. 'What's up, Fi? What has happened?'

She looked suddenly as if she would burst into tears again, and my trembling increased. Her usually red lips looked almost bloodless and she pushed her straight brown hair back from her face with hands that shook. She whispered dismally, 'Oh, Helen. I did a terrible thing. Mother and Father are furious. And they're awfully cross with you, too, for not being here . . .'

In my opinion, Fiona never did anything wrong, so probably it was my fault. As she started to cry, I quickly reviewed the family. Everybody seemed well; nobody appeared to have been hurt.

Fiona was nearly as tall as me, and I put my arm round her lanky frame. 'What is it, Fi?' I asked, through chattering teeth. But she just put her head on my shoulder and cried harder, long, slow sobs, silent like mine usually were, but sobs that seemed to be wrenched out of the innermost depths of her. My own despair was forgotten in the new fear of what had happened to upset her so much.

'What is it, Fi?' I implored again.

She gave a huge snuffle and began to mutter into my ear.

'Well, some men came with a big van – and they hammered on the front door until I simply had to answer. And they said they had come to collect the furniture because we were behind in our payments. And both Mummy and Daddy are so angry because I let them in and they took it.' She lifted her face towards mine, and then said desperately, 'But I couldn't help it, Helen. They were so big – and one of them put his foot in the door so that I couldn't slam it shut. I was so scared, Helen.' And she began another flood of tears.

'They really took it away?'

'Yes. The front room is empty.'

I began to chuckle quietly, so as not to draw Daddy's attention.

'It's nothing to laugh about, Helen,' Fiona whispered forcefully. 'It was terrible.'

'There now, Fi. Don't cry. Don't you see? We don't have to pay for it any more. That is five more shillings a week in the house. It's glorious. Think, five shillings will buy at least twenty more loaves a week. That's two loaves a week each. Cheer up, love.'

Fiona wiped her eyes with the back of her hand.

'Oh, no,' she said harshly, her voice heavy with sarcasm. 'No such luck. Father says we have to go on paying, whether we have the furniture or not. It's in the agreement.'

My trembling ceased entirely at this sudden revelation. I looked at her unbelievingly.

'Pay for what we haven't got? What nonsense.'

In my innocence, I knew nothing of hire purchase agreements or how they were abused by some companies doing business in the city. Many, many people were caught up in this vicious system, and many of them paid for years, because they either failed to read the small print in the agreements they signed or they did not understand the jargon in which they were couched. There were, of course, many reputable companies who stood by the spirit as well as the letter of their agreements. But my parents had apparently fallen victim to the blandishments of some salesman who was, perhaps, himself desperate for the commission he would get on the sale.

'We do, Helen. We have to pay.'

I looked wildly round me, for someone or something on which to vent my frustration.

'Where was Alan when all this happened?' I asked savagely. 'Couldn't he have helped you keep the door shut?'

'He wasn't home from school. It wasn't his fault. I left Avril with him and ran on ahead. I wanted to have the tea ready for you when you came home.' She looked piteously at me and sobbed again.

'Never mind, Fi, dear. You did your very best. Don't cry any more. I have to go to night school. And I must get Edward and Avril off to bed.'

I patted her on the shoulder, took a large breath and strode into the living-room. 'Bybyes time, darling,' I said to Edward, and with a laugh swept him up off the imaginary ship. A few minutes later, I forcibly dragged Avril away from the game to have her face, hands and knees hastily wiped before popping her into bed. Brian and Tony began to quarrel as to who should be thrown overboard to the sharks. Father told them irritably to get ready for bed, and Alan asked equally irritably if he would ever be allowed to do his homework in peace.

I had brought my books down from the bedroom after hearing recalcitrant Avril's prayers, and now I picked them up and ran out through the back door. Fiona was washing her face under the tap and I shouted goodbye to her as I went by.

Two quiet, orderly hours in school restored me.

# Chapter nineteen

The next morning, a few minutes after I arrived, breathless and hungry, the Presence sent for me. I was still very upset from the bitter recriminations of my parents, which had burst forth from both of them as they rushed between living-room and kitchen getting themselves washed and dressed for work. Mother had gone out the previous evening to the pawnbroker and had pawned all the clothes which Mrs Fox had sent, except what I was wearing, and this had added to my distress. It was a very miserable and frightened young girl who crept into the Presence's office, and stood humbly waiting for her to speak.

She looked up from her desk and in a few crisp, sharp words she dismissed me for inefficiency. She gave me a week's notice.

My small world, my new hopes, shattered round me. It was as if they fell like tinkling glass from a broken window, leaving me naked to a winter wind.

As I stood dumbly staring at her without any idea of what I should do, she turned the pages of a file on the desk in front of her. Gradually my eyes focused on her long, shrivelled fingers and following the line of them, I saw that the file was marked 'Forrester', in large capital letters.

In the silence, the significance of the file slowly dawned upon me. At some point, my parents must have applied to my employers for help. And a file on our family must have been sitting on the shelves in the outer office, available for all the girls to read. I felt so mortified at the idea of a social worker's report on our poverty-stricken home being read by the other girls that I wondered how I would manage to face them during the week's notice the Presence had just served on me.

She was speaking again. 'Miss Finch will be promoted to telephonist. I am prepared to give you another chance as office girl in her place. Her salary is ten shillings a week.'

Reprieve! I snapped up the offer.

Ten shillings would pay Alice. And people got rises in pay, didn't they? Perhaps I would, if I could last out long enough.

She lifted the telephone receiver. 'I will speak to Mr Ellis. Report to him.' She gave me a grim, small smile of dismissal, and I crept out of the room. Her manner was cool and distant, and yet I felt that, amid the many worries of her day, she had tried to help me.

I did not look at any of the other girls, as with eyes downcast I went over to Mr Ellis's desk and stood by him, waiting to be noticed. He was saying, 'Yes, yes. I understand,' down the telephone. Finally he hung up the telephone receiver, and swivelled round towards me.

'That's a proper mess now, isn't it?' he barked.

I hung my head and said nothing.

While I waited, crestfallen, he reorganised his staff, so that Miss Finch could spend the day showing me what to do. Then I was borne off by a naturally triumphant Miss Finch to hurry into our outdoor clothes again.

All letters addressed to destinations within approximately one mile of the office were delivered by hand, as were urgent ones to more distant addresses. One of the sights of the city was the vast number of small office boys and girls trotting about, delivering letters. Their wages were cheaper than the cost of postage.

I knew the city well and soon sorted the letters into a round, and Miss Finch and I set out together. In and out of lawyers' offices, shipping offices and shops we tramped. There was even a letter for the Liverpool Playhouse, which we excitedly delivered at the stage door, hoping against hope that we might catch a glimpse of one of the actors. But we were disappointed. A joking, cheerful doorman took the missive from us.

Mary warned me that the lift men in some of the buildings were not to be trusted, and several times she insisted that we walked up the stairs, once as far as the sixth floor.

I did not understand the import of her warning until the next day, when I did the round on my own. Two men pawed me, while with one hand they pulled the rope that carried the lift upwards. I shrank into the far corner where I could not be reached. This did not deter one of them who, with a grin, stopped the lift at a deserted top floor and pinned me into the corner.

Instinctively I screamed at the top of my voice, and pushed away the exploring hands with all the force I could command. The letters scattered over the floor of the lift. I was panic-stricken, though I could not have said what I was frightened of.

When I shrieked the man let go of me. He turned and angrily flung open the iron gates, and told me to get out and walk. He picked up the letters and threw them after me, as I shot past him on to the landing. I snatched up the letters and scampered down the staircase to the floor I needed. I was sickened, as he slowly followed me down in the lift whispering obscenities which I had previously only come across scribbled on the walls of public lavatories and had never quite understood. His leering face, seen through the iron gates as I passed them on my way down, haunted my nightmares for several days.

This was the first time that anyone had made a sexual advance to me, and, since I did not really understand what the threat to me was, I was filled with nameless terrors for a long time, and learned to run upstairs like a rabbit. Practically all the novels I read ended with a first kiss and I imagined that a happy marriage was a life of gentle tenderness. That there was a physical side to it was unknown to me. I had washed my brothers often enough to know that there was a difference between boys and girls, and Edith had always washed us and dressed us in front of each other, so it all seemed perfectly natural, as did the fact that elm trees and oak trees had different types of leaves.

I had once watched a bull amongst a herd of cows and understood from the cowman that they were making calves. I vaguely understood that babies were carried in their mothers' stomachs, because some of my brothers and sisters had been born at home; and I had picked up from scurrying maids a little of what was happening, but how the baby got there was unknown to me and I presumed that its beginning was spontaneous, though I gave it surprisingly little thought. I knew I was too plain for marriage so would not be having any babies anyway.

During the past two years, while I had been developing into a woman, I had been entirely cut off from the speculative gossip of young girls. Mother had not seen fit to explain anything to me or to warn me of any danger to myself. Yet I sensed now a real physical danger and I gave a wide berth to all lift men and commissionaires.

When Miss Finch and I returned to the office, we dashed up the stairs to the kitchen to make the morning tea. A tray was spread for the Presence, kettles were filled and cups and saucers were assembled on other trays. A box of biscuits was opened and a biscuit put on every saucer.

While Miss Finch delivered tea to the Presence and to the people working on the same floor as the Filing Department, I ran down the innumerable stone stairs to the basement, carefully balancing in one hand a cup of tea for Miss Lester, who took the names of the clients when they first entered.

The stench in the badly ventilated cellar room was appalling, as I handed the cup of tea to the blue-clad girl seated at a tiny table facing the clients. She thanked me, while about twenty pairs of eyes watched silently. I paused by the table, expecting Miss Lester to make some light remark or other. Gossiping, however, was a major sin in the eyes of Mr Ellis, so she said nothing.

I looked out over the clients and they stared back at me. There were fat women in black shawls, black skirts and white aprons. They were Liverpool Irish, I knew. Once or twice, while sitting in the park watching the children play, I had spoken to such women shyly about their children, and found them kind and responsive. Some of them still had the high colour of country women, but most of them looked white and drained of strength.

There were also a few women in coats and hats, shabby and grey. A number of men in stained working clothes sat quietly, with their cloth caps held neatly on their laps. One or two children fidgeted fretfully on the wooden benches or sat on the coconut matting which covered the stone floor. Low-watt bulbs cast a poor light over the well-ordered crowd.

Perhaps it was their quietness, their resignation to the long wait for attention, which was most depressing. They seemed people who had lost all hope, and my heart went out to them. I understood why they smelled, the exhaustion which made them so very quiet. The organisation, I guessed correctly, had not enough money to enable them to offer their clients a cup of tea. Thoughtfully I stole back up the stairs to the kitchen.

'You were a long time,' complained Miss Finch impatiently. 'Take this tray down to the first floor. Give each of the interviewers a cup – and don't forget the volunteer at the centre table.'

I took the heavy tray of filled cups and carried it carefully down to the first floor. Balancing it on one hand, I pushed the landing door to open it. A youth as thin as a broomstick held it open for me as I passed through. I saw his face light up at the sight of the tea tray, and I felt dreadful because I could not give him a cup.

It was another waiting-room which smelled equally badly and was equally gloomy. There was only one light hanging above a centre table round which a screen had been set. A well-dressed lady sat at the table, a neat row of files before her. At the side of the table on a wooden chair sat an ancient bundle of bones hunched under a thick blanket shawl. Her tiny face, dark from lack of washing, peered anxiously out from the shawl, like a mouse peeping out of its hole. Little hands clutching the shawl across her breast were equally mouselike. She watched me put a cup of tea down by the voluntary worker, and I felt for a second the old woman's clemmed stomach, the agony of the smell of the tea.

A number of small rooms ran off this waiting-room. These were the interviewing rooms, where in reasonable privacy the clients could at last whisper out their difficulties. It seemed to me sometimes that the whole place ran on whispers, as if it were a scared place where one dared not speak in a normal voice for fear the gods might be disturbed.

I took a cup of tea to each lady in a green overall in the interviewing rooms. In every room was an old-fashioned roll-top desk with a number of baskets of files at the back of them. The baskets were marked 'Visit' or 'Letter' or 'In Hand' or 'Filing'. The clients were seated on wooden chairs at the side of the desk, and they hardly paused in their recitals to the interviewer as I brought in the tea. In one room, Dorothy Evans was riffling through the file baskets, looking for a missing file. The interview was continuing despite Dorothy's presence, and I soon learned, like her, to be quiet and unobtrusive in such a situation and never to say anything except, 'Excuse me.'

When my tray was empty, I scurried up to the kitchen on the top floor. Miss Finch was filling another cup.

'Take this down to Miss Dane – her office is next to the Cash Department.'

Miss Dane, I discovered, was the Assistant Presence. Since she was not quite so weighed down by responsibility as the Presence herself, she had time to stop her perusal of a mountain of correspondence to ask me if I was the new office girl,

In case it was not obvious, I said, 'Yes, madam, I am.'

She was a pretty, dark-haired woman, and she smiled sweetly at me, as she said, 'I hope you will be happy here,' as if she really meant it.

'Thank you, madam,' I replied warmly, and became her devoted slave.

Tea having been served, Miss Finch and I leaned thankfully against the kitchen counters and had tea ourselves. At that time, Mary Finch was sixteen years old, a year and a half older than me, and this seemed a big gap to bridge, so our conversation was desultory.

After a few awkward minutes, we did another run up and down stairs to collect the dirty cups, and then washed them up. Our overalls still showed wet splashes from our washing up, when we again presented ourselves to Mr Ellis.

'The index cards are ready for filing,' he said. 'Get on with it.'

We obediently sorted the cards into alphabetical order and filed them. Then we took another trip to the basement waiting-room to relieve Miss Lester, while she fled upstairs to the cloakroom.

Two new girls to look at caused the clients to rustle in their seats and murmur to each other behind shielding hands. There were no magazines for them to read, so their boredom must have been intense.

Miss Finch sat down at the table and I stood by her and looked around me. One wall was shelved and was packed with fat, dusty envelopes set upright.

'They're old files,' explained Miss Finch. 'If you can't find a file upstairs, it may be down here.' And as if to justify her words, the phone rang and she was requested to check if a certain file was on the shelves.

It was. And to save Miss Barker, K to Z, coming down for it, I was sent hurrying upwards with the grubby envelope. The staircases were rapidly beginning to feel like Mount Everest to me, they were so long and steep.

When I returned, a woman in a faded cotton frock and grey cardigan was standing in front of Mary. She was holding a baby and her stomach was already swollen with another child. Mary wrote down her name and address, and handed the slip to me.

'You phone it up,' she said lazily.

I took the slip as if it might bite me and reluctantly went to the little cubbyhole where the phone was. Slowly, I lifted the receiver.

Immediately came the soft hello of the volunteer temporarily manning the switchboard.

I gave the name carefully, spelling it out to make sure that it was correctly recorded.

'Thank you,' said the voice from the switchboard very clearly.

I hung up the receiver on its hook and stood looking triumphantly at the phone. I had managed to use the instrument and I could hear on it. Joyfully I went back to Miss Finch. Perhaps, one day, I would be able to manage the switchboard.

# Chapter twenty

After our visit to the basement waiting-room, Miss Finch and I spent an hour sorting and filing index cards under Mr Ellis's eagle eye.

As her fingers flew along the drawers of cards, Miss Finch explained to me in a whisper that at half past eleven we had to go to a famous cake shop and restaurant to collect a sandwich lunch for a committee, which would meet in the Committee Room on the top floor during the lunch hour. We had also to make coffee for the members, and lay the table.

The walk to the restaurant was not very far, but after all the stairs I had climbed in the course of the morning, it seemed a long way. Still, the fresh air blowing off the river and the bustle of the city were welcome. In this district there was little hint of the frightful effects of the Depression upon Liverpool; just an occasionally empty shop, and a larger number of offices to rent than usual. The businessmen hurrying up and down the street were well dressed, and no unemployed men hung about the street corners.

The lunch was not quite ready, so we waited unobtrusively in a corner of the cake shop and watched the fashionable crowd passing through to the restaurant at the rear. Ladies in flowered or feathered hats with veils drooping over their eyes were greeted by men in immaculate dark suits, their neatly rolled umbrellas hooked over one arm, black felt hats held in their hands, as they ushered the ladies into the dreamland beyond. I remembered when Mother had been just such a lady meeting one of her men friends in a restaurant for lunch. She sometimes took me with her, as a sop to propriety, I presume.

My eyes wandered to the display counters. Behind the glass there was a wonderful collection of cakes, chocolate éclairs, *babas au rhum* topped with cream, *petits fours* in delicate pink, white or mauve icing, French sandwiches oozing with raspberry jam and cream and smothered in icing sugar. There was a fruit cake with at least an inch of marzipan resting on its top. It was flanked by chocolate swiss rolls, and my mouth watered. It all seemed part of a dream of long ago.

'Here, take this,' ordered Mary Finch.

She thrust a large confectioner's box into my hands and balanced another on top of it, while she turned to pay the shop assistant with money given her by the cashier.

'Be careful,' Mary warned, as we struggled through the lunchtime crowds. 'We'll get into trouble if the cakes are squashed.'

In the kitchen, we set out on plates the pretty cakes and the tiny rolls filled with different meats and wisps of mustard and cress. Then we laid the long, narrow table and made a pot of coffee, wrapping up the latter in tea towels to keep it warm.

With a last glance at the inviting table, Mary Finch hustled me out and down one floor to the silent lift.

'Committee members are allowed to use the lift,' she explained. 'You'd better know how to run it.'

I was dreadfully hungry and this announcement threw me into immediate panic. I foresaw another débâcle, like that of the switchboard.

Mary showed me how to start and stop the lift, and then said, 'Now, you try.'

Gingerly I closed the gates at the main floor, pressed the handle and, with a sense of shock, found that instead of going up we had descended to the basement waiting-room. The astonished clients – they were, according to Mary, always to be referred to as clients – had seen all those preceding them sent up to the Interviewing Floor by the stairs and they were obviously surprised at this sudden arrival of a lift.

'Stupid,' hissed my teacher, who must herself have been both tired and hungry. 'Turn the handle the other way.'

I did so, and we shot upwards, passing a bewildered gentleman in a bowler hat standing on the ground floor.

We were at the top again and the lift automatically clanked to a stop. The door of the Filing Department opposite flew open. The Presence's typist, her face forbidding, asked, 'Why are you running the lift? The Secretary wishes to know.'

Trouble again. I opened my mouth like a codfish, but it was Miss Finch who answered smartly, 'I'm teaching the new girl how to run it, ready for the Committee.'

'I see.' The typist returned to her desk.

'Phew!' exclaimed Mary. 'The old geezer's got the ears of a cat. Now run the lift down, and stop at every floor. Try to get it level.'

We sailed straight down to the basement again, and I whispered to Mary, 'Caves, catacombs and coal mines, bargain floor.'

Mary started to giggle.

The man in the bowler hat must have decided to walk up the stairs, because the main floor, opposite the tea merchant's door, was deserted.

'Graveyards, grizzlies, golliwogs, gamps, goats, tea shop, main floor,' I announced gravely.

Mary laughed, and waited expectantly for the next floor.

'Overalls, olive oil, ostriches, offal, first floor,' I said, in the same sing-song voice of a department store lift girl.

'Secretaries, sausages, soap, Somalis, shoes, Simnel cakes.' I flung open the gate at the second floor, stepped out and bowed to Miss Finch as if she were an honoured customer and I a shopwalker.

But Miss Finch looked past me, her face immobile. I whirled round. The Assistant Presence was watching me, her eyes twinkling with amusement.

Horrified, I waited for the guillotine to fall. But she was laughing, as she wagged an admonishing finger. 'The Committee will be arriving. I saw Mr Thompson walking up just now.'

'I'm sorry, Miss Dane,' said Mary, and with silent grimaces to each other we descended to the ground floor, while Miss Dane walked up to the Committee Room on the top floor which was not served by the lift.

There was a sound of running feet in the hall, and a young man carrying a briefcase almost flung himself into the lift. He was breathtakingly handsome, and his immaculate white shirt showed up a regimental tie to perfection. Before I could close the gates, he was joined by two white-haired ladies wafting a soft perfume with them. They greeted each other; and, after peeping out to see if anyone else was coming, I carefully closed the gates. The three passengers turned towards the gates and waited in silence as we travelled upwards, like a small congregation listening to a priest reciting the Creed.

At the top, I positioned the lift with a series of sharp little ups and downs, and then let the passengers out. None of them had said anything to either Miss Finch or me. The ladies loosened their furs and walked slowly up the remaining flight of stairs, while Miss Finch and I, like little marionettes, ran the lift up and down, ferrying other Committee members. Later, I learned that many of these people were members of old Liverpool families famous for their charities through several generations. They were all concerned by the sad state of their native city, and they gave generously of both time and money in an effort to help their suffering fellow citizens.

As I watched them from under lowered lids, it sometimes felt odd to me that my grandmother and grandfather had probably wined and dined with these people or their parents, had done business with them, had attended balls and concerts with them; and, there I was, so hungry that I could have eaten all the lunch waiting upstairs, running a lift for them as if I was part of the machinery.

# Chapter twenty-one

I had been tired at the end of the first day of work, but by the end of the second day it seemed as if every muscle had its own particular ache. My imagination boggled at the thought of how many stairs had been climbed, how many miles walked. Even Miss Finch, who was a strong, well-fed girl, looked worn out; and I had done the same amount as she had on less food than a prisoner of war could hope for. As I trailed home, I realised that on the following day I would have to do the same work without Miss Finch's help.

At the end of the day one of the duties of the office girl, I discovered, was to collect any remaining outgoing letters from their various signatories, put them into their envelopes and take them to the nearby General Post Office and drop them in the letterbox. There was always a flurry on the part of the stenographers to bring down last-minute letters for signature by the Presence.

The Presence was a very hard-pressed woman and was frequently in the middle of phone calls or interviews when the letters arrived. The stenographers laid the letters on her desk, thankfully put on their hats and coats and went home. The little office girl stood outside the office and waited for the letters to be brought out by the Presence's secretary, who was a volunteer; and on some evenings she waited and she waited.

The office clock would tick remorselessly on towards Edward's and Avril's bedtime and the hour of night school. My stomach would tighten with fear of Mother's temper if I was not there to help. And night school teachers could be very sarcastic if one was late for class.

Finally, the letters would be brought out. The pretty secretary would help me put them into their envelopes. Those to be delivered by hand were put on one side. With a smile of relief, the secretary would hand me the ones to be posted; and I would run down the stairs, across the busy streets, and dutifully drop them into the post office's mighty maw.

At home at last, I took off my hat and coat and hung them on a peg in the hall. There was no night school on that second day of work. But there was homework to do, English essays to write, arithmetic problems to solve, shorthand to practise. Then there were the beds, left from the morning, waiting to be made, dishes to wash up, Edward and Avril to wash and put to bed, clothes to be washed or sponged and pressed, all the thousand and one tasks of a large family. I sighed as I entered the living-room.

The room looked different.

Everybody was present, except Fiona and Avril whom I could see through the window. They were skipping in the back yard.

The window!

It was shining clean and the grubby net curtain which usually covered it had been washed.

I glanced around. The big, old-fashioned iron grate with its side oven shone with blacking. The battered wooden chairs had been polished till all the nicks and chips in them appeared covered. The upturned paint drums had been scoured. The mantelpiece, usually littered with bills and replies to Mother's begging letters, was dusted and tidied, the papers neatly stacked under a well-washed stone; and the alarm clock ticked merrily in the dead centre; it seemed to be sticking out its chest with pride at its pristine green paint and its twinkling glass. The worn linoleum on the floor was speckless and the piece of coconut matting in the centre had obviously received a good beating.

Mother was sitting by the fire. She had changed her work dress for a shapeless, grubby cotton frock and her bare feet were thrust into a pair of old carpet slippers. The varicose veins on her legs showed in sickening knots, and her face was lined with fatigue. She had started to darn the boys' socks ready for them to put on again in the morning, and she was frowning heavily as she pushed the big needle in and out. She looked up as I entered.

'Goodness, Mum,' I exclaimed, as I looked round admiringly. 'You have been busy. The room looks lovely.'

'Humph.' She looked down at her darning again.

I eased around the *Liverpool Echo* and gave Father a cautious peck on the cheek, in the hope that I was forgiven for going to work. And then I leaned over and gave Mother an equally careful kiss. But Mother, for once, did not seem angry with me. She said, 'Hello, dear,' rather absently and went on darning.

I picked up Edward and gave him a hug. He laughed at me as I put him down, and then scrambled away under the table, where, judging from the dialogue, Brian and Tony had established a castle. Their imaginations were so fertile that they were able to create a whole strange world out of almost nothing, and it probably saved them in some degree from the effects of the savage reality of our life.

Mother said very mildly, 'There is some dinner in the oven for you, dear.'

Alan looked up from his book, and said, 'Hello. It's sausages.' He sounded cheerful and his red-rimmed, bright blue eyes were, as usual, friendly in their expression.

I grinned at him, and then I looked back at Mother. Sometimes I was more afraid of her when she was being kind than I was when she was not. Carefully, I moved round the back of her and opened the heavy oven door. Two sausages sat on a plate accompanied by a good tablespoonful of dried-up cabbage and a whole potato. I whipped the hot plate over to the table, found a knife and fork and thankfully sat down to eat. From time to time, I took a peep at Mother's clouded face.

'The dinner's nice,' I said appreciatively. This brought no response, so I added, 'You must have worked awfully hard today, Mum.' I looked again round the room and wondered where she had got the soap, the polish and the blacking from. There had never been any money for such things while I had been keeping house. The floor must have been scrubbed with a scrubbing brush, which we did not possess, before it could be shined as it had been.

Father rose, picked the teapot off the hob and brought it to me. He looked down at me with an odd expression on his face – as if he were trying to warn me. 'Here you are, old girl,' he said kindly, as he put the pot down on the table. 'Have some tea.'

What had I said that I should not have said?

'Thanks, Daddy.'

Mother stabbed a sock to death. 'I have not been working here,' she announced icily. 'I have been in Lewis's all day, demonstrating automatic toasters.'

Alan did not look up from his book, but the eyelid furthest from Mother went down in a clear, slow wink.

'That must have been interesting,' I said firmly, as I poured a cup of well-boiled tea. 'I've never seen an automatic toaster.'

'I hope I never see another,' said Mother with feeling. Then her rage burst out of her. 'Alice – that Alice – had the temerity to walk into this house this morning, without permission, and clean this room.

'She actually let herself in. It's outrageous!' Mother rolled up a pair of socks and flung them into the fruit punnet we used as a sewing box.

'Alice cleaned it?' I exclaimed.

'She did and I am furious.'

'She did a marvellous job,' I said, with honest admiration.

Mother's chin quivered and her thin chest heaved, as she seized another sock and thrust her hand into it.

'I will decide when my house needs cleaning. I will not have a peasant walking in and out of here, as if she owned the place.'

I was so tired, and I thought how marvellous it would be to come home every day to a clean, tidy house, so I said pacifically, 'You know, Mummy, if she did not charge very much, it might be worth getting her to do it regularly. It would save us both.'

'She didn't charge anything,' interjected Alan. 'When she brought Edward home, she said it gave her something to do while her mother was having a nap and that Edward liked being in his own house.'

'What nonsense!' Mother said angrily.

'Where did she get the blacking from? And the polish?' I inquired, as I scraped my plate.

Alan laughed. 'She brought her own.'

Mother caught her breath and I looked quickly across at her. She was biting her lower lip and a tear ran down her face. Suddenly I understood her humiliation, and instinctively I jumped up and went over to her. I put my arm round her shaking shoulders.

'Try not to cry, Mummy,' I urged. 'Everybody knows you have been ill and she probably thought she was being kind and helpful. I know that people round here help each other a lot. They always seem to know where help is needed, because they gossip so much.'

Mother nearly choked. 'I don't want them gossiping about me,' she shouted. 'When I want help I will pay for it.'

Father had been watching the scene over his newspaper, and now he said exasperatedly, 'You should not be upset. The girl meant well. She's not going to do it again, I am sure.'

'She certainly will not,' snapped Mother. 'As you observed, I settled that point once and for all.'

I felt as if Mother had stabbed me with her darning needle. 'Don't let it be so, O Lord. Please!' I almost whispered aloud.

But it *had* happened. Alice had been dismissed as firmly as I had been the previous day. And I had yet to tell my parents about my dismissal and reinstatement.

'What about Edward?' I asked, trying to keep calm.

'Oh, you will have to stay at home. This idea of going to work is ridiculous. See what an upset it has caused to all of us. And you are worn out.'

I *was* worn out. Mother so rarely looked at me unless I had done something wrong that I was surprised that she had noticed. But the gulf opening in front of me was so abhorrent to me that I gained a fresh surge of strength. And I fought back as if defeat would mean certain hanging in the morning.

Every member of the family joined in the battle. Mother had hysterics, Father roared, Edward howled. Avril, stretched to her full thirty inches of height, shook her finger at us all and demanded in frantic tones that we stop. Alan took my part with reckless abandon. Fiona wept and screwed her piece of skipping rope into knots as she swore she was not going to stay at home, as I suggested. From the castle under the table, the sounds of knights preparing to go out to slay a dragon ceased and two scared faces peeped out.

'Who is going to see that the boys don't get into trouble?' Mother asked dramatically, as they emerged.

'I will,' shouted Alan.

'They're big enough to look after themselves,' I screamed, most unfairly.

Brian and Tony began to bellow as they, poor innocents, suddenly became the focus of the quarrel. They must have felt that they were being abandoned by all of us.

Sometimes, in those difficult days, I identified myself with an alley cat which I had once seen engulfed in a football crowd racing down a train platform from a football special. Slipping, sliding, slithering in and out amongst the hob-nailed boots, fearing all the time that small paws would be crushed, wispy tail agonisedly trodden on; expecting any moment to feel a steel toe in the ribs flinging it over the platform edge into dark, unknown depths of misery; finding, for a second, shelter by a pile of luggage in which to lick quickly at bruised sides; only to be caught up again in the ruthless rush; looking madly for a wall up which to race or a kindly hand to sweep it up and tuck it inside a shirt, away from the terrible boots.

This time I thought that Minerva had forgotten her stepchild.

The abuse was largely verbal but the threat of physical punishment was always there. The elder children had when young all felt the weight of a cane and sound spankings with a hand; and occasionally both Father and Mother would strike out quite hard at one or the other of us. I do not think it occurred to any of us, even Alan who was growing quite tall, to strike back.

I would not yield. Mother said she would go to see the Presence and would demand my dismissal. The organisation had not, after all, purchased me, she said acidly.

Suddenly I remembered the Presence's words about a week's notice. Presumably, on my side, a week's notice would also have to be given before I could leave. I announced this triumphantly as fact.

'What rubbish,' shrieked Mother. She was thrashing round the small room like a tiger, and the children moved mechanically to get out of her way as she advanced on each one of them.

Father, who was still sitting in his chair, as if it offered a modicum of safety, the newspaper crumpled in his clenched fists, said in a more normal voice, 'She is correct. Either we pay a week's salary to them or she must work the week.'

Fiona wailed loudly, 'I don't want to stay at home.'

'You'll have to,' I said mercilessly. 'Fi, you'll have to. I have done my bit. You must take a turn. It's only till Edward is big enough to go to school.'

'I won't,' she screamed. She flung her skipping rope to the floor. 'No.'

'No,' Mother flashed at me. 'Oh, no. You are not going to push your responsibilities on to poor Fiona. She is much too frail, poor darling.'

# Chapter twenty-two

The need to give notice saved me.

Fiona was ordered to stay at home with Edward for the following two days. Mother's contract with the toaster manufacturer expired on Thursday night; she would start a new contract at another store the following Tuesday. This, I argued, would give her time to arrange some fresh care for Edward.

Poor little Edward. Poor Fiona, red-faced and deeply resentful. Mother actually smiled, however, when I presented her with my total earning for the week, less fourpence for contributions to National Health and Unemployment Insurance and another penny contributed to a hospital fund. She hardly heard me when I explained that the following week I would be earning only an office girl's pay.

In the office, I ran so hard and whispered so softly that my appointment was confirmed, despite my gauche manners and poor grooming.

A few weeks later, the other girls asked me to accompany them to the cinema. Bashfully, I refused, owning up that I did not have the money. They looked at me askance and did not ask me again for a number of years; perhaps they thought I did not like them.

Night school came to an end and I passed the examinations. This gave me more time to help Mother at home. The office staff, in turn, went away for two weeks' holiday to the mountains or the seaside. They usually went with their parents and came back with breathtaking stories of the boys they had met. They giggled behind the stacks of files until Mr Ellis roared at them to return to their work. He seemed to be the only person who spoke above a thin whisper.

I had no adventures to share with the girls. I was not entitled to a holiday that year, and my world of screaming family rows, of creditors, of pawnbrokers, of the lack of the most basic human needs, seemed to be so divorced from the experience of the staff that there was no common ground. I was obsessed with the need to survive, with simple worries, like how to squeeze a pair of rayon stockings out of Mother, or even darning silk with which to mend the ones I wore. I was totally dependent upon the whims of Mother. She seemed to take it for granted that anything I earned was hers, and this idea stayed with her throughout my working life. Girls did not need money for expenses; boys did.

One day, the Presence told me sharply to tidy up my hair. It was pay day and, in despair, I took out of my nine shillings and sevenpence a single bright shilling. A comb cost twopence, some hair clips a penny. Ninepence would buy a good, stout pair of rayon stockings.

Mother was so infuriated that she tried to snatch Joan's old handbag off me in order to extract the shilling, but I whisked it under me and sat on it and, tearfully, refused to move.

Father came home and walked into the middle of the scene, and I appealed to him, because sometimes he did seem to regard me as a human being, even if I was a girl. Without any hesitation, he said I should keep the shilling, and have one each week, so I thankfully fled with my handbag to the kitchen and left my parents to fight it out.

The weekly shilling was usually spent on second-hand articles of clothing. But I soon learned not to leave any pieces of clothing at home unless they were wet from washing, because they would be immediately pawned; stockings or gloves would be used by Mother herself or given to Fiona. On days when there was nothing to take for my lunch, I would buy a penny bread roll from Lunt's bakery near the office.

An overwhelming ambition in those days was to be able to afford from Lunt's a roll packed with cheese. These cost twopence, however, and I had to content myself with buying them for other members of the staff or just looking longingly at them through the bakery's steamy window.

And so I struggled blindly on from day to day. The trees in Princes Park, where on Saturday afternoons I took Edward to play, turned yellow and carpeted a neat circle of grass beneath them with curled-up leaves. Wet days became more frequent, and I delivered the letters each morning in shoes that became quickly sodden; the cardboard put into them to block up the holes disintegrated, and tender bare soles were exposed to the pavement. I caught so many colds that the days when I was without one became ones of rejoicing. Liverpool air is always damp and, in those days, was filled with black particles from a myriad of chimneys, so that nasal catarrh and bronchitis were endemic and gave rise to the famous, snuffly Liverpool accent. Like many of the population I blew my nose through my fingers on to the pavement, and kept my single handkerchief for neat dabs at my nose in the office.

Alan reached the age of fourteen in November and left school shortly afterwards. I was plunged into bitter and unfair jealousy, as I watched him set out for his first job as office boy in a new suit bought for the occasion from Marks & Spencer's. In his pocket he carried a bit of lunch wrapped in an old margarine paper and a penny for the tram, so that he would not have to climb the long hill home. He was given pocket money as a matter of course, so my battle evidently helped him. He was intelligent and quick-witted and very articulate. He had snatched the job from dozens of other applicants and deserved all the help my parents could give him.

The life of an office boy was very hard. In a tall, gloomy, Victorian building, he worked from eight thirty in the morning until six o'clock at night and until one o'clock on Saturdays, for a wage of seven shillings and sixpence a week. Office boys were commonly hit when they made mistakes or if they dared to answer their seniors back, and the tight-lipped bookkeeper who taught him how to keep accounts was very heavy-handed. He was still far from being fully developed and, like me, was painfully thin. Since he spoke 'with an olly in his mouth', he had been in many fights at school – it is not only sparrows who attempt to destroy those different from themselves – and sometimes, in the absence of the bookkeeper at lunch, a general fight would break out amongst the young men in the office. Though he fought back fairly skilfully, I can remember seeing bruises across his buttocks where he had been beaten with an old-fashioned rounded ruler.

Attached to the church was a troop of Boy Scouts and Alan had joined this. Although we were certainly not the poorest family in the parish, the Scoutmaster must have found it impossible to obtain money from my parents for a uniform for him, and, therefore, provided him with one. He once went away to camp with them and returned looking strong and rosy and very freckled, but the fair skin soon became white again and the beguiling freckles faded, to be replaced by acne in its worst forms. Great boils covered his face and neck. A cheerful expression helped to compensate for this affliction. His tousled cowlick was neatly slicked back with the aid of brilliantine and the black pocket comb tucked into his jacket pocket. His pale skin gained a slight ruddiness as, like me, he ran through the streets of Liverpool, in and out of horse and motor traffic, delivering letters and messages.

Like me, Alan suffered from the lack of a raincoat and from inadequate footwear. Liverpool shares with Ireland not only Irish inhabitants but Irish weather. When it is not actually raining, there is still a misty dampness which seems to penetrate one's bones. Older people always seem to be complaining about 'me rheumatism' or 'me arthritics' and say that they 'hurt something wicked' on wet days.

Alan, Brian and Tony all played cricket in the street, often with a beer bottle as a wicket and a piece of board as a bat. Alan had had the advantage, when quite a small boy, of playing the game in better circumstances. A couple of professionals had taken an amused interest in the little eager beaver who haunted their practice ground and had coached him. This acquired ability had led him into the school team. One of his older colleagues at work gave him his old cricket bat and pads, and this enhanced his chances of playing with other teams after he left school. He got a lot of pleasure from these games.

He also went to night school. He always says he learned a lot there. But he did not stay in the system very long, and he probably learned much more in the Auxiliary Air Force, which he joined a few years later.

I rejoiced in his good beginning in the business world. Because my parents kept pressing me to stay at home again and be the unpaid house-keeper, I was most unchristianly envious of the interest and encouragement lavished on him by both Mother and Father. I cried for hours through freezing winter nights, and prayed frequently and earnestly for strength to keep my temper. I was convinced that most of my misery was caused by lack of self-control over envy and bad temper. It was a long time before I realised that there is a limit to anybody's self-control; and that the only sin I had committed was to be born to my mother at a time when she would otherwise have divorced my father. She could never forgive me for it.

# Chapter twenty-three

As autumn merged into winter the children began to look forward to Christmas, having been reminded of its coming by Brian and Tony's extra choir practices. For years, Fiona and I secreted all kinds of bits of wool, old socks and cotton scraps, and out of them we manufactured gifts for the family. Golliwogs and rabbits emerged from the socks, hand-hemmed handkerchiefs, handkerchief cases, pincushions and hair tidies, prettily covered boxes and pyjama cases were made from the cotton scraps. I once made Fiona a doll's bed out of a shoe box; it was complete with little blankets and a bedspread, and she joyfully put her tattered doll into it. The doll was her only treasure from our old home. It was dreadfully dirty, and its papier mâché feet and hands were nearly worn out; but its glass eyes still opened and closed and it still had some hair.

Another time, I made a horse and cart for Edward. The horse was made out of corks found in the street. It had wobbly legs made out of slivers of firewood. The cart, which was a carton from a box of matches, had high wheels made from the tiny lids of ointment tins, also found in the street gutters. Though it was not a very robust toy he played with it for several days before it fell to bits.

From their choir money, Brian and Tony bought little gifts for everybody. One of my most treasured possessions is a pottery black cat given me by Tony and, until recently, I had a tiny pottery donkey with a red pincushion on its back, bought for me by Brian. When, after forty-five years, I recently smashed the donkey I stood over the scattered bits and cried. Both these treasures travelled halfway round the world with me. Another treasure is a crocheted red and yellow egg cosy made for me by Avril in one of her earliest sewing classes. Sometimes I take it out and think of the small, determined little girl stabbing away with a crochet hook too big for her fingers.

Alan's shilling a week was strictly for pocket money, so he bought us all kinds of delightful gifts, like bottles of perfume and talcum powder from Woolworth's.

My parents always tried to make Christmas pleasant for the younger children. Only the first two Christmases in Liverpool were without any real effort at celebration, and for both of those we enjoyed one of the

Christmas boxes of food distributed to the poor of Liverpool during the festive season.

For two Christmases after I began work, a mysterious stranger telegraphed us five pounds. We never discovered who sent it but it provided a dinner and a stocking full of small gifts for the little ones.

Alan and I, like all working people, had two days' holiday. Such was his exhaustion that on any holiday Alan slept until midday. For Fiona and me, however, there was never such a luxury. Boys needed rest; girls could manage without. Brian and Tony had to be got up and given their breakfast in time for them to sing at the Christmas services. Edward, like most little boys, was awake at sun-up, as was Father. On Sundays and holidays, Mother stayed late in bed and Avril slept late, too. Holidays for me were not a time for relaxation, and I was always thankful to escape back to work. At work, people occasionally said, 'Thank you.'

In February, the cold and the lack of food caught up with me, and I fell ill. I staggered round the spinning office, dumbly terrified that if I said I was ill I would be dismissed, as girls in shops sometimes were. There was the further fear that if I had to stay at home, Mother would find means of keeping me there. She looked after Edward on days when she had no work; occasionally Fiona would be kept at home to mind him, and on other days he was handed round to various neighbouring women to be watched for a few hours. The problem was solved when he reached the age of four and could run along to school with Avril. Nothing seemed to disturb him much. He was used to a large family and seemed to add any strangers to that family. He was obedient and had a tranquillity which the rest of us lacked. Perhaps he realised that, despite the fights which raged over his head, he was never attacked and we all loved him very much.

Though the gulf between Mother and me had, since infancy, appeared to me to be unbridgeable, she had recently begun to talk idly to me as if I were a woman. Only the surface of her mind seemed to be engaged in the conversation; somewhere deep underneath lay the real woman, with true passions and motives. But it was better than nothing. Despite this small break, I still dreaded that she would again pass over her family responsibilities to me. So that in overwhelming fear I fumbled about the office making tea, sorting index cards, going out to deliver letters, while Mr Ellis ranted that I was more than usually slow and stupid. My chest hurt and my throat hurt and I ached all over as I sought to please him. On the second day, like an Edwardian heroine, I collapsed quietly into a chair.

Everybody was concerned and kind. Smelling salts were thrust under my nose, tea was made; and, when I could get up, Mary was instructed to escort me to the tram. I was not very clear about what was happening and was shivering as Mary bundled me into the vehicle.

I sat down by a workman in torn work clothes, and took out my last penny from Joan's handbag. I dropped it, and it rattled away down towards the front of the vehicle. The workman looked up from his *Echo*, while I sat aghast, feeling that even if I could find the coin under the feet of all the other passengers, I would collapse if I bent over to retrieve it.

The middle-aged workman next to me was staring, as the skinny conductor, rattling his money bag as warning, came down the aisle to collect the fares. I sat silent, waiting to be thrown off at the next stop because I did not have the fare.

The man folded up his paper and proffered a sixpence to the conductor. 'Two woons, lad,' he said.

The conductor punched two tickets, handed them to him, and wandered on down the aisle. The man handed one of the tickets to me. ''ere ya, luv,' he said, his rough red face beaming.

My voice seemed to come from far away, as I said, 'Thank you. Thank you very much. You are most kind.'

'Aye, that's all right, luv.'

He looked down at his folded paper and I looked down at the stubby fingers holding it; they were scarred from many cuts about the knuckles and the nails were broken to the quick. The memory of them and of their wonderfully perceptive owner stayed with me through the illness that followed.

Contributions to National Health Insurance entitled workers to the services of a doctor. When my parents came home and found me shivering in my bed, they sent for the general practitioner with whom I had registered my name.

He came marching into the smelly, bug-ridden bedroom, went straight to the window and flung it open, waited for a moment and then closed it partially. In the light of a candle held by Mother, he examined me and diagnosed influenza and tonsillitis. The tonsillitis had caused an ear infection. He ordered that more covering than the single blanket and old overcoat on my bed be put over me, a fire be made in the bedroom, the window kept slightly open. He painted my throat with tannic acid, put drops in my ears and ordered aspirin to alleviate the influenza. He was a handsome man with a very white skin and a large black moustache. He was exceedingly kind to me over the three weeks of my illness, coming in daily to paint my throat, and assumed an almost godlike character in my romantic mind.

He also ordered a light diet of milk, eggs and orange juice. This seemed to be out of the question. But Mother did make bread and milk for me, and for the rest I had Oxo cubes dissolved in hot water, toast and tea. When there was enough coal, a fire was made for me by Father, but most of the time we were too short of fuel, despite the fact that my kind employer continued to send my wages by mail and Mother cashed the postal orders.

For days I lay in my cold bed watching the sleet and rain of February through the dusty, finger-marked window, too exhausted by fever and pain to think. The children were used to my retiring temporarily to bed with bouts of tonsillitis and rarely came to see me except at bedtime. Edward had been moved from my bed in case of infection and shared my parents' bed; but as soon as the fever had departed Mother used me as a baby-sitter for him, which meant I dared not sleep during the day.

Once I could walk about the house, I asked the doctor to certify me as fit. I told him that if I was away much longer, I might lose my job. This was such a common reason for going back to work before one was fit that he signed the certificate. I washed and ironed my blouse and panties, mended my stockings and the next day reported to work.

It seemed as if the staircases had grown longer in my absence and the distances I had to walk to deliver letters seemed to have expanded to infinity. Several times I had to lean against a wall until bouts of faintness passed.

It took such a very long time to walk home that Father became anxious and set out to meet me. We came face to face beside the Philharmonic Hall, where he had paused to glance at the tattered black and white posters announcing their concerts.

His cheap navy blue suit shone at the elbows and seat, and it hung on him. He looked cold and forlorn without a raincoat, and his thin, lined face showed anxiety, as he hastened towards me.

'Where have you been?' he inquired, as he took my elbow and turned towards home. 'We have been worried about you.'

'I had to wait for the letters to be signed before I posted them,' I muttered, my breath coming in short gasps after the effort of climbing the hill.

'You should have taken the tram home,' Father said. 'You're not fit to walk.'

'I didn't have any money,' I wailed suddenly, all the misery of years bursting from me in one long, subdued howl.

'Good God! I thought it was arranged that you should have a shilling a week for pocket money and fares.' He stopped and looked into my woebegone face.

'Mother didn't have any of my wages left, when I asked her this morning,' I sobbed.

He clicked his tongue in annoyance. 'Dear Lord!' he exclaimed in exasperation.

This was the first time for many years that Father and I had been together without any other member of the family present, and it was as if he came out of his usual absent state and really looked at me. The sight seemed to have some impact.

I continued to wail softly as we inched our way along dark Myrtle

Street and turned into Catherine Street, while he supported me by the elbow.

My sobs receded and I turned towards him. His large, high-bridged nose was scarlet from acne roseola, the rest of the skin an unhealthy yellow. His shirt and collar had reached an off-white colour from too much washing with too little soap, and his trousers badly needed pressing. His expression was so sad that I nearly burst into tears again. When he was not absorbed in a book or quarrelling with Mother, he could be quite light-hearted and very witty, but now I was again reminded of a butterfly caught in a rainstorm. With horrid clarity, I saw, not a vague, exasperating figure called Father, but a defeated man; and for a moment I walked with him through the morass of despair into which he had fallen. There seemed nothing left of the cheerful young man, described to me by Grandma, who had gone off to war, despite his short-sightedness, and ended up in the forests of Russia. My first memories of him had been of a voice screaming with terror in the night. He suffered scarifying nightmares of his war experiences while he tried to re-establish himself in a post-war world, which was fed up with returning soldiers and their needs. He was a cultivated man, clever in his way, but now he worked as a clerk for the city, earning more than he handed over to Mother, but still very little. With the rest of the family, he suffered very much from the lack of intellectual companionship as well as lack of food and comfort.

As we slowly made our way along Catherine Street, we began to feel comfortable together, like walking wounded helping each other along. Though we did not talk much, because I was too exhausted, a feeling of understanding began to grow between us.

Before we entered the house, Father took a sixpence from his waistcoat pocket and pressed it into my hand.

'Come home on the tram every day,' he ordered.

I stared down at the tiny silver coin, too tired even to thank him, and then nodded agreement and slipped the coin into my handbag.

He pulled the string hanging from the letterbox and released the latch of the front door. He swung the door open and stepped back on to the pavement with a little bow, to allow me to pass in first. Poignantly, that polite gesture brought home to me, more than anything else, how different he was from the men who lived round us. Little Avril once expressed a similar idea. She said, 'I love Daddy. He is so gentle and he is the only man in the street who wears a collar.'

# Chapter twenty-four

I soon gained strength again and, through long days, slid silently between the patient, smelly clients, carrying cups of tea or files or messages. Sometimes I felt like advising the quietly courteous interviewers that our funds would do as much good if they were simply scattered in the back streets and left for the inhabitants to pick up. In large areas of Liverpool there was barely an inhabitant who was not in distress. Workless, half-starved, they were packed into deteriorating houses lacking proper toilets or running water. They were often shiftless and stupid, many spent their money on drink and some on drugs, but their need was blatantly manifest to anyone who cared to walk down the long treeless streets and through the narrow courts. Born and bred in such shocking conditions, who could blame them for seeking at every opportunity the garish warmth of the public houses on almost every corner?

It was pathetic to watch the clients doing their best not to use coarse language before the gently bred ladies of our organisation. Their usually loud voices were lowered to the whispers of the confessional, as they hesitantly chose words that would please, not offend. They never laughed.

In fact, nobody laughed, except the shorthand typists in their isolated nest on the top floor. It was not an environment calculated to raise the spirits of a sad and sick fifteen-year-old.

Grandma had, however, taught me to read out of the Bible, and I believed firmly in miracles. I had also not yet totally lost my belief in fairies, particularly Robin Goodfellow, a wicked sprite who sometimes snatched cups from my careless fingers and smashed them on the floor or who lost my pencils and dropped the hairpins out of my hair.

When the Presence sent for me one sunny May morning, therefore, I was expecting to be upbraided for the breakage of a cup and saucer, Robin Goodfellow having been rather busy the previous day. Instead, she performed a miracle.

I stood humbly before her desk, blue overall crumpled and splashed, greasy hair untidily knotted into a bun at the nape of my neck. Fortunately, she was too busy to look up at me.

She had a letter in her hand and she announced, as she read it, that I was entitled to two weeks' holiday that summer and had been granted a free holiday in a place called Kent's Bank. Mr Ellis would tell me when I could go, and a train ticket would be sent to me by the charity concerned. It did not strike me at the time that she might have asked me if I would like to go. I was ordered to depart for Kent's Bank on a date to be arranged.

Beside myself with excitement, I thanked her and fled back upstairs to the kitchen, where I stood quivering in front of the sink. A holiday! An undreamed-of luxury. A miracle.

Later, I cautiously inquired of one of the filing clerks if she knew where Kent's Bank was. She looked derisively at me for a moment and then sniggered. That little choking laugh told me that a recipient of charity was contemptible, and that she knew why I asked.

'It's on Morecambe Bay,' she said, and turned superciliously back to her file sorting.

Terribly hurt, I slunk back to the kitchen.

As I ate potatoes and cabbage and gravy, saved for me from the hot meal Mother had made at teatime, I told her about the holiday.

'It's all free, Mummy. Even the train ticket. Except I think I would simply have to have a nightgown and some walking shoes – if you could get them, Mummy.'

'I can't afford them,' said Mother simply. She was sitting in the easy chair, Edward on her lap, and smoking a cigarette.

'It is time you provided things like that for yourself, now that you are at work.' She took a slow pull at the cigarette and exhaled the smoke through her nostrils. 'You must have had a rise in salary since you started. You have been working for over a year now.'

Startled, I blinked at her. I had hardly given a thought to pay increases. I had concentrated solely on retaining my job.

'No, Mummy. I've never had a rise – only a reduction the first week. I'm still the office girl.'

Mother's eyebrows rose. 'That's absurd. You must have had an increase.'

'Honestly, Mummy I haven't. I would have told you if I had.'

Her lips twisted and she stared hostilely at me. It was clear that she did not believe me.

My throat constricted. Then I said stiffly, 'I don't cheat, Mummy.'

'They don't have money to give increases,' interjected Father, looking up from his book, laid on the table in front of him beside a half-drunk cup of tea. 'Helen should go. She still doesn't look well. Perhaps we could get a one-pound cheque to buy the things she needs. Try. See what you can do.'

While they argued and Mother fretted about the peremptoriness of the Presence, who had obviously not considered that my help might be needed at home, I rescued Avril from a fight on the front pavement and put her and Edward to bed. Avril always wanted to be included in the boys' games; and this time they had not allowed her to join in a game of marbles and she was in a howling tantrum over it. She transferred some of her furious frustration to me, as I hauled her into bed and told her in true sisterly fashion to shut up.

It was a further miracle which found me standing on the doorstep of a fine stone mansion in Kent's Bank run as a guest house by an organisation which used its profits to provide free holidays for the less fortunate. The June sun warmed my back and the clear, sharp smell of the sea wafted round me. In my hand I held a brown paper bag containing a clean blouse and panties, a nightgown and a toothbrush. On my feet I wore a second-hand pair of boy's shoes. Fiona had volunteered the loan of her raincoat which was a little short on me, but made me look quite neat. All the children had been delighted that I was to go on a holiday, though it was clear from their wistful faces that they wished they could come, too.

In answer to my timorous knock, a middle-aged man, swarthy and black-haired, ushered me in and up a fine, well-carpeted staircase, to a large bedroom containing six single beds.

'You are the first arrival, so choose whichever bed you like,' he said with a cheerful grin. 'You can put your toilet things on the dressing-table there and clothes in the wardrobe.' He gestured towards two enormous pieces of shining Edwardian furniture.

'I'd enjoy being by the window,' I replied shyly, pointing to the furthest bed which stood close to a tall light window draped in white net curtains. Through the window I could see pine trees waving in the breeze and a dazzling glimpse of the sea.

'Fine,' he said. 'Come downstairs to the lounge and have some tea, as soon as you are ready.'

I smiled my thanks and he went away.

Feeling very nervous, I put the paper bag in the wardrobe, and then like a cat in a new place I walked round the room, examining the peerless white pillows on the beds, looking down at the highly polished linoleum on the floor, and finally stopping to wash my hands in a tiny basin in a corner. I combed my hair and redid my bun in front of the spotted dressing-table mirror, and then cautiously opened the bedroom door and ventured downstairs.

The lounge was full of chattering men and women, who all seemed much older than me, and I hesitated in the doorway while the scene came into clearer focus.

An elderly gentleman was sitting on a settee directly opposite the doorway. When he looked up from his teacup and saw me, he smiled, and evidently realised that I was feeling very shy. He motioned me to come over and sit by him, which I did, perching nervously on the edge of the settee.

He had a large, grey moustache and heavy black eyebrows under which bright blue eyes twinkled merrily. He took a pipe out of his mouth and said, 'Just arrived?' I nodded, and he put down his teacup. 'I'll get you some tea. Do you take milk and sugar?'

I assented with another shy nod, and he went to the tea table and returned with tea and three biscuits. He pulled a small table forward and set the cup in front of me.

'There we are,' he announced. His voice was deep, with a pleasant Welsh sing-song to it. He sat down beside me and took up his own cup again. He had put his pipe away in the pocket of his finely cut tweed jacket.

'My name is Emrys Hughes,' he said. 'And that's my brother, Gwyn, over there.' He gestured towards the mantelpiece against which leaned a tall, thin man, also grey-haired, talking to a lady in a green dress. 'What's your name?'

I told him, and, while I sipped my tea, he asked where I came from and whether I was still at school. Each question came out in such a breezy, cheerful manner that I was soon relaxed and laughing with him. He told me that he and his brother owned two big drapery shops in North Wales, that he himself had had a heart attack at the beginning of the year, so he had come to Kent's Bank for a holiday. He had prevailed upon his bachelor brother to come with him, and they had left the businesses to the tender mercies of managers.

The teacups were removed, and still we gossiped. For the first time for many years, I was among people who knew nothing about me and judged me by what they saw. Gwyn brought the lady in green over to us. She proved to be a schoolteacher, who had already been at Kent's Bank for a week. Emrys looked at a heavy gold pocket watch which he took out of his top pocket, suggested that we all go for a stroll in the grounds and then eat dinner at the same table. So, much to the amusement of the older people, I spent a happy half hour running about among the trees, trying to get close to one of the many squirrels, and arrived at the dinner table glowing with the fresh air and the happy anticipation of an adequate meal.

The staff who served the meal seemed to be accustomed to very hungry people, and I ate my way through three plates of meat and vegetables and two of pudding. Emrys, who had to keep his weight down, he said, leaned back in his chair and watched me speculatively, while Gwyn and Margaret, the schoolteacher, chipped me about how such a small person could find room for so much food.

Having lived so much with Grandma, I felt quite at home with older people. I lost my nervousness completely, my usual gauche manners gave way to the good conduct instilled in me as a child, and I felt so happy I thought I would explode. Emrys had a way of sitting quietly and giving complete and careful attention to what was said to him. He would run his tobacco-stained fingers through his thick, grey hair, worn rather longer than was then the fashion, and smile, and comment or argue carefully on any subject discussed with me, as if I was an adult whose ideas were important to him. I was unused to anyone giving me their full attention and if I had been less innocent, I might have been troubled at such affability. But as I responded to his good-humoured teasing I knew only a great gaiety and lightness of heart. A liveliness I did not know I had began to emerge.

The first two days of the holiday were taken up with long, organised walks in the countryside, broken in the middle by a picnic lunch. The guests were divided into two groups, those who could take very long walks and those who preferred easier ones. Since both Emrys and I had been ill, we chose the easier walks and Gwyn and his schoolteacher came along with us.

I now shared the bedroom with five mill girls from Rochdale. All of them had been ill and said frankly that they, too, were enjoying free holidays. They all had several changes of clothing and enough money to buy tickets for the bus trips, later in the week, and to purchase endless sweets and ice cream cones from the village shop. They ignored me, and kept up a raucous conversation amongst themselves. Though I had often heard foul language in the streets of Liverpool, I had never lived with people who used it, and I was frequently shocked and sickened by them. They also came on the easy walks, but fortunately stayed within their own group.

I danced along beside Emrys, through forest glades dappled with sunshine or along the sides of fields waving silvery green with growing oats. Occasionally, Gwyn would make us stop, while Emrys sat down to rest. He carried a piece of macintosh in his pocket and when a convenient wall or bench did not present itself, he spread the macintosh on the ground and sat on that. While he regained his breath, I would cast around, picking wild flowers or small sprays of fresh green foliage, which one of the staff would put in a vase on the dining table for me. Emrys did not know the names of many of the plants, but I had learned their names from Edith and was able to identify them for him.

Though I had handed to Mother three weeks' salary paid in advance, she had not seen fit to give me any money. I had only a few pennies in my purse, because I had spent most of the three weekly shillings on stockings. This made it impossible for me to buy tickets for the coach tour arranged for the third day.

Emrys and Gwyn had not yet come down to breakfast, so I ate the meal rather soberly in the company of Margaret and another middle-aged lady. Margaret was herself convalescing after a dose of influenza and we compared our respective illnesses and then talked about books.

'See you later,' she said gaily, and I nodded. I went up to the empty bedroom and wondered how to employ the day. I heard the arrival of the motor coach and the bustle of departure, as I sat with a copy of Lytton's

*Last Days of Pompeii* in my lap. I had already read the story twice and this seemed to hold true of all the books in the lounge downstairs. Finally, I tossed it aside. I would have a bath. I had tried several times since my arrival to do this, but the bathroom had invariably been occupied. Today, however, all the other guests had gone out so I could take my time about it.

The bath was a huge Victorian tub, left over from the time when the house had been a private home. I turned on its great brass taps and let the water thunder in until it was quite deep. There was a large, used tablet of soap in a wire basket stretched across the bath. Quickly I stripped off and stepped in.

This was the first bath I had had for four years and the water rippling across my stomach felt odd. I looked down at long, slender legs wavering beneath the water, at a stomach which stuck out too much like that of a hungry child, at surprisingly prominent young breasts, at arms so thin they looked like sticks. The skin was a dull yellow, almost bronze in places. I had not looked at myself properly since I was a child, in that long-ago world which we had left so precipitantly. As I soaked in the hot water, I remembered how Father had told his biggest creditor to sell up his house and its contents, and how he had walked out of it, allowing us to take nothing with us, except the clothing we were wearing and a blanket to cover his sick wife and newest child. He knew nothing of his rights to clothes and bedding, to the minima of existence. With this one quixotic gesture, he had deprived the family of all that even the most hopeless debtor was legally entitled to. His last money had been spent on train tickets to Liverpool, his home city, which did not want him.

I kneeled up in the water, dipped my head in and then soaped it thoroughly. Three times the brown locks were soaped and rinsed. Then the thin body was soaped until it looked like a snowman. The water was covered with grey soapsuds.

Like a dripping muskrat, I climbed out, emptied the bath and began to refill it.

The door burst open and a young, male member of the staff rushed in, pulling off his apron as he came. He was well into the huge bathroom before he realised that I was standing there naked, one hand on the brass tap.

He stopped, his startled face registering shock. Then he blushed hotly.

'I say, I am sorry!' he exclaimed, and turned and fled.

I was so used to being intruded upon by my brothers in a house where all washing had to be done in the kitchen that I was undisturbed. But I did for a moment wonder why he should be so flabbergasted. A girl in her skin was nothing special as far as I could see.

I repeated the scrubbing and, when I finally emerged from the bathroom, hair wrapped in a towel like a turban, I was scarlet from head to heel.

I drew back the net curtains and sat down by the window to dry my hair in the breeze. Such quietness enfolded me as I had not known before. Leisurely I combed the wet hair over my shoulders, and watched the sun glancing on the sea. I could smell the salt and, closer to hand, the pine trees in the garden. For the first time for years I had nothing to do. It was as if every nerve slowly loosened and relaxed. Three nights of deep, warm sleep and two days of stacks of food had helped to heal both mind and body.

I sat on the hard bedroom chair for a long time, the two rows of carelessly made beds behind me, the fine view framed by the window in front of me. My mind was empty. There was no past, no nagging family, nothing. No future, except the happy anticipation of welcoming Emrys Hughes and the other kindly guests when they returned, and then eating and eating and eating.

A train arriving at the nearby station roused me. I got up and went to the spotty mirror to arrange my hair in a bun again.

I peered short-sightedly at the image in the mirror and was surprised at what I saw. The hair, usually so straight because of its greasy coating, now waved softly down each side of the thin cheeks, its mousy brown carrying in it a rich red burnish. Surprised, I coaxed it into deeper waves.

From under smooth black brows, large green eyes, no longer bloodshot, stared sadly back at me. A few lumpy spots marred a complexion which was surprisingly white. I smiled cautiously at myself. The teeth were not straight and were tinged with yellow. I had scrubbed them well but I had no toothpaste. With newly awakened vanity, I decided I had a nice smile. I wondered if make-up would cover the spots, and then sighed because there was no money for such luxuries. Telling myself to stop playing Narcissus, I put my hair up, taking care, however, not to draw it back too tightly and spoil the waves.

Lunch was not served in the holiday home to guests, so I went without. It was probably as well, as it gave an over-taxed digestive system time to recuperate. I spent the rest of the day washing my spare blouse and panties and ironing them dry with an iron borrowed from the kitchen. Then I went for a long walk.

The lanes had all the bright greenery of June, but last year's leaves lay sodden at the bottom of puddles formed by overnight rain. They reminded me of winter.

I dreaded the winter. Another year of cold, sopping wet feet, of piercing wind, of long stone staircases to be climbed, of shivering in a freezing bed. Another winter, too, of incredible loneliness.

Fiona is growing up, I comforted myself. She will be company. Yet instinct told me that Fiona would never really communicate with me; she was too crushed, too determined never to be caught out of character, as a passive, pliable, inoffensive, obliging person, guaranteed not to answer back. The steel which I felt lay deep within her would be used for her own self-defence. She would crouch behind it, hiding any real feeling lest someone take offence. Just as I had been cast as a maiden aunt, she had been cast by my parents as a lovely girl who would make a good marriage which would help to raise the family again to its former stature. And yet, sometimes, I thought that Fiona might surprise my parents more than I ever could. As with the rest of the children, I could give Fiona love, but she was incapable of giving me friendship.

After my walk I tidied my windblown hair and then went down to the lounge. There was a number of women's magazines in a magazine rack and I curled up on a settee with these in excited anticipation.

Except for *Peg's Paper* which Edith had allowed me to read when I was small, I had not seen any women's magazines, and I soon was engrossed in enthralling stories in which the heroine was always blonde and invariably won the hero over the machinations of a dark, sultry villainess. The kisses were passionate.

# Chapter twenty-five

The bus disgorging a noisy crowd of returning guests put an end to my quiet day. I reluctantly uncurled myself from the settee and put down the magazine I had been reading. Emrys came puffing into the lounge, grey raincoat flying behind him, pipe aglow like a watchman's stove. He was followed more slowly by his brother, Gwyn.

'Why didn't you come?' he asked. 'We missed you, didn't we, Gwyn?'

Gwyn smiled kindly down at me. 'Yes, we did,' he assured me.

I went pink with embarrassment, and said, 'I thought I'd have a quiet day. Did you enjoy the trip?'

'I'd have enjoyed it a lot more if you had been there,' Emrys replied roundly, and playfully pinched my cheek.

Now I was blushing at the compliment. He evidently saw it as he struggled out of his coat, and laughed.

'Well, I've made sure you come on the other trips. Gwyn and I have bought tickets for all of 'em for you. Now you *have* to come.' He gusted with laughter, and Gwyn chuckled and said, 'Well, we hope you will.'

'That's immensely kind of you both,' I told them, laughing myself, because I could not help it.

While Gwyn helped Margaret off with her coat, Emrys stood in front of me, sturdy legs apart, while he struck matches to relight his pipe. He had told me that he was not supposed to smoke, but he could not give it up. As he gossiped about the lakes they had seen, I wondered what he would think if he saw my poverty-stricken home. Both brothers were obviously prosperous; both had gone to the prayer meeting held in the lounge each evening and both had joined earnestly in the prayers that were offered; kindness and thoughtfulness in small things was obvious in every move they made. They were very different from anybody I had ever met before. I could well imagine them behind their drapery shop counters, cheerfully and patiently dispensing everything from two pennyworth of buttons to forty yards of damask for curtains.

As the fortnight progressed, my friendship with Emrys deepened. I began to feel a real affection for the man, but such was my innocence that I never considered what he might be feeling. He was so much older than me.

Once, when he held my hand during a bus trip, some of the ladies saw it. They teased me and said I had made a conquest. This embarrassed me, because I felt that anybody could see I was incapable of conquering any man; I was too plain.

He never overstepped the bounds of propriety, however, and I never felt frightened with him. A couple of days before the holiday was due to end, he wrote out his home address for me, and said he hoped I would come to see him.

'My wife died three years ago,' he said simply. 'Gwyn and I keep house together in a flat over one of the shops. But my sister lives nearby, and you could stay with her.'

I doubted in my mind that I would ever manage to travel as far as North Wales, but the idea gave me much pleasure, and I said with genuine enthusiasm, 'I would love that.'

He looked at me very soberly for a moment, and then said, 'Would you?'

I nodded.

He grinned at me. 'Then we'll arrange it.'

On the last day of the holiday, we all went to see Cartmel Priory, and were ambling round the old church, behind our guide, when Emrys stopped suddenly and began to gasp for breath. He clutched his chest and turned and stumbled into a pew to sit down. The rest of the party had moved on ahead a little.

I leaned over the side of the pew and put my arm round his shoulder. 'What is it, Emrys?' But I knew what it was. I had seen it happen to Father when he was a young man. 'I'll get Gwyn. Just keep sitting.'

I ran over to Gwyn, and whispered to him. He spun round, at the same time taking a small bottle out of his jacket pocket. He fumbled in his top pocket as he ran back and produced a worn tin spoon.

He pushed into the pew, and asked me to support Emrys's head, while he poured out a colourless liquid and forced it into the gasping man's mouth. Some dribbled down Emrys's chin, but most went in. Then, after he had put the cork back into the bottle, he stuck it down on a pew shelf, while he rolled up his raincoat and made a pillow.

We laid Emrys along the pew seat, while the other guests, suddenly aware that something was wrong, came thronging anxiously over to us.

Slowly, Emrys's face lost some of its agony, the breathing became more normal. I crouched in the narrow space beside him and chafed his hands anxiously. Someone lent a coat to put over him. The verger was asked to telephone the guest house and arrange for a doctor to be called.

Emrys's eyes had been tight closed, but as he relaxed he opened them and looked at me. 'Helen.'

As soon as he felt he could bear to be moved, two men in the party made a seat with crossed hands and carried him into the bus and laid him down on the back seat. Gwyn cradled his head, and I knelt by him and held him, so that he did not fall off. He lay quietly.

The bus driver manoeuvred the bus very carefully over the narrow lanes, and as soon as we reached the guest house, two of the staff came running out with a wooden chair with arms. Emrys was lifted from the bus into the chair, despite mild protests that he thought he could walk. He was not a heavy man and the two young men made short work of carrying him up the stairs and into his room. He was closely followed by a doctor carrying a black bag and by his anxious brother. I stood forlornly at the bottom of the stairs, and then reluctantly went to my room to wash before dinner.

Everybody in the dining-room seemed to be talking about the fatal heart attacks they had witnessed, and I was very cast down, though Margaret did her best to cheer me up.

Gwyn did not come down to the meal, so when we had finished Margaret and I went into the hall and, after a moment's uncertainty on Margaret's part, went to the office to inquire if they had news.

We were told that while we were at dinner an ambulance had come and Mr Hughes and his brother had gone to a hospital in a nearby town. Margaret and I looked at each other, and then in silent consent went to the prayer meeting.

I did not sleep much. I was filled with a strange emotion such as I had not experienced before, a fear of the loss of a loved one.

The next morning, before breakfast, I plucked up enough courage to go myself to the office to inquire if they had news of Emrys. They had not, but the manager allowed me to use the telephone to inquire from the hospital how he was.

Mr Hughes was resting comfortably, I was told primly. He was not yet allowed visitors.

At breakfast I passed this information to Margaret. Despite my depression, I ate a huge breakfast and while still at table said goodbye to Margaret, because she had to leave immediately in order to catch her train home. I went up to the bedroom and silently put my few belongings back into their paper bag, while the turmoil of the packing being done by the five mill girls went on around me. There was a strong smell of dirty washing and violet perfume, and I was glad to escape.

I said goodbye to the staff and to several other guests, and caught the train back to Liverpool and to reality.

# Chapter twenty-six

The family were quite pleased to see me back and asked many questions, which I answered frankly. I told Mother about the Hughes brothers, and she made a little grimace with her mouth, and asked, 'They didn't touch you, did they?'

'Emrys held my hand,' I said.

She laughed in a deprecating way, and I was unaccountably incensed.

'They were very good to me,' I said defensively, and retreated to wash the dishes before I was provoked into saying more.

Such an excellent holiday gave me a lot more strength, and I formed the ambition of learning to type. The evening schools did not give courses in typing; my shorthand speed was rapidly increasing, but without a concomitant skill in typing, it was not much use to me.

I went to see Miriam in the attic. She very willingly allowed me to use her typewriter in the lunch hours and showed me how to manipulate the machine. She saved wastepaper so that I could use the back of it for practising. The three typists crammed into the little room took turns in instructing me how to set out letters, agendas and minutes. The head typist also showed me how to use the big Gestetner duplicating machine with its huge tubes of very black, very sticky ink.

Emrys was constantly in my mind and I daily hoped for a letter to say he was well again. But there was none. I told myself that I was such a small, unimportant person that perhaps I had been only someone to amuse him while he recuperated from his earlier heart attack. But I would see him again in my mind's eye, teasing, talking, laughing with me, and thus reassure myself that we had been really good companions and a true friendship had been formed.

At the end of the month, I plucked up courage, took a piece of copy paper from Miriam's store and, one lunch hour, wrote to the address he had given me, to inquire how he was.

Again, I began to watch for a letter, but still there was nothing. My new-found strength began to fade under the constant pressure of work at home, work at the office, work at night school, and the everlasting hunger. I fell into a quiet depression and found it hard to concentrate on my studies.

One hot sultry August day, when I arrived home to find the family, as usual, just finishing their evening meal, I was greeted by Mother with the information that my friend had died. She said it not unkindly, as she tossed an open letter across the table to me.

I slowly turned back into the hall and hung up my hat and coat. I did not want to touch the letter; I did not want to have the shocking news confirmed. I stood panting in the hall trying not to cry. People did not die; they got better from heart attacks, didn't they?

Mother was saying, 'Have a look at your letter.'

Reluctantly I picked it up. First I looked at the signature. Gwyn Hughes.

It began, 'Dear little Helen' and for a second I was tripping along beside a rushing river, and Emrys was saying, 'Be careful, little Helen. Don't fall in.'

Gwyn apologised for not writing to me earlier, but he had had so much to do that it was only now that he was able to attend to his personal correspondence.

Emrys had recovered sufficiently from his heart attack for the hospital doctor to say that he could make the journey back to Wales in a private car, if they broke the journey frequently enough for him to rest. At the moment of leaving the hospital, he had been stricken by another massive attack which had taken his life. His body had been taken home and had been buried beside those of his wife and his son, who had died when he was twelve.

Gwyn was sorry to have to send me such bad news. My companionship had been a great pleasure to both of them, and Emrys had been determined not to let the friendship lapse. He was going to write to me as soon as he returned to Wales.

With quivering hands, I put the letter back in the envelope. I was too shaken to complain about the letter's being opened. All I wanted to do was to go to bed and rest, shut myself out of life for a while.

Brian and Tony, those great companions, were staring at me uneasily. Probably death frightened them, too.

I smiled wryly at them. 'He was quite old,' I reassured them. 'It was natural.'

'I'm sorry,' said Father. 'They sound like very nice people. Very kind.'

I put the letter in my handbag. 'I will write to thank him,' I said.

'You should,' said Mother. 'Come and have your tea, dear.'

Fiona silently gave up her chair to me, and Alan passed over the bread and margarine. Mother brought me a small plate of lettuce and cold meat. For the first time that I could remember, I was aware of an aura of kindly sympathy throughout the family. Very slowly, in a dazed way I began to eat.

# Chapter twenty-seven

I knew Emrys Hughes for only two weeks, but he left me a legacy which changed my whole life. He taught me that I was worthy of love and respect. He revealed to me that, given normal circumstances, I could be a cheerful, merry companion. He gave me self-respect, a belief in myself. This change in attitude did not reveal itself immediately because I was locked into circumstances beyond my control. But it was there, tucked away in the back of my mind to give me strength of purpose when the time came.

The raunchy cotton mill girls had also done something for me. I had not at first understood their conversation, because I did not know the words they used, but constant repetition soon made their meanings clear. They talked of nothing but sex, and their lurid discussions soon knitted together for me much that I knew subconsciously before. Then the reading of a great number of files and observation of the prostitutes in the streets greatly added to my understanding. One is supposed to be shaken by such revelations, but it all seemed quite normal to me and I accepted it without being disturbed. Perhaps because I was so starved, I had almost no feelings myself. My days were choked with work that had to be done, giving little time for contemplation of anything other than the next essay to be written, the next cup of tea to be provided.

I did not think of sex in connection with Emrys Hughes. He was a dear person, very careful of me, and I gave him the same kind of affection that I gave my grandmother, uninhibited and unthinking. Only years later, in the ripeness of womanhood, I realised that he might well have fallen for an innocent slip of a girl. He would not have been the first man to love someone thirty years younger than himself. But that last fortnight of his life was not wasted. It enriched mine immeasurably.

One of the more understanding ladies dressed in green overalls was a psychologist, a Mrs Croft, and, unlike the others, she would sometimes talk to me when I took her in a cup of tea at a time when she had no client with her. She knew that I attended night school and was learning shorthand. She asked me if I could teach another girl this subject.

The girl lived too far from the city to attend evening school. She could, however, take a lesson immediately upon finishing work and before going

256

home. I could use Mrs Croft's husband's office as a place to give the lesson, and could charge about one shilling and sixpence each time.

So once a week, on an evening when there was no night school, I went to Mr Croft's office for an hour and gave a lesson to a languid, uninterested girl a little older than myself, while the cleaning staff mopped and dusted round us.

Probably because I was not a very good teacher, the girl quickly lost interest. But I earned enough money to enable me to put an advertisement in the *Liverpool Echo*, and acquire another pupil. A boy of about sixteen, suffering from epilepsy, asked to be taught at home. He was a very different kind of person, eager and enthusiastic. He practised assiduously and, by the time his parents moved with him to a milder climate, he was writing steadily at forty words per minute.

My parents approved of this tutoring, though Mother grumbled because I would not be available to help until late in the evening. I said that I proposed to keep the one shilling and sixpence a week that I was earning, towards buying lunches and some clothes.

At first, Mother frequently borrowed what I made, by riffling through my handbag and taking the money out. She never considered it necessary to pay it back. Finally, I made a stout little cotton bag to hold the precious pennies, and hung it round my neck by a piece of string. Once a week, I went to Woolworth's cafeteria at lunchtime and bought a threepenny bowl of excellent soup and a roll. It was a treat to look forward to.

Before I thought of keeping my teaching money in a bag round my neck, and had managed to accumulate a few shillings, the shoes I had worn on holiday got to a point where there was so little sole left that I could not keep the pieces of cardboard from falling out. Finding shoes for all the children must have been a nightmare for Mother, and the best she could do for me was to give me her summer sandals which still had a little wear in them.

I woke up one morning to a black city suddenly made into a wonderland by an early fall of snow. I spent my last penny on a tram to work, but still my feet were sopping wet and freezing before I arrived at the office.

I sat down in the office kitchen, took off the sandals and wiped them with the floor cloth. Then I rubbed the stockinged toes with the same cloth.

The letters for hand delivery that morning were fortunately all for nearby offices, and I was just about to set out with them when the Cashier sent for me.

This forbidding lady always frightened me and she was not in the best of moods. She had a letter to be delivered to the Dental Hospital about a mile and a quarter away. It was still snowing, so I asked if I might take the tram.

'No,' she snapped. 'We haven't any money to waste on tram fares.'

By the time the local letters had been delivered, the snow was nearly up to my ankles and I was in real pain. Before setting out for the long trudge up the hill to the Dental Hospital, I sat down on an office stairway, took off the sandals and knocked the snow out of them, then brushed off the ice clinging to the stockings. I was weeping, and I wondered if I took the letter back to the office and refused to deliver it, I would be dismissed.

I decided that I probably would lose the job, and I dreaded this more than anything else. So up the hill I went through almost deserted streets, delivered the letter, and came down again at a stumbling run, crying all the way with pain in my feet. I envied Alan the new pair of shoes that had recently been bought for him. But he also got his feet wet that day.

Back at the office, I stripped off shoes and stockings, filled a sink with water and, teetering on one toe, plunged each foot in turn into the hot water. Then I tried to dry them on the roller towel, an impossible feat. So I left a trail of water leading to the kitchen, while I went to dry them on the floor cloth.

As I put on the wet stockings again, I began to laugh shakily at the idea of the Presence surprising me with one foot caught in a roller towel. She was kind enough that, had she known about it, she would probably have been very upset at my being sent so far in such bad weather.

I was still shivering as I ran to make the tea and then fled up and down the eternal stone steps to deliver it, but probably the exercise helped to restore the circulation. I was left with only a very bad cold.

That lunchtime, Miriam offered to lend me a portable typewriter for a week, so that I could practise at home. She was a member of the Communist Party and did all she could to attract other members. Another of the stenographers was an equally ardent member of the Roman Catholic Church and also keen on converts. So between the two of them, I received a lot of attention. Life was such a struggle for me, however, that I had neither time nor strength to consider their arguments and remained totally uncommitted.

The loan of the typewriter was most kindly meant and I wanted to hug Miriam in gratitude. She brought it to the office the next day and I took it home, with some scrap paper, and put it in the empty front room. The children all wanted to try it, but I told them it had to be taken special care of because it was on loan. I joyfully practised far into the night, much to the irritation of Father, who could not sleep because of the steady tapping. I was myself always short of sleep, because I did my homework in the early mornings before the family got up, or late at night after they had gone to bed, provided that there was a penny to put in the gas meter to obtain light, or a stump of candle.

When I had finished my long practice, I returned the typewriter to the safety of the front room, put a penny from my handbag into the gas meter ready for the morning and crept up to bed. I was filled with hope that a good typing speed would help me to get a better job.

# Chapter twenty-eight

The following evening I had to go to night school, so I was too busy to practise on the typewriter. On the third evening, I hurried through my work and then ran into the empty front room to fetch the machine.

There was no typewriter.

Perplexed, I looked in a built-in cupboard by the fireplace, but it held only the gas meter.

Mystified, I went back into the living room, where Mother was sitting by the fire reading the newspaper. Edward and Avril were playing on the coconut matting, squabbling over a few cigarette cards they had found.

'Mummy, did you move the typewriter from the front room?'

Mother looked up with studied casualness, and I knew instinctively that something was wrong.

'Yes, I did,' she said carefully.

'Well, where did you put it?' I asked impatiently. 'I want to practise.'

'It is not here.' Her cultivated voice was without expression.

The fearful apprehension in which I spent most of my life suddenly reached swamping proportions.

'Mother! What have you done with it? You haven't sold it, have you?'

'No.' She was looking at me with a kind of lazy indifference. I felt as if she had me impaled on a pin and that in the back of her mind she was enjoying the situation. My childish belief that parents always did the best they could for their offspring had long since vanished, and I was very frightened.

'Mother,' I whispered. 'What *have* you done with it? Are you teasing me – joking?'

'I never joke,' said Mother, and I realised that that was true.

She got up from her chair with a slow graceful movement, walked past me and into the hall. Through the open door, I watched her leisurely put on her hat and then her coat.

'Where is it, Mother?'

'In pawn.'

'Oh, my God! For how much?'

'Three pounds.'

I gasped. 'But I've got to return it in a couple of days!'

'Oh, don't worry. I'll get it out in due course.' She turned towards the front door.

'By Friday?'

'Oh, I doubt that.'

'Oh, Mummy!'

'Don't be so melodramatic,' she fumed irritably, as she opened the front door. 'You must make an excuse to keep it another week. It's time Avril and Edward were put to bed.'

The cold was thick in my head and my throat was so sore and constricted that I could hardly ask the next question.

'What shall I do if Miriam says she needs the machine?'

She snapped back angrily, 'That's your headache. You should be able to manage something like that.'

I stared speechlessly at her as she stepped out on to the pavement, slamming the front door after her. All the horrors that could possibly befall me if the machine was not returned flew through my head. Accusations of theft, of court proceedings, loss of my job. I could tell Father, but what could he do? He had no money to speak of.

There was no one to help me. I wished that the dirty, linoleumed floor would open up and swallow me, so that I did not have to face poor Miriam.

My terror was so great that it blotted out everything else. I failed to hear instructions given to me in the office, and was constantly in trouble for forgetting small errands which the filing clerks pressed upon me. I forgot to take a voluntary worker a cup of tea. I accidentally put a 'By Hand' letter into the post box; the firm it was addressed to telephoned to complain about having to pay the postage. I carried a big tea tray carelessly through a doorway and knocked the spouts off two teapots. I stood, appalled, while tea gushed all over the floor, and the Cashier ranted that I would have to pay for new teapots. I nearly laughed at her. At night school, I sat at my desk and saw and heard nothing. The essays and assignments set me remained undone.

'Whatever is the matter, Helen?' each teacher, in turn, demanded testily.

Miriam reluctantly agreed to allow me to keep the typewriter for another week.

At home, I moved like a zombie through the usual routine of baby-sitting, shopping, cooking, cleaning, washing, ironing. The children were used to my being quiet, except when embroiled in a fight with my parents or a rare spat with Alan or Fiona, so I doubt if they noticed much change. Father lived in his dream world, went most evenings to the library and on Saturday and Sunday went out for a drink with a colleague. I saw no point in asking Father's help; it would spark another family row. Only Mother knew, and she made no reply when I pestered her to redeem the machine.

I had never considered that children might love their mothers. I always feared mine.

I think that sometimes, when I was little, Mother felt guilty at pushing me on to Grandma or to Edith, and it was then that she would send for me. She would listen to my reading or give me a sweet and ask me about school. But she did not really hear me when I replied, and I would thankfully rush back to Edith or close my eyes and look forward to the next visit to Grandma's house.

At the end of the second week, Miriam said she needed the typewriter. Her rich brown crown of shining hair swung round her pixie-like face, as she looked up at me with such a friendly grin that I wanted to cry.

'I'll bring it in on Monday,' I promised, my voice strained with the cold and sheer terror.

At home, Father was out, and I had a fearsome row with Mother to no purpose, and retired to bed crying hysterically.

On Tuesday, Miriam, her expression a little puzzled, inquired again.

I apologised for forgetting to bring the machine in the rush of getting to work. On Thursday and Friday, I muttered the same apologies. She just nodded and looked curiously and unsmilingly at me. Undoubtedly, she had begun to worry about her prized possession.

I was saved from having to face her on Saturday morning. One Saturday each month was free, and I stayed at home and did the washing.

Dressed in an old cotton frock, I was carefully washing my work skirt in the kitchen sink when there was a polite rap on the iron door knocker.

Mother was cutting bread and margarine for tea, so, with hands still dripping, I went into the empty front room and peeped through the piece of net curtaining we had pinned across the windows.

Standing on the pavement looking up at the decrepit brick house was Miriam.

I flitted back to the kitchen.

'Mother!' I whispered in a panic. 'It's Miriam! She must have come for the typewriter. What am I going to do?'

Mother looked up from her bread cutting, knife poised in mid-air.

'Don't answer the door,' she said simply.

'But she must have come all the way over from the north end of town specially.'

'I said, "don't answer".'

I wrung my hands, as I hissed back, 'But, Mummy . . .'

She was implacable. 'Don't answer.'

I was panting with fright and stared at her helplessly for a minute. Then I said angrily in a normal voice, 'I *will* answer. I can't bear it any more. I will tell her exactly what has happened.' My voice rose in hysteria. 'I just can't endure it any longer.'

Fiona, the only other person at home, came in from the lavatory in the back yard. She stared at us in scared apprehension.

Miriam rapped again, louder. I started for the living-room through which I would have to pass to reach the front passage.

'Oh, no, my lady.' Mother dropped her knife, swiftly slammed the door and put her foot against it. She glared at me. 'How dare you?'

I stopped. I wanted to strike her to make her move, but it was so alien to me that I could not.

In a fever of fear, I shouted, 'I will tell them in the office on Monday and then they will know you stole it.'

Mother went white. 'You would not dare to tell such a lie,' she retorted, as the knocker sounded once again.

But I did not care what happened, as long as the intolerable burden was removed from me, and I replied determinedly, 'It is not a lie and I certainly would dare.'

'All right. I will speak to Miriam. You remain here.' She was bristling with anger.

She opened the living-room door and marched through to the front of the house.

I clung to the kitchen table, hardly able to stand, while the sound of the front door opening and then Mother's delicate voice echoed through the house.

Mother and Miriam had not met before, so Miriam first explained who she was and then asked politely if she could have the machine back, because she had some work to do on it. Mother said enthusiastically how delighted she was to meet her and how grateful she was for her kindness to me. I closed my eyes and prayed, wondering what she would say next.

The well-bred voice was explaining that she herself had ventured to use the machine yesterday. Unfortunately, one of the letters had fallen off and needed soldering on again, so she had taken it up to town to have it repaired.

'Oh, dear,' exclaimed Miriam. 'Where did you take it?'

'Um, you know that place on Dale Street? I took it there. They said it would be ready on Tuesday.'

Miriam sounded very relieved as she replied, 'Oh, that's not too bad. I could pick it up myself.'

Mother's voice chimed in with measured charm. 'Oh, I won't hear of it. I must pay for it. I will arrange for Helen to bring it into the office on Wednesday. I am so sorry that up to now she has been so delinquent about returning it. I will make sure that this time she does not forget.'

There was a mumble of polite, friendly argument, then goodbyes were said, and the front door was softly closed.

I was so shaken that I wanted to vomit.

'What was that about?' asked Fiona, as she took her skipping rope off a hook on the back door.

I did not reply for a moment, and then I said wearily, 'It's so complicated, Fi, I can't explain it. But everything is O.K. now.'

# Chapter twenty-nine

Mother had barely shut the front door when the string on the latch was pulled and the door again swung open. Brian and Tony came bursting in from playing football in the street. They were excited because it had begun to snow heavily, and they thought that later on they might be able to make a snowman. They were followed almost immediately by Avril and Baby Edward, who had toddled down to Granby Street together, to buy a pint of milk; the milkman had refused to deliver any more until his bill was paid. Giggling together triumphantly, they handed me the bottle.

Since the children were there, Mother said nothing to me, but, as she picked up the bread knife again, her contemptuous look spoke volumes. Feeling wretched, I returned to the sinkful of washing.

As I was hanging the garments over a piece of string strung across the kitchen, Father and Alan came through the back door, laughing and shaking the snow off themselves.

I must tell Daddy, I thought. I simply have to. But not now, because of the children. Mother will turn on me, the minute I open my mouth. But three pounds is a huge sum to raise. How does Mother imagine she is going to do it?

Mother was very quiet during tea. By silent consent nothing was said about Miriam before the children.

I had to give a shorthand lesson that evening, so immediately after tea I prepared a protesting Edward for bed. I borrowed Fiona's macintosh from her to put over my cotton dress, because my skirt was not dry and my own very light macintosh was neither windproof nor waterproof. I would have to talk to Daddy in the morning. With a quick glance at the clock, I snatched up my shorthand books and ran to catch a tram outside the Rialto Cinema. To reach my pupil's home, it was necessary to take a tram to the Pier Head and another one out again to his district. There was no question of being able to walk the distance in a reasonable time.

The snow was coming down in great fleecy flakes and my feet were soaked before I reached the end of our street. The bright lights of the cinema seemed to be floating amid the flakes, and a drift was forming across its curved front steps. The clumsy trams looked like glittering ghosts as they churned their way slowly along Catherine Street. Few people were about, and for a second I considered turning back. But I needed money so badly that when my tram arrived, I swung on to it without hesitation.

'Lousy night,' remarked the conductor as I tendered the fare.

At the Pier Head, the wind was driving the snow in whirling sweeps across the stone sets, almost obliterating the Royal Liver Building and the squat Cunard Building. The Church of our Lady and St Nicholas was lost amid the white downpour. As if from nowhere, the sounds of the foghorns and the harsh bells to guide the ferry boats came floating round my head. One or two shadowy people scurried past me.

Surrounding the tram superintendent was a tight knot of drivers and conductors, red ears sticking out from navy blue caps and glowing cigarettes drooping from their mouths. They were arguing about stopping the service. I was shivering, and clutched the macintosh collar round my neck to stop the snow trickling down inside, as I waited for their decision. The wind from the river seemed to penetrate my bones.

The superintendent vanished in search of the telephone.

I blew my nose on a square of newspaper, then shoved my bare hands into my mac pockets in an effort to keep them from freezing. The heavy flakes clung to my hair and I brushed a rosette of snow off my bun. The drivers and conductors climbed back into their respective trams to get out of the wind. I did not dare to follow one of them for fear I missed my own tram, which had not yet arrived.

Long before I saw the tram I needed, I could hear the driver pinging its bell with one foot, as he edged the great vehicle slowly round the curve of Mann Island. Between the sharp pings of the bell came the sound of the slap of the river water around the floating dock behind me, the sound of the Mersey which lay between Grandma and me. For a moment, I felt like chancing my tram fares on a ferry fare instead and running away to her.

'Don't be a fool,' I told myself sharply. 'You haven't got the fare for the bus on the other side – and an eight-mile walk in this storm is impossible.'

The supervisor, bustling with importance, came towards the newly arrived tram. The driver stepped down to meet him; he did not want to take the tram out again. The supervisor irately pointed out that on his return journey he normally picked up men coming off a night shift in an outlying factory. After some argument, the driver reluctantly climbed on to his platform, and I thankfully clambered into the back, shaking myself like a collie dog. I sat down on the wooden bench which ran the whole length of the car, bent over and lifted an almost solid crown of snow from the top of my head. It splashed all over the ridged floor as I dropped it. The interior of the vehicle was comfortingly warm, but I continued to shiver and my feet were bitterly cold. I was the only outgoing passenger and I stared glumly at the empty bench opposite, until the conductor came to collect my fare.

265

The driver slammed open the intervening door, letting in a great gust of snow-laden air. He shouted down the length of the car to the conductor that they would be lucky if they saw their beds that night. He was not going to be responsible if the bloody tram got stuck; he'd told the bastard back there that they would never make it up the hill. These remarks did not cheer me up. The tram was already far behind schedule and I would be very late for the lesson.

At Pembroke Place the points of the track were solid with ice and did not yield to the driver's poking at them with a metal bar. The conductor climbed down and a committee of two was held over them. Then, shaking themselves free of snow, they climbed back in again. The driver eased the brake off and let the tram roll slowly backwards down the hill for a few yards. Then he took the line up London Road. We were off the proper route, but not so far that I would not be able to run to my pupil's house.

As we crawled along, the thin, underclad conductor came into the body of the tram and closed the back door. He sat in the far corner from me, silently smoking cigarette after cigarette.

I was heavy with the cold which I had caught nearly three weeks earlier and had failed to shake off. As the chill from my waiting at the Pier Head wore off, I gradually began to feel stiflingly hot, and I almost envied the driver out in the wind. My head ached abominably and I laid it against the cold windowpane and closed my eyes. I suffered greatly from headaches, partly, I think, from eye strain, so another one was nothing to worry about.

After what seemed an interminable time of grinding noise as the tram laboured onwards, I was jerked awake. The tram had stopped. The lights were still on and the motor was throbbing.

The driver pushed open his door and came in, puffing and blowing, his face nearly purple between his peaked cap and great muffler. The conductor looked up.

The driver addressed me.

'Can't go no further, miss,' he announced.

'God spare us,' exclaimed the conductor, and threw his cigarette butt angrily on to the floor. 'Where are we?' he asked.

I picked up my wet shorthand books from beside me, as the driver replied, 'West Derby Road, near Green Lane. I thought I could work my way round, like, to me proper route. But I couldn't turn at Shiel Road like I hoped. Had no luck at all. And now there's two abandoned trams on the track ahead of us. I can't see no sign of drivers or conductors.'

West Derby Road! I was miles from where I should have been and at least three miles from home. I looked in alarm at the two men discussing what they should do. They seemed to be fuzzy round the edges. I got up from the seat. My legs wobbled, and I sat down again quickly. I was suddenly afraid of the bitter cold outside.

The driver said, 'We'd better all get home as best we can. If I can find a phone box on the way, I'll phone the boss to say where the tram is.' He took off his big scarf as he spoke, and shook a shining cascade of snow off it. 'Could try taking the bloody thing in in the morning, when I'll be able to see better.'

Trams can be driven from either end. They do not have to be turned, so I asked, 'Couldn't you drive it back again to the Pier Head?'

'What for, luv? There's nothing there but wind and water.'

The conductor peered ineffectually through a bit of window he had rubbed clear of steam. 'Snow's so deep, we'd probably stick anyway. Best get home, like you say.'

I nodded and the pain jabbed through my head. How was I to find my way through a maze of narrow streets, snow-choked and deserted? Yet there seemed nothing else to do. Once the driver turned off the power, the tram would quickly become very cold indeed.

'Do you know how I can get to the Rialto Cinema?' I asked.

They looked at me appalled. 'Eee, you do have a way to go,' exclaimed the driver.

Again, a committee of two was formed. The driver lived in Holt Road, the conductor in Old Swan, which in normal circumstances was no great walk from where we were stranded. The conductor decided to leave us. He turned up his overcoat collar, said 'Ta-ra, well,' very dolefully, cautiously stepped down into the street and plodded away into the night.

The driver, sighing heavily, decided to drive the tram back along the route he had come to the nearest point to his home street or until the vehicle stalled. This would help me, too, and he said he could direct me home from where he lived. He floundered outside again and succeeded with difficulty in reversing the trolley on the overhead wires, and then heaved himself into the rear of the tram to drive it.

He left the communicating door slightly ajar, so that he could talk to me, and I moved up to the end of the bench closest to it. We sailed slowly down the same side of the street up which we had travelled. I hoped we would not hit another vehicle which might be coming towards us. There seemed, however, to be no other thing moving in the city, and our tram finally refused to go any further after reaching Shiel Road.

The driver slammed the vehicle's doors shut, and took my arm. Together we struggled on foot along Shiel Road, while the wind blew the snow into our faces, down our necks and up our coat sleeves. The driver had boots, an overcoat, a cap, a scarf and gloves. I had on a cotton dress, a macintosh and a second-hand pair of walking shoes which I had bought from the pawnbroker for two shillings. My head and hands were bare, and rayon stockings did not offer much protection. I was also very thin, with no proper layer of fat to help ward off the cold. I regretted bitterly ever having set out.

By the time we found the driver's brick terrace house, with his wife peeping anxiously through the tiny bay window, the wind had eased and the snow was thinning.

His wife invited me in to rest and shelter for a while, but my mind seemed to be fogged up and all I could think about was the desperate need to get home and into bed. Stupidly, I said that the snow was easing and I could manage to walk home.

She nodded doubtfully at me, as her husband stamped about behind her in the narrow hallway, and she closed the door slowly as I moved away.

Durning Road to Tunnel Road, from dim gas lamp to dim gas lamp, alternately freezing and perspiring, I struggled on, through totally deserted streets. This was not a district of private cars, but here and there a van or truck had been abandoned and snowdrifts were rising round them. Each windowsill I passed had a neat traycloth of snow on it, each doorstep its unbroken drift.

I was beginning to think that I would have to knock at the nearest door and ask for shelter when I suddenly found myself at the junction of Upper Parliament Street and Smithdown Road. And through the unearthly silence, came unexpectedly the distant rumble of a tram. I looked quickly down Smithdown Road from where the sound seemed to come. I saw the electricity spit and its reflection flash across the snow as its trolley crossed a wire. I half stumbled, half ran towards it.

The driver – there was no conductor – was astonished to have a passenger suddenly emerge from the storm. He stopped, and let me on through the front of the tram.

'Eh, miss. You must be frozen. Where you tryin' to get to?'

'The Rialto,' I gasped, as I felt down my chest and eased out my little money bag, to get a penny from it. A pain like a knife wound was shooting through my back and my throat was swelling in its old threatening manner.

'Eh, you don't have to pay t' fare,' he said, through the slightly ajar front door, near which I had thankfully taken a seat. 'I'm trying to get that far for me own sake. I got a flat in Catherine. But I reckon points will be frozen, so I won't be able to turn.' He jerked his head to indicate the way he had come, and added, 'It was bloody awful back there. I let me conductor off by his house.'

I nodded dumbly. In the warmth of the tram, my head was whirling as the snowflakes had been, and all I could think about was home.

The snow had stopped when, about fifteen minutes later, I pulled the string on our door latch and stumbled in, into my father's arms.

# Chapter thirty

I have a dim remembrance of Father rolling off my stockings in front of the fire and putting my feet into a basin of lukewarm water, to restore the circulation; of Mother holding a cup of scalding hot tea to my lips, and of being surprised at the anxiety in her pale blue eyes. Then I was in bed with Edward's hot water bottle pressed to my back and Father was cursing as he tried to make a fire in the bedroom fireplace.

Faces came and went in the candlelight. Or was it sunlight? Medicine was forced down my throat, a poultice applied to my back. Fiona helped to hold me on a chamberpot placed on the bed. Once it seemed to me that Edith was there and I called out to her, but she faded away. I dreamed that Minerva came down from her seat on the top of the town hall and shook her spear at me for being so foolish. Then there was a great nightmare during which I was arguing with the pawnbroker about the return of the typewriter. I kept shouting at him that he must give it to me because it was stolen property. I had long spasms of coughing, when all of me seemed racked with aches and pains. I was dreadfully hot and kept throwing off the bedclothes, but they were always tucked round me again.

Then, quite suddenly, I was shivering in the light of the pale Liverpool sun coming through the bedroom window. My feet were sticking out from under the coverings, and I pulled them up close to me. The movement sent a shooting pain through them. A cold hot water bottle lay at my side and I tried to push it away, but somehow my hands would not obey so I lay still.

After a little while, I opened my eyes again and turned my head. A small fire was smouldering in the grate, and in the double bed on the other side of the room lay Brian. He was tucked up tightly in a pile of bedding and coats. His hair stuck up like the hairs of a shaving brush and the face beneath was yellow with two bright red spots on the cheekbones.

I tried to ask him what had happened, but when I moved, such a pain shot through my head from both ears, and my throat seemed so swollen, that I barely got the first word out.

He seemed to understand, and one small, chilblained hand crept out of his covering and he pointed to his throat. He managed a wry little smile.

Mother came slowly in. Her feet dragged as she came over to me. Without make-up and without her hair combed, she looked faded and pinched. She must have been exhausted, after having two invalids to care for, particularly since I would normally have taken a lot of the load from her.

She saw with obvious relief that I was awake. To allay the pain, I lay perfectly still while she put her hand on my forehead to check the temperature.

'How are you feeling?'

I tried to smile. 'Ears hurt – and throat and legs,' I croaked. 'Brian?'

Mother nodded. 'He has quinsy, poor boy. He is going into hospital this afternoon, to have it cut.' The lines on her face deepened. Brian was one of her favourite children.

'Where is he going?'

'The Ear, Nose and Throat Hospital.'

Very carefully, I turned my face towards the other bed. Despite his illness, Brian's eyes crinkled up cheerfully at me.

For a long time, I lay looking at the cracked, grey ceiling, trying not to weep with weakness and pain, because crying only constricted the already painfully tight throat. Mother brought both Brian and me a cup of tea and supported us in turn as we drank.

The doctor came in the afternoon and dispatched Brian, still stoically cheerful, in an ambulance to the hospital. Then he turned to me.

'I was beginning to think I'd have to send you in, too,' he said, as he probed round my neck with his fingers.

I smiled weakly. 'What have I had?'

'You've had a nasty attack of bronchitis – in fact, it is still with you – but I think you will mend now. You also managed a bad dose of flu. And now we have to tackle your throat and ears.'

I nodded, while he took a camel-hair brush out of his bag and a bottle of tannic acid, so that he could paint my throat. After he had done that, he put drops in both ears. He was very gentle, his handsome young face filled with concern. Afterwards, I learned that he did not charge for his visits to Brian, since he was already in the house to see me. Brian's hospital stay would be covered by charitable contributions to the hospital, he told Mother. He came every day, twice, to paint my throat and check my ears.

All I could eat for a while was a cup of Oxo with bread mashed into it or a cup of tea, but I slept a lot.

Two days after my delirium left me, I remembered Miriam's typewriter. I lay sobbing quietly for hours in great fear about it, while Mother did an afternoon stint in a department store.

Father was home first. I had heard Fiona come in, followed by the other children, but she was making the tea, judging by the sounds that floated up the stairs, and had not come to see me. Father came straight upstairs and still had his hat in his hand as he sat down on the bed, careful not to shake me.

'Well, how's my girl?'

'Not bad,' I whispered.

He patted my hand, and I asked him eagerly, 'Daddy, do you know about the typewriter?'

He looked grim, as he said that he did.

'Were you able to get it back? Has Miriam got it?' It seemed as if my whole life hung on the answer.

He gave a little snort, with a hint of laughter in it. 'Yes, dear. She has.'

'Thank God,' I muttered. 'Thank God.' The burden was off me.

He sat staring sombrely at the empty fireplace – we had run out of coal. After a minute, I asked huskily how he had done it.

'Well, your mother had applied for a five-pound cheque to buy some clothes for the boys – and the finance company granted it. So we bought everything we could on it and pawned the lot. And we didn't pay the rent, so that made enough. Your mother took the machine into the office – and I understand that Miriam was very nice to her.' He sighed heavily, and then said, 'Don't worry any more. You should have told me immediately it happened. I doubt if I would have known about it at all if you had not shouted your head off over it while you were in delirium.' He looked down at me and laughed suddenly. 'There was quite a rumpus.'

I could imagine the row there must have been between Mother and him, and I grinned back at him.

'And I was out of it all,' I chuckled. My throat hurt and I stopped suddenly. 'It's a dreadful load of debt.'

'Nothing new,' he said, with the same sort of optimism that Alan sometimes displayed. 'You are not to worry. Just get well.'

'How long have I been ill?' I asked.

'Eight days.'

'When can I get up?'

'It will be some time yet.'

I laughed again, this time a little more carefully. 'Fiona still has to hold me on the chamberpot – so I suppose it will be a while.' Then I began to cough and to wince with pain in my chest and head. The smoke from his cigarette had got into my throat.

One day, the doctor asked Mother to refrain from smoking in the bedroom. She was very offended and railed against him as soon as he had gone. He had also lectured her on the necessity for getting some weight back on to both Brian's and my wasted bodies. He ordered cream, butter, potatoes, fresh vegetables, liver and eggs – and rest, lots of rest and fresh air for both of us.

Mother listened, and bowed her head politely from time to time, as he urged her quite passionately to stuff us with food. But when she had quietly closed the front door on him and had returned to the bedroom to give me a dose of cough mixture, she first fumed about his rudeness in asking her not to smoke, and then said crossly, 'And where does he think I will get the money from for cream?'

Tears of weakness forced themselves through crunched-up eyelids, as I lay back on the pillow. I remembered the slice of bread for breakfast, the lack of lunch until I had managed to buy myself a bowl of soup or a roll and butter, the tiny plate of dinner kept from the hot meal Mother made either at lunchtime or teatime, according to her work schedule. She did not eat much herself, but I was still growing; my needs were at least as great as Fiona's. I thought of Alan, able to go to the cinema on the strength of his pocket money, of the lunch he carried each day, of his new shoes and his tram fares. Why could not I have had the same?

And the answer seemed obvious. Because you are a girl old enough to be more useful at home than at work; a girl, moreover, whose very existence was resented from the day of her birth.

People, least of all parents, do not analyse their attitudes to children; and I am sure Father and Mother saw me only as a recalcitrant, disobedient offspring who had to be brought to heel. Their lives had been ruined and they were too exhausted to think their children's problems through. Mother used quantities of aspirin to sedate herself and Father, when he got the chance, vanished off for a drink. And they both smoked incessantly. They had neither time nor inclination to give sober, careful thought to what was happening to me.

Mother did, however, begin to bring me plenty of bread and margarine and big bowls of porridge with a little sugar and milk. But a great lassitude enveloped me. After a few mouthfuls, the throat seemed choked and I could not eat any more. Frequent small helpings were difficult for her to arrange because she worked a half-day on most weekdays, and she was herself tired to death.

Fiona helped me to use the chamberpot and she and Mother washed me. At first I accepted these attentions with about as much response as a rag doll would give. Then, as I grew a little stronger, the wells of gratitude were loosed and I would thank them effusively for every service, however small.

I began to worry that such a long absence would mean dismissal from my job. And how long would it take me to get strong enough to face those awful stone stairs and heavy trays again? And my night school work would be weeks behind.

I asked Fiona to bring me my text-books and I lay with them on the bedclothes, too weak, too tired to lift them up and read them. When Mother went to the library, she very kindly brought me a pile of novels and these were the first books that I read, as I grew a little stronger and was able to sit up.

As the fear that I might die receded, Mother began to get impatient with my slow recovery. She was weary, weary beyond words, after coping with Brian's and my sickness, her own periodic jobs and all the tasks that I normally did. Fiona had been pressed into service, but Fiona was as good as Mahatma Gandhi at practising passive resistance; she had no intention of inheriting my domestic shoes. She learned quickly that trade union habit of working to rule. And who could be angry with such a gentle, helpless, blue-eyed beauty? None of us could.

When Brian returned from hospital, and, after a week's convalescence at home, was allowed to return to school, Mother seemed to feel that I should automatically have recovered as well.

I was unable to oblige, though our patient doctor had managed to bring down the inflammation in my throat, and the abscesses in my ears had burst and were healing. I was also able to sit on a chair, though I found a hard wooden one difficult to sit on because I had no fat on my buttocks.

Christmas was nearly upon us, though I had given no thought to preparing gifts and my parents had not mentioned it, when Fiona brought a letter up to me. Though the letter was addressed to me, it had been opened. It was from the Presence.

The Presence announced that she was very concerned that I had been so ill, and she would call to see me at three o'clock in two days' time.

The thought of such an important visitor as my employer coming into our bedroom threw me into a panic. What would she think of the stuffy dirtiness of it, of the lack of bedspreads, even enough blankets? How would she regard a room furnished only with two beds, a candlestick, a wooden chair and an unscoured chamberpot? She was a gentlewoman, I reminded myself. She would be horrified.

'What shall I do?' I asked Mother when, later, she brought me a cup of Oxo.

'I think you had better see her downstairs,' said Mother. 'The doctor said you can get dressed for a little while tomorrow, so you can probably get down the stairs all right.'

I agreed fervently. If Mother tidied up the living-room it would look much better than the bedroom did.

'How long did they pay my wages for, Mummy? Did they send any?'

'Oh, yes. They're still paying them. A money order comes every week. I cash it at the post office.'

'That's awfully kind of them,' I said.

'Well, they're a charity. They should be charitable,' Mother said, with considerable venom in her voice. She picked up my medicine bottle and shook it.

The sudden elation in me died at her remark. I shivered. How cold charity could be.

As I sipped the scalding Oxo, I told myself that I was stupid, inept, untrained and deserved the impatience of the filing clerks and Mr Ellis, the irritability of the Cashier who had the unenviable task of making the charity's ends meet. Two of the social workers, the ladies of the green overalls, had, at my first Christmas with them, given me gifts, one of sweets, the other of a bottle of lavender, which I had promptly used as gifts for Mother and Fiona; so they knew I existed. There were days, however, when I wondered if I was really a person to the staff or whether I was just an inefficient piece of machinery. Mother had never regarded her servants as people; perhaps they thought of me like that.

I sighed, and dismissed the depressing subject. Anyone as unwashed, smelly, ugly and generally repulsive as me, I assured myself, was bound to suffer the opprobrium of those who could afford hot water and soap.

But the Presence realised I was a person. She had apparently ordered wages to be sent to me, and now she was going to call on me. She had sent me on a miraculous holiday which had given me the affection of Emrys Hughes, draper, during his last few weeks on earth.

At the thought of Emrys, tears of weakness began to flow. The battle to survive seemed too great to be borne and I wished I was with him.

'What are you crying for?' asked Mother. 'Come along, now. Take your medicine.'

# Chapter thirty-one

Mother seemed anxious that we should make a good impression on the Presence; and on the day of her visit, she brought the tin basin from the kitchen and washed me all over with warm water. She had ironed my work skirt and she lent me one of her own blouses to wear. I was too weak to endure having my hair washed, so she combed it out and pinned it back from my face with a hair clip. All the time my heart went pit-a-pat at the thought of facing my formidable employer, and I was glad to rest before Mother supported me down the stairs.

To my surprise, she opened the front-room door instead of the living-room door. Obediently, I tottered into the room and stared, unbelievingly, around me.

A small fire blazed in the hearth and gave a pleasant glow in a room made dark by an overcast afternoon. A pretty beige and green rug covered the floor; the windows were draped with pale green silky curtains. In front of the fire stood a new, beige settee, and at either side was a matching easy chair. In the window was a softly shining bureau. Over the mantelpiece hung a glittering plate-glass mirror. Reflected in it was a watercolour painting hanging on the opposite wall. The picture was one painted for Mother when she was a young girl, and she had snatched it up when leaving our home; it was all she had of our earlier, more prosperous life, and she had never pawned it.

'Good heavens!' I exclaimed. I was so startled that my weak legs gave way and I sat down suddenly on the settee.

'It looks nice, doesn't it?' said Mother, her face glowing. 'It's a little bare yet, but we'll soon add some more pieces. They delivered it on the Monday after you were taken ill.'

I replied truthfully that it looked extremely nice. I had more sense than to start a fight regarding the other ideas which shot into my mind. 'It's charming,' I added.

'I wasn't sure whether to choose beige curtains or green ones. But the green brocade seemed such good quality that I bought those.'

'They look lovely,' I assured her. 'Thanks for making a fire here.' My head was whirling with the effort I had made to get dressed and come downstairs, and my chest felt constricted and painful with the effort not to burst into helpless tears.

Mother smiled. 'I'll just go and tidy myself before your visitor arrives. It's fortunate that I did not have any work today.'

She closed the door quietly behind her, and I leaned back against the new upholstery. Mother was an intelligent, well-educated woman, but when I looked around me I doubted her sanity.

How many shillings each week was this new extravagance going to drain from us? I wondered. And if they felt compelled to buy something for the house, why not start with blankets and sheets or towels? Our beds still lacked the basic necessities to keep us warm and clean – and they had gone out and bought a drawing-room full of furniture. I sobbed inside, not daring to cry aloud. And how much longer was I to go hungry – and to a lesser degree the other children, too – until the damned stuff was paid for? I knew that we had not yet finished paying for the furniture that had been repossessed. Would they never learn to be practical? I whimpered in feeble anger.

There was a quiet knock at the front door, and I hastily dashed errant tears away and sniffed. I had not got a handkerchief.

There was the sound of soft, refined voices in the hall, a familiar, slightly shuffling step. I eased myself round, with some difficulty, to face my employer as she entered. Somehow she did not look so awesome in these surroundings – just a frail, small, elderly lady with a genuine look of concern on her face, as she held out a little gloved hand to be shaken.

'How do you do?' I inquired politely.

Her eyes looked dreadfully tired, but she said, with a little smile, 'Very well, thank you. And how are you?'

'Better, thank you,' I managed to gulp.

Mother asked her to sit down on one of the easy chairs, and she did so. She loosened the fur collar of her dark winter coat, arranged her black handbag on her knee and crossed her ankles neatly.

Mother swished down into the other easy chair, and the Presence looked me up and down earnestly.

'You seem to have been very ill,' she said. 'You have lost a lot of weight.'

I nodded nervous agreement. I wanted to lie down, but did not dare to move.

'Has the doctor told you yet when you will be fit for work?'

Mother intervened. 'This is her first venture downstairs, so I imagine it will be a few weeks before she can do much walking.'

'I imagine so.' The Presence continued to gaze thoughtfully at me. I had the feeling she could have given a police description of me after such an intense scrutiny.

There was an embarrassed silence, finally broken by Mother, who inquired, 'Would you like a cup of tea? You must be cold after coming so far. Helen usually has a cup at this time.'

The Presence was drawing off her leather gloves. She glanced up at Mother, who had risen from her chair. 'I would enjoy one very much. Thank you.'

That got rid of Mother for a few minutes, which I had had an instinctive feeling the Presence wanted to do. She smoothed her wrinkled gloves between absent-minded fingers, as she looked round the room. I noticed that her thin face had fine, premature lines round the eyes and at each side of the firm mouth. She wore no powder or lipstick, and she had the quiet, deft movements of a nun.

'This is a pleasant place for you to sit, isn't it? I am happy that your family seems to be getting on to its feet again.'

I wanted to lean forward and put my head into her tweed-covered lap and bellow tearfully that, in my opinion, the whole room was an outrage to reason. Instead, I whispered, 'Yes, it is a nice room.'

'You have been with us for two years, now,' she said with sudden briskness. It was a statement, not a question.

I nodded, and she sighed as if the fact was cause for woe.

'We need an extra girl in the Registry Office, to look after the index cards and to help with the filing. Such a girl would have to relieve the telephone operator at lunchtime. I understand that you can now manage the switchboard; and it has been decided to give the new position to you. Er – Mr Ellis is agreeable to this.' She looked at me expectantly, a suggestion of a twinkle in her eyes.

The sense of overwhelming relief I felt was so great that, at first, I could not speak. I opened my mouth and no words came. A promotion! No more making tea or having to go out in the snow, and less running up and down stairs.

'Oh, thank you,' I finally gasped, with such sincerity that she really smiled this time.

'Your salary would be twelve shillings and sixpence, payable monthly.'

I was in ecstasy. 'That would be splendid,' I whispered. I wanted to shout it from the rooftops, dance in the street. Life was beginning to move forward at last.

'You can tell your parents about it yourself,' she added, in a tone of voice which hinted something which I did not at first grasp. Then, as I heard the rattle of teacups in the back room, I realised that she was being very forbearing. In a period when children of the middle classes remained children until their majority, it would have been quite possible that she would discuss this promotion with Mother before telling me, particularly as she herself belonged to a still earlier generation. She had, however, left me the choice of telling my parents about the salary increase, or not. Did she, I wondered, understand something of the misery I was going through?

'You are very kind,' I said warmly.

Because our crockery was chipped and ugly and we lacked many essentials, like milk jugs, Mother brought the Presence a cup of tea with milk already in it, and proffered the cheap glass sugar basin with its tin spoon.

The tea was graciously accepted and consumed, the bad weather discussed and good wishes expressed for my early recovery.

'We will see if we can arrange another holiday this summer,' the Presence promised, as Mother took her cup from her.

Mother made no comment. Her smile was thin and polite. With a jolt, I wondered if she would try to keep me at home again, on the excuse of chronic ill-health. Perhaps I would never return to the office. Perhaps she was just willing to accept the payment of my salary as long as the organisation was prepared to pay it.

I must have gone even whiter at the idea, because the Presence said suddenly, 'Helen is exhausted. I must go.'

Hands were shaken, and Mother showed my kind visitor out. I thankfully lay down on the settee.

If Mother and Father could buy over a hundred pounds' worth of sitting-room furniture, I meditated bitterly, then they did not need the extra half-a-crown a week I would be earning. I desperately needed to be able to buy soup for lunch each day, instead of once a week. I needed shoes and second-hand woollens to keep me warm. The money I was already giving to Mother was more than adequate for the small amount of food I received, for the coal and gas I shared, and for a small contribution to the rent. I determined that Mother should have the next rise in pay I received, but not this one.

'And if you think I am going to stay at home, you can think again,' I muttered to myself acidly.

Mother had been quite patient while nursing me, but, from sad experience, I doubted if that patience would extend past the day I managed to walk about.

# Chapter thirty-two

The doctor feared that the infection of my ears would cause a loss of hearing, and he insisted that I should see a specialist. So, a few days before Christmas, Mother managed to bundle me on to a tram, and we went to the Ear, Nose and Throat Hospital.

Since I was very weak, we arrived early, in the hope of being seen without much delay by the specialist, who donated his services to the hospital.

When I looked up at the building, it seemed to touch the pale blue sky. Its tall, narrow windows, the stonework beautifully carved by long-dead masons, seemed to be slender fingers pointing upwards. Mother propped me against the wall, as close as she could get to the pollution-blackened doorway, where a shabby crowd awaited the opening of the Outpatients' Department. A cold wind fluttered the stained raincoats of the men and the bundly overcoats of the women, some of whom hugged beshawled children to them. The wind pierced my own macintosh and Mother's woollen cardigan which I was wearing beneath it, and I shivered convulsively. Mother had on a second-hand leather coat, which she had bought to keep her warm while doing a short spell as a door-to-door vacuum saleswoman.

Every so often I would feel faint and would start to reel, and Mother would pin me against the building's wall so that I did not fall. After waiting about half an hour, just when I felt I could endure no more, the door was opened by a probationer and the motley crowd poured in, elbowing each other in an effort to be first.

We found ourselves in a large waiting-room with lines of wooden benches, and we sat down, not sure what we were supposed to do next.

I fainted against Mother's shoulder and, when I came round, I heard an angry rumbling from the waiting crowd. Apparently, Mother had asked a passing nurse for a glass of water and the girl had said coldly that it was not necessary, that I would come round quickly enough.

This indifference had riled the outpatients and they spent some time talking to each other and to Mother, in furious whispers, about other hospitals where they felt they had been treated equally uncompassionately.

We sat for a long time and nothing happened, until a nurse came and sat at a desk in front of us. Mother left me in the care of an elderly lady sitting next to her, and went to inquire when we might be seen.

'The specialist usually arrives about eleven,' the nurse said. 'You will just have to wait.'

'Could my daughter lie down somewhere?'

'Ask the patients if they will move up, so that she can lie on the bench.'

But the room was packed, so I leaned against Mother in a lethargy which passed occasionally into complete oblivion. I was so bony that it was also very painful to sit on a wooden bench for such a long time.

Finally a young physician and a nurse arrived, and began to sift through the patients, to discover their reasons for attending the hospital. Our kind neighbour held me again, while Mother went to the desk to explain our presence. By this time I was so exhausted, I did not care whether I saw a doctor or not. All I wanted to do was lie down – on the floor, if there was no other place.

'You should not have to wait much longer,' the nurse told Mother. 'Doctor arrived a few minutes ago.'

At about twelve, having left home before eight o'clock, we finally were ushered into a lofty, poorly lit office. A thin, grey-haired man in a white coat, a man with the gentlest voice and the kindest manner I ever remember, was seated on a little stool, scribbling on a note board held across his knee. Since I had come about my throat and ears, his elderly nurse took my coat from me and sat me down in a straight-backed chair.

The doctor, a famous surgeon, smiled at Mother when she handed him a note from our physician, opened the envelope and read the description of my illness.

He put the note down on a nearby table, and, while he looked at my face, he asked Mother a few questions about the duration of the infection. I sat with eyes cast down, hoping I would not fall off the chair.

'Well,' he said, as he picked up a torch. 'Let me have a look.'

He peered very earnestly down my throat, and then with another instrument down my ears. I winced as the ears were stretched slightly by the insertion of the cold appliance. He then felt carefully round my neck.

Mother volunteered the information that I had been subject to ear infection ever since I had had the measles at the age of five. His expression as he turned to Mother was a bit puzzled; perhaps the exquisitely enunciated words from such a battered-looking woman surprised him.

He turned back to me and said gently, 'Helen, I would like to examine your chest. Nurse will take your blouse from you and help you with your underwear.'

I nodded, and unbuttoned the heavy cotton blouse, to expose the naked, bony chest beneath. I handed the blouse to the waiting nurse.

Both doctor and nurse gasped. The doctor glanced at Mother in a puzzled way, as if to include her in their shock. I was suddenly afraid that the doctor had spotted some deadly disease.

'Nurse, bring a gown,' ordered the doctor sharply. 'I think I had better take a look at Helen generally. Help her slip off the rest of her clothes.' He looked at me and smiled. I must have appeared to him to be scared beyond measure, as I gazed at him, pop-eyed, because he said soothingly, 'There is nothing to be afraid of, my dear.'

Mother had not expected that I would have to strip, and I saw her flush slightly, as I dropped my skirt off, leaving me garbed in a pair of worn, off-white knickers held up by a pin and a pair of rayon stockings supported by rubber bands.

Almost tenderly, the nurse slipped the stiff white gown round my shoulders, and her carefulness frightened me more.

The nurse laid me on an examination table and the specialist checked me over, part by part. I must have looked ugly to him, with only a slight rise of young breasts above ribs that stuck out, a distended stomach with a fluff of pubic hair at its base, legs that seemed all bone. I could not see my own buttocks, but I knew that there was little fat on them. He pinched me in several places very gently. Then he wrapped the gown round me, and the nurse helped me to sit up.

The specialist turned to Mother, and in a voice which indicated a rage ill-controlled, he asked her, 'Mrs Forrester, what *has* happened to this child? An illness such as your physician describes could not have reduced her weight to this extent.'

Mother said uneasily, 'She does not have a very good appetite.'

'She is half-starved.' He was furiously angry, and his voice rose. 'You will lose her unless you find some means of getting food into her. No child should have to suffer like this. What is the City thinking of? Is your husband on Public Assistance?'

'No,' muttered Mother. 'He works for the Liverpool Corporation.'

'And Helen?' He turned to me. 'Have you got work, child?'

I told him the name of the organisation which employed me. The nurse had put me into a chair, and I sat staring at him, aghast.

Hunger was painful at times, but most of the time I felt lethargic and weak. I thought I was lazy, and I was always pushing myself to complete the work I had to do.

'I can't understand it, Mrs Forrester. You are, I imagine, an educated woman, and should understand something about nutrition. Your physician *has* expressed to me his anxiety for her general condition, though he sent her to me, of course, because of the ear and throat infections. But unless she can eat more and put on some weight, she will be subject to all kinds of illness. Her ears will heal – your doctor will explain that to you. Even in this city, however, it is some time since I saw such a shocking case of malnutrition. Did your doctor recommend a special diet?'

During this diatribe Mother had stared at him with an expression of blank disbelief. Now she flared up suddenly.

'Yes,' she snapped. 'And I have done my best to give it to her – but she doesn't eat it.'

In an instinctive defence of Mother, I interjected, 'I haven't been able to eat very much, doctor. My throat hurt and so did my ears when I swallowed.'

He looked at me almost contritely, as if ashamed of his outburst, and said to the nurse, 'Take Helen into the other room – there's an easy chair there. You can help her dress in there, while I talk to Mrs Forrester.'

The nurse picked up my clothes and wrapped the white gown round me. She put a hand under my elbow to help support me as we went towards the door. At the entrance, I paused, reluctant to leave someone who cared so much that I was thin and hungry.

'Thank you, doctor,' I said, forcing back tears of weakness.

I never saw him again.

As the nurse helped to dress me and told me what a wonderful doctor my new-found friend was, an outburst of words rumbled through the closed door. I could not hear what he was saying, but when Mother joined me she was weeping unrestrainedly, and this distressed me. I took her arm, to comfort her, while the nurse said briskly, 'Doctor will be writing to your G.P. You should go to see him in a few days' time.'

Without a word, the two of us went very slowly back through the hall and out into the street to catch a tram.

'Mummy, I'm so sorry. Please don't cry. What did he say?'

No matter what battles we had fought, Mother had suffered so much herself since we arrived in Liverpool that I could not bear to see her reduced to tears by a stranger. The careworn woman, whose arm I leaned upon, was totally different from the pretty, fashionable lady I had known as a child. I wanted passionately to erase whatever bitter words the specialist had used when speaking to her in my absence.

Mother did not answer me at first, but heaved me up the steps of a tram which arrived as we emerged from the hospital. She handed the conductor two pennies and received our tickets, before she finally spoke.

'He is going to write to our doctor,' she said finally, with a trembling sigh. 'He will make some recommendations. You have nothing to fear. You have no disease.'

And that was all the information I could extract from her.

A few days later, I managed to walk the short distance to our own doctor's house, and spent a happy hour reading all the old magazines in his waiting room, and talking in laboured German to two German patients waiting to see him. They told me such horrifying tales of what was going on in Germany under Hitler that I felt my own suffering to be very small.

The doctor checked my ears, throat and chest again. The specialist's report, he said, had been optimistic about my hearing and he hoped I would not have much hearing loss. Afterwards, he sat down at his desk, and said very earnestly, 'Helen, you must eat as much plain food as you can obtain. Don't spend your pocket money on sweets – buy an orange or an apple. Clean up your plate at meal times.' He grinned cheerfully at me.

'Yes,' I agreed. How could I tell him that I had had no sweets during the four years I had been in Liverpool, except one or two which had been given to me? How could I tell him how empty my dinner plate had been for so long?

'And I want you to go to bed early and rest as much as you can during the next few weeks.'

Rest? With so many children pestering me with their constant needs? And I was now terribly behind in night school – my only hope for a better future; I would have to catch up somehow. Then I remembered the new job – that would be easier. So I nodded agreement again.

'And during the weekends you should walk in the park whenever it is sunny, to get fresh air. Perhaps go to New Brighton sometimes and walk there – that would be nice, wouldn't it?'

Poor, benighted man. Didn't he realise that the ferry boat to New Brighton cost twopence? Princes Park was there, however, and I often took Baby Edward and Avril for walks in it. So again I agreed.

As he scribbled on his prescription pad, he said, 'I wish your mother had come with you. I would have liked to discuss your diet in detail with her. Tell her what I have said, and come to see me again next week.' He handed me a prescription. 'Have this tonic made up and take it regularly.'

I thanked him and went out and walked slowly down the steps into Parliament Street. After such long confinement, Liverpool seemed a beautiful place in which to walk. My eyes ran appreciatively along the fine symmetry of the big terrace houses which lined the street. Father said they had been built from money gained from the slave trade with America, but they were still beautiful to me. Even the stolidness of the brick Home for Incurables seemed lighter, more cheerful, than usual. The whole district was bathed in a mid-afternoon hush, that pause which occurs in suburbia before the homeward rush from the city. The only other person I saw was a woman on her knees scrubbing the marble steps of the Rialto Cinema and Dance Hall, and I paused on the other side of the road to watch her. Perhaps, I thought wistfully, now I have a rise in pay I could go to the cinema. People said that the floor of the dance hall was a particularly good one, and I imagined myself in a long dress twirling round it in the arms of the Prince of Wales, now a troubled exile, to the strains of a Strauss waltz. It doesn't cost anything to have dreams.

# Chapter thirty-three

Many years later, Alan told me that one day, while I was out, some people came from the child welfare authority and threatened to take us all into care. He cannot remember the date of this, but I think it must have been during my convalescence, perhaps while I was at the doctor's surgery. It is hardly likely that our doctor or the outraged specialist would have left such a case of malnutrition unreported. It is also possible that my astute employer may have goaded officialdom into action. Brian's skinny condition had quite likely been noted during his stay in hospital. So several complaints were probably made.

Whenever it was, my parents must have talked their way out of it. In those days, few would believe that neglect or ill-treatment of children occurred in any but working-class homes; and once my parents' original social status had been established there would be a tendency to believe anything they said. From the day on which we saw the specialist, however, Mother saw that I received the same amount of food as the other children, and it was obvious that she gave priority to the buying of food over other needs. We still did not have enough to eat, but there was an improvement. I became concerned that in an effort to feed me, she would go without herself, and this caused a reciprocal concern for each other, which improved our relationship.

As soon as I was able to stay up for most of the day, Mother began to use me as a housekeeper again, and I was dreadfully afraid that, once again, I would become the family's unpaid general factotum. I never grudged helping in the house, but I did not want to be permanently at home.

Little Edward was now nearly four and could talk well. He was a pleasant, confiding small companion, always asking questions, like Tony did. I would sit with him on my lap, his untidy brown hair against my cheek, quivering inside at the thought of being shut into a kind of slavery without any rewards.

Long before I returned to work, I had taken out my text-books and begun to study again. I pressed Fiona into reading aloud to me, so that I could practise shorthand and not lose speed. This bored Fiona terribly – she hated reading anything, but she was very good-natured and, on my behalf, she stumbled through business letters from the text-book and the first few chapters of *Jane Eyre*. She would put down the book after two or three minutes, during which my pencil had scampered frantically across my notebook, and would ask bewilderedly, 'How can you stand it? Why bother?'

I would smile at her and say I liked it. Embryo maiden aunts must be able to earn, I felt, though I could not have explained it to her. I did not want to end up a nervous ghost in the house of one of my siblings, caring for their children, dependent on them for the smallest need.

Sometimes, when Edward or highly strung Brian had difficulty in going to sleep, I would sing irregular French verbs or German declensions to them. Brian chuckled at the strange words, but Edward only needed a comforting hum and did not miss Little Bo Peep or her friends.

Three of the children had not been up to the bedroom to see me at all while I was ill. Fiona, Avril and Edward tumbled straight into the big double bed on the other side of the room and usually fell asleep immediately, but I had not seen Alan or Tony, and Brian only immediately before he was sent to hospital. Now I was downstairs again, they looked as if they had all grown enormously during my absence.

Brian had recovered quickly, and he and Tony had found good friends amongst neighbouring shopkeepers' children; they played in their houses or in the street. They also went to choir practices and to the church services.

Alan had made friends with one or two other office boys and clerks, and his pocket money was sufficient to enable him to go to the cinema, to boxing matches and to play cricket.

Fiona did not make many friends. Like me, she had little money. She was also very slow-moving, so that getting herself to and from school, keeping her scanty clothes clean and joining in an occasional game of tag or skipping with other girls in the street practically filled her day. Occasionally, on a Saturday afternoon, Alan kindly took her to the cinema, or she beguiled Mother into giving her twopence to go by herself. Continuous performances in the cinema had just begun to be common, and she sat all through the afternoon and two evening performances, seeing the same two films offered, over and over again. She would return about eleven o'clock at night, silent and bemused. As she approached her fourteenth birthday, she began to put her hair into rag curlers and to take a deep interest in her appearance. Boys in the streets around whistled after her, and she would run into the house blushing and bewildered.

Because I had such intense pain during my menstrual periods, a pain which could not be hidden from the rest of the family because I used to scream with it, she dreaded the onset of this natural cycle, but when it came it was painless and she was much relieved. When I saw this, I asked the doctor if my pain could be at least reduced, but he laughed and told me to take a couple of aspirins, assuring me that it would go away when

I was married. Through the years I got the same reply from other general practitioners.

Avril, short for her age though sturdy-looking, still raged helplessly when our parents quarrelled or whenever she was in any way frustrated. Like me, her birth had been bitterly resented, and in her first years she had been left almost entirely to the care of servants. Now, however, I noticed that Mother had begun to recognise a fellow spirit, for they were surprisingly alike, and the little girl clung to her mother in a very moving way. Yet another stray cat had attached itself to our household and Avril seemed to get some comfort from cuddling it and pretending that it was a baby. It submitted very patiently to being wrapped in a piece of blanket and held upside down.

As I waited for my lethargic body to gain strength, I watched the children come and go, each intent upon his or her own business. I began to realise that life does change; nothing lasts for ever. When I had first come to Liverpool and had been plunged into sudden, frightful poverty amongst coarse and scarifying people, it seemed as if we would always be small and helpless. But it was not so; the children were growing vigorously, despite poor food.

All growing things push against each other, each fighting for air, space and sustenance, and large overcrowded families are no exception. And I observed that, as each child grew in strength, it fought quite ruthlessly for a place for itself, giving very little thought to the plight of the others. I saw that the family unit was not as tightly locked together as my parents were fond of imagining. And I was plunged into melancholy when Mother preached to me the need to go without, give up my life to the care of the children. Why could they not help, too? I would ask angrily. And the retort was always the same, 'You are the eldest.'

But, in truth, they were better at avoiding it. Alan was the eldest boy and automatically more privileged; he was my father's hope. Fiona pretended to be much more stupid than she really was, and she was more frail. Brian and Tony kept out of the way, and Avril had such a colossal temper that even Mother was silenced by it. Amongst us toddled Baby Edward, serene and self-assured, too small to have to worry.

Too sick myself to do a great deal, I sat and watched them, corrected them if they seemed to be doing anything of danger to themselves, made the meals and the fires, and wondered once if they would go hungry for my sake.

The answer, I believed, was that of Shaw's Pygmalion, 'Not bloody likely.'

# Chapter thirty-four

When I returned to work, the mood of the city seemed more cheerful. The previous winter it had been hung with crape for the passing of King George V; Edward VIII, my adored Prince Charming, had come and gone, and was an exile with his Mrs Simpson. Now we all looked forward to a coronation, that of George VI and his plump little Queen, Elizabeth. It seemed also that there was a trifle more work available, though the lines of unemployed were still very long.

I said a mental 'Hello' to Minerva, looking down from the dome of the Town Hall. Belief in ancient gods never quite dies – it remains, mixed with the myths and legends of one's people, in the background of one's mind; and I believed that Minerva would help her people, if she could, and even, perhaps, an ugly little stepchild like me. It was not an active belief to be expressed in prayers; but just a cosy feeling like that given by a St Christopher medallion or the ownership of a black cat.

I was still very weak, and was thankful that I now worked most of the time on one floor of the office, though I was constantly under the subduing eye of Mr Ellis. I was allotted a wooden chair and a corner of a table on which to do my work. I became very quick at the tasks given me; and, whenever I had the chance, I would retire behind the stacks of files on the excuse of helping to put some of them away, to read, spellbound, the files' contents. They were moving stories of human suffering, sometimes covering many years, set down in unemotional prose by succeeding social workers. In some cases, I was acquainted with the family concerned, and it was interesting to see a social worker's opinion of them. I chuckled sometimes, because the priorities of the family and those of the social worker were often at odds. Most of my neighbours had the aim of surviving with as little pain and as much immediate enjoyment as they could obtain.

I learned the names of the women I had observed on the way to night school. They allowed men to play with their bodies in the same way as cows allowed a bull. Now the files told me that this was wrong; it was sinful. And I began idly to wonder about the relationship of men and women and about love. Surely there was something more to it than the conversation of the mill girls I had met on holiday had led me to think. I came across the words fornication and adultery, Bible words that I had not previously thought about. The dictionary was not very helpful.

I remembered the knowing laughter of Cristina Gomez when she had referred to Alonzo's goodness as a husband; perhaps she meant more than the fact that he gave his wages to her each week. Perhaps the wild, unearthly dreams I sometimes had were prompted by my coming into the beginning of womanhood; I blushed when I remembered them.

In my isolation from anything that most other girls had, friends, affection, parties, dances, I had missed the usual slow discovery of sex. Whispered stories told between girl friends, the hints of it in magazines, discreet warnings and indications from mothers, had not been part of my experience. No boy had ever approached me. I had never worked out why Emile Zola's Nana was so wicked; all she seemed to do was stay in bed. In our early days in Liverpool I could have been raped and I would not have understood what had happened to me. Perhaps it was fortunate that I had been so dirty, so grey in looks, that I merged with the grey-black city around me and had thus walked unscathed through streets that for centuries had been very unsafe. Now, I began to knit together the romance of the many novels I had read with the facts that the files and the mill girls had brought to my attention and to understand the happiness of Cristina and her husband. The thought of the Gomez couple brought home to me that whatever physical relation there was between husband and wife it could be an enriching experience. And I imagined that lonely single men bought that experience from prostitutes.

Now that I was in the office most of the time, I came into closer contact with other members of the junior staff.

We could find no common meeting ground.

I was still grubby and untidy, though our landlord had had our house fumigated and I no longer feared passing bugs to the other girls. Even the fleas in the house had been reduced. Occasionally I caught head lice from the other children, who picked them up at school; and once I had to go to work with my head smothered in a heavy ointment to eradicate them; this caused a lot of stares and some open laughter, because my hair was pasted down against my skull, like a boy's.

Like any youngster, I wanted to be included in the girls' conversation, much of which hinged on the films they had seen, the boys they had met and the radio programmes they had heard. Though I had not been to the cinema in Liverpool and we had no radio, I had read a great number of popular novels which had been made into films, so I could analyse the plots and discuss their themes. I sometimes broke into their gossip with an observation, which was usually received with stunned silence; and the conversation would be resumed, as if I had not spoken. This made me feel hopelessly stupid and I would be quiet for some time afterwards. When I made a mistake, however, they would address me brusquely.

The first purchases I made with my increase in salary were a bar of soap and a packet of soap flakes. These were used up within a day or two by the rest of the family, but now, with a little money, I tried very hard to collect a few more clothes and to keep them clean. I hunted through the oddments table at the pawnbroker's and I saved up for a pair of shoes from Marks & Spencer's.

I soon discovered that to have spare clothes was very difficult. Frequently, I came home to find the garments pawned or on Mother's or Fiona's back. This made me furious and my wicked temper would rise and for days I would be in disgrace for the outburst. I rarely borrowed from Mother and always asked specially; she had several hats and sometimes I would beg the loan of a change of headgear. I was confused. How did other girls cope with such situations? I wondered. What should I do?

And the weakness from my illness persisted, despite the slight improvement in diet. The tremendous inborn strength which had carried me through years of hardship was gone. I was racked with pains in my legs and sometimes in other joints, and the throat still tended to acquire threatening septic spots in it. I gargled with salt and water in the hope of clearing them, but it was only partially successful.

So the strain for the first few weeks after being ill was very great, and I did not take much notice of my successor, Sylvia Poole, except to help her a little until she knew the office girl's work. I was afraid to say much to her, because I expected to be snubbed. She had eyes as blue as speedwells, which stared, with considerable perspicacity, through thick, horn-rimmed glasses. Though much shorter than the rest of the staff, she seemed uncowed by them or even by the formidable Mr Ellis.

I lived all my life in fearful apprehension, but she seemed to view life with a calm confidence. She had a firm, though light tread, and all her movements were deft and certain. I could not imagine a voluntary worker daring to complain to her that the tea was cold or that there was too much milk in it. Such complaints used to send me racing up to the kitchen in nervous haste, to fetch a fresh cup.

In the privacy of the top-floor kitchen, where at first I helped her make the tea, she asked me, 'Have you been here long, Miss Foster?'

'Forrester,' I corrected.

'Er – Forrester. How long have you been here?'

'Two years.'

'As office girl?' The blue eyes glanced sharply up at me, as she rattled cups on to saucers. The pretty red lips curved in a grimace. 'I wouldn't like to do this job for long.'

I did not know how to answer. All the underlying terror of losing my job and not being allowed to take another seemed impossible to explain to someone of her temerity.

Her smile was sweet and friendly, however, and gradually I began to relax with her. She had a very pink and white complexion and the suggestion of a double chin, which indicated plenty of good food. She had a charm, a gaiety about her which I longed to emulate.

Finally, I answered her question.

'Yes, as office girl. The job seems to offer a future, Miss Poole.'

Again she made a disdainful moue with her mouth. She was a year younger than me, but her fearlessness and her self-assurance made me feel the younger of the two of us. To my astonishment, she did not seem to think my conversation stupid; and slowly I began to talk to her about all kinds of subjects.

I had theories of history, and she patiently submitted to their being unloaded on her. I had done considerable background reading on the current political situation in Europe and I read every newspaper I could, either at home or in the library, so that, however misguided my ideas may have been, I had many of them. I had recently acquired two pen-friends in Germany, who told me something of what they were being taught. Their letters were loaded with references to 'our beloved Fuehrer', and we shared surprise at anyone so monstrous being beloved. The basement waiting room held an ever-increasing number of terrified refugees from all over Europe, sent to us for aid, so we were more aware than many people of what was happening to Jewry, to trade unionists, to honest priests, under the beloved leader.

When I described to her birds that I had seen or a flower peeping up between paving stones or how lovely the Greek church looked in the early morning sun, she did not snigger. And gradually the barriers went down.

Sometimes we would walk out of the office together to catch our respective trams – walking to and from work was impossible for me at that time because I was too weak – and conversation would pour out of me in torrents. All the pent-up knowledge, ideas, theories, came flowing out, to be tried against a cool and clear intelligence. In fact, for a long time I forgot the difference between a monologue and a dialogue. When I expounded on an idea that was particularly far out, she would respond, 'But don't you think, Miss Foster . . .' and I would automatically correct her, 'Miss Forrester'. She would politely repeat, 'Miss Forrester . . . don't you think that . . .'

And my idea would begin to take a more sensible outline.

Life suddenly began to be exciting, interesting. I could hardly wait to meet her again and share another reflection with her. Every joke, every amusing incident had to be recounted.

Her parents had managed to keep her in school until she was fifteen and encouraged her to go to night school; her desire for better education was nearly as great as mine. She wittily reduced the office staff to size for me, and I ceased to be afraid of them. Her respect for my ideas added a little self-esteem to that already implanted by Emrys Hughes.

One day, she became the target for the scorn of the other girls. She arrived with her straight brown hair transformed into a soft blonde, waved and curled about her face. The improvement in her looks was remarkable and I said so. But to bleach one's hair, however good the result, was simply not approved of by lower-middle-class society, and the staff retired behind the stacks of files to laugh and condemn.

As she helped me sort index cards, she said with a scowl on her pretty face, 'I don't see any reason to look dowdy all my life. I'm going to make the best of myself.' And undeterred by Mr Ellis's startled looks, she added, in the days that followed, a subdued make-up to her already good complexion.

I was fascinated by the transformation.

Instead of buying soup in Woolworth's restaurant, I spent one lunch-time examining the contents of their cosmetic counter, and, greatly daring, bought a tin of Snowfire foundation cream and a box of face powder. Unfortunately, when I applied them, before the broken mirror stuck in our kitchen window, they did not transform me immediately into a beauty. The washed-out, sallow complexion was made somewhat whiter and the red acne boils were a little less apparent, but the black rings around my eyes looked even blacker, as did the thick black eyebrows. However, I hopefully applied these aids to glamour again when I went to work the next day. Nobody seemed to notice any difference.

When I discussed the matter with Miss Poole, like an old granny solemnly discussing a funeral, she looked carefully at my efforts, and said, 'What about buying a lipstick and some rouge?'

This shocked me. Mother had always used both rouge and lipstick and, when she was younger, heavy eye make-up. But I remembered the servants saying that she was fast. I did not want to appear fast.

'Wouldn't it be rather – um – fast?' I asked timidly.

'Of course not,' Miss Poole assured me firmly. 'I use them. Everybody does now.'

So I went without another lunch and spent sixpence on rouge and lipstick. They were the wrong colour for me, and I did not place the rouge correctly. With my hair combed back in a bun and two feverishly red spots painted on my cheeks, I looked like a Dutch doll.

This time, Mother noticed. And she laughed at me. Cross and crest-fallen, I went to wash my face.

But Fiona, much less cut off from other girls than I was, had borrowed some women's magazines which showed how to apply make-up. In exchange for a chance to paint her own face, she brought these magazines out from under her mattress and let me read them. When Mother was out, we both tried to follow the instructions, vying for peeps into the bit of mirror as we worked. There was a special diagram showing how to place rouge on a long, thin face. I was surprised at the improvement, though the magazine confirmed that the colour was wrong for a brown-haired, green-eyed person with a yellow skin.

When I looked at Fiona's more successful efforts, I realised, with a shock, that she had grown up. She laughed at my expression of astonishment. Perfect teeth flashed between the gaily painted lips. She had carefully removed, with a wet finger, the surplus powder from her huge eyelashes and smooth, long brows, and her dancing violet eyes were greatly enhanced by the powdered skin.

'Fi, you look gorgeous,' I exclaimed.

'Do you really think so?' she asked shyly.

'Oh, yes,' I assured her.

She looked down at her grubby, little girl's clothes, and sighed. 'Thank goodness, Mummy's going to buy me some decent clothes to start work in. She's going to get a cheque so that I can have a new coat and hat and everything.'

Such a pang of jealousy went through me. I remembered the exhausting battles I had fought and was still fighting to be able to work, to have a few clothes, even to get enough to eat. Here was Fiona taking it for granted that she would have no such difficulties.

'She hasn't asked you to look after Edward until he starts school in September?'

'She knows I'm no good at that sort of thing,' she replied placidly, as she took down the mirror and tried rearranging her straight hair in a more sophisticated style.

It was true that Fiona had always appeared very helpless, when asked to help in the house. I looked at her sharply. She had picked up the family comb and was contentedly combing her hair. I had an uneasy feeling that she was much smarter than me.

'Good for you,' I said, trying unsuccessfully to keep acidity out of my voice.

Fiona put down the comb and turned to me.

'They can afford to pay someone,' she said calmly. 'There will be five of us at work, when I start.'

'Tell that to Mother,' I snapped bitterly.

# Chapter thirty-five

As promised, the Presence arranged another holiday for me. This time, I had to pay my own fare and one pound towards the cost.

'Since you will receive a month's salary before you start the holiday, there should be no difficulty about that,' she said to me very pleasantly.

I was most grateful and thanked her effusively. I nearly danced out of her office. A holiday like the one I had had before would make me strong again, take away the pains in my legs. And I could, if I wished, sleep and sleep and sleep, until my head stopped aching and my eyes lost their bloodshot hue.

Filled with excitement, I dashed into the house when I arrived home and poured out the thrilling news to my parents, who were seated at the table, bickering as usual. It took a lot of effort on the part of both Father and me to persuade Mother that she could provide the necessary one pound.

'I'll save up my fare,' I promised, as I ate a slice of bologna and several pieces of bread and margarine, followed by gulps of sweet, weak tea.

In the weeks that followed, by halfpennies and pennies, I saved the fare, two shillings for pocket money and enough to buy some stockings, knickers and a petticoat, the first petticoat I had owned in Liverpool. The day before my departure I bought the ticket, put my few clothes together in a shopping bag, and talked gaily to a silent Mother about the beauty of the Lake District.

On the Friday night I handed her my month's pay, less the rise which the Presence had quietly given to me. This latter money I had to keep for fares, stockings and soup when I returned. Mother slipped the money into her handbag, without a word.

An hour before the train was due, I asked her for a pound to pay to the Holiday Home.

'I haven't got it,' she said.

I could not believe her. But it was true.

On the previous evening, while I had been fetching some milk from the dairy, the agent who collected for the finance company that provided the cheques with which she purchased clothes, had called. She was, as usual, behind in her weekly payments, and he had threatened court action; so she had given him my wages. She added coolly that, since I would not now need the ticket for the train, she would like to have it, so that she could get a refund on it from the railway company.

I spent my holiday sulkily watching Edward, while Mother commenced a full-time job as the representative of a sweet firm. Edward would go to school in September, and she felt she could undertake regular work. I began once more to fear that she would try to keep me at home.

Within two weeks her accounts were, as she put it, in a muddle, and she was dismissed. I breathed a sigh of relief as she returned to her demonstration work in shops, and the children cheerfully ate her samples.

In an effort to improve my wardrobe, I bought two black dress lengths from the pawnbroker and a sixpenny pattern from Woolworth's. I found that I could not cut the dresses out with the blunt, curved nail scissors which were all we had, so I begged a razor blade from Father and cut them out with that. It took me some weeks to hand-stitch them, but when they were finished, they fitted well; and even Mother said they looked very nice.

I had also bought from the pawnbroker a thick brown coat. It was a nondescript garment which had suffered from being bundled up in his loft, but it was warm. And though it was summertime, I seemed to feel cold every time the wind blew, so I wore it daily.

Mother called at the office one day and asked for me. Since I was in the basement taking clients' names, Sylvia Poole asked if she could help. Mother said she wanted my coat and, in front of the other girls, a bewildered Sylvia gave it to her. I was even more bewildered, when Sylvia told me about it. And I was hurt by the gleams of amusement in the eyes of the other young staff members.

I was outraged when I returned home to find that the coat and my second, newly stitched dress were in pawn. But heated argument did not get it back, and I shivered into the autumn before I had saved enough money to redeem it.

I was again plunged into embarrassment at the office when Father sought an interview with the Presence. He wanted help to keep our many creditors off the doorstep. I am not sure what kind of a miracle he expected her to perform on his behalf, but he lost his temper and so did she. Their raised voices came clearly through the door panelling into the office in which I worked. She told him that, with five people working, his family was far better off than most.

'But there are seven children,' he spluttered defensively.

'One should not father children one cannot keep,' she retorted tartly.

The office was convulsed with laughter. Even Mr Ellis managed a subdued haw-haw, as he wrote in his big record book. I wished that the floor would open and close over me. I bent over the index cards and sorted them feverishly, while the private exit to the hall from the Presence's office was opened and slammed shut again.

Father raged, off and on, for days afterwards, and vented much of his frustration on me, as if I was responsible for my unbending employer.

I feared greatly that the Presence would lose patience with such a trying family. But she did not. On the contrary, she was particularly kind whenever she met me in the hall or on the staircase, and would stop to ask if I was well or how night school was proceeding.

A few weeks later, she was asked by the British Broadcasting Corporation if she could find someone who would give a talk on managing on a small budget. This was not an easy request to fill, because most of our clients were far from literate, and she asked me if I thought my mother could do it.

Mother was delighted. The offer meant a day trip to Manchester, lunch provided, and a fee for the broadcast. We all encouraged her.

She spent hours writing out likely lists of expenditure, and then screwing them up and throwing them impatiently into the fire. Though she was very good at letter writing, the talk had to be written in a manner suitable for verbal delivery; and this she found extremely difficult.

I watched her struggle for several evenings, as I went about my household tasks. Then I asked her timidly if she would like me to try to write it for her. Much to my surprise, she thankfully agreed.

Since every day I read several files which gave detailed lists of family expenditures, I was able to compose a likely-sounding budget, based on Father's supposed salary plus my earnings. Then I wrote this into a chatty format and read it out, timing it by our solitary clock. It was a little short, so I added a recipe for fried herrings as a recommended standby for impecunious housewives – fishmongers nearly gave away herrings in those days.

While I stood nervously by her, Mother read it, and, with a sigh of relief, said it was excellent. I basked in her unexpected approbation.

She had a most enjoyable day in Manchester and delivered the talk without a hitch. It resulted in several complimentary letters from listeners and was reported in the *Liverpool Echo*. Because we had no radio, we could not hear her, but most of our neighbours did own radios and they were most impressed that anyone in our district could speak on it. They ceased to regard Mother as 'bloody stuck-up', and Mother found herself talking to respectful women wrapped in shawls or old overcoats, all of them anxious to discuss her wonderful budget, which actually balanced. Their questions confused her, since she had not made up the talk, and they must have been puzzled by some of her answers. The unexpected status that the talk gave her in our bedraggled community, however, helped her greatly. She was forced to communicate with our many kind neighbours and her isolation was broken. She had had to approach one or two of them before, when asking them to care for Edward, but this new relationship opened up their world and their suffering to her, and, though she often made sardonic jokes about them, she tolerated them much better.

Some of the mothers of the girls at work had heard the talk and reported it to their daughters. The daughters spent a considerable part of their lunch hours and tea breaks arguing with me that it was a pack of lies, and I found myself in the unenviable position of having to defend it as gospel truth, despite Father's request for help from the Presence. I said loftily that the debts Father had come to see the Presence about were old ones, and finally they retired to their respective gossip corners and left me once more alone. Sylvia Poole said nothing, for which I was profoundly grateful. Perhaps her mother did not hear it.

The unexpected success of my composition set a seed in the back of my mind which was to lie dormant for many years before it finally sprang to life, and flowered.

# Chapter thirty-six

Pressed by youngsters who wanted to share the experiences of other children, Mother began to take us, on fine Bank Holidays, to New Brighton, a small holiday resort on the other side of the River Mersey.

Father refused to accompany us to its crowded beach, washed with the effluent of both Liverpool and Birkenhead, so Mother and I packed paper shopping bags with banana sandwiches and beer bottles filled with lemonade made from a concentrate. Down the sides we stuffed old pairs of underpants or shorts and our always dirty towels, so that the children could bathe.

We took the tram down to the Pier Head and caught the New Brighton ferry. The floating pier, pulsating gently beneath our feet, was always packed with people, anxious to spend a day away from Liverpool's heavily polluted air; and we held the children firmly by their hands lest they stray beyond the confining link fence and fall into the heaving tidal waters.

When the ferry boat's gangway slammed down, the crowd pressed forward while the passengers hurried off. Then, using prams and elbows to make a path, they charged on to the boat. Frantic voices floated out of the crowd screaming to our Aggie or our George to 'come 'ere afore you fall in.'

Pushing and jostling, we poured on to the upper deck in search of a seat in the sun, so that we could nurse Edward and Avril. Edward invariably broke into howls of fright at the uproar and had to be comforted by having the pretty seagulls pointed out to him and the lovely shiny waves.

Then there was the excitement of watching the funnel belch smoke. One of the boys invariably got a smut in his eye, which had to be hooked out with the corner of a handkerchief or by carefully pulling down the red-edged lid.

Sweet air from the sea blew straight up the estuary, ruffling the surface of the great river. The Royal Liver Building and the Cunard Building, trademarks of the Port of Liverpool, receded, and the New Brighton tower, the lighthouse and the sturdy battery jutting into the river loomed up. The children went mad with excitement and rushed up and down the companionways and along the crowded decks, like small, wingless gulls.

At New Brighton pier, the mob poured off like black pepper out of a pot. It was a miracle that nobody fell off the gangplanks into the water.

The beach always seemed to be full before we arrived, and yet, somehow, boatload after boatload of people were absorbed.

Heavy on the air were the odours of beer and fish and chips. Fathers and young men made straight for the public houses beyond the parade, while mothers spread old blankets to mark their patch of sand. The children flew down to the water like startled seals.

Ice cream men dispensed dripping cornets, and Alan and I sometimes bought one each for the younger children, if we had money left over after paying our fares.

Occasionally, Mother sent me to a booth to buy a pot of tea – one shilling deposit on the teapot – and we drank hot tea, while the children guzzled the overly sweet lemonade straight from the bottles.

While a towel was held round the middle of each child in turn, they wriggled out of their clothes and put on the old pants we had brought with us, and then went dancing into the filthy water. It was remarkable that nobody caught any deadly disease from the sewage- and chemical-filled stream.

They came out shivering, splashing the water from their skinny bodies, their feet caked with a mixture of sand and mud, and stood round us while they devoured the sand-impregnated sandwiches. Then they would play tag in and out of the seated crowd. To go to the fun fair was beyond our resources, but the children were happy to be freed from constraints of traffic and narrow streets, and to be allowed to yell at the tops of their voices.

My grandmother had always forbidden me to go to the beach near her home on Bank Holidays, because it was filled with similar trippers. Nice people, I was taught, stayed at home on such days. I wondered privately what she would think of her grandchildren if she could see them.

To my mother, these trips must have seemed unbearably noisy and smelly, the people round her crude and boorish. Yet, in a way, the change did her good, too, and she always returned from them much more talkative and cheerful.

In the late afternoon, we made the long trip home, sun-reddened and weary, Edward and Avril tending to be fretful and quarrelsome, Brian and Tony still bouncing. Fiona, Alan and Avril, being very fair-skinned, were usually as red as pillar boxes, and blistered by the unaccustomed strong sunlight. They groaned ruefully about it and, whenever possible, we bought a twopenny bottle of calamine lotion and sponged it over their backs and arms, while during the next few days they peeled painfully.

One August Bank Holiday, we spent the day at New Brighton in a crowd so thick that it was literally impossible by late afternoon to find a square foot of beach on which to sit. We were lucky, however, and the children stripped off and tumbled away into the water. The next day, on the front of a national newspaper, was a large close-up of the Forrester family, half undressed, with a caption describing the record-breaking crowd. Though we were not named, we were easily recognisable.

This made fuel for both Alan and me to be baited by our colleagues at work, and, as far as I was concerned, this seemed to confirm their poor opinion of me. The gulf between us widened. It made no difference, however, to my developing friendship with Sylvia Poole. Miriam, also, continued to be very kind to me, and she took me one Sunday for a hike into North Wales. I found that I did not have the strength to walk very far because my legs began to ache intolerably. We sat comfortably under a hedgerow, however, while she expounded to me the philosophy of Karl Marx and Engels. I discovered that we were both victims of The System; but her ideas seemed too radical for me to comprehend. I did learn, however, through this and many subsequent conversations, quite a lot about human beings caught in a radical belief, how the mind can be closed to argument, the path followed so narrow that even the biblical 'eye of a needle' seemed wide and liberal. I remained obstinately politically uncommitted.

Another unexpected pleasure came into my life when we discovered that the Central Hall on Renshaw Street held showings of old films. In an effort to give the poor of Liverpool an alternative to the public house, they offered a long programme for the price of twopence, and people flocked in from all over the city centre. I used to accompany Mother on any Saturday evening on which I was not giving a shorthand lesson, and it became a treat I looked forward to throughout the week, because it did not matter how shabby one looked; nobody was in a position to sneer.

Then Sylvia asked me to go for a walk with her one Sunday afternoon and to have tea with her family.

'I'll ask Mother,' I promised, rather desperately.

She seemed surprised that I had to ask permission to accept the invitation, but I could not tell her that I had been taught obedience like a performing dog, and I rarely moved without permission.

I broached the subject to Mother, as I did the ironing on the living-room table, while the rest of the family was out and Father was reading peacefully in the cold front room.

Mother was sitting by the fire with her feet up on a pouf made out of an old tin can, and she looked up quickly from the newspaper she was reading.

'What kind of a girl is she?'

Dread question. Miriam's degree had made her acceptable, but Sylvia had no such advantage.

'She's pretty – and she's clean – and she has nice clothes – her mother makes them,' I floundered, as I eased the iron round Father's second shirt; he had only two shirts, with four loose collars.

'Mm?'

'She speaks nicely.'

'Does she?'

'Yes.'

If she doesn't give me permission, I will go anyway, I silently swore to myself.

I set the iron on the fire to heat up, while Mother folded up the newspaper.

'Well, that sounds delightful,' Mother said warmly.

I stared at her, shirt cuff half folded back. Then I gasped, 'Oh, Mummy! I'm so glad you think so. I'm sure you will like her.'

Mother made a slight, disparaging gesture with one hand, as if to indicate she doubted that liking would enter into it. She had accepted the acne-pocked youths with their strong Liverpool accents who were Alan's friends, and the fact that Fiona occasionally played with rowdy local girls in the street. Tony, Brian and Avril sometimes sounded as if they had been born in the narrow street in which we lived, because remembrance of their former home had practically vanished. Perhaps Mother realised at last that we could no longer be exclusive, that she could not prevent her children adapting to their new circumstances, however unpleasant it was to her.

Now I had to approach the problem of getting a suitable dress out of pawn. Mother kept in her purse all the tickets for the many bundles of donated clothing and bedding that the pawnbroker had piled up in his loft for us.

'I could afford two or three shillings to redeem something, Mummy,' I said meekly.

'Yes,' Mother replied, a sudden razor sharpness in her voice. 'You have plenty of money.'

A year earlier such a remark would have stung me into a quarrel. Now, I was better able to keep control of myself, and I said as gently as I could, 'I'm trying very hard, Mummy, not to ask for anything, to pay for everything, so that you have one less person to worry about.'

Mother slapped down the newspaper and got up. 'You seem to be doing very well. You seem to have money for everything.' Her whole stance was unexpectedly filled with boiling resentment, as she shuffled over to the fire and poked the coals crossly.

I began to tremble at the sudden change in attitude. To gain time, I took the iron off the fire and wiped the soot off it with a piece of rag. I was clumsy and managed to sear my thumb against it. I winced, dropped the rag and popped my stinging thumb into my mouth.

I wanted to shriek at Mother that every penny spent for fares, every threepenny-bit for a bowl of soup at lunchtime was painstakingly considered. I wanted to remind her bitterly that the last ninepenny pair of rayon stockings that I had bought had been taken from under my mattress and worn out by her. In consequence, I had had to appear at work with long black lines on my stockings where I had overstitched ladder after ladder. I was still smarting from the giggles of the other girls and Mr Ellis's tart inquiry, 'Where d' yer buy stockings like them from?'

I bowed my head over the ironing again.

'Well, sometimes I do better – when I have a shorthand student.'

'Humph.'

She put down the poker and moved slowly round the room, picking up and putting into a pile odds and ends left around by the children. I looked at her back with pure hatred for a moment. Her legs were grievously lined with bulging blue varicose veins and her shoulders were hunched like those of an old woman. Too much starch in her diet was beginning to make her fat around her waist. The anger in me gave way to pity.

Perhaps, better than all her children, I understood what had happened to Mother. I could remember her in the heyday of her beauty, when, at every function, she was surrounded by admirers. The sight of her now easily moved me to compassion. It was, however, like being compassionate towards an angry wasp.

As I began to get a grip on myself again, I wondered what she was thinking about, as she trailed around the grubby, ill-lit room.

The silence lengthened between us, till I felt the tension relax a little. Then I asked, 'Could I get my overcoat out? And the dress with the gold spots that I made?'

'I'll give you the ticket for the coat – it's in a bundle by itself. That dress is not suitable.'

'I don't know what else to wear.'

'There's a blue wool dress in one bundle. I intended to wear it for work – it came in a parcel from Mrs Walsingham some time back. You could borrow it. It fits me, so it will fit you.' She spoke in a weary, dull voice, and she did not look at me.

So the bargain was struck. I could borrow the dress once, for the price of its retrieval. I could have my coat back if I had the money to pay the pawnbroker.

I thanked her humbly.

# Chapter thirty-seven

Sylvia had on a well-fitting, grey pin-striped suit. Her golden curls peeped out from a tan-coloured sailor hat. Her immaculate shoes, gloves and handbag matched the wide-brimmed hat. The heels of her shoes gave her height, and she looked charming.

I was agonisedly aware of my old overcoat and lack of gloves. I wore the hat that Mother had had on when we arrived in Liverpool, a battered beige cloche. The coat was still badly creased from its sojourn with the pawnbroker, despite my frantic efforts with a hot iron. Underneath it, Mrs Walsingham's dress hung on my slight frame; I consoled myself with the thought that it was a very good dress, excellently cut from a soft blue wool. I had had more success in ironing it than I had had with the coat.

We walked soberly for an hour along silent Sunday streets. Occasionally, we met a young couple, dressed in Sunday clothes, strolling arm in arm, or pushing a pram with a befrilled baby in it.

Finally we arrived at a terrace house, similar to the one in which I lived. There was, however, a great difference in its aspect. The panelled front door had no dust on it; the windowsills were likewise clear of dust. The front step had been swept and washed.

Sylvia took her key out of her handbag and let us both into the gloomy hall. The house smelled sweet, I noticed, as I took off my crumpled coat and gave it to Sylvia to hang up on a peg in the hall.

She ushered me into a living-room, smaller and darker than ours. It was stuffed with furniture, but its general air of cosiness reminded me of pictures on Christmas cards. All it lacked was a row of brightly coloured children's stockings hanging along the high mantel shelf, in expectation of Father Christmas's arrival. Instead, in front of the old-fashioned fireplace with its big cooking oven, stood a little, stout lady in a navy blue dress with a tiny pattern on it. Her grey hair was combed softly back into a bun. Her complexion was rosy enough to suggest high blood pressure. Her hands were clasped in front of her, and her wedding ring was deeply imbedded in a finger swollen slightly, perhaps from years of washing with a scrubbing board. She seemed to me the epitome of all that was kind and motherly.

And mother me, she did. I was plied with tea and bread and butter and jam and homemade cake. I was warmed by the fire, and in a quiet, shy manner made to feel very welcome. I had talked without stopping to Sylvia during our walk; but now I felt shy, and Mrs Poole had to help me out with a question or two to keep the conversation going.

At one point, Mr Poole rushed in from another room. He was in shirt-sleeves and waistcoat, his scant hair rumpled, his glasses slipping down his nose. How was he going to finish preparing his sermon when there was no more paper to write on? he demanded.

My presence was pointed out to him and he was introduced hastily, but his mind was not on visitors and he shook my hand absently. As soon as more paper was produced from a drawer, he vanished immediately.

Mrs Poole told me that her husband was a lay preacher, in addition to his normal work as a city electrician. I did not know exactly what a lay preacher was, but was too shy to ask to have it explained to me. She added that there was one other member of the family, Sylvia's elder brother, who was out for the afternoon. She sighed and indicated that she was in some way worried about him. As she talked, I began to realise that I knew him.

Just before my fourteenth birthday, the Liverpool Education Committee had discovered my existence and had ordered me into school until I reached my birthday. Sylvia's brother had been a pupil in the same class as me. There were forty-five or more pupils in the class and discipline was, of a necessity, rigid. I remembered Chris Poole vividly, because he was a target for the sarcasm of every teacher who entered the room, and yet he did not seem to be particularly naughty. If there was talking on the boys' side of the room, it was invariably he who was reprimanded, though he might be one of several offenders. If a pencil was not returned to the teacher, he was the first to be checked for its disappearance. If the class fidgeted or something was noisily dropped on the floor, it was he who had to stand in front of the class as punishment. And the class was so conditioned that they took his guilt for granted, and laughed at his discomfiture.

I recognised a fellow scapegoat and felt a sneaking sympathy for him.

I was never in trouble during that period of schooling. I was thankful for the orderly lessons and was happy to put in a phenomenal amount of work. But Chris, with all the exuberance of a thirteen-year-old, obviously hated the inflexible confinement to a desk, hour after tedious hour.

If anything went wrong at home, it could be guaranteed that I would be the first person blamed; in the classroom this happened to Chris. In Germany it was happening to the Jews. I had just begun to realise that majority groups will always find convenient scapegoats for their own shortcomings; the scapegoat is usually a small minority. In families it can be a minority of one.

So I understood Mrs Poole's general anxiety about her son better than she realised and could feel sympathetic about it. And by many small threads of congeniality a friendship grew up between Mrs Poole and me which was nearly as deep as that between her daughter and me.

I felt so enriched that I walked home from their house in a dream, feeling as if I was floating a foot off the ground.

# Chapter thirty-eight

He was a short man, padded with layers of hard fat under his well-tailored grey suit, a man with a chin always blue, however well shaved. He stood silently staring at the ceiling of the lift while I took him up to the Committee Room, and I marvelled at the announcement that the Presence had that morning made regarding him. He had never spoken to me. How could such a rich man understand a very great need of the small person who politely opened and shut the lift gates for him? A need for entertainment. As he climbed the final staircase up to the Committee Room, I stared at his broad back with awed amazement.

'He's Greek,' said Dorothy disparagingly.

'He's in shipping,' Phyllis told me. 'He made a fortune.'

And I thought, very humbly, He's remembered how empty of fun life can be, if you have principles and no money.

'Sylvia,' I whispered behind the files. 'He's giving us three shillings and sixpence each. The Cashier is going to give it to us.'

Sylvia's brow wrinkled up in doubtful surprise.

'It's true. It's a present to all the staff, so that we can go to the theatre. It's supposed to be the price of the very best seat anywhere. The senior staff are going to get more.'

Sylvia pushed a cardboard folder into the file, while she considered this information.

'You know, it's only sixpence to go to the Playhouse,' she said thoughtfully.

'Really?' I breathed.

'Yes. You queue up at the side of the theatre – you can't book.'

'I used to do that at home,' I said, without thinking. 'At the matinées.'

'Home?'

I giggled sheepishly, and did not answer. Liverpool was home, wasn't it?

The slip was revealing. Was I still waiting to go back home to the small southern town from which we had come? To a house now occupied by others? To a nanny who must have long since married and gone to live in the sixteenth-century farmhouse her fiancé owned?

305

Sylvia was waiting for an answer, another file held ready to push into the stack.

'Oh, I used to go by myself to the theatre – when I was about ten. Mother sometimes allowed me to go to the cinema if there was a suitable film – but I never went.' I laughed at the recollection, and added, 'There was a theatre in the town which had all kinds of shows – travelling ones – and I used to go there. I sat right up at the top of the topmost balcony.'

Sylvia laughed, and said she wished she had been there, too.

Mr Ellis heard the unseemly laughter, and reprimanded us. But later on I told her about Mother's lovely singing voice and how she had always belonged to amateur operatic or dramatic groups. When Brian was born and Edith had complained about the work load, Mother had formed the habit of taking me with her to rehearsals. I was a very quiet child, not much trouble to Edith. But it was a gesture on Mother's part and Edith had to be satisfied with it.

At first I sat and fidgeted in the frighteningly empty theatre and did not understand what was happening. I watched while adults walked about the stage with books in their hands and talked in loud, artificial voices. A gentleman seated in the front row sometimes shouted at them, and someone else occasionally rushed on to the stage and rearranged the players and told them how to behave. But gradually I became fascinated as a story began to evolve in front of my eyes. There was nothing very experimental in the plays they performed and a child could understand them. Once I discovered the existence of dress rehearsals, I used to look forward to them very much. Sometimes, as I grew older, Father took me to the opening night. He always had a formal bouquet of flowers to be presented to Mother at the end of the performance, when the bows were taken; in fact, sometimes the stage looked like a garden because of the number of bouquets presented to the principals.

Father also arranged for me to go to the pantomime each year, whenever one was within reasonable journeying distance. And what pantomimes they were, filled with singing and dancing, magical illusions, uproarious Dames whose red and white striped pants always fell down below their skirts, and, of course, noble Principal Boys like Dick Whittington and lovely Princesses in silver gowns. A magic world, a paradise for children.

Since the kindly Greek had intended that his gift should be spent at the theatre, Sylvia and I decided that we would spread the money as far as it would go. By sitting 'up in the Gods', as the gallery was called, we could see seven plays at the Liverpool Playhouse.

Probably no one would have appreciated our solemn efforts more than the benevolent donor. We queued patiently, leaning against the side of the building. We always hoped to see the actors and actresses arriving at the stage door, but we never did. Instead, we were entertained by a tattered crew of mouth-organ players, concertina players, clumsy tumblers, and even an elderly tramp who would slowly put a brick down on the muddy street, lay his head on it and gradually raise his legs until he was standing on his head. He would remain poised uncertainly on the brick while a beguiling small boy ran up and down the queue with a cap held out hopefully. It was some years before Sylvia or I could afford to give him anything.

When the gallery door was opened, we would pay our sixpence and make the long, long climb up the stairs to the top of the building. Crouched on a bench, with our knees knocking the heads of the people in the next row, we waited for the curtain to rise. Coffee could be purchased at the back of the gallery, and I was torn with doubt as to whether our Greek shipowner would mind if I spent some of his money on a cup. I finally decided that it would not be honest to do so, and sometimes I used my soup money for coffee instead. One could become very cold and wet while waiting in the queue, and if I did not warm up quickly, my treacherous throat would begin to swell and the pain in my legs intensify.

But the excitement, the magic, was a tonic to a starveling like myself. Neither Sylvia nor I realised that we were watching the early efforts of some of Britain's greatest actors and actresses, who were being nursed along by a famous director, William Armstrong. Michael Redgrave and Rachel Kempson, Geoffrey Toone and Lloyd Pearson, peopled the shabby theatre with kings and queens and princes, and I fell hopelessly in love with each handsome face, as cloaks were swept over shoulders and swords were flourished.

I told my parents I had been given tickets for the theatre. I did not dare to say that I had been given money; it would have inevitably been squeezed out of me, by reminders that there was nothing in the house for breakfast or that Baby Edward had no socks; and I would have felt so guilty that I would have handed it over like a lamb. I kept the money from my occasional teaching earnings, and the extra half-a-crown that the Presence paid me, in a bag round my neck. But often the need was so great at home that I would have to give part of it for some necessity, and go without lunch or some other small luxury. Since my illness, it had been a grim necessity to hold on to sufficient money for tram fares; it was over a year before I was strong enough to walk to and from work again.

Minerva, sitting on top of the Town Hall dome, smiled particularly on the Liverpool theatres of those days, as if to encourage specially her actors to create for two young girls a world of wonder which helped to make endurable the soot-blackened city outside the theatre walls. In those precious hours in the stuffy Playhouse gallery, tucked up comfortably beside Sylvia, I was happy as I had never before been happy in Liverpool.

Thank you, dear Minerva. Thank you for all that sweet content. I knew you'd help me.

*By the Waters*
*of Liverpool*

*To dear Robert*
*who helped so much*

# Chapter one

I was seventeen going on eighteen, and I had never been kissed by a man. It was not surprising. Who would want to court the favours of a gaunt, smelly beanpole? I was five feet four inches tall, and that was real height in underfed Liverpool.

As I strode primly along Lime Street, on my way to evening school, the men who hung about the entrances of the cinemas hardly spared me a glance. I was most unflatteringly safe. And this, in a world where women still took it for granted that they would get married, was very depressing. Girls did not look for careers – they worked until they got married. If a woman was not loved and cherished by a man, she must be hopelessly ugly or there must be something else wrong with her.

I tried not to care that no young man had so much as winked at me. I stuck my proud Forrester nose in the air and vowed to make a career for myself as a social worker in the charity which employed me. Dorothy Parker, the famous American writer, had once remarked that men seldom make passes at girls who wear glasses; and I had a pair of too-small horn-rimmed spectacles perched on my nose. There was nobody to suggest to a shy, short-sighted girl that she might occasionally take off the ugly impediment to show the sad, green eyes behind.

'Perhaps your yellow skin will improve, as you get older,' my childhood nanny, Edith, had suggested; and she scrubbed my face harder still with Pear's Preparing To Be A Beautiful Lady soap. To no purpose. All time and our subsequent poverty had done was to add a revolting array of acne spots, spots that were made worse by the lack of soap, hot water and clean towels at home.

And here was the year 1937 rolling along. Soon I would be eighteen. And nobody, I felt, really cared what happened to me. To my mother I was a trying daughter who brought in a wage each week; to the rest of the family a pair of hands, very useful for cooking and darning socks.

It was seven years since Father had gone suddenly bankrupt, plunging us into a poverty so great that I was frequently surprised that the nine of us had survived it, seven skinny children of whom I was the eldest, and two equally thin parents.

I sighed as I trudged up the hill. Though Mother and Father now both had work, they were very poor managers, and we were still cold and hungry most of the time, surrounded by the unpleasant odour of neglect and poor nutrition.

I handed my small wages to Mother every pay-day, except for three shillings and sixpence. This totally inadequate sum was supposed to clothe me, pay for lunches and tram fares, make-up and all the small things a girl at work was expected to have. Mother was bent on making me give up my employment and once again stay at home to keep house, something I dreaded; so she made it as difficult as possible for me to go to work.

I found pupils to coach in shorthand in the evenings, but I earned very little because my free time was extremely limited.

I was doing very well at evening school, I comforted myself. One day I might be promoted and earn enough to live on. My ugly, kind bookkeeping teacher had assured me recently that, if I took one more course, I would be able to become a bookkeeper. She had added that parents were always glad of a girl at home who brought in a wage; it contributed to their comfort in their old age.

She had put into words something I dreaded, something only a husband could save me from. I could be faced with spending the rest of my life maintaining and waiting on two irritable, shiftless, nagging parents, the usual fate of the daughter who did not marry. Because I was plain and shy and frightened of my mother, I knew I could be bullied into being a nobody, a nothing.

Some women with gentle parents found their care a labour of love. Not me. I knew I would be crushed as flat as a shadow. I had already had a spell as housekeeper, from the age of eleven until I was fifteen. It had been a nightmare, looking after six young children and two quarrelling parents. Mother had, before Father's bankruptcy, never had to care entirely for her children. We had had servants. In fact, I hardly knew her until we were plunged into a slum together. She escaped from her unruly brood by working as a demonstrator in department stores.

In a frantic effort to escape myself, I had at the age of fourteen raged and threatened, as only a fourteen-year-old can, until I got permission to attend evening school, to repair in some part my lack of education.

At fifteen, with the unexpected help of Miss Ferguson, a deaconess at the local church, I had fought another battle to take the job I at present held. Housekeeping was divided between a very angry mother and me.

I called Miss Ferguson my Fairy Godmother, and it was of this devout, cultivated lady that I was thinking as I kicked a stone up Copperas Hill on the way to evening school. The street was quiet in the fading spring light, the misty air balmy – and I was shivering with pure fright.

Miss Ferguson had laid on my shoulders a fear worse than that of death, the fear of hell, Dante's hell.

How could she do such a thing? I wondered miserably, with a super-stitious shudder. She was my Fairy Godmother.

She had first visited the family in order to recruit my two middle brothers, Brian and Tony, into the church choir. She knew them because all the children attended the church school. She had seen my situation as unpaid maid-of-all-work, and, perhaps to give me an hour or two of rest, she had pressed Mother into allowing me to go to church on Sunday evenings. At first I had no suitable clothes to go in, but once I could look at least neat, I thankfully attended.

We were Protestants, an important point in a city where the division between Protestants and Catholics was bitter and sometimes bloody. Children were aware from the time they could speak which side of the fence they stood on, and the implanted bigotry is to this day not entirely rooted out.

No amount of churchgoing could erase the vaguely erotic dreams which haunted me occasionally, or a terrible sense of empty loneliness. Ignorant, innocent, half-starved, practically friendless, my flowering body was trying to tell me of needs of which I had little notion. Almost all the myriad of novels I had read ended with the hero kissing the heroine for the first time. I had never considered what happened next. I felt a kiss would be the ultimate height of happiness.

But it was churchgoing which was causing my present unhappiness. As I turned into the big, gloomy evening school, which I loved so much, I was trembling with fear. Unable to concentrate on the shorthand teacher's rapid dictation, my mind was filled with scattered pictures of what had happened the previous Sunday.

Unaware of impending trouble, I had crept out of the back pew in which I normally hid my shabbiness, and battled my way up Princes Avenue through a brisk north-westerly carrying with it a spray of rain.

I was going home to a mother almost unhinged by her fall from considerable affluence, and to a fretful, delicate father, an underpaid, overworked city clerk. Liverpool was awash with the unemployed and the underpaid, and this governed all our lives. To a plain girl hurrying through the dusk, life seemed very hard. There was little physical strength in me. I was frail and always hungry, and I hugged my worn brown coat tightly round me for comfort.

Thankfully I pulled the string hanging from the letterbox of our row house. The latch lifted, and I was glad to step inside, away from the wind.

Miss Ferguson, Fairy Godmother and deaconess of the church, was seated in our old easy chair by the fire in our living-room, undisturbed, it seemed, by the fetid atmosphere and the dirty chaos surrounding her. She must have been quicker than me in leaving the service and making her way over to our house, because she was already deep in conversation with

Mother as I edged my way into the cluttered room. Her square pallid face with its cherry-red nose wrinkled up into a smile as I entered.

'Good evening, Helen.'

'Good evening, Miss Ferguson. Hello, Mother.'

Mother was seated on a straight-backed chair opposite Miss Ferguson, and was smoking with long, deep puffs, the smoke like a fog round her head. Miss Ferguson seemed to be the only person able to penetrate beyond Mother's polite façade and fight her way through to the real, suffering woman beneath, and Mother was listening intently as Miss Ferguson continued their conversation.

Dressed in black, with wrinkled woollen stockings and flat-heeled shoes, her hair covered by a black coif, Miss Ferguson was very different from Mother's fashionable friends of so many years ago. But she was a cultivated woman, like my convent-bred mother, and it was a pleasure to listen to the hum of her soft voice.

I picked up an old fruit basket full of mending from beside the hearth and began my nightly task of darning the family's socks and stockings. Everybody's woollen socks or rayon stockings seemed to spring a hole or a ladder each day, and because we had so few pairs, they had to be darned ready for wear the next day.

At first, as my needle flew in and out, I did not take much notice of the conversation. Then Mother's voice penetrated. She sounded pettish. 'Helen's at evening school three times a week. And she is often out on Saturday evenings – either at the theatre with her friend, Sylvia, or teaching her shorthand pupil. Then church on Sunday evening – she's hardly home, to help me.'

I looked up quickly, just in time to catch a resentful glance from my tight-lipped mother.

Dear heaven! Now, what had I done? My needle slowed. Miss Ferguson knew how much washing, mending, ironing and cleaning, not to speak of child care, I managed to tuck into the time before and after work and during the weekends. She visited regularly and had seen me always busy. She now favoured me with a quick wry grin, and let Mother's complaints pass.

I looked at my flashing fingers as I darned. Broken nails and soot-ingrained cuticles, half-healed cuts and burns, all told of fires made, sooty saucepans scoured and food prepared. At work I hid my hands as much as possible.

'It is really time dear Helen was confirmed – I should have mentioned it before,' Miss Ferguson said persuasively. 'The Confirmation lessons don't take very long – in fact, she may already know all that is required.'

So that was it. Well, I was quite happy to be confirmed if it pleased my Fairy Godmother, and thereby become a full member of the Church.

'I suppose it is,' replied Mother. She flicked the ash of her cigarette into the tiny fire, which was almost lost in the huge, old-fashioned kitchen range. 'It is the time for the lessons – she really has to spend more time at home. I need her help.'

I let them continue to discuss the merits of Confirmation and the first Communion which would follow it, and went on darning and dreaming. Suddenly my heart jolted, when unexpectedly Miss Ferguson said, 'Of course, the dear child has never been to Confession. If she is to take the sacrament, she will need first to go to Confession. It would be a good idea, don't you think, if she got into the habit beforehand and went this week. Perhaps young Alan should think about it, too.'

I could feel myself going clammy all over. At that moment all the history books I had read, written almost entirely by Protestants, seemed to contribute to the sense of horror at anything which savoured of Catholicism – and Confession was surely a Catholic institution. In my nostrils there was suddenly the smoke and smell of the burning flesh of Protestant martyrs, made beloved by many a story; ordinary men and women, lords, priests, yokels, who had bravely faced being burned alive rather than acknowledge the Pope or the Mass – or confession to anyone but God.

I was weak on the theology of it, but I knew that Catholic Bloody Mary was the most hated Queen in British history, because she had tried to burn out of existence all signs of Protestantism. This unthinkable suggestion of Miss Ferguson's went against everything I had ever learned of my church. In a city riven down the middle by religion, it seemed incredible that a Protestant deaconess should ever mention Confession.

Needle poised, I burst into the conversation with a frightened squeak, a squeak of genuine horror. 'But we are Protestants. We say the General Confession during service. We make personal confessions only to God. I thought that was what being a Protestant was all about.'

Mother laughed, her delicate, superior, crushing laugh. 'Helen, we are High Anglicans. It is by accident that you have never been to Confession before. By chance, most of the places we have lived in have only low churches, so that when you were little you were taken to them.' She drew on her cigarette, and then added a little sharply, 'You seemed to have enjoyed going to a high church recently.'

'In all the many months I stayed with Grandma I never went to Confession,' I protested. 'If she had gone, I am sure she would have taken me with her.'

Mother did not like being reminded of her mother-in-law, who had washed her hands of her shiftless son and would no longer have anything to do with us.

'Your grandmother was too old to walk further than the village church – and that church was low church.'

I pushed my fist into one of Brian's smelly socks and attacked another hole. My voice trembled, as I said flatly, 'Well, I'm not going.'

315

Miss Ferguson looked nonplussed, and her hands with their black cotton gloves fluttered helplessly.

Mother's heavily made-up face began to darken. 'Don't be ridiculous, Helen. It would do you good to go, to come face to face with your arrogance and bad temper. It might teach you to honour your parents, which would be a welcome change.'

Me? Confess? Tell some strange priest that there were times when I felt like murdering my mother? Times like this moment. Tell him that I had dreamed that I took all my clothes off in front of a man? I couldn't. I wouldn't. I could tell God Himself these things in the course of the General Confession, because He had made me and probably understood His faulty work. But not a priest – not a man!

Much that I had let pass during my recent churchgoing suddenly fell into place. I had puzzled that the ministers of the church strode the streets in cassocks with black birettas on their heads, that servers assisted at the altar, that incense was used, the whole elaborate ritual. Now, the theatrical beauty of it, which had so impressed me, seemed suddenly to hide a basket of vipers.

Shivering but determined, I put down the darning into my lap and turned to Miss Ferguson. Her short-sighted eyes darted from Mother to me.

'Miss Ferguson, I couldn't do it. If I have to go to Confession, I might as well become a Catholic and do it properly. There wouldn't be any difference.'

Miss Ferguson found her voice and said rather hoarsely, 'There is a great difference, Helen. We do not accept the supremacy of the Pope. Our King is head of our church.'

Mother nodded agreement, her mouth pinched with her disapproval of me.

I felt as if I had been backed against a wall by a member of the Inquisition. I had never thought about the legitimacy of being allowed to worship as one pleases. I had no profound knowledge of my own faith. Most of my age group did not even attend church, though the majority, if asked, would say that they were either Protestant or Catholic – so great was the religious division in Liverpool.

To Liverpool Protestants, Catholics were people who lived in the worst slums because they did not know any better, and their greatest entertainment was attacking Protestant religious processions. They were not ordinary, kindly people at all.

I saw through Miss Ferguson's suggestion only the tortured faces of my own beloved martyrs. I ignored the fact that Protestants had, in their time, done their share of roasting hapless Catholics.

Miss Ferguson saw the need to reassure me, and she leaned forward and patted my knee. 'The first Confirmation classes will be held in a fortnight's time, my dear. Come along to the vestry. I am sure the good

Father can explain to you much better than I can how good for the soul Confession is.'

'But – but ...' I spluttered helplessly. 'Miss Ferguson, I can't – I just can't.'

The good Father! Not the Vicar. Childhood memories of gentle, vague scholars in clerical collars sipping tea in various drawing-rooms made me want to rush back in time to them. I seemed to recollect that they only extolled the basic virtues. Where had they gone? I must have been asleep during the weeks I had been attending Miss Ferguson's church.

Mother was saying brightly that, since Miss Ferguson thought it wise, time would be found for my attendance at classes.

With her usual outward charm, she saw Miss Ferguson out of our grubby living-room, into the narrow hall and finally out to the littered street. I knew very well that she would attend to me later in a very different fashion.

Though doubtless learned clerics were already discussing and challenging the concepts of hell and damnation and other long-held beliefs, eternal punishment for the heretic was a very real threat to a girl brought up by ignorant country servants and subsequently cut off from her contemporaries as I was. To defy one's parents for any reason was bad enough. To defy one's church was, in my opinion, likely to be much worse. As I contemplated Brian's tattered sock, l was shaking with fear of the spiritual forces which might be ranked against me. I wondered if I would be struck dead if I argued with the priests, actually raised my voice in a church building. And death was only the beginning of trouble for those cast out of the Church. I might burn in hell for ever afterwards.

Nevertheless, quivering like a mouse before a cat, I determined on a last squeak.

# *Chapter two*

I could remember Mother at the age of twenty-four, an elegant beauty with fashionable short black curls and large, pale blue eyes. Her fine legs were sheathed in the latest pure silk stockings, her skirts daringly short, so that a sudden flip of them would give a glimpse of ruffled silk garters trimmed with tiny roses or pearls, or French knickers heavy with lace. She attracted a great deal of attention from Father's war-battered friends, and Edith said she could get anything by merely fluttering her eyelashes. It did not work, however, when I tried fluttering my scant lashes, and I decided it must be something magical, known only to grown-ups.

The slightest argument or objection, the smallest frustration, would unleash her ungovernable temper, from which shell-shocked husband and servants would fly. I was terrified of her and would cling to Edith, seeking safety in her starched white lap. Edith always said comfortingly that she did not care a tinker's cuss about Mother's tempers; the job was handy for her. We lived conveniently close to the young farmer who was Edith's fiancé, and we frequently escaped to the warmth and laughter of his mother's farmhouse kitchen. Alan, who was the child next to me in age, was also wheeled in his pram to the farm and got bounced merrily on many a rustic knee.

Now Mother was a middle-aged harridan, worn down by the illness she had suffered when my smallest brother, Edward, was born and by the privation we had all endured since Father's bankruptcy. Her figure was shapeless from eating too much white bread, her lovely legs horrible with varicose veins, hands ruined like mine, from washing, scrubbing, blackleading fireplaces, and lack of gloves. We rarely had hot water or soap, either for cleaning or washing ourselves, and face or hand creams were luxuries to look at through the chemist's window. All that remained of Mother's earlier self was a great charm of manner and a quick intelligence, when she felt like using either of them. Her scarifying temper had been further fed by her total unhappiness at her present state.

Like alcoholics, an improvement in my parents' lives could be brought about only by their facing their problems squarely and themselves determining on a new and careful path, in their case a financial path. But, like many alcoholics, they could not do it. So we all continued to suffer, despite the fact that five of us were at work.

Alan worked as an office boy in the city, and most of his small wages were handed back to him for tram fares, lunches and pocket money. Similarly, my pretty fifteen-year-old sister, Fiona, worked as a cashier in a butcher's shop. She earned the same amount as I did, but, unlike me, most of her wage was handed back to her for her expenses. Her clothes were bought for her, new, by paying for them by weekly instalments through a system of cheques. Companies issued cheques, commonly for five pounds, and with these one could buy clothing or household goods of one's choice at any store on the company's list. The clothing was often shoddy and expensive, but Fiona was at least as well dressed as any other girl travelling to work on the trams with her. I struggled to keep myself in clothes by buying them from the pawnbroker's bargain table.

Paying the cheque man was as much a worry to Liverpool housewives as finding the money to pay the rent, and it drained our income. We were permanently hungry, frequently cold and not very clean. Cleanliness is expensive. Our landlord had freed us from one plague of slum living. He had had our house stoved, so that we were no longer verminous, and our relief from bug and lice bites was wonderful to us.

Brian and Tony, who came next to Fiona, had inherited their parents' brains and they also had some of Mother's earlier vivacity and physical strength. Brian had won a scholarship from the church school to the Liverpool Institute, and I was very envious of him. Earlier, I had won a scholarship to the Liverpool City School of Art, but I had not been allowed to take it up. I had to stay at home to keep house.

Also at school was short, determined Avril, almost unnoticed unless she had a temper tantrum like Mother, and little Edward, beloved baby of the family, whom I had nursed along since infancy. Though Edward was not very strong, probably because of the lack of adequate food in early childhood, his mind was clear and he had the ability to apply himself with great concentration to whatever he was doing. He could already read well, and Father hoped that both he and Tony would also win scholarships. Neither Mother nor Father gave any heed to Avril's possible abilities as a scholar. She was only a girl.

The only other members of the family to attend church were Brian and Tony, who for nearly three years had sung in the choir and had enjoyed a remuneration of a shilling and eightpence per month, which they were allowed to keep. Now they sometimes acted as acolytes. Nobody, as far as I knew, had pressed them to go to Confession. They were, however, the cleverest of passive resisters and even if pressed would probably have placidly failed to turn up for it. Brian's hazel eyes and Tony's calm blue-grey ones could look as blank as a factory wall, with an innocence and incomprehension of stare usually seen only in the subnormal. They were a pair of cheery scallywags, most unlikely to be faced with the inner qualms and soul-searching which always afflicted me.

I was dreadfully troubled when Mother ordered me to stop being such a fool, and to attend Confirmation classes. I made no reply, because I had long since learned not to do battle when I knew for certain that I could not win. For several days I fretted fearfully, about what I should do.

'Them as don't obey goes straight to hell,' Edith had assured me, whenever I was being particularly perverse.

And there was Grandma's soft voice whispering, 'Good children go to Heaven, dear. Only the wicked burn in hell.'

And the Bible from which I had learned to read, under Grandma's tuition, was full of the horrors of what happened to those who did not obey the will of God.

As I sorted files in the office, I tried to comfort myself. 'It doesn't really happen nowadays. It is an allegory.' But the fear in me was almost a primeval one; it stuck in the back of my mind and refused to be shifted.

Mother was obviously used to the idea of Confession. It must have been reinforced when she was a child, because she had been brought up in a convent, the only Protestant amid a sea of Catholics. It was waste of time to appeal to her.

Walking home through the April rain, I prayed to God to tell me what He wanted me to do, and got no immediate reply. Confused, afraid, with a mind filled with myths, I turned to the only other person I could think of who might advise me. I would ask Father.

# Chapter three

To get a little time alone with Father would, I knew, be difficult. A big family in a tiny house has almost no privacy.

I pulled the string hanging inside the flapless letterbox, in order to let myself in. I had worked late and then gone straight to evening school and had not eaten since morning, but I paused for a moment in the doorway to watch some men playing ollies in the gutter. The little white balls skittered over the rough roadway, almost invisible in the light of the street lamps. These men used to say disparagingly about our family that we talked 'with ollies in t' mouth'. Refined Oxford accents were extremely rare in slums.

The smell of the house hit me as I went into the little hall, a smell of warm, damp, much used air, with strong overtones of the odour of vomit.

All the family was crowded into the small back living-room. Old-fashioned wooden shutters had been closed across the curtainless windows and secured by an iron bar. A small fire blazed bravely in the big iron kitchen range, and by it Father was seated bolt upright in the solitary easy chair.

His usual yellowy complexion was flushed red, and he was pounding his delicate, almost feminine fist on the arm of the chair, as if to emphasise forcibly something he had already said.

As I paused by the door, he almost shouted, 'I will not tolerate such an abomination. It is disgusting beyond words. She must leave at once.'

He was answered by an unintelligible babble from the family.

I thought for an anxious second that he was talking about me. I lived in constant, gnawing fear that my parents would withdraw me from my job and make me stay at home again to keep house; they were quite capable of taking such a decision without any prior discussion with me and of handing in my resignation directly to my employer. I was still under twenty-one.

With some trepidation I eased my way through the half-open door and into the room itself. The children's upturned faces looked sickly in the light of the single, unshaded electric bulb, and Edward turned his heart-shaped face, pinched with fatigue, towards me. He said simply, 'Bed.'

Though he was nearly seven, he was no great weight and I picked him up, and said, 'Yes, love.' He and Brian were the only children I ever knew who asked to go to bed. It was as if their strength ran out suddenly. I smiled at him, and added, 'I'll put the kettle on to heat and help you wash your knees and neck as soon as it is hot.' I looked cautiously round him at the family.

The centre of attention was Fiona. She was standing in the middle of the group, facing Father, and her wide eyes with their enormous fringe of long lashes showed signs of tears. She was almost cringing, her toes turned slightly inward, her arms across her breast as if to protect herself.

She said in a watery voice, 'It's not that bad, Daddy. I didn't go. I wouldn't dream of it.'

Nobody took any notice of me, except Alan, who grinned at me as I stumbled over his feet, on my way to the kitchen with Edward. 'I think it's funny,' he said to Father.

There was some hot water in the kettle sitting on the greasy little gas stove, so I poured it into the washing-up bowl and commenced to wash Edward. I could hear Father's choked voice. He said furiously, 'It is *not* funny. It is horrible. At the least, it shows a total disrespect for the dead – at the worst, it is perversion. They ought to be put out of business.'

Mother was laboriously cutting her nails with our single pair of blunt scissors, letting the ends drop into the hearth, and she murmured, 'It makes me shudder.'

I paused in my preparations to wash Edward's dirty knees, and left him sitting on the kitchen table drying his face, while I went to the intervening door and asked, 'What's happened, Daddy?'

'Pack of sickening necrophiles!' Father exploded again, turning to me.

Brian and Tony were sitting at the table, elbows on open exercise books. I saw Tony's eyes light up. A beautiful new word to be learned, to be used incessantly for at least a week, while he turned it over in his mind and tried it in every possible way.

Mother greeted me with a worried, 'Hello, Helen. We'll explain it later. Put Avril and Edward to bed – it's getting late.' She turned to the students at the table who were obviously most intrigued by the conversation. 'Hurry up, you two. Put your books away.'

'It's something about looking at dead people, Helen,' Edward whispered to me, as I returned to him, and rolled down his knee-high socks. His knees were very dirty and I scrubbed them with a piece of cotton cloth. There was no soap.

Avril had followed me out, and stood waiting for her turn to be washed. She said nothing, but her plain, round face beneath the straggling blonde hair was white, and I wondered if she was ill.

Edward struggled out of his woollen jersey and proffered a far from white neck to be washed. 'It's nasty,' he muttered.

Both children looked so bewildered and scared that I answered them with forced cheerfu.ness. 'It doesn't sound very respectful, I know. But I'm sure there's nothing to be afraid of. Dead people are just people who have shed an overcoat which has worn out. And the real people – their souls – have gone to Heaven. They are happy. It is only the people who get left behind who are unhappy – it's natural – they don't like being left.'

I tried to be soothing and matter-of-fact, while Avril perfunctorily washed her hands and face in the same pint of water.

Protesting crossly, Brian and Tony put their books together and heaved themselves between furniture and family towards the staircase and bed. Tony asked sulkily, 'How do you spell necrophile?' and was told angrily by Father not to be impudent.

I took the candle from the kitchen and eased Avril and Edward along after the boys. Mother looked overwhelmed with fatigue, but she was not too tired to fire at Fiona, as I passed her, 'For goodness' sake, be quiet, girl.' Fiona sank down on an upturned paint can, which we used as a chair, and continued to whimper miserably.

Upstairs, I heard Avril and Edward say the small prayer which our nanny had taught me long ago, 'Gentle Jesus, meek and mild . . .' Then I tucked Avril into the bed she shared with Fiona and me, and put Edward into the one he shared with Brian and Tony, and left them shivering under the thin blankets to their individual nightmares.

Brian and Tony stumped grumpily round the room, pulling off their outer clothes and tossing them on to the bed rail. I put the candle down on an orange box, which had been made into a dressing-table by draping an old curtain over it, and told Brian to blow it out before he got into bed. 'Quietly, boys,' I pleaded. 'Let Edward go to sleep.' Then I ran downstairs again to the living-room.

Alan had picked up a book and was flicking through it. Father and Mother were staring into the fire, Father rubbing his chin with quick, impatient motions. Fiona sat, her back against the wall, still crying. I was dreadfully hungry and quite apprehensive about what might have happened, but I went first to her and put my arm round her shoulders. She laid her head against my threadbare skirt. We never talked together – we had little in common except our sisterhood; yet we were often a comfort to each other.

'Daddy, what *has* happened?'

'She has to leave her job,' said Father, beating an impatient tattoo with his fingers on the arm of his chair. Mother nodded agreement. Alan put down his book and watched the scene with a look of morbid fascination, glancing expectantly from one to the other of us.

'Why?' I inquired, puzzled.

'She must,' Mother agreed, and then added crossly, 'It is not fit for a young girl – it is not fit for anyone to be there.'

Alan interjected with an unexpected chuckle, 'You could put it down to professional interest – after all, it's all meat.'

Mother was shocked. 'Alan! How could you say such a revolting thing?'

Alan grinned wickedly and folded his arms, as if enjoying the family's evident distress.

Father groped for words and finally said carefully, 'The butcher's shop in which Fiona is working is opposite an undertaker's. Sometimes the undertakers invite the butchers over to look at the corpses. I cannot believe that it is the undertaker himself who does this – I think it is some of his employees.'

Fiona lifted her face. 'It is, Daddy. They do it when he is out – and the butchers always wait until our boss has gone to market.'

'How awful!' I exclaimed. 'Imagine being stared at in your coffin by a pack of strangers. How morbid!' I looked down at Fiona's tousled head, and said to her, 'Perhaps you should look for another job.'

Fiona turned her face up towards me. She was so white that I thought she might faint. She said, 'They had a young girl there this morning – and she wasn't in her coffin – or even wrapped up. She was naked – and they were whispering and laughing afterwards about how they played with her. It sounded awful. So I was sick suddenly over the cash desk – and they laughed. After I had cleared up the mess, they sent me home early.'

Nausea began to overwhelm me. Vague tales I had heard, whispered amongst the beshawled women beside whom I had sat on front steps or in the park while watching the children play, began to surface in my mind and come together. I had always discounted their mutterings as rubbish. Now I realised that it was not rubbish. They had been disapproving about something which had really happened. I took big breaths to control my surging stomach. How could men be so vile?

'Heavens, I'm glad you told Daddy,' I muttered.

'I had to,' responded Fiona flatly. 'I was thinking about it again just before you came in – and I was sick over the floor.'

'Humph,' Mother almost grunted, 'I thought it was something else, but I was wrong, thank goodness.'

For a moment, I looked at her blankly and then remembered her bouts of morning sickness before every birth, and I said indignantly, 'Fi would never get herself into trouble. She's not that kind.' But a sudden, different fear for Fiona had been planted in my mind. Did she know anything about sex? I was still vague myself about the precise details of this mystery, but since I never expected to have a boy friend it did not matter in my case. It did matter for Fiona. I knew that she was already meeting a local youth secretly and going to the cinema with him.

Father had been brooding during this exchange. Now he fumed, 'They should be reported.'

'Who to?' asked Mother.

'The police, of course.'

'Could the police do anything?'

'Oh, yes. It is a serious matter.'

'Oh, Daddy,' wailed Fiona. 'If you do tell the police there'll be such a rumpus in the shop. The men will say I'm a lying troublemaker, and the boss won't want to give me a reference.' She rubbed her wet eyes with the backs of her hands. 'The story will go all round the local shops, and then what will I do? With no reference, I won't stand a chance.'

She clung to me and I suddenly leaned limply against her. I was beginning to feel faint with hunger.

# Chapter four

Fiona's situation was grave. When fifty youngsters were competing for even the most menial of jobs, lack of a good reference could be crippling.

'You can stay at home and keep house,' Mother said briskly. 'You spend all you earn – I never see much of it.'

'Oh, Mother, Fi only gets fifteen shillings a week, and she pays all her expenses – even buys some of her clothes,' I intervened vehemently.

Fiona's hands clutched convulsively against my hips. She, too, feared becoming the family's forgotten, unpaid maid-of-all-work.

Mother fumbled in her handbag for a cigarette and lit it from the fire with the aid of a newspaper spill. 'She would be more use at home,' she reiterated.

Father got up from his chair and moved restlessly up and down the narrow space between table and hearth which formed a passage between the front hall and back kitchen. He was very thin, and his grey tweed office suit with its shiny seat and elbows hung loosely on him. He looked haggard, as if this new problem was too much for him, and his face and prematurely bald skull shone pale yellow in the poor light. He took off his bent, gold-rimmed spectacles and rubbed eyes that were red-lidded and bloodshot.

'If I want to leave,' sobbed Fiona, 'I *have* to give a week's notice on pay day – that's Friday, and it's Friday night now. So it means I have to work almost another two weeks. And nobody is going to give a reference to a girl who leaves without notice – and how can I tell the boss the real reason I want to leave? It's too horrid!' She continued to dampen my skirt, as I held her.

Mother looked scornfully at her two daughters, her lips curled in disdain. 'Really, Fiona! All this fuss, when you could make yourself useful at home for once.' She turned to Father, and almost shouted, 'For goodness' sake, stop prowling.'

Father flung himself back into his chair, while Fiona cried, 'No.'

'She cannot mix with such dreadful people any more,' Father sounded off determinedly. 'What is the world coming to?'

'They leave me alone most of the time.' Fiona turned her puffy face towards Father. 'I sit in the cash desk and lock myself in. It has glass all round it. They tease me but they can't get in.' She moved uneasily against me. 'Only when I go to the loo sometimes . . .' Her voice trailed off.

Father started up. 'What?' he exclaimed. 'What happens then?'

'They chase after me and pinch my bottom,' she announced baldly.

'Oh, Lord!' Father was really shaken, as if he himself had never in his life pinched the bottoms of our maids.

Alan burst out laughing. 'That's better than being whacked on your rear with a ruler, like I am.'

'Alan!' exclaimed Mother. 'What a lot of louts they must be.'

Father looked at his pretty daughter, speechless for a moment, and then said firmly, 'You will stay at home tomorrow, Fiona. Helen can phone from her office to say that you are not well. Then we will say later that you are not fit to go back. You can look for other work.'

'I'm not staying at home.' Fiona could be as woodenly obstinate as Avril and me, but she never seemed to draw her parents' wrath as fully as we did. 'I just have to get through the next two weeks as best I can. Then I'll leave. After all, I've put up with them for nearly a year now.'

Father looked at her aghast. 'You mean all this has been going on for a year?'

'Not all the time.'

'How frequently?'

'You mean going to see the – the . . . ?'

'Yes.'

'Oh, they run over every time the undertaker has a nice-looking one.'

'And have they been pinching you all that time, too?'

'No, Daddy, only just recently.'

'You must have encouraged them, Fiona.' This from Mother.

'Oh, no, Mummy. I suppose they notice me when they've nothing much to do. Anyway, how can a *derrière* encourage anybody?' she asked innocently.

This made Father smile, even in the middle of his disquietude. Fiona's flawless figure, now burgeoning, would in years to come cause many a heart to throb and provide a good deal of temptation.

Father's voice was very gentle as he looked at his younger daughter. 'I am sure you don't encourage them, my dear.' He smiled knowingly at Mother, who did not smile back.

Alan began to whistle softly to himself and moved restlessly against the table.

'If I had a sheet of the butcher's notepaper,' said Mother suddenly, her face brightening, 'paper with his heading on it, I could write an excellent reference for Fiona.'

'Mother!' I exclaimed, scandalised. 'That would be forgery.'

'A new employer might phone the butcher to check it,' suggested Alan.

'I don't think so,' replied Mother, ignoring my outburst. 'As a demonstrator going from shop to shop, I carry written references – I've heaps of them, because all my jobs are short-term ones. I don't think anybody has ever telephoned to check them.'

Fiona looked up quickly, and then mopped her eyes agitatedly with my hanky which I had handed to her – it was the only one I owned. 'Mummy! Could you do it? Really?'

Mother looked as pleased as a Cheshire cat. 'I don't see why not.'

'If I go to work tomorrow, I can get the paper easily. I have some in the cash desk.' She straightened up, sniffed and rubbed her nose hard with the hanky. 'I could start looking for a new job on Monday.'

It took Mother and Fiona some time to convince Father that it was the most sensible way out. But he was genuinely worried about his favourite daughter, and he finally gave in.

Alan thought it was a huge joke, and asked Mother if she could do anything about forging pound notes. I thought she would strike him, but instead she laughed.

Though it seemed to me to be wrong, that it might be better if Father had a quiet talk with the butcher himself, I did not want to start a family row, so I held my tongue.

On Saturday, Fiona went to work as usual and returned triumphantly with the required sheet of notepaper. Mother concocted an excellent letter for her, written in a round, illiterate hand quite unlike her usual beautiful penmanship. She ended it with a phrase popular amongst tradesmen, 'And oblige your obedient servant', followed by a flourishing signature.

Father often bought a *Liverpool Echo* on his way home from work. The day's copy was lying on his chair, so Fiona and I spread it out on the table and conned the Situations Vacant columns very carefully, though it was nearly midnight.

We found two advertisements for office girls, and Fiona begged Mother's penny pad of notepaper from her, took the cork out of the ink bottle and sat down at the table, pen poised. She looked up at me expectantly. To my dictation, she wrote in a round schoolgirl's scrawl letters of application to both companies.

Mother looked disparagingly at her handwriting. 'Really, Fiona, I should have thought you could write better than that.'

But Fiona could not, and never did. The teaching of handwriting in the elementary schools was so poor that few people seemed to leave with anything better than an ugly, irregular hand. Good, flowing handwriting, like the right accent, marked one's place in the social scale, and Fiona's laboured, round letters indicated a girl with a poor background, in a world which was very snobbish. Only Alan, who had been taught in preparatory school, wrote the same exquisite Italian hand as my mother did.

Fiona had a natural refinement and an endearing gentleness, without a hint of snobbery. She floated amongst all kinds of people without difficulty. Her letters, however, did not produce any replies, despite the fast postal service which we enjoyed, and Fiona became very depressed. Mother thankfully set her more and more household tasks each morning, and then borrowed her fares and lunch money, which meant that even if she obtained an interview with a firm, she would probably have to walk to it.

I encouraged her to keep on writing applications and, as my office was close to the *Liverpool Echo*'s office in Victoria Street, I dropped her replies each day into the newspaper's letterbox.

I had hoped to have a talk with Father on that busy Saturday, because both he and I finished work at one o'clock on Saturdays. Every time I thought about the coming Confirmation lessons, my stomach clenched with apprehension and I longed to unburden myself to somebody. But he had spent the afternoon at the public library, and after he had eaten his tea, he went immediately up to bed. He had had a heart attack when I was a little girl, and occasionally pain in his chest sent him hastily to lie down.

## Chapter five

'Why can't I sign on at the Labour Exchange?' asked Fiona fretfully. 'They might have a job for me.' She was helping me to clear the breakfast dishes, and without make-up she looked tired and not very well.

Mother was putting on her lipstick in front of a piece of broken mirror wedged into the frame of the back kitchen window, and at this remark she paused and said to Father, 'She might be entitled to Unemployment Insurance.'

'If she was, she has forfeited it by voluntarily leaving her position.' Father was running backwards and forwards between kitchen and living room like a demented hen. 'Where can my hat be? Have you seen it? I'll be late.' He called to Brian who was about to go out of the back door to school, 'Brian, wheel the bike round to the front door, there's a boy, while I find my hat.'

'I'll be late if I do,' complained Brian, his dark, heart-shaped face sulky, as he clapped his school cap on to his head.

'Oh, rubbish,' replied Father. 'Go and get it. And don't wear your cap in the house – you are not a workman.'

Brian slammed down his satchel on to the floor, flung his cap on top of it, and went to do as he was bidden.

'Why can't I?' reiterated Fiona, plaintively.

'Do you want to stand in a queue with a mass of unwashed, vulgar girls?' asked Mother. She quickly licked her forefinger and ran it over her eyebrows to remove the surplus face powder clinging to them. 'There is no point anyway. They would try to put you into domestic service. Do you want that?'

'No,' muttered Fiona dejectedly. Neither she nor I had ever considered going into domestic service. Even in my most deprived days, when I began to fear I would die from hunger, I had never considered this way out of my misery. Both of us remembered the servants in our own house when we were small. With the exception of their weekly half-day off and on alternate Sundays, they were never free from six o'clock in the morning until eleven at night.

No. No domestic service for Fiona. Being at home was a shade better than that; at least one could have a good cry in the privy at the bottom of the back yard.

Father found his hat under the living-room table, where the boys must have been using it as dressing-up material. He grabbed the bicycle from a fuming Brian at the front door, and pedalled creakily away to work.

'Never mind, Fi,' I comforted. 'What about writing to some of the big shops in the city – they like to employ under sixteens. I'll deliver the letters – or Alan can.'

Fiona's face lifted a trifle. 'Who should I write to?'

'Um – er, try Lewis's or Blackler's.'

'I'd love to work for Owen Owen's or Boots.'

I was hastily getting into my coat and hat. Given good advice on how to improve her appearance, Fiona would have fitted well into these higher-class shops, but she was untidy and grubby, despite the fact that Mother bought her new clothes as often as possible. I said with caution, 'You could try them.' I picked up the letters that she had written the evening before. 'I'll put these into the *Echo* office for you.'

'Come on, Helen,' shouted Alan from the front doorstep.

Mother told Fiona what to give the children for lunch and fled through the back door to catch her tram. Suddenly poor Fiona was left standing alone in the dirty, cluttered living-room.

Some time back, I had been very ill and for two years had not been strong enough to walk to work. Recently because I felt better and, anyway, could no longer afford the tram fares, I had begun to walk again. Alan had always been provided with tram fares, but he started to accompany me. This long march to and from the city was hard on shoes. We both had pieces of cardboard poked into our footwear to help to fill up the holes in the soles. I had painful ingrowing corns on the bottoms of my feet from the exposure of the tender flesh to hard pavement. At times it was like walking on knives.

We always went along the side of the Anglican cathedral. It was the last of the big Gothic edifices to be built in Europe, and clearly on the morning air one could hear the tiny taps of the stonemasons' hammers, as if a band of elves were hard at work. In pouring rain the great building looked like a huge red sandstone peak, and I loved looking at it, though I had never yet plucked up enough courage to enter it – I feared I was too shabby. Alan did not share my catlike interest in new territory, so when I suggested that we go into it together, he shrugged and asked, 'Whatever for?'

Along Rodney Street, with its charming Georgian frontages, its trim white front doors and gleaming brass plates, he made me stop several times. It was a street of medical specialists, whose cars parked in the street reflected their owners' status. Alan would pause to touch reverently a polished door handle or a new shiny mascot sitting proudly on a bonnet, and would point out to me the merits of the various makes.

Sometimes he would talk enthusiastically about the cricket matches which he played in the park. He was always the hero batting steadily against the opposing team's wicked bowlers.

Occasionally, he would ruefully rub his bruised bottom and mutter maledictions against the ruthless bookkeeper under whom he worked as an office boy. Older men were heavy-handed with their apprentices. They believed in knocking a young man into shape. They had never heard of bruised egos, and a bruised bottom was just one of the hazards of being young. Boys of fourteen found themselves a small minority amid older men and they learned their trade and how to behave, whether they liked it or not. Perhaps that is why in those days there was less vandalism and less theft. In big, soulless places like the docks, however, theft was a fine art.

I rarely talked to Alan about my own affairs. I was, after all, a stand-in mother to him. I listened. It was unusual for me to talk very much to anyone except my friend, Sylvia Poole. I never seemed to be able to stop talking to her. Ever charitable, Sylvia always said she learned a great deal from me. She certainly received a great number of lectures on British and French history.

Neither Alan nor I mentioned the necrophiles amongst whom poor Fiona had found herself working. To me it was another sickening facet of human behaviour to be shunned, condemned and put out of my mind. Alan had made a joke of it, and I wondered if he really thought it was funny. It must have been in his mind, because he said suddenly, as we hurried down fashionable Bold Street, 'You know, Fi is very dumb. She was lucky she didn't get raped in that place.'

'She's not so stupid, really,' I replied. 'She had enough sense to lock herself into the cash desk – like a doll in a glass case. She's so pretty. Too nice to be pushed around.'

I caught my breath as a stab of pain went down the side of my stomach. A familiar dull ache spread down my back.

My step faltered, and Alan paused to ask, 'Something the matter?'

'No. Nothing much. Just a little spasm. It will go.' I clutched one arm across my waist, to try to contain a second wave of pain.

'You look awfully white.'

'No. It will go,' I reassured him, and moved forward again, pressed by the crowd behind me hastening to work.

Alan must have been aware that each month I was seized by terrible, clawing pain lasting some eight to twelve hours. It was impossible to hide it, because I would faint from time to time. Yet I could not bring myself to tell him what the trouble was. Our National Health Insurance doctor assured me that it would disappear when I married, which was not much comfort to a born spinster. He never examined me. I took aspirin in large quantities. Mother bought me ground ginger to take in hot water and, if the pain struck while I was at home, I had the use of Edward's hot water bottle to hug. Nothing helped much. I wondered how I would ever crawl through the day's work. I had no sanitary towel with me to use, and no money to buy one. We used bits of old cotton cloth which we washed over and over again.

I did not consider returning home. People who missed too many days of work tended to be dismissed at the first excuse, and I had lost a lot of days through illness already. If I fainted in the office it would be all right. Women frequently fainted from overwork, lack of food and all kinds of untreated illnesses.

I felt a stab of another kind as we moved slowly onward. The pin holding up my panties had opened and scratched me, and in seconds they slid down my legs and lay round my ankles. Alan giggled, as did one or two passers-by.

Proud as hell, I felt so humiliated that I started to cry quietly as I stepped out of them. It was not the loss of the panties that bothered me; it was their grey raggedness. They were tattered beyond repair, elasticless, patched on patches, in a world where a good pair could be bought for sixpence – and they were already stained. I did not know how to endure the look of disgust on the face of one nicely dressed woman who stepped round me. I wanted to scream at her that it was not my fault that I was not clean.

'Pick them up quick and put them in your bag,' said Alan, a grin on his face.

I did so, hastily cramming them down into the old-fashioned handbag, and we moved on quickly. Alan produced a hanky and I surreptitiously wiped my eyes. The pain was coming in low-level, steady waves.

'Thanks,' I murmured, as I handed it back to him. The handkerchief was grey from poor washing. Sometimes it seemed as if we lived in a world which was made up entirely of shades of grey and black.

We came to the corner of Whitechapel and Church Street. Here our ways parted.

'All right?' Alan asked.

I hesitated for a second, wondering if he could lend me three-halfpence for a tram ride home. Fear of piling up more absences than my employer would tolerate made me say, 'Yes, thanks. 'Bye.'

I shuffled up to the office. What was I going to do? I would have to ask one of the girls for help. Would they again think me to be a disgusting object, lacking even basic common sense to provide myself with ordinary sanitary requirements?

Filled with consternation, beside myself with pain, I climbed the six flights of stone steps to the cloakroom on the top floor.

# Chapter six

There was no one in the cloakroom and it gave me the opportunity to attend to myself as best I could. I replaced the errant panties, pinning them firmly this time.

With eyes closed in pain, I washed my hands. The water belched forth from the tap, gloriously hot, and I thought how heavenly it would be to lie in a bath full of it, to ease the cramping pain. And the soap – how lovely it smelled.

There was a quick tap-tap of high heels on the linoleum on the landing. The door burst open and in flew the Head Cashier. She was a small woman, swathed in a green overall, a rigid disciplinarian. Today, her forbidding expression boded ill for anyone she met. I hastily busied myself drying my hands.

She ignored my good morning. 'Where are the girls?' she demanded. 'Everybody is late.'

I trembled. Without exception, all the younger employees dreaded this ferocious lady. Her assistant was never known to open her mouth, and her junior clerk was so frequently reduced to tears that her eyes seemed permanently lachrymose and her nose was red from much mopping.

'Well?'

I started to say that I was going downstairs to work immediately, when such a sharp, tearing pain hit me that I clutched the white roller towel and let out a moan more like the shriek of a woman in childbirth.

'Good gracious, girl! Whatever's the matter?' Her usual bitter expression vanished.

My senses were leaving me, and I whispered, 'It's my period.'

She was much shorter than me, and elderly, but she said firmly, 'Pull yourself together. Now, put your arm round my shoulder. I'll help you into the Committee Room. You can sit down there.'

Eyes clenched shut, mouth open as I continued to groan and gasp, I thankfully put my arm round her shoulder and she supported me into the adjoining room. She dumped me on to a wooden chair and then put three other chairs together, and assisted me to lie down on them. The wood of the curved seats was not comfortable, but it was better than having to stand.

334

A couple of books from the bookcase were put under my head. She arranged me on my side with knees tucked up in a foetal position. Then she stood back, hands on hips, and surveyed me.

I could not control the deep, primeval groans that burst from me, as the pain surged in ever greater waves. Tears would come later, when the agony was gone and I was left exhausted.

'Poor girl,' she exclaimed suddenly. 'It's worse than childbirth.'

Childbirth was something I hardly understood at that time, but much later in life I found that indeed she was correct.

'I'll get the office girl to make some strong tea,' she promised, 'and I'll send up some aspirins.' The scarifying Department Head had vanished completely and a very understanding woman had emerged. She did not waste time telling me to be brave or to stop the noise I was making. 'You lie here and try to relax yourself – it might help.'

I whimpered, 'Thank you – but aspirins don't help much.'

'They should if you take enough. We'll try what four tablets will do.'

I curled myself up tighter, as another roll of pain went through me. 'Mr Ellis . . . ?' Mr Ellis was the head of my department, a man of few words, usually very tart ones.

'I'll deal with him,' she promised, and whisked out of the room.

It seemed a very long time before the door opened slowly and the office girl slid in with a tray of tea things. The girl was a replacement for my friend, Sylvia Poole, who had left to take training as a chiropodist. I wished frantically that Sylvia was with me. She was so sensible. I was very cold and was lying on my back, knees up, swaying them from side to side, unable to find easement, and threatening to fall off my perilous perch. As each peak of pain was reached, I would put my clenched fist against my mouth to muffle a shriek, and then moan, a noise which came from the depth of my being and had nothing to do with will.

The tea tray was put on another chair drawn close to me, and the frightened little girl, a mouse, aged fourteen, fumbled in the pocket of her blue overall. 'She said I was to give you these.' She handed me four aspirins from one pocket and then, very shyly, a sanitary towel from the other pocket. 'She said I was to help you while you put it on.'

That meant I had to get on to my feet and make a trip to the cloakroom. I lay with eyes closed, wondering if I could do it.

'She said to tell you to take big breaths,' announced the girl, watching me pop-eyed, as if I were something in a cage.

'Ask Miriam Enns to come and help me,' I winced. Miriam was a stenographer, one of three who worked in a small office next to the Committee Room. She was in her late twenties and had been very kind to me. A dedicated Communist, she tended to attempt to recruit quite ruthlessly, so I had begun to avoid her, since I was not politically minded. I was too engrossed in trying to stay alive, to sidestep Mother's terrible tempers, to educate myself, to be a good employee. To survive was all I asked of life.

Miriam came running. 'Whatever happened?' she asked. Her reddish hair drooped smoothly round a pixie face. She had a big mouth which could curve into a smile so sweet that one could hardly believe in the strong Party worker lurking within. But she had the physical strength I needed very badly.

The moment she saw my contorted face, she understood. I had taken refuge before in her little office on several occasions when I had been struck like this while at work.

Miriam looked down at the tea tray and sent the office girl away. 'O.K., love. Have the tea first. Have you got any aspirin?'

I opened my clenched hand, to show the four tablets.

She raised her eyebrows. 'That's a lot.'

I took a large breath, as instructed. 'The Cashier said – take four,' I gasped.

'Well, I suppose she'd know.' The Cashier was never referred to by name, only as She or The Cashier. I called her Madam when I had to speak to her.

'Oh, Miriam!' I nearly screamed.

'You'll be all right, dear.' She poured the tea and held it to my quivering lips, while I swallowed the aspirins. Then she sat by me and chafed my hands and talked about seeing a doctor.

'I did, Miriam, and he just laughed – said I'd be all right when I married.'

'The stupid fool,' she exploded. 'Consult someone privately.'

'Miriam, I don't have money for things like that.'

She was referring to doctors who practised outside the National Health system. I was registered with a National Health doctor and it was difficult to change one's physician under this system. I felt I was lucky to have one doctor on whom to call, never mind anyone else. In suggesting a private physician, Miriam was, for once, allowing her middle-class instincts to outweigh her socialistic convictions.

I choked down the aspirin, and then we staggered to the cloakroom like a pair of drunks. Miriam kept one foot against the door, so that no one could enter, while she helped me wash myself.

Back in the Committee Room, she rearranged the chairs and I lay down again, while she ran downstairs to take dictation from one of the senior staff.

The pain did not go, and I longed for home. I suppose that the charity could not afford a taxi to send me home – they were very short of funds – and I certainly could not go on the tram. The society did own a car, but it was in use all day taking workers to visit clients in distress.

For a while, I continued to lie on the chairs, but then removed myself

336

to the linoleum floor, where I could move more easily. The floor was very cold, but it was flat. Nowhere in the building, which housed some twenty-five women, if one included the employees of a tea company on the ground floor, was there a couch or easy chair for staff use. There was no place where one could eat a packed lunch, except for the minute kitchen adjacent to the Committee Room. Truly, the tailor's child is the worst clad, and we lacked facilities which were increasingly being provided by thoughtful employers.

Halfway through the morning, the Cashier sent the office girl in with more tea and two more aspirins. Thirty grains of aspirin in little over an hour and a half did have some effect. The top edge of the waves of pain was less sharp. I lay with eyes crunched shut and wondered if the pain was a judgment on me for refusing to go to Confession.

I could not eat the slice of bread and margarine I had brought for lunch, but I drank eagerly a cup of coffee which Miriam poured for me from her own thermos flask. Miss Short, the Head Typist, kindly provided two more aspirins.

Forty grains of aspirin. I was not sure how much one could take without poisoning oneself. I knew that a hundred aspirins would cause death – it was a popular form of suicide amongst women. Mother took as many as twenty in a day. She had no physical pain to assuage, but she said they soothed her nerves; suffering from nerves was a socially acceptable ailment – Liverpool women often referred to 'Me poor nairves'. Mother also smoked twenty to thirty cigarettes a day, as did Father.

The pain finally lessened, and when the other clerks returned from their lunch break, I went downstairs and reported shyly to Mr Ellis.

'Oh, aye,' he said absently, when I said I was feeling better. 'Take t' index cards and sort them – there's a lot.'

I sat down at the corner of a table which was my place in the crowded room, and spent the rest of the afternoon sorting the little white cards into alphabetical order and then standing to file them in long wooden drawers. The aspirin and exhaustion combined to make me feel sleepy, and sometimes I felt as if I was floating on a sea of distant pain.

When the office girl brought in the afternoon tea, she also carried a message from the busy Cashier, who worked in the next room. How was I? Would I like some more aspirin? She spread out her grubby little hand to show two tablets. I swallowed them gratefully with the tea.

The secretary to the Presence – the Presence was my name for my austere employer – thundered away on her typewriter at the other end of the table, but on seeing me take the aspirin, she paused to inquire what the trouble was. Through tightly clenched teeth, I told her I had a monthly pain. She nodded sympathetically and renewed her thunder. The other clerks running about with piles of files in their arms had no time to stop to ask after my well-being.

It was the longest of afternoons. The noise and vibration of the typewriter in front of me, the sound of the buzzers and bells of the old-fashioned telephone switchboard behind me, the filing clerks pushing behind my chair as they ran to and fro, made the close-packed room almost unbearable. Clients crept in and out, to see the Presence in her office which led off the room I was in. Chairs were dragged across the floor for them to sit on and even that vibration went through me and made me hurt all the more.

It did come to an end, however, like everything else in life, and I had to admit to Mr Ellis that I had not completed my day's work.

'Humph, then we shall have to work faster tomorrow, shan't we?'

I agreed humbly, and put the remaining cards in the table drawer.

In the cloakroom, I met Miriam struggling quickly into her overcoat. She stopped to inquire how I was.

'Better,' I said. With my eyelids drooping with fatigue, I turned to hang up my overall.

'You usually walk home, don't you?'

'Yes.'

She buttoned up her coat and picked up her handbag. 'You'll take the tram tonight?'

'No.'

'For heaven's sake, why not?'

I forced myself to look at her and said dully but honestly, 'I don't have any money.'

'Oh, child! Why didn't you say so before? I'll lend you twopence – you can pay me on pay day.' She rustled round in her handbag and proffered the coins. I took them gratefully. I had been troubled all the afternoon wondering whether I would manage the long climb up the hill to home.

Liverpool trams swayed like a ship in a storm and I began to feel nauseated. I was glad when the vehicle came to a stop at the Rialto Cinema and I could descend, while its motor hummed like a hive full of angry bees as if to say it could not wait to let me off.

As I stood on the corner of Upper Parliament Street waiting for the traffic to clear so that I could cross the road, my eyes began to dim and I knew that I would probably faint. But where to take refuge on such a busy corner, with its lounging groups of unemployed men gossiping idly?

Facing me stood the Rialto Cinema and Dance Hall. It had a wide pillared entrance and a sweeping curve of steps. l could lean against one of the pillars, I thought, under the supervising eye of the girl in the cash desk. If I actually passed out, she would undoubtedly call for help for me. Two or three people obviously waiting for friends to join them were already standing on the steps. People would think I was waiting for a boy friend to take me to the cinema.

The Commissionaire glanced at me. He was a shrimp of a man in a gilt-trimmed uniform too big for him. I leaned against the wall of the entrance at the furthest point from him, and closed my eyes.

'You O.K., love?'

It was a man's voice. Wearily I opened my eyes. A man neatly dressed in a light raincoat, tightly belted, and a trilby hat rakishly tipped over one eye was standing in front of me smoking a cigarette.

I knew him by sight. He seemed to spend a lot of time hanging around that corner. Once, while I was buying groceries, he had come into the shop to purchase some cigarettes, and after he left the shopkeeper called him a damned pimp when speaking to another woman customer. 'Got three girls, he has,' she had said.

He had, however, the pleasant smile and easy manner of so many smart alecks making a living in the streets, and I answered, with a sob in my voice, that I was quite all right, thank you. I winced and turned my face away. He did not leave me. Instead, his voice quite compassionate, he asked, 'Like a cigarette?'

The steps of the cinema looked wavy when I again opened my eyes, and my legs threatened to give way. I glanced at the proffered case. It was finely worked silver.

'No, thanks, I don't smoke,' I responded.

'Try one of these,' he urged, poking at some small brown cigarettes in one side of the case. 'They're great for headaches – make you feel on top of the world.'

I sighed. 'It's all right, thanks very much. I'll be O.K. in a second or two. I live quite near.'

He helped himself to an ordinary white-papered cigarette and threw the stub of the old one into the street. He tapped the new one on his thumb-nail before putting it into his mouth, then closed the beautiful cigarette case and stowed it in an inner pocket. He produced a matching petrol lighter, lit the cigarette and exhaled leisurely through his nose. 'Yeah,' he said. 'I know you. Seen you often.'

At this I stared, pain forgotten. Then I realised that if I knew him by sight, it was very likely that he knew me as a local inhabitant. I smiled wearily and straightened myself up. His cigarette had not lit properly and he flicked his lighter on again. The tiny flame showed for a moment a coarse but not unpleasant face, with calculating black eyes. I felt I was being weighed up.

'What do you do, like – work?'

'I'm a clerk.'

He nodded, and I said good night, and slowly walked the short distance home.

It is strange to think that if, in the acuteness of my pain, I had accepted the Indian hemp which he had offered me and it had created sufficient euphoria to dull it, I would have wanted to obtain it again. Undoubtedly, he would have approached me again, anyway, in the hope of my becoming hooked. Then he would have promised me clothes, food and a flat if I would work for him, and I would have slowly sunk into the dregs of Liverpool.

But I knew from reading and from one or two cases I had seen at work what hashish could do to people, and almost instinctively I had refused.

# Chapter seven

The back living-room seemed packed with people all talking at the tops of their voices. The family had long since finished its tea and, normally, I would have quickly eaten whatever had been kept hot for me in the oven which lay alongside the fire. Then I would have cleared the dishes and washed them up and put Avril and Edward to bed before going to night school. Tonight I had no strength left.

Mother, in a soiled house dress, was sitting in Father's easy chair, reading the *Echo*, her bare feet on a wooden chair – to rest her veins, as she always said.

'Hello, dear,' she greeted me amiably, glancing over the newspaper. Then she put the paper quickly down on her lap. 'Are you ill?'

Sometimes I was more afraid of Mother when she was being considerate than when she was quarrelsome. I answered carefully, using the polite expression for what had happened to me. 'I was unwell.'

'How are you now?'

'A bit better, thanks. I won't go to night school tonight – I'll hand my German essay in on Wednesday.'

I took out of my handbag the crumpled confectioner's paper bag which held the uneaten lunch of bread and margarine. 'I'll take this for tomorrow's lunch,' I added as I laid it on the table.

'Gosh,' exclaimed Fiona. 'You must be hungry.' She went quickly to the oven and lifted out a plate, using the hem of her skirt to protect her fingers from the heat.

I smiled at her gratefully, as she put the meal down in front of me, a tablespoonful of stewed minced beef, a potato and the inevitable pile of frizzled-up cabbage.

'Mother bought some jam tarts and we kept one for you. Here it is.' She pushed towards me a second plate with a little tartlet in a paper case sitting on it.

Mother was watching me as I sat down, and I asked if she could spare two aspirins.

'Of course,' she said, and got up to find them in her handbag. 'Would you like some hot ginger?'

Even in pain, this horrible thick concoction of ground ginger mixed with hot water was something to be avoided, so I refused it with suitable expressions of gratitude for her kind thought.

'Eat your tea and go to bed,' she advised, and returned to her perusal of the paper.

Edward put his tousled brown head out from under the table where he and Tony and Brian were playing cards. 'You can use my hottie if you've got a tummy ache,' he offered. He loved lending his hot water bottle to other members of the family. Some kind soul, responding to the begging letters Mother wrote quite regularly, had sent it with a parcel of clothes. Since it was unpawnable, Edward had always had his bed warmed by it.

I laughed for the first time that day and thanked him, as he ducked back underneath the table. The healthy noise of play in the room was a godsend to me. So often my parents fought or the children squabbled and howled. Amity was something to be cherished.

Avril was playing by herself at her favourite game of dressing our latest alley cat in an old baby shawl and putting it to bed in a box. She was talking softly to the patient animal.

Mother had dropped the aspirins by my plate, and Fiona brought some weak tea, made by pouring fresh water over the old leaves in the pot. Mother leaned forward and poured a cup out for herself and for me. Absently, she popped two aspirins into her own mouth and swallowed them.

Father and Alan were seated on old paint cans, trying to rewind the thread neatly round the handle of a time-worn cricket bat that one of Alan's colleagues had given him. Both had nodded to me when I came in; now they started to argue as to the best way to secure the thread.

'Snap!' came a delighted shout from Tony under the table. 'I've won. I've won!'

'No, you haven't,' responded Brian indignantly. 'Something's wrong. All the Kings have been played before. There must be an extra one in the pack.' He had a most retentive memory, but neither Edward nor Tony would accept his contention. An altercation broke out as they scrambled round in the tiny space, while they checked the incredibly battered pack of cards with which they always played.

I ate my tartlet, while Mother leaned down from her chair and shouted at them. The raised voices vibrated through my racked body. The tartlet did nothing to assuage my hunger, and I considered eating the lunch which I had brought back home. But I was not sure that there was enough bread in the house to provide me with lunch the following day, so I left it wrapped up in its old margarine papers.

I went upstairs and took a piece of cloth from a pile at the back of a dusty built-in shelf in the bedroom. These rags had been accumulated from bits of sheeting and garments bought from the second-hand shop and torn into squares. Mother, Fiona and I used the same collection for our periods, washing them again and again. We were always nervous of running out of them.

The pain was rapidly easing now, and I went downstairs again, through the living-room where a fight between the boys seemed about to break out, through the little back kitchen with its clutter of unwashed dishes, into the tiny back yard, lined with brick, to the lavatory by the far wall.

We were lucky to have a flush lavatory to ourselves. There was still a number of courts in Liverpool, surrounded on all sides by houses containing a family in each room, where all the inhabitants shared two lavatories set in the middle of the court.

Ours was a dank, cold outhouse, and its pipes or its tank froze every winter, causing bursts which sometimes took our aristocratic landlord weeks to repair. Copies of the *Liverpool Echo* lay on the long wooden seat, for use instead of toilet paper.

When I returned, Fiona had filled the hot water bottle for me and I thankfully took it and went up to bed, leaving the family to cope as best they could with the work I usually did.

The bed I shared with Fiona and Avril now boasted a bottom sheet and three pillows with pillow-cases. The linen was grey with poor washing with insufficient soap, and sometimes with no soap or hot water; but it indicated an improvement over earlier days when I had slept on a wad of newspaper covering a door set on bricks, with an old overcoat to keep me warm.

I crawled on to the lumpy, smelly mattress and drew the two thin blankets up to my chin. I placed the hot water bottle carefully on my aching stomach; it was so hot that it seemed as if it might skin me. The rest of me was very cold despite the comparative mildness of the weather, and my knee joints and ankles hurt quite sharply whenever I moved.

Then the tears pent up during the day exploded and I cried bitterly until I could cry no more. I cried from weakness, from cold, from hunger, from despair that life would never get any better, a holocaust of loneliness, of frustration, which seemed to pick up brief pictures of the pain-filled day and whirl them maddeningly in my head. Despite my fear of burning in hell if I did not go to Confession, I began to pray passionately to be allowed to die.

But God evidently had other things in mind for me, because I continued to survive.

# Chapter eight

I slept so deeply that I did not hear Avril or Fiona get into bed, but when Father's alarm clock clamoured its warning of six o'clock, I was automatically out of bed and on my feet in a flash, anxious to get into the kitchen before the others, in order to wash myself in private.

Father trailed down the stairs ahead of me dressed in the tattered remains of a camel-hair dressing gown his sister had given him for his sixteenth birthday – the only garment apart from what he had been wearing that he had brought from our old home. He went straight to the kitchen range to rake out the cinders and build a new fire, while I put a kettle of water on the gas stove for his shaving and for Mother's early morning cup of tea.

I filled the washing-up basin with cold water from the tap, stripped off and quickly washed myself from head to foot. Mostly I had to make do with water and a cotton rag – occasionally there was soap for my face. When the kettle boiled, I padded across the tiles, naked, filled a cup and handed it to Father through a crack in the door. He then shaved, without a mirror, in the living-room, using an old-fashioned cut-throat razor and a stump of shaving soap. As soon as I had some clothes on, he would enter the kitchen and make Mother's tea, occasionally holding the razor dripping with soapsuds in his left hand, half his face still lathered, the other half shining clean. The early morning offering of tea was one of the few things Mother appreciated about Father. She always thanked him and drank the weak, scalding liquid slowly, while shouting instructions about clothes or breakfast to various members of the family.

Fiona was usually the main target of her criticism in the mornings. In all her younger days Fiona never managed to prepare her clothes or lunch for the following day. The fact that the boys took it for granted that their clothes, books and lunches would be prepared for them and that they could, therefore, be considered equally inefficient was lost upon Mother: girls were capable of looking after themselves; boys were not.

If the fire that Father had made did not catch, I tried again with it, while he washed in the kitchen. First, old copies of the *Echo* were crumbled up to make a base, then a small pyramid of wood chips, bought from the chandler in neat wire-bound bundles, was built, upon which small coals were laid.

A match was set to the paper and, if the wind was in the right direction, the chimney would draw the flames upwards and the fire would catch. In addition to coal, we burned vegetable peelings wrapped in newspaper, worn-out shoes, anything that would burn was burned. I had long since given up collecting rubbish from the streets to keep the fire going, because I felt we should be able to afford enough coal to give us a little fire, morning and evening. Nevertheless, despite five of us having work, the coal cellar was often empty, particularly in the autumn and spring, when Mother felt we should be able to manage without heating. At such times we kept the windows tightly closed and the damp, badly constructed house acquired an icy stuffiness, an unwholesome exhalation of nine half-washed bodies.

This morning, Fiona, wandering about in her grubby nightgown, kindly laid the breakfast table for me and fed Edward and Avril.

Alan had recently very proudly begun to shave with a safety razor. He was rather slow at it, because his face was a dreadful mass of acne spots, great pustules painful enough in themselves without an added nick from the razor. Sometimes the pimples came up on the back of his neck and the pressure of a stiff collar band aggravated them, until they became big open sores that took a long time to heal.

While Alan shaved, Brian and Tony washed themselves. They pushed and shoved against each other, as each tried to insert a finger into the tap, so that they were doused by the resultant spray. The stone tiles of the kitchen were often running with water by the time they had finished.

Avril and Edward, having been perfunctorily washed in warm water before they went to bed, got a quick wipe around their mouths with a damp cloth and a flick of the comb from either Mother or me.

Except for Mother and me, everybody ate a small dish of cornflakes with milk, followed by a slice of bread and margarine, sometimes with a little marmalade. Weak tea was the drink of the whole family. In the interests of economy, Mother and I ate a piece of bread and margarine only.

Quite frequently, Mother did not work in the mornings, so often the children came home at lunchtime to a hot meal, usually of minced meat or of eggs, with potatoes and cabbage or carrots. When she did work before noon, a meal of bread and margarine and cold meats was prepared by Mother or me and left on the table for them, and we tried to provide something hot for them at teatime.

Father and Alan took a lunch with them of bread, margarine and cheese. Since I made up the lunches, I always made mine last, and there never seemed to be any way in which I could divide the small amount of Canadian red cheese so that I could have some without leaving them short. The severe illness I had suffered two years earlier had left me very apathetic about myself; it was enough for me if I could crawl through the day without incurring either Mother's or Mr Ellis's wrath and perhaps get a kind word from my dedicated night school teachers.

Mother was a demonstrator. She took short contracts with department stores who wanted to launch new kitchen gadgets, and she stood in the store and showed people how to use them. Occasionally, she did door-to-door selling for vacuum cleaner companies, family photographers, Christmas card publishers or sweet firms. When doing outside work, she wore an all-enveloping leather coat which she had bought second-hand. This protected her from Liverpool's damp, cold wind, and, despite its bulk, she still managed to look elegant in a faded way. She had a lovely carriage and an authoritative voice with a pure Oxford accent. She was a very good saleswoman.

Her supervisor in a vacuum cleaner company, who once called at the house, said admiringly, 'She could steal your front door key off you and sell it you back before you knew it had gone.'

Father received this doubtful praise in stiff silence, while his guest threw a cigarette stub into the hearth and smoothed his curled moustache.

I do not know what Mother thought of some of the men with whom she worked, but it is doubtful if their crassness bothered her much. She was so sure of herself, so certain of her social superiority despite our current circumstances, that she was to a degree armoured against them.

Father was different. He was abject in his failure and very easily hurt. His public school training, followed almost immediately by war service in Russia during the Revolution, had given him little preparation for a world which had changed completely by the time he came home. He might have survived better had the Depression – and a large family – not added to his difficulties. Like many soldiers returning from the First World War he was emotionally and physically drained by its unremitted horrors; there was little real strength left; and I could guess at the cold flame of hatred in his heart when faced with a runt of a salesman, who was probably doing rather better than he was as a city clerk.

Mother came downstairs with the coarse white teacup in her hand, and paused when she saw me in the hall to ask if I felt better. I said I did. How could I complain of overwhelming fatigue to someone who looked like a haggard ghost herself?

As we stepped out of the house into a beautiful, rain-washed morning, glad to be away from a fetid, crowded home, Alan offered to pay my tram fare to work. He was shy about referring to my aches and pains of the previous day, but he was well accustomed to their occurrence.

'No, dear,' I said. 'I shall be all right. In fact, the exercise is good for me.' And I marched beside him down the street as if I had not a care in the world. I could not take his pocket money; but I loved him for the sheer kindness of the offer, and our conversation held more than its usual friendly warmth.

'The man from the furniture shop came last night – after you'd gone to bed,' he informed me, as we paused to look in the window of the bicycle shop at the corner of Bold Street; and he sighed over black enamelled frames and racing handlebars.

'Oh, dear!' I exclaimed. 'What now?'

'Threatening to take it away again.'

'Haven't they been paid lately?'

'Suppose not,' he replied gloomily.

'Oh, blow. It's such an appalling waste, Alan. Mummy and Daddy make the weekly payments for a while. Then the stuff is repossessed – but we still have to pay for it – it doesn't get us off the hook. It's so stupid. Really, they're absolutely crazy.'

'Humph.'

He was not very interested. He never used our front sitting-room. His friends did not come to visit – he always met them on the cricket or football field or in the park, where they would sometimes kick a tennis ball about in an impromptu game.

I was very interested, because payments for the furniture represented a heavy drain on our income. It was money that could have been spent on food and coal. Mother always hankered after some semblance of prosperity, and this was the third room full of sitting-room furniture she had bought on the hire purchase system, while ignoring our frantic need for bedding and beds, coal, hot water and food. It was easy to obtain furniture for a very small down payment and weekly payments, laden with interest. Failure to pay resulted in prompt repossession of the furniture, without releasing the buyer from his financial commitment. So the loss could be a heavy one, particularly if one had nearly completed the payments. The three separate firms we had to pay or face being sold up entirely by the bailiff swallowed enough money to have fed us well. Twice the sitting-room had been emptied by phlegmatic furniture removers, well used to pushing their way into the houses of debtors. Now it seemed that it might happen again.

# Chapter nine

The great port of Liverpool lies on a series of hills rising from the waterfront, and each day I climbed the long slopes from the city centre, on my way home. I passed concert halls, hospitals, surprisingly finely built Edwardian public houses, rows of little shops and tasteful Victorian houses, some of which were falling into decay. Every so often there was a newsagent's and tobacconist's shop, and I depended upon the hastily chalked newspaper headlines displayed on boards outside their shops to alert me to the big news of the day. They currently dealt with the crises of the Spanish war, about which Miriam frequently held forth passionately in the office. She foretold quite accurately that it was but a dress rehearsal for a much bigger conflict. They also announced the forthcoming coronation of George VI and his plump little Duchess, Elizabeth. Some of these shops were decorating their windows with souvenirs, coronation mugs, flags and brooches. A number of defiant people still wore pins and brooches with the insignia of Edward VIII, to show they thought that he should be the king, despite his intention of marrying an American divorcée.

I never saw a billboard that dealt with Liverpool's fearful slums, some of the worst in the country, nor the hunger in them. Occasionally an increase in the number of unemployed was mentioned, and a great march by workless men who walked all the way to London got some attention. The slums with their suffering inhabitants had always been part of the Liverpool scene; they were not interesting.

Trudging homeward through pouring, slashing rain, I had no particular desire to arrive. Too often more problems, more worries awaited me.

This evening, to my astonishment, there was good news. Fiona had received a letter asking her to go the following afternoon for an interview with a magazine-distributing agency. She was as agitated as an aspen in the wind, and while I ate my tea, she discussed with Mother what she should wear, as if she had a wardrobe full of clothes instead of a single blouse, a skirt and two dresses which were almost outgrown.

Mother was being most cooperative. She offered to lend her a hat which had recently been refurbished with the aid of a bright yellow feather and a new ribbon into what was known as a Robin Hood style. Mother knew that when a shorthand student had paid me a few days earlier I had bought a pair of rayon stockings, so she lent her those as well, despite my protests that the pair I had on could not be mended any more; they were laddered beyond redemption.

After returning from night school, I spent a couple of hours fuming as I oversewed ladders and darned heels, and then lengthened one of Fiona's dresses for her. It was after midnight before the hem was finally hand-stitched and pressed, but Fiona who had never learned to sew was touchingly grateful.

There were times when I wished that Grandma had not taught me how to use a needle. When I was a child I used to stay with her for long periods of the year in her house on the other side of the Mersey river, but she no longer had anything to do with us, because Father had quarrelled bitterly with his family.

Mother had learned from nuns who brought her up how to do fine embroidery for copes and altar cloths, but she was not adept at other sewing. She sometimes darned socks if I was too busy to do them or if I had, in a rage at the pressure put upon me, temporarily struck work. Nine people in near rags produced a lot of sewing, by necessity to be done by hand. My eyes were always tired from short hours of sleep, constant reading for night school and from my daytime work, all done with the aid of spectacles long since outgrown and in need of replacement. Quite often the work was done by candlelight, because we did not have pennies to put into the electric and gas meters.

Apart from Fiona's letter, there was a letter for me to give me pleasure. To improve my German I had a pen-friend. He was the son of a school-master and lived, as far as I could judge from the map on the wall at night school, about forty miles from Munich. The idea was that I should write to him in German and he would write to me in English, so that we would both benefit. However, he soon fell into the habit of writing in German. This had for me one fortunate result. Because Mother did not know German, she gave up opening and reading my letters before allowing me to have them, something which I had always bitterly resented.

In early April, he had sent me some violets, carefully pressed, from his garden. His letters had taken a slightly sentimental turn, and he wanted a photograph of me. It was very thrilling, though Hitler's stern limitations on foreign travel and my poverty made it almost certain that we should never be able to visit each other. As a young boy, he had already visited England on an exchange plan, and that was how I originally met him.

When this pen-friendship first commenced, I had had the utmost difficulty in finding money for stamps out of the shilling a week allowance I had squeezed out of my parents. Miriam in the office had willingly contributed sheets of typing paper and some envelopes, and I usually wrote to him in my lunch hours, using the office kitchen counter as a desk because it was clean. I had a tiny pocket German dictionary which my German teacher had given to me, and as my grasp of the language improved I wrote with its aid ever-lengthening letters.

Too shy and ashamed to tell him of the grim poverty into which we had fallen, of the filth, hunger and vermin which were my daily companions, I wrote as if we were still living in our old home and I was attending the local high school – a private school which took girls of all ages. I described the house, the servants and our social life. My grandmother and her home, shared with two aunts and a cousin, were also sources for description of English life. As time went on, I wrote of my hopes of becoming a qualified social worker in Liverpool, and he responded by saying that he would become a schoolmaster, like his father. We had lively discussions on books which we had both read and on religion, but he soon discovered that if we touched on politics or if I sent newspaper cuttings, the letters were not received, indicating censorship of both inward and outward mail, presumably in Germany.

I had also acquired a girl pen-friend in Stettin, through an offer, in the correspondence column of a Sunday newspaper, to put children in touch with each other. Judging from her photograph, she was exceedingly pretty, an ash blonde, and was the daughter of some small government official. She was impatient of my bad German, which was very good for me, but she gave me such long and involved explanations of German grammar and idioms that I sometimes did not understand all she said. She was one of a class of students who had been encouraged by their teacher to seek English pen-friends, and both sides seemed to get quite a lot of fun out of it. What neither side knew was that we had been drawn into a minor spy network, and this was to cause me no little distress when the war began.

Ursel, aged fifteen, and I were blissfully ignorant of all this and discussed the scary prospect of her father arranging a marriage for her, when she was passionately in love with a boy who travelled on the same bus as she did each day. When she was not correcting my grammar, she wrote pages on every detail of the young man. They had never got beyond smiling at each other – but for nearly a year her hopes ran high. At the age of sixteen, a marriage *was* arranged for her by her father, to the minister of her church, a man of forty, and the last letter I received from her a few days before the war broke out was from a young girl broken-hearted and pregnant. It would have moved even a bored censor. Poor Ursel – and the war with its repression of the clergy and its ruinous fighting was yet to come.

# Chapter ten

Fiona went for her interview. Father provided her with threepence for the tram fares to and from the city, and she returned glowing with excitement.

'I think I've got it,' she said, as she took off the Robin Hood hat with its bright yellow feather and handed it back to Mother. 'They said they'd let me know – they want to see one or two other girls before deciding.'

She did not return my stockings, but she was so relieved and happy that I did not want to spoil things for her. I did not tell her that the phrase 'We'll let you know' was the stock dismissal of an unsuccessful candidate. She would learn the sad facts of job hunting in Liverpool by experience. She had been fortunate in finding her first job, because few girls would want to work in a butcher's or a fishmonger's shop, and she was probably by far the smartest fourteen-year-old to apply.

I went on sweeping the living-room's tiled floor and then worked my way over the small piece of coconut matting in the middle, briskly brushing the dust and debris towards the hearth.

'What kind of work is it?' Mother inquired. She was seated at the table, writing pad and bottle of ink before her, and she did not look up from her composing of a begging letter. She still occasionally wrote to perfect strangers asking for financial help, and quite frequently received compassionate replies enclosing a welcome pound or two.

Fiona sat down on the easy chair and clasped her hands in front of her. She replied eagerly, 'They would teach me to use a thing called an addressograph. It makes the labels to put on the magazines they send out. They've got hundreds and hundreds of magazines, lovely ladies' magazines and story ones – everything. They send them out to subscribers. They've got so many that they even have to have a van to take them to the post office.'

'Are there many on the staff?'

'No. Two gentlemen saw me – and an old lady who does the books. I don't think there was anyone else.'

'What's the pay?' asked Alan.

'Twelve shillings and sixpence a week at first, and then in two months' time – if I get quick at managing the machine – they'll give me fifteen shillings. Isn't it great?'

Alan looked amazed. 'Holy Cain! You lucky thing! I'm only getting seven and sixpence – and Helen's been working nearly three years – and she's only getting twelve and sixpence.'

I was actually receiving fifteen shillings, but I dared not say so. The precious half-a-crown difference was what had paid my fares during the time I had not been strong enough to walk to and from work, and now it sometimes bought me a bowl of soup in Woolworth's cafeteria when there was nothing left at home for me to take for lunch. My shorthand student, when I had one, paid me enough to cover my pair of rayon stockings every other week and the bits and pieces of clothing from the pawnbroker's bargain table.

Fiona laughed, looking suddenly like Mother when she was young and full of vivacity. 'I'm so excited.'

'It's lovely,' I agreed heartily. 'Lift up your feet, people.' They all automatically raised their feet off the floor, while I swept neatly in and out of the chair legs. Like an army, they put their feet down on the floor again in perfect unison when I reached the hearth and picked up the pile of dust between my hands. I threw it into the fire and there was an immediate outcry from the others at the horrid odour of burning hair, as it hit the hot coals.

Father had been sitting silently on a wooden chair at the opposite end of the table from Mother, while he drank a cup of tea left over from our meal. He rested his head on his hand and, except for the red acne rash across his nose and cheeks, his face was pale. Now he said, 'I'm very glad about the job, Fiona. What happened this morning about the furniture?'

All the joy was immediately wiped off Fiona's face. She said sadly, 'They came and took it – like they did before, Daddy. They just pushed past me and walked in when I opened the door.'

'Pack of bullies,' said Father angrily. 'And to think that we've already paid two-thirds of it. They might have waited.'

Personally, I thought the furniture company had shown the patience of Job waiting for their money at different times. But I knew enough to keep my mouth shut. I put the broom away and went upstairs to get my account books, so that I could do my bookkeeping home-work.

When I returned, Mother was saying, 'We could let that room. Nobody is going to let us have more furniture on the never-never plan for a while.' I smiled at her use of Liverpool's name for the hire purchase system, which never, never seemed to get paid off.

'Well, it might help to pay the furniture instalments,' said Father wearily. 'Some business girl who has her own furniture, perhaps?'

I sat down by him and opened my ledgers. 'She'd have to pass through this room and the kitchen every time she wanted to get water or go to the lavatory,' I pointed out.

'Oh, you always look on the black side of things,' Mother grumbled. 'I don't suppose such a girl would be home very much.' She folded up her letter and put it into the envelope. 'I'll advertise it in the newsagent's window. I wonder what rent I could get?'

'A small room rents for about seven shillings a week,' I told her, as I carefully made entries in my collection of books.

'How do you know?' Mother was cross. She licked the envelope and rubbed her hand impatiently across the back of it to seal it.

'Well, Mummy, I see details of dozens of people's incomes and expenses at the office. The first thing an interviewer does is to fill out a form about the client with all kinds of details.'

'I think that's about right,' Father agreed. 'I see plenty of them, too. With no bathroom in the house, we can't charge much.'

'I'll try for ten shillings,' Mother said firmly. 'After all, this is a very respectable house.'

She wrote an advertisement on the back of an envelope and immediately went out to see the newsagent, who would, for twopence, exhibit it for a week in a glass case hung on his door.

Fiona had had an early tea before going for her interview and now announced that she was going to see a girl friend. Alan drifted off to play cricket with the other boys in the street. I should have gone to call Avril and Edward to come in because it was their bedtime, but for the moment I was alone with Father. He had picked up his library book and was looking for his place in it. I laid down my pen.

'Daddy, could I ask you something?'

'Yes, dear.' He closed his book again and peered at me through his spectacles. I noticed that the gold frame was bent, so that one eye was not looking through the middle of the lens, and it gave a curiously lopsided appearance to his face.

I reminded him of Miss Ferguson's desire to see me confirmed, and that she expected me to go to Confession before taking my first Communion.

'I've been so worried, Daddy. What is it all about? I never dreamed of having to go to Confession. I thought old King Henry the Eighth and Queen Elizabeth did away with such things in the Church of England? I'm so frightened, Daddy – is it wrong to refuse to go?'

He chuckled. 'Good Lord, no. There's nothing to be frightened about. The Church of England allows considerable latitude within its ranks – you must know that.' He sighed heavily. 'Both your mother and I were brought up as High Anglicans – in fact, you probably know that your mother was actually brought up by Roman Catholic nuns, despite her being a Protestant.'

'Hm,' I agreed.

'But then there was the war. And, you know, it was difficult after that to believe in anything. We rarely went to church after that, except to get you children christened.'

'You go to the cenotaph every November the eleventh, no matter what,' I reminded him with a little smile.

'Yes, I do. But that's just so that my old friends – my dead friends, wherever they are – know that I remember them, that I have never forgotten them.' His voice was suddenly shaky. 'There were only three survivors, you know, from my old regiment – the three of us who volunteered for the Russian campaign.'

I could not bear the stricken look on his face, and I selfishly recalled him to my own predicament by asking, 'Must I go to a High Anglican church, Daddy? Couldn't I be confirmed somewhere else? Edith always took us to the village church – and they had very plain services, I remember – and neither you nor Mother said anything.'

Again he sighed, and then he looked up at me with a little smile. 'As far as I'm concerned, dear, you can go to any Protestant church you like, if it gives you comfort. I know you are trying to live a good life – and church will help to keep you out of mischief.'

Mischief was the last thing I was ever likely to get into, and I laughed, a laugh tinged with great relief.

'Really? Would it be all right? Could you talk to Mother about it?'

'Of course. Your mother won't mind, and I expect Miss Ferguson will get over it; she will probably be offended at first, though, because you always seem to have been a protégée of hers.'

'She's been a fairy godmother – and I'm truly sorry if she becomes angry about it, but even for her I can't face Confession.' I picked up my pen and chewed the end of it, and then said passionately, 'I'd burn first.'

Father laughed. 'You're a real Protestant – but I'm glad for you that you seem to have a clear belief, God bless you.'

Such a weight rolled off my shoulders. The smell of sulphur and brimstone, the smell of hell, which had haunted me uneasily for days, rolled away.

I jumped up from my chair and leaned over to kiss his bald pate. 'Thank you, Daddy.'

He caught my hand and squeezed it, while he looked up at me earnestly. 'Religion is a private thing – remember that. If you can find a path to God which suits you, take it. I wish I could, but I am not able to feel anything any more – as I said, it was the war.'

I put my arm round his shoulders and sought in my mind for comforting words. 'Perhaps you will change as time goes on, and the memory of the war becomes less.'

He nodded. 'Perhaps.' But he never did.

I was the one who changed. Starting from Father's unexpectedly wise counsel, I began to look at others' religions with a wider and more inquiring mind, as I moved about Liverpool and met people of all beliefs and all nationalities. Edith was fond of remarking that the gentry had too much book learning and not enough real learning, and it took a while for me to remedy this imbalance.

The ice between Father and me had been broken. Older now, I was more able to forgive and understand his weakness and, in reaching out for his aid when I was so afraid, I think I had restored to him in some small part a sense of being wanted, being needed for more than the wages he brought in.

Whether his talk with me had alerted him to the possible code of behaviour of his sons, I do not know. He began, however, to check on where they went in their spare time and what they did. He made them all promise to tell Mother or me their destination whenever they went out. Nobody thought of Fiona and Avril. The boys all had lively, inventive minds and were fairly well-mannered. They tended to draw friends to them, whose parents were glad to have them play in their houses, where they were under supervision. The boys also frequently played together, and this helped to keep them out of bad company.

Father's new interest in his children was wonderful to me. One of the most scaring things in childhood is the lack of an older person to turn to, to depend on for guidance and advice. Now, in a diffident, irregular way he was beginning to make his presence felt in the family, as if the trauma of the war and his financial ruin was beginning to be sloughed off. Though, in fearsome battles, Mother still shouted him down, he persisted quietly, using a strong sense of humour which I had not realised he possessed.

# Chapter eleven

Two women came on separate occasions to view our empty front room. One of them was an elderly widow and the other a shop girl in crumpled black – black was the uniform of work in those days. The lack of a bathroom and an indoor lavatory made them both turn it down with supercilious sniffs.

A few days later, a young Irish labourer, cap in hand, came to see it.

'I'm sorry, I am not prepared to let the room to a man,' Mother said, beginning to close the front door on him.

'It's not for myself only,' pleaded the youth. 'It's me wife and me baby.'

It is doubtful if anyone, except the poorest slum landlord, would have considered such a tenant. Labouring in Liverpool meant casual work at rock bottom wages – and a consequent difficulty in paying the rent. A baby meant noise and a lot of washing to be hung out. And Irish people did not have much of a name for cleanliness.

I saw Mother hesitate. The careworn white face with its red-rimmed, pleading eyes must have touched some chord in her – perhaps she remembered when she had canvassed from door to door, trying to find a landlord who would accept seven children. 'Is your wife with you now?'

'She's waitin' at t' corner.'

'Ask her to come. She'd better see it, too.'

Joyfully, he turned and bawled up the street, 'Mary, coom 'ere.'

A plump, cheery woman wearing a black shawl, with a young baby wrapped in the front of it, came panting up to the doorstep. Her rosy face, and thick light brown curls bobbing round her shoulders, reminded me of Edith, our nanny. They both had the same country-fresh look. Her expression was one of sudden glowing hope.

Fiona and I were longing to see the baby, which seemed very small, and when we had all trooped into the bleak front room, from which even the curtains had been removed by the hire purchase company, Mother asked if we might see it. Its tiny puckered face under a clean, frilled bonnet was tenderly admired by all of us, as it placidly slept.

''E's only six weeks,' his mother announced proudly as she wrapped the shawl back over him.

Mother stood in the middle of the unvarnished square of wooden floor, where the carpet had lain, and explained the disadvantages of the room. The young couple were irrepressible.

'Och, I can keep a couple o' buckets o' water in t' room. And Pat will be gone to work before most of yez is up.'

'We're all away during the day,' Mother informed her, 'except for a little while when the children come home to lunch.'

'To be sure,' responded Mary, with a wide, sweet smile, 'I can do me washing and cooking while you're all away.'

'You can hang the washing out to dry in the back yard,' said Mother. 'Come and see.'

We all went out to view the tiny, sooty yard with its lavatory near the alley door.

'We could keep our coal in the corner here,' suggested Pat. 'I could roof it over with a bit of a tin roof, like.'

'Where are you living now?' asked Mother, as we returned to the house and entered our living-room.

'We're living with me mam,' replied Pat. 'It's too hard on Mary, though. Me mam isn't an easy woman, I know. When we was in Dublin we was living with her mam, and that was all right, wasn't it, Mary?'

Mary nodded agreement, and sighed. We all understood. In Liverpool-Irish families, daughters frequently brought their husbands to live in their family. Husbands escaped from their mothers-in-law by going to work and then in the evening going down to the local pub for a drink. The young wife, however, had recourse to no such escape route if faced with her husband's mother – and the result was battles so bitter that they sometimes spilled out into the street and caused a street fight, a welcome entertainment to the onlookers, but unpleasant for the combatants.

As we showed the young couple round, I had become more and more resentful of Mother. I believed that she was raising the couple's hopes, without having any intention of giving them the room. Now, to my astonishment, a bargain was struck: a rent of ten shillings a week, plus one shilling for electricity, payable in advance.

'If you want to use the gas stove in the back kitchen, you will have to put your own pennies into the gas meter,' Mother instructed them. It seemed fair, but in practice we were more likely to benefit from gas left over by them than they were from us, because we always seemed to run out of gas and money before we had finished cooking. We had to try to complete the job on whatever bit of fire we might have at the time.

'We'll bring our gear over on Saturday afternoon,' Pat said. They both thanked Mother gaily, and through the undraped window we watched them laughing and talking together, as they hurried up the street.

Mother was the strangest person, I thought. There were layers of her character of which one caught only a momentary glimpse. Our tiny house would now have twelve people living in it, all using the same outside lavatory and the same cold water tap. The inconvenience of people trailing through our crowded living-room and kitchen at all times of the day and night would be indescribable. Our frequent bitter family rows would be heard clearly by these strangers, the details in due course to be gossiped to the neighbours. The clash of uneducated Roman Catholic Irish with upper-class Protestants was something I dreaded. Yet, watching Mother's drawn face, I was sure she had taken the family in out of compassion. Admittedly the rent was more than half the rent of the entire house, but nothing could compensate for the overcrowding and loss of any small privacy we had.

Mother and I went back to the living-room and were met by a barrage of questions from the children, who had watched in silence the small procession to and from the back yard.

'Yes, they are coming to live with us,' Mother told them. 'You will have to be quiet so as not to wake the baby – and be polite to them.'

Alan raised his eyebrows and made a rueful expression at me, while Fiona just shrugged her shoulders. Father was out having a drink with a young colleague with whom he had recently become friendly. Fortified by several glasses of beer, he received the news optimistically when he came home. Perhaps he felt, like me, that a week of such an arrangement would see the end of it.

# Chapter twelve

To my surprise, Mother accepted my diffident announcement that I would prefer to be confirmed by another church with only a fretful, 'What am I going to say to Miss Ferguson? Really! Don't you have any consideration?'

I was much too shy to go to see Miss Ferguson myself, and I do not know what explanation Mother gave her. I never saw her again, though I did hear her once when Mother sent me to borrow a shilling from her, with the plea that we had nothing for breakfast – which was true. Mother had already coerced out of me the few pennies I had, so feeling very sick at heart I had trudged to her flat, through dark streets, where the gas lamps gleamed dully through a sea mist.

The lady with whom she lived answered the door. She did not know me, and when I inquired for Miss Ferguson I was told that she was having a bath. Fearing Mother's scathing tongue if I returned without the shilling, I nervously whispered the reason for my visit. She left me standing in front of the open door while she went to consult the bather. There was a mumble of voices in the little apartment; then clearly I heard Miss Ferguson say, 'Better give it to her. Get it out of my bag – it's on the dressing-table. I'm tired of that woman – she never pays back.'

I wanted to turn and run. Miss Ferguson probably lived on a pittance, unless she had private means. The stranger was, however, hastening down the hall towards me, at the same time feeling inside a small black handbag. When she reached the door, she unsmilingly handed me a silver coin and shut the door on my muttered 'thank you very much'.

I stood looking at the offending woodwork and wanted to throw the coin at it. Mother had lost a good friend for the sake of a shilling – which she could have easily saved had she not smoked.

Mother received the money with triumphant relief, and sent Avril out to buy bread and margarine, milk and cornflakes.

So kind Miss Ferguson vanished, as far as I was concerned, into a dish of cornflakes. Fairy godmothers do tend to depart when their work is done.

When Pat and Mary and the baby arrived, it was clear that they regarded Mother as a fairy godmother. They brought their bits of furniture on a handcart; it took two journeys. An iron bed frame was put together in the room, with much bumping and rattling of metal slats which had to be woven across the base. A wool-packed mattress tied with string was banged down on it, making the slats again vibrate in tuneful protest. A wash-stand with a marble top, innumerable galvanised metal buckets, a pile of enamelled wash basins with a few dishes laid inside the top one, two chairs and a small table, some iron saucepans, a tea chest of assorted garments and blankets with a chamberpot perched on top, a fine old handmade cradle on rockers, all were piled into the room. There was only one small cupboard, which had once held a gas meter, and I wondered how everything would fit in.

Mary pinned up over the small bay window a pair of dusty-looking lace curtains. They did not give much privacy when the light was on, but they looked fairly tidy from the outside. It was only from occasional glimpses through the curtains when I passed in the evening that I was aware of the muddle of their lives. Nobody to my knowledge entered the room.

The young couple evidently decided that to make the situation bearable for both sides, they should be as invisible as possible. We were barely aware of Pat, except as a shadow going out to work through the front door as Father and I came downstairs each morning. He spent half of Sunday in bed with his wife, judging by the giggles we heard and the pinging bed slats. Mary once said primly, 'Men must have their rest on Sundays.'

To use the lavatory in the yard, they went out the front way, walked past three houses and then down a side alley which led into our back alley, and came back in through the yard door to the privy. They rarely pulled the chain, but at least they did not come through our living quarters. Nobody commented on this long tour they had to make so often, and I doubt if the family appreciated their consideration.

While we were out, Mary cooked huge quantities of stew in an enamelled wash bowl on the gas stove. I sometimes saw her hurry through our living-room with this vast amount of steaming meat and vegetables, smelling so savoury that I was envious. I think she cooked enough at one time to last two or three days and that she heated portions of it on the fire in their room. I once caught a glimpse of the room's interior when I opened the door for her when she was thus laden. Three big pails of coal and three of water were ranged against a wall. A pile of washing was flung into a corner. The baby's cradle stood close to the fire. The wash-stand was littered with utensils for cooking, the mantelpiece laden with anonymous bottles and jars. The table and chairs were, I knew, set in the bay window – I had seen them as I passed – and the rumpled bed was against the hall wall, behind the door. The wooden floor was bare and grimy, but it had been swept. A thick effluvia of human living rolled out, a mix of stew, onions, baby's faeces, sweat, urine, and steam from the washing drying on a string hung from the mantelpiece. It added itself to the neglected grubbiness of our part of the house. I hastily shut the door after Mary's, 'Thanks, luv.'

After a few days, we discovered that Mary had found an old built-in wash boiler in a corner of the coal cellar. Rather than use a similar one in the corner of our kitchen, she had carried water downstairs and had boiled her washing in it by making a fire in the tiny grate underneath. She did all her washing down there amid the clammy smell of coal dust and cats. Then she hung the clothes to drip in the back yard, before bringing them to finish drying in her room. She was very resourceful.

I probably saw more of her than the others did, because I was almost invariably the last person to go to bed. I often did my night school studying after everyone else had gone up to bed. She would slip apologetically through the room several times, carrying buckets of coal and water or a pile of washing from the back yard. She also emptied buckets of dirty water down the kitchen sink.

Occasionally, while I was studying by candlelight because we could not afford a penny for electricity – candles cost a halfpenny – she would hasten in with a penny because they also were plunged into darkness. I always continued with my candle, because I felt it would be unfair to switch on the light and help use up their pennyworth.

On Saturday night, Pat, with a shy grin on his face, would knock on our living-room door and hand to whoever opened it eleven shillings. They had no rent book and never asked for a receipt. Their trust was moving.

Because of the poor quality of the building, any raised voices could be heard in the next room, and they must have suffered from the continual squabbling of the children and the bitter, screaming rows between my parents.

Sometimes they themselves quarrelled. In their case, it was not always a verbal spate. There were the sounds of screams, scuffles and thumps, while the baby howled untended. Fortunately, perhaps, our children found it funny rather than frightening. Most of the time, the baby was quiet, cosied against his mother's ample breasts or rocked in his warm cradle by her foot on the rocker, while she knitted.

Occasionally, Mary would stop in her late-night promenade to ask me what I was doing. She smelled strongly of milk and perspiration, but she had a glowing life about her, an eager effervescence that I wished was mine. She was endlessly curious about us and boundless in her praise of Mother. I began to see Mother in a slightly better light. 'To be sure, she's a great lady,' Mary would remark at times, and I wished I could feel the same about her.

One night, I had been wrestling with a difficult task which my English master had set me. I was to read a book of essays by William Hazlitt and comment on it. I was very tired and could not concentrate and was asking myself why I bothered, since it would make no difference to my marks, when Mary, carrying a pile of dirty washing, entered without knocking.

She paused, smiled and asked, as an opening gambit, 'How are yer, luv?'

Relieved to be temporarily delivered from Hazlitt, I put down my pen and pushed the cork into the ink bottle.

'Not bad, Mary. How are you?'

She looked at me hard. 'You bin cryin'?' she inquired solicitously.

I had cried, after everyone had gone to bed, letting the tears drop on to my books. Mother had paused on her way to bed, and had asked me with a hint of contemptuous curiosity what I was going to wear for my forthcoming Confirmation. Her attitude was cold, as if she were poking idly at a half-dead beetle on the floor.

I had never seen a Confirmation, and it was with a sense of shock that I received the information that I would be expected to appear in a white dress and veil – a fact which was confirmed by the head of the church's Sunday school, the following week, when after the evening service she announced to the congregation that veils would be loaned by the church.

In a world which still judged people by what they wore – a moment's consideration of a person's dress would establish his position socially – I was in a difficult dilemma. To buy odd garments to cover me was hard enough; to buy a dress for a single occasion was impossible. I would, presumably, need white stockings and shoes as well, which would never be worn again.

Mother had not offered any answer to her query, so there was not much hope of help from her. I said, tight-lipped, that I did not know what to do, but I would think about it, and opened my books and got on with my homework as best I could with a mind in a nervous flutter. Life never seemed to get any better and this additional problem made me cry with dumb despair.

'We all have a little cry some time or other, Mary.' I tried to smile.

'Oh, aye,' she agreed. 'I like a good cry myself sometimes. Relieves you, like.'

I nodded and piled up my books. I would have another try at Hazlitt tomorrow during my lunch hour.

Mary shifted the washing round in her arms. It reeked.

'What's to do?' she persisted.

I sighed. 'Well, Mary.' She was always Mary, never Mrs O'Neill, to all of us. It marked the difference in class. 'Well, Mary, I'm going to be confirmed.' And I went on to explain the problem of the dress.

Mary was thrilled. Confirmation was a great event, she burbled, though in her opinion it should have taken place when I was seven. 'Och, you'd look like an angel, in white,' she assured me, looking my beanpole figure up and down. 'Surely your mam will get you a frock?'

'She can't afford it,' I defended Mother. 'And I don't have a penny,' I added frankly.

Mary clicked her tongue. '*My* mam got me one – and for sure we didn't have much money. It's a very special occasion.' She glanced down at the washing in her arms. 'Look, luv, just let me take me washing down. We got to think how to do this.'

She tripped down the stone steps to dump the washing in the copper. When she came up she had a coal smudge on her apron and was dusting it off impatiently. She stopped in front of me, and announced almost defiantly, 'If you can't get a dress any other way, I'll lend you me wedding dress.'

'Oh, Mary!' The offer was so kind, but Mary's figure was rotund and anything of hers would have hung on me. Yet her dress must have been almost a sacred relic to her amid her present hard circumstances. I hesitated.

She must have read my mind. 'It's proper nice – and it'll fit near enough,' she said. 'I was real thin when I was married.' She looked down at her enormous bosom and giggled. 'Marriage agrees with me. I'll have a word with your mam.'

When I came home the next evening, Mother greeted me with such enthusiasm that I was frightened. But, according to Avril, Mary – dear Mary – had indeed been talking to her, pointing out that other than my marriage or my funeral, Confirmation was the greatest day of my life, even if it was to be performed by a Protestant bishop.

Before I even got my coat off, Mother was saying, 'Just come and look.'

Laid on a chair, with a sheet of newspaper under it so that it was kept clean, was an open dressmaker's box with a large pile of white tissue paper in it. Mother carefully parted the tissue, took out a dried sprig of orange blossom and laid it on the table, while she gushed, 'Isn't that sweet? It's from her wedding bouquet.' Then she carefully lifted out a pile of lace and shook it. It was a charming, long-sleeved white dress.

I gaped as I looked at its shimmering whiteness, its absolute purity of line. 'Mother! It's lovely. It's perfect. They must have spent a fortune on it.'

Mother laughed. 'Well, you should know by now that a working-class wedding is a great event. And they spend money on them.'

Mother carefully folded the dress back into its tissue. As she lifted the package and handed it to me, a few grains of lavender fell from it. I bent over the box's contents and sniffed. It smelled like Grandma's sheets and dresses, with a lovely perfume of fresh lavender.

'Mummy's going to buy you some white shoes and stockings – and a petticoat,' interjected Fiona. 'Aren't you, Mummy?' She said it firmly, as if to reinforce the decision.

'Of course,' said Mother, without blinking an eyelid. Fiona winked at me. Mary, she told me afterwards, had swept Mother along on such a flood of excitement that Mother had said she would apply to the finance company for a cheque for a pound, to cover the purchase of these accessories.

To persuade Mother to buy me anything was little short of a miracle and, with the box still in my arms, I knocked on Mary's door, and went in to thank her. She blushed as I kissed her. Then heaved her baby round on her lap to offer it her breast, and muttered, 'It's nothing, luv. Nothin' at all.'

So, for the first time I entered the echoing hollowness of Liverpool Cathedral. It was overwhelming. Soaring pillars of tawny pink sandstone, huge stained-glass windows, their myriad colours reflected on the smooth grey stone floor, a welter of beauty for a sensitive seventeen-year-old, a fitting place for God to dwell. Surely, I thought, God Himself is present here.

Mother and Fiona had entered by another door, and I stood alone for a moment almost afraid to advance into such a place. Then a lady from the church fussed forward, led me into a corner, pinned a veil over my newly washed hair and straightened my dress. 'You haven't got any gloves!' she exclaimed, throwing up her hands. I looked down at my work-reddened hands and then at the hands of the other boys and girls, standing soberly near me. Everyone had on white gloves, except me. I blushed to the roots of my hair. All the sense of oneness with the beauty around me vanished. Would God ever forgive the lack of white gloves?

It was my fault. I had never thought of gloves. I blamed myself, never thinking that Mother, experienced in all things appertaining to etiquette, might have reminded me.

'I suppose you'll have to go without,' said the lady testily. 'Pull your sleeves down as far as you can.'

Hanging my head, I stood alone in a corner, waiting to be marshalled into a procession according to height, and tried to turn my thoughts again to the spiritual aspect of the ceremony, but I could not recapture it. All the pleasure and hope of my beautiful dress was lost, all the tender belief that I was approaching God like a bride ready to offer what little virtue I had to His service was gone, shot down by an impatient woman and the lack of a sixpenny pair of gloves. Ironically, I could have bought them myself, one of my shorthand students having paid me the night before. I began to shiver.

Two by two we advanced towards the old bishop sitting in front of the altar. We knelt before him and he placed his hands firmly on our heads, so that we should not rise prematurely. He said in a loud sonorous voice, 'Defend, O Lord, this Thy child with Thy heavenly grace, that she may continue Thine for ever; and daily increase in Thy Holy Spirit, more and more, until she comes to Thy everlasting kingdom. Amen.'

I was so innocent that I expected to feel different after the magical words had been spoken. But I did not. I was still shivering, disconcerted by the importance of outward and visible signs – like gloves – as against the inward and spiritual grace which I had hoped to acquire that day.

Mary had said firmly to Mother that I must have a photograph of myself, to celebrate the event and as a keepsake, so the sixpence which could have been spent on the missing gloves was expended at the local photographer's, who took the first picture of me since I was a little child. Until I looked into his mirror when tidying myself ready for the photograph, I had, of course, no idea what I looked like, because at home we had only a small piece of broken mirror. The photograph was better than I had hoped.

The photograph shows a slender girl with small curves in all the right places. She is dressed in a plain lace gown with the uneven hem which had been fashionable a few years earlier. She has long slender fingers, delicate ankles, and small feet encased in white satin shoes. Her face, clothed in horn-rimmed spectacles too small for her, is as plain as the back of a Liverpool tram.

# Chapter thirteen

I was now eighteen, going on nineteen, a plain, silent girl still struggling to stay alive, no longer quite so devoted to the Church, deeply distrustful of the motives of those whose lives touched mine, a young woman without hope.

I had been promoted to the Stenographers' Room, working side by side with Miriam, thankful to be at last delivered from the sniggering girls downstairs. My shorthand was almost perfect, thanks to good evening school teaching; my typing was still very faulty because I had taught myself. I had consequently not received a rise in salary, just an improvement in status.

Miriam had for a long time worked very hard to raise money for the volunteers among her Communist associates who went to fight against Franco in the Spanish Civil War. Now, as her fingers flew over the typewriter keys, she raged that the war was lost to the Fascists and soon Europe would be plunged into a much bigger war. She threw herself impetuously into aiding the many Spanish children who had been sent to safety in England and into consoling the wounded, disillusioned returning volunteers.

There was a number of active Communists on our staff, earnest women toiling as social workers in the depths of Liverpool's appalling slums. Despite their desire to recruit to their party, I kept well back from their political endeavours, partly from the fact that my personal life was so full of work that I could not cope with anything as abstract as political beliefs, and partly because of the scarifying stories Father had told me of Communist excesses he had seen during his military service in Russia.

Several stenographers had come and gone during my employment with the charity, but the Head Typist was still the devout Roman Catholic who tried regularly to save Miriam from her misbegotten ideas and me from the clutches of a heretic church. She was a dear and almost everybody was fond of her, no matter how cross she got about hanging participles and bad spelling. Between her and Miriam I learned to disagree with other people's beliefs and yet have respect for them.

At one point the charity was so short of funds that she instituted a fine of one penny for every sheet of paper that Miriam and I wasted as a result of typing errors. Miriam promptly said, 'Not bloody likely!' and since I had little money to spare to pay fines, we smuggled screwed-up balls of paper containing our typing sins out of the room, by quietly stuffing them into our overall pockets or down our necks. Occasionally, we had the most remarkably lumpy figures.

My life had settled into a dull, fatiguing rut. Ever fearful of unemployment, I clung to my job. Each January or February, I went down with influenza or bronchitis and, in my emaciated state, usually took a month to recover. The Presence always sent my wages to me, no matter how many weeks I was away, a rare generosity in those days.

A few more jobs were becoming available in the beleaguered city. Shadow factories were being built, with an eye to war; and an army of bricklayers and other building workers, though thankful for a small pay packet, cursed with pain as their blistered hands and aching backs got used to working again.

I began to have a faint glimmering of hope that, despite my lack of education, I might be able to find a better job or, by continuing my evening school studies, become well enough informed to join the more privileged green-overalled social workers.

Students came to our office from the Social Science Department of the university, to do some practical work. Our workers gave them lectures, taught them how to interview and took them to see our clients in their homes. Some of the students were horrified at what they saw and were afraid of visiting alone.

In the Committee Room a large bookcase began to be filled with volumes on the theories of social science. Whenever the lecturer forgot to lock the bookcase, I borrowed books for a night or two and read them, slipping them back into the bookcase when the room was empty. Sometimes the theories and the interpretations of statistics made me laugh, and I thought of the shrewd exploiters of social assistance amongst whom I lived. Some of our neighbours knew every trick and used extremely agile brains to obtain what they needed from the many agencies in the city; it was almost like a business to them. They were all poor, but it was often not the most needy who received the most help. Now, three generations later, this swindling has become an art, and some people live very comfortably with it. They would probably do equally well if they turned their astuteness towards earning a living. Crying poverty, however, can be a good excuse for shrugging off the weight of responsibility for one's life.

The books opened up to me the world of theory, and I began to understand that there were people who spent their lives trying to find the underlying principles upon which society and nature itself were built. Pondering upon theological questions was something to which my history reading had introduced me; now I became interested in what might be going on in the university. It was further intensified by a casual conversation with one of our older students, who told me that he had been a weaver for twelve years and had, during that time, managed to study enough to matriculate. He had also saved enough to put himself through university. For a moment my ambitions soared. Then he said, 'I couldna ha' done it without me mam and dad. They just asked a bit for me food – and they gave me a room to work in – you need a room of your own to do aught. Me dad was really good. He went without to buy me books and me mam took in washing. Soon I'll be able to help them.'

The ambition flopped like a balloon with a leak. My parents took from their girls; they did not give. They might occasionally encourage verbally, but they would not help. Any money they had, any ambition they felt, was channelled to the boys. Fiona, Avril and I were always just useful wage earners.

Alan, nearly six feet tall, though very thin, joined the Auxiliary Air Force and clumped about in strong black Air Force boots. He shone them to a jetty perfection every Sunday morning. He had an Air Force uniform, with brass buttons which were also polished with the aid of endless tins of Brasso. He learned to press his uniform himself, a radical decision brought about because once when pressing his trousers I had burned a hole in them.

Every Saturday and Sunday, he went to an airfield to be trained, first in ordinary drills and physical fitness programmes, then to work, as he said, on *real* aircraft with *real* tools. The planes were Hawker Hind biplanes, which went all of one hundred and seventy miles an hour. He was thrilled, and concentrated on the work with passionate intensity. His thin wrists strengthened as he learned to use tools, and the regular exercise broadened his shoulders. He began to walk with more self-assurance. He was paid for his service and was allowed to keep the money in addition to his pocket money.

He was generous by nature, and he would often treat the younger children to the Saturday matinée at the Rialto Cinema. They ate ice cream sandwiches during the intermission and had a wonderful time shrieking encouragement to film heroes like Tom Mix as, on his white horse, he galloped after the 'baddies', who always rode black horses.

Fiona, after spending two miserable weeks in suspense, had been engaged by the magazine dealer and was very happy, working the addressograph and, when business was slack, reading all the magazines, from *True Confessions* to *Good Housekeeping*, not to speak of a number of American magazines for men, which, she told me, were utterly shocking. Her employers treated her like one of the family. She was soon earning fifteen shillings a week, the same as me. She paid half of it to Mother for her food and kept the rest for travelling expenses and pocket money. Mother still bought her clothes, which put her away ahead of me financially.

Every night she went to bed with her hair in curling rags, until she could afford a permanent wave. I wanted such a wave, too, but had not the faintest hope of being able to afford it. I had no time to put my hair in rags, so I still had long hair pulled back into a bun.

Her boy friends multiplied, so her entertainment was paid for by a series of devoted swains. Sometimes, she would beg me to tell a more ambitious one at the front door that she was out, while she slipped through the back door to meet someone else. Her social life became one of the first family jokes at which we all laughed.

It was apparent to me that Father was now earning more than he used to. He, too, began to have a modest social life, when he met his colleagues at various public houses in the city. Several times he went to concerts at the Philharmonic Hall, newly rebuilt after a disastrous fire, which Brian and Tony had enjoyed watching. He managed to buy a suit and an overcoat and occasionally shoes and shirts. Cinemas bored him, so he did not go to them. He did not give any more money to the home, which caused constant flare-ups between Mother and him. His main argument was that to retain his job he had to have a minimum of clothing, which he would certainly never get if he did not buy it himself. To that end he had to save some money. Mother would come flying back at him, that he smoked and drank too much, to which he would promptly retort that she spent most of her evenings at the cinema – she went at least twice a week – and that she also smoked like a proverbial chimney. Then they would rake up every possible transgression since the day of their marriage, and accuse and counter-accuse until the family fled or was reduced to tears and impassioned pleas to them to stop.

Though Mother was now very strong physically, she was feeling the effect of the change of life, something I had never heard of until Miriam mentioned it in connection with her mother. Mother's temper was so unpredictable that if she was more unbalanced than usual we did not notice it. She complained, however, of being overly hot and she sometimes looked as if she had fever. Miriam called these attacks hot flushes and advised me to be patient with her and encourage her to rest. I made a great effort to hold my tongue when she was being particularly vicious in her remarks, and tried to help more in the house when she obviously did not feel well.

At nearly nineteen I was an adult and better able than I had been to assess soberly what was happening to any of us. Once Mother realised that I understood what was happening to her, she seemed glad to be able to speak frankly to me about it. I encouraged her to see the doctor from time to time, and though there was no real aid then for this intense physical upheaval, he was able to comfort her by assuring her that it would pass.

Rest was possible, because she did not work full time, and when all the children were at school she could go to bed in the afternoon and get up late in the morning. Whatever cleaning and washing there was to be done was usually achieved at the weekend when I was at home. She began again to read regularly, and drew real enjoyment from the great storytellers of the time – Edgar Wallace, Jeffrey Farnol, P. G. Wodehouse, Rafael Sabatini and many others. She had been a librarian before her marriage and she liked to discuss what she had read. In me she found a willing listener.

Through her guardian, who owned a string of private libraries, she had met many of the early twentieth-century writers and in those days had read much more deeply than she did in her later years. It dawned on me that her knowledge of literature had in part guided me, because every time I was ill – which was at least twice a year – she would bring me her own choice of books from the public library to read in bed. It was she, I recollected, who had brought me the first books I read on Japanese and Chinese history and travel books on South America, a continent I had never thought about before then and a fascinating area for further study.

This shared love of books formed a slender bridge between us, and I began to find it easier to talk to her, though on a shallow level, about other concerns in which I was interested, like the war we were all afraid would break out and about the refugees pouring in from Europe.

Mother feared for her sons. She dreaded them being butchered as her own generation had been, though I once heard her remark that she had 'done her duty to the nation by producing four sons.' The idea that to produce soldiers was the duty of a mother shocked me beyond measure, but to women of her age, of the officer class, it must have seemed natural.

As a result of the battle-axes being laid down between us, though never buried, at the time of the office Christmas dance I felt brave enough to say that for once I would like to attend.

'Do you think you could help me buy a second-hand dress?' I begged humbly. 'I have never been to the office parties before, and Miriam thinks I should – I might meet some of the Committee members – and that might help me with promotion later on.' Miriam was nothing if not practical, despite her ideals.

Mother pondered over this, and said, 'I'll see.'

A few days later, she came home with a long white rayon taffeta dress, which she had bought from a girl she knew in one of the stores. My share of the cost – five shillings – was paid in two instalments, as my shorthand student paid me. The material of the dress was delicately patterned in fine red and green stripes and at the back it had long ruffles running from waist to hem. The sleeves were short and puffed and the low V-neck had a diamanté clasp tucked into it. Though it was not particularly fashionable, it fitted me and Fiona said it looked quite pretty.

The white stockings bought for my Confirmation had, because of their colour, survived Fiona's marauding so they were ready to hand, and Mother gave me the pawn ticket so that I could retrieve the white satin slippers and the petticoat from Uncle's.

The pawnbroker was Jewish, portly. What hair he had was curled tightly round a bald patch. The light of the bare electric bulb above his high counter shone on his olive face and made his heavy watch chain glitter. He was an old friend.

While the apprentice went up into the loft to retrieve the cloth-wrapped bundle, I told him shyly about the dance, and then confided that I had not been to a dancing class since I was eleven and feared I might not be able to dance.

'T' boys'll soon learn yez,' he assured me with a grin. 'Eee, now, I wish I could coom meself. But me wife'll never let me off the hook, yer know. Proper hard case she is.'

I laughed. 'I think the girls are allowed to bring a boy friend – but, of course, I haven't got one.'

'Aye, give yerself time, luv. You'll soon find one.'

I smiled, feeling suddenly a little flattered by his pleasantries, though I did not think that boy friends were likely to enter my life.

I sat quietly on a chair at the edge of the dance floor for the entire evening, watching the colourful dancers.

'What else can you expect?' I asked myself. The other girls had each brought a partner. Miriam did not come, having Party affairs to attend to. Except for an elderly gentleman, who, after bowing and making a polite inquiry, brought me a dish of ice cream and a glass of lemonade, I was left alone. After a few moments of laboured remarks about the inclemency of the weather, the gentleman was drawn away by a more thoughtless and equally bored Committee member. I ate my ice cream and sipped the lemonade with what I hoped was a look of jaded sophistication, and at about half past ten I went to the ladies' cloakroom and retrieved my old brown coat and outdoor shoes. After putting on these shabby garments, I put a carefully reserved silver threepenny piece in the attendant's saucer. She looked up from her knitting and said, 'Thank you, miss,' a slight surprise in her thick, Liverpool voice.

It was drizzling as I dawdled back up the hill from the city restaurant in which the dance had been held. I held up the long dress from the wet pavement and the satin shoes hung from the fingertips of my other hand. Occasionally, I heaved a great sigh. The whole great expense had been for nothing.

Only Mother was up when I entered the living-room. She was sitting with her feet braced high against one side of the big kitchen fireplace, her dress slipped back above her knees, to ease her veins. She laid her book down on her lap, and asked, 'Well, how was it?'

'A flop,' I replied, laying the precious slippers carefully down on a chair. 'I didn't get a dance.'

'You didn't stay till the end? It's only eleven now.'

'I could not sit there – through the night – until one in the morning – it would be too humiliating. Not one of the girls even spoke to me.'

Mother bit her lips. 'I'm sorry, dear,' she said, and she sounded as if she really was. Then after a moment, as I peeled off my coat, she added some sound advice. 'You'll have to stop looking like a frozen rabbit. Men don't like plain girls – and girls who look both plain and dull never get anywhere. You must smile – look gay.'

I sighed, and tried to smile. 'I expect you're right,' I agreed.

The next day the pretty dress, the petticoat and the beloved white satin shoes were bundled up in a white cloth and returned to Uncle.

# Chapter fourteen

Nineteen thirty-eight was the year that Mr Neville Chamberlain, our Prime Minister, sold Czechoslovakia down the river, in order to gain time for us. The word 'appeasement' entered our vocabulary, appeasement of a raving lunatic called Adolf Hitler, who with his Panzer divisions was mopping up the map of Europe. It seemed that after every visit Alan made to the cinema, he would remark that the Paramount news reels had shown the takeover of another country.

At first we all felt a sense of relief when an ailing Mr Chamberlain, supported by his black umbrella, came home from Europe and announced, 'Peace for our time.' It was peace bought at the expense of Czechoslovakia; and it seemed that gradually in the city a great sense of shame welled up. 'Letting a pack of bloody gorillas loose on them,' I heard a station porter say angrily.

The sacrifice *did* gain us time, we all knew that, time to mobilise the fleet, time to extend the barracks just off Princes Road, to fill factories at Speke with the machinery of war, expand the fire brigade, plan the evacuation of the city, time to write innumerable pamphlets which fluttered through our letterbox on what to do in an air raid, gas attack, food shortage, petrol rationing, evacuation of schoolchildren – it went on and on.

A pile of gas masks in neat cardboard boxes arrived on our living-room table, to make the children giggle and shiver nervously as we tried them on, and were suddenly converted into anonymous, long-snouted aliens.

It was taken for granted that if we had to go to war our cities would within a few days be flattened by air raids. Liverpool was our paramount western port, a legitimate target. I found that I was not much afraid at the prospect of death, only of being half dead beneath a mountain. of rubble. I wondered if in such a situation I could commit suicide by swallowing my tongue as it was said the poor suffering Ethiopians did. Death – to be dead – did not seem to be much worse than being alive.

Mother fervently thanked God that only Alan was old enough to be called up. Alan was wildly excited, and spent every moment he could at the airfield. Father, who had fought the war to end all wars, looked particularly pinched and sad as he read the headlines in the *Echo*. He went out and bought himself a small atlas from the local tobacconist, and with more perception of the future than our army generals, spent evenings plotting the advance of the Japanese in China, a fray which had been pushed to the back pages of the papers.

I had my usual dose of flu during February, and it left me with a cough which was a nuisance to the whole family. I determined to try to save up for a holiday. I discovered from a book at work that there was a Girls' Holiday Home on the seafront at Hoylake in the Wirral, across the river. They charged about a pound for a week's stay, not a very large sum, though it would take me a long time to save it, and the shilling or so train fare.

I instituted an iron discipline. No trams at all, no twopenny cinema shows of old films at the Central Hall, only a penny bun for lunch instead of a threepenny soup, and, most difficult of all, making my easily laddered rayon stockings last longer – the main difficulty was keeping them out of the clutches of Fiona and Mother. They cost ninepence a pair and were my biggest single expense. I relooped ladders with the aid of a darning needle, an eye-straining, time-consuming job. I darned and redarned the heels, which badly fitting second-hand shoes tended to wear through very quickly. The money saved was carried in a little cloth bag on a string round my neck, and no matter how much Mother whined I never admitted its existence.

After a bitter battle, Mother managed to squeeze out of me a further two shillings and sixpence from my small wages. This left me with exactly one shilling to cover all my needs, and in a desperate position. Any money for my own existence had to be earned by teaching shorthand to pupils in their homes.

Six or seven shillings would feed a woman quite well. What I ate at home would cost about three shillings, so Mother was doing quite well out of me. My one joy during this period was going to the theatre with my friend, Sylvia, the money for which was provided to all the staff by a kindly Greek interested in the work of the charity which employed me. I used to live for those evenings spent tucked up on the topmost bench of the Liverpool Repertory Theatre, one of the finest repertory theatres in the country.

The village in which the Girls' Holiday Home was situated was the village in which Grandma lived. I had spent many months of childhood with her. I used to cuddle up by her side while she taught me to read from the Bible; and, from dog-eared sheets of music, how to read the notes.

Grandma was short, plump, and always dressed in black silk or satin, skirts almost touching the floor, a boned, white lace modesty vest filling the neckline in a long V-shape from her tiny pink ear tips to her waist. She had a hearty, merry laugh and could be very witty. As she shook her head the front curls of her snowy wig bounced gently on her forehead. When she went out to shop in the village a huge hat was skewered with long hat pins on to the top of the wig. The hat was always heavily trimmed with black, grey or white satin, sometimes held by a large diamanté brooch or by a bunch of dark red cherries – very dashing – or black feathers. Because going to Liverpool to buy a new hat was an exhausting operation, my two aunts who lived with her would periodically retrim her hats for her. I accepted as natural that her clothes were always black, as were those of her very dignified circle of lady friends. Widows wore black, and a few of the older ones wore tiny black bonnets like Queen Victoria's, with a black veil which could shroud the face or be flung back, according to the official depths of one's mourning. Victoria had set the fashion for widows, a fashion nearly as repressive as that for widows in India. Grandma had been a widow for forty years. In its almost unbearable boredom, it must have seemed to such a lively woman like a life prison sentence.

Dare I go to see Grandma while I was in Hoylake? I wondered. I had dreamed for years of doing so, had wanted to run away to her when first I faced the appalling poverty of Liverpool. Father had not attempted to get into touch with her, as far as I knew, since their final quarrel when he went bankrupt, and of latter years I had refrained from visiting her because of his bitter remarks that I would not be welcome. But Father was her baby, who had arrived long after his nearest sister, and they must sometimes have wanted very much to see each other. He had also managed to quarrel furiously with his two sisters who lived with her. They did not approve of the gay life he had led nor did they approve of Mother, who, they felt, was not quite a lady, having worked for her living.

During our early years in Liverpool, a small parcel postmarked Hoylake would arrive from time to time. It always contained a pair of very soft, finely knitted children's combinations; there was never any note. Avril or Edward would rejoice for weeks in the warm comfort of the garments. Mother always wrote a polite thank-you note to Grandma - nothing more. I wondered sometimes what Grandma thought about during the long afternoons when she must have sat, as was her custom, in her sunny lace-curtained sitting room, cat on knee, and knitted. Did she grieve? Or was she sustained by righteous indignation? Had she any inkling at all about what was happening to us, that we looked like children who had suffered in an Indian famine?

After a noisy row with Mother about my duplicity in saving for a holiday and about my grim determination to go on it, regardless of the fact that Edward needed new shoes, it was with mixed feelings that I carried a shopping bag containing a change of clothes down the long slope of King's Gap to the sea. It was said that King William's troops set sail for Ireland from here, to fight the Battle of the Boyne, a battle celebrated annually by Liverpool Protestants with a great procession, in defiance of Roman Catholic wrath.

The wind from Liverpool Bay blew my hat off as I turned to walk along the Promenade. Along here, in a bright red brick house which was a nursing home, I had been born in a bed relinquished to my labouring mother by a wounded soldier, who lay on the floor in the passage while I yelled my first unhappy breath. Because the nursing-home staff were swamped by wounded men, this man tended my mother and washed my nappies for her, while Father fought in Russia and did not know for a long time that I was born.

I ran my hand along the iron rail of the Promenade. Here, as a six-year-old, I had squeaked delightedly when a young fisherman picked me up and ran agilely along the top of the iron railings while the incoming tide lashed at the wall below us. From here, I had once or twice sailed out in his fishing boat with his brothers. The boat was a bouncing cockle of a craft which stank of fish. No wonder I am never seasick; my introduction to the sea was so happy. Grandma must have wondered once or twice why my discarded clothes smelled so badly. I never told her because officially I was spending the day with a lonely small boy who lived on the seafront. I did not like him, so when sent trustingly down the road to his house, I just went on to the beach and messed about amongst the fishing fleet, if it was in.

As far as I could see, there was no fishing fleet any more, not a sign of a sail or a net; only small pleasure craft heeled half over in the sand, waiting for the tide to come ripping in past the Hoyle Bank and round Hilbre Island and set them dancing.

The Holiday Home was spartan, but I rejoiced in clean sheets and shining floors. I was allotted a small windowless cubicle in which to sleep. It was stuffy with much use, and the whole building smelled of a mixture of floor polish, cabbage and cats.

I left the door of the cubicle open and sat down on the narrow bed and read innumerable notices on the wall telling me not to sit on the bed, to turn off the light, to be in at ten p.m., not to smoke, to come to meals promptly, etc. I wondered what to do. Girls cursing under their breath stumbled past to other cubicles, pushing heavy suitcases ahead of them.

The near darkness of the cubicle was becoming depressing when suddenly the suitcases of two girls jammed in the narrow passageway. They swore ripely and richly in strongly accented German. Then they stood and laughed at each other. I jumped up eagerly to lend a hand, and between the three of us we managed to move the cases, though we left a long scratch on the varnished wall of the passage.

The girls were the daughters of Swiss hoteliers. They had been working in England for nearly a year as servants, in order to perfect their English. Their employers had sent them to the Holiday Home while they themselves took a vacation. They, too, had very little money. We were reciprocally pleased with each other. I could understand their German and they could follow my accentless English. It was a joy to me to show them the Wirral.

At low tide, carrying our shoes and some sandwiches, we paddled out to Hilbre Island, stopping to watch the shrimps tickling our toes, and the local people bent double as they dug for cockles and mussels. We watched the sea roar in again round the tiny island, while we hunted for seashells along its shore. In the evening, when the water had silently retreated, we strolled slowly back across the wet sand, while the hills of North Wales went purple and the lights of West Kirby began to wink out ahead. As we walked, I pointed out to them the stumps of a great primeval forest sticking out of the sand, and we imagined tiny brown men in coracles drifting round the mouths of the Dee and the Mersey.

Puffing in the boisterous wind, we walked the length of the great sea wall which held back the tide from the villages of Moreton and Leasowe. Behind the wall rich market gardens showed neat squares of different shades of green. Dutch dike specialists came from time to time to inspect this great sea wall and it was much admired. Father used to say that the best cure for a cold was to walk its length and let the wild clean air from the bay blow the germs out, which probably was not quite what the builders had in mind.

We scrambled down into an abandoned quarry, in the hope of finding some of the nests of the innumerable birds who made it their home. We did not find a nest and we had a panicky few minutes before we managed to haul ourselves out, dusty, breathless and laughing. There were no birds except sparrows in our street in Liverpool, and the riotous singing in that quarry was like a Polish choir going full belt.

Inland, we discovered small villages in winding lanes, and we would walk along them singing softly together, enjoying the great swishing trees and eating penny ice creams bought from minute village shops.

I was happy with my gay companions. Good though very plain food helped my famished body, and the cough lessened. But all the time I thought of Grandma.

One day we passed along the road in which she lived, three giggly, gawky girls, two in light sleeveless summer dresses, one in a winter skirt and crumpled blouse, and I glanced quickly, almost frightenedly, at the house which meant so much to me.

It looked exactly the same as I remembered it. Lace curtains draped round the windows, wrought-iron gate, straight red-tiled path to the front door, carefully swept and washed, and a patch of neatly cut lawn with a few recalcitrant daisies scattered on it like stars.

I do not know why it is that some front doors look more closed than other shut doors, but to me Grandma's door looked that day particularly blank and forbidding. I did not sleep much during the night as I wondered whether if I knocked and it were opened, there would be any welcome inside.

Towards the end of the week, the two Swiss girls became acquainted with two young men who had been caulking a rowing boat on the shore. I had walked up to the village to buy a small gift for Mother, a peace offering.

On the Friday, the girls received an invitation from the boat caulkers to go out for a row, so I had my last afternoon in Hoylake to myself. At first I sat in the gloom – on my bed – and read the notice which said that one should not use the bedroom in the daytime. I felt very lonely in the deserted Home, and chewed my thumb unhappily.

Then, as if propelled by instinct alone, I got up and quickly washed my hands and face in the communal bathroom, changed my blouse, galloped down the stairs and ran along the Promenade, not pausing for breath until I was faced with the slope of King's Gap. My battered handbag was clutched in one hand, while with the other I tried to stop the hairpins falling out of my hair in the playful breeze.

Breathless, I opened the gate and ran up the familiar path, as if afraid that if I were observed from the windows someone would stop my entering.

I knocked.

There was no response. Perhaps everyone was out.

Shyly, I knocked again, and there was the sound of the well-remembered step of one of my aunts.

She opened the door, looked at me blankly, and then smiled. 'Why, Helen!' she exclaimed.

Still panting, I asked, 'Is Grandma at home?'

My aunt hesitated, and then said, 'Yes, she is. Do come in.'

I entered and paused in the doorway, while the feeling of the house rushed over me. The grandfather clock was still ticking its friendly tick, the house still smelled sweetly of flowers, polish and women's perfumes. No odour of tobacco or cooking. The antique china pieces still decorated a small shelf above the sitting-room door, through which my aunt had vanished, her pink-striped Macclesfield silk dress flicking behind her, as she shut the door after her.

As breath returned to me, panic also invaded. What was I going to talk about?

My aunt was back in the hall, and saying, 'Go in, Helen.' She gestured with one thin, delicate hand. She closed the door behind me as I went in, and I could hear her going upstairs. I felt the same fear that I always did when the Presence sent for me to scold me for typing errors.

The room was shadowed in comparison with the bright sunshine outside, and for a second I could hardly see the figure seated near the fireplace in one of the chintz-covered easy chairs.

I caught my breath sharply, as if someone had stabbed me with a pin.

A tiny, shrunken person, swathed in black, seemed engulfed in the chair. Beneath a white wig which appeared too large, two dim blue eyes smiled at me in a face hung with paperwhite folds of skin. The familiar brooch

378

on the lace under her chin looked big and clumsy. Hands which seemed only bone and blue veins rested on a shallow china bowl of green peas, and on a small table by the chair was a basket full of pea shells and a brown paper bag, which presumably held more of the vegetable.

I stood awkwardly in front of her. 'Granny,' I said, while inside my heart cried. I had forgotten what great age did to the human frame. To me she was eternal. I was suddenly and brokenly aware of all the years that I had missed being with her. She was in her nineties, and though I did not care very much about death for myself, I wanted her to live for ever.

'How very nice,' she said, in a weak but clear voice. 'Come here, dear.'

I went to her and carefully kissed the papery cheek. She smelled sweetly of Yardley's lavender, as usual, and her lace modesty vest was fresh and white. 'Sit down, dear, and tell me about yourself. Bring that chair close to me.'

So I brought a straight chair and sat knee to knee with her. While we shelled peas together, I told her about the Holiday Home and about my job and how I hoped one day to be a social worker. Somehow, I could not bring myself to tell her about the frightful privation we had endured, nor about the steady hunger and cold, the lack of blankets, woollens and coal from which we still suffered. She had obviously been ill and I was not too certain that she comprehended all that I was saying to her.

When the peas had all been shelled, she leaned her head against the back of the chair and closed her eyes. I stopped talking, and she reached out her hand. I held the fragile fingers, while she rested, and thought about a small girl whose hand she had held through many a walk to the village. Now, it was I who was holding her hand.

After a while, my aunt came briskly into the room, and said, 'It's time for your walk, Mother.' She picked up the bowl of peas, the brown paper bag and the basket of shells. 'Perhaps Helen would like to go with you.'

'Certainly,' I agreed.

Grandma opened her eyes and looked at me. There was a slight twinkle in them. 'Yes. We'll go together. It will give Aunt Emily a rest.'

A long black coat was brought in by Aunt Emily and the old lady was eased into it. Carpet slippers were exchanged for tiny button shoes, which Aunt Emily did up. A hat as monumental as I ever remembered, trimmed with a touch of white – Grandma's only acknowledgment of summer – was carefully pinned on by Grandma herself. Then she sat down on a straight chair for a moment to recover from the exertion.

'How long for, Auntie?' I asked.

'About half an hour. Keep off the Promenade. The wind is too much for her.'

I nodded, and she opened the door for us. Grandma carefully crept across the rugs, and I eased her down the single step. She shuffled forward along the red-tiled path.

It seemed a terribly long way to the gate, and miles to the end of the road. However, Grandma silently concentrated on walking, and we turned into King's Gap, away from the sea. After about five minutes on the gentle slope, Grandma gasped, 'I think I have to sit down, dear.'

'Oh, goodness!' I looked wildly round for a bench or a low wall. The nearest place was a wooden seat about a hundred yards away. I pointed it out.

Grandma was panting, her mouth a little open. 'It seems a long way.'

'It is closer than returning home, Granny. I could carry you.'

She smiled up at me with the bright flash that I had known as a child, as if her mind had reverted to its old clarity. 'No, no. Don't be afraid, my dear. We will do it a step at a time.'

It was the longest hundred yards I have ever walked, but we finally got there and sank thankfully on to the weathered seat. I put my arm around Grandma's shoulder and she leaned against me and closed her eyes. It was like holding a small sheaf of wheat, the same sense of easy crushability.

I looked down at the top of the satin-trimmed hat, now pushed askew because she had laid her head on my shoulder. My old enemy, despair, washed over me. Memories shot through my mind, a belief in her inherent goodness, gratitude for the skills she had passed to me. She had taught me more subtle things than reading and sewing, to put on a cheerful face so that one does not depress others, to face with fortitude what cannot be changed, daily courtesies, which always surfaced when I was with people of my own class. My aunts, too, had been very patient with a silent, obstinate little girl.

Now I knew in my heart that Grandma had come close to the end of her allotted span, and I did not know how to face the idea. I wanted to wrap her up in cotton wool, like something infinitely precious that must be preserved at all costs.

But nothing I could do would stop the remorseless march of the years – and it was obvious that the aunts were caring for her very well.

The return was accomplished by slow shuffles and pauses, a trifle more easily since the mild slope was downwards. Grandma did not say much, except for an occasional deprecating chuckle at her own inadequacies as she stopped to pant.

The front door opened as we approached up the path, and I pushed Grandma ahead of me up the step. She stopped for a second when safely landed, and then toddled into the hall. My aunt said, 'Thank you very much indeed for taking her out. She has to rest now.' She began to close the door, and added, with a bright smile, 'It must be your teatime by now.' Then she quietly shut the door.

I looked dumbly at the blank piece of wood in front of my nose, hardly able to believe that it was truly shut. A slow burning flush flooded my face and I turned angrily away and marched down the hill to the sea. The wind rushed up to meet me and helped to cool the fury within. I dropped over the railings of the Promenade on to the deserted powdery sands, and turned towards my favourite place, the Red Rocks.

Until the water began to lap close, I did not think of the tide cutting me off. I hastily took off shoes and stockings and paddled quickly the last few yards. Such was the respect for property instilled into me that it never occurred to me to climb the sloping walls which protected the private gardens running down to the beach, and walk through to the road, and so save myself from the icy water.

I sat down on the rocks at a safe elevation and wrung out the hem of my heavy skirt. Then, cross-legged, chin in hand, I watched for a long time the tide race in and the sailing boats set out from Hoylake and West Kirby. I forgot about tea at the Holiday Home and was aware only of the pain inside me.

The sun sank slowly down in the centre of the sea, leaving an emerald green and bright pink sky. Grandma had a little oil painting which she said Turner had painted of that sunset. The painting was dark from years of being too close to the smoke of the fireplace, but as a child I had loved to run my fingers round its elaborately carved gilt frame.

With twilight, it became cold, so, shivering, I put on my shoes and stockings and clambered over the rocks to the road, and with head bent with grief and no little sense of humiliation I plodded along the almost deserted road back to the Home.

# Chapter fifteen

At home, Mother had recovered from her vexation at my daring to go for a holiday. She was further mollified by the gift which I had brought her, a pretty box covered with seashells. Both she and Father were intensely interested when I told them that I had been to see Grandma.

'Did she ask about us?' inquired Mother.

I looked at them both sadly, and had to admit that she had not asked a single question about the family, not even about Father.

'She's very weak,' I defended. 'I'm not sure that she is quite aware of what is going on around her. And, of course, I got cut off rather abruptly from her, when the door was shut on me. I had imagined that we would talk more over a cup of tea – or something.'

Father's voice was acidulous. 'I'm surprised they let you in.'

In June of 1939, a strange man presented himself at our door. He was small, dressed in a belted raincoat and a trilby hat. Father had answered the door and thought he was a salesman. He was just about to say, 'Not today, thank you,' when the man said, 'You must be Mr Forrester?'

Father agreed that he was.

'I am sorry to tell you that your mother has died,' the stranger baldly announced. He then went on to say when the funeral would be held.

I had been standing on the staircase watching the scene, and the cold words bit into me. I wondered how much more they must have hurt Father. He looked very white, as he ushered the visitor into our living-room.

Our tenants in the front room had recently found a house and left us, so our home smelled a lot better – but the sitting-room was still bare of furniture. I followed them into the living-room. Mother was introduced as the visitor edged his way into the crowded room, and when they were all seated Father asked how Grandma had died. My eyes misted, as I leaned against the door jamb. I remembered the little wraith with whom I had walked. It would not have taken much to blow her out of this life.

'She died in her sleep – from a stroke,' the visitor said. He went on to explain that she had had a stroke a year earlier and then, more recently, a series of smaller ones.

Father and Mother sat quiet for a minute. Then Father realised he had not inquired who the man was, and now he did this. The man gave his name and said he was a friend of the family. He had business in Liverpool, so had been asked to convey the news of the death to us.

Father closed his eyes. Despite the gravity of Mother's expression, there was a bright gleam in her eyes, which I did not understand.

Father said he would attend the funeral and looked inquiringly at Mother. Mother nodded negatively. 'Mrs Forrester will not attend.' He looked unhappily at me. 'If my eldest daughter wishes, she will accompany me.' I lowered my eyelids and made no response. I had not thought about the funeral.

Politenesses were exchanged and the man was ushered out. 'Unfeeling bastard,' exclaimed Father, as he came back in. He sat down slowly on his battered easy chair and put a shaky hand over his eyes.

'I'm sorry, Daddy,' I said gently. 'After all, he was a stranger – he didn't *have* to come.'

After some dithering, I decided not to go to the funeral, though as a child I had been very fond of my aunts. I was afraid they would think ill of me, because I had no mourning clothes and no money to buy any. I said to Mother, 'I would have to ask for a half day off – and every office boy who wants to go to a football match says he needs time off to go to his grandmother's funeral – and I've had so much sick leave that they might feel I was imposing on them by asking for more.'

Mother sighed, and agreed. 'Remember your grandmother as she was, dear, when you were little.'

She had understood, and she had called me 'dear'. I was grateful to her.

The day of Grandma's funeral was overcast and rainy in Liverpool. Mother stitched a black band of ribbon, culled from an old felt hat, round the left arm of Father's overcoat, a sign of mourning for those who could not afford black clothes. He shaved slowly and carefully that morning and gave his shoes a tremendous polish in a kind of dumb honour to his mother. I checked that his socks did not have holes in their heels, and wept all the way to work.

When he arrived home in the evening, he was emotionally exhausted. For once, Mother fussed round him. She made him tea, and put more coal on the fire to dry the legs of his trousers, which were soaked, as were his muddy shoes and socks which were put inside the fender to steam on the hearth. He had walked all the way to and from James Street station, because he did not have enough money for a tram, after paying the train fare to Hoylake.

'Did they give you anything to eat?' I asked, as he sipped the scalding brew from his cup.

He nodded negatively.

While Mother sat with him, I went into the kitchen, made toast, and in some bacon fat fried the solitary egg sitting on the shelf. Fortunately, all the children had gone out to friends' houses to play, so the house was quiet.

Father was not accustomed to so much attention, and after he was warmed and fed and had returned to sit in his easy chair, he cheered up a little.

'They all stood on one side of the grave – and I stood on the other. I felt like a pariah. Nobody spoke to me, except the solicitor, who said I had better come back to the house with them for the reading of the will.'

Again I saw the sudden gleam in Mother's eye – and this time I understood it. Grandma had quite an estate to leave. The unlit cigarette between her lips quivered.

Father sighed heavily. 'You will remember that years ago, my brothers and I signed an agreement that the contents of Mother's home should not be broken up but would be left to my sisters, so that they were assured of a home.' He paused and took off his spectacles to rub his eyes. Then he laughed, a small deprecating laugh. 'That was before your uncles died – and in the days when we had a home worth speaking of.'

Mother nodded. She tore a piece of newspaper from the *Echo* on her lap and started absently to fashion it into a spill.

'Well, of course, that still holds,' continued Father. 'Then in her will she left all her own property – that's the dowry she brought with her when she married Father, to the aunts, so as to give them a better income to live on, I suppose – I don't think they have a great deal themselves.'

Mother leaned towards the fire to light the spill and then with the flame she lit her cigarette, puffed and blew the smoke towards the blackened ceiling.

'What about your reversionary interest?' she asked.

'What on earth is a reversionary interest?' I interjected.

Father turned to me. 'Well, dear, you know your grandfather died when I was a little boy. He left all his property to your grandmother for her lifetime. This meant that she enjoyed the interest – rents – whatever else he had – but she could not touch the capital. The capital was to be divided between his children or their heirs, after your grandmother died.'

I knew my grandfather had been far from poor, and I gasped. 'Does that mean we actually get some money?'

'Well, I had hoped so, though I think that the estate has not prospered because of poor management by his executors. Anyway, the thing is that when you were young, I borrowed from one of your aunts against my interest. Not against all of it by any means.'

He stopped and stared into the fire. Then he took out a cigarette, leaned over and lit it from Mother's.

'Well, what happened?'

'I signed a legal agreement in which I promised to pay interest on the loan – I had expected to pay the loan back quite quickly. I could not repay

– and I forgot about the interest until today. She claimed the interest for ten years – and that wiped out my share.'

'Good God!' exclaimed Mother, cigarette halfway to her mouth. 'Did she really?'

'Yes.' Father sighed again. 'She was legally entitled to it. Only it never struck me that a sister would actually charge interest.'

I made a face. Father was so unbelievably innocent at times that I wondered how he had survived at all so far.

'Well,' I said slowly, 'I suppose if she had had the money invested all these years, she would have got interest on it – and if she had not spent it, her capital would have increased substantially.'

'True,' said Father sadly. 'She was entitled to it.'

Mother clicked her tongue in exasperation, and unthinkingly stabbed her half-finished cigarette out on the bars of the fireplace. She flung the stub angrily into the unusually cheerful blaze.

And I sat quietly thinking of my usual obsession – cold. I thought of a frigid bed, where I lay with aching limbs beside a restless Avril, whose feet seemed always to be icy, and a patient Fiona who folded her arms tight across her chest and never complained. I dreamed of white sheets and a pile of fluffy blankets piled on top of us – and, yes, a hot water bottle each. And of the boys, inadequately clad, despite their school uniforms paid for by the city, often with wet feet and no gloves. Alan at least had his Air Force boots and a really thick Air Force uniform, so that he was warm during the weekends, but he must have been cold in bed, too. Our house was jerry-built and the heat of our single fire was soon dissipated.

I thought wistfully that a small capital sum, if my parents used it sensibly, would save us so much misery – though I had to admit that our present circumstances were a little better than they had been.

'Never mind, Daddy,' I tried to reassure him. 'One of these days, we will have all the basics of life again and be quite comfortable.'

He smiled at me, looking suddenly very like his mother.

Mother looked as if she were about to cry.

A few days later, a small parcel came by mail for me. It contained a watch, and it had come from Hoylake. I presumed it was Grandma's and was delighted that she had remembered me. It was a neat gold one, with a black moiré ribbon wrist band, and I put it on with tender pleasure. I never left it off my wrist, so it was never pawned.

Early in the war, when I had enough money to afford it, I took the watch to a reputable jeweller to be cleaned and adjusted. He asked my name, opened the watch and took it into a back room. A moment later, he returned very fast, his face most forbidding. 'We sold this watch to . . .' and he named my cousin. 'Please explain how you come to have it.' He waited, lips pursed, eyes accusing.

My mouth fell open with shock at the abrasive tone. I licked my lips and swallowed, not knowing what to say. I knew I still looked like a skivvy, the kind of person who would never normally have been in his shop.

'It was left to me by my grandmother,' I faltered. 'The lady you mention is my cousin who lived with her.'

'When?'

I gave the date of my grandmother's death. I was very frightened. I feared he might call the police and accuse me of theft.

'What is your cousin's address?'

I gave my grandmother's address, where I presumed she still lived, and said, trembling, 'She probably bought it as a gift for Grandma.'

The address obviously tallied with the one he had, so he said slowly, 'I see.'

He pulled out a receipt, made it out in my name and, without apology or explanation, handed it to me. 'Ready in a week,' he said.

Badly shaken, I went out of the shop and stood on the pavement and watched unseeingly the rush of lunch-hour pedestrians. Because I was obviously so poor, I had been treated as a possible thief. I was outraged.

I never forgot the arrogant jeweller, and I felt a most unchristian satisfaction when his shop was blown up later in the war.

# Chapter sixteen

I was nineteen going on twenty and I had never been kissed by a man, other than an occasional peck from Father. I had never gone to an adult party and only once been to a dance. I had never since I was eleven played any games, did not know the meaning of the word *fun*. It seemed as if there was nothing but work in the world. The only real pleasure was my regular visits to the Repertory Theatre with Sylvia and an occasional walk with her.

The dogs of war who were to eat my generation were howling through the streets of Europe. The basement waiting room of the charity for which I worked was packed with woebegone, nerve-racked Jewish and trade union refugees from every country in Europe. Upstairs, in the Interviewing Department, lay a Dictionary of the Languages of Europe and this was handed to non-English-speaking clients, so that they could at least establish for us which country they came from and which language they spoke. We could then obtain an appropriate interpreter. My French and German, though far from perfect, became suddenly useful.

In the parks, trenches were dug as air raid shelters. I remembered stories my father's friends had told, when I was little, of flooded trenches rotten with corpses and preying rats, and I felt sick.

For my twentieth birthday on 6th June, 1939, Friedrich, my ever-faithful German pen-friend, now a young officer in the Luftwaffe, sent me a small ivory edelweiss on a gold chain; in his part of Germany the edelweiss was, in the olden days, given by a boy to his prospective bride. It was a lovely gift, the first piece of jewellery that I had ever owned, except for Grandma's watch, and I sighed regretfully over it – an English woman would certainly not be approved of as a wife of a Luftwaffe officer – and I wished that he had followed his original intention of becoming a schoolmaster. With the gift came a charmingly sentimental letter. In answer to a rather depressing letter from me, he assured me that his beloved Fuehrer would never plunge Europe into war. All Herr Hitler wished was to see all German-speaking people united under one flag. One day German travel restrictions would be lifted and we would meet each other and how wonderful that would be.

It could, of course, be that Friedrich was right and all our newspapers were wrong. As an Air Force officer, he might know more than I did of what was happening. Sometimes the *Express* gave the same view as Friedrich, and it was a big newspaper – it should know.

With the edelweiss in my hand, I dreamed wistfully. He had no inkling of the many other problems which I faced. The previous Christmas I had wanted to send him a present, a real challenge for me. I solved it by buying a torn sheet from the second-hand shop, for a few pennies. The sides of the sheet were still good, and from that material I had cut six handkerchiefs, and hem-stitched them. The drawn-thread work was trying to the eyes, but the result was attractive. Then I embroidered Father's initials on three of them and Friedrich's on the other three. I had ringed Friedrich's monogram with a ring of tiny roses, all done with white cotton. Both recipients had been delighted.

What on earth would Friedrich think, I wondered, with a wry grin, if he knew where his gift had come from? What would he think if he saw my home?

Our sitting room had once more been furnished on the hire purchase system, and we had finally managed to pay off the debts for which we were still responsible on the earlier sets of furniture which had been repossessed by the furniture stores. Father had also bought, on the same plan, a radio which was a great joy to all of us.

The radio ran on batteries and we had periodical crises when new batteries were required. The wet battery had to be recharged about once a week; and I soon learned, after carrying it down to the shop to have this done, to walk down the street with bare legs. The acid from the battery tended to slop down one's legs and burn them. Legs heal eventually – stockings do not. I still carry faint marks on my legs from those acid burns.

Despite the fact that five wages were now coming into the house, none of us earned very much. My parents still had little idea of how to manage a small income, with the result that we were still very poorly fed, often cold, and lacked proper changes of clothing. Shoes still got lined with cardboard to fill the holes in the soles, and I still sat at work with my feet firmly on the floor so that the other girls would not notice the holes.

Mr Ellis, with his formidable tongue, had been replaced by a gentle elderly lady, who was invariably polite and kind to me. Without saying anything, she seemed to understand a little of what was happening to me and the consistent effort I was making to educate myself. She sometimes asked me what plays I had seen – she also received theatre money, as it was called by the staff – and what books I had read recently.

Perhaps it was because of her recommendation that one morning the Presence sent for me.

'Oh, my goodness,' I groaned to Miriam. 'What have I done now?'

The Presence smiled, actually smiled, when after knocking timidly I entered her office.

'Sit down, Miss Forrester,' she ordered briskly.

Nervously I perched on the edge of her visitor's chair. If I had to sit down to hear it, she must have something quite devastating to say.

'Miss Forrester, we are expanding our Bootle office. The District Head at present runs it with the aid of voluntary workers. She does, however, need someone on whom she can rely to assist her. We have decided to appoint an Assistant District Head, and I would like to send you out there.'

I gaped. Presumably I would be a kind of Girl Friday – but the designation of the post put me close to the rank of the long-envied green-overalled social workers. The post could lead to further promotion. Perhaps a living wage.

'The salary would be seventeen shillings and sixpence a week, Miss Danson added, and swivelled herself round to look at me for the first time.

A rise in pay of half-a-crown would just cover the additional long tram journeys out to the north end of the city. It would not stretch to anything more. But it was a break at last.

I smiled. 'I would like that very much,' I assured the Presence enthusiastically, putting to the back of my mind how much the tram journeys would add to my already incredibly long working day.

Full of excitement I broke the news to Mother. She refused to believe that the rise in pay had been so little. 'It amounts to nothing, really,' she fretted. 'They must have given you at least five shillings?'

'They didn't, Mummy, I assure you. But I will get training in actual casework – and that is worth something.'

So, for half-a-crown more than I would have received had I been unemployed, I took on considerable responsibility and continued to live largely on hope.

Bootle had more unemployment, more overcrowding, more pollution, more ignorance, more huge Roman Catholic families floundering in poverty than I had ever seen before. It was even worse than the badly hit south side of the city. No wonder the patient, delicate-looking District Head needed help. With only the society's small funds available to us, it was like being asked to shovel out a rubbish dump with a teaspoon.

I plunged in to help, but found the greatest difficulty was within myself. I had been so crushed by the staff of the Head Office that I tended never to do anything which I had not been asked to do. I had little natural initiative; only a kind of slavelike mentality. And this had, with much trial and error, to be slowly overcome. If I was to join the green overalls, all of whom had degrees, I realised sadly that I had a long way to go.

One night, as I sat huddled on the tram from Bootle, I pondered over my inabilities, not at that time very clear about what ailed me, knowing only that change I must from the frail, drained woman for whom nobody cared very much, into a more dynamic person. Otherwise, I feared, I did not have much to look forward to in the future.

Left alone with Father one Saturday afternoon, I asked him tentatively if he could think of any other kind of work to which I might aspire. Without a second's thought, he came up with a very good suggestion. 'You might be able to pass the entry exams for the Civil Service by now – they give you quite a wide choice of subjects, you know.'

Half believing, I made inquiries and found he was correct. Father became interested, and I found a schoolmaster willing to coach me in Geography, the weakest subject amongst the rag bag of subjects which I could offer. For five shillings a lesson, half of it contributed by Father, he came to the house in the evenings, and began to teach me about winds, tides and currents and how they affected the layout of the world. And I was hooked. Nobody in my childhood had taught me anything beyond the names of rivers, cities, countries, seas and where they were. Night school was finished for the season, and, fascinated, I studied earnestly from the books he lent me. He came four times. Then I received a brief note from his wife that he had been called up. Reluctantly I returned the books.

A few weeks later, the Civil Service cancelled its examinations for the duration of the war. Nobody seemed to know at that time how they would recruit any staff they would require.

Frustrated, I threw myself once more into an effort to improve my social work.

# Chapter seventeen

As war began to breathe down the back of our necks, our socially isolated family received unexpected visitors.

A fussy, elderly man who lived in the next street arrived to show us how to put on our gas masks. He was apologetic to the ladies because their hair-styles were likely to be disturbed by the straps, since it was essential that the masks fit tightly. He recommended our keeping our hair short. He also warned us that mascara was liable to melt and run down our faces while we had our masks on.

Fiona was the only member of the family who used mascara, and she continued placidly to brush it on in front of the piece of mirror wedged into the kitchen window frame. It made her already huge eyelashes even more seductive. She brushed her hair up into the newly fashionable high sweeps round her face, and at the back bouncing curls fell to her shoulders.

My bun got so tangled up with the straps of the mask that it was as well that there never was a gas attack.

The air raid warden knocked peremptorily on our door. He lived a few doors away from us and had been unemployed for years. He had a reputation for being utterly lazy, but he took his present duties very seriously, and demanded to see our blackout curtains.

We had none. We had no curtains at all upstairs, except for a short net curtain across the front bedroom window. We did have, however, the original big wooden shutters of the house in the downstairs rooms, and had always used these instead of curtains in the living-room. The warden agreed that these would make excellent blackout and a good defence against flying glass. He tutted like a maiden aunt over the bare bedroom windows, and ordered us to buy black cloth and make curtains.

'Or yer can paste double layers of brown paper over t' panes. Another thing you can do is make wooden frames covered with thick paper and fit 'em into t' windows each night, like.'

Mother said frostily that we would just have to manage without candle-light in the bedrooms. She was not going to blot out the daylight with brown paper, and she could not afford curtains or frames.

The warden stuck his blue chin in the air and replied that the windows must be covered – by law – in case the flare of a match or other casual light flashed out of them and brought German bombs down upon us.

Mother was not going to take orders from any local oaf, and retorted, 'What rubbish!'

The warden stood firm. 'I tell yez, you'll be fined if you don't cover 'em,' he warned, his dark Irish face grim as he held his temper in.

Muttering maledictions, Mother went out to buy blackout material for the front bedroom. Then, in the copper in the basement, we dyed two of our few sheets and pinned one over the back kitchen window, which lacked shutters, and one over the window of the boys' bedroom. The girls' bedroom window remained bare and, since we could not show a light, we had to fumble round in the dark when going to bed.

The warden was not satisfied. The windows should have sticky tape crisscrossed over them, to stop shattering glass from flying into the rooms. Mother said she would see to it, but she never did, and the patient warden finally acknowledged defeat. Resignedly, he recommended that we sit on the basement steps during raids, that being the safest place in the house.

A schoolteacher came to explain the need to evacuate Brian, Tony, Avril and Edward to the country, in the charge of their teachers. She was a faded, middle-aged woman in a worn tweed suit, and the children stood around the room and stared at her as she spoke.

She inquired if we had any relations to whom they could be sent. 'You might prefer that to their going with the school.' Her artificial teeth clicked as she pushed them into place with her tongue.

'No,' replied Mother. Father cleared his throat.

'There are the aunts at Hoylake,' I suggested tentatively. 'Could Avril go to them?'

'I doubt if they would take her,' Father interjected, and it was finally agreed that the children would leave with the school.

Dismayed at the thought of filthy, lousy evacuees from Liverpool or Birkenhead being billeted on them, the aunts had the same idea as I did, and the next day a letter arrived suggesting that they should take in two of the children. Father roared with laughter at the thought of how suddenly important their long-neglected nephews and nieces had become. He turned the letter over and over in his hand, and remarked, 'I can't remember when one of them wrote to me last.'

Mother looked as if she had been caught between the devil and the deep blue sea, and I tried to reassure her.

'They were always very kind to me when I was a child,' I said quickly. 'None of the children will come to harm with them.'

So, as German tanks ploughed across the Polish border, Tony and Edward, with a pitifully small amount of luggage, went off with a schoolteacher, to meet the aunts they had never seen. I will never forget their tight, white little faces. A stony-faced Avril, determined to be brave, went with them, to live nearby with a friend of the aunts; and for the first time in her memory knew what it was to have good, new clothes bought for her, sleep in a properly equipped bed and be decently fed. Brian, like a young soldier, went with the school to Wales and lived with a postman who was also exceedingly good to him. Despite much kindness, none of the children came through that traumatic time without scars.

The government provided an allowance for the evacuees' board. But later on, they demanded that parents contribute to this cost. On the day they announced this, Mother decided that she could not bear to be parted from her darlings any longer, and they were brought home. If she had to maintain her children, they might as well be at home, air raids not-withstanding. When the raids became very heavy, under pressure from the school they were re-evacuated, this time to strangers, and they were very unhappy. However, when the government again demanded money, Mother brought them home. They were thankful to return, despite the danger.

In June, 1939, Alan went gaily off, for the second year, for his annual training camp with the Auxiliary Air Force. It was to be two weeks long and was to be his holiday. We knew that, like the first one he had attended, he would be out in the countryside at a Royal Air Force base being well fed and would be enjoying himself working with tools. He would also be paid, and would return home looking well and with pocket money to spend. Before he went, he bought himself a new sports jacket and trousers, so that off duty he would look smart, and we teased him before he went, about all the feminine hearts he would break during his free evenings. He was happy.

He did not return. There was no letter to say what had happened, and Mother was in a panic. Father said that a number of young men from his office had also not returned from various military training camps where they had gone as Territorials for their summer training. It was part of the national call-up.

About a month later, the postman delivered a small sack containing Alan's unworn sports jacket and trousers. Mother wept. 'He must be dead,' she mourned, and pawned them next time she was short of money.

Father reminded her that the Forces were very good at telegraphing the news of deaths. No news was good news.

Three or four months later, he arrived home on forty-eight hours' leave. He looked even thinner than when he had left us, but it seemed as if he had grown a foot. He had finished an arduous square-bashing, through which all regular recruits had to go, and was now again thankfully working on planes. He was tired and slept most of his leave, but he was still enthusiastic and went back to his base quite cheerfully.

He had obviously had a tough training period, so we refrained from reminding him that we would have been glad of a letter to say where he was. Now we had an address, both Mother and I wrote to him regularly.

Mother forbade me to write to the evacuated children or to go to see them. I was very angry about this, but gave in sulkily when she said, 'Seeing someone from home will upset them.' Despite her argument, she went out to Hoylake to see them and she would never say how she got on with her in-laws. I could not really understand her objection to my going, but she may have been jealous for a long time of my particular position as surrogate mother, and wished to reassert herself with them.

Anyway, I obeyed. I was finding it increasingly hard to face up to Mother. My new job amid appalling squalor, in addition to the long journey out to Bootle, was draining a character already crushed and exhausted.

It seemed as if the whole population of the country was on the move, as men were called up and women shut down their homes and went back to live with mother, as the children vanished into the countryside, and drafted workers got sent to distant war factories. Lonely youths far from home spent much time cultivating girls who would invite them to their homes, to compensate a little for spartan Victorian barracks or bare, comfortless workers' dormitories. Fiona's dates multiplied exceedingly, and into our emptied house began to drift a curious assortment of men of all nations and all social classes, to eat our rations and warm their wet feet at our single fire, to have their socks darned and their buttons stitched on. Mother was in her element as a hostess, and we all hoped, as the war progressed and the other boys were called up, that somewhere in the world Alan, Brian and Tony were being taken care of, too. I think this was the best contribution that Mother ever made to society, as she tried to feed and comfort the strangers at our door.

# Chapter eighteen

To say that in the summer of 1939 we were scared would have been an understatement. Almost everybody in Liverpool was obsessed by a dread of the unknown. The tenseness of men's voices and their slightly hysterical laughter, the grim shut-in look of women whose sons and husbands were being called up, the problems of beleaguered city officials suddenly faced with putting into effect elaborate programmes, which had been concocted by equally harassed civil servants sitting at desks in far-away London, all contributed to an almost unbearable tension as we waited.

Much preliminary work had already been done during the year of time bought for us by Mr Chamberlain during the infamous meeting in Munich in 1938. Now, there was a great urgency, and everybody's life was thrown into confusion.

Father was transferred by the City to work amongst the increasing number of refugees from Europe, who were arriving in Liverpool. He was shortly to be nearly overwhelmed by the arrival, in waves, of battered contingents of the Polish Army and Air Force. Later, he was transferred to the staff dealing with the inadequate Rest Centres provided for the bombed-out. They had originally been meagrely provisioned to discourage people from settling down to live in them rather than seeking new accommodation. The frantic needs of bewildered households, often without menfolk, could not be met. The more houses that were damaged, the more people crowded the Rest Centres and the less likelihood they had of finding alternative accommodation. Father worked like a demon.

In the meantime, we waited, fearing the future and yet unable to visualise what it would bring. Mother had been working as the representative of a greetings card firm. In August, she found herself politely dismissed, in the expectation that the paper for such a business would be severely rationed. She decided that she could, now the children were away, take a full-time post, and she was thankfully snapped up by a big bakery firm, whose bookkeeper, a Naval Reservist, had vanished into the Navy. Mother could keep books because, at one point, during the First World War, just before my birth, she had taken the place of a man in a bank, and she said that she was the first lady cashier in Liverpool. The salary offered seemed enormous in comparison with what the rest of us were earning, and she was able to buy herself some new clothes and send some extra clothing to our frightened little evacuees at the aunts' house. We now had five fewer mouths to feed, and this made a great difference. I had cornflakes for breakfast as well as a piece of bread and margarine, and occasionally marmalade, which I had not tasted for many years. There was no shortage of food in the shops and we were not rationed until several months later.

This better salary which Mother was able to command made me even more ambitious to join the ranks of the green-overalled social workers. But the longer I worked in the Bootle office the more I realised that lack of education was going to hold me back. Anyone new coming on to staff had a degree. It was not that I could not do the work. I understood only too well most of the problems that bedevilled our ever-increasing flood of clients, and as the war came closer I could sympathise with the middle-class women who began to consult us.

Men in good positions were called to the army, where they earned fourteen shillings a week, seven shillings of which they had to allot to their wives, so that they were eligible to draw a dependant's allowance. These allowances were so pitifully small that they hardly paid the rent for many people. Women threatened suicide as they were increasingly bullied by hire purchase firms, mortgage companies or rent collectors because they could no longer pay. A few employers sent their employees' wives sufficient money to bring the allowance up to their husband's wages, but many, faced with profound changes in their businesses due to the war, were unable to do this. My colleague and I read up the laws on contracts till our eyes glazed and learned to find technicalities upon which we could break hire purchase agreements and so release our desperate clients. Finally, organisations such as ours were able to press the government into declaring a moratorium upon serving men's debts, and so keep the wolves from the door until the end of the war.

So experience poured in upon me – but at the back of my mind there was always the nagging thought that if I was ever to make progress in the world of social work, I would need that precious piece of paper, a degree. And I had not had the opportunity to matriculate.

On 1st September, all the lights of the city were turned off. It created a darkness which townsfolk had not faced before, and we blundered about like people suddenly blinded, and were touchingly grateful for a lighted match or the spark from the trolley of the electric trams to give us a bearing. At first we endured the blackout with shivery, laughing fortitude, but after a while it became a frustrating curse, a maddening tedium. It was dangerous, too, as traffic tried to move about in such dense darkness and pedestrians stumbled over unexpected steps and hazards, like the fire hydrants, wandering dogs and cats, and parked bicycles. I once walked into a letterbox and went home with a streaming, bloody nose. We learned how beautiful the stars were and, until the bombing began, rejoiced in moonlit nights.

All schools were closed, because in principle all children were evacuated with their teachers. This meant that for the first time for years, I not only had no children to care for, I had no studying to do. All places of entertainment were also closed, with the exception of public houses which were small and had only a limited number of people gathered in them. I was accustomed to cramming my life with study, with house cleaning, with care of many of the children's needs and with tutoring in shorthand. My current shorthand student, a cripple, had been evacuated to Southport and I had not yet found a replacement, so although I worked long hours I sometimes found myself, late in the evening, sitting with Mother over a cup of tea, not knowing what to talk about. If I introduced a subject, I could never be sure that she would not take offence and begin one of her irrational rages, so I tended to sit in dismal silence, and leave her to talk if she wanted to. Her favourite subject was Father's backslidings or some incident in the office when she had bested an adversary. I felt sorry for the office.

Mother was herself undoubtedly at a loss. She was not in the least interested in me and, I think, endured my presence as best she could. Her usual retreat, the cinema, with its long programmes and two new films a week, was closed to her. She had no friends – I do not recollect her ever having a bosom friend, though in our palmier days she had many close acquaintances and admirers. Father sometimes asked if she would like to go with him to his favourite pub, Ye Hole in Ye Wall in Hackins Hey, and have a drink. She would always respond tartly that, 'Ladies do not go into public houses.'

Looking back, I find it odd that neither of us at that point volunteered our help as wardens, telephonists, first aid personnel or anything else. Half the town was enrolled in some service or other, while we sat stiffly over our tea. For my part, I think it was both mental and physical exhaustion. Having to walk most of the distance to and from work and spend the day coping with other people's woes, many of them quandaries unheard of before, was a heavy strain. I rarely reached home before eight o'clock, a home where I still never had enough to eat. There was a limit to the number of the world's woes which I could take upon my skimpy shoulders.

In Mother's case it seemed as if there was a whole section of her which did not function at all. She never managed to bring any real order into her life, never mind into ours. The bright and intelligent mind, of which I sometimes caught a glimpse when she cared to talk about books, seemed to have been buried amid the wild, superficial gaiety of the post-war years and the disasters which had subsequently befallen us. Perhaps she was hopelessly drained, too.

So there she sat, drinking tea and popping aspirins into her mouth, while Poland was decimated and we waited for our turn.

Father bought two second-hand suitcases. The few spare clothes we had were packed into these, together with family papers, like birth certificates, marriage lines and army discharge papers. One case was kept by my parents' bed and one by mine, so that if the house caught fire from incendiary bombs, we could run outside with them. When the air raid siren went, we shot out of bed, grabbed our clothes and the cases and fled to the doubtful safety of the cellar steps. There were several false alarms at first, when the sirens howled, the anti-aircraft guns in the park rumbled, searchlights swung across the sky and part-time wardens ran along the streets, pushing everyone indoors. Still the bombers did not come.

We began to feel safer.

Mother bought some cheap dress material, striped in green and tan, and I stitched pretty covers, complete with shoulder straps, for our gas mask boxes. I also made each of us a matching turban and scarf. Mother, Fiona and I sailed out in these feeling very smart and up-to-date. After a while, like everyone else, we discovered what a convenient receptacle the gas mask box was. We left the gas masks at home and used the box to carry make-up, lunches and the inevitable cotton pocket handkerchief. When rationing commenced, Mother found that the ration books fitted very conveniently into hers.

With no student to tutor, I had very little money of my own. I not only walked to town, which was the first stage of my journey to work, I walked halfway to Bootle as well, trudging a couple of miles along Scotland Road, a dreadfully poor area, and Stanley Road, to reduce the amount of the tram fare. I cut out lunch, except when there was enough bread in the house for me to take a slice of bread and margarine.

Rumours went about that one could earn huge sums in the new factories out at Speke, which were going into war production. I thought about this and then decided that after the war I could be out of work and walking the streets with hundreds of other unskilled workers. To become a qualified social worker as quickly as possible still seemed a good idea, if I could achieve it.

No one could complain to us that our work was not essential. Daily we filled an ever-widening gap between official mandates and the protesting, unhappy victims of them.

I missed very much my fellow typist, Miriam Enns. She lived too far away from me for us to meet socially, and anyway I had no money to pay for coffees in city tea shops, which would have been one way of seeing her. Gradually, I lost touch with her.

Sylvia Poole was working for a firm supplying medical aids, like bandages and cotton wool, and her company became very busy. We did, however, manage to go for prim little Sunday walks together, and, because of the slackened pressure in our house, Mother agreed that she should occasionally come to tea. Tea was a simple meal of bread and margarine and jam, followed by a cake bought from a shop which sold leftovers from a big bakery. Much to my delight, Sylvia and Mother got along famously, and Mother began to look forward to her coming, and would suggest that I ask her.

It was ironical that the commencement of a world war which threw the lives of millions into turmoil should at first give me a little more leisure. During the long walks home, I began to think of myself as a person in my own right and tiny independent wistful longings floated in the back of my mind. I had always had it drummed into me that I was a possession of my parents, to be moved around, fed or not fed, bullied or ignored, as they saw fit. I had fought against it instinctively for years, but I had always lost, excepting in regard to going to night school and obtaining my current job. Now, in little flashes, I began to wonder if one could not, after all, exist without somebody else's permission. But I was an exhausted bag of bones, worn out with years of intolerable strain, and the slave mentality which I had acquired was not going to be easily shed.

On Sunday, 3rd September, 1939, Father kept the radio on from early morning. He did not go for his usual walk. Mother and I went about our normal Sunday tasks of cleaning, cooking, washing and ironing, feeling particularly subdued. Even Fiona, who took little notice of anything which did not directly concern herself, got up earlier than usual, and wandered restlessly about the house, while we waited to see if Hitler would continue the war in Poland, despite the Allies' ultimatum. A tremendous, ominous silence lay over our old black city as people stayed close to home. No children played in the street and no traffic passed along it. The old men who played ollies in the gutter did not come out for their customary game.

I read again a comforting letter which I had received from Friedrich the previous day. Our dear Fuehrer was apparently still uniting the German race and I was not to be afraid, just to keep on writing to his home address. Earlier in the week, I had received a hysterical letter from Ursel. Her husband, a minister, had been arrested for a sermon he had given defending the Jews, and she was terrified. How the letter got past the German censor is beyond me, unless they had become a little less efficient as a result of Germany's having to supervise so many newly acquired countries.

At eleven o'clock, we gathered in the living-room to listen to the BBC. The tired voice of our Prime Minister, Mr Chamberlain, announced that we were at war. As we all stood up while the National Anthem boomed over the radio, we looked at each other. Mother and Father, veterans of that war to end all wars, Fiona, beautiful in spite of her hair curlers, a face as blank as the page of a new exercise book, and me with Friedrich's letter still in my pinafore pocket, all of us assured by our newspapers that we would be buried under the ruins of Liverpool within hours of the declaration of war. Would

Friedrich be one of the bomber pilots, I wondered, fingering the gentle letter? Or was he at this moment too busy killing innocent Poles?

It seemed incredible, impossible. The weight on my chest was unbearable. I said in a grating voice, 'I think I'll make a cup of tea.'

# Chapter nineteen

A few evenings later, mildly surprised, like everyone else, that I was still alive, I languidly hung up my coat in the hall, the same old brown coat so often pawned, now near the end of its days.

The door into the living-room opened suddenly and I blinked in the light from the room's bare electric bulb. Fiona, with a piece of toast in one hand, stood in the doorway, and said with something like awe in her voice, 'Helen, you've got to go down to see the police.'

'What?'

She was obviously intrigued at this unexpected call for her eldest sister, and with a cheek swelled with toast, she repeated, 'You have! To see the police.'

Thoroughly alarmed, I forgot my hunger and hastened into the room. Father and Mother were seated at the table. They had just finished their evening meal, and thick white plates rimmed with bacon fat were scattered round the soiled cloth.

'Mother! What's wrong? I haven't done anything.'

Father answered me. 'Only Fiona had arrived home when they came. They left a message to say that you should go down to a place in Lime Street – and take with you any correspondence you have received from Germany.'

'Oh, my God!' I muttered. 'What would they want that for?'

Mother put her knife and fork neatly together on her plate. 'We don't know, Helen. We hope it isn't serious.'

'Am I supposed to go tonight?'

'It is nearly eight o'clock,' Father replied. 'They can wait. I'll take you down tomorrow evening. Try to get home early.'

Throughout the night I tossed sleeplessly, racked by nervous fears. Had I broken the law in writing to Germany? Would they shut me up in an internment camp? Should I burn all the carefully kept letters and say I had none to show them? Friedrich had been courting me by mail. What would they say about that?

In the morning, as I washed myself in cold water in the kitchen, using a bit of Father's shaving soap since there was no other soap, and Father built the living-room fire, I shouted to him to ask his advice. I made a clean, blushing admission of Friedrich's sentimental advances. As soon as I had my underclothes on, he came into the kitchen to wash his hands and get his razor. While I made Mother's early morning tea, he slowly lathered his face and thought about what I had said.

'We'll take the letters with us,' he finally decided. 'They will look so innocent – I am sure the police will understand. If you destroy them, they may become unduly suspicious – people do usually have some of the letters they receive, lying in drawers or desks.'

'O.K.,' I agreed reluctantly.

Because father was a little behind in his shaving, I took Mother's tea up to her, and she broached the same subject as she huddled in the meagre bedding.

'Your father and I were talking about your going to see the police. He says you must look nice. What are you doing about your clothes?'

Only twice before had Mother discussed clothes with me, at the time of my Confirmation and when she had helped me to buy the dress for the office dance. Now she sounded quite anxious.

I saw the point. A nicely dressed middle-class girl would be treated with greater respect.

'I hadn't thought about them. My coat is a mess, and I haven't needed a hat since the warmer weather started. No gloves. Social workers don't have to look smart, thank goodness. The turban and scarf I made for the spring don't look bad, though – I could wear those.'

Mother sipped her tea. 'Your father is very worried. Could you buy a coat in your lunch hour? I have a pound that you can borrow.'

I was flabbergasted. I never looked for help from Mother – and now she was suddenly offering it. She *must* be worried. She earned very much more than I did, but I had not expected such a sudden change of mood.

'I could try, Mummy. C and A Modes might have something in their sale.'

'I don't think there is anything in the pawnbroker's which will fit.' Mother sipped the scalding hot, greyish brew thoughtfully.

Suddenly, I wanted a new coat passionately. I forgot about the police. I remembered only that I had never had a *new* overcoat since I was a child. 'I'll try, Mummy,' I said eagerly. 'I can pay you back bit by bit as soon as I get a new shorthand pupil – you'll remember that Miss Bennett was evacuated to Southport last week – but I have advertised for someone else.' I whistled under my breath. 'I'll have to go into town from Bootle, in my lunch hour. If I'm late back, the office will just have to put up with it for once.' I felt reckless in my longing for a coat.

At lunchtime I had about ten minutes to find a garment at half-price in which to impress a suspicious police force, an impossible task.

Breathlessly, I looked through the racks of new stock – heavy winter coats just put on display – until a white-haired lady asked if she could help me. 'I've a pound to buy a coat,' I confessed frankly to her, and she was unexpectedly sympathetic. She suggested a lined mackintosh, and my face must have fallen, because she said, 'Come over to the back here. There are one or two items which were missed when we were putting away the summer stock after the sale yesterday.'

And there it was, a soft woollen coat, beige, with a narrow braid trim in orange and green round the collar. The top front button was missing, a loose thread marking where it should be.

'Try it on.'

I did. It fitted neatly on the shoulders and round a twenty-inch waist. I twirled slightly, and the flared skirt swished round legs that I was astonished to see were slender and shapely. The turban, a hemmed length of tan cloth touched with green flecks, which I had made from a design in a magazine which Fiona had brought home, blended very well with the coat. The assistant tightened the belt slightly and stepped back.

I glowed, and inquired carefully, 'How much is it?'

'Nineteen shillings and elevenpence – marked down from thirty shillings.' She rubbed her chin thoughtfully, as she surveyed me. 'I think I can find you a similar button. The collar would nearly hide it, if it doesn't quite match.' She went to a table, opened a drawer and ran her fingers through an assortment of buttons and belts. She turned triumphantly with a beige button between her bright pink fingernails.

I apologised to my superior at the office for being five minutes late, and plunged into work. Later, when a moment of calm arrived and I had made a cup of tea for both of us, I told her that I had to go with my father that evening on some special family business and asked if I could leave promptly.

She sighed and the weary lines under her eyes deepened. 'Of course,' she said. She was only about seven or eight years older than myself, and I wondered suddenly if our clients were worth the sacrifices she made for them. Since leaving university, she had given all her young days to them, given them her life, working far into the evenings and at weekends to try to find help for them. And I wanted to do the same thing. Or did I?

Father had to pay my tram fares into the city, because I had spent my last travel money for that week on the additional trip going to and from the dress shop. In a brown paper bag lay practically all Friedrich's letters and most of Ursel's passionate epistles, including the last terrified cry. The pride in the new coat had gone and had been replaced by feelings akin to panic.

Father was grave and, at first, silent. On the tram, he murmured to me to answer any questions put to me, and then he qualified the remark by adding, 'And don't say anything more than that. I will introduce us.'

We were passed from a uniformed constable, to a sergeant and then to a plain-clothes policeman, as we worked our way into the bowels of a building in Lime Street. This was not the police station – it bore all the marks of makeshift offices hastily set up. Father had assumed like an overcoat the quiet air of authority and the cultivated language of the public school man that he was, and this outweighed his cheap clothes, and had its effect. The higher one was in the social hierarchy the more carefully the police handled one.

Finally, we were seated at a small table sheltered by a cloth screen, which looked as if it might have started life in a hospital fifty years before. The room was a large one, containing a number of tables similarly set up, and men and women sat round them whispering and shuffling papers, like relations going through desks after a funeral. I stared up at a high ceiling, finely moulded as if for a ballroom, but covered with dust and drooping spiders' webs. Pale green walls were discoloured from ancient water leakages and the passage of many people.

Two new plain-clothes men joined us. One sat opposite me at the table, the other one perched on a stool slightly at a distance half behind me. Nervous as a new climber faced with a precipice, I clenched my hands on my lap and braced myself for whatever might come.

It was an ordeal. The fear of internment, perhaps imprisonment, haunted me, though at no point was either mentioned by my interrogators. At times I thought I would surely faint before it was over.

Once our relationship and our names were established, Father sat quietly. I produced the letters and laid them in two neat piles before the man at the table. He was middle-aged, with deep lines criss-crossing a craggy face. Small, hard blue eyes glittered between reddish-gold eyelashes. Thin, tightly curled hair had been plastered down each side of his head with a heavy application of strongly scented pomade, an odour combined with the heavy smell of stale cigarette smoke. He and the man behind me smoked incessantly, and the pile of cigarette butts rose in a dirty white saucer on the table. I was offered a cigarette, but whispered that I did not smoke. A battered packet of Player's was offered to Father, and he took one and smoked it slowly, while he listened.

A young man in a shabby blue suit had pulled another chair forward and sat down. He had brought with him a small pile of writing paper, some folders and a couple of well-sharpened yellow pencils. He had arranged a shorthand notebook on his knee and was taking notes of everything that was said. This threw me into further alarm. I shifted myself fractionally, so that I could see what the young man wrote. My own shorthand was first class and I had often transcribed from the other typists' work. I had no difficulty in reading what he wrote, even at an odd angle. If he doesn't get it down correctly, I will correct him, I promised myself, like a terrier prepared to defend its territory from a Great Dane, all bombast and no clout.

Age? Place of birth? All the addresses I had ever lived at – Father had to aid my memory about this one. Jobs? Schools? My short time at school was explained by Father as being because of Mother's bad health – but these were not school officials, they were detectives. Religious affiliation? Friends?

Friends? Had I really only two? Miriam and Sylvia? Boy friends? Only Friedrich? Was I sure? No casual men friends that I met only occasionally?

'No,' I snapped indignantly. 'I'm too busy.' Why could not they see that that was a stupid question to a girl who looked like me?

'Why did you study German?'

I looked at him dumbly. Why did one study anything? Because one wanted to know.

'I wanted to make up my lack of ordinary education,' I told my grim interrogator cautiously.

'Most people learn French.'

'I am learning French as well.'

'Humph.'

We sat silent for a moment, looking at each other. The blue eyes were cold and hard, mine a little moist because I felt physically weak and helpless. Why were they bothering me like this? I wanted to ask. But Father had warned me only to answer questions, not to ask them.

I half closed my eyes, so that the detective should not see the tears threatening. Under my lids I took a quick look at the shorthand writer's notebook. On his current page, the record was correct, right down to the exact wording of Father's interjection about my schooling.

The detective was reading Friedrich's letters. Apparently he read German easily and was flicking from one page to another quickly.

'How did you come into contact with Friedrich Reinhardt?'

I half smiled. I was immediately whisked into a train lumbering northwards towards Crewe. I was travelling alone, as usual, on my annual visit to Grandma's. On the window seat next to me sat a boy about two years older than me. He was dressed in a grown-up suit of unusual cut, rather shabby. He was slim, hair dark and slightly wavy, with a heart-shaped face and a flawless white skin.

The train was a local one which stopped at almost every station, and at each stop the boy would peer anxiously out of the window. Two adults in the compartment, a middle-aged husband and wife, had, after staring at both of us, opened newspapers and retired behind them.

Very shyly, the boy had turned to me and asked, 'Pardon me. Where are you travelling?' His accent was foreign.

Equally shyly, I had peeped up from under the brim of my panama school hat, and whispered, 'Liverpool,' as if it were important that the other travellers did not hear me.

'I must the train at Crewe leave. A man comes for me there.'

'I change at Crewe. I will tell you when we arrive.'

'Much thanks.' He relaxed his vigil of station watching, and I sat the doll I had been nursing down on the seat beside me and arranged its skirts modestly. He smiled at it, rather patronisingly, and I smiled at him. Boys never understood what a friend a doll could be.

It was the beginning of a long friendship, all of two hours. I left with a note of his address and the promise to write. It was a simple address, the name of a village near Munich. Neither of us did write, of course, and the slip of paper was lost before I returned from Grandma's. But the address was not lost. It stayed in my mind with the picture of a beautiful youth and a lovely train journey through the green Midlands of England. When I began to learn German and the class was encouraged by the teacher to find a German pen-friend, I had remembered it like a nursery rhyme and all the other odds and ends which children keep in a mental rag bag.

'How did you get the name and address of Reinhardt in order to write to him?'

I jumped at the sharp repetition of the question. The granite face before me was formidable. I told him.

'You have a remarkable memory.' The tone was heavily sarcastic.

'Children remember all kinds of things,' I responded woodenly.

'What was he doing in England?'

'He was going to stay with English friends of his father's – friends from long ago before the war – to improve his English. It was already quite good. He could talk about almost anything – but not correctly.'

'Where was he going?'

'To Manchester.'

'And where had he come from?'

I was getting fed up and snapped back, 'I didn't ask him.' Father cleared his throat reprovingly.

I thought I was being grilled thoroughly but when, after what seemed hours, we finally got down to Ursel's letters, questions about Friedrich seemed nothing.

I had been put into touch with Ursel when I had replied to a letter in the Sunday *Observer*, which Father had once bought. The letter offered to put children in touch with pen-friends in Germany. I had asked for a girl friend. The detective told me that my letter of so many years earlier had been found by the police in the file of the man who wrote the letter to the *Observer*, a known Fascist.

I stared at the detective unbelievingly. 'Who on earth would bother to retain such a letter? And why are you interested in such a silly thing as two girls writing to each other?'

The detective did not answer. He was reading one of Ursel's letters. Perhaps he did not like his work being considered silly.

Then he launched his attack. Question after question. Small things that Ursel had asked about, matters I had long since forgotten. How had I replied? What did this paragraph or that one refer to? Questions until I was dizzy and bewildered. Finally, Father intervened to remind the detective reproachfully that I was only a young girl.

'Twenty is not a young girl,' retorted the detective tartly. 'Please be quiet. I have my work to do.'

Father was obviously getting very upset. But he did keep quiet.

Nine o'clock. Ten o'clock by the timepiece on the wall. I began to think we would never be allowed to go home. And I still did not understand what all the fuss was about. I was floundering in bewilderment.

At about eleven, it came suddenly to an end. The man who had been sitting quietly nearly behind me said, 'I think that will do, Tom.' He swung his heavy body round to look at me. 'We will have a summary typed up. You can sign it and then you can go. If you change your address you must let us know immediately.'

The curly-headed detective stood up and stretched himself. Unexpectedly, he asked quite pleasantly, 'Would you like a cup of tea?' He picked up Friedrich's and Ursel's letters, shuffled them into a neat pile and put them into a folder handed him by the stenographer.

I nodded silently. Father said, 'Thank you.'

The three men went away, and I turned to Father. 'What . . . ?' I began in a quavery voice.

Father said very softly, 'Don't say anything.' He made the smallest possible gesture towards the screen half surrounding us, and mouthed, 'Listening.'

I swallowed, and said in a normal voice, 'I hope they bring the tea.' If they were listening, they might as well be reminded of their promise. Then I sat with hands crossed on my lap, like a tabby kitten tired of play, and watched people coming and going through the door.

After a little while, a bald-headed elderly constable in uniform brought two cups of tea, with Marie biscuits tucked into the saucers. 'There you are, miss, sir,' he said politely, as he put the cups down on the table.

We ate the biscuits and drank the tea in perfect silence, while we listened to the rise and fall of innumerable muffled conversations in the huge room. Men in uniform, men in civilian clothes, occasionally women of various ages and classes, were ushered through. How late did the police work? I wondered.

At five to twelve, the curly-headed detective returned, bearing several sheets of closely typed paper. 'Sorry you had to wait so long,' he said quite cheerfully, and plunked himself down on his chair once more. He started to read the closely typed sheets very carefully, running his forefinger along each line. I noticed that he had lost his little finger and I sat watching the slight movement of the stub as the non-existent finger tried to adjust to the movement of the others.

The stenographer and the second detective joined us at the table, their faces looking nearly as rumpled as their navy blue suits.

The summary of the conversation was handed to me, with the request to read it and sign it.

Father uncrossed his legs and leaned towards me. For the first time he looked tense.

'Read it very carefully, Helen. If for any reason you feel it deviates from what was said, I am sure the officer will have it altered.'

The officer sighed and looked at his watch. He blew through his lips, making a soft pooh-poohing sound, and then agreed, 'Yes, it can be altered.'

I was no lawyer but I was used to reading contracts, new laws and government directives and interpreting them to our clients. The stenographer had composed a very fair summary of what had transpired. A lawyer, no doubt, would have queried every sentence, but I did not have such an adviser. In fact, it never occurred to Father or me that we could have demanded the presence of a lawyer, though I cannot imagine how we would have managed to pay him anyway.

I borrowed Father's fountain pen, and signed.

# Chapter twenty

The signature had a galvanising effect. The stenographer, hovering in the background, was dismissed. The detective who had been the observer at the interview seized a weather-beaten trilby from an old-fashioned hat stand nearby, clapped it on his head, said 'Good night,' to us, and 'See you in the morning, Tom,' to my diligent questioner, and fled after the stenographer.

The big room seemed suddenly nearly deserted. Tom leaned back in his chair and stretched himself. He rubbed his eyes and grinned like a schoolboy at Father and me. The rocklike hardness of his expression vanished completely and we were faced with an average Liverpudlian, who might have been a small businessman of some kind.

'How are you going to get home?' he asked Father.

Father did not have a watch, so I looked at Grandma's watch and said to Father, 'It's half past twelve. We shall have to walk.'

Father rose and nodded to the detective.

'Like to wait a few minutes? I'll drop you in my car.'

Father was looking completely worn out and both of us had to be up by six the next morning, so I smiled impulsively at the detective, and said, 'That would be lovely.'

The detective gazed slyly at me through red eyelashes. 'Forgiven?' he asked.

My smile died. 'You have to do your work,' I replied. 'But I wish you'd tell us what it is all about.'

He stood up, moved around the table and then perched himself on the edge of it, facing Father. 'Well, I can tell you this. Your daughter is not what we are looking for. We are quite satisfied about that.' He stopped, and again blew his soft pooh-poohing sound. 'We're checking everyone known to have any association with Germany. We could have a Fifth Column here, ready to betray us – you must realise that. Your daughter's letter about a pen-friend was found in the files of a known Nazi, when we picked him up. He had a neat little espionage system going, you know. Linked up children in one district in England with a single class in a German school.'

I gasped, and he grinned at me.

409

'The English letters addressed to one school in Germany were read by German Intelligence before delivery.' He paused, and shrugged. 'You can appreciate how it would work. Kids write about where they live and what their father does for a living – whether he has been called up or sent to work in a new factory. Undoubtedly, questions were suggested to the German children for them to ask their pen-friends; I've checked enough piles of correspondence like Helen's to realise this. If they had enough letters they would get a very good picture of what was going on in a given town in England – and Liverpool, being a big port, would be of particular interest.'

'Good Lord!' exclaimed Father. 'You mean that Helen had actually become part of this?'

'Yes.' He turned and grinned down at me. 'But her pen-friend had left school early to be married. I gathered from her letters that she was married at sixteen?'

'She was,' I agreed sadly. 'She was terribly unhappy. Her husband was a minister in her church – and he was nearly forty.'

'So, you see, she could not be prompted in her questions – without telling her how she was being used. And from her last letter I gather that her husband was in deep trouble with the Nazis.'

I sighed, and nodded agreement.

'But why put me through all this . . . ?' I gestured helplessly.

'Had to be certain, my dear. And you work in a place where many of the staff are highly politically minded.'

Dumbfounded, I stared at him. I thought of Miriam and her high ideals – and then I remembered that only the month before Russia had signed a non-aggression pact with Germany. I whistled under my breath, an unladylike habit learned as a child from a shepherd.

'From Communists, Conchies, Catholics and Cranks, good Lord deliver us,' the detective was saying to Father. He glanced again at me, sitting frightened in my chair. 'What's a pretty little thing like you doing, working in a place like that? You should be out enjoying yourself – dancing.'

I was deeply offended and said loyally through gritted teeth, 'The ladies I work with do a wonderful job. I sometimes think they prevent this city from bursting into riots from sheer misery. At least people can talk to us about their troubles.'

His red eyebrows shot up and he made a face. 'Well . . .' He swung off the table, and abruptly changed the subject. 'I'll get the car. You know your way to the front door?'

We agreed that we did, and we stole down quiet corridors where lights still burned behind closed doors, to wait in front of the building.

At first, after the light inside the building, we faced a wall of complete darkness, but gradually our eyes became accustomed to it. Familiar Lime Street began to emerge. The outline of St George's Hall loomed against the sky in front of us. Intermittent flashes from the shaded lights of cars lit up for a moment the squat block of the War Memorial or the finely cast fish whose tails held up the lamp-standards. Other than the occasional sound of a car engine the busy city was absolutely quiet, and I jumped violently when above my head a sleepy pigeon cooed once.

'I'm glad we don't have to walk home in such darkness,' I remarked to Father. I was deeply angry at the detective's derisory remarks, but the safety of his car would be welcome.

'I should buy a torch,' replied Father, 'and you should get one, too.'

I shrugged. When would I be able to afford a torch? I wondered suddenly if Father knew that Mother received practically all my salary, and that to all intents and purposes I worked for nothing.

'Could you lend me fourpence for my fares tomorrow?' I inquired hopefully. 'Now I'm out at Bootle, it is too far for me to walk. I'll pay you back as soon as I get a student.'

'I can,' Father replied. 'I won't have to pay our fares back tonight, thanks to friend Tom.'

A small car swooshed around the corner and drew up at the kerb. We felt our way carefully down the steps. The door was opened from within and the front seat tipped forward, so that I could clamber into the back seat. Father sat by Tom, and as we swept through the empty streets, they talked fitfully about the invasion of Poland by the Germans and the sinking of the *Athenia* by German submarines.

When we stopped in our deserted street, I leaned forward and asked, 'May I have my letters back some time, if I come for them?'

Tom laughed. 'Not till the end of the war, luv – round Christmas, probably. They have to stay in our files until it's over.'

'That's not quite fair, is it? You said I wasn't what you were looking for.'

'Can't be helped, luv.' He turned round to look at me over his shoulder. 'You should forget about your German boy friend. Find yourself a nice English lad.'

I drew in my breath crossly. I resented Friedrich being termed a boy friend. It seemed to belittle him. But one does not argue with the police. Father had got out of the car and was holding the front seat forward for me. I slid out as gracefully as I could, and paused for a second to shake my skirts straight again.

The detective leaned across the front seat towards us. I saw the flash of his teeth as he grinned. 'Remember what I said, young lady. Cranks, Conchies, Communists and Catholics – get out of it. Enjoy yourself while you're young.'

I seethed with anger. Father bent and shut the door, after saying good night and thanking the man for the lift.

'The abominable bigot!' I exclaimed furiously to Father, as he felt around in his pocket for the house key. 'I had no idea police could be so narrow-minded. I could cheerfully have shot him.'

Father sighed. 'They are like the rest of us.'

Father had been so good about coming with me to the interview that I did not want to argue with him, so I swallowed my flaring temper and did not answer him.

The letters never were returned to me. They probably still lie in some dusty crate of wartime files of the CID, a gentle record of innocent young people touching each other's lives across a mighty gulf.

# Chapter twenty-one

'Mummy, I haven't got enough clothes,' wailed Fiona, oblivious of small matters like a full-scale war. 'I can't wear this dress *again*, going out with Reg.'

So Mother retrieved some bundles from pawn. Since they contained all kinds of garments, I benefited by the addition of a summer dress and a blouse to my small wardrobe. Both Mother and Fiona were considerably plumper than I was and these garments were too tight for them. This did not stop them 'borrowing' them – and anything else of mine left clean and folded on the shelf in our bedroom. The resultant burst under-arm seams were left for me to repair, which I did with savagely bad temper. I had also to wash and iron the garments.

When I turned on her in anger, Fiona would say mildly, 'But your things are always ready. I don't have time to see to my clothes.' And it was with difficulty that I refrained from hitting her.

Mother always helped herself, with the remark that I was welcome to borrow anything of hers. But she, like Fiona, rarely washed or pressed her clothes until she had nothing fresh left to wear. Anyway, both Fiona's and her clothes hung on my wasted frame.

The absence of the children and Alan considerably eased the financial strain. Mother's excellent salary meant that there was a little more food in the house, though frequently it was not the most nutritious kind. I still lacked lunch quite often, but a proper, though modest, breakfast helped me through the day, and there was a little more on my plate at night. There was far less work to do at home, no studying and no student to teach, so the awful strain on me began to slacken, despite long hours of work and travel. Yet I was totally miserable.

One weekend, Mother brought home some cheap wallpaper with a garish pattern of bright red cherries and green leaves printed all over it, and we covered the dingy grey walls of the living room with it. Emboldened by the improvement, Mother bought some cotton curtaining in similar colours, but emblazoned with roses, and we stitched curtains and, also, padded seat covers for the upended paint cans which formed some of our seating. The effect was very cheerful.

We still lacked sufficient bedding and sheets, and as the autumn crept on the increasing cold began to make my legs ache abominably. The bedding from the boys' beds had been pawned the day they were evacuated.

A general boredom set in as the fear of being bombed to death receded. I spent some weekend evenings with Mrs Poole and Sylvia. Mrs Poole, a professional dressmaker, showed me the proper way to cut out and fit a dress. But I could not afford to buy any material.

It seemed that nobody was interested in learning shorthand in such uncertain times. A small advertisement in the *Liverpool Echo*, paid for with the last fee of my evacuated student, brought no result.

Despite my anger at the derogatory remarks of the detective, he had sparked in me the idea of looking elsewhere for a better-paying job, and I began to scan the Situations Vacant columns of the *Echo*. I wanted a position in which I could use my burgeoning experience in social work. I did not particularly want to be a secretary, for which type of position I was quite well qualified, unless it could be to a private person. There were still a few people in those days who had live-in secretaries, and in a big private house I felt that to a degree I could return to the kind of life which I had known in childhood. I wrote in reply to several such advertisements and received one response from Chester. An interview was arranged in the Adelphi Hotel. I did not get the job. My poor clothes, despite the new overcoat, and my generally neglected and unhealthy looks, together with a gauche, painfully shy manner, made it certain that I would never obtain a post in a private house. A more cultivated and presentable young woman would be essential.

With time to think, my inadequacies became even more painfully apparent to me. Yet I seemed shut into a situation of such acute penury that it was impossible to alter myself very much, and I cried myself to sleep a number of nights.

I had never discussed the situation at home with Sylvia. I shrank from trying to explain to anyone the hardships we had been enduring and the weird, bewildered lostness of my parents. Much of the time they seemed to float in a mist through which they were incapable of finding their way, though, as I pondered, I realised that Father had been trying recently to reach out to his children. Looking back, it is clear that Sylvia and I rarely discussed our personal feelings or our emotional life. We fed each other with talks about political events, books, theatres, history – a lively intellectual stimulation, almost bereft of the giggles and gossip of ordinary youngsters. Perhaps Sylvia had other friends who fulfilled this youthful need, but I did not.

There was no one to whom I could confide my shy desire to look chic, to learn to behave appropriately, become a normal middle-class girl again, groomed and cared for. Even the working-class girls who lived round me knew how to take care of their hair and their skin.

Wistfully I thought that if I had a little money to spend on pins and setting lotions, Fiona would show me how to do my hair. Mother spent a lot of time showing Fiona how to use hair tints and face creams and make-up. She bought her a fair amount of clothing and all this, added to a natural beauty, made her stunning to look at. All she had to do was smile in a lift or in the café where she had her lunch and it did not take long for well-heeled young men working in the city to find a polite way of approaching her and making a date. She was introduced by them into a circle of young people where she was accepted and was invited to parties, balls and dances. She soon learned from the more refined girls that she met how to deport herself, and this, added to her normal gentleness, made her quite popular amongst them. She sometimes amused me in bed by telling me of small incidents that indicated that she had succeeded where I had failed; she was on an upwardly mobile path. I wondered if I would ever learn to put a teacup down on a table without upsetting it, enter a room without tripping over the rug, the small social etiquette of when to take off gloves and hat, when to shake hands and when to greet a girl with a kiss; such small things, yet so important in a world still ruled by etiquette.

At twenty I was still wearing the glasses bought for me ten years before. The frames were hopelessly small and had not been improved by several poor repairs. A few years later much of my clumsiness disappeared when I was able to buy a new pair and see properly again.

But I had no money for hairpins, never mind expensive things like spectacles, and now no money for make-up or lunches or even stockings. Few people in those days had the courage to ask an employer for an increase in pay, and I lacked the courage of a mouse. My fear of unemployment had been enhanced by the lack of response to my tentative efforts to obtain another post. And I still owed Mother the pound she had lent me for the coat, about which she had reminded me caustically only a week before.

The visiting of clients in their homes, which I had been doing since my transfer to the Bootle office, had taught me that, though many of them were in dire straits, a great number of them lived far more comfortably than we did. They were simply better managers. Strangely, the war had not made much difference to the number of unemployed, but increasingly they seemed to be finding ways of earning small sums to augment their parish relief. They talked quite frankly to me about these little jobs, trusting me not to make a record of the information. If I had reported them, any money they earned would have immediately been deducted from their meagre allowance from the Relieving Officer. The women cleaned the homes of the more prosperous, the men did gardening, worked as handymen and sometimes as casual labour on building sites. No matter what time I called, there usually seemed to be a fire in the grate. What they most suffered from was overcrowding in dilapidated, verminous houses, lack of bathrooms, hot water and indoor lavatories, things that they could not themselves do a great deal about. Their rents were controlled at such a low level that it was in many cases impossible for landlords to find the money for repairs, renovations or fumigation.

At home, we never learned to manage so successfully.

One Saturday, after a visit to a client, I had to spend twopence in a public telephone box to check something for the woman concerned, with my superior in the office. Afterwards I was in great distress when I realised that, though I would have the twopence returned to me eventually, I now had no money to pay my fare back to the centre of the city. I would have to walk there, and then the rest of the way from the city centre up the hill to our house. I was already sorely troubled that I had no fares left for the following week also.

I thought I would never reach home as I trudged along Stanley Road. I was dreadfully tired and still badly undernourished. At St Luke's Church, I sat down on the steps because I felt I could go no further. People passing glanced at me curiously, so I shut my eyes until the world had stopped swimming around me.

It was a mild day, sunny enough for the rays to fight their way through the cloud of pollutants that veiled Liverpool on the few days when it was not windy. I should be able to manage four or five miles, I told myself, now that the situation at home had eased.

Jumbled, chaotic thoughts wandered through a dulled mind, as I sat trying to get my breath. The detective had suggested that I should enjoy myself, go dancing. He must have been crazy. Things like that cost money. Even to volunteer, say, as a part-time air raid warden, which would have given me new friends, would need a few more pennies for fares, for the odd cup of coffee, possibly for uniform. Eyes still closed I put my head down on my handbag on my knee, and laughed.

'Are ye all right, luv?'

An elderly newspaper seller had shuffled across the road and was bending over me solicitously. I looked up, startled. Small kind eyes stared at me through cheap metal-framed glasses balanced on a bulbous red nose.

'Yes, thank you. Yes. I had to rest a moment, that's all.'

'Thought you was goin' to faint.'

I smiled up at him. 'No. I'm fine now, thank you very much.'

He grinned and toddled back to his little table of newspapers.

With gritted teeth I made myself climb the hill.

At the Rialto, leaning one trench-coated shoulder against a stucco pillar, lounged the pimp who had once offered me a cigarette. I wondered if his girls felt much worse than I did. He said good night as he always did, tipping his rakish trilby hat as he did so. He must have found me rather a joke, because I looked so prim, yet despite his despicable occupation, I always smiled and replied politely, 'Good night.'

This night I was almost shaky enough to ask him for a cigarette, to quell my hunger and soothe the great tide of unhappiness which was threatening to engulf me. It beat in my head, choked my throat. Years and years of suppressed misery welled up; thoughts of all my lost girlhood, all the possibly happy, irresponsible years lost in grinding poverty and an incredible weight of work, marched past me and jeered at me, as if to say, 'You think you were *entitled* to live and laugh and be happy? Don't kid yourself. You've got years and years of semi-slavery before you – and nothing much else.'

The house was incredibly quiet as I entered. I shivered. Without the children, I felt bereft of a reason for living.

Father and Mother sat on either side of the fireplace reading the paper. For once, they were not quarrelling. The puppy recently brought home by Brian slumbered unheeding on the coconut matting, his back braced against the warm fender, the current stray cat curled comfortably on top of him. It was a great friendship. Fiona must long since have gone out with a date.

Both parents looked up and said, 'Hello.'

I responded with a small, tight 'hello' back, and went straight to the kitchen to fill the kettle at the sink. When I twisted a knob on the gas stove, gas hissed out of one of the rings and I thankfully lit a match and put it to the ring. I could make tea quickly.

There was a slice of commercially cooked ham on a plate in the kitchen, and I called, 'Is the ham for me?' My voice sounded as if I were being strangled.

'Yes,' Mother called back, and I heard the rustle of the newspaper as she turned the page, and it grated on my raw nerves. I took two pieces of bread from a packaged sliced loaf, dabbed some margarine on them and put the ham between them. When the kettle boiled, I asked Mother and Father if they would like tea; if so, I would make a full pot. They both decided to have some.

With agitated hands, cups were somehow rinsed under the cold water from the tap and assembled on the table with the ham sandwich. I sat down in front of them and looked at them. My throat felt tight to choking point. Within there was a rising feeling of panic. In a minute, I thought frantically, I am going to scream – and scream – about nothing.

That was it. Scream about nothing. Scream about the void which was me. About a non-existent person, with no meaning to anyone else but me – or perhaps Sylvia. My God, how I wished she was there.

Moving like a zombie, I poured and distributed the tea. I bit at the sandwich and rolled the cotton-wool bread with its stringy piece of ham round my mouth. I chewed, but could not swallow it, trying all the time to control the irrational hysteria rising in me.

I took a big breath, then sipped some tea to help the sandwich down. I choked.

417

Hand to mouth, I fled to the kitchen sink and succeeded in spitting out the offending piece of sandwich. I began to cry.

It was as if a well-locked lid had suddenly burst from a gas tank, because of uncontrollable pressure from within. I could hear myself groaning and screaming, as I clung to the edge of the sandstone sink, frightful primitive cries of a creature beyond help, writhing as if in pain.

Pain it was. All the pain, all the suppressed grief of nine dreadful years, coming to the surface, now that some of the intense load had been lifted, the revolt of a human creature nearly pressed out of existence. Screams of awful mental anguish.

# Chapter twenty-two

In a flurry of dropped newspapers, Mother and Father were beside me in a second.

'Good God, Helen! Whatever's the matter?' Father's face was shocked.

But I could not answer. I was far away, outside the tortured being standing at the sink, totally unable to take command again of my normal territory. I shrieked like an air raid siren out of control.

Mother took my arm and shook me. 'Stop it, Helen! Do you hurt somewhere?'

Hurt? I hurt all over. The shrieks became wild laughter.

Father seized me by the shoulders, turned me towards him and administered a great slap across my face.

It was partially effective. Mind and body snapped together again. With a hand to my stinging face, I continued to cry helplessly, bellowing like Avril in a tantrum. But I no longer laughed or shrieked. And this was no tantrum. It was like the cries of someone just bereaved. Mother put her arm round me and led me into the living-room. 'Sit down,' she ordered, and parked me on a straight chair by the table. I laid my head on the table and continued to cry helplessly. 'Tell us what is the matter.' Her voice was unexpectedly concerned, and somehow the unusual tone caused greater paroxysms of tears.

Father, standing anxiously beside me, produced his dismally grey pocket handkerchief, and proffered it. I took it and wept into it.

Mother pulled up another straight chair and sat down. 'Are you ill?'

I nodded negatively. I could not put into words what ailed me. How can you say to the person most responsible that you are broken-hearted?

'Perhaps you'd feel better if you lay down for a little while,' suggested Father. In the Victorian and Edwardian world from which he came, women were entitled to have the vapours, a tearful manifestation of low spirits. They were usually persuaded to lie down and have smelling salts and brandy administered to them, until they could rise and face their terribly narrow world again. The connection struck me immediately and caused fresh storms of sobs.

'Nervous breakdown?' Mother whispered to Father, and I wanted to scream again.

'I hope to God not,' replied Father, as if I was not there. And that was the root of the trouble. To both of them most of the time I was not there – I did not exist. I rubbed my face on the dirty cloth and howled.

Mother patted the back of my head. 'I think bed is best. Come along upstairs, and when you are rested you can tell us what the trouble is.'

I was too far gone to care what happened, so I was led upstairs, kicked off my shoes and lay down on my bed. Mother brought a blanket to cover me, as I continued to cry. It was as if I would never be able to stop.

Father sat on the edge of the bed, while Mother went to fill Edward's hot water bottle.

'What's the matter, old lady?' Father asked, while Mother was downstairs

'It's all too much,' I nearly shrieked. 'I'm so tired. So tired and so lonely. I work hard – I never stop – and I never get anywhere.' I wept on, while Father sat, quiet, on the bed.

'I feel so weak – and I'm always hungry. And I've no money to buy anything at all – and I wonder if I ever will have. And nobody seems to notice or care. Nobody cares a tinker's cuss.'

I turned on my face and roared into my knobbly pillow.

Father caught one flailing hand in his own tiny hands, which went white at the slightest cold because his heart was so bad.

'Don't say, that, dear,' he responded, as if hurt to the quick. 'You're my Helen Rose. I care.' He started to unclench my fist and to rub my hand as if it were cold. 'Things are much better than they were, dear.'

'They are for everybody else,' I wailed. 'Not for me.' He continued to rub my hand. 'I wish I was dead,' I raved.

Mother came in with the hot water bottle. I took it from her and put it instinctively to my stomach, where the pain usually was, and curled up round it in a foetal position. I began to hold Father's hand as if it were a lifeline.

The room was nearly dark, so Mother lit a candle and put it on the mantelpiece. Then she, too, sat on the edge of the bed. There was silence, except for the sound of my weeping. The concern of both parents was undoubted, but in a corner of my mind which was beginning to function it appeared to me that it was the fear of the scandal of mental illness, rather than concern for me as a person, which bothered them. Probably this was unfair, but such was the distrust built into me since infancy.

I do not know for how long I cried. The storm began gradually to retreat, until I was sobbing occasionally, eyes sealed tight. The warmth of the blanket and the hot water bottle began to relax me, and I lay exhausted.

I lay quite still, too drained and fatigued to speak. Father still patiently held my hand, waiting for me to recover. Mother began to fidget round the room. 'Feeling better?' she inquired.

I looked dully at her silhouette against the candle. 'Yes, thank you,' I muttered, and then added hesitantly, 'I'm sorry.'

'That's all right, dear. You rest now. I'm going to attend to the blackout, and then I'll make some fresh tea and bring it up.' She turned briskly to Father, and said, 'You had better stay with her.'

'Of course,' Father assured her, and gave my hand a little squeeze. He must have been getting cramp from my holding on to his hand for so long, but I felt that if I let go, and lost the human contact, I would slip back again into hysteria.

I heard the big shutters in the living room being slammed and the iron bar being threaded across them, and then the ting of the rings on the blackout curtains which we had so painstakingly hand-stitched; there were small thuds as Mother put some books along their hems to hold them flat against the window, so that light did not seep through. I began to cry again. The thought of the war made me feel even more helpless.

Father carefully put my hand down. 'I'll blow the candle out – the warden may spot it.' He went over and blew out the small flame, and the odour of the smoking wick permeated the room. I watched him, still sobbing. He turned and looked out of the window through which the faint last afterglow of the sunset filtered. Over the chimneys of the houses huddled close to the back of our home, the thin pencil line of a searchlight swept slowly across the sky.

Between huge, shuddering sobs, I said, 'I'm sorry to make such a fuss, Daddy.'

He turned and came slowly back to me. Seated on the bed, he faced me and asked, 'What happened?'

I tried to compose myself, and in unhappy gasps, I answered, 'It's nothing really, Daddy. I'm stupid. I spent my return fare from the office on a telephone call for a client. So I had to walk home from Bootle – and it seemed the last straw. I'm so tired – I feel I want to die with it.'

'You've had a lot of illness, I know. But I thought you were quite well.'

'I suppose I am.' Still weeping, I pulled myself up to a sitting position.

He sat looking anxiously at me, while I tried, not very successfully, to control myself.

'It wasn't exactly being without the twopence to come back to the city – it was the whole thing. Everybody in the family – all their needs – seem to be considered – but never me. I haven't a penny. I can't find another student to teach. No lunch, no make-up, no clothes. I'm desperate for new stockings.' My voice rose with a hint of hysteria again. 'If it wasn't for the Greek gentleman who gave us theatre money again this winter, I would never have been able to do anything. Even to visit Sylvia costs tram fares.'

'Have you told your mother?'

'Oh, Daddy! Ever since I went to work, she has done her best to make it impossible for me to stay there. She wants me home as a cheap housekeeper. She wouldn't give me a penny.' I put my head in my hands and cried some more.

'She paid for a coat for you recently.'

'She *lent* me the money – and she wants it back,' I nearly screamed in fury. 'And I only got that in the hope of not having the police on our backs – that would have been a real scandal, wouldn't it? Nice families don't get called in by the police, do they?' I put my head on my knees and lamented like a wind on the moors.

Father put his arms around me, the first time I ever remember him doing so, and did his best to comfort me.

A very subdued Mother brought me tea, which I drank. Then as my sobs subsided, she suggested that I try to sleep. Still shuddering, I thanked them both and obediently lay down like an exhausted rabbit in a thorn bush.

# Chapter twenty-three

Through my troubled sleep, I was aware of a first-class uproar in the living room below. The battle between Mother and Father was joined again while I lay in bed on Sunday morning – the first Sunday I ever remember staying in bed, except when I had been ill.

Shattered and demoralised, I lay by Fiona, crying softly and listening to the enraged voices going back and forth. I wondered if I was indeed losing my reason.

A little more food had come my way. We had a fire more often, and usually there were enough pennies to provide a minimum of gas and electricity. These were solid gains, for which I should be grateful. I did not realise that it is not the actually starving who revolt – they are too weak – rather, it is the underfed, the underprivileged, who feel that the system could provide more for them. My system – my family – had taken my money, my work, my affection – and had given very little. I felt betrayed and forgotten by those who should have had my interest at heart, and I wept on.

Fiona stirred, stretched and shivered in the bedroom's clammy stuffiness. She heard my snuffling into the pillow, whipped around and lifted the blanket cautiously off my shoulders.

'What's the matter, Helen? Have you got a tummy ache?'

Slowly, I turned my face towards her. She looked quaint with her hair neatly rolled up on hairpins secured under a net – Europe might be in flames, but Fiona set her hair every night without fail. The deep, violet-blue eyes looked down at me with alarm.

'I don't really know exactly what is the matter, Fi. My tummy's all right. I just can't stop crying.'

She rolled close to me and put an arm round me. 'It must be something.'

I curled up close to her and cried into her shoulder, while she made soothing noises and stroked my long straggling locks.

Between sobs, I began to tell her about not having a student to teach and my resultant penury. She was a good listener and by no means as stupid as she sometimes led our parents to imagine. 'This last few days I've realised, Fi, that without an education – with no degree – I'll never be able to be a real social worker. I might do the same work, but I would not be as well paid. And night school doesn't provide degrees.'

Fiona smiled. 'You're clever – and you can write shorthand and type. You could get a really good secretarial job.'

'Not the way I look,' I lamented. 'My clothes are all right nowadays for social work – one shouldn't look too smart. But a secretary must look really nice.'

'You should ask Mummy. She'd buy you some clothes – she's got plenty of money – she buys all mine.'

I felt the hysteria returning. I burst into further muffled wails. 'Mother expects me to manage.' I did not want to remind her that both she and Mother preyed on me for the bits of clothing I managed to obtain for myself.

Fiona pushed my hair back from my face and said earnestly, 'I didn't think you were interested in clothes and things like that. You're always too busy.'

'Nobody thinks,' I shot at her bitterly. 'I just don't really exist where most people are concerned.'

She stared at me uncomprehendingly, as the tears came down on her nightgown in rivulets.

She hugged me tightly. 'Please, please, don't cry, Helen. If clothes are the trouble, it's easy enough for Mother to get them.'

'It's not only that,' I wept. 'I want to have fun and go dancing, like the detective said.'

This made Fiona lean back and look at me in astonishment. 'Really?'

'Well, of course I do,' I nearly bawled.

'I thought you liked studying – and books – and helping people.'

I gave up, and cried on, and a bewildered Fiona held me tightly, until her nightgown was thoroughly wet.

Downstairs Father's footsteps echoed in the hall and a moment later the front door slammed. The key hanging from the letterbox by its piece of string made a protesting rattle against the wooden panels. Father, I guessed, was going for his usual Sunday morning walk and drink at Peter's, a famous public house near Catherine Street.

Mother's slippers flip-flapped up the stairs and I clung closer to Fiona. Over me crawled my infantile fear of Mother, primitive, childlike, ridiculous, but nevertheless overwhelming.

'How are you feeling?' she inquired to the back of my head buried in Fiona's shoulder. 'Crying again? Come on, that won't do. There's no need to weep so much.' The voice was kind, a little weary.

Fiona, bigger and stronger than me, pushed me away from her and eased me round to face Mother.

I made an effort to check the waterfall, and sniffed and said, 'I'm sorry, Mummy.'

Fiona burst in. 'Mummy, she's feeling miserable. But all she really needs is to look nice to get another job – and have some boy friends – and things.' She spoke cheerily and patted me. 'Isn't it, Helen? That's all.'

In part she was right, so I nodded. How could I explain my frantic need to feel that someone cared, that another adult loved me enough to really care what happened to me?

Mother had not yet washed, and she looked as badly as ever I did, with her dyed black hair in a ruffled mop and the lines on her pasty-white face looking as if they had been etched in. But she laughed, an unusually natural laugh, and sat down with a bounce on the bed. She spoke with determined cheerfulness.

'Your Father and I have been discussing the matter,' she announced.

I tried to stop crying and to listen. I did not know that I had frightened them both very much by my sudden collapse, which they feared was the beginning of a complete breakdown, with all its future slurs on the mental stability of the family. In those days one was, to most of the population, either sane or insane – and insanity marked the whole family, not just the victim.

'We think that you and Fiona must be treated alike.' I felt Fiona stiffen beside me – and suddenly I wanted to laugh, in spite of her sympathy. Did she fear being reduced to my circumstances? Mother continued, 'Daddy and I can manage if you pay into the house the same amount as Fiona does – and we'll get you some clothes out of pawn.'

I gazed at her dully. I wanted her to take me in her arms. I didn't care about the physical help. I was mentally begging her to love me, to tell me that she would do what she could to help me, sympathise, comfort.

She was waiting for my reaction, and shrugged her cardigan up closer round her neck. She became uncomfortable under my gaze and said suddenly and defensively, 'You were always so keen on managing alone.'

I was astonished, and I stopped crying. How could she rationalise the situation like that? But there was no strength in me. After all, hadn't I wanted to be treated like Fiona? And, as far as physical needs were concerned, that was what she was offering.

I had no stamina left. One cannot argue a person into loving one, so I ignored her last remark and said, 'Thank you. It would help a lot if I paid like Fiona – and I would be grateful for some clothes.' I leaned against Fiona and tried by closing my eyes tight to stop a further flood.

There was silence for a moment, while Fiona hugged me close, and then Mother said, 'Your hair is a mess. Lady Fayre is having a sale of perms. They're down to three and sixpence. I'll stand you one, if you like.'

Fiona burst in enthusiastically. 'You should, Helen. You should. Betty is a wizard on hair.'

I crushed down the pain within, and said, 'That's very kind of you, Mummy. I would love to have my hair done professionally.'

Mother really was trying to be supportive; I realised it, and I added, 'Thanks, Mum,' while I clung to the comforting warmth of Fiona, and I lay quietly while the two of them swiftly planned my physical rebuilding.

# Chapter twenty-four

I sat bolt upright in the hairdresser's shabby white wooden chair, while Betty, a plump and gloriously brassy blonde, first removed the too small, black-rimmed glasses and then pulled out the hairpins which held my bun in place. She ran her fingers through the tumbling locks and spread them on my shoulders.

'Goodness, you've got lovely hair, miss. So thick. I'll put a brightener in the rinse.'

I had given Betty *carte blanche* as to how she did my hair, so I smiled and said, 'Thank you.'

She took her scissors out of her pink overall pocket and snipped and shaped. Rolls of nut-brown hair joined the piles from earlier customers, drifting about the floor. She leaned me over a grey sink, which smelled of old soap and hair, and scrubbed my head with light experienced fingers, and then towelled it half-dry. Strand after strand was rolled on metal curlers, which hung round my head like so many small clock pendulums. Cotton wool was then poked between them to protect the skull. I gasped as the curlers were doused with a chemical that smelled like ammonia, and I snatched the towel from the sink edge, to protect my smarting eyes.

Betty laughed, and threaded the curlers into plugs dangling from electric wires attached to a kind of chandelier hanging from the ceiling. She turned on a wall switch and after a second or two a strong smell of burning hair was added to that of the ammonia-like lotion. I peeped over the towel. Wisps of smoke were rising from the curlers. 'Good heavens!' I exclaimed in alarm, and instinctively tried to jerk my head away, but I was firmly suspended from the ceiling.

'Be careful,' warned Betty, 'or you'll bring the whole thing down on your head.'

Quite undisturbed by the smoke, Betty had seized a broom and was shoving the mass of cut hair into a corner, while she sang under her breath. I froze in my seat and was relieved to find that the curlers ceased to smoke.

I began to relax, and Betty went to gossip with her apprentice, who was setting another customer's hair. The apprentice looked most fashionable to my untutored eyes. She wore her hair parted down the left side, smoothed back from her face and caught in a hairslide. A loose wave nearly covered her right eye. At the shoulder the hair was turned under in what was called a page-boy. Her eyebrows had been plucked to a pencil-thin line, the expressionless face powdered to a smooth whiteness and the lips painted with a purplish lipstick to a full pout. I sighed.

My mind was dull and lethargic, sodden with weeping, which from time to time tended to burst forth without warning. I felt I never wanted to face another whining client, no matter how pitiable her state, never open another book to study, never do an iota more of housekeeping or child-caring, never ever have to face another fight.

But life does not stand still. It has to be faced, somehow dealt with. I was shamefacedly silent before the family.

On the Monday evening after my collapse, Mother had announced that she was going to the pawnbroker, and had enrolled a protesting Fiona to act as parcel carrier. 'Somebody I know might see me,' she wailed ineffectually. Now a pile of crumpled garments awaited washing and ironing or sponging and pressing, to get the smell of the pawnbroker's loft out of them. I was grateful but still leadenly depressed.

That same evening, Father had gently suggested that we might go for a walk together, and I had thankfully accepted. Numbly, I had walked beside him down the hill towards the town. We strolled along Bold Street, looking in the shop windows. It was still light enough to see their contents. Because of the blackout, no illumination had been turned on, and, since rationing had not yet begun, the windows were still filled with goods. It did not seem to have occurred to shopowners that, if we were bombed, the glass would be blown out and their careful displays ruined or looted. Wholesale looting by fellow townsmen was as yet an unbelievable idea.

Father began to play his favourite game of If I Had a Million I Would . . . With this million, he would build and furnish a huge house. I slowly began to join in. We chose furniture and curtains and rugs out of Waring and Gillows'. We filled the larder with peaches in brandy and caviare from Cooper's in Church Street, and the butler's pantry with silver knives and forks and serving dishes from Russell's. Russell's clock struck as we walked, its little figures coming out and performing as the strokes went on, and I felt a poignant need for Baby Edward, who loved this clock, and was now trying to be a model small boy for his aunts.

We went up Lord Street and filled our imaginary wardrobes with clothes from Frisby Dykes and the many gentlemen's shops; passed the statue of Queen Victoria standing firmly above Liverpool's most popular public lavatory, and down James Street. Here we were amongst the offices of the great shipping and food companies which had their business in Liverpool. Each door had a pile of sandbags round the entrance.

The city was very quiet, as we continued on. Its peace and the pleasant conversation, my father walking by me as he had done when I was a child, had its effect. I began to feel more cheerful.

'Let's go right down to the Pier Head,' I suggested, quite unaware that this small decision was to make a big change in my life.

The sharp wind, clean and bracing, blew up from the river, sending little eddies of abandoned wrapping papers scurrying across the sets of Mann Island.

Father held his trilby firmly on his head and I took my hat off, as the playful breeze struck us while we walked along Georges Landing Stage and watched the busy river glinting in the sunshine. A transatlantic liner was moored by the Princes Landing Stage, and, by common consent, we went to peep at it through the open gates. A good-humoured guard warned us that we must not go through the gateway, unless we had business with the ship. I looked with awe at the great Cunarder, a queen of the Atlantic.

'Nice old girl, isn't she?' remarked the guard, nodding his grey head towards the ship. He laughed ruefully. 'Not that I'd recommend a trip on her at present. It's much too lively out there for comfort.'

My hairpins were falling out in the wind, and I held on to my loosened bun while I smiled at the guard and nodded, though the thought of the German submarines lurking in Liverpool Bay was no laughing matter. Some men standing near looked as if they might be crew from the ship; they were laughing and talking as if they did not have a care in the world.

Suddenly, as Father chatted with the guard, my hair rolled down my back and was lifted up by a particularly strong gust of wind. I snatched at it and knocked off my glasses. The same gust blew up my skirts, and to the amusement of the men talking, I tried to grab at the falling glasses, the flying hair and the revealing skirts.

One man, standing with feet giving to the rise and fall of the floating dock as if used to it, laughed at me and came forward and rescued my glasses, fortunately unbroken. He was a burly young man, heavy-shouldered, and with a big fair moustache, unusual for those days. As he handed me the spectacles, he looked so jolly that, unhesitatingly, I laughed back when the errant wind flicked the ash off his cigarette on to his suit. Struggling with my flying locks, I thanked him, and with Father turned towards the protection of a shed on Georges Stage. I screwed up my bun again, and we took the tram home.

It was a happy walk and I suddenly felt much better. I forgot the young man. But he did not forget me.

Betty undid a roller and tush-tushed over it, rolled it up and slipped it back into its electric outlet. 'Won't be long now,' she remarked, as she leaned against the sink and lit a cigarette. Through the cigarette smoke, she looked me over in a casual, friendly way. 'Yer sister says you never go anywhere. But, yer know, yer could do quite well for yourself – if yer wanted.' She turned to her assistant who was standing turning the pages of a magazine, while she waited for her customer's hair to dry under a noisy machine. 'Couldn't she, Dawn?'

Dawn flicked her cigarette ash into the sink and strolled over to look me over, as if I was a pony up for sale. She nodded, and smiled at me. 'You got lovely legs.'

'Wait till I've finished her hair. You won't know her,' promised Betty. 'If you like, luv, I'll make your face up, too. Just so you can see what a difference it can make.'

'O.K.'

Underneath still surged a fearful depression hard to control, despite Mother and Father being so helpful, an emptiness of spirit, a lack of hope.

I was unable to talk truthfully and naturally to my parents, was certain in my mind that as soon as I seemed better, their interest would wane again. I missed the children and the letters from Friedrich and Ursel, all of whom had at least diverted my mind from our grim surroundings. I had not seen Sylvia for some days and determined that some of my new pocket money would be spent in order to see more of her. But even with her, there was a holding back, a reserve, a sense that I would never make her understand what the years had done to me. That trust was to come later on, but its time had not yet arrived.

I was thrust under a spray and Betty's scarlet-tipped fingers scrubbed away the ghastly-smelling solution. In apprehension I watched her brush out the tiny tight curls until I looked like a South Sea Islander. 'Goodness, Betty. What are you doing?'

Betty laughed, and sloshed highly scented setting lotion over my head. Cold trickles ran down my neck. 'Haven't you ever had a perm before, luv?'

'No,' I admitted shyly. 'I've not been to a hairdresser before.'

'Well, I never. You wait. Proper pretty it will be.'

And proper pretty it was. Soft curls finally haloed my thin face, a deep wave disguising the high forehead.

Betty stepped back and looked at me, head on one side. 'Now, when it grows, I'll set it for you with a bush of curls at the back – you could put a big slide in to hold them. T' perm'll last a few months, if you vary the style a bit.' She leaned over me, and picked up a pair of tweezers from the shelf in front of us. 'Now hold still.' She put a heavy hand on my forehead, and gave a quick series of painful tweaks with her tweezers. 'See, I took a few hairs out between your brows – makes a difference, doesn't it?' It did.

She took her own make-up from out of her handbag and swiftly rubbed vanishing cream into my face, touched the cheeks very lightly with rouge, carefully crayoned the lips with a slightly mauve lipstick, added a little length to the heavy black eyebrows with a dark pencil, and stood back.

'Come and see, Dawn. What she needs is very soft make-up, looking so young, like.'

Dawn, her customer combed out and sent on her way, strolled languidly over. 'Very nice,' she opined. 'Boy friends won't know you.'

I blushed under the rouge. 'I don't go in for boy friends.' Then at their startled looks, I added, 'Never had time.'

'For crying out loud!' Betty exclaimed. 'You've missed your vocation – you could do real well for yourself. You look as nice as the next girl – and you walk a lot nicer. Why, Nick was only saying the other day, you got style – only needs bringing out.'

Astonished, I asked, 'Who's Nick?'

'Oh, you know him. Everybody does. He knows you. He was in this morning, fiddling with everything as usual. Saw your name in the Appointments Book. He knows every girl in the place – it's his business.' She giggled.

'But I don't know him,' I insisted, preparing to get up from the chair.

'Oh, yeah, yer must do. He's often around the Rialto – wears a light-coloured mac most of the time – proper smart.'

Enlightenment dawned. 'Oh, yes. He says good night sometimes.' I paused, and looked at her distrustfully. 'But he's a pimp.'

The girls grinned knowingly at each other. 'Sure. He's set up a lot of girls in his time. Buys 'em clothes. Finds them flats. He's fair. Trades under a lamp-post, he does. Yer should get to know him better – you'd do fine with him. He moves his best girls into real good districts.'

I was shocked. 'Oh, Betty. I'm not that kind.'

Betty's face lost its smile, and hardened. 'We're all that kind, luv, when times are like they are. Better'n slaving in service or standing on your feet in a factory all day – or being so clemmed like you are.'

I looked at her steadily. There were lines under the heavy make-up. I got slowly up from the chair. Did she find it better than being a hairdresser who had to cut prices to the bone? 'Thank you, Betty,' I said very gently, and I took out from my otherwise empty handbag the three and sixpence which Mother had given me, and handed it to her, while Dawn drifted back to her magazines.

Betty smiled very sweetly at me, as she put the money into the drawer of a chipped white counter. She replied a little sadly, 'There, luv. Don't be offended. You take care of yourself – and keep that innocent face of yours. Some nice lad'll know a good thing when he sees it – and take proper care of you.'

'You're too flattering, Betty,' I teased her. 'I'm not cross.' She meant to be kind and I did not want to leave her with the feeling that I condemned her way of life. I knew from my work that, too often, it carried with it its own tragic punishments.

# Chapter twenty-five

I went back to work on the Tuesday after my collapse, and did my best to cope with the mob besieging our waiting room. It was a week later, however, when I walked into the office with hair permed, face made up, dressed in a good blue tweed suit and a plain white blouse, and caused a modest sensation.

'My goodness,' exclaimed my patient colleague, her pale face turned upwards from a mass of untidy files lying on her desk. 'I can see you won't be with us long, if you go on looking like that,' she added archly. 'You look very pretty.'

The inference that I might be whisked off to the altar at any moment made me smile weakly, as I teetered on my second-hand high-heeled shoes towards the door, and hung one of Mother's old hats on the back of it. The hat was navy blue and Fiona had donated a bunch of artificial sweet peas to retrim it. Both Mother and Fiona had been unexpectedly kind in helping to renovate a crushed young woman. But the inner woman remained squashed.

It would be nice to be able to say that we lived in amity ever after. Far from it. Mother continued to nag at Father and rage at me, between short bouts of better humour. Father still drank more than he could afford, still lost his temper over small details. Mother and Fiona, rushing to get ready for work, still purloined any clean clothes I had. But the total of garments between us was greater.

The amount of expense money and pocket money seemed wonderful. It bought a meagre lunch, stockings, and make-up from Woolworth's. I bought some much needed panties and a petticoat, all as yet unrationed. I was close to having the comforts of the working-class girls who sat facing me on the long benches of the trams, as I went to work. I was servilely grateful to my parents.

I was so afraid of offending people, particularly Father and Mother, that I was finding it increasingly difficult to show any originality, to use my own judgment. For years, I had continued a deadly routine of night school, of being an exact and obedient employee, an inoffensive helper at home – except when human nature had its say and I burst into a temper.

Now at aged twenty I wanted to strike out, find a new life for myself.

To learn to act, not just react. I had been brainwashed too long into the idea that I lived by courtesy of other people. Touched as yet lightly by the first ripples of tremendous social change which was to affect all women, I determined to change myself not only in appearance but in character, to assert myself, to be a whole woman in my own right.

'I am me,' I cried inside. 'And I want to be me.'

Mother agreed to Sylvia's coming to tea. I wanted to learn from this most faithful friend's outlook on life. She was so balanced, so sensible.

Sylvia came. Her hair was, as usual, carefully blonded, swept upwards from the back to form a crown of curls on top of her head. The fairness complemented speedwell-blue eyes and a dimpled, merry face. She talked with Mother and made her laugh. They got on splendidly.

Sylvia had always taken a course or two at night school, and because all schools were closed she was wondering, like me, what to do with her spare time. Now, as she sat like a neutral zone between Mother and me, I made a great effort to advance an idea made possible by the advent of some pocket money.

'You know, Sylvia, how clumsy I am – I'm always dropping things or falling over something. And I was wondering if I learned to dance – that would help me. After all, you learn to be precise in your movements when you dance.' I paused doubtfully. I did not dare to say in front of Mother that the detective had left with me this idea of dancing, having fun. I feared her scornful laughter, in spite of her recent efforts on my behalf. 'I wondered if we could go together?'

Sylvia drew in a deep breath. She was a nonconformist by religious persuasion, and with a sinking heart I remembered suddenly that nonconformists do not dance. Perhaps I've shocked her, I thought miserably.

Fiona interjected, 'I never had to *learn* to dance – I just picked it up.'

I ignored Fiona. I hoped that dancing was all her devoted retinue had tried to teach her, but in my jealous heart I always knew that, though Fiona seemed so pliable, her escorts would not be allowed to step out of line. She had a firm fastidiousness bordering on the prudish – she enjoyed the turmoil she created, but she would laugh and slip away from any man who presumed too far.

I concentrated on Sylvia. She was happily ladling jam on to a thin wafer of bread and butter. A quarter of a pound of butter had been bought specially for her, and the bread had been cut as it used to be cut in our long-ago world of cooks and housemaids.

'Everything is shut,' she said ruefully.

'There are two or three dance studios tucked into old houses round here,' I reminded her. 'One of them says on its noticeboard that it charges only a shilling for a group lesson.' What was Sylvia thinking? Was she feeling wicked at the idea of dancing?

'I used to go to ballet school when I was little,' I went on, 'until a wardrobe fell on top of me and injured my foot – and it was great fun. After that I dragged the foot a bit, but I should be all right for ballroom dancing.' I could not mention that such a corrupt person as Nick said that I walked well – and had style.

She made a little moue with her mouth. 'That must have hurt. Of course I'll come if you would like to go.' She giggled as if she thought it might be fun.

'You can dance already,' Mother protested. 'Why waste money? We sent you to learn ballroom dancing, when you made such a fuss about not going to ballet school any more.' She looked at me accusingly, as if I should now emerge, twelve years later, a perfect dancer – like a moth crawling out of a chrysalis and taking flight.

I did not say anything. I sensed the beginning of a fight which I had not the strength to undertake.

'Oh, she'll have forgotten,' Sylvia assured Mother briskly, as if she understood my need to be rescued before I fled back down my mental burrow. She turned to me, and added firmly, 'See what day they take beginners, and give me a phone call at the office. I'll come.'

# Chapter twenty-six

The black taffeta dress with tiny gold spots on it was redeemed from pawn and carefully pressed. I had made it several years before from a length of material bought from the pawnbroker. It had been cut out with a razor blade and hand-stitched. The taffeta smelled old, but the dress had not split anywhere. New black lace frilling was sewn into its neckline. Also redeemed were the white satin slippers I had worn at my Confirmation. I dyed them black. They had satin bows on each toe, and I was entranced by them, they looked so delightfully frivolous. Cinderella was about to go to the ball.

Cinderella, however, was not actively expecting to meet a prince. At the back of her mind lay the memory of the pleasure of moving rhythmically to music, a faint picture of a small girl in a short black velvet tunic standing in front of a mirror and slowly rising on her first pair of points, a child dreaming of being a cygnet in *Swan Lake*.

The cygnet was still rather like a duck, as she climbed the stone front steps to the porticoed entrance of the dancing school. The paint was peeling off the front door, and the steps looked as if they had not been swept for a generation.

Emboldened by a tiny crack of light from under the door and the distant sound of a gramophone, Sylvia rang the bell.

The door was opened by a thin man in a light grey business suit. Hair was plastered back from a middle parting, above a rather sickly face. Grey eyes, as sharp as the warden's when looking for illicit cracks of light, surveyed the two of us.

We both smiled politely, while the unfriendly stare continued. Then suddenly the man grinned. 'Come in, come in,' he invited, and led us into a big, dimly lit hall from which a wide staircase led upwards into total darkness. He closed the door quickly behind us, and inquired, 'Are you beginners?'

We assured him that we both had to start from scratch. 'Well,' he exclaimed jovially, rubbing his hands. 'Tonight's the night. We'll soon have you on your feet.' He pointed to a cupboard under the staircase. 'Put your coats in there. Bring your handbags with you – we mustn't lose things, must we? Then you can give Doris here your shilling.'

As we took off our coats, I observed a smiling middle-aged woman in a frilly dress covered with a pattern of large orange flowers. She held a record in her hand, and put it down on a small hall table, while we paid her.

'Ever been dancin' before?' she inquired in a friendly voice.

'No,' we murmured bashfully.

'Oh, you'll enjoy yourselves here. You'll like the people. We're fussy who we have in. No trouble – ever.'

Trouble in connection with a dancing school had not occurred to me, and I wondered timorously what she meant, but the man came bustling in from the hall saying, 'I'm Norm,' and led us further into the ballroom.

The ballroom had been contrived by the removal of the walls between the dining room, sitting room and breakfast room in the original house, so that the dance floor ran from front to back of the building. Three sets of windows were heavily shrouded with blackout curtains. The walls were a faded, frowsy grey, and battered bentwood chairs lined two sides. A large glass-fronted cabinet stood in an alcove at one end. On a small table, by the door through which we had entered, stood a big wind-up gramophone, flanked by an untidy stack of records. Two girls in summery dresses sat, legs crossed, on the far side of the room. Cigarettes dangled from their fingers, and they glanced casually over at us, and then continued their animated conversation. A couple of young men in neat suits with wide flowing trouser legs and big, gaudily striped ties were sprinkling chalk on the hardwood floor which, alone, showed evidence of care. The surface had been lovingly refinished and the wood glowed.

Norm seated us near the other girls, and said, 'I'll be back,' as the doorbell rang. Doris put on a record, and the young men rubbed the chalk lightly with their feet along the line of dance.

Men and women in their twenties and three or four much older couples began to fill up the room. Most of them seemed to know each other, and, while they waited, they gossiped in thick nasal Liverpool accents. Doris changed the record to a quickstep, winding up the gramophone like a mangle. She and Norm then swept out on to the floor and danced, while everybody watched. Since this was only the second time I had seen adults dancing, I was no judge, but the couple made a production of a basically simple dance. An infinite number of graceful variations was introduced, and, oblivious of their audience, they smiled at each other as if sharing some rapturous experience. It was a wonderful exhibition of perfectly coordinated, flowing movement; the shabby room was for a few minutes a theatre. I did not know then that I was looking at two of the best ballroom dancers in the north.

With hands clenched tightly on my lap, knees and ankles primly together, I sat on the edge of my chair, mesmerised by the charm of the dance. Now Doris and Norm gave a little bow, the audience clapped, and they retreated towards the gramophone. After a moment of consultation with his partner, Norm strode into the middle of the room, rubbed his hands together, and said, 'Now, most of yez learned the basic steps of the waltz last week. Now I want you to try out what you learned, and then we'll learn how to do a turn. Take your partners, please.'

The two girls smoking near us screwed their cigarette ends into a saucer of nub ends on the floor by their chairs, and rose to partner each other. I flashed a tiny, scared smile at Sylvia, who was sitting leaning back in her chair with a bright smile on her face. A young man, immaculately neat, acne scars all over his face, crossed the floor to her, and, with work-roughened hands clasped before him, bowed and asked her, 'Would you like to dance?'

She blushed, pushed her handbag surreptitiously further under her chair with her toe, and with a cheery grin at me, announced, 'Well – er, I can't dance.'

The young man went pink, and replied that he could not either. Undaunted, they went out on to the floor, and the young man put his arm round her waist, clasping her as if she might run away at any moment.

I was alone, feeling a little rejected. Would nobody ask me?

Norm was checking his flock, and when he found everybody paired off except me, he bowed and said, 'Let's dance, love.'

I remembered how to stand, and put my hand correctly on to his shoulder. He smelled nicely of carbolic soap and brilliantine. 'Now, everybody,' he called, 'remember, one and two, one and two, one and two.'

A very firm hand at my waist and an equally firm grasp of my right hand led me off correctly, without a word being said, except for the chanting count of 'one and two'. We circled the floor. After the first few steps the beat of the big band music relaxed me and I allowed myself to flow with my partner. 'Good,' he murmured approvingly, and twirled me into a simple variation. 'Very good.'

'You can dance already,' he said puzzled, 'and you're very light.'

I blushed to the roots of my hair, as if I had done something wrong. 'Well, I learned as a very little girl, but I thought I'd forgotten,' I confessed. Then I got up enough courage to say shyly, 'I think that it is your good guidance. I've never seen anybody dance like you and Doris. I wish I could be that good.'

He seemed as pleased with the compliment as if I had presented him with yet another gold cup, to add to the collection in the cabinet. Then he said, 'Oh, aye. You might be if you stuck at it.' He added earnestly, 'You'd have to find yourself a good partner, though. We've got a few silver medallists as come here – working for their golds, they are – and we've got one gold medallist – other than ourselves, that is.'

As the record came to an end, he led me over to Doris. 'We'll try the turn now,' he said to her. Then he added, 'Been telling this young lady, what's your name, luv, that she could win a silver if she worked.'

Doris nodded. 'I was watching you.'

I said shyly, 'My name is Helen Forrester. I didn't know one could get medals for dancing.'

'Of course you can,' replied Doris. 'A silver means you're good – and a gold you can teach.'

I looked at her open-mouthed. She had just bounced right at my feet a most interesting, brand-new idea of how I might earn a living. Long ago, a country doctor had broken it to me very gently that I could never be a ballet dancer, because I was going to walk always with one foot turned slightly in. My dancing teacher confirmed it. I was sent to learn ballroom dancing, because every middle-class girl was expected to be able to dance. I had been very unhappy amid hordes of other little girls, and small boys dressed in sailor suits with whistles hung round their necks or in Eton suits with stiff white collars. Nobody had seemed to notice the turned foot – and neither, apparently, had Norm or Doris.

Doris was saying proudly, 'You should look at our cups in the cabinet there – proper collection of 'em we've got. Going to try for the world championship soon.'

None of us seemed to think it strange to talk about entering dance competitions, when we expected to be bombed out of existence before too long.

'How exciting!' I exclaimed, with genuine enthusiasm.

'Needs a lot of work,' Norm said, as he sifted through the worn records. He picked out a record and handed it to Doris to put on to the gramophone. While she was doing this, he leaned against the table to rest his feet, and said to me, 'If you're serious, you should come for lessons at least twice a week, and then come to the dance on Saturday night for practice with different partners. See how you get on, like.' He smiled at me, and I agreed, and then said shyly, 'I think I'd better go back to Sylvia.'

Sylvia was making rueful remarks about broken toes to the girl next to her. I sat down primly on the edge of the chair beside her. I was determined to continue the classes, and I hoped she would come with me, so I said soothingly, 'Never mind. A few lessons and we'll all improve.'

My dance with Norm had not gone unnoticed, and the moment we were told to take our partners to learn the turn, a gawky young man with a nervously bobbing Adam's apple was at my elbow, bowing with old-fashioned politeness to ask me if I cared to dance.

I jumped up eagerly, like an unpopular child suddenly asked to join in a game.

Norm, I discovered, was a stickler for good ballroom manners, and he stormed down the room towards one youth who asked a girl in a pink blouse, 'Worm, come and wiggle.'

'If that's how you're going to address a nice young lady, you needn't bother to come again,' he snapped.

The nice young lady immediately sat up straight, folded her hands in her lap and lowered her eyes.

The boy made a wry face, swept her a low bow, and inquired, 'Madam, would you care to dance?'

She nodded assent and rose gravely, leaving her cigarette balanced on an ash tray. Satisfied, Norm turned to his class.

Sylvia's pretty face and cheery manner assured her of partners, and I sat out only one dance. From this predicament I was rescued by Doris, who took the man's part and guided me very well through the basic steps of the slow foxtrot, which I had not danced before.

As we groped our way carefully through the unlit streets, towards the stop where Sylvia could catch a tram home, I was animated, flushed with excitement and exercise, yet scared that for some reason I might not be able to afford to go to the class again.

Sylvia's face was scarcely visible, but from the tone of her remarks she seemed to view the evening with an easy good humour and would tolerate another evening like it. My spirits sank a little, and I wondered if she could possibly understand what a lifeline it seemed to me.

# Chapter twenty-seven

After a couple of weeks, Sylvia gave up attending the dancing classes, because of the long distance she had to travel in the blackout.

I went on my own. All the girls there were very nice to me, though they never gossiped with me or shared their jokes. Norm and Doris were conscientious teachers; and I began to gain a little self-confidence.

The dancing of the silver medallists at the Saturday evening dance showed a finish which owed much to almost daily practice. I was astonished at how much time working-class people were willing to spend on it, unlike the upper classes, who had many other sources of entertainment. Amongst Norm's pupils were older married couples who had met at a dance club, and had danced together all their adult lives.

To dance had been my first ambition in life and the first to be crushed. Its relaxing rhythm now began to heal the wounds that earlier years in Liverpool had so painfully inflicted upon me.

If I wanted to continue to dance, I had also to learn to be courteous and sociable. Such skills are normally learned within the family and their circle, while playing games, attending parties or church or clubs. By extreme poverty and the need to be a surrogate mother, I had been cut off from all the contacts that a young girl could normally expect to enjoy. Now, at twenty, I was an ignorant novice, trying to pick her way amid people who would have roared with laughter at most of the ideas with which my brain was cluttered. It was not easy.

The young men must have had many quiet laughs at my clumsy efforts to be agreeable. I was painfully shy with them, and soon became aware that they treated me a little differently from the other girls present. It was subtle, but it was there. I was an oddity.

I never lacked partners, because I swam on to the dance floor with the ease of a baby duckling learning to swim. All of them wanted a good partner with whom to practise, regardless of whom they eventually escorted home after the dance.

One brave youngster, curly-haired and with the physique of a boxer, did one Saturday evening ask if he could take me home. I looked at him with short-sighted bewilderment and assured him that I was quite capable of seeing myself home. He looked stunned for a moment – perhaps he had never been refused before – and then he grinned in a friendly way which seemed to indicate approval, and said, 'That's O.K., luv,' and went to ask somebody else. Word of this rebuff must have gone round the class, because nobody else ventured to ask.

I went to the classes as frequently as I could afford. At first I was too shy to go to the Saturday night social dances, feeling that my dress was too shabby for a formal dance. The other girls seemed to have innumerable dresses.

I was so accustomed to working as a social worker amid a sea of unemployed that I had never realised that even if unemployment was 33 per cent, that still left over 66 per cent of people in employment.

Now I was entering a new world of highly skilled artisans, where the division of the sexes was amply demonstrated by the fact that the women, whether married or not, congregated on one side of the room, while the men stood on the other side. Occasionally, bored by the lack of conversation, I would talk with Norm and Doris and learned much about their dancing careers and their hopes of expanding their business when the war was over – maybe after next Christmas.

I discovered that I was supposed to talk to my partners while dancing, and I spent anxious moments trying to think of something to amuse men whose main interests were football, football pools, girls and learning to dance so that one could meet more girls.

Finally, I hit on the question, 'Do you work round here?' This usually got an immediate answer, and then I would ask what their job was. This usually called forth a monologue which lasted until the dance ended. As I was escorted back to my chair, I would assure them that it had been a really interesting conversation and I had no idea before how hard men worked. It was true. Many of them worked very hard in hot, dirty, dangerous places, and I soon admired their tenacity, and the fact that they never seemed to realise how brave they were. One of them had spent most of his working life setting the stones of the Anglican cathedral, and was very angry at having been brought down to street level by a government call-up, to build air raid shelters.

I met mechanics and carpenters, electricians and apprentice plumbers, machinists, pattern makers, draughtsmen, shipyard workers, slaughtermen, engineers of every description, bakers and others who worked in Liverpool's huge food industry, occasionally a man in an ill-fitting uniform home on his first leave; very rarely, a seaman or two. They were all scrubbed from head to heel, hair clipped close to their heads like Roman soldiers, dressed in well-pressed Sunday suits.

The top earners were girls who worked for Vernon's and Littlewood's, the companies who ran the football pools. Other girls were shop assistants, waitresses, factory hands in the biscuit factories or stocking works or the Dunlop Rubber Company. They dressed most elaborately, and I gathered from overheard conversations that they spent hours shopping for exactly matching hats, gloves and shoes, and in setting each other's hair. Like the girls I had worked with in the head office of my employers, they talked only of men, films and clothes.

On Sundays, I often went for a walk with Father. He gave me not only time but long and stimulating discussions of subjects which interested him. There was little that he had not studied of the life and times of Louis XIV of France, le Roi Soleil. We would discuss the King's policies, his strengths and failings, the details of his palace of Versailles, which Father had visited a number of times in his youth, and the lives of his advisers.

At night, we turned on our rickety radio, and Mother, Father and I listened to the nine o'clock news, as if it were holy writ. Then we would sweep the seeking needle slowly across the dial, while we tried to pick up news from France and Germany; and more than once I heard Hitler making a speech which sounded all the more terrifying because I could not always understand all of it.

Both Father and Mother benefited from a quieter home. Father never said whether he missed the younger members of his family and he never went to see them, probably because he flinched at the thought of having to meet his sisters if he did.

So, while Poland fought for its very existence, I danced my way back to a modicum of mental health, and we all waited for the holocaust to begin. The thought of it sat at the back of everybody's mind, a weight only hinted at by some stray remark – but there, all the same. At that time in the war, it was as if a conductor had raised his baton ready to begin a symphony, and the tiny pause before the orchestra played the first chord went on and on and on, the players frozen in their seats.

# Chapter twenty-eight

People who did not drink were thankful to find some entertainment still open to them, and Norm was having to turn people away. 'T' floor might collapse and land us all in t' cellar, if I get too many dancing at the same time,' he explained, his thin face earnest. His skin looked yellow from too many late nights, on top of a job in a grocery during the day.

To me, the vibrations of the floor suddenly became something in which to take a personal interest.

Normally the Saturday night dance brought out the best dancers, Norm's treasured silvers and gold, and they now became fretful at the overcrowding. He consoled them by quietly opening up on Sunday night for them. Fortunately for him, the police had plenty of other work on their hands.

I still occasionally went to church on Sunday evenings, though the religious ardour of my early teens had gone. There was still enough natural light for the services to take place. The days of services in semi-darkness, as the winter approached, were yet to come. I would sit in the back pew, as usual, and wonder how I should make a life for myself, and sometimes ask divine help. Ever since I had arrived in Lime Street station at the age of eleven, torn from all that was familiar to me, I had seen clearly the need to obtain an education, despite my parents' objections, and then find an occupation to make me financially independent. What else could a plain girl look forward to? Now the war had made life even more complicated. Though I had not been able to find other employment, there was a steady flow of women, bereft of their menfolk, leaving their homes to take men's places in the work force. There was a call for volunteers for the women's services, in the Army, Navy and Air Force; but because I had no formal educational qualifications, I shrank from being thrown into the lowest rank to do unskilled, menial tasks. Less and less, I wanted to spend my whole life in the sea of sorrow in which I was at present working. I was recovered enough to feel compassion for the flood of widows caused by the sinking of the *Athenia* and the *Courageous* and a myriad of small ships which had been caught far from home at the outbreak of hostilities, and were now trying to creep back to Britain through seas menaced by U-boats. But sometimes I longed for laughter and cheerfulness. And so, while the collection clinked into the church plate, I fretted absently.

443

August and September saw Fiona's young escorts increasingly likely to be in uniform. It was clear that *my* dancing partners were going to be the war's privileged class; their skills were needed in the factories, much too precious to be wasted on the battlefield. It seemed that the war was going to be actually fought by the upper classes and by life's eternal losers, the unskilled.

It was Saturday, the day on which Hitler and Stalin formally abolished the country of Poland; and the clear moonlight made a fairyland of black Liverpool, beating its slate roofs into silver sheets, softening the ugly row houses, making the grubby windowpanes glitter and the eyes of the many slinking cats in the alleys into blazing emeralds, as if there could not be a war in progress. It was a night of calm in which to look at the newly rediscovered stars.

Swinging my dancing shoes on two fingers, I strolled leisurely along the avenue to the dance club. Except for the bottom step, the imposing front steps and porch were in deep shadow, but I ran up them absently with feet that had become familiar with them, and stumbled clumsily into a small group of people waiting to be let in.

'Ow!' exclaimed a male voice, as, confused and apologetic, I stepped back on to a foot.

A shaded torch flashed for a second on my face, and then was turned downward to aid the shuffling and giggling group to see.

The owner of the torch assured me, 'It's all right. I think I'll live.' I was aware of a solid rock of male figure leaning against the portico.

''lo, Helen,' one of the waiting girls who had seen my illuminated face greeted me.

'Hello, Gloria,' I replied, smiling into the darkness. 'How are you?'

She did not have time to answer, because the door was opened by a grinning Norm, apologising for being so long. 'Had to go upstairs and turn a light off,' he explained.

Seven of us, four men and three women, hurried into the dimly lit hall. Though the electric light was swathed in red tissue paper to dull its rays, Norm shut the door quickly, before the ever-vigilant warden could complain.

The gramophone was playing a scratched record of 'Three Little Fishes and a Mother Fishie, too', as we took off our coats and changed our shoes – woe betide anyone who stepped on Norm's precious floor in anything but dancing shoes. I always put on my little satin slippers with a feeling of pure joy.

I did not know the other people who had entered with Gloria and me, so I wandered into the ballroom with her. The dance was already in full swing and the floor was crowded. Doris looked up from her gramophone records and remarked, 'You're lucky. There isn't room for any more.' She surveyed the crowded room, and then added, 'This won't last, now the big dance halls are opening up again.'

'Why not?' I queried. 'It's a friendly place.'

She sighed. 'Well, we depend on regulars, and if they keep on transferring men around the country, like they are doing, there won't be anybody left for you to dance with, luv. Our John's got to report to some dump in Hull tomorrer. And he hasn't even got a place to stay.'

Our John was her brother, a pattern maker, so I commiserated with her, while the old house shook gently with the boom of the music and the movement of the dancers.

Gloria and I were soon claimed by men who knew us and were swept away into the mêlée of dancers. Above the music, I could hear Norm greeting some of the people who had come in with me, as if they were prodigal sons. 'Where you been all this time? What you doin' now?'

My partner deposited me, breathless, on a chair on the far side of the room from the door, where the reunion was continuing with much back-slapping and laughter. My perspiring partner, the bricklayer who was really a stonemason, bowed and left me, to join the male cohorts near the door. I smiled briefly at the girl sitting next to me, but did not talk. She was with her mate, her close girl friend, and absorbed in a deep conversation about what *he* did and what *he* said last night.

I was still panting when I thought I heard my name mentioned in the group of which Norm was the centre. I looked up quickly, just in time to see Norm hastily lower a finger pointing at me. Apparently slightly embarrassed, he turned his back to me and continued the conversation, in which Doris was also included.

The cigarette smoke made the room blue, hazing faces, dimming lights and adding a further deposit to the walls and ceiling. After a slightly longer break than usual Norm shouted, 'Take your partners for an old-fashioned waltz,' and after a doubtful start the strains of 'The Blue Danube' filled the room.

Two young men were standing before me, both wishing to dance. One was a stranger.

'Like to dance?' asked the old acquaintance, with a surly look at the newcomer.

I was about to rise when the stranger said shamelessly, 'Little Miss Helen promised this one to me when we came in.'

I opened my mouth to rebut this indignantly, but he had already leaned down and put his hand firmly under my elbow to help me up. Before I even had time to look at him properly, I was out on the floor, making apologetic faces to the other man over my partner's shoulder.

What the man lacked in finesse, he made up in energy. An old-fashioned waltz takes more vigour than its later counterpart and was always a test of endurance for me. Nevertheless, I was laughing breathlessly by the time

The Blue Danube managed to reach the sea and come to an end. We had not spoken a word, and I had hardly glanced at my partner's face, except to note that he must be in his thirties. Lines, which would soon look like seams, etched a ruddy skin lightly, and there was little of the softness of youth. The face was vaguely familiar. The arms guiding me were extremely strong.

With a final spin, he whirled me to the narrow end of the room with its case of golden trophies. We flopped on to two rarely used chairs, and he pulled a handkerchief from his top pocket and mopped a perspiring brow. Blue eyes beneath fair, bushy brows laughed at me over the damp cotton. I was panting like a Pekinese and could not speak. The eyes were so merry, though, that I had to smile back. It was as if we suddenly shared some naughty secret.

'Well, little Miss Helen, how was that?'

'Fun,' I gasped. 'But really, you told an awful lie.'

'I spend nights dreaming of meeting her again – and she calls me a liar when I do.' He slowly tucked the crumpled hanky back into his pocket, then leaned back in his uncomfortable chair, hands lying loosely on his thighs. He looked at me, with a slight smile curving under a heavy, though neat moustache somewhat yellowed by tobacco smoke. Strong stubby fingers showed faint signs also of cigarette smoke, as did most people's.

Though subjected to a fairly intense examination, I did not feel shy – only bewildered that he claimed to have met me before. He was so relaxed, however, that he conveyed it to me, and when I had regained my breath, I said perplexedly, 'I'm sorry, but I don't remember meeting you before – yet you knew my name?'

'A girl on the steps called you by it – and, anyway, Norm sent me over to dance with you – thought you'd like me. Do you?'

I burst out laughing, embarrassed by the question. I did not know what to reply. 'Well . . . well . . .' I looked again at him, and then added bravely, 'Of course.'

He grinned, more at my confusion, I think, than at the reply.

'Did I . . . ? Were you . . . ? Did I tread on you on the step?'

'Yes,' he responded, with a twinkle. 'You trampled on me. I'm very hard done by tonight.'

I was sober. 'Did it hurt very much? I'm so sorry.'

'I thought I was crippled for life.'

'At least you didn't swear.'

'I save that for recalcitrant machinery – and occasionally for other things. Are you accustomed to men swearing at you?'

'No. But they do swear sometimes – under their breath. And at work I've been sworn at by angry men once or twice.'

'Have you? Where do you work?'

'Well, I'm a social worker – and sometimes men don't like the advice

446

you give them – or the advice you give their wives – and they get very miffed.'

The smile had gone from his face, and he said, 'Well, I'm blowed. You don't look like one.'

'Like what?'

'A social worker.'

'What's wrong with them?' I asked sharply. But a quickstep burst from the ever-faithful gramophone and, without answering, he got up and held out his hand to me to dance.

He held me quite closely and guided me into one or two variations which I think he had invented himself. His suit was navy blue and I was careful not to brush my powdered face against his shoulder. After we had circled the floor in silence, he asked me in a genuinely puzzled tone, 'What's a nice girl like you doing in a place like this?'

I turned my face up to his. 'It's most respectable,' I parried.

'Aye, it is. Norm takes care of that. But you're different. You don't belong here.'

His accent was that of a north-country man, but he did not have the thick nasal Liverpool accent of the other men present. I grinned wickedly, and inquired with deceptive quietness, 'And what is a nice man like you doing in a place like this?'

That made him jump. 'What? Me?' I felt the quiver of laughter in him. '*Touché*,' he replied.

We danced halfway round the room before he answered. Then he said, 'I came with one of my friends and his wife. I sometimes do in winter. They're great dancers – they learned here.' He twiddled me into one of his fancy variations, and I felt the smallest sigh go through him. 'I rent a room in their house – to keep my gear in – and to sleep in when I'm in Liverpool.'

I glanced up at his face again. The mouth under the moustache was set and he looked suddenly weary. He became aware of my gaze and looked down at me, and smiled.

I was feeling tired myself, so I asked, 'Would you like to sit out the rest of the dance?'

Pure mischief glinted in the blue eyes. 'That's an idea.' He guided me round until we reached the door, and under the benign eye of Norm leaning against the gramophone table, he danced me into the empty, chilly hall, and sat me down on the carpeted stairs. They smelled of dust. He squeezed in beside me. There was just room for the two of us, and he put his arm round me, ostensibly to make more space. It was exceedingly comforting, quite the snuggest feeling I had ever experienced. And I felt quite safe. Norm was only a few feet away. It struck me that Norm had allowed this man to do something he would never tolerate in anyone else. Nobody was allowed to linger in

447

the dark hall. Everybody was kept firmly under his paternal eye in the ballroom.

'Do you know Norm and Doris well?'

'Pretty well. Been coming here occasionally for years. Makes some company when I'm ashore, if all my friends seem to be out.'

He wriggled himself more comfortably in beside me. 'Mind if I smoke?' I assured him that I did not mind, so more wriggling ensued while he retrieved cigarettes and matches from his jacket pocket. Before flicking out the match, he held it and it lit up his face. It was not a particularly handsome visage; it was somewhat battered, though full of laughter lines. The nose looked as if it had been broken long ago. The eyes were lively and intelligent. The match, of course, lit my face as well, and I wished suddenly that I was as lovely as Fiona. I had never sat alone with a man other than my father, and never close to one except Emrys Hughes during a holiday when I was about fifteen, a charity holiday obtained for me by the Presence. And Emrys Hughes had been old enough to be my father. This man was young and I wanted to continue sitting by him; it felt very nice. He had already slipped the packet of cigarettes into his top pocket, when he said contritely, 'I forgot to ask if you'd like one. Would you?'

'No, thank you. I don't smoke.'

There was a small silence between us while he drew on his cigarette, which I broke by asking, 'Do you go to sea?'

'Yes, miss. Engineer. Got my Master's, though. And how did you know?'

'You walk like a seaman. And what is a Master's?'

'Master's Certificate. One day – maybe – I might get a ship of my own.'

'Master of your fate?' I teased.

'And Captain of my soul.' The voice had an odd, defensive note in it. The hall was cold and I began to shiver.

His arm tightened round me, and he exclaimed, 'You're getting chilled. Come on, little lady, let's dance.'

So we danced, and I heard a great deal about the problems of being an engineer. Then he was silent as he led me round the room. I forgot that there were other men with whom I normally danced. I was content to let myself float in the arms of this most peculiar man, a man who looked as tough as an old boot, yet with a speech that was almost as civilised as my own.

I remembered suddenly that he had not told me where he had met me before, and I wondered if perhaps it was a long time ago, when I had stayed with my grandmother. He might have lived in the same village.

# Chapter twenty-nine

Norm put on the record with which he always closed off the evening, a waltz called 'Who's Taking You Home Tonight?'

My partner was very quiet as we slowly circled the floor. He looked down at me and asked, quite humbly, 'Can I see you home?'

I was suddenly flooded with shyness. 'It's all right,' I murmured, turning my face away. 'You don't have to bother. I'm quite safe by myself.'

My face felt flushed. I looked up at him and was subjected to a sober, searching look. He sighed, and agreed, 'You're quite right, my dear. When are you coming here again?'

'Tuesday, all being well.'

'Well, I'll see you here. It'll be a day or two yet before we sail.'

The information that he would shortly leave Liverpool, perhaps sail out of my life as swiftly as he had sailed in, was not pleasant. I was suddenly painfully aware of the U-boats sitting outside the bay, reminded of the mourning women in the waiting room. I licked my lips and smiled up at him. 'I'll be here – but I may be late.'

'That's my girl,' he said more cheerfully and did a flamboyant, wild spin which would have made Norm wring his hands in horror had he spotted it.

'I don't know your name,' I ventured.

He laughed. 'God bless my soul! You don't, do you? Well, it's Harry O'Dwyer. And Doris said yours is Helen Forrester, right?'

'Yes,' I whispered. What was I doing? I must be crazy.

He whirled me into the corner reigned over by the collection of gold cups, and stopped. The last few bars of the music slowly trailed to an end, and Norm turned off the lights, except for the one over the gramophone table. He always said it was romantic to do so.

For a moment he held me close to him. It seemed to me that life had stopped, and he and I were suspended in a warm, cosy space of our own. Then, slowly he let go of me, and said, 'It's been a good evening, hasn't it?'

I came out of my trance, and agreed. 'It was fun.' With my hand still on his shoulder, I laughed softly, and asked, 'Before you go, tell me – where have we met before?'

449

'Don't you remember?'

'No.'

'Dear me. And I always thought I was such an unforgettable character!' He chuckled. 'Remember walking on Georges Landing Stage with an old man – your dad, I imagine?'

Enlightenment dawned. 'You were the man who kindly picked up my spectacles? And you wanted to meet me again – you said something about it earlier this evening? You really did?'

'Of course I did, dear, innocent little Miss Helen,' he mocked gently. He took my hand and led me over to the door, through the crowd making its way into the hall. He gave a small old-fashioned bow, and said, 'See you Tuesday.' He went away to join his friends and the crowd closed round him.

In a daze, I went to retrieve my shoes from the untidy pile in the big hall cupboard.

'My, my!' exclaimed Gloria, while she poked in the pile of shoes. 'You *have* made a conquest.'

I was offended, stood up straight suddenly and hit my head on the chin of a girl jostling me from behind. I apologised, and then said to Gloria, with a quiver in my voice, 'What nonsense! Me? I may have made a friend, Gloria.'

We crawled out between the pressing bodies, each with shoes in hand, and she said, as she wobbled on one foot while she put a shoe on the other one, 'Why not? Don't be upset. You're a proper nice girl – always said so. Keep yourself to yourself. And he's a fine-looking fella.' She jabbed an elbow in my side, and added, 'Wish you luck, I do.'

Disarmed, I laughed self-consciously. 'Oh, Gloria.'

She giggled at me as, with shoes on, we straightened up. 'Lovely hair he's got.'

'Who's got lovely hair? Have I?' Her husband came from behind and put his arms round her waist, while I tried to remember what kind of hair Harry had.

'Not you, you old so-and-so,' she replied affectionately. 'You're going bald on top. That man Helen was dancing with.'

My face was scarlet. I heaved myself into my coat. I wanted to escape from their frank appraisal.

Her husband took his face away from its resting place on his wife's back, and gave her a push. 'Get away. You've got the girl all upset. She's as red as a beetroot.' He turned to me, his plain pasty face friendly. 'Don't take any notice of her. She's always looking for romances.'

I did my best to smile, but my lips were tight. I was nearly dead with embarrassment as I said, 'Good night,' and followed the crowd down the dark steps.

The blush slowly dissipated in the sharp September air, and I marched steadily home in the moonlight, trying to face the fact that the evening had been different from any evening I had ever spent – and that I could hardly wait until Tuesday. Common sense was saying, 'Don't be a fool. He's a sailor. Girls in every port. Experienced. And you're not much of a catch, despite Mother's efforts with clothes and things. Perhaps he won't even be there on Tuesday.'

Mother was still up when I arrived home, but I could not bring myself to tell her about the strange engineer. I feared her sarcastic tongue and the amused discussion that would probably go on behind my back. And suppose he did not come on Tuesday – I could not bear public humiliation. Mother, however, was anxious to discuss Fiona's latest escort. 'She's gone out to dinner at the George and then to dance,' she announced. 'He's a fully fledged General from the barracks. Said he saw her every morning waiting for the tram and had wanted to ask her for ages. So suitable, don't you think?'

'How exciting,' I responded absently, as I poured a cup of tea from the pot on the hob. I wondered if Mother realised that Generals, usually men of good family, did not pick up girls from tram stops with any particularly honourable intention. I was anxious. Mother babbled on, however, and finally with no further comment I went to bed.

Probably Mother did not see Fiona's General in the same light that I did. She would think of him as an equal making himself known to an equal, a situation where he would tend to be much more careful of Fiona. I hoped wildly that Fiona was as big a prude as I thought her to be.

As I shivered in bed, I ticked myself off for being so stupid as to spend money on dancing, when what I really needed was a pair of thick blankets on my bed. I was as stupid as my mother, I upbraided myself. I determined to try to save up for this very expensive item, and the ache in my legs the next day reinforced the resolution. And then I remembered that if I bought a blanket, Mother would pawn it the first time she was short of money.

That week I cried for a city. Warsaw, brave, defiant old city, faced its final martyrdom, as German troops entered it. No point any more in trying to find its valiant voice on the radio. Another tragedy to add to that of the submarine, *Thetis*, which at that moment lay in Liverpool Bay while frantic efforts were made to raise her, though her crew were long since dead. In the office, my senior colleague faced not only supplicating hordes, but an ever-growing pile of government instructions which had somehow to be read and understood and explained to our volunteer helpers. Her eyes were nearly as blackly ringed as mine. She scarcely stopped to eat and took a load of work home every night.

I often worked late at the office, but I never took work home. I could not face it. I walked a razor's edge. Though slowly recovering from years of privation, I was still by any normal standards in very poor health, still not well fed or properly warmed. Dancing had proved a real mental therapy but I tired easily. The war added its daily strain of perturbation. I worried about Alan and fretted about the children, though they were probably better looked after than if they were at home.

On Tuesday, as anticipated, I worked late. The trams taking me home seemed to crawl through the darkness. I ached with impatience. The house was in darkness, and I was greeted by an ecstatic dog and a note from Mother, who had thankfully gone to the cinema now it was open again. 'Gone to Rialto. Boil an egg.'

I duly boiled an egg, shared a slice of bread and margarine with the importuning dog, washed up a collection of dishes and made up the fire. It seemed as if invisible hands pulled at my skirt and made me slow. I washed carefully and then, holding the candle in my left hand, I made up my face. In its flickering light, I combed my curls softly round my face, peering anxiously into the piece of broken mirror wedged into the kitchen window. Would he be there?

Norm had left the front door unlatched, as he usually did on lesson nights, so I let myself in. I stood quietly in the big hall, shoes still dangling on my fingers, and stared through the open ballroom door.

He was there. Draped over a chair by the gramophone, if such a solid block of manhood could be said to be draped. He was talking to Norm. Neither man noticed my entrance, so I took a good look at him, and such a wild delight filled me that I wondered for a moment what was happening to me. Gloria was right. He did have nice hair of a nondescript fairness. He wore it a little longer than was the fashion. Without brilliantine, it curved comfortably round his forehead, a forehead which already had fine lines in it. Even relaxed, he radiated a considerable self-confidence. It was quiet, but it was there. It offered no direct threat, yet it suggested a powerful personality. Despite his easy manner and his light banter with me, he appeared a man not to be trifled with, either by a drunken seaman – or a flighty young woman.

I bit my lip, feeling hopelessly inadequate, and wondered if I should tiptoe out again. Where did he come from? Who were his people? His speech put him a cut above Norm's other customers, yet he was not what Father would have called a gentleman.

The sound of his hearty laugh rolled through the door, and plucking up courage, I changed my shoes and sidled in diffidently. I could already feel a blush rising up my neck. What was one supposed to say? How should I behave?

He had seen me. He immediately got up and came over and ushered me in. 'Hello, little puss,' he said, and grinned all over his face, emphasising the lines on it.

He was so totally friendly that, as I opened my handbag to pay Norm, I smiled back feeling more relaxed, and said, 'Hello.' He might call me little puss, but he himself was not unlike a dignified, amiable St Bernard dog. If he had had a tail I am sure it would have wagged in big, slow sweeps.

He put his hand over my bag and clipped it shut. 'It's fixed,' he assured me.

'Oh, but I can't . . . you can't,' I flustered. I looked appealingly at Norm, who assured me, 'Gentleman's privilege, luv.'

I swallowed, and said doubtfully, 'Well, thank you,' and allowed myself to be led to one of the chairs at the side of the ballroom, out of the way of the stumbling tango beginners. He sat down beside me, one arm curved along the back of my chair. 'I was afraid you weren't coming.'

I apologised for being late and said I hoped he had danced with someone else.

His response was scornful. 'With that bunch?'

'They're nice girls.'

He pursed up his mouth. 'Not my cup of tea.'

'Why do you come, then?'

'I came to please my landlord's wife last time. This time I came to see you.'

'Really and truly?' I smiled at him, flattered.

'Well, of course.' The gramophone struck up a quickstep. 'Would you like to dance?' he asked, unenthusiastically.

We danced. He was very quiet, and at the end he asked, 'Couldn't we go somewhere and get a cup of tea – and talk a while? There aren't any really nice places round here, but I know one which is very respectable.' He looked round the shabby, smoke-filled room. 'We'll never be able to talk much here – and I'm sailing Thursday night.'

I looked up sharply. I was suddenly afraid for him. Fear must have shown on my face, because he said, 'Don't be scared. I'll take good care of you. Ask Norm – he's known me off and on for a long time.'

'Mother will be expecting me home soon after eleven,' I dithered, while my pulses beat madly.

'I'll get you home in time. Promise.'

He looked so wistful and inside me was stirring a crazy pleasure at being singled out by him. 'Please, little Miss Helen.'

'I'll get my coat and shoes,' I said, trembling inwardly.

# Chapter thirty

We sat down opposite each other in a steamy little café. We were the only customers. A fat, white-aproned woman stood behind a small counter laden with two hissing gas rings with bubbling kettles on them. An assortment of plates covered with glass domes held sandwiches and buns. The woman came over to our plain deal table, and said, ''lo, Harry, me luv, what is it tonight?'

Harry looked inquiringly at me, and I said primly, 'A cup of tea would be very nice.'

Harry ordered two teas.

'Would your young lady like something to eat? I've got some fresh bath buns – or you could have something hot?'

I was, as usual, hungry, but I had no idea of his financial situation, so I said with a smile at the friendly soul waiting in front of us that a bun would be lovely. His young lady, indeed!

Harry was grinning at me like a small boy. He nodded towards the retreating female. 'Come here for years for most of my meals, when I'm ashore. It's quiet. Jack's wife gives me breakfast – I eat my other meals out, so as not to intrude on them. He's First Mate, and it's like a permanent honeymoon there when he's home. Ma here keeps me well fed, don't you, Ma?' He looked across at the counter, where a large pot of tea was in the making. Ma looked up and smiled and said she did her best.

'Why do you have to work so late?' he asked, stirring two spoonfuls of sugar into the cup of tea I had poured for him.

I bit into the huge bun brought me on a thick white plate. 'It's the sinking of the *Athenia* and the *Courageous*. Every boat that goes to sea seems to have Bootle men on it – and we're looking after their widows.' Then I remembered, as his face sobered, that he went to sea, too, so I added hastily, 'I'm sorry, I should not have mentioned it.'

He sighed heavily, and put his elbows on the table and clasped his hands, big well-shaped hands with scarred knuckles and very short nails, broken in places.

'That's all right,' he said and was quiet, biting absently on his knuckles. 'I'm a Bootle man myself. My mum and dad still live there. Dad's retired. He went to sea – ship's purser.'

'You don't stay with them?' I inquired, guardedly.

'No.' He appeared to be cogitating over the question and continued to chew his knuckles. 'I'm too old to be bothering them now. I got used to living away from them – for a while Mam wouldn't have such a limb of Satan over the doorstep.'

'What?' Despite a mouthful of glutinous bun, I had to laugh.

'It's true,' he said ruefully. 'She's still a bit edgy with me.'

Still laughing, I asked, 'Whatever did you do to offend her so?'

'Decided I'd never make a priest – so I went over the wall.'

It was a totally unexpected answer, and I stared at him in astonishment. 'Really? A priest?'

'Yes. Why not?'

I nodded. Why not? So many Catholic families hoped to have one child enter the Church, either as a priest or nun. The child would be brainwashed almost from infancy, so that it would never consider doing anything else. But this was the first rebel I had ever met – or even heard of.

'Did you study for it?'

'Yes. At first I thought I'd make it. Then it was as if part of me was dying inside. Don't know how to explain it. Like being slowly strangled, if you understand.' He was spreading out a watery ring on the table, and the blue eyes glanced up at me, as if to judge how I was taking his admission. 'I guess I didn't have the necessary discipline.'

'What did your teachers do?'

'Oh, them. They were very good. They made me mull it over good and plenty – because it costs money to educate a priest – and I think some of them really cared. But they don't want discontented men, and finally I left – with their blessing. They did it without making me feel guilty. But my mum – that was a different matter.'

'What about your father?'

'Oh, he's a real old philosopher. Nothing gets him. But he does what Mum says while he's home. He's got to live with her! Neither of them takes kindly to him being home all the time. She's used to running the place – because of him being at sea all the time.'

I had seen enough seamen's wives to understand the matriarchal set-up. 'So what did you do?' I asked.

'Never even unpacked after I came home from the seminary. Got shown the door. God, she was furious. I went to stay with my married brother for a day or two. Then I got a job sweeping out a warehouse. I didn't know what to do – jobs are as scarce as hens' teeth. Then I met a pal – a lad I'd known at school – and he got me a job with him aboard a miserable little tub – goddamn awful boat – excuse the language – and I was as sick as a dog the first week. It was rough – my God, it was. But having a pal aboard a bit older than me made all the difference – saved me from the worst, till I got to know the ropes.'

'Are you always sick?' I asked. I wondered with dim horror what the worst was. All the seamen I had ever interviewed spoke of vermin, poor food and low wages.

'No. Never been sick since, oddly enough.' He smiled at my empty plate, and signalled Ma to bring another bun.

'Don't you go to see your mother?'

He sighed. 'Yeah. But she's never forgiven me and never lets me forget it. So I don't go every time I'm ashore. I give her a little allotment, so that if ever I stop one she'd get a bit of a pension. See my dad more often and my brother.'

I looked at the old, young face in front of me, the openness and geniality of it, and wondered how any woman could be bitter enough to show a son like that to the door.

'Your mother doesn't realise what she is missing,' I said impulsively.

'Och, you're a sweetheart,' he said with sudden cheerfulness, and drank up his tea.

'Being used to study must have helped you pass your exams to be an engineer – though it is so very different.'

'Well, I had to start from scratch. But grammar school is a good place for learning to learn – and the Fathers at the seminary certainly reinforced it. They wouldn't have any backsliding. You can learn anything if you're really set on it.'

The room was hot, and he opened his navy blue jacket, to show a creased waistcoat with a watch chain across it. He also wore a wrist watch with an expanding gilt band. Inwardly I smiled at the creases on the waistcoat. I could not remember seeing a merchant seaman whose clothes were properly pressed. I suppose, if they took them to sea, they kept them rolled up. And this man had no one to look after him ashore. He picked up the conversation again, and continued, 'I don't drink, except the odd glass of wine – tried as a youngster, of course, and threw up a good many times before I gave up. So I've time to read – makes you a bit cut off from your mates at times – and I saved – so it was easy for me to take time out for courses.'

'It's unusual for a seaman not to drink. I thought they all *lived* on rum, more or less.'

He laughed. 'Get away. There's always a few that don't. My father never did.'

'Well, what do you do when you're in a strange place?'

'Sometimes there's a Sailors' Home or some place, where you can get a game of billiards – or you can go to a show or a match or into the bazaars. There's another chap, a Methodist, and he doesn't drink either, so we sometimes go together.' He looked at me slyly, and added, 'Pick up a girl occasionally.'

'Do you consider that you picked up me?' I asked tartly.

He grinned, hesitated, and then said, 'No. I hope I've made a permanent acquisition.'

I was so happy that I simply glowed. It must have been obvious to him, because he caught my hand across the table and gave it a hearty squeeze. For a moment we were united, and then bashfully I withdrew my hand, and asked shyly, 'What else do you do?'

'Well, not a great deal. Often enough, you're too busy to have much time ashore. I read a lot – take a pile of books with me. Get fed up at times – particularly not having a home to go to.' He lit a cigarette and blew a neat smoke ring into the air. 'Enough of this old man. How about you?'

This was a question I had been dreading. What should I tell him? How could I explain my odd parents? If I explained my origins, would he think I was swanking and despise me?

My unease must have shown on my face, because he said gently, 'It doesn't matter, luv. I can see you've had a bad time – it's written all over you.' Then he leaned forward and took my hand again. 'I don't care what you are – or anything. I know a good thing when I see it. I did when I picked your specs up off Georges Landing.'

He astonished me. Did I really show what had happened to me? Or what did he think I was – something dreadful? I sat looking down at my hands clasped over my handbag on my knee. I had to acknowledge an overwhelming desire to keep his interest, and was mortally afraid of not being able to do it. I wanted so much that he should think well of me.

He was sitting, elbows on table, a long ash on his cigarette, as quietly as if he were waiting for a badger to emerge from its burrow in the evening light.

The silence between us continued, until he began to smile at me, and as if to help me, began to talk again.

'You know, a man in my position doesn't often get the chance of meeting a decent woman like you – unless you strike lucky. When you don't have a home base, you can be cut off, like. And when you start out to be a priest, you try not to think about women – in that kind of way, if you know what I mean,' he muddled on, going a bit pink himself.

I smiled back at him. 'Yes, I understand. You wouldn't be taking out the girls who lived near you – the ones you'd normally meet – when you were in your teens, for example.'

He chuckled. 'Right.'

Suddenly I felt more at ease. 'Well,' I said, 'I've been cut off in a way, too.'

He looked at his wrist watch. 'Do you feel like walking home?'

I nodded agreement, and he signalled to Ma. She eased herself round the counter and he paid her. With his money in her red hand, she smiled down at me in a most approving way, and winked at Harry. I blushed yet again, and, as I rose, I thanked her.

Harry ushered me through the narrow door of the café and somehow his arm stayed round my waist as we slowly walked up the hill. He had a sailor's eyesight and steered me safely in the dark, overcast night. The whole city seemed still.

'Tell me how you came to be cut off, too,' he demanded.

It was easier talking in the dark, to a comfortable, warm presence strolling by me. A man I felt to be honest deserved honesty, so slowly, sometimes with pain, I told him what had happened to our family and its consequences to me.

He heard me through, with only an occasional exclamation. As we neared our street, I fell silent. What is he going to think of such a crazy family? I wondered. So unbalanced, not established, unpredictable except in their stupidity.

'You poor kid,' he said compassionately, and tightened his arm round my waist.

At the top of our road, he stopped and turned me to him. He paused, as if considering something for a moment, and then very carefully kissed me on the cheek. 'What's your office phone number?' he asked. 'I'll be busy now. Won't be able to see you until we dock again. I'll phone you as soon as I'm back – and we'll make a proper date. Officially, I'm not supposed to know where we're going – allow five weeks. O.K.?'

I was trembling in his confining arms, with a scarifying, overwhelmingly strange feeling within me.

'Yes,' I whispered.

'Which is your house?' he asked.

'It's the seventh – no, the eighth – down on this side.'

'Right. Just in case I can't get you on the phone, I'll know where to find you.'

'Do you have an address?' I asked nervously, trying to sound normal when I felt far from normal.

He immediately gave me the address of his lodgings. I wanted instinctively to put my arms around him and beg him not to go, but I was too shy.

A number of short voyages and happy reunions later, he told me that to gain my full confidence was harder than making friends with the disillusioned ship's cat, who regarded the cook as his sole friend, and then persuading the beast to come on to his lap.

# Chapter thirty-one

Five weeks seemed an interminable time. When the thirty-five days were over and there was no telephone call I was nearly distracted. Harry had told me the name of his ship, and certainly no one had come into the office to claim a pension because the ship was lost – in those days of official silence about the total number of our losses, this was the most likely way I would have known if it had gone to the bottom.

On the forty-first day I could bear it no longer, and with elaborate casualness I asked Norm if he had heard anything.

Norm dusted one of his records, and said that almost certainly if Harry's pal from the same ship was missing, he would have heard about it – so the ship was still afloat. If it had docked, Jack's wife nagged him so much to be taken dancing that they would have been in the room that minute. He grinned knowingly at me. 'He's a proper nice lad, isn't he? I knew you'd like him.'

I nodded and smiled – and sighed.

'Don't you worry, luv. He'll be back like a homing pigeon. He needs a girl like you.'

But I did worry. Something wonderful, something precious, had plunged light-heartedly into my miserable existence, and I could not bear to lose it. I knew of so many little ships limping home damaged, or lost at sea. I realised to the full what many of the stony-faced women who came to our office for advice were going through.

Fiona, secretive and sour-faced, announced to Mother's disappointment that she did not like her General and had dropped him. Fiona had more sense than she was ever given credit for.

She stayed at home one night and set my hair for me. I was tempted to tell her about Harry. Yet, as she chatted on about films she had seen and dances she had been to, I thought better of it. Surrogate mums listen; they are not expected to have anything to confide. Secretly, I dreaded ever having to introduce a man friend to Fiona. Her charm, her sex appeal, were overwhelming, like Mother's in her younger days. I would not stand a dog's chance against such competition.

Mother was fretting over a government demand that parents contribute towards the billeting allowance made to the hosts of evacuees. The sum

459

suggested was six shillings for each child, a little over half the allowance. Both parents grumbled that they could not afford it, though they could now afford to smoke, to drink, to attend the cinema or concerts. They had grown used to having money in their pockets, as I had with my little allowance.

I dreaded being returned to my earlier impossible penury, and I again advertised for a shorthand student, still without result. I had continued to apply for jobs advertised in the *Liverpool Echo*.

Unemployment was still very high, and employers could obtain stenographers who had matriculated. Few of the men who interviewed me bothered to examine the sheaf of certificates which I had received for my night school endeavours. I was also still very poorly dressed in comparison with other girls who worked in offices, though I had now taught myself to make and alter underwear and dresses quite successfully. Not that I had the use of what I made for very long. All too frequently painstakingly hand-stitched petticoats and renovated dresses were borrowed by plumper Mother and Fiona, to be left dirty and with seams burst. I raged impotently and tried hiding my single change of underwear under the mattress. To no avail. I was a rotten, greedy, bad-tempered daughter and sister who did not trust her relations. My despair about Harry did not improve my patience.

Another worry was that Mother began to justify avoiding paying the billeting charges for the children, by saying her darlings must be homesick and want to return. It certainly would have been cheaper to have them at home, because the price of food was still low – and we did not eat well anyway.

I brought a storm of recrimination down on my head by reminding Mother that, though Liverpool had not yet been bombed, there was no guarantee that it would not be soon. I wondered bitterly how much real affection she had for her children; she did not seem to really miss them very much. This idea strengthened my mistrust of Mother, despite her keeping her word to me regarding her share of my salary. I found myself even less able to talk to her, except for common courtesies.

After forty-two days I gave up. Either Harry's ship was lost, or he had abandoned the clumsy hobbledehoy he had picked up. Probably the latter, I told myself acidly. Moodily I slammed files on to shelves, typed letters and was sent out to visit invalids or the elderly, who were always remarkably sweet to me.

'Miss Forrester,' called my colleague, holding up our solitary telephone. 'A call for you. Make it quick, because I have a lot of phoning to do.'

I blenched with the surprise of it, and almost snatched the instrument from her. 'Hello,' I murmured.

'Little Miss Forrester?'

'Yes.'

'Harry here. Look, sweetheart. We've just berthed. It's going to be a quick turnaround this time. Could you meet me at Mrs Ambleton's place – you know, the little café we went to – tonight, seven thirty, eh?'

'Yes,' I breathed. 'Oh, yes, of course.'

'Wait for me if I'm late?'

'Yes.'

'I'll be there. 'Bye.' The phone clicked as he rang off.

In a dream I handed the receiver back to my intrigued colleague, who was smiling questioningly at me. 'Thank you,' I said, and then added, 'I'll check how the waiting-room is doing.' And I fled, down to the unused basement of the house which was our office, pushed open a creaking door into an old kitchen wreathed with cobwebs, shut myself in, and burst into tears with relief.

# Chapter thirty-two

While my colleague was out visiting a difficult case, I made a fast call to Fiona and asked her to tell Mother I would not be in for tea. 'We'll be sending out for some sandwiches to eat in the office while we work,' I lied merrily. Fiona had obviously been expecting a call from someone else, because her lively 'Hello' turned to 'What, you?' when she heard my voice. She promised, however, to relay the message.

'Where's Harry?' asked Ma through a cloud of steam from her kettles.

'He's coming,' I puffed, as I took off my darned woollen gloves and loosened my coat.

'Like a coop o' tea while you're waiting, luv?'

'Yes, please.' My eyes were on the narrow door. I was dreadfully hungry, but I was so happy, so wonderfully, wonderfully happy.

Eight o'clock came and went, and slowly my hopes shrivelled. Three men went out, and a man and a girl came in and sat down to a meal. The smell of sausages was tantalising.

He came in slowly and, for a moment, until his crumpled face broke into a lively grin, I hardly recognised him. He was dressed in beige twill cotton trousers, a blue shirt open at the neck, worn under an open black leather jacket. His face was almost without colour, except for red rings round eyes so weary I wondered how they stayed open. In one hand he carried a flat white paper bag. He came towards me eagerly, whipping off a navy blue peaked sailor's cap, as he approached.

'Eh, I'm that glad to see you,' he said, putting his arm round my shoulder for a second, before turning to swing into the chair opposite me. 'Thought I'd never get loose. How are you, luv?'

I was all curled up inside with pure joy. I wanted to hug him, and I am sure my face glowed as I said, 'Oh, I'm all right. What about you?'

He looked exhausted, as if he should have been in bed, instead of meeting a stray girl in a café; and my happiness flowed out in compassion for him.

He grinned, and said, 'Well, I'm starving. Have you had your tea?'

I nodded negatively while my eyes dwelt on him, and he called to the beaming, fat lady, 'What have you got, Nell?'

She offered steak and kidney pie or sausage and mash, with steamed treacle pudding to follow.

Over a huge helping of pie, I repeated my question. 'What about you? You look worn out.'

'Been chasing all over the bloody Atlantic, if you'll pardon the language.' He began to eat quickly, as if he were indeed starving. 'Convoy got scattered – it was slow as a company of snails, anyway. We made it home on our own – we're fast compared to most freighters.'

A shiver of dread went through me. I refrained, however, from asking any more questions. Time enough to talk when he had eaten his dinner and unwound a little.

Between mouthfuls, I kept glancing up at him, amazed that he had thought of me first when he came ashore, that he really was sitting opposite me.

He caught my questing eye. 'Never stopped thinkin' about you,' he said, with a piece of kidney balanced neatly on his fork.

The tell-tale flush flooded my face. I wanted to say, 'I never stopped thinking of you.' But I was too proud to commit myself. This kind, comfortable man might soon get fed up with my long silences and my gauche ways.

'I'm so glad you got back safe,' I finally managed, a bit primly.

He leaned back and laughed. 'Wasn't too bad, luv. I was thankful to see Blackpool Tower, though, I can tell you.'

I thought about the sea mines being laid by both combatants, of surface raiders, of the dreaded U-boats, as yet only flexing their muscles. Suddenly I felt the icy Atlantic waters with their surface mist drifting over struggling men. I felt the choking water in my own lungs, and I asked impulsively in a strangled voice, 'Do you have to do another voyage? Can't you stay ashore – do something else?'

His eyes were intent on me, speculative. 'No, little Helen. We all have to go back. Even if I decided to swallow the anchor – and I might – I can't do it until this little ruckus is over. What about some pudding?'

I tried to console myself with a piece of steamed pudding big enough for a hungry lorry driver.

Steamed pudding did not help much. I was in love. I knew it. In love with someone I was seeing for only the third time. It was ridiculous, absurd, stupid, certainly unwise. Then I told myself piteously that there was no harm in loving, as long as one did not expect anything in return. As always with the children, perhaps I could give him love without consideration of what I would get out of it. Physical love I would have to be careful about, but that was only part of it – it was the commitment which mattered.

I need not have worried about being left with an infant to care for. I was dealing with a most unusual man, who, however he felt, was very much in command of himself. It was almost disappointing not to have to fight for one's honour.

We spent the rest of the evening riding backwards and forwards on the ferry boat, crossing and recrossing the Mersey river. Tucked in the curve of Harry's arm, it was a good place to talk and get to know each other.

On the first trip, he put the white paper bag on my lap. 'I brought you a present,' he announced.

Surprised, I picked up the bag hesitantly. 'May I look?'

He nodded expectantly, and I opened the bag, touched material and carefully drew it out.

It was a dress, and I did not need to totally unfold it to know that it was a very good dress. The colour in the poor light was either tan or dark red. It had tiny pin tucks running the length of the bodice on which was pinned a discreet leather flower touched with gold. It had long sleeves, and could, I guessed, be worn for any occasion.

'Harry!' I exclaimed, blushing. 'It is too – too much – you should not have done it – but, oh, it's beautiful. Thank you very much.'

His arm tightened round me. 'Didn't know your vital statistics, but I found a girl the same size, I think. Like it?'

I shook it out and admired its fine leather belt, its plain skirt, and turned starry eyes up to him. 'It's perfect,' I said. 'I've never had anything so beautiful before.'

Our faces were very close together and I thought he would kiss me, but he didn't. Just hugged me tighter.

'Thought you'd like it. Went down to the garment district in Manhattan and looked around. My pal often buys things there for his wife. They've got everything there - stuff that goes to the good shops.'

I was overwhelmed. 'You shouldn't spend so much on me,' I protested.

'Humph. And who else would I be spending it on? That's the trouble with me. Never had anybody I wanted to buy presents for, for years.'

I laughed, and carefully folded up the dress and put it back into the bag. How I was going to explain it to Mother and Fiona or stop them from borrowing it, I had no idea. I could not explain my happy acceptance of it even to myself – and from a Roman Catholic, to boot.

We sat talking together, warm and happy, two odd, extremely lonely people, neither of whom had had very much out of life except work, and yet matched like a pair of gloves. I wondered what had happened to my passionate belief in my church, feelings strong enough to make me refuse Confirmation from a church which demanded that its members go to Confession.

This remembrance made me turn to him and, snuggling close, say, 'Harry, I have to tell you – you know, I'm a Protestant.'

He chuckled unexpectedly. 'I thought so. Do you feel very strongly about it?'

'I'm not sure. I used to feel that no other religion was a true one. But the more I see the more I realise that nobody can really say that.'

'Well, not to worry, my dear. Times they are a-changing. We'll talk about it some more another day.'

Nevertheless, we continued to talk about beliefs, though not very deeply, and then about ships' engines – very deeply and far out of my depth. Finally, we came round to the war, which was always at the back of everybody's mind, and in this regard Harry said, 'Y' know, I've never been out of work since I went to sea – and I've saved. Since the war began I've been getting danger money – and it is going to add up. So I was thinkin' of buying a house – I know it sounds daft – but I'm fed up with not having a place of my own. I want a decent place and I've been bickering with a chap out at Allerton who's got a few new houses for sale. Would you like to come some time and look at one with me?'

I was a bit staggered, and my mind leaped ahead with all kinds of wild hopes. Remember, I told myself, don't expect anything. 'I'd love to,' I assured him. 'It must be miserable not having a home.'

'It is,' he said, looking at me positively wickedly.

To be able to buy a house – to have the money to do it – seemed to me an almost impossible ambition. Presumably, however, he knew what he was doing.

'When do you sail again?'

'Couple of days,' he replied soberly. 'Real quick turnaround. Never know what they'll do next. They're even shifting crews around to other companies, as if they were ruddy pawns.'

'It's happening ashore, too,' I said.

He eased himself around, in order to look at me directly. 'Like to come dancing tomorrow night? I can get loose for a few hours – they owe me plenty. We can go to the Rialto, if you like.'

'Let's go to Norm's,' I suggested. The Rialto seemed suddenly a cold and alien place.

'O.K., and I'll try to think of a nice place for coffee afterwards.'

He said he would get the overhead railway back to the dock, and saw me on to the tram with only a gentle peck on my cheek. It was very disappointing. He told me later that he was so afraid of scaring me off and yet his time ashore was so little.

I did not have to account for the new dress, because everyone was in bed when I arrived home, and the next morning they all rushed off to work without remembering that they had not seen me the previous evening. While Fiona was washing herself in the kitchen, I hid the pretty garment on a hanger under my old brown winter coat, which was by this time too decrepit even to be pawned and was sometimes used as a bed cover.

465

I tore home that evening and shared tea with Mother and Fiona, because Father was working late. It was unusual for me to lie, but that night I lied like the proverbial trooper. I said I had bought a new dress from a well-known second-hand shop which dealt in high-class clothing, and was going to press it to wear to the dance club that evening.

When Fiona saw it, her eyes widened. 'You lucky thing!' she exclaimed. 'Do you think they'd have anything to fit me?'

'Probably they would,' I responded non-committally, as I carefully ran the flat iron over it on the kitchen table. To press such a garment without an ironing board was a skill learned from patient experiment.

It was a tan shade which suited my sallow complexion, and it fitted very well; too well, I hoped, for either Fiona or Mother to get into it. 'It *is* a nice dress, more like an American fashion than an English one,' Mother said quite innocently, leaving me tight-lipped and silent. 'You should go and have a look, Fiona, and see what they have.'

I could imagine what Mother would say if she knew a man had given it to me, and particularly if later that man dropped me. I could not face such humiliation. The less said the less humiliation there would be.

He was there, waiting for me, joking with Norm and Doris, all dressed up in creased navy blue. He whistled when he saw me. I had not been able to see myself in the dress, because we lacked a long mirror.

Doris said, 'Golly, you look nice, Helen!'

I looked across at myself in the long ballroom mirror and knew that I looked good. And I felt good, more sure of myself. The girl in the mirror was much as I had imagined myself growing up to be, if disaster had not struck the family first. I had agonised over having to wear black shoes and carry a black handbag with a tan dress, but they were an elegant contrast.

We danced and we danced until the end of the evening, oblivious of anyone else. He looked less weary and I was so happy.

Afterwards, five or six of us stood in the misty moonlight outside the front door, chatting casually. I was carrying my walking shoes, meaning to go home in my dancing shoes. Harry offered to put the shoes in his raincoat pocket – there was no doubt that I was going to be escorted home this time.

One of the girls laughed, looking at my satin-clad feet. 'Goin' to dance home?' she asked.

'I could dance all night,' I replied lightly, glancing up at Harry. 'I could dance the length of the avenue.'

'Get away, now.'

I laughed. 'Bet I could.'

'Bet *we* could,' said Harry, joining in the laughter, and he put his arm round me and, whistling a slow waltz, he turned me away from the cheerful little group, and we danced away down the pavement.

I was shyly quiet in the warmth of his arms. The other young people called, 'Ta-ra, well. Enjoy yourselves,' and their voices faded as they walked in the other direction.

'I'd like you to meet some of my friends,' Harry remarked, as we danced to our own peculiar music down the empty avenue. 'I've a few old friends, mostly married, round Bootle.'

'I'd like that very much,' I said.

'We'll do it next time I'm home. They're more like your kind of people than that bunch are.'

I was no longer sure what my kind of people were, so I did not answer. But I felt that any friend of his was likely to be pleasant to know.

Only the sound of our shifting feet broke the silence. I was afloat in happiness. There was no beginning to life and no end, only the perfect now in the arms of a semi-stranger who meant everything to me, a stranger who was already planning to introduce me to his friends, take me into his life.

Halfway down the avenue he stopped, and holding me tightly, lifted my face and kissed me, a kind of kiss I had never imagined and I never wanted to stop. But he did stop it with a quick sigh, and a resumption of our slow progress, while all kinds of wild and wonderful feelings raced through my slender body.

'Love, I know this is too quick. But I want to marry you, if you'll have me – soon as I can get a house ready to put you in safe and sound.' He ignored my gasp, and went on, 'I'm askin' you now, because I'm away so much that I could lose you to somebody else.'

I was struck dumb, and he urged, as he stopped dancing again, 'Be my girl – I'll never let you down, I promise. I've always wanted a wife like you – someone I could really talk to – and so pretty.'

'Are you sure, Harry?'

He laughed. 'I know a good thing when I see it.'

'Then of course I will. I can't think of anything I would like better. And I'll try to be a good wife – I know how to keep house – and, oh, Harry, I want to make you happy.'

Instinctively, I lifted my hand from his shoulder and touched the tired face, and whispered, 'I love you.'

'My girl – my little Miss Helen!' He swung me off my feet in a happy whirl, and then we went on dancing, dancing down the avenue into the Liverpool mist.

# Lime Street at Two

The generals, the institution can
select a strategy, lay it all out,
but what happens on the battlefield
is quite different.
  *Count Lev Nikolaevich Tolstoy 1828–1910*

*To my husband*

# Chapter one

The huge clock still hangs in Lime Street station, Liverpool, and marks a convenient spot for travellers to be met. During World War II, almost every girl in Liverpool must have written to a serviceman coming home on leave, 'I'll meet you under the clock at Lime Street.' There were always women there, dressed in their shabby best, hair long, curled and glossy, pacing nervously under that indifferent timepiece. Every time a train chugged in, they would glance anxiously at the ticket collectors' wickets, while round them swirled other civilians, and hordes of men and women in uniform, khaki, Navy blue, or Air Force blue, staggering under enormous packs and kitbags. Some men wore foreign uniforms, with shoulder flashes of refugee armies, navies and air forces. No matter who they were, they all shared the same expression of deep fatigue.

This huge vortex of uprooted humanity was supervised by stolid-looking military police standing like rocks against a tide. Some of them were American Snowdrops, so nicknamed because of their white helmets. Occasionally a single English civilian policeman stood out amongst all the other uniforms, a reminder of peacetime and sanity, when a quiet, 'Now move along there, please,' was enough to reduce a pushing crowd to order.

The station may be rebuilt, the generations pass, but the ghosts are still there, ghosts of lovers, husbands, sons, withered like flowers on distant battlefields long forgotten, and of mothers, wives and sweethearts long since dead. Amongst those kindly shades stands Harry O'Dwyer, the fiancé of my youth, a ship's engineer, lost at sea in 1940.

I do not know how I got through that dreadful summer of 1940, after the news of Harry's death, or the long, hopeless year of 1941. It was a period when the Merchant Navy was decimated by German submarines and aircraft. Once a man was at sea, there was not a moment when he was not in acute danger. Over the bar, in Liverpool Bay, the U-boats waited, like cats at a mousehole, for the slow, ill-defended freighters entering and leaving the ports of Liverpool and Birkenhead. If they survived the submarines, they could strike acoustic mines, magnetic mines and other menaces plopping about in the heaving waters.

Even snugly moored in dock, ships were often the target in air raids; and the homes of their crews, packed in the dockside areas, were frequently destroyed.

I lived within a mile of the south docks, with my father and mother, four brothers and two sisters. I was the eldest child. We were a most unhappy family, our lives fraught with the bitter quarrels of our parents, and our considerable penury.

When I was a child we had lived in comfortable circumstances, but in 1930, my father had gone bankrupt, as a result of the Depression. In an effort to find employment, Father had brought us to Liverpool, his birthplace. Like most of the people living in the south of England, he had no notion of the horrifying effect of the Depression in the north. The unemployment rate was 33 per cent and there was almost no hope of work. We had sunk into an abyss of poverty, which I have described in earlier books. By 1940, however, we had begun to climb out of the pit into which we had fallen, though we were still very poor.

My parents were still filled with the public school snobbery of their youth, so I had told them nothing of my engagement to Harry O'Dwyer. They would have immediately condemned such a union as beneath me. Harry was from a respectable Irish working-class family and a Roman Catholic, originally intended by his family to be a priest. Since I was a Protestant, we had agreed to be married quietly in a registry office soon after I was twenty-one, when I would not need my parents' consent. Harry had bought a little house, which was not quite complete when he was killed. I was twenty-one years and two months old when his mother told me of his death, under the very odd circumstances that she did not know she was talking to her son's fiancée.

In 1940, I was a neophyte social worker in Bootle, a small town sharing a common boundary with Liverpool. It was a Roman Catholic area tightly packed with overcrowded terrace houses, factories and timber yards, hedged in by the docks along the river. Though the poverty was very great, Harry was proud to say that he was a Bootle man; men had sailed from Bootle since the Anglians settled there in AD 613, and perhaps even before that.

One morning in August, our waiting-room at the office was packed with the widows of men lost at sea, who wished to seek our advice regarding claiming pensions. Among them sat Harry's mother, long since estranged from him because he had refused to enter the Church. She was now bent on benefiting from his death by claiming a pension. I thought I would faint when she explained her business, and I quickly referred her to my colleague, Miss Evans. Then, deserting the waiting crowd, I fled to the unused cellars of the old house in which the office lay, and there in the clammy grime of a disused coal cellar, I stood shivering helplessly, so filled with shock that I hardly knew where I was. When, after a few minutes, my mind cleared a little, I was nauseated at a woman who could order her son out of their home because of a religious difference, and yet could coolly try to get a pension at his death.

I heard Miss Evans calling me and automatically I ran back up the stone steps. She met me on the upper staircase and scolded me for leaving clients waiting. Like a zombie, I moved to obey her orders. I did not cry.

I did not want to know this cold, grasping woman, Harry's mother, nor did I say anything to my own parents; there was no point in facing their probable derision at such a humble marriage. I could almost hear their cultured voices ripping apart a man I had loved dearly, and I could not bear that they should do it.

Somehow, I kept my mouth shut, but the unexpressed grief was like a corrosive at work inside me. It caused such damage that I never truly recovered from it. In a body made frail by much illness and, at times, near starvation, it worked its will. In a character already very introspective from childhood, filled with fear of grown-ups, its effect was devastating.

As a little child, I learned early that my parents were simply not interested in me, and that I had to face all the fears of childhood alone. As a young adult, I continued that early attitude of solitary suffering, and it was reinforced by the loss of the one person I trusted implicitly.

Though I did not consider it at the time, I had lots of fellow sufferers and, as a social worker employed by a charity working in the dock areas, I had to help to look after them. Our waiting-room was daily filled by rows of weeping mothers and wives; every ship that went down seemed to have a Bootle man aboard. My mind is filled with memories of the overwhelmed resources of our little office, when the *Athenia*, the *Courageous*, the battle-ship *Royal Oak*, and hundreds of others, big and small, were lost in 1940 and 1941.

Sometimes the position was reversed, and a seaman's family was lost in an air raid.

My senior, Miss Evans, and I often faced a stony-eyed or openly weeping merchant seaman or a serviceman, sent home on compassionate leave because his home had been bombed and his family killed. Commanding officers did not always tell them why they were to go home. A few would go straight to their house, see the wreckage and realise what had happened. But quite a number reported directly to our office, as instructed by their commanding officer, and we would have to break the news to them. Because extended families frequently lived in adjoining streets, a man could find himself left with only a badly injured infant in hospital, and neither sister, aunt nor mother left alive to help him to care for the baby.

These heart-rending cases intensified my own sorrow to such a degree that I could not bear it any longer, and I decided I must try to obtain other work. Not only was I grief-stricken, I was also hungry. The salary that the charity was able to pay me was so small that I could not even afford lunch; I was poorer than most of the clients who thronged our waiting-room.

# Chapter two

Even in 1940, there was much unemployment in Liverpool, and the competition for any job was still very keen. At first, when the war began, the number of unemployed was increased by firms going out of business as a result of the war. For example, my mother, so acid-tongued at home, used her superior-sounding Oxford accent to good effect as the representative of a greetings card firm. The company was suddenly faced with an acute paper shortage, and, in order to remain in business, they had to turn to printing products essential to the war effort; they did not need a sales force. Mother, by this time very experienced and quite nicely dressed, soon found a new job as an accountant in a bakery.

Girls like me, however, were in direct competition with a large population bulge made up of babies born after the servicemen came home from World War I. We were now in our early twenties.

Though by this time I was a skilled shorthand typist, as well as having had experience in social work, I was turned down again and again when I applied for secretarial posts.

The supercilious head clerks and typing pool supervisors looked me over as if I were a horse up for sale, often asked the most impertinent questions and always demanded references as to my moral character. They also asked about my education, and I had to own up that I had had only four years in school.

'Why?' they would snap suspiciously. 'Were you ill?' and I would have to reply that my parents had kept me at home from the age of eleven, in order that I might keep house for my parents and my six younger brothers and sisters; it was essential to impress on them that I was extremely healthy, because no employer would consider a person who might miss days of work through ill-health.

They looked disdainfully at a sheaf of evening school certificates showing high marks, and then would often change the subject by making disparaging remarks about my poor appearance.

I could not help the way I looked. My complexion was a pimpled white from insufficient food. My homecut hair hung lankly from lack of soap. In spite of working days and evenings, I could not earn enough to dress myself properly, even in second-hand clothes. When I could manage it, I bought little tins of Snowfire make-up from Woolworth's at threepence a tin, to improve my looks, but often enough the expense was too great for my limited funds. I was neatly shabby to the point of beautifully stitched patches on patches, darns on darns.

Seventeen shillings and sixpence a week, which was what I earned, was only two shillings and sixpence more than I would have received on unemployment pay. Before I received my wages, deductions were made by my employer for National Health and Unemployment Insurance and for hospital care. The remainder was demanded of me by Mother. In those days, many mothers believed that they owned not only their daughters, but also everything their children earned, and my mother was no exception.

Money for my own expenses was earned in the evenings, by teaching shorthand to pupils in their homes.

I always fell into a panic when I lost a pupil, because it often meant that I had no tram fares and must walk the five miles to work in Bootle, through quite dangerous slums. In winter, the walk had to be done in the dead dark of the wartime blackout.

Mother was not prepared to help me. She had at that time no intention of ever being a full-time housewife herself. Before Father went bankrupt, she had always been able to afford help with the children, had never had to care for them herself. She used every pressure she could think of to make it impossible for me to work, so that I would stay at home and be a free housekeeper. Even during the time that my younger brothers and sisters, Brian, Tony, Avril and Edward, were evacuated, she nagged and made my life a misery on this subject, presumably in order to have me ready at home to care for the children when the war ended. This remorseless battle between us had gone on for years, but I had always refused to give in.

I was quite sympathetic about Mother's preference to go to work, but I never could see why I should have to shoulder the burden of her responsibilities and become, once more, an unpaid, unrespected slavey to an uncaring bunch of siblings and two indifferent parents.

Perhaps Mother's lifetime repression of me had become a habit and closed her mind to the possibilities of other domestic arrangements. I knew from infancy that my very existence was a trial to her – she had always made that point extremely clear to me – and I tended to apologise continually to her as if I had no right to live.

Some time back, when, because of her callous attitude towards me, I had nearly suffered a nervous breakdown, she had become suddenly afraid; mental instability was much feared as a dreadful blot on a family's reputation. She promised she would treat me exactly as she did my pretty, compliant sister, Fiona, the third child of the family, now aged eighteen. Until I could command a better wage, she promised, she would take from me only about seven shillings a week, which would cover amply the food I ate.

She soon forgot her promise and fell into a series of tremendous rages, until I again gave up all my wages.

Fiona, three years younger than me, earned the same amount as I did, but the money was, in practice, left with her for her expenses and clothing, as was often done in middle-class families. She always looked well dressed.

Alan, the brother next to me in age, was in the Air Force. Out of the miserable fourteen shillings a week which he was paid, he allotted seven shillings to my mother. I felt that this, also, was pressing too hard on someone who had very little. I was unwise enough to say so, and Mother blew up like a time bomb.

'It's the only way in which I can claim a government pension, if he is killed,' she stormed.

As far as I was concerned, this remark put her into the same cold-hearted category as Harry's mother.

Before he was killed, Harry, my fiancé, had been on several voyages to New York, and at different times had brought me three very nice dresses from the Manhattan garment district. Anxious not to give an indication that I was engaged, I had told Mother that I had bought them in a second-hand store. Together with a pair of satin slippers, bought for my Confirmation and subsequently dyed black, the frocks enabled me to look appropriately dressed when I went to a local dancing club. Mother and Fiona often borrowed them. Since both of them were bigger than me, the seams were now showing signs of splitting.

Despite Mother's ruthlessness, from the spring of 1940 I had endured my lot more philosophically. I would be twenty-one in June and would marry Harry in the summer, when he hoped to have earned enough to furnish his house with the essentials, so that we could move into it.

Now I was alone again and so distressed that I believe that sometimes I was out of my mind. I would cry as I walked home through the darkness, and often cried through the night, while Fiona slept contentedly on the other side of the bed, and poor little Avril, aged twelve, squirmed uncomfortably between us.

One very hungry day, I inquired at the Employment Exchange about joining the Wrens, the naval service. I saw myself trim and smart in the navy blue uniform and tricorn hat of an officer.

The clerk told me sharply that, with my qualifications, I might get into the A.T.S., the women's service attached to the Army; they needed kitchen help and drivers. I could not drive, and my present work demanded more skill than cooking for the Army, so I turned down this suggestion.

Feeling crushed and lonely, that evening I spent an extravagant shilling and went to the dance club, where I had first met Harry; I craved warm, friendly people round me.

Norm, the owner, had a new record of 'In the Mood' on his wind-up gramophone, and over the cheerful noise of it, he greeted me genially.

At first those dancers who had known Harry and me were a little shy about asking me on to the floor. When they discovered that I was not going to weep for him on the padded shoulders of their best suits, I was never short of a partner. They were nearly all skilled workmen, for the moment exempt from military service; they were earning bigger wages than they had ever enjoyed before and had money to spend.

As a joke, I mimicked the pompous clerk in the Employment Exchange, who had so mortified me when I asked about joining the Wrens. A group of us were waiting for Norm to change the record, and the men gravely assured me that for a girl to join the Services was a fate worse than death.

With eyes averted, one man said, 'It's not suited to a nice girl like you. You'd have a rotten time.'

Another said with a grin, 'Nice girls don't leave home; they stay close to their mams.' He nodded towards his friends, and added, 'When these lads get into uniform it brings out their tomcat instincts; regular tigers, they are.' He exchanged playful punches with the others, and the conversation became ribald, so I left them. Truly, I thought, there is no one so conservative, small c, as a skilled craftsman. I trusted them enough, however, to feel that I should keep on trying for work as a civilian.

One of Harry's acquaintances escorted me home, and left me politely on my doorstep.

During that night, as I lay sleepless, I think I began to realise that I could not live my life alone, and that I hoped to meet someone a long time in the future, who would fill the frightful gap in my life. I was used to a large family round me. Homes were, indeed, more crowded in those days. Sometimes there was a grandparent or other relation living with a married couple with children, and a lodger or two; single men frequently rented a room and were boarded by their landlady, who sometimes became the target of malicious tongues. Elderly women, widowed or single, occasionally doubled up and also endured the disparaging remarks of their neighbours, in these cases with regard to their sexual preferences. The concept of birth control was barely beginning to penetrate the densely populated area in which I lived; and in Bootle, a Roman Catholic district, it was almost unknown and, in consequence, families were huge.

If I could keep myself, I thought rather pitifully, one of my brothers, when they married, might allow me to live with him, if I were still single. At least then I would have some male protection. In the meantime, it was necessary for me to earn sufficient to satisfy my mother, and have enough left over to buy a decent lunch each day, pay tram fares, clothe myself and, if possible, put away something for my old age. I rarely dreamed of anything more, except to be able to go to a dance or to the theatre occasionally. The idea of holidays or of buying books, pictures or music never entered my head – they were untold luxuries.

During the following few weeks, kind, familiar faces began to vanish with alarming rapidity from the dance club. Though many members were exempt from military service, Ernest Bevin, the Minister of Labour and leader of the powerful Transport and General Workers' Union, was redirecting skilled manpower to war production, often in other parts of the country. The men's places on the dance floor were taken by soldiers from the nearby barracks, and they brought in women picked up from the streets. These new members of the club were harder for the owners, Norm and Doris, to control; they were transients with no local reputation to maintain.

Very shortly after, a tight-lipped and disapproving Norm and Doris announced the closure of the club. They would both go to work in a munition factory and would reopen their business after the war. Their dancing shoes were put away and they passed out of my life, two kind people who believed in a certain standard of conduct and refused to deviate from it.

It was only when I saw the hastily scrawled note pinned on the dusty black door, *Closed for the duration*, that I realised how much I had depended upon the club for company. Because it was so late before I got home from work, it had been my sole source of social life, except for occasional visits to the Playhouse theatre with a friend called Sylvia Poole.

After reading the note, I stood looking up at the door with its blistered paint and soot-covered portico, and I felt again, for a moment, the same scarifying loneliness of my first days in Liverpool as a child of eleven.

A savage air raid was in progress, but, despite the whistling bombs, I had, on my way home from work, crossed the double width of the parallel boulevards of Princes Road and Princes Avenue, to look once more at the old house where I had first met Harry. It had brought me such intense, though short-lived happiness. A greenish flare, dropped by a German bomber, lit up every detail of its simple, graceful architecture and gave it an almost dreamlike air.

'Goodbye, youth. Goodbye, happiness,' I muttered bitterly, as amid hissing flak I crossed back over the road and the avenue, and went home to face the inner loneliness, the sense of being lost, which is the lot of the bereaved.

I wanted to die.

# Chapter three

Alan had been in the Air Force since July, 1939, and I missed him very much. I did not see much of Fiona, who came next after Alan in the family. She worked as a clerk in a magazine distributor's office and had a number of men friends who took her out in the evenings to dinners, dances or the cinema. My parents rarely spoke, except to quarrel. The four younger children, Brian, now aged seventeen, Tony, aged fourteen, Avril, twelve, and Edward, aged nine, had in August, 1939, been evacuated to the country for safety, but early in 1940 Mother brought them home again, because the government had demanded a modest financial contribution to their upkeep while they were away.

Brian finished school that year, and went to work for a shipping agent in the city. He also joined the City Police A.R.P. Messenger Service, a group of boys with bicycles who, when the telephone lines were blown down during air raids, acted as messengers between hospitals, police, air raid wardens and rescue squads, and rest centres for the homeless. Father used a bicycle to get to work, and Brian borrowed the machine at night.

On their return to Liverpool, the youngsters faced almost immediately four sharp, frightening air raids. No damage was done in our district.

I had suggested to Mother that, with the fall of France, it would be easier for the Germans to bomb the north of England, and perhaps we should leave at least the younger children in the country, where they were being fairly well looked after by my father's sisters and, in the case of Avril, by a friend of my aunts. Mother would not hear of it; it was cheaper to bring them home.

Now she said to me, 'See, the Germans are only interested in bombing the north end of the docks. We are quite safe, down here at the south end.'

I held my tongue.

Fortunately for our children, the government had reopened the city schools. At the beginning of the war they had been closed, because their teachers had to accompany the evacuees to the country. Some children, however, were never evacuated; they ran wild in the streets, and vandalism and theft became widespread. When the trickle of children returning from evacuation became a torrent, many teachers were recalled, and the small predators went back to learning to read and write.

It says a great deal for the dedication of the teachers at that time that despite the upheavals in their own lives and the dislocation of being evacuated, they managed to teach Tony and Edward well enough for them to win scholarships to grammar school. This made it possible, later on, for both boys to gain university degrees.

Nobody seemed to give much attention to little blonde Avril, the second youngest member of our family. She was only a girl, equally frightened of being re-evacuated and of the air raids. In a chaotic world, she plodded on through elementary school as best she could.

The return of the children made Mother reopen, yet again, the question of my giving up my work and staying home to look after them.

As I washed the dishes and she dried them, she said without preamble, 'Now the children are back, Helen, I expect you to stay at home. You can give your notice in on Friday.'

The idea of keeping a daughter permanently at home, often denying her marriage, died hard. But I felt I had endured enough in my early teens when I had been forced to keep house and, as the housekeeper who did not have to go to work, found myself reduced to a point bordering on starvation – the workers were fed and clothed first, the children next, and the woman at home was often left with nothing.

I did not, at first, answer Mother. This was before Harry's death and I was buoyed up by the thought that in a very few months, I would have only a loving husband to care for.

'I don't think it is necessary, Mother,' I replied carefully. 'Couldn't we manage the house between us? I'm getting good training as a social worker – it should lead to something better.'

Mother put the last pile of plates on to the kitchen shelf, while I emptied the washing-up bowl. She said scornfully, 'You'll get nowhere without a degree, so what's the use?' She glanced impatiently round the tiny, stone-tiled kitchen, with its greasy deal table, and sandstone sink with a solitary cold water tap. 'Now, where are my curling tongs?'

'On the mantelpiece in the living room,' I replied mechanically, and I followed her into it, as I shook out the wet tea towel, ready to hang it to dry on the oven door of the old-fashioned range. The range took up nearly the whole of one wall of the room, and I noticed that its iron frontage badly needed blackleading.

Mother found her tongs and thrust them into the fire, and I silently draped the tea towel over the oven door. While the tongs were heating, she combed her hair quickly, in front of a piece of mirror balanced on the mantelpiece.

'You know very well we can't manage, Helen,' she began again. 'It was difficult enough to manage when the children were evacuated.'

'They're not babies any more, Mother. They could all help. Brian and Tony are big enough to queue in the shops, or even help with the cleaning. Or why can't Fiona take a turn at keeping house?'

'Fiona is too frail – and she doesn't know how. And boys can't do domestic work. How stupid can you be?'

'Well, why can't they?'

Mother paused with hot tongs poised to make a curl at the side of her face. She said angrily, 'Helen, you are being impudent. When I say you are to do a thing, you do it, my girl.'

'No, Mother,' I responded with unusual temerity. 'I am not staying home again.'

I thought Mother was going to strike me with the hot tongs, and I stepped back hastily.

'Don't talk to me like that. I won't have such nonsense. I'll talk to your employer. I'll have you dismissed.' Her face flushed with anger, and she seized a piece of her hair and rolled it on the tongs, as if she were about to pull it out.

I was scared. I had no idea what the ladies at work might do, if approached by an angry mother. They might very well agree to let me go to get rid of a shouting harridan on their doorstep. Mother saw her chance in my frightened face, and she pointed the tongs at me, and said, 'You have to learn, my lady, the facts of life. You can't choose what you want to do. You have to do what I say.'

How I wished Harry was there. I would have turned and run to him, begged him to find me a place to shelter until we could marry; it was, after all, only a little while until we would be married. But Harry was at sea. I thought of Father, the weaker parent, and burst out, 'I think we should talk about this with Father.'

But Mother was not listening. She was ranting about feckless daughters and how she would be worked to death, as she continued feverishly to put curls in her hair. Occasionally, she would pause in her endeavours to shake the tongs at me, as I stood like a paralysed rabbit in front of her.

I was saved by Edward's coming in. He had fallen down and grazed his knees. They were bleeding and I took him into the kitchen to wash them, while Mother went upstairs to find a piece of old sheeting we kept for bandages.

By the time we had mopped up the blood and the tears, it was time for Mother to go to the cinema, and with a sharp, 'I'll talk to you later,' she put on her hat and coat and shot out of the house. I was left to put Avril and Edward to bed and to wonder whether I should, perhaps, just capitulate, and leave when I married.

We might have been able to afford a little help in the house, between all of us, but my parents were great fritterers of money. They both smoked heavily, and my father drank. There was always money for Mother to go to the cinema, which she did twice a week at least; always money to buy, for show, a piece of furniture for the sitting-room, paid for on the hire purchase system, a most expensive way to buy anything; money for clothes for Mother and Fiona. But there was never enough for good, plain food, for coal, blankets, soap, for underwear for the younger children. We were always short of necessities, and I knew from experience that, made to stay at home, I could be the most deprived person of all.

A beshawled neighbour of whom I had once asked the time, because our single clock had stopped, had said to me disparagingly, ''Asn't your dad got a watch? All lace curtains and nothin' in the larder, that's your mam and dad.' And she had sighed, as she looked me up and down.

A scared waif of a girl, I had not known how to answer her, so I had hung my head and shuffled away with Baby Edward in his squeaking pram.

Whenever Mother was short of ready money, she would collect any spare clothing lying about or some of our sparse bedding, and pawn it. Because I took great care of my few clothes, it was the shelf in the girls' bedroom which was first raided.

I was frequently reduced to the clothes I had on, and then had to save up, penny by penny, to retrieve the rest from Uncle Joe, the pawnbroker.

It was a game I could not win. Years later, however, I bought very cheaply a chest of drawers which had been badly seared by fire. A kindly man friend, aware of the problem, made a key to fit the old-fashioned locks on the drawers. Mother had one of her bigger tantrums on the subject of these locks, and she immediately demanded a key. I refused her, and carried the single key threaded on a piece of string round my neck, with Harry's ring.

When I heard from Harry's mother that he had been killed, I was devastated not only by grief, but, in the background of my pain, also by the knowledge that I had lost my sole defence against my mother. As my friends in the dance club had sharply reminded me, nice girls did not leave home – they might have added, except, of course, to be married.

Sometimes, in those early weeks after Harry's death and after the row I had had with Mother about being the family housekeeper, I would stand behind the high shelves of files in the office of the charity for which I worked, and hold my head, while I shivered helplessly. Father had tried to act as peacemaker between Mother and me, by saying we should first try if we could manage without someone at home. Mother had reluctantly agreed, but she continued to nag at me about it. I wondered if between sorrow and Mother and hunger, I would go mad. Then I would renew my efforts to find better-paid work. At least, I thought, that might settle the problem of being always hungry.

# Chapter four

Mother had many small ways of trying to make it impossible for me to go to work. One was to pilfer any money I had, so that I had no tram fares for the five-mile journey to Bootle where lay the office of the charity which employed me.

I kept a close eye on my handbag, but sometimes not close enough. I also tried secreting tram fares in the bedroom which I shared with Fiona and Avril, but a room furnished only with a double bed, a single shelf and no floor covering does not offer many hiding places. Several times, I put a week's fares up the chimney, getting very sooty in the process, but she either found the money herself or, perhaps, Fiona mentioned it to her as an idiosyncrasy of mine.

Fiona was always *asked* if she would lend money and always wailed miserably that she had none. Her ability to burst into floods of tears, her gorgeous light blue eyes welling up piteously, always defeated Mother, whereas my verbal fury merely bred acidity in return.

A few weeks after Harry's death, of which, of course, Mother knew nothing, she had done one of her lightning swoops on my belongings and had pawned them. The blouse and underwear which I had been wearing that day had to be washed and dried overnight, ready to put on the next morning. In a world where washers and dryers had not yet been heard of, this meant putting on damp clothing every morning. Frequently there was no washing powder or soap, so my white blouse had, in Liverpool's polluted air, become grey.

It was some time before I managed to save up two shillings (ten pence in today's money) in order to redeem a change of garments from my old friend, the pawnbroker.

The only method of saving which I could think of was to walk most of the way to and from work. My two shorthand pupils paid me one shilling and sixpence a lesson, but I had recently lost one of them when I tried to increase my charge to two shillings. To get another one, I would have to advertise in the *Liverpool Echo* or *Evening Express*, and I had yet to find the money for that.

At the same time, as the Battle of Britain progressed, air raids became frequent.

The raids usually began about six o'clock in the evening and lasted until eleven or twelve. It was everybody's ambition to be safely at home, or wherever they were going to be in the evening, before the air raid warning howled its miserable notes across the waiting city. This was usually an impossibility for me, because, as the raids gained in intensity and the bombed-out sought our aid, the load of work in the office increased proportionately.

We worked later and later. My colleague, on whom devolved the ultimate responsibility for the office, looked ever more careworn; her skin was pasty from lack of fresh air and her eyes black-rimmed. She was a wonderfully caring person who gave of herself unsparingly to our distraught clients.

The five miles to work seemed to take a lifetime to walk. I went down the hill and through the city, and out again, along Byrom Street, Scotland Road and the eternity of Stanley Road, through some of Liverpool's worst, festering slums. Like many English people who commonly travelled long and inconvenient distances by public transport to their employment, I arrived already very tired. Because roads were blocked by fallen debris or railways were out of commission, many others beside myself were forced to walk. A walk which I would have cheerfully undertaken, however, if it had been necessitated by an air raid, depressed me beyond measure because it was totally unnecessary.

Only people who have had to walk without a torch or cycle without a lamp through the total darkness of a blackout can appreciate the hazards of it. Innumerable cats and dogs trotted silently through it, to be tripped over by cursing pedestrians; pillar boxes and fire hydrants, telephone poles and light standards, parked bicycles and the occasional parked car, not to speak of one's fellow pedestrians, all presented pitfalls for the unwary. Many times I went home with a bloody nose or with torn stockings and bleeding knees from having tripped up. Another problem was the ease with which one could lose one's way; it was simple to become disoriented while crossing a road or a square and end up on the wrong pavement, hopelessly lost.

A new hazard appeared later in the war, and was the cause of Father's having a painful fall, when the batteries of his flashlight failed. Lack of sufficient water pressure to douse the fires raised by incendiaries had necessitated the laying of extra water pipes directly from the river. The pipes ran along the street gutters or the edge of the pavements, and even in the daytime, people occasionally fell over these unaccustomed barriers. Father, one night, tripped over a newly laid pipe and bruised himself badly. He lay on the pavement in the dark, too shaken to get up, until he heard footsteps approaching.

He cried for help, and was immediately answered by a male voice. He was located, helped up and asked about his injuries. Father said that he was all right, that the fright of the fall had given him heart pains which had now ebbed.

'I'm lost, however,' he said.

The stranger asked his address, and Father told him it.

'Oh, that's easy. I'll have you home in a couple of shakes,' promised the man. 'Put your arm in mine.'

'Have *you* a torch?' inquired Father, very puzzled at his rescuer's self-assurance in the total darkness.

The stranger laughed. 'I don't need a light,' he said. 'I'm blind. Didn't you hear my stick on the pavement?'

'No, I didn't,' Father answered. 'Do you think we could find my spectacles? They fell off, as I went down. They must be just here somewhere.'

The stick was used to sweep the pavement round them, and the spectacles, fortunately unbroken, were returned to their owner. A very grateful Father was safely deposited on his own doorstep by a man who, in ordinary circumstances, would have been regarded as seriously handicapped.

Bearing in mind the distances I often had to walk, it was as well that I had inherited my mother's stamina, if not her temperament; even so, the strain was very great.

In the safe knowledge that no one could see me, I would stumble along in the dark, weeping openly, and wishing I was dead. Yet, when a stick of bombs began to fall nearby, and the whistle of each succeeding missile became closer, I would instinctively duck for shelter in the nearest shop doorway and crouch down, hands clasped over head, until the last resounding bang. I discovered that to survive is a fundamental instinct of all living things, and in such situations instinct takes over.

Sometimes the planes would dive fast, one after another, and other pedestrians would dash pell-mell into my refuge, to huddle tightly round me, like sheep in a storm, until the danger had retreated. Then, with shy apologies and light jokes directed to unseen faces, we would issue forth again into the street.

While we sheltered, the blackness was occasionally lit by the unearthly green glow of flares floating slowly in the sky, while the Germans tried to locate their specific targets. For a moment we would see fellow shelterers in the greatest detail, and all of us would feel naked and helplessly exposed to our enemies in the sky. The flares and bursts of tracer bullets were in one way useful, however, because they gave us a sufficiently good view of our route that, when we all set out again, we were less likely to have a fall.

The flares also showed up A.R.P. messenger boys racing recklessly along on their bicycles; regardless of danger, they sped from air raid wardens' posts, to hospitals, to fire stations and rescue squads, wherever a message needed to be delivered. Most of the boys were under seventeen years of age, too young for military service; yet nightly they took chances which even the military would have considered risky.

Motor traffic crawled along with heavily shaded lights; ambulances and fire engines rang their bells continuously.

Lorry drivers, tram and bus drivers normally kept going until a raid was overhead, when they would park and take refuge in the nearest shelter. There were few private cars on the streets, because of petrol rationing; those out at night were, for the most part, carrying walking casualties, rescue squads, tradesmen like telephone men and electricians, air raid wardens and medical personnel. More than one vehicle ended up in an unsuspected bomb crater in the middle of a road, the driver and passengers killed or injured.

So when my mother riffled through my handbag with her tobacco-stained fingers, to take my fare money, she created cruel hardship for me, and it was not only for my lost love that I wept.

# Chapter five

When attacking convoys, particularly at night, the Germans began to use packs of U-boats working in unison, rather than single submarines. Although the escort ships of the convoys now had a listening device, called Asdic, with which they could detect the presence of submarines, the noise of the convoy itself often confused the listeners and made it difficult to identify a submarine with certainty. It was also ineffective if the U-boat was on the surface.

To avoid the Asdic device, the U-boat commanders would come up steeply into the middle of a convoy, and, in a few moments, create havoc. Then, still on the surface, they would race away into the darkness, outrunning the escorting corvettes.

Once my first grief over Harry's death had become more controllable, I again began to feel very deeply for the frantic mothers and wives of merchant seamen and Royal Navy men, alike, who died during September, October and November of 1940. The women threatened to overwhelm our little office, with its limited resources.

During one dreadful Saturday morning, when weeping women stood in the waiting-room because all the chairs were full, and queued along the passageway and stairs, I was so distressed that something seemed to break inside me, and I cried out in fury to a startled voluntary worker, 'It's madness to send men to certain death like this!'

The words rang through the crowded, untidy room, and all the voluntary workers stopped their bustle and turned to stare at me. My weary colleague, Miss Evans, seated at her desk at the hub of the turmoil, put her hand over the mouthpiece of the telephone, and said sharply, 'Miss Forrester!'

In the ensuing dead silence, I mumbled, 'I'm sorry.'

I snatched up a pile of files and began feverishly to put them back on their open shelves, my fury unassuageable. The tears coursed down my cheeks. Why couldn't seamen have enough sense to stay ashore? I raged inwardly. Most of them had skills which would have given them protected jobs in war factories. On the other hand, Harry had said that, if he had come ashore, he would have been called up, sooner or later, for the Army or the Navy; he might just as well remain a merchant seaman, and earn better wages.

Based on my utter frustration, a dull anger at Harry surged in me. He was old enough not to be amongst the first to be conscripted. We could have been married by now and had some happiness together; I could have been carrying his much desired baby. The fool! The stupid idiot, to go and get himself killed! I was terribly, unreasonably furious at him.

In those wild moments, I gave no thought to the fact that unless freighters went to sea, to carry on the country's trade, we would soon starve. I also forgot that, though Harry often complained about the conditions under which seamen lived aboard ship, basically he enjoyed going to sea; like everyone else, he hoped the war would soon be over. Few civilians knew enough of the true situation to realise that it was bound to drag on for years. Wars are very easily started; the problem is in bringing them to a close.

Now Harry was gone, and I had not the faintest idea what to do, as I struggled to help women equally distressed. My mind refused to concentrate; my body longed for rest, preferably eternal rest. Normally I was always hungry; now I sometimes found it difficult to eat.

Even Mother noticed my unusual dullness and told me to stop looking so sulky. 'Laugh and the world laughs with you,' she would say, so truly, 'Cry, and you cry alone.'

It's easier for her, I would think sullenly. She's doing quite nicely now. I forgot that she had been through an earlier war, a war which had been in many ways much worse.

'Why aren't you going dancing?' Fiona asked. I looked at her blankly for a moment, and then replied, 'I'm too tired – the office is so busy.'

I don't think that Father noticed anything much. He tended to live a life of his own amongst his friends from the office; Mother never accompanied him either to the public houses or to the concerts and plays to which he went. Sometimes he would inquire of Tony or Brian what they were doing in their spare time. Not infrequently, he had a tremendous row with Mother, usually on the subject of money.

He may possibly have noticed that, at that time, I was not quarrelling much with Mother, and consequently the house was quieter. I was too exhausted to face her verbal barbs, and no matter what she did, I accepted it and did my best to cope with the consequences.

On the Saturday on which I had exclaimed so explosively in the office about the lunacy of the war, I worked all day, and arrived home just as Mother was putting on her retrimmed, turban-type hat before going to the cinema. She was peeking at herself in the broken piece of mirror on the mantelpiece. It was still the only mirror in the house and was consequently very precious. During the war, mirrors were hard to obtain.

She nodded to me, buckled up the belt of her leather overcoat and picked up her handbag. 'Back at eleven,' she threw over her shoulder, as she went through the back door.

As I took off my own coat, I listened to the click-click of her high-heeled shoes on the stone flags of the back alley. I remembered how, as a child, I would lie in bed after Edith, our nanny, had tucked me up, every limb tensed, eyes screwed tight in case those clicking heels came upstairs. Nothing made her crosser than to find that Alan and I had failed to go to sleep promptly at six o'clock. An extremely nervous child, I was afraid of the dark, afraid of the flickering shadows made by the candle which Edith always left on the dresser, but, most of all, I was afraid of my stormy mother.

While I put together a meal for myself, Father leaned back in his chair and closed his eyes. It was a habit he had acquired after a heart attack which he had suffered at the age of thirty-three. Now, he was dozing while he waited for the arrival of his friend, Tom, a schoolteacher, still in his late twenties. Before Tom had gone to attend a teachers' training college, he had worked in Father's office, and, despite the difference in age, they had interests in common, including Father's long-standing study of French history; they also argued about politics by the hour.

I knew that they would go to town, to drink in The Vines in Lime Street and in other public houses. Ye Hole in Ye Wall was another of their favourite haunts. Once Tom took Father to Ye Cracke in Rice Street, and subsequently, if Father was alone, he always went there. It had a tiny parlour with a transom labelled 'The War Office' over its entrance. Men used to sit there and refight the Boer War, and no doubt Father refought the First World War in the same place. He really enjoyed exploring the many quaint taverns in Liverpool. He would come in about eleven o'clock, gravely drunk, and proceed, with care, upstairs to bed, to sleep it off in time for his Sunday morning pint at nearby Peter's, another of his favourite public houses.

Father woke up from his nap, and sat cracking his fingers for some minutes. He looked up at me. I was seated at the table, a sheet of cheap writing paper in front of me.

'Are you not going to a dance?' he asked.

'No. I thought I'd write to Alan. He must be having a terrible time at Biggin Hill; it's been bombed like anything.'

Father nodded agreement. Though he could write well and amusingly, he rarely wrote to any of his children while they were away, and I think that in many other houses this task was left to the womenfolk.

'He's ground staff; he should be able to take cover,' Father said heavily.

I wondered at Father's indifference to the danger his sons were in while they were in the Services. Perhaps, after the horrors of trench warfare in the First World War, bombing, aerial combat and the dangers at sea seemed petty in comparison.

Mother had heatedly forbidden me to write to or visit our little evacuees while they were away. 'You'll do nothing but upset them,' she had accused me.

Despite my protests, she was so vehement that I never did write.

Alan was my old and trusted friend, as well as my brother, and she knew better than to come between us. I wrote to him as often as I could. He did not always reply, for reasons which were painfully obvious from the headlines in the newspapers. The Battle of Britain was in scarifying flood. His base, Biggin Hill, was an airfield of crucial strategical importance and a frequent target of the Luftwaffe. He had continued to be trained as ground crew, had been promoted to Leading Aircraftsman, and did not normally fly. Our inadequate number of Spitfires and Hurricanes had, however, at all costs, to be kept in the air, and boys like him worked like devils to do it; at night he often slept under the aircraft on which he had been working, because time was so precious.

In the gorgeous summer of 1939, he went away a gangling youth. When we opened the door to him on his first leave in January, 1940, it was as if a young giant stood on our doorstep. He seemed to have grown a foot in height, his shoulders had broadened, and his face was that of a man. Though thin, he was healthier than I had ever seen him.

As we sat around our frugal fire, he told us that he had done six months of square-bashing, drilling very much as if he had been in the Army; then he had gone for further training in the maintenance of aircraft.

On his more recent leave, he had divulged, 'Some of the crates we have to deal with look more like colanders than aircraft when they land. And we have to get them back up again within hours.'

'And the crews?' I asked.

'We're losing an awful lot,' he replied, his face strained and sad.

I had guessed at the losses; we were getting Air Force families in the office, as well as those of seamen. Tears welled at the back of my eyes.

During his leaves, we gave all his clothing, which was usually soaked with oil, a thorough wash, and Mother fed him with everything she could cajole out of arrogant shopkeepers. He brought his own ration card, but it was inadequate, and, as well, we gave him our own rations of cheese, bacon and meat.

He seemed happy to be at home, and yet, by the end of the week, it was always apparent that he would be glad to return to his R.A.F. station. Though war is horrifying, it brings excitement and drama into dull lives. As yet, he was only a Leading Aircraftsman, hardly trained, but his uniform gave him a certain prestige; and he always performed at his best when facing a high level of stress.

So, seated at the scratched, living-room table, I tried to forget my own pain and to put myself in his position. I wrote as cheerfully as I could about the neighbourhood, as yet little damaged by bombs. I told him about

Nickie, our tan and white mongrel, who knew the sound of the air raid warning and the all clear, and came and went, without any direction from us, to his own private air raid shelter, which he had established in a little cupboard by the side of the fireplace.

My second brother, Brian, had brought the animal home, some years before. A publican had thrown it out of the door of his public house, and the tiny whimpering puppy had landed at Brian's feet. Dreadfully upset at its obvious hunger, Brian brought it home to a house where hunger was endemic; yet we were unanimous in adopting it, and it shared our meagre meals and learned to eat anything. Faithful and intensely loving, it lay on my feet as I wrote.

I did not mention in my letters the nightly air raids we were enduring; they seemed small in comparison with the battles that the Air Force were fighting.

On the 30th and the 31st August, Biggin Hill received two dreadful poundings which nearly put it out of action. Planes were damaged on the ground, as well as in the air, and there were numerous casualties.

Alan, not yet twenty and with less than a year's full-time experience, had, like all the other youngsters there, to cope with repairs that would in normal times have called for skilled engineers and mechanics. Above their heads, pilots who were no older fought to break up the waves of German bombers and Messerschmitt fighters, as Goering tried to wreck the Royal Air Force, and thus open up Britain to the invasion armies then gathering in French ports.

The fall of France had been devastating for Britain. The German Air Force was now operating from French airfields just across the English Channel. Based in French ports, the U-boats could hunt the eastern Atlantic to their hearts' content. As I wrote, I realised, with a pang, that it was probably one of those very U-boats from France which had caught Harry's ship. I knew that Alan, too, was now in deadly peril; but letters must be optimistic.

Optimistic? Most of Britain was in a state of quiet despair. The British Army had been thrown out of Norway. Our men had been pushed out of France, though, to console us, the saga of the rescue from Dunkirk of the remnants of our army was on everyone's lips – once or twice, I heard of men who had arrived on their mothers' doorsteps, filthy, bloody, ragged and exhausted, rifle still in hand, having come straight home after landing; a few of them never went back – protected by their families, they simply deserted.

Now London was being bombed unmercifully, and there was a steady trickle of Londoners fleeing the capital. Some came to Liverpool, only to be caught in the lesser, though still frightening, raids on our city.

Almost everyone suffered nightmares at the thought of a German invasion, and superhuman efforts were made by the Home Guard and civilians to be ready for it. So that the Germans would not be able to find their way, signposts were uprooted and names of railway stations painted over. Nobody seemed to realise that a professional soldier would, in thirty seconds, make any hapless civilian he came upon say exactly where he was. All that happened was that, throughout the war, people got lost like pennies running down a sewer drain. Fortunately the Air Force did not need signposts to know where it was; otherwise, they might have got lost, too, and the war would have had a different ending. The Army was not so fortunate, and many times, during my long walks in the Wirral, I directed lost, khaki-clad lorry drivers. Once I came upon a stranded tank, its flustered crew kneeling over a map at the roadside. They not only wanted to know where they were but where they could get a cup of tea!

There was a rap on the front door, and Father got up to let in his friend, Tom.

He came into the living-room and stood uneasily fingering his trilby hat, while Father put on his overcoat.

'Good evening, Helen.' I smiled up at him rather shyly. I did not like him, because I felt he was responsible for Father's drinking so much. This was not fair, because Father had always drunk quite heavily, perhaps to soothe his shattered nerves when he returned from the First World War, a shell-shocked neurasthenic.

Tom was a big, heavily built man, a little under thirty years of age, extremely dark, his well-shaven chin still almost black from a threatening fresh growth.

He said to Father, 'I got my call-up papers this morning.' He ran the brim of his hat nervously through his fingers.

Father stopped buttoning up his coat. 'Well, I'm blessed! Army?'

Tom did not look as if he regarded it as a blessing. 'Yes,' he replied. 'Have to report next week.'

'Ah, well, I suppose it was bound to come. At least you're single. No family to worry about.'

'Mother's very upset.'

'I'm sure she must be.' Father sighed, as he picked up his hat. 'I shall miss you very much.'

Tom half-smiled. 'Thanks. Are you ready?'

They both said goodbye to me, and left me to my letter. I could hear Avril laughing in the back yard, as she played a game of ball against the house wall, with another little girl. She did not laugh often enough, I thought.

Nickie put his nose on my knee and I patted him absently. Apart from the disintegration of my personal life, the further world around me was changing fast. The war kept nibbling at unexpected aspects of life. Men like Tom were being whisked away, and women like his widowed mother suddenly had to face a society which did not care much what happened to them, a society from which fathers, husbands and sons had given them a good deal of protection.

I tried not to think about my own unhappy situation, but the fact that I did not have the money for a stamp for Alan's letter reminded me forcibly of my dire financial straits.

What should I do? What *could* I do when I had so little formal education?

I had recently been for two interviews for secretarial jobs.

I was turned down immediately it was obvious that I had hardly been to day school at all. My experience in a charitable organisation did not, I discovered, rank very high. Charities were, in the minds of head clerks interviewing me, run by bumbling amateurs, do-gooders, cranks, a lot of old women. Humbled by the sharp tongues, I had thanked the gentlemen for their time, and had gone home.

# Chapter six

On 7th September, 1940, London suffered a dreadful bombing; it went on day and night, until the news was that the city was on fire from end to end. As verbal descriptions of it were passed from mouth to mouth and reached the north, we became more and more apprehensive that our turn would be next.

In a hastily scribbled letter, Alan told me that about five hundred bombers were involved, and that the raiders were very well protected by fighter planes.

Londoners hardly had time to recover before the Germans, on 9th September, mounted another huge operation, in which they stoked up the fires still burning from the earlier raid. On the 11th they hit Buckingham Palace, which seemed incredible to many Liverpudlians. Who would dare to hit the palace of a king? The King seemed almost thankful that he himself had been bombed out; he said that he could now look homeless East Enders in the face!

Liverpool was under nearly continuous nightly attack. Alan said he never went to bed for weeks during that period, but neither did we. We nodded on the basement steps, trying to get what rest we could, while the diving planes screeched overhead and the guns in Princes Park roared unceasingly. I learned a lot of German irregular verbs during those long, sleepless nights, in an effort to continue studies that I had pursued through seven years of evening school attendance. Such schools had been closed at the beginning of the war.

Working in the dock area, I could see that it was daily becoming more difficult to keep the port of Liverpool open, and Bootle, lying immediately to the north, was to have, for its size, the doubtful honour of being the most heavily bombed area in the British Isles. The ingenuity of the population in keeping going amid the ruins was a wonder to behold.

The civilian casualty lists began to lengthen. Amongst other places, the lists were posted outside our main office in the city, and I remember so clearly the tired, anxious faces of the people scanning them. But the faces of a few readers had an expression of morbid fascination, eyes glazed, lips parted, as they read – the same expressions that you can, nowadays, see in the faces of onlookers at an accident or a street murder or rape; they

495

just stare and do nothing about it, getting pleasure out of other people's agonies.

For many of us, life was solely long days at work, work which in the Bootle area consisted largely of trying to continue normal operations amid the wreckage of a factory or office or warehouse or dock. Then a quick rush for home, into the air raid shelter – if one was available.

As I write, I can feel the burning tiredness of my eyes at that time, and the acute discomfort of the ridged stone basement steps. I can smell the odour from the cellar of damp coal and of cats. I can see the flaking whitewash on the stairway's walls and a century of cobwebs hanging from its ceiling. It never seemed to occur to any of us to make some cushions to sit on – we had none in the house – or brush down the dirty walls, perhaps rewhitewash them, to cheer the place up. We were singularly unenterprising and simply endured the long, chilly nights.

If we were lucky, we would get an hour in bed, before we had to get up at six o'clock to go to work. I often felt worse after that hour in bed than if I had stayed up; but it did help to reduce the swelling in one's feet, which came from never putting them up.

Picking one's way to work in a long procession of pedestrians winding through shattered or blocked streets is a memory which must have remained with many people. It always astonished me how clean and neat we managed to make ourselves, despite interruptions in the water supply and the appalling dust raised by the bombing.

Because I had frequently to walk onwards to Bootle, in the north, I was often amongst the earliest people to set out from the south end of the city. I found myself part of a long line of much older women, their heads wrapped in turbans or kerchiefs, a pair of old shoes under their arm or sticking out of a shopping bag. They plodded along stolidly on swollen feet, their varicose veins lumpy under their woollen stockings. Occasionally, they would shout, 'Mornin',' to each other or stop for a word or two, but for the most part they walked in silence, putting first one cautious foot over scattered chunks of brickwork or electric cables and then lifting the other one over. Sometimes they paused to stare back at some unusual object, like a bath, lying in the road, or to watch the firemen and rescue workers at a particularly large scene of destruction.

They were the cleaning ladies of Liverpool, often leaving homes that had been damaged in the previous night's raid, to go into the city to make ready the offices and shops before their staff arrived. Increasingly frequently, they found nothing left to clean, only a dangerous mountain of rubble or a burning skeleton of a building. Many businesses, however, had reason to bless them, when the building was still standing, but all the windows and doors had been blown out and stock or papers were scattered everywhere. Imperturbable, they would pick up, shake and sort, until they had the floors fairly clear. Then, if the electricity was still working, they would plug in their vacuum cleaners and assail the all-enveloping dust. If there was no electricity, out came brooms and mops, buckets and floor cloths. To the nervous, excited clerks and shop assistants, when they arrived later, these women were quiet symbols of stability.

As the winter crept in, loss of windows became hard to bear, both at home and at work. The sweeping rain soaked many a home and office, despite people's efforts to keep it out by nailing old rugs or linoleum over the gaping frames.

Our office in Bootle was no exception. I arrived one morning to find snow thick on the ugly brown linoleum of our second-floor office, and a great drift up against my desk.

With icy fingers, I carefully shook the flakes off the precious files on the top of my desk and that of Miss Evans. I lifted the telephone receiver and wiped it. Immediately a sharp voice asked, 'Number, please?' I thanked heaven that it was working, as I quickly put the receiver down again.

Using a piece of cardboard, I shovelled the freezing piles out through the glassless windows. But there was still a lot on the floor when the rest of the staff arrived. 'Be careful not to slip,' I warned our voluntary helpers, as they tiptoed through the puddles.

As the day progressed, the remainder of the snow melted under tramping feet, leaving the office dank and miserable for days afterwards.

I learned to be very afraid of looters.

On the ground floor of the old house which was our office, we had a room filled with clean, second-hand clothing, for the reclothing of the bombed out. Not only were people sometimes clad only in their nightclothes, when their house came down about their ears, their day clothes could be ruined by such a catastrophe; every stitch in the house could be torn, impregnated by glass or ruined by spouting water pipes and thick dust. Everything had to be replaced – and Bootle was poor, terribly poor.

One frosty morning, as I hastened up the street, I saw that the office had again lost its windows during the night. My exhausted colleague had succumbed to influenza, and I wondered who I should talk to in the Town Hall in order to get a fast replacement of the glass.

As I unlocked the front door I heard the sound of voices. At first I thought it was the women who ran another charity on the ground floor, but then I realised with alarm that it was men's voices I was listening to.

The door of the clothing room was ajar, and I ran forward and flung it wide.

A sheet had been spread over the centre of the floor and two men and a woman were tossing clothing on to it.

'What on earth are you doing?' I asked indignantly.

One man paused and looked up at me. He was burly, in shirtsleeves, with huge muscular arms covered with black hairs. A docker, I guessed.

'You get out of here,' he growled. 'And mind your own business.'

'This is my business.' My voice rose in anger. 'You don't belong here. Get out yourself before I call the police.'

The three dropped the clothing they were holding, and looked uncertainly at each other. They did not move.

'O.K. I'll call them.' I moved towards the door.

'Oh, no, you don't.' Both men advanced on me, their feet tangling in the pile of clothing lying on the sheet.

I quickly pulled the door shut in their path. The lock was broken, but it might hold them up for a second or two.

Light and fleet, I sped up the stairs, thrust the key into the lock of our office, slipped inside and locked it from the inside. I seized the telephone and thankfully asked the operator, 'Police, quick.'

After a solid night of bombing, the police number was engaged. The men were pounding on the door and shouting threats. 'Call the A.R.P. There are probably more people there,' I told her.

Though she had been afraid of interrupting a police telephone conversation, the operator unhesitatingly broke into the conversation on the A.R.P. phone, and asked for help.

The men outside must have heard the relief in my voice, as I said, 'Thanks very much.' By the time two volunteer wardens pounded up the stairs, the looters had fled.

I was still trembling when the first volunteer member of our staff arrived. I asked her to re-sort and hang up the clothing again, and a little later on, presumably as a result of the wardens' report, our windows were boarded up by workmen, who arrived unbidden by me.

We had some funds which could be lent to men who had lost their tools in a raid or to replace smashed spectacles, and alleviate similar woes, which were not covered by any governmental source. Ready cash was kept in an old-fashioned cash box, locked in a cupboard overnight. On a bleak November day, while my superior was still sick, I put the cash box out, ready, on the desk, and went to the waiting-room to check the number of people there.

A boy passed the waiting-room door. I presumed he had brought a message from his family; it was a common occurrence, and I went back to deal with him.

The boy had flitted silently out, taking the cash box with him.

I was appalled, and immediately sent for the police.

Two plain-clothes men, they sat and warmed themselves by our dim electric fire, and sighed and rubbed their hands.

'Normally we could pick 'im up as quick as light,' one of them said. 'Anybody with that much money to spend sticks out like a sore toe. But now . . .' he shrugged, 'with all the high wages . . . well.'

The thief was never traced. It was a sore loss to our small organisation.

During my harsh days of mourning, I learned a lot of sad truths. It was a revelation to me that the poor would steal from the poor. Working-class solidarity had been preached to me consistently by Communists working in the main office; the poor stood shoulder to shoulder against the wicked, exploiting upper classes. But, in truth, they prey on each other, with a ruthlessness which was, and still is, hard to swallow. Who has not seen decent city-built housing, built specifically to help those who could not afford much rent, stripped bare as a skeleton, of tiles, fittings, lead for the roof, by people who must have been close neighbours to know even that the house was not yet occupied?

There is a saying in Liverpool, 'If it isn't nailed down, sit on it.' I now understood what it meant, and I became very careful.

Particularly during the war, great targets for thieves were the gas and electric meters in the cellars of damaged houses in the poorer areas. These meters had to be fed either by pennies or shillings, and their cash boxes were temptingly full of money. In peacetime, they were often rifled at night. A slender youth would lift the manhole in front of the street door, normally used for the delivery of coal directly into the cellar, and slide through the opening. He soon prised open the drawer in which the money was collected, and was then hauled quietly out by an accomplice.

Though our house was not damaged at the time it happened, we twice had our meters broken into, and found, to our sorrow, that we had to pay the gas and electricity companies all over again.

One exasperated old man near us had had to pay a huge gas bill because thieves had robbed his meter. Afterwards, he carefully tied a ship's bell to the underpart of the manhole cover.

One early morning, as I was washing myself in the kitchen, I heard the sonorous ding-dong of the bell, and about half a minute later, shrieks and curses in the street. The old man had caught a youth and was giving him a sound beating with a broomstick, a far more effective punishment than a lecture from a magistrate.

# Chapter seven

It was October, and nearly five months since I had bid Harry a hasty goodbye, when he embarked on his last voyage. I still felt very forlorn and terribly alone, despite a large family. I had spent this Saturday afternoon walking over to see the pawnbroker, to retrieve a cotton-wrapped bundle containing two of my dresses, a skirt and cardigan, which Mother had pawned. My return journey took me past the house in which we had rented two freezing attic rooms, when we first came to Liverpool.

Seated on the stone steps which led down from the pavement to her basement home was Mrs Hicks. Bundled up in a series of woollen cardigans, she was enjoying the late October sunshine.

She was an old friend, and when she saw me, she got up from the steps and dusted her black skirt with her hands.

''Allo, luv,' she greeted me in surprise. ''Ow are yer? Come in. Haven't seen you in ages.' She pulled open the cast-iron gate which protected the steps.

I smiled at her and carefully eased myself past the gate and on to the narrow steps, to follow her down and through the heavy door under the sweep of steps that led up to the main entrance of the house.

The basement rooms in which she lived had originally been the kitchens of the house. Thick, vertical iron bars still guarded the windows, and the interior still smelled of damp and much scrubbing with pine disinfectant.

The sun did not penetrate her home, and in the gloom, she beamed at me, every wrinkle and crease of her face suggesting battles won or lost, patience learned. She had been very kind to all of us in the bitter days when, up in the attic, we had nearly starved.

Brian had been her particular friend, and she asked after him, as she shut the outer door. I told her he was well and had work.

'Sit down, now. We'll have a cuppa tea. See, the kettle's on the boil,' and she pointed to an iron kettle on the hob, belching steam like a railway train. 'And how've *you* bin, me duck?'

While I sat down by the fire and put my bundle on the floor, she moved swiftly round the room on tiny booted feet, while she collected the tea things and put them on a table beside me.

'I'm all right,' I lied. 'And how are you? It's lovely to see you again.'

'Och, me? Never nuthin' the matter with me. And me hubbie's a lot better, now he's workin'.'

Mr Hicks, I learned, had become a timekeeper at a new factory in Speke, and Mrs Hicks said that, after so many years of unemployment, it felt strangely nice to have regular wages coming in, although it meant a long bicycle ride for him each day.

I congratulated her. Provided they were not bombed out, people like Mr and Mrs Hicks benefited greatly by the war.

Mrs Hicks finally came to rest in the easy chair opposite me, and, as we sat knee to knee, she stirred her mug of tea vigorously, and remarked, 'You don't look at all well, luv. Has your throat bin botherin' you again?'

'No, Mrs Hicks.' My throat was husky, but not with the tonsillitis which plagued me from time to time. I put my mug down on the little table, put my head down on my knee and burst into tears.

In a second I was pressed to Mrs Hicks's pillowy chest. 'Now, now, dear.' She stroked my hair, which I was again growing because I had no money for hairdressers. Then she turned my face up to her. 'What's to do? Has your mam been at you agen?'

No love had been lost between Mother and Mrs Hicks; she must have heard Mother raging at me many a time.

'No, Mrs Hicks. It's not that.'

Gradually she wormed out of me my loss of Harry, and I said tearfully, 'I don't know what to do, Mrs Hicks. I just don't.'

'You're not expecting, are you, luv?'

Mrs Hicks was a most practical woman, and I had to smile at her through my tears.

'No, I'm not. We – we agreed we would wait. But I wish I was. I'd have something to live for, then.'

'Nay. It's better as it is – you'll see that later on. And him bein' an older fella, he sowed his wild oats years ago, I'll be bound. He knew what he was about – he must've really loved you.'

'He was awfully good. He didn't want me to be left single, with a child, like so many.' Fresh tears burst from me.

She let me cry, and it did me good. The tea went cold, but when I gently loosed myself from her arms and leaned back in my chair, full of apologies for being such a badly behaved guest, she wiped my face with a corner of her apron, and then made me sit quietly while she made a fresh black brew. 'I don't blame you for not telling your mam; hard case, she is, if you'll forgive me for sayin' so. Will you tell her now?'

'I don't think so, Mrs Hicks. It's past now.' I sipped my new cup of tea gratefully. 'You know, she'd dissect the whole thing and be so disparaging – mostly about his being a seaman. You know her.'

'Humph. What's wrong with goin' to sea?'

501

The question was rhetorical; I did not have to explain my mother's snobbery to Mrs Hicks; she had suffered from it herself often enough.

'Have you bin to see his mother?'

I had already told her how I had met Mrs O'Dwyer when the lady came to my office to consult the society for which I worked about claiming a pension. Now I added, 'She seemed so hard and bitter, Mrs Hicks. Harry said she never forgave him for leaving the priesthood; and yet, there she was, trying to benefit from his death. Frankly, it made me feel sick.'

The tears welled again.

'Aye, dear, dear. What you need is a body and a good wake. Gives you a chance to cry yer head off.' She sighed. 'There's lots like you, luv, and all they can do is light a candle.'

I agreed wanly, and often, in later years, when I saw forests of candles twinkling before bejewelled madonnas, I thought of all of us who did not have the privilege of burying our dead.

I said, depressedly, that I must go home, and she rose and put her arm round me as I walked across the room. 'Now, you come and see me again – any time you like. And I won't say a word, if I see your mam. I won't say nuthin' to nobody, if it comes to that.'

'Thank you, Mrs Hicks.' I put my arms round her and kissed her.

I went to see her two or three times. Then I lost touch with her when, on the sudden death of her landlady, the house was sold, and she had to move. Nobody seemed to know or care where she had gone. The new owner of the house simply shrugged his shoulders and said, 'Half the world's on the move.' When I stopped the postman on his round, to inquire if he had a forwarding address, he remembered the old lady, but he nodded his head negatively. 'They didn't have no letters to speak of. She couldn't read, you know. Nice old girl, she was; let me shelter in her hall, once, when it were raining.'

# Chapter eight

Being able to talk frankly to Mrs Hicks during several visits helped me immeasurably. She encouraged me to cry and talk as much as I wanted, and she never used the platitudes that come so readily to the lips of those trying to comfort the bereaved. Illiterate she might be, but she understood people very well, and I began to accept that I really had to pick up my life again and go on living.

Everyone in Liverpool needed as much strength as they could muster. That autumn, we endured over fifty consecutive nights of air raids. Brian, Tony, Avril and little Edward looked washed out and old, because of fear and lack of sleep. They never complained, however, and the three younger ones went to school daily, no matter how late they had had to sit up. Fiona was rarely at home during these raids; she continued her social life as if the bombings never occurred. She would return home after the raid was over, with stories of playing cards in hotel shelters or eating in a restaurant while the lights dipped from time to time, as the building rocked.

We worried when Brian was on duty during a raid. The more intense the attack, the more likely that telephone wires would be brought down, and the more messages he would have to carry through the pandemonium of the streets. A cyclist has not even the protection of a vehicle roof over his head; and, for once, Mother and I were united in our worries. He would turn up, however, soon after the all clear had sounded, covered with dust, eyes bloodshot, triumphant and cheerful, after having helped the police and wardens dig out victims.

After one particularly heavy raid, he breezed in rather later than usual, saying casually to our horrified mother, 'Sorry I'm late. We had to find the heads.'

Without the production of the head of a victim, a person could not immediately be pronounced dead – arms, legs, even torsos, did not count, and this caused boundless difficulties to many families. So, quite phlegmatically, seventeen-year-old Brian had been hunting heads at the site of a bad incident.

I wondered if the highly strung, imaginative little boy had really grown into an iron-nerved man, or whether he had just learned, of a necessity, to live with his fears. In any case, his experience as a police messenger must have helped to prepare him for the greater horrors he saw later in the Royal Navy. He never lost his compassion, though; the small boy who took pity on a whining puppy and brought it home grew into an immensely understanding man.

Sometimes I was myself caught in a raid, while still at the office or when walking home; once or twice, when the siren sounded, I was at a dance with my friend, Sylvia Poole.

I had known Sylvia for a number of years. She had a lively mind and we enjoyed discussing topics of the day. I was interested in the forces that shaped history, and in individuals, like Churchill and Hitler, who seemed to be born at a pivotal moment in time. Did they shape our history or had our history shaped them? Ideas about the economic forces surging beneath the surface of the news turned my attention to appropriate books and newspapers, as did the plight of European Jews.

I knew more than most people about the dreadful situation of European Jews, because since 1933 I had seen a steady stream of refugees go through our office, and each of them had his own shocking story. When I put the individual stories together and saw the general trend of them, I was both horrified and terrified.

After the war, when I talked to demobilised friends who had served in the army of occupation in Germany, men and women who had seen Belsen and other death camps, I knew that even my worst imaginings had underestimated what had happened. I had been taught that the Germans were the best-educated, most advanced people in Europe; yet they had condoned genocide.

Sylvia and I never discussed our personal affairs. Looking back, I do not really know why not. Girls are supposed to giggle and confide in each other. I never did. Sylvia was precious to me because of the way we hammered out ideas.

Sometimes, during that hard winter of 1940-41, I accepted a date with the acquaintance of Harry's who had escorted me home on the day that the dance club closed. I was glad of company, and had no thought of anything more than that; indeed, I found it hard to think beyond the day I was living. He was a pleasant, shy young man in a reserved occupation, but when he wished to deepen the friendship and began to speak of a possible engagement, I sent him on his way. Though I liked him, I could not love him.

There was an inner core of me which was extremely fastidious. Though I was a passionate young woman, I lived in a time when many girls would not settle for less than marriage; and for me marriage had to have real love as one of the ingredients.

As a good dancer, I had the opportunity of meeting throughout the war a great number of young men. Far from the roots of home, men who normally would not have been seen dead in a ballroom, sought company on the dance floor. Friendships and romances flourished, but for me the chemistry was never right. And I further longed to meet the kind of cultivated man who visited our home in the long-ago days before Father went bankrupt. Though Harry had fought his way up from nothing, he had had the company of scholarly men during his youth; he knew how to study and he read widely. His mother might be a most unreasonable woman, but I think it must have been she who taught him good manners, and this, added to a naturally kindly character, made him a very pleasant person to be with.

On 8th October, the *Empress of Britain* was sunk, and on 5th November, the armed merchant cruiser HMS *Jervis* went down while escorting an Atlantic convoy. Despite brave efforts by the *Jervis* to defend the convoy, five other boats joined her at the bottom. In December, U-boats off the coast of Portugal played havoc with several convoys. The sorrow caused was reflected in our office, the names of ships whispered by weeping women becoming a monotonous litany.

We became expert at guiding womenfolk, many of whom could hardly read or write, through the voluminous red tape in which they became enmeshed when they applied for pensions. Some women took a double blow; they lost a husband or son to the German navy and, during the air raids, they lost their home, and, sometimes children, as well. It became a relief to deal with more ordinary problems, like a cripple's special needs or a bastardy case.

Increasingly, I sought diversion during the long hours spent seated on the cellar steps, when there was nothing to do except consider how sleepy and how miserable one was. So I continued to study my German grammar book, until the humour of it struck me; then I laughed and put it away – I never wanted to speak to a German again. Crouched on the steps with a lap full of cotton reels and darning wool, I sewed and mended. Whenever I had a few pence, I went with Sylvia to a new dance club or to the theatre, regardless of the heaviness of the raid.

I danced mechanically with anyone who asked me, glad when the man was a good dancer, so that I could give myself over to the rhythm of the music and find some relaxation. While exchanging the usual pleasantries, I would, over my partner's shoulder, watch the door, look at the other men on the floor, always hoping, half believing that Harry would be there. Outside, I searched the faces in the bus queues and in any group of seamen walking in the town; wherever there were men, my eyes hunted automatically. I began to understand Mrs Hicks's remarks about the need for wakes and funerals, to be convinced of death.

The owner of the new dance club which Sylvia and I attended converted his lessons into a permanent wake. He had lost his wife in the blitz and had had her body cremated; her ashes were put into a fine vase, and the vase was set on a special shelf in the ballroom. The idea was so macabre that we ceased to go there and, in fact, neither of us ever went to a dancing class again.

Father asked me to write periodically to his friend, Tom, now training with the infantry. To please him, I did write for some considerable time, giving news of Liverpool and, since he was a teacher, sending press cuttings about the plight of teachers, which I thought might interest him. Perhaps Father hoped for a match between us, but I found him as dull as a January day. His replies were pedantic and grammatically perfect; I used to scribble *Ten out of Ten* on the bottom of them.

Father was very disconsolate at losing his drinking companion. He used to go alone to the concert halls and public houses they had previously frequented, but, since he was a sociable man, he probably found people to talk to.

He was on friendly terms with his colleagues at the office, but they had other interests. In their spare time, many of them were air raid wardens, and some joined the Home Guard when it was set up. Most took the government's instruction to Dig for Victory very seriously and, according to Father, raised mammoth crops of vegetables on what had once been their lawns. We had only a brick-lined yard, so gardening was not possible, but, in any case, Father's bad heart precluded his doing much heavy work.

There is no doubt that during those years he was often very lonely. Mother and he were never the good companions that older people can become. At best, they carped at each other continually.

Father was a clerk in the Liverpool Corporation. He was transferred by them to work in the administration of Rest Centres for the bombed out and of warehouses used to store the possessions of the dead or of the temporarily homeless.

When members of the Polish Army straggled into Liverpool, he was sent for a few days to help to take the history of the ragged, disillusioned men. Some who could not speak English could speak Russian, and the language he had learned under such painful circumstances in the Russian campaign in the First World War was suddenly put to use. He enjoyed the work, but he would come home to sit in his ancient easy chair, eyes closed, hands trembling with fatigue. Like all of us, he lacked sleep; and I think, also, that the company of soldiers in such adversity reminded him of his own anguish in the Great War.

The constant barrage of the guns during the raids also wore him down. I could see his face grow steadily more grim, as the nights progressed. He would sit very quietly on the cellar steps, while overhead the racket was continuous. Occasionally, however, he would bury his face in his hands, and once he muttered that it was exactly like being on a battlefield with a jammed machine gun, unable to return the fire.

There was little that I could do for him, except let him talk to me whenever he felt like it. He enjoyed telling his war stories over and over again. They were excellent vignettes of the lives of primitive Russian peasants, who had rescued him from certain death when he lay half frozen amid his dead comrades in the bloodied snow. He told me of sharp encounters with the enemy, in pathless forests, where his greatest fear always was that he would get lost. Many of his wounded friends died, when a shed made into an improvised hospital was set alight by the enemy during a raid. He still shuddered at the memory. 'It was a hopeless inferno in seconds,' he said. He spoke with praise of a Japanese unit which, at one point, served with him, of the utter savagery of the Russian Revolution, of the people of Archangel dying of starvation and the smallpox. He was himself immune to smallpox, because his mother had caught it while she was pregnant with him; so he helped to nurse and to bury the victims of the disease. He had innumerable scarifying tales of the personal agony of war and revolution, so often forgotten amid cold statistics. He taught me that revolution rarely solves anything.

When the noise of the bombs was very bad, he would give a shaky laugh and say, 'And we thought we had finished with war!'

'It will be over in a few months,' I would say to him. He would smile faintly – he knew better – from experience.

Once he said with great bitterness, 'It will never be over – it will go on and on.'

How right he was. The war died down amid exhausted European populations, only to blaze up in Korea, Vietnam, India, Afghanistan, Iran, Iraq, Egypt and Israel, while embers smoulder and threaten Africa and strange outposts, like the Falklands.

In October, Sylvia celebrated her twenty-first birthday with a party, one of the first grown-up parties I attended.

Her plump, patient little mother must have collected bits of rationed food over many months. Someone had contributed a bottle of blackcurrant wine of surprising strength; unaccustomed to alcohol, we all became quite merry.

On my twenty-first birthday, the previous June, Mother's employer, a baker, hearing that I was approaching my majority, baked for me an exquisite little birthday cake. It was a rich fruit cake, which he had decorated himself with delicate flower wreaths of white royal icing. It was illegal to make such an extravagant cake, and he must have taken the ingredients from some illicit hoard stored away at the beginning of the war. He presented the cake to Mother as a gift.

The family had joined together to buy me a leather shopping bag, popularly known as a zipper bag. In these bags, carried by almost all business girls, were transported make-up, lunch, a change of shoes and stockings for wet days, a novel to read on the bus or train, and innumerable oddments like safety pins and aspirins. I was delighted by the gift; they must have hunted through most of Liverpool's many shops to find such an article.

I arrived home from work, that evening, about eight o'clock. The family had given up hope of my arrival, assuming that I was working late and was having a snack in the office. They ate the sandwiches and scones which Mother had kindly provided to celebrate the day. The cake, however, was kept untouched.

I remember being moved almost to tears at the effort that had been made to find me a gift and a cake. I immediately cut the cake and passed it round the family. It was strange to eat cake for my birthday – but no dinner!

# Chapter nine

Small financial problems which, looking back, seem laughable, presented me with dreadful headaches.

In the early part of the autumn I forgot to switch off the cloakroom light before leaving the office.

The room had no blackout curtaining, and the light blazed forth across the old, walled garden at the back of the building. Our outraged warden reported it, and the society was fined seven shillings by the local magistrate. This amount was deducted from my wages at the rate of one shilling a week, and for nearly two months my already penurious state was reduced to near disaster; I remember being torn between a decision to walk to work and thus wear out my precious stockings, which would have to be replaced, or nurse my current pair of stockings along, by hooking up the ladders with a fine crochet hook and darning and redarning, so that I could ride on the tram to work. It was a very long seven weeks.

It always astonished me that Mother never got fined for similar offences. The warden frequently remonstrated with her about the lack of curtaining over our back bedroom windows and the consequent glow of candlelight through them, a glow which in his opinion would guide the Luftwaffe straight to us. Perhaps because he was a neighbour he was loath to report her. Towards the end of the war, she did buy some second-hand curtains and put them up, but I suspect that she rather enjoyed baiting the unfortunate warden.

It was on a foggy day in late November that, after a heavy raid, I was very tired and decided to travel the whole distance to work by tram. On the first tram I took, to the city centre, the clippie told me that the whole system had been disorganised by the air raid, and that I might get a tram to Bootle more easily from the Pier Head.

At the Pier Head, the Transport Supervisor was about to dispatch a tram to my destination. It was evidently the first tram which would travel along Derby Road that morning, and I heard him tell the driver, 'The police say the timber yards is burnin' fierce. I tried to telephone, but the wires must be down 'cos I couldn't get through, and nobody seems to know what's really happening. So you mayn't get to the end of the line.' He paused uncertainly, and then ordered, 'Go as far as you can. There's no end of people as will be going on and off shift at the other end.'

The driver, his face almost purple from constant exposure to the elements, wound a huge scarf round his neck and climbed wearily on to his unprotected platform. He tinged his bell irritably with the toe of his boot, and his clippie threw away her cigarette end and skipped quickly on to the back platform. I followed her more sedately. The rush hour had not yet begun, so I was the only passenger.

The clippie was a gaunt woman in a navy blue uniform, too short at the sleeves. She collected my fare and handed me a ticket. Then she closed the door of the passenger compartment and sat down opposite to me, to have a cosy gossip on the hardships and dangers of being a tram conductor.

'I'm that scared sometimes at night, with no proper lights, like, and the pubs let out. It's all right if they're merry drunk, if you know what I mean; the worst that'll happen is that they'll be sick all over the floor. But if they're bevvied and ready for a fight, or if they start to slobber all over you, well! And me man away in the Army, an' all.'

I sympathised with her. I wondered if I could do her job. Cope with drunks, and the impertinence she would endure as a woman doing a man's job? I doubted it.

While, out of the corner of her eye, she watched the scenes of destruction that we passed, she smoked incessantly. 'Lot of fires,' she remarked, and then added with a sigh, 'I'd rather be in an air raid, at times, than face some of the men as gets on this tram.' With the heel of her flat, laced-up shoe, she ground a cigarette end into the floor.

'Couldn't you get a better job?'

'Well, it's handy, 'cos I do split shifts, and in between I can get home to see to the kids. And the pay's good – for a woman.'

When the tram slowed, at a point where men were still hastily clearing pieces of debris from the tram lines, she got up abruptly.

'I'll ask Hisself how he's doin',' she said, and strode forward between the bench seats, which faced each other the length of the vehicle. She shoved back the door which connected with the driver's platform, and smoke rolled into the passenger compartment; the poor driver must have been nearly blinded by it. I hastily pulled out a cotton handkerchief and dabbed my smarting eyes. In seconds, I could barely see anything myself.

The tram stopped.

Shadowy firemen and wardens bobbed round the vehicle and shouted up to the driver. As the result of their encouragement, the driver edged the tram forward, tinging his strident bell persistently.

As we sailed slowly past, a warden called up to him, 'The overhead wires is still up all the way. It's a bloody miracle.'

The tram stopped again. From behind the hanky pressed to my nose, I peeped at the stout back of the driver. A warden had swung himself up on to the platform beside him. The warden's face was black with soot, his eyes and mouth a startling red.

'I can't see a thing in front of me,' the driver protested.

'I'll get down and walk in front of you,' the warden offered. 'I'll watch for anything on the line.' He hopped down on to the road again, and shouted up to the driver, 'Now, mind you listen hard for me – and don't, for God's sake, run me down. You can see better than you think – it's more steam than smoke now.' Then his voice came more faintly from the cloud of vapour. 'Couple o' hundred yards and you'll see all right. And they'll have this bit o' trouble damped down by the time you come back.'

Once again the tram eased forward. It seemed a very long two hundred yards.

When visibility improved, the warden left us with a brisk wave of his gloved hand, and the driver accelerated. Timber flamed and crackled as we passed the yards, and sometimes waves of heat swept through the open door at the front.

I should have been frightened, and yet I was not.

I was let down at the stop nearest to the office, and, as I walked up the side road to the dilapidated building, I was thankful to find that the immediate area appeared undamaged. It was extremely quiet, and I met no voluntary workers hurrying up the road at the same time. These middle-aged ladies were normally extremely conscientious about being prompt, and I put down their absence to the transport system being disorganised by the raid. No clients were leaning against the front door, waiting for me to let them in. Sometimes, however, if the raid had been severe, they would come streaming in from the Rest Centres later in the morning.

I unlocked.

The postman did his morning round very early, so I emptied the letter-box, and slowly climbed the stairs, sifting through the letters as I went.

I unlocked the rooms the organisation occupied and put on the lights. The silence oppressed me. The raid must have been so bad the previous night that people were not yet able to move around, I decided, or were still having breakfast in the Rest Centres.

The mail consisted largely of government circulars, which would have to be studied, so that we could advise our clients of the latest foibles of civil servants, on the subject of servicemen's debts, rationing, pensions of every kind, and so on. Many civil servants were tucked away in huge mansions or commandeered hotels in different parts of the country, and were in a fair state of confusion themselves; this was reflected in the muddled bureaucratic gobbledygook of their epistles.

After the letters had been scanned and sorted, I wandered round the office and went into the waiting-room, to open the only window which had any glass in it. Though the air that rushed in was smoky, it smelled better than the fetid atmosphere of the room, and I leaned out to see if the buildings at the back had been damaged.

Below me, amid the weeds of the brick-walled garden, squatted a solitary soldier. He was bent over, as if taking cover.

I smiled. From the back, he looked like a Home Guard practising guerrilla tactics, and I expected that in a moment I would see one or two more of them sneak over a broken part of the wall, rifles at the ready; retired men or men on night shifts would sometimes get together in the daytime to do this. Like mothers-in-law they were a favourite cartoonists' joke, but they tried very hard to prepare themselves to face the Germans' professional invasion troops.

The soldier stood up slowly and signalled with a wave of his arm to someone outside my line of vision. In response, two other soldiers appeared, carrying spades instead of rifles.

The first soldier moved aside. And then I saw the object of their interest.

A dull metal pillar box was resting half on its side, much of it buried in the earth. After circling slowly round it, the men with spades began very gingerly to dig it out.

A bomb disposal squad ! And a very large unexploded landmine which, presumably, the first soldier had now defused.

But if it were damaged, it could still explode.

The instinct of self-preservation sent me across the room and down the stairs quicker than the bomb could have blown me. Coatless, hatless, out of the front door I flew into the cold, smoky road.

An unattended army lorry was drawn up by the side gate, presumably waiting to transport the bomb to an open area to be exploded.

In the middle of the road, I paused uncertainly.

An angry shriek came from further up the road. A warden beckoned me wildly. I ran towards him, where he stood behind a rope tied across the street.

He lifted the rope for me to duck underneath it, as if he believed that the rope itself would protect us from the possible blast.

Furiously, he thrust his thin, bespectacled face close to mine. 'And how did you get down there? When we cordon off a place, it's cordoned, and you're not supposed to go there. You might be killed.' He was genuinely concerned.

Gasping for breath, I muttered, 'I came into work from the Derby Road side. I didn't see any barrier. Perhaps the soldiers undid the rope to get their lorry in, and forgot to tie it across the road again. No wonder I didn't have any clients or staff in the office. I *think* it's defused now.'

'Well, you stay right here, young woman, till they've taken it away. It can go off, defused or not defused, if some of its innards is ruptured.'

It is strange how strong the instinct to live is. I stood shivering by the warden for nearly an hour, until we saw the lorry roll slowly down the other end of the road, with its horrid burden in the back.

While I waited, I thought about Coventry, which, on 14th November, had been decimated in one enormous raid. I wondered if we would be the next victims.

Raids did continue, though none as heavy as that which destroyed Coventry. Amid the turmoil that they engendered, the problem of Christmas asserted itself.

We were determined to give the younger children the best possible Christmas. To Mother, it meant squeezing out of a reluctant butcher one of his few turkeys; to me, it meant contriving from nothing a gift for each child; and to all of us, it meant we could get a good sleep some time during the daytime hours. The Germans, however, had other ideas. On the night of Friday, 20th December, we endured a very heavy air raid, with an even more severe one on the 21st. On the Sunday night, we shared a third intense raid with Manchester.

After the first raid, I went out and stood in the middle of our empty street, while the all clear howled eerily round me. Though there was no sign of damage in the street itself, the sky was suffused by the reflection of fires, and I wondered what would be awaiting me in the office that Saturday morning. Shivering with cold and apprehension, I went back into the house, to snatch a couple of hours of sleep before setting out on my long journey to work; I was thankful that my kind superior at the office had, at last, returned after her long battle with influenza. The raid had lasted ten hours, ten solid hours of bombardment. What a mess there would be for us to clear up. What a tremendous number of ruined lives to try to put together again.

Despite having to take several detours, the city bus and tram service was working very well. We passed scurries of activity where fires still burned, victims were being dug out, and dangerous, teetering walls pulled down. The Adelphi Hotel, the pride of Liverpool, had suffered badly from blast, and my fellow passengers on the tram viewed it with surprised exclamations, as if it should have been exempt from damage.

'It was a landmine,' the clippie told us. 'Fell at the side of the building – in Copperas Hill.'

Copperas Hill was a narrow street of early nineteenth-century houses, some boarded up as uninhabitable, a few used as offices, the rest still lived in by very poor people, who would that morning be a lot poorer – if they were still alive.

Feeling physically and mentally drained, I left the office very late that Saturday evening. The Luftwaffe had already been extremely busy for some hours.

I dithered on the office steps. The roar of flames, the whistle of bombs, seemed concentrated in Bootle and in the north end of

Liverpool itself. I would have to pass through the area in order to get home.

Miss Evans had decided to work later, to catch up with her records, and then to sleep in the office. She insisted, however, that I should go home. 'There isn't much you can do to help me now – you'll be safer at home,' she said.

She was very brave. Looking up at the sky, all too full of shrieking, diving planes, it seemed likely that the office would not survive. Very reluctantly, I left her in the cold, empty building.

I walked up to Stanley Road, to see if, by chance, there was still a tram running to town.

The whole normally busy road was almost deserted, though in the distance I could hear the bells of a fire engine and, as I crossed the street, a van nearly ran me down. I listened for the answering guns in their emplacements in Bootle, but could not hear them. The searchlights were busy, though, flicking like metronomes across the sky.

In the light of flares, fires, tracer bullets and searchlights, it was easy to see. I felt cross; I was not going to be kept from home by any German planes. I began to walk.

When the even explosions of a stick of bombs seemed to be coming very close, I dodged into doorways, pressing myself tightly against whatever door presented itself. Twice I found a public shelter, crowded with people, some singing, some praying, rosaries in hand, and was urged by wardens to remain there. But I was obsessed with the need to get home, and immediately there was a slight pause in the racket, I slipped out and pressed onwards. At several points, the raid passed right overhead at a time when there seemed no place to hide. I went down on my knees in the road and then flattened myself against the kerb, face tucked into the tiny corner of protection that it offered; and listened to hasty footsteps running on the pavement, as others tried to find a refuge, while I eased myself slowly along the gutter. Further down the road, I heard someone cry out in pain and the sound of anxious voices, as a person was struck, presumably by flak. A series of bombs appeared to hit the next street, and I was suddenly glad that I had been faced with a blank wall on my side of the street, and was consequently sprawled in the gutter; if there had been a house or shop doorway in which to shelter, I could well have been speared by glass slivers bursting from the windows.

On the theory that a moving object was harder to hit than a stationary one, I ran like a frightened alley cat, in the hope of avoiding an incendiary bomb or heavy piece of debris falling on me. Incendiary bombs, though quite small, were deadly if they fell on someone, and flak from our anti-aircraft guns, or flying pieces of rubble and glass from bombed buildings, were more of a menace than the chance of being caught directly by an exploding bomb. Another great danger was from falling power lines, still live and spitting like angry dragons.

At the junction of Cazneau Street with Scotland Road, which is the continuation of Stanley Road towards the city, I hesitated. The violence of the raid had momentarily decreased, and the blackout appeared to have taken over again. If I went up Cazneau Street, I could bypass the city centre which was probably under attack. Cazneau Street was, however, a fearsome slum with which I was not familiar, and I feared that once I crossed London Road, a main artery which bisected that particular line of streets, I would get lost. Mind made up, I trotted along Scotland Road. I was shivering with nervous determination to outwit the Luftwaffe and get home safely.

As I neared the city centre, there was more traffic about and more pedestrians; raucous male voices called after me as they glimpsed the outline of a young female. I increased my speed and panted onwards towards the Old Haymarket, a vast open space into which the Mersey tunnel debouched from under the river.

I'll cross William Brown Street, where the Picton Library is, and skirt around the wall of St John's Garden. It'll give me a bit of protection, I told myself. By doing this I avoided the wide open spaces of this handsome part of Liverpool and would be less likely to be hit. I would also bypass most of Lime Street, still the main walk for prostitutes in the city, where I had no doubt it would be business as usual, blitz or no blitz; it was not the ladies I feared, but their pimps and hangers-on.

The city was in turmoil, with service vehicles zipping recklessly through the battered streets. There seemed to be a very big fire at the beginning of Dale Street, and behind the buildings past which I ran up to the far end of Lime Street, there was obviously another heavy conflagration, which I afterwards was told was St John's market burning. Roasted in it were most of the turkeys which Liverpudlians had dreamed of eating on Christmas Day, and to hear the talk in the shopping queues after the holiday, one would imagine that the loss of the turkeys was more deeply mourned than the loss of three hundred and fifty-six men, women and children who died during the three days of the blitz.

As I ran, incendiaries fell like rain, and magnificent St George's Hall was alight; I was told later that there were hundreds of people sheltering in the cells underneath it, unaware that the building above them was in flames. Though I was aware only of a blizzard of bombs, flak and hazardous litter on the pavements, a short distance away a bomb fell in front of the Court Theatre, and a fire engine, racing to a call, fell into the crater, killing the entire crew of seven; so much for speed in such a situation. I was lucky that I did not fall over something or into something myself.

I felt naked as I left Renshaw Street behind me, and climbed the hill towards Catherine Street. To my right, the Anglican cathedral was outlined against a rosy sky. It seemed less noisy here, and was totally deserted. The quiet rage, which had sustained me through the city, began to drain, and I was aware of intolerable fatigue.

There were several hospitals at the top of the hill, where cars and ambulances were coming and going steadily. I wondered if I should give up, and take refuge in one of them. But I was very close to home, and hospitals could be hit, too. In fact, during that night the Royal Infirmary and the Mill Road Infirmary were severely damaged.

I dragged onwards slowly, bothered by the smoke and dust in the atmosphere as well as by the sound of bombs whistling down on the city centre.

At the sound of the front door being opened and closed, Father, his face filled with anxiety, came up from the cellar steps. 'God! Whatever happened to you?' he exclaimed.

I licked my parched lips. 'I walked,' I said simply.

He caught my arm and led me to a chair, where I sat un. . I regained my breath. I remember the flashes of light from explosions, coming through cracks in the wooden shutters over the window, as I sat there.

Mother came up, the inevitable cigarette in the corner of her mouth, and despite the scream of bombs and diving planes overhead, she cut bread and margarine and boiled a precious egg for me, while, at the kitchen sink, I washed under our single cold water tap. Mother was extraordinarily brave under fire; I do not remember her once showing any sign of fear, and she accepted my ghastly appearance without comment, while she prepared a meal for me. I was grateful to her.

As I crouched on the cellar steps and ate from a tray balanced precariously on my knee, I told the sleepy family what I had seen.

Mother heaved a big sigh. 'I hope Brian and Fiona are all right – Brian is doing his messenger service, and Fiona went to a Christmas dance at the Grafton, with some of her friends.'

For the benefit of the three younger children present, I said cheerfully, 'I'm sure they will have taken cover and be all right.' Mentally, I was angry with myself for having described in front of them so vividly what I had seen on my walk home. I must have frightened them. They did settle down again, however, on the mattress which Mother had put down for them on the coaldust-laden floor of the cellar.

When small snuffles indicated that they had fallen asleep, I told my parents of the incident which had most upset the office. 'It isn't in our district – it's in Sandhills – but we had people inquiring about it at our office – some of them relations of those trapped. It's in Bentinck Street, where the railway line crosses it. There is – there was – a row of four or five railway arches there, really well built – solid; a first-class air raid shelter, where lots of people slept every night. And last night, you know, Mum, it got a direct hit and the arches came hurtling down on the shelterers.

Most of them are dead, but it is believed that some are alive – and they can't get them out – the stone blocks of those arches are so big that they have nothing they can move in which will lift them.'

'What are they going to do?' asked Father.

'Last thing I heard, they are going to bring something in to split the blocks, to make them moveable. But by the time they've done that, it will be too late. Even if some are alive, they'll be horribly injured; they'll wish they were dead. Every time I think about it I feel sick.'

'Poor souls,' Mother whispered.

'One of our wardens told me that there isn't a hope in hell for them – somebody built that bridge all too well.' I crunched up my eyes. We all had a kind of faith in the heavy rescue squads, that we would always be dug out. Now that trust was shaken. I wondered how long it would take the living to die.

I sighed. 'I can't imagine what Bootle will be like after tonight. I'll go back first thing tomorrow.'

'On Sunday?' exclaimed Mother.

'Well, of course. What else can I do?'

About six in the morning, Brian returned, as filthy as I had been. His grin was as great as ever when he said, 'Helped to dig out at Mill Road Infirmary.'

He was followed almost immediately by a white and shaken Fiona, who had managed to get a taxi from the Grafton, after agreeing to share it with three other people.

'It was awful, Mum. We'd hardly got there – I'd just walked into the ballroom and was looking for the others, when there was a most horrendous explosion. A whole chunk of the roof blew off, and bits came raining down round the alcove in which the band sits. Poor Mrs Hamer – you know, the lady who conducts – dived under the grand piano! It's funny now.' She gave a sheepish giggle. 'But it was really scary, and I turned to run outside; I was afraid of being buried. One of the men hanging around the door stopped me. He said I'd get hit by flak, and to stay put.'

'That was wise,' said Father, as he helped her off with her coat.

'Well, I'm glad I stayed. Mrs Hamer picked herself up, and the band went on playing as if nothing had happened. They tidied up the floor a bit, and we all danced until the all clear went, around five o'clock. We had a good time, though sometimes I was a bit frightened when I could hear the bombs dropping nearby.'

Mother was bustling round, making early morning tea. 'You shouldn't be out on nights like this,' she scolded.

'Oh, Mummy, I might as well be there as here; they could easily have attacked the south side instead.'

'I get worried about your getting home, as well.'

'That was easy. There was this young army officer wanting to get back to the barracks here. He got a cab from somewhere and shared it with three of us; he was really nice.'

Still gossiping, everybody went to bed and I had my breakfast and went to work.

# Chapter ten

That chilly Sunday morning, for the first time, I had to show my special identity card, which indicated that I was a social worker.

I was stopped by a police constable on duty near the Rialto Cinema, where Princes Road, Upper Parliament Street and Catherine Street all meet. I had hoped to pick up a tram or bus there.

'Nobody allowed in the town this morning,' he told me, as he handed the little green card back to me. 'Where was you wanting to go?'

'Bootle.'

'Ye gods! Ye'll have a job.' He watched me put the card safely back into my shabby handbag, and then looked past me. ''Alf a mo', they might give you a lift.' He signalled someone approaching from behind me.

A police car, with two constables in it, drew up beside us.

'This young lady's with the welfare. She's got to get to Bootle – to work. Could you take her?'

'Goin' down to Dale Street,' answered the heavy, red-faced officer at the wheel. He turned to me. 'Could drop you at the corner of Scotland Road, or rather Byrom Street, for starters,' he offered.

A police car would certainly be allowed through any road blocks, so I gratefully accepted. Though there were few civilians about, air raid and fire personnel were clustered round dusty heaps of rubble, some still smouldering, and our driver had to edge his way through several streets which were littered with debris from homes and little shops ripped open from top to bottom, to show an assortment of wallpapers looking garish in the dancing light of lanterns and torches carried by the air raid wardens and rescue workers. It was the coldest and darkest time of the year, the worst time to lose one's home. I hoped it would not snow.

At the corner of Byrom Street, along which I had flitted through the blitz only a few hours before, the driver honked his horn at a W.V.S. canteen van. The van drew into the kerb.

'What's up?' the lady driver shouted.

The constable in the passenger seat leaned out of the car's window and bellowed an inquiry as to their destination.

'Bootle.'

'I guessed right,' the constable said to me, with some satisfaction, and it was arranged that the W.V.S. driver would give me a lift.

Sandwiched between two volunteers, both housewives who had been up most of the night and were now taking food to stricken Bootle, I heard their stories of the raids.

When I saw the office still standing, I muttered, 'Thanks be.'

Miss Evans and the first voluntary worker to come in were already besieged by bewildered people, many of whom had been bereaved the previous night and had lost their homes. A greater number of dusty, dishevelled inhabitants had homes only partly damaged. They had, however, had their little store of food ruined, tins squashed or pierced, bread, milk and margarine filled with dust or sand, and their handbags or precious ration books lost in the mess. They had no money to buy fresh food and did not know where to get a new ration book on a Sunday.

One elderly lady, brought in by a neighbour, had lost her spectacles and could barely see. A man's tools had been blown away. Neither had money to replace their loss. Harassed mothers, the usual representative of families, told us that their whole families were so covered with soot falling from the chimney that they were hardly recognisable; there was no water to wash in and they had no change of clothing. And almost every person complained of cold, because, at the very least, their windows had been blown out.

As the day progressed, our small funds were rapidly depleted and our store of clothing shrank.

Apart from giving help ourselves or directing people to other sources of aid, we represented the Red Cross Society. The Red Cross had set up a system by which a letter of twenty-five words could be sent to a prisoner of war, who otherwise rarely got any news at all from Britain. It was always a surprise to me that, after an air raid, many of our clients gave first thought to reassuring their husband, son or lover in a German prisoner-of-war camp that they were safe. It was as if they expected that news of a raid on a man's home town would be immediately transmitted to him by some unknown means.

I marvel at how much love and caring was conveyed in those twenty-five-word messages, by semi-illiterate women often carrying an unbearable burden themselves.

The most pressing need that Sunday morning was water; water to wash people in, water to wash clothes, water to make tea, water to wash out houses filled with dust and debris. I was told that the municipality opened the public swimming pool, provided soap and towels, and invited the soot-covered bombed-out to come to have a bath. We still had a water supply in the office, so our small stock of coal was used to make a fire in the old basement kitchen range to heat it, and we were able to bath a number of children in the big, old-fashioned iron bath, which still stood in our cloakroom. Then we dressed them from the store in our clothing room.

People were strangely quiet and very practical. We had odds and ends of families much in need of comfort; two young girls, who had slipped down the street at the beginning of the raid, to visit friends, had stayed while the bombing continued. They had returned to a hole in the ground where their home should have been, and no family survivors; an unknown baby picked up in the street and howling lustily for food was brought in by a young boy, who did not know what to do with it; an electrician still in pyjamas, anxious to get to work the following morning, despite his flattened home, had neither clothing nor tools left; two elderly women needed doses of special medicines, their supply having been lost in the ruins of their homes. And so it went, all day long.

At four o'clock, my colleague, who had worked most of the night, and I, who had had little sleep, were both exhausted. We went together to the waiting-room and said sadly that we could do no more. 'Could any of you come back in the morning?' we asked in despair.

Everybody sat firm; they were equally desperate. One woman said kindly, 'You go and have a cup of tea, luv, and rest a bit. We'll wait.' Everybody nodded gently in agreement.

We sat quietly by our one-bar electric fire, while a volunteer in a rather better state of repair than we were made tea. We shared the bread and margarine I had brought from home and a chocolate bar provided by the volunteer; we drank our tea in quick, scalding gulps. Then we went on again.

We closed the office at seven o'clock. By that time bombing had recommenced, and nobody fresh had come into the waiting-room since the air raid warning had blasted out over the ruined little dockside town. We dealt with everyone remaining, and then set out for home.

My colleague had the use of a little car owned by the charity, so I presume she went home in that; the society's petrol ration was so small, however, that there was no possibility of her driving me home to the south side of Liverpool. A tram trundled slowly along Stanley Road and I thankfully swung myself on to it. In the harried city centre, however, there seemed to be neither tram nor bus going in the direction of the Rialto Cinema, so, drunk with fatigue, I walked the rest of the way home.

Though all around me an orange sky and persistent explosions proclaimed more disasters, the need to get home was paramount, and I concentrated on putting one weary foot in front of the other.

The whole family came up from the cellar steps, to greet me. Each vied with the other to tell of the devastation they had seen during their Sunday walks. They were electrified by the drama of it all.

'It's too bad,' Father exclaimed, 'St Nick's has gone.'

The loss of the Sailors' Church, Our Lady and St Nicholas, hurt. It was part of our waterfront, part of our heritage.

'And Wallasey!' Fiona chimed in. 'Not Liverpool at all – across the river. It's got nothing to do with the war – it's just houses. And it was bombed like anything! What would the Germans want to do that for?'

I shrugged helplessly.

'The biggest bang was Evans, Sons, Lescher and Webb going up,' announced Tony, in reference to a chemical company for whom my old friend, Sylvia Poole, worked. 'They said it was like an enormous firework display!'

'Poor Sylvia,' I said. 'That will put her out of work.'

I drew up a chair to the living-room table and hastily ate a very dried-out Sunday dinner, which had been keeping hot for me in the oven of the big iron range, since midday.

'Where's Brian?' I asked, suddenly realising that he was missing.

'The fool's gone upstairs to bed,' Mother snapped crossly. 'He refused to take cover on the steps with us – the stupid boy said he was too tired. I'm worried to death about him, up there. Supposing the bedroom window is blown in? He'll be cut to pieces.'

I did not reply. While Mother poured herself another cup of tea and took it back to the cellar steps, I took my dinner plate and cup to the kitchen sink and washed them under the cold tap; a rime of gravy refused to come off the plate, so I left it to soak.

Suddenly, my senses began to reel and I clutched at the draining board for support. Then I staggered to the open cellar door.

The family looked up. In the warm candlelight their faces reminded me of a mediaeval painting; the children's innocent looks, their parents' careworn visages, could have been the detail filling the corner of some great canvas from Siena.

'I'm sorry, Mother,' I said flatly, 'I have to lie down; otherwise I'll collapse. I'm going to bed.'

At the foot of the cellar steps was a single mattress on which Tony, Edward and Avril would soon curl up together. Behind it lay a small pile of softly glittering coal, and to the left I could see the dim outline of a big clay and brick wash-boiler, and in front of it an open space. It was not considered safe to put another mattress in this space, because of the weight of furniture in the room above it. So the older members of the family always sat on the steps during raids.

Followed by Mother's fretful clucking, I staggered through the living-room and up the stairs. Through the uncurtained window of my bedroom the sky looked like Guy Fawkes Day. I kicked off my shoes and fell on to the bed. I did not hear the all clear sound, but the next morning, Monday, I was up at six and went back to work. In Bootle, there was no sound of carols in the streets, no busy last-minute shopping for Christmas amid bright lights. Instead, there was dire need amid the almost total darkness of the blackout.

The Germans left us alone during the Christmas holiday itself. I imagined, with a wry chuckle, the entire Luftwaffe, all overweight and ash blond, standing round Christmas trees and singing 'Holy Night, Silent Night'. I did not wish them joy. I was at work throughout that time. If the family had a Christmas dinner, I did not share it. I left my humble gifts on the living-room table for them to find on Christmas morning. I suppose they must have given me gifts, but I have no memory of them. I was so exhausted that I forgot my own grief.

# Chapter eleven

A girl named Belle, whom I was to meet later in the war, was in Mill Road Infirmary when it was bombed during the Christmas blitz. She told me how scarifying it was to lie helpless after having her appendix out, not daring to move in case she burst her stitches and bled to death, while bits of plaster from the ceiling fell on to her bed and she expected the roof to cave in on her any moment.

'When the nurse came and put my pillow over my face, I thought I'd suffocate,' she said. 'But she was only trying to save me from being cut by flying glass. As if a pillow was much good – I've seen glass slivers go right through a mattress!'

The memory of the bravery of the nurses remained with her for many years afterwards; they were true heroines, and it was the same at the Royal Infirmary.

I wondered why they – that almighty They – did not paint red crosses on the roofs of hospitals; and then I realised that it would be difficult in the case of our hospitals; most of them had been built in Victorian times, with fancy turrets, twisting chimneys and steeply sloping roofs, not a very practical surface on which to paint a cross.

When I suggested this to Father, he laughed cynically.

'They wouldn't show any mercy, anyway,' he assured me. 'There isn't much mercy in hand-to-hand fighting. And killing from a distance, as they are doing? I don't suppose they feel the slightest qualm.'

I thought of the babies born during the blitz – life going on, despite the fear of death. There were some hair-raising stories of babies being born in air raid shelters, and at least one made his way into the world under the counter of his parents' tiny corner shop. When her birth pangs began, his mother crawled into the shelter of its heavy oak slab. The midwife, when she arrived after cycling through the raid, crawled in after her, and delivered the baby by the light of a candle. We actually had a terrified girl begin to give birth to her baby on our office floor. Mothers in shock sometimes produced a dead child, which was an added grief, and in Bootle a lot of miscarriages were blamed on the frightening experiences of expectant mothers whose homes were damaged or demolished.

Doctors were another group who, with wonderful courage, remained at their posts. Raids began in the middle of operations; lights failed when crackling electric cables were knocked down; floors caved in under them or fell on them, incendiaries falling slantwise came crashing through roofs and windows at the most inopportune moments; injured civilians buried under menacing piles of fallen masonry had, somehow, to be reached and their agonies assuaged. More than one gave his life for that of his patient.

On the Boxing Day of that sad blitzed Christmas, our old alarm clock clanged at six in the morning, and I shot out of bed. I had to go to work.

While the rest of the family slept on, I ran downstairs. In order to see what the weather was like, before I put the light on, I folded back the heavy wooden shutters of the living-room window.

It was bitterly cold and the unheated room still smelled of soot from a bad shake which our house had received, when a bomb had fallen a few streets away and had brought down all the soot from the chimney. I lifted the window in the hope of letting out some of the sooty odour, but the still air outside was so full of fine dust particles from the raids that it did not smell any better.

I leaned over the sill and looked up at the sky. It was still very dark, and the dust haze made it worse; it seemed to me, however, that there was some cloud cover as well as dust.

Dear God, I thought, if you are up there, send us some snow. Send it now, while we've got the people under cover at least – before we get more homeless on our doorstep.

Snow would clean the air. Snow would blur the image of the city, partially camouflaging it. If the snow were heavy enough, flying would become difficult and the Luftwaffe might be deterred from a further raid.

Shivering with cold, in my nightgown, I leaned out and prayed passionately, 'Snow, O Lord, snow! Enough to give us time to clear up a bit before the next raid, please.'

And it *did* snow, fine, soft flakes sizzling into the still glowing furnaces which had been buildings, covering churches and public houses, shops and warehouses and homes. It covered our wounds and made everything virginally beautiful with its glittering whiteness.

Few people were about, as the trams I caught took me out to the office. I sat and sewed as I travelled. I always carried with me either knitting or embroidery, and in this way made little gifts for the family, for Christmas and birthdays. With a few scraps of old garments or bed linen, I could make soft toys, handkerchiefs, clutch handbags, nightdress cases and matching hair tidies – hair tidies were small embroidered or lace-decorated pokes, hung by a ribbon from dressing-table mirror stands. All the loose hairs from brushes and combs were put into them, and they were emptied when the room was cleaned. No bedroom was complete without a pretty hair tidy. From second-hand wool, unravelled from worn-out sweaters, I knitted mittens, gloves, scarves and berets.

Often, when I travelled after air raids, I went into the unknown. Telephones were so few that it was rarely possible to ring to inquire from a friend or a business or an institution how they had fared during the night, to ask, for example, if a train or bus was still running. Very often, what few telephones there were were unreachable, because the lines were down. In my working-class world, nobody had a telephone, except the doctor or the chemist. There were, as yet, no public telephone boxes in our district, and the instant transfer of personal news and reassurances was far in the future.

When public transport was disrupted, it was not very easy to communicate with the shorthand pupils I taught in the evenings. The students never replied to letters, although the Post Office was still extraordinarily efficient. Increasingly, when I arrived on my students' doorsteps, after a difficult journey, I would be told that our Em, or our Marjie, was working overtime and would not be home for her lesson. There was also a growing feeling, well expressed by one of my pupils, originally a shop assistant and now in a munitions factory. She tossed her brilliant golden mane, and said, with a shrug, 'I'm earnin' that much on munitions, more'n any typist. What's the point in lairnin'?'

I suggested gently that, after the war, she might be glad of shorthand and typing skills.

She laughed. 'I'll be married afore then. I won't have to work.'

Knowing that without money from teaching shorthand I would not be able to continue working in Bootle, I renewed my efforts to find more lucrative employment.

A cold, depressed New Year came and went. Slowly Bootle picked itself up, and the office returned to near normality. There were further sporadic bombings, but nothing so terrifying as the Christmas blitz.

One blustery February morning, after a short, sharp raid, I found on our doorstep a flurry of faded yellow pages from a large book. The script was alien to me, so, out of curiosity, I made a neat pile of them and took them inside to show Father.

Father spread the pages on the table and turned them over carefully. He was as intrigued as I had been.

'I think it's Hebrew.' He rubbed a page gently between his fingers. 'The paper is very good, and, see, the pages have been hand-cut with a paper knife; you don't see that very often nowadays. The book must have been quite old.' He pondered over my find for a moment or two, and then said, 'I wonder if the book belonged to Mr Cohen. He was killed last night, you know. Direct hit on his shop, poor old man. His daughter survived, though. She's in the Royal Infirmary – the warden told me, when I went out to have a look round after the all clear went.'

'Do you think she'd like to have them?' I asked. 'They could be all that she has left, in connection with her father.'

So, in the hope of bringing some small comfort to a badly injured elderly Jewish lady, Father and I combed the adjoining streets and alleyways and asked our neighbours to look in their back yards for any further pages. We collected quite a number. We wiped the dust off them, dried them where necessary, and made a neat parcel of them.

Since it was the weekend, and Father did not have to go to work, he undertook to cycle over to the Royal Infirmary to see Miss Cohen.

Miss Cohen was still under the anaesthetic after surgery for her injuries and was, therefore, not able to receive a visitor. Father explained to the Ward Sister the purpose of his journey, and she undertook to give the parcel to Miss Cohen, with a hastily scribbled note from Father. 'If the book is not hers, the pages can be thrown away,' Father told the nurse.

Weeks went by and we forgot about the incident. Then Father received a letter written in a stiff, upright hand. Miss Cohen had been touched beyond measure by Father's kindness; the pages did, indeed, belong to the book her father had been reading during the raid. As we had suspected, the pages were the only thing left from her old home, and she would treasure them always. She was in a convalescent home in Wales and was now walking with the aid of sticks.

Father and I looked at each other. Though we did not say anything, it was obvious that we were both struck by her quiet acceptance of what had happened to her. I wondered what it was like to have to begin again when one was about fifty-five years old.

Another person who had unexpectedly to begin again was Fiona. She received a week's notice to leave, from the magazine agency which employed her. The agency was closing down for the duration, because its subscribers were now so scattered, and it was also difficult to obtain the magazines normally ordered for them from the United States.

'What am I going to do?' she wailed. 'They were so nice to me.'

'You'll have to report to the Employment Exchange,' Mother told her briskly. 'Perhaps they'll put you in the Forces.'

Fiona was aghast. Though she had stayed at school until she was fourteen, she, like me, had not much education, and she was scared at the thought of where she might be sent by the omnipotent Employment Exchange.

# Chapter twelve

Fiona was directed by the Employment Exchange to work in a factory in Speke, a suburb on the south side of Liverpool. The factory manufactured components for aircraft. The journey to work was not difficult but, since her shift began at eight o'clock, she had for the first time in her life to get up early.

She was most excited at the prospect of earning the much higher wages offered to her, and enjoyed the period of training she was given.

'The girls are very rough,' she told me. 'Their language is unbelievable.'

'Did the Employment Exchange give you any other choices?' I inquired.

'No. Except that I could have gone into the A.T.S., if I could have passed the army medical. And I didn't want that, really. At least I can come home at night, if I'm in a factory.'

She really was not very strong; we had always protected her from heavy work, and I hoped the job she was given would not require great muscular strength.

Another change was pending in the family. The severity of the Christmas raids had, at last, been enough to convince Mother that the younger children should have remained in the country. Tony was now over fourteen though, and she felt he should remain in Liverpool. During his earlier evacuation he had, like Brian, won a scholarship to the Liverpool Institute. The Institute had originally been evacuated to Wales, so he had gone there to join it. Because so many boys returned home, the Institute had been reopened in Liverpool, so when Mother arranged for his return home, he was able to continue school.

Now, once more, Mother wrote to the aunts, my father's sisters, who lived across the river, to ask if they would again accept little Edward and Avril into their home.

Because the aunts originally faced having Liverpool slum children billeted on them, they had asked that some of their nephews and nieces be sent to them, to be their evacuees. We had thankfully accepted their offer. Tony and Edward had been well cared for by them, and Avril had been most kindly looked after by a friend of theirs.

We all waited impatiently for a reply to Mother's request. Despite the disruptions of the war, we could reasonably expect an answer within forty-eight hours.

No reply came. Then Father discovered from files in his office that the authorities had decided that the aunts' village, Hoylake, was now considered too close to badly bombed Birkenhead and Wallasey to be safe for evacuees; the aunts were, therefore, exempt from billeting.

A subsequent letter to their friend who had looked after Avril elicited a polite reply saying that they had another child staying with them.

A scattered raid which damaged property near to us finally prompted Mother to consult the children's schoolteachers. Within a couple of days, Edward and Avril were whisked away to Wem, a small village in Shropshire.

There they really suffered. Billeted on poor families with few facilities, people who also did not want them, they were even colder and more hungry than they had been at home. The local school had to accommodate the village children as well as the evacuees, so pupils were taught in two shifts, which meant a very early start to the day for our young ones. They had a long walk to the school and back, and then a dreary afternoon when they were not wanted in their hosts' houses and yet had nowhere to go. Far more than the heavy raids they had endured in Liverpool, the bitter experiences of their second evacuation were ingrained in their minds for the rest of their lives. I could cheerfully have shot Mother for removing them from the comfort and safety of their original billets.

Tony had never talked much about his earlier experiences in Wales, except to say that he was first billeted with a very old lady, who lived alone in a huge, neglected house. Though she was kind, she had no idea how to manage a strange little boy. He must at first have been very frightened, but he never complained of being unhappy. Perhaps his life there was marginally better than it was at home, and his unquenchable sense of humour carried him through. When the subject of re-evacuation was brought up, he said simply, 'I won't go.'

Once the two younger children were re-evacuated, our household was reduced to Father and Mother, Brian, Tony, Fiona and me. Except for Tony, all of us had work. Mother's irritation at my refusal to become a full-time housekeeper was reduced to a steady grumble. I still did my share of housework and standing in queues. My days were very long, however, particularly those on which I had to walk to work. In an effort to cope with the needs of our war-weary clients, the staff continued to work long into the evening and through the lunch hour.

During this period, as I tried to overcome my sense of hopeless loss, to stop myself glancing along the rows of anxious faces in the waiting-room, in the hope of seeing one cheerful, broken-nosed, beloved countenance, I began to understand better the turmoil within an apparently coherent, calm client; I looked for the real person behind the mask. Later on, it gave me strength not to flinch, when faced with a pilot whose face had been burned off or with frightfully misshapen civilian cripples. I sought the valiant, hurt personality within the shattered frame, the truest bravery sitting silently, uncommunicatively, in a wheelchair.

In my mind, also, the difference between black, white, yellow and brown people lessened. I lived in a district with a fairly large black West African population and the Chinese community was not far away. Bootle itself had a number of seamen from the Far East, some Indians and Negroes; most of them had white wives and gorgeous-looking children. As the bitterness of the blitz drew us all closer together, I learned that we all shared the same needs, the same fears, the same bigotry; we were simply the human race.

At the time, having met hundreds of fleeing Jews, I found it difficult to include Germans and, later on, the Japanese in the human race! In the face of the licensed cruelty and murder of a war, it is hard to stand back and view the faults of one's own beleaguered nation, and then judge.

Though ignorant and very innocent, caught in the trap of a lonely, narrow life, in a few months I seemed to grow from adolescence to maturity, just as the boys who went into the Forces suddenly became men.

I often wondered what a normal life was like. Was there such a thing? What was it like to live all one's life in one house, go to one school for twelve years, be trained for a profession or go to university? I could not recall what it was like to eat three meals a day as a matter of course. What was it like to have friends you had known all your life, people you never had to explain anything to, because they knew of, and had shared, many of your experiences? Go out to dinner? To parties? I had been to only one adult party in my life – Sylvia's twenty-first birthday celebration. What was it like to stay in the house of a friend? How should one behave in such circumstances?

The novels I read dealt with the crises of life, not the humdrum everyday. Being moved about as a child, like a tiddly-wink counter being neatly pinged into ever-new cups, was not a great deal of help to me in answering these questions. A child visitor was not treated in the same way as an adult. One was often put to sleep in the corner of someone else's bedroom, someone who, often enough, found a child a nuisance. Frequently, in my grandmother's house, I was very lonely and fell back upon a morose charwoman for company. Above all, I was expected to be quiet, which immediately stifled many of the questions a child might have asked in normal circumstances.

Moving to and fro, from Grandma's house to my parents' house, parents who often moved themselves, meant that I was, during my few years at school, usually 'the new girl', and I grew ever shyer and more diffident as I moved from school to school.

My parents and their friends, caught up in the mad gaiety of the early

Twenties, after the First World War, had lived a life separate from that of their children. We were penned up in a nursery with a nanny. Except for glimpses of other children's parents when we went, occasionally, to play with families like our own, grown-ups and their behaviour were something of a mystery to us. Grandma, two aunts and an older cousin, who lived together, were probably more familiar to me than any other grown-ups, but I was always acutely aware of being an outsider amongst them, and, looking back, I am surprised how little I really knew them.

In the long, noisy nights of the blitzes, when it seemed that we might all be dead before morning, I pondered for hours on these gaps in my knowledge.

I knew my crisis-ridden clients quite well. I had seen their dreadful poverty, though it was not as acute as mine had been. I admired their bravery and resourcefulness. But their world was totally different from the world from which I had sprung. They had deep-rooted family ties. Most of them had always lived in the same street and had a strong sense of neighbourliness. They worked in the same places that their fathers and grandfathers had done. They belonged to trade unions and benevolent societies and to churches and chapels. They had networks.

Normally, was it like that in the middle classes?

Was Grandma's household, where I had spent so many healing months as a little child, a normal household? No man lived in that house, and a male visitor was rare indeed. Did not the four staid women who lived there have wild desires like me? How did they subdue them? What had lain behind their gently smiling faces?

Being a surrogate parent from the age of eleven had cut me off from ready discussion with my siblings, of their experiences and ideas. To me they were our children, whose needs must be met; I never thought of them as people in whom I could confide or ask difficult questions of. The three younger children, Tony, Avril and Edward, had no memory of our earlier life, and Brian had very little; theirs was a totally different upbringing. Only an occasional word dropped by Fiona and Alan indicated their remembrances, and their lack of shared early experience with the rough, though quite friendly, youngsters living round us.

I never dared to ask Mother what she would regard as normal. She could demolish me with a word. When Father felt like communicating, he talked like a Canadian on the telephone, a flood of words which could last for an hour without stopping to take breath. He was interesting and witty but a difficult person of whom to ask straight questions.

Legally and in truth, I had become an adult, an adult without the experiences of my class or status. I was anxious to blend into my odd world as I found it, not to be thought of as unusual by my acquaintances at the office or by the neighbours, most particularly not to be thought of as uneducated. Though quite loquacious, I tended to avoid any expression of my own deeply held beliefs and ideas, and would often agree politely with anything people said to me, no matter what I felt; it was as if I papered over the cracks and voids of personality and experience with what I regarded as suitably patterned wallpaper. To many observers the result must have been quite eccentric.

Though my parents seemed unaware of the fact, Fiona, too, was grown up. She was becoming increasingly resentful because, like many parents, Father and Mother tried to dictate to her who should be her friends. They had one idea in mind, that she should make a good marriage. At nineteen, she was bent on pleasing herself, and it seemed to me that she chose quite well. She was not nearly so stupid as she pretended to be, and she had inherited Mother's ability to play a part if she wanted to – to avoid the persecution I endured from Mother, and to avoid taking a turn as family housekeeper, she had most successfully played for years the part of Mother's darling, empty-headed little girl. I did not blame her in the least; I wished that I had been that smart. Now, however, she wanted to be her own woman.

Many years later, it was interesting to see her on stage in amateur dramatic performances. She was unusually adept at interpreting a character, and I felt sad that she had not had the opportunity to exploit this gift in the professional theatre. With this ability and her great beauty, she might have become a popular actress.

Now, feeling more independent as a result of her good wages, this usually placid, inoffensive young woman rebelled.

One raidless evening, while the rain beat down outside, she announced to my parents, seated finishing a last cup of tea after the evening meal, that she was considering becoming engaged to a young watchmaker, whose politics were known to be far left.

Father slapped down his newspaper, knocking over his cup, and blew up like a ruptured gas main. Mother, for once in total agreement with her mate, was equally noisy. 'Fiona, how ridiculous! He's not a nice young man at all, and you must know it!'

I could not remember ever seeing Fiona so angry as she became that night. Dry-eyed, but flushed, she said furiously that she would live her own life and make her own mistakes. Irritation, suppressed for years, came bursting out, and I realised how alike we were, except that she had had the self-control which I lacked. She suddenly ceased to be, to me, a rather distant saint, who, according to Mother, was always perfect, and became infinitely more loveable in her distress.

Finally, she snatched up her macintosh and handbag, and stormed out of the house.

My parents were left facing each other, nonplussed and panting with rage. I had been in the back kitchen, washing the dishes. Not wishing to be caught up in the row, I had watched through the open door while I continued the greasy, sooty job. We were always short of soap, and a small kettle of hot water is not enough to clean saucepans used on an open coal fire. Dish detergents, now taken for granted, were still being tested in the laboratories; in any case, we probably could not have afforded them.

Now, I wiped my hands on our single murky tea towel, and came into the living-room. For once, my parents looked dumbfounded, unsure of themselves. As I sat down, facing them at the table, I felt almost sorry for them. It was as if some quiet grassy slope had suddenly blown up under their feet, leaving a gaping hole.

'Don't be too upset, Mummy. Fiona will cool down in a little while, and you'll be able to talk to her again.'

Neither parent answered me; Fiona had said too many bitter things to them. Home truths that they would have accepted from me as being just my vicious, bad-tempered character, came hard from a daughter noted for her gentleness.

I tried again. I was very anxious that Fiona should not marry in haste, out of defiance. 'She may not marry him, you know. Engagement isn't marriage – and they are often broken, nowadays.' I paused. The silence was oppressive. 'Try not to be too upset. Just wait and see what really happens.'

Mother suddenly collected herself. 'You mind your own business. Keep out of this. We will decide who she marries.'

Father, also, had recovered a little of his usual equilibrium, though he drummed his fingers on the table, as he always did when upset. He gave me a warning look, and then said to Mother, 'She is under age, don't forget. She can't marry without my permission.'

I nodded agreement, and sighed wearily. Then I edged my way round the back of Father's chair, to get at the fruit basket, which held the socks to be darned. I wondered wryly if I would ever be freed from mending woollen socks each night; even a husband would need his socks darned, and I thought, with a sudden pang, that a seaman would have needed warm, hand-knitted ones – but that would have been a labour of love.

Rescue from these monotonous tasks was on its way; a wonderful thread called nylon was already being used for the manufacture of parachute silk; it would, in time, rescue women from hours and hours of work.

I studiously avoided meeting Mother's eye, by concentrating on threading the needle, as she got up impatiently from her chair, and flipped back and forth in the tiny space of the room, muttering, 'We have to stop this.' I thought how wise I had been to say nothing about Harry to them.

While they verbally tore the ill-starred watchmaker apart and discussed possible strategies, my needle flew swiftly in and out of sock heels. I said not a word.

I felt Fiona creep into our double bed late that night, but I feared Father or Mother might hear me if I said anything much, so I just asked, 'You all right?'

She whispered, 'Yes,' and I turned over to sleep again.

She must have risen very early. I did not hear her. When Father and I went downstairs to start the fire and the breakfast, there was a note addressed to me lying on the table.

'I am leaving home,' she had written. 'I am so fed up. Don't worry about me. I will phone you at the office.'

# Chapter thirteen

'It's all your fault,' Mother shrieked at me.

She stood in her nightgown in the middle of the living-room, while my harassed father dodged round her, as he gathered newspaper, a bundle of wood chips and a bucket of coal, in order to build the fire in the Victorian grate, a task he undertook each morning, provided we had coal.

Normally, long before the rest of the family got up, the living-room was warm and cosy, and hot kettles of water stood on the stove, ready for them to wash in. So that the room continued to keep warm for the children returning at lunchtime, Mother would bank up the fire with damp slack before she left for work.

Both Father and I appreciated being able to hold our cold hands over the flames before we went out, he because his circulation was very poor and I because I was cursed with rheumaticky pains in both hand and leg joints. Though I got up at six o'clock, I had such a long journey to work that I could not wait to heat water before getting washed, and I always washed in cold. This also chilled me.

Now, as Father struck a match and put it to the kindling newspaper, I went into the kitchen to wash myself. Angry that I had not replied to her, Mother flew after me.

'You've encouraged her to leave. Why else would she leave a note for *you*? Really, you're nothing but a troublemaker!' She flourished Fiona's note at me.

I ran cold water into the washing-up bowl, and stripped off my nightgown. As goose pimples rose all over me, I wished that the gas stove would work properly, so that I, too, could have hot water; but I dared not waste time waiting for a kettle to boil.

Father had put a cup of water in a tiny pan on the only gas burner that worked reasonably, so that Mother could have early morning tea. Now, spitting like a fighting cat, Mother dumped the water into a small teapot and stirred vigorously. I gritted my teeth, partly to stop them chattering with the cold and partly to hold back the sharp tirade I would have liked to let loose at Mother.

I scrubbed my face and neck, and icy trickles went down my flinching back. Then I said carefully, 'Mother, I haven't had anything to do with it; I've hardly seen the boy. But we do know that they've been friends for a long time – and that he'll inherit his father's watchmaking business, so it could be worse.'

Mother poured herself a jam jar of tea; we had no cups. We had commenced the war with very few, and kitchen casualties had taken their toll. It was well-nigh impossible to replace them, so great was the china shortage in the shops.

Before turning out the gas, Mother stuck a cigarette in her mouth and deftly lit it by poking it into the flame; she occasionally lost part of her eyelashes and eyebrows from this habit.

'Humph,' she snorted. 'She *must* have had encouragement.' The tiny scullery was filled with smoke, as she exhaled.

'She's grown up, Mother. Nobody can tell her what she can do and what she cannot. Certainly, I have never given her any advice,' I replied, as I dried my goose-pimpled flesh on our grubby towel – the only advantage of being the first person to wash in the morning was that the towel was dry; everybody else had to use it damp.

'The minute she phones you, get her address. Then telephone your father at the office, and he can go to bring her home.'

I sighed. Without answering, I slipped on my knickers and petticoat, and went into the living-room. I laid the towel on the fender in front of the fire, in the hope of drying it a little for Father.

Father had heard what Mother had said, and now he told me, 'You must tell us. I am really worried about the girl. Nice girls do not leave home.'

There it was again – the idea that women could not manage alone. And yet the whole population seemed to be on the move, either by government decree or, equally involuntarily, because of the bombing of the cities.

Father gave the coals a careful lift with the poker and the fire blazed up cheerfully. He laid the poker in the hearth, and then took his razor from the back of the mantelpiece behind the alarm clock. I had left my newly pressed blouse and skirt on the back of a chair near the fire on the previous evening, so that they would air overnight. Now I put them on. They still felt clammy. My stockings hung beside Mother's, laid over a piece of string stretched between nails across the mantelpiece; they were rayon, and I washed and mended them each evening. They, also, were still a little damp, but I hauled them quickly up my long legs, and rolled the tops over a pair of elastic garters; it was customary to wear an elastic foundation garment with suspenders, but mine had worn out and I saw no hope of replacing it, so I was reduced to garters and continual, surreptitious hitching up of my stockings throughout the day.

Father had gone into the kitchen to shave and wash. Now he called, 'Did you hear what I said, Helen?'

'Yes, Daddy. But, Daddy, she must be very unhappy – otherwise, she wouldn't have left.'

Father did not reply.

Privately, I was filled with admiration for Fiona's temerity. But then, I told myself wistfully, she can easily afford a bed-sitting room with cooking facilities. I had considered following her into the factory, but I knew that the minute the war ended we would then both be out of work. She would easily find a husband, but I would not – I would always have to earn my living, and I must have skills and experience to enable me to do this. Moreover, she was not very happy in her new employment.

'The girls are horribly crude,' she had told me, 'and the men! They keep trying to catch you in dark corners, so that they can fondle you.'

'Good heavens, Fi!'

'Well, I haven't much choice; I don't suppose it's any better in the A.T.S.'

'Be careful.'

'Oh, I am. I just mind my own business and try not to leave the assembly line, except with other girls. And the money is good.'

As I laid the breakfast and Mother took her turn to wash in the kitchen, she continued to grumble at what she called Fiona's ingratitude and lack of consideration.

Brian, yawning and red-eyed, wandered into the room, and inquired, as he heard Mother's complaint from the kitchen, 'What's up?'

Shaking cornflakes rapidly into six assorted bowls, I told him.

'What's the fuss? She'd have to leave home anyway if she were directed into one of the Services.'

'God forbid,' exploded Father, as I pushed a bowl of cornflakes towards him. 'At least she can live at home where she is. She was stupid to have accepted work like that – they could have found her an office job.'

Brian sat down to eat his breakfast. 'Looks as if they're going to call up all the girls, any time now,' he remarked.

I quickly made a cheese sandwich for Brian's lunch, wrapped it in the greaseproof lining from the cornflakes packet, and handed it to him. Then I scraped margarine over a couple of slices of bread to take to work myself. While I hunted through the sideboard drawer for something to wrap my lunch in, I asked Brian, 'Do you really think we'll all be called up?'

'Well, everybody's talking about it at the office,' he said.

My heart sank. With so little education, I would get the Army's most dirty, menial jobs to do. It was not a cheerful prospect.

A quick rat-tat on the front door announced the arrival of the postman; a faint rustle came from a letter being stuffed through the broken letterbox.

Mother had gone into the hall to get her hat, which she always put on immediately after arranging her hair, so that it did not get ruffled. She picked up the letter and brought it into the room.

'It's for you,' she said to me, suspicion in every line of her. As if there was something wicked about it, she added, 'It's a typed letter.'

She tossed it across the table to me.

# Chapter fourteen

The letter was from the Petroleum Board, a consortium of oil companies formed for the duration of the war. The letter asked me to go for an interview at their Dingle Bank installation, less than a mile from my home.

For the first time since Harry's death, I felt a tingle of real excitement. Nothing could bring Harry back or ease the pain of loss, but employment close to my home would alleviate the great strain and constant worry over getting to work each day.

On the morning of the interview, I telephoned the Bootle office and told Miss Evans I did not feel very well, but would be there in the afternoon. She was accustomed to the disruption caused by the acute menstrual pain I endured, and accepted my excuses. I felt a little ashamed at deceiving her; she had always been most kind to me, and it was not her fault that I was overworked and hopelessly underpaid.

I had washed all my clothes the previous evening. Now I scrubbed myself, and set my hair neatly; it was now shoulder length and I curled it with Mother's curling iron and pinned it back from my face. The result was an untidy mess, so I tied a shoelace round my head and tucked it into a neat roll, a fashion made common by the lack of hairpins and clips on the market.

The Installation lay next to the Herculaneum Dock, and, as I walked down Dingle Lane, a high wall on one side and neat, small houses on the other side, the wind blew freshly off the river; it smelled sweet after the acrid, fire-laden air of Bootle.

Shyly, I approached the policeman guarding the entrance and explained my business.

He smiled amiably down at me and inquired, to my astonishment, 'Got any cigarettes, lighter or matches on you?'

'No. I rarely smoke.'

'O.K. Go to that office over there.' He pointed to a brick building more like a small house than an office. 'And good luck,' he called after me, as I picked my way across a rutted lane.

In a glass-walled office, I was interviewed by a snappy little man in rimless glasses. Despite being indoors, he wore a bowler hat. His business suit was of a blue which Father would have instantly condemned as vulgar. I disliked him on sight.

He did not offer me a seat, but after standing in front of him for a couple of minutes, in a flash of anger I seated myself on the visitor's chair by his desk. As he fired questions at me regarding my experience, he looked me up and down, from ankles, neatly crossed, to the turban on my head.

Occasionally, the telephone on his desk rang and he barked instructions down it, while I looked around me.

Through the glass, I could see a number of people working at high desks. One of them was using a machine I had never seen before. He would tap the keys of it and then pull a handle. I learned afterwards that it was an adding machine, and very precious – like everything else, they were difficult to replace.

After one telephonic interruption, the man swivelled round to look at me again, and said, 'You'd be working in Wages.'

I answered primly that I had hoped to work in a personnel department, where my experience in social work might be useful.

'Well, Wages is Personnel, isn't it?'

I did not answer, and he continued, 'You'll be classed as a stenographer – two pounds, seven and sixpence a week, to start.' He turned back to the telephone and picked up the receiver. 'You'd better be tested,' he told me.

My heart sank a little. I did not want to be only a stenographer. Yet the wages seemed excellent – and I would have no travelling expenses. I did not know that the salary offered was not particularly high; throughout the war, Fiona was to earn much more than I did.

'Miss Hughes'll come and test you,' the man said, as he slammed down the receiver.

While we were waiting for Miss Hughes and the telephone was put to good use, I decided that if the post was offered to me, I would take it; the relief of having enough salary to enable me to buy lunch would be very great. I rationalised my decision by believing that I would gain experience which would lead me to a personal secretaryship one day.

Miss Hughes came quietly in and stood by the desk, until my interviewer deigned to notice her. She was a middle-aged woman with dull brown hair done in the same style as I had done mine. Her homely face was politely expressionless. Instinctively, I felt she shared my dislike of the man in the bowler hat.

'Take this girl and test her; she's for Wages.'

Miss Hughes's face broke into a friendly smile, as she took me into an empty office, dictated an ordinary business letter and left me to type it on a dusty Remington as heavy as a tank.

When she returned, she seemed satisfied with the result, despite two rubbings out.

'I am sorry about the corrections,' I said. 'I usually do better than that.'

There was a trace of cynicism in her laugh as she said, 'I don't think Mr Fox decided to take you on because of the quality of your typing!' She looked down at the letter, and added in a kindly tone, 'But your typing is quite good.'

She left me sitting by the typewriter, while she went to confer with Mr Fox, and I wondered what her rather odd remark meant. I had been at work on the Installation for some weeks before I discovered that I had been chosen to join Mr Fox's Young Ladies, every one of them picked because they had nice legs! The steady stream of young women coming to take the places of men called up would have made a good chorus line, as far as legs were concerned, and most of them had the prettiness of youth.

I walked home feeling like a prisoner enjoying his first few moments of freedom. For the first time for months I was almost happy. No more nightmare worries about how to get to work. No more teaching shorthand at nights and on Saturday afternoons. No more going without or with only little lunch. I could even go to the theatre a little more often, something which had been a rare treat indeed up to then.

At the end of March, I said goodbye to my kind colleague in the Bootle office, and, without a qualm, put behind me seven years of gross overwork and exploitation, the unhappiest years of my working life.

# Chapter fifteen

Despite my hopeful anticipation, I was as scared on my first day at the Installation as if I were about to be guillotined. I think that, when my friend, Belle, joined the staff a little later on, she, too, must have been quite nervous. She had had a wearying series of illnesses, and was in Mill Road Infirmary when it was hit during the Christmas blitz. Needless to say, she had lovely legs, and a very pretty face. She was vivacious and had a wicked sense of humour.

The policeman at the gate recognised me. He stood, arms behind his back, swaying gently backwards and forwards on the heels of his heavy black boots, and asked, 'So you got in?'

I smiled up at him. 'Yes, I did.'

'Well, that's very nice. Got any matches or smoking materials?'

'No.' I paused, and then, perplexed, I asked him, 'Why do you want to know?'

'Well, it's in case of fire. No smoking allowed. Everybody has to leave their matches and pipes and cigarettes with me.'

'Oh, I see. Thank you.'

Though it was early, Miss Hughes was already at her typewriter in the small brick building where I had been interviewed. When I inquired where I should go, she instructed me to follow the lane from the entrance until I came to the end of it. 'It's the building on the left,' she said.

So, on that fine spring morning, I followed a narrow, deserted, macadamised road which ran through the entire Installation. At intervals, I passed other small buildings, like the one in which Miss Hughes worked. Each one had the name of a famous oil company on it; presumably, they were, in peacetime, the local offices of their companies. Between them and behind them towered great round storage tanks, with a narrow ladder running up the side of each. Each tank was moated, so that if they leaked, the petrol or oil would be confined. Between the tanks ran pipelines over rough grass. Near one tank, two old lilac bushes were putting out buds, and other flowering bushes suggested that the area had once been a large garden. A high stone wall, patched with moss and lichens, marked the Installation's boundary. It, too, looked as if it had belonged to a garden.

At one point, I peeped into a huge garage, where it appeared that tanker lorries were being repaired. A man in greasy overalls looked down from the top of one of these behemoths and whistled after me as I passed.

I blushed and averted my gaze; I had never elicited a whistle from anyone before.

The sun shone brightly on the strange, circular storage tanks, making them look like abandoned pieces of ancient desert architecture. On the road before me, sparrows twittered and pecked, to rise and flutter away as I approached them. Seagulls sat on the edge of the tank tops and shrieked warning as I passed. Over all, hung the heavy, sickening odour of petrol, a very different smell from the close stench of Bootle slums. Above the boundary wall, I could see the chimneys of houses crowded near the adjoining Herculaneum Dock. I was a little shocked that such a volatile commodity as petrol was permitted to be stored so close to people's homes; a well-placed bomb on a single storage tank could, I felt uneasily, set off such a violent series of explosions that the entire Installation could be ignited in seconds. Such a holocaust would take with it the whole neighbourhood.

It was the knowledge of this possibility which, during a particularly vicious raid, made a quiet family man on the staff climb the deadly tanks near our office and heave off their floating roofs a series of incendiary bombs, for which incredible bravery he most deservedly received the George Cross.

I finally reached the last building on the road. Behind it loomed the boundary wall. It had a padlocked gate in it, which presumably led into Grafton Street and gave access to the Herculaneum Dock. I looked up at the little office, and paused. About thirty years later, in a novel, I would make that building into a tiny cottage, facing the river, and I would break down the boundary wall, so that the inhabitant of the cottage had access to Grafton Street. The tenant's name and the name of the book would be *Liverpool Daisy*.*

In front of the building was a large yard with a series of petrol pumps in it. Two big tanker lorries were being filled, and a man stood on top of one tank, dipping it, to check the level of its contents. Several men in overalls stood near the tankers, gossiping and shuffling papers in their hands. Such a strictly rationed commodity involved much paperwork, as the petrol passed down the lines of distribution. Not even the most involved checking system, however, prevented occasional theft, and there was a lively black market in petrol.

A youth of about seventeen, also in overalls, was placidly sweeping the yard, and whistling like a blackbird; he was the first *young* man I had noticed on the Installation. He was to be called up shortly and would

---

* First published by Robert Hale Ltd, as *Liverpool Daisy* by June Bhatia. First issued in Fontana Paperbacks, 1984.

become, before he was demobilised, a Wing Commander in the Royal Air Force, a feat which caused many earnest arguments amongst his fellow workers about the waste of talent during the Thirties, and how he might have spent his life as a labourer, had there been no war.

Shaking with nerves, I mounted the steep front steps and knocked at the door. Then, taking a big breath, to stall my sudden sense of panic, I turned the knob and walked in.

Though the lives of all my future colleagues had been upset by the war, I sometimes think that opening that door allowed me to leave a world of nightmare and enter a normal world. Yet I was truly terrified, particularly when I caught a glimpse, through an inner doorway, of two men working. It brought home to me that I had, in giving up social work, left a segment of society run almost entirely by women, a whole way of life based on caring for others. Now I was entering a man's world, in which women played only a subordinate role, a world run solely for profit.

How was one supposed to behave? It was one thing to dance or converse with men, be pleasant for a few minutes; quite another to work alongside them. Fiona was having a difficult time, I knew, amongst men who regarded her as a sexual object to be preyed upon, not as a fellow worker. I wanted to turn and run. Better the devils of hunger and privation which I knew, than the devils I did not know.

But it's too late to turn back, I reminded myself, as I stood awkwardly before two girls a little older than myself.

At the sight of me, one girl swung out of her seat behind a desk. She was tall, rosy-cheeked and merry-eyed, uncannily like my childhood nanny, Edith.

As she came towards me, she said, 'You must be the new shorthand typist. You're just in time for tea. What's your name?'

I told her, and she showed me where to hang my hat and coat. One of the men, who proved to be the Departmental Manager, came from the inner office. He told me where to sit, and suggested that I try the typewriter for a few minutes. Then he would dictate some letters to me.

Two other small offices yielded the peacetime manager of the oil company which normally occupied the building, and his quiet, unobtrusive secretary. Their work involved the design of a pipeline to run under the English Channel, and I did not see much of them, except when the secretary was ill. I then deputised for her. Because we laughed and talked so much, the two of them must have been acutely aware of the invasion of their peaceful building by the Wages and Personnel Department of the wartime consortium of the oil companies. They were, however, very patient with us.

Over a cup of tea, I relaxed a little, but I had been so cut off from my own age group, so alienated by privation, that it was months before my voice lowered its nervous, defensive pitch, to its normal, deeper key. It was months before I understood the department's racy, youthful badinage; in fact, I doubt if I ever did truly understand its more subtle inferences. I suspect that my bewilderment was a source of much good-natured amusement to all of them.

I found, to my dismay, that amongst my duties was the calculation of a payroll. At night school I had, in bookkeeping classes, been taught only how to keep a simple set of account books; and, on the side, one teacher had tutored me in basic arithmetic. I had had little practice at either. In all my years in that office, I doubt that I ever got the weekly payroll absolutely correctly put together. The men whose wages I mixed up were extraordinarily kind and patient with me, and the Departmental Manager was never more than wittily caustic about it. I was, however, deeply ashamed of my inability to do basic arithmetic. Once again, the lack of schooling had caught up with me.

To a generation brought up in a period of pocket calculators, the urgent need to be able to do mental arithmetic quickly and accurately must seem strange. Yet without mechanical help one needed such an ability at every turn, and I am sure there are still elderly people who can add up a column quicker than their grandsons can do it with a calculator. Certainly the girls in my office were very accurate.

I dreaded being dismissed as inefficient. Probably, with all the red tape which would have had to be waded through to dismiss anyone under wartime regulations, it was easier to put up with me. It came as a great surprise at the end of the war, when employers and employees were freed from government restrictions, to be offered employment by one of the oil companies.

Throughout that summer, and for many summers after, I wore to work the three dresses Harry had given me – up to then I had always regarded them as being for best occasions only. From New York, they were beautifully cut and far superior to anything the other girls wore. Two of them were black, trimmed in subdued colours, and to me they were mourning dresses. Ironically, I had no decent underclothes to wear with them.

Out of my improved wages, I gave Mother thirty shillings a week, more than I would have had to pay a landlady in our district for dinner, bed and breakfast. At last, her pressure on me to stay at home to keep house eased; I was rapidly becoming a financial asset. We managed the home between us, and I thankfully stopped teaching shorthand at night.

The first six weeks of my new employment seemed very leisured. Despite the battle with the payroll each week, the weight of work was negligible, compared with the tremendous load carried in Bootle. The extreme fatigue began to seep out of my tired limbs and exhausted mind.

During that six weeks, I did three wonderfully exciting things.

In all my life I had never been to a dentist, and during our years in

Liverpool I had, like the rest of the family, endured some excruciating bouts of toothache. Because of a poor diet and lack of a toothbrush, Mother had lost most of her teeth – they simply loosened and fell out. Some of mine were loose and several had large cavities. When they had ached, the holes had been stuffed with a tiny piece of cloth dipped in bitter oil of cloves. Feeling very daring, I made an appointment with a local dentist. It was taken for granted that a visit to a dentist was always painful, so I had to screw up my courage, as I waited in the front room of his house for my turn.

He must have been used to neglected mouths, because he simply listed a formidable collection of fillings to be done, and two extractions, one because a tooth was beyond repair and a second because it was too loose to be filled. 'They also need a good scraping,' he told me, as he filled a needle to lessen the pain of the two extractions.

It was enough work to keep a modern dentist busy for half a dozen appointments, but this was in the days before dentistry was covered by health insurance, and the dentist had to keep his fees within the bounds of what the patient could pay. He therefore did the extractions immediately. They were painful and I bled sufficiently to cause him anxiety, probably because I was so ill-nourished. The following Saturday, he drilled and filled and scraped and polished until my mouth was sore and my head spinning.

'Come in next week, and I'll give the fillings a final polish,' he ordered, as he scrubbed his hands in a tiny corner wash basin.

When the final grinding was done, so that the fillings matched the teeth above or below them, I was so happy at being free of pain at last that some of my exuberance was communicated to the dentist, and he grinned under his grey moustache, before he opened the door of his surgery to let me out. 'Feel better?' he asked.

'I feel wonderful.'

'Good.' His smile faded, as he surveyed his crowded front room. He must have been very tired. So many dentists had been called up that the weight of work on older men must have been very heavy, but not so heavy for him that he failed to remember ingrained, old-fashioned courtesies, like opening the door for me. I was touched that he should bother to do so.

Marks and Spencer's store was to me an Aladdin's Cave. There, I bought a pair of glistening black shoes with higher heels than I had ever worn before, all of one and a half inches high, and two pairs of rayon stockings – I had never before been able to buy *two* pairs at one time – and I felt very rich.

The purchases proved to be a good investment, because shortly afterwards all clothing was rationed.

Except for a pair of satin dancing shoes, bought for my Confirmation in the cathedral, these were the first new shoes I had had for ten years. I had always managed with second-hand ones.

Lastly, I opened a Savings Account at the post office nearest the Installation. I would put money into it each week. Post Office Savings Accounts had the advantage that one could save in them as little as sixpence a week. The customer was provided with a book into which he stuck sixpenny stamps, as he was able to purchase them. The money was to be accumulated for new spectacles. I was still wearing, at twenty-one, the glasses prescribed for me when I was eleven. The frames were too small and had been mended and re-mended through the years, and the lenses distorted my vision. I tended to manage without them. Now, faced with the tightly packed figures on the payroll, I suffered frequent headaches.

I carried the Savings Bank book in my handbag, and guarded the bag from Mother as if it held the Crown Jewels. Though she could not draw money from the account without forging my signature, I felt that she might easily do this, or, if she knew I had any money, she was capable of making my life such a misery that I would finally give it to her.

Many goods we take for granted were either no longer available, or were kept under the shop counters for specially favoured customers. Amongst these were make-up and hairpins and hair clips. The American seamen on the tankers docking at our Installation soon discovered this. Nylons, lipsticks and all the other small pleasures of life were soon circulating round the Installation and were eagerly bought by the girls. No Customs officer at the exit gate of the Installation had time to bother about a single lipstick or pair of stockings carried out in a girl's zipper bag; their staff was so depleted by the call-up that they were already harassed enough. I bought a lipstick and some hair clips, and felt very wicked indeed.

Occasionally, as cigarettes, also, vanished under counters, I bought Mother a packet of Camels. She always thanked me politely for them, and would then complain steadily, as she smoked them, that, compared to Player's Navy Cut, they were horrible.

We were, of course, not allowed to smoke on the Installation because of the fear of fire, so we looked forward to a morning cup of tea instead. A tea break in the morning, however, was expressly forbidden by the management. It was considered an unnecessary indulgence. Nevertheless, we always made an illicit morning cup.

Because the office staff was scattered across the Installation in the numerous small offices owned by the individual oil companies, it was difficult to supervise us, but the trying little man in the bowler hat would zip around the entire complex between ten and eleven o'clock, in an effort to surprise us sipping tea.

He roared into our little office one morning, like an autumn gale. While banging the space bar of the typewriter noisily with my right thumb, I hastily slipped my contraband cup of tea into the stationery drawer of my desk.

The resultant slop ruined a pile of typing paper and dripped with a noise that seemed unnaturally loud, on to the brown linoleum beneath my feet. I typed nonsense industriously to cover the persistent tip-tap.

I do not know where the Departmental Manager hid his cup or what the other girls did, but the picture of unnatural industry which we all presented was a miracle of instantaneous reflexes.

He said nothing, just snorted, and strode through the rooms, rattled down the basement steps to ensure that none of the yard staff was being so intemperate as to take tea and biscuits down there, came up again, glared at us and bolted out of the front door. We could hear him outside loosing his frustration on the unsuspecting yard men. We rescued our teacups and put the kettle on again.

Something had to be done, we all decided. We enlisted the help of the telephonist on the central switchboard in the main office, where the bowler hat had his glassed-in desk, at which I had been originally interviewed.

This lady was regularly informed by the wardens of the district, before the siren went, that an air raid was imminent. It was her duty to telephone each office to alert them to the impending danger. One of us would answer her ring, and she would announce, 'Yellow Alert,' or 'Red Alert,' according to the closeness of the German planes. Occasionally, she would say, 'Purple, purple,' which meant that the raid was likely to be upon our area. On receiving such warnings, we were supposed to take shelter in the basement, with the yard crew. Warnings in the daytime had, however, become very infrequent, so we took over this system.

When the bowler hat moved out of his office, all the offices on the Installation got a whispered, 'Yellow!' Other offices would report sighting him to the operator, and the girl would hastily ring the phones of offices it seemed likely he would visit. She would say, 'Hurry, it's red!' And tea would vanish and biscuit crumbs would be swept into the wastepaper basket. The dreaded Purple warning was reserved for the manager of the entire Installation. When, with suitable ponderous gravity, he emerged from his office – a rare occurrence – the whole Installation was on Purple Alert, as if the entire Luftwaffe was overhead.

It is very important that management be sometimes blind, and to separate an English woman from her teacup, even when it contained the anaemic-looking brew of wartime, takes more business acumen than it is worth spending. The bowler hat knew when he was defeated and gave up.

Though they were spent in a maelstrom of war, those six weeks were for me a time of recovery, and of learning to laugh and to enjoy the light-hearted company of my own age group. They were, in a sense, my first unworried, happy times, as I adopted my fellow employees as a second family. It seemed that the worst had already happened to me and was gone. I was moving forward into a new world.

And then came the May blitz.

# Chapter sixteen

As a result of the Lend-Lease Agreement with the United States, Liverpool was one of the primary ports through which flowed help in the war effort. The May blitz, which commenced on 1st May, 1941, was a week of night bombing aimed at destroying completely the city and its satellite towns. It was also the headquarters of Western Command, and the eradication of such an important command post would, alone, have made the attack worthwhile to the Germans.

Since previous raids had usually begun about six o'clock in the evening, I was thankful to be working close to my home. The office normally closed promptly, a luxury I had rarely enjoyed before, and I trotted through the fresh spring greenery of Princes Park as quickly as I could in order to be home before a raid began. A secondary reason for my haste was that there were soldiers in the park. They manned the anti-aircraft gun emplacements and, because there were few civilians about during the week, I was a little nervous of them.

Throughout the previous four months, there had been scattered raids causing a fair amount of damage. But we had slept undisturbed for a week or two before the May blitz, and had been lulled into a false sense of security.

We were all in our night clothes, and Brian and Tony had been in bed for some time, when, on the first night, the siren went. The clatter of incendiaries, the sound of bomb explosions and the roar of guns all seemed to come together immediately after the wail of the warning, and we tumbled down the stairs to shelter on the cellar steps. Now we shivered in the dank cold, heads on knees to protect our faces – of all injuries, young people seemed to dread most being blinded or having their faces disfigured. The family were shivering but none of them panicked, and we talked and made jokes to sustain each other, though our voices sounded oddly muffled through pyjamas and nightdresses.

After a stricken moment or two, I remembered the sound of incendiaries and that I was on fire duty that night, so I left the top step on which I was sitting and, with a muttered explanation to Mother, went through the shaking house, snatched up my overcoat from its peg in the front hall and slipped it over my faded pink nightgown. Then I cautiously opened the front door. No one was in the street and there was no sign of flares on the opposite roofs. Keeping my head down between my shoulders, I ran across the road, bare feet pattering clearly in tiny breaks in the noise. I looked up at the roofs on our side of the road.

Nothing.

Very thankfully, I ran back into the house, through it and out of the back door, to look at the rear of the houses in the next street. They seemed all right, so I opened the yard door and went into the smelly alley which ran between our yard and the adjacent ones of the next street. I looked up at our roof and the other roofs in the block. All were dark, though the sky above looked like a coronation firework display.

Sickened by the odour of urine round me and acutely aware of my bare feet in the filthy alley, I turned to go indoors again, and bumped into someone else.

I was more frightened by the sudden contact than I was by the raid itself, and I nearly fainted. A pair of arms were pushed under mine and I was unceremoniously heaved to my feet again.

'Aye, luv, what's to do?' asked our faithful air raid warden.

'Oh,' I said in relief. 'I was checking the roofs. It's my turn tonight.'

'Miss Forrester?'

'Yes.'

'You was falling. Are you faint?'

'You frightened me so much,' I laughed shakily.

'Sorry. You get indoors. I'll shout, if there's need.'

'Thanks.' I felt my way back to the door. Before entering, I scrubbed my feet thoroughly on the bit of coconut matting which served as a door mat. Not even the zooming planes above and the sharp rap of ack-ack fire outweighed the sense of sick revulsion at what I had probably walked through in the alley.

The tremendous throbbing of aeroplane engines above our heads and the quick response of the guns immediately after the warning, told us that this was probably going to be a very heavy raid, and so it proved. Both sides of the Mersey were pounded.

As the house shuddered over us from a nearby explosion, and a slate slid down the roof and shattered in the street, Mother said, 'I hope Fiona is all right.'

'I hope so, too,' I agreed through the folds of my nightgown covering my knees.

As promised in her parting note, Fiona had telephoned me at the office, and had given me her address, a bed-sitting room in a southern suburb, not far from the factory in which she worked. She had made me swear that I would not tell our parents where she was, and I had unwillingly agreed, knowing very well what a fierce family battle there would be if Mother suspected that I knew her address. All I told Mother was that Fiona had said, over the telephone, that she was living in a most respectable house.

Now, feeling sorry for Mother, I said hesitantly, 'She's living well away from the city centre.'

'I am glad.' Mother's voice sounded flat and tired. She had always leaned on Fiona for company because she was hopelessly isolated from her own kind.

It obviously had not occurred to my parents that they could have traced their errant daughter through her employers. Perhaps a factory seemed so huge and alien to them, a place where anonymous employees were simply swallowed up every morning, their identities unknown, that it seemed an impossible task. While I sat listening to the fierce detonations outside, I decided that one night I would tell Mother I would be working late, and then go to see Fiona; I wanted to be sure that she was really taking good care of herself.

As the clock crawled towards midnight, we became very silent, each one of us nursing his own fear, afraid to say anything lest we lose our courage and become hysterical.

We all jumped with surprise when, soon after one o'clock, the all clear sounded. While the rest of the family stumped back up the stairs to bed, Father and I followed our usual practice after a night attack, and went out into the street to take a look round. Several of the neighbours were doing the same thing.

Towards the city centre the sky was red, sparks eddying amid heavy clouds of smoke, while white pillars of flame from broken gas mains lunged upwards.

The streets on either side of us and our own street were apparently undamaged, and we whispered to our neighbours our relief that it should be so, as if speaking in normal voices would wake the neighbourhood. If there were anyone left asleep after such pandemonium as we had just endured, it would have been the sudden silence that would have woken him!

Like everyone else, Father and I were very shaken by the intensity of the raid, and before he went up to bed, Father sat down to smoke a cigarette. Knowing from childhood how even a thunderstorm could evoke again in his mind the roar of the battlefield, and reduce him to tears, I was loath to leave him, so I pulled a chair out from beside the table, and sat down to gossip a minute or two. He offered me a cigarette, and I laughed and took it. He had to demonstrate to me exactly how to smoke it, and I found it soothing. After that, I kept in my handbag a packet of cigarettes, mostly American ones culled from the purveyors on the Installation, and I smoked through the long, boring periods of waiting which a war brings. I smoked in innumerable queues, fish queues, sausage queues, greengrocer's queues, and bureaucratic queues for ration books or government information, for stamps or a turn in a public telephone booth. Sometimes I smoked while waiting for dates under the clock in Lime Street station.

Walking to work through Princes Park the following morning, it was as peaceful as untouched countryside. The guns stood silent amid their camouflage, and, overhead, silver barrage balloons floated like cuddly toys put there for the amusement of children. Outside the park the tranquillity was not so apparent. An ambulance came out of a side street where there was a flurry of uniforms. The driver was going very slowly, indicating that she was ferrying someone in great pain, and I trembled at the amount of suffering being endured. It must have been a bad incident, I decided.

Incident had become a word which, to me, made little of death and destruction. There had grown up a sickening gobbledygook, as the government, to avoid panic, sought to minimise what was happening. The upbeat stories in the newspapers were often nauseating in their hyperbole. The true bravery of the survivors and the dying, in the face of appalling suffering, was often overlaid by a description which made a raid sound like a football match we had unfortunately failed to win; better luck next time.

Sadly, I marched on to work. In the office, we silently looked round the desks, a quick glance by each arrival to see who was missing. When all the desks were full, we settled soberly down to work. Each day of that dreadful week we did the same. If someone was late, our hearts sank, and we would see the same worry in each other's eyes.

Towards the end of the week, our office boy who lived considerably further up the coast, in Southport, failed to arrive.

'He's as safe as houses up there,' we told each other. 'He must be ill.'

He came in after lunch, fair hair rough and uncombed, the rest of him smudged and untidy. He grinned broadly when he saw our anxious faces. 'It took a bit of time to dig us out,' he announced casually.

A bomber with a fighter in pursuit had jettisoned its remaining cargo; a bomb had hit his home. They had lost everything, but had survived themselves, unhurt.

The outside staff and the roster of firewatchers for that week had a very busy time, trying to avoid fire on the Installation. Even though we had our own fire brigade, a lot of help was needed to watch for incendiaries, or unexploded bombs or shells, falling amid the tanks. It was while on fire duty during this week that a member of the outside staff won the George Cross for his outstanding bravery.

One night, the end of the Installation's jetty was blown off. Here, American tankers were tied up and their contents pumped through pipelines running the length of the jetty, straight into the storage tanks. When the river end of the pipes was damaged, oil spewed into the water before the flow could be stemmed, and the Mersey suddenly became a deadly menace.

Wardens ran from house to house, and the news was spread by telephone from dock to dock along the river, not to so much as strike a match for twenty-four hours, while two tides swept up and down the river and cleared the spill.

As the week progressed, the national newspapers reported nonchalantly that there had been a raid on a north-west town. But by word of mouth, ominous stories reached us, even in our rather isolated workplace. We could see the heavy pall of smoke over the city centre, and on the wind came the smell of burning rubber, roasting wheat and peculiar chemical odours, and over all, and lasting the longest, the smell of wet ruins of plastered walls.

Officially, the city was not under martial law. The Board's lorry drivers reported, however, that soldiers were on guard in a number of places and were helping with the rescue work. They said, also, that the roads into the city were jammed with fire engines, caterpillar tractors and lorries, and buses full of workmen.

After several nights, I stopped in the yard one morning to ask a group of drivers waiting for their tanker lorries to be filled whether any of them had been to Bootle.

One took his cap off to me and said he had.

'What's it like?' I inquired. 'Is the damage very great?'

'It's bad. Very bad. Supposed to be eighty per cent of the houses flat or damaged. Have you got friends there, miss?'

I sighed, as, in my mind's eye, I saw the packed waiting room and the weary, ragged queue on the staircase. 'Yes,' I replied. 'I have a lot of friends there.'

'Sorry, miss.'

I smiled up at his deeply lined face, eyes almost lost in wrinkles with much driving. 'Thank you.'

Considering how great even its normal need of help was, there were very few social workers in Bootle. Now, the inhabitants must be desperate. So often, after being rescued from their smashed homes, it was middle-aged women who had to trail about on foot, children clinging to their hands, to find a place to live, to get new documentation – like ration cards, or pension books for the elderly, visit those members of the family in hospital or arrange burial for those who had died. And frequently they had no money whatever.

I knew that, at first, they would be defiantly cheerful, though shaking with shock. Their sorrow and despair would strike them a few days later.

As the week progressed, I thought of the fatigue of the police, the firemen, the wardens, the Women's Voluntary Service, the First Aid and the rescue squads. During that week, most of them never had a proper wash or took their clothes off, and they had, of course, no knowledge that the seventh consecutive raid would be the last of the series. The Germans afterwards turned their attention to London and Glasgow. The Luftwaffe was also being regrouped for the invasion of Russia – a piece of news which left us speechless when we were faced with it about six weeks later.

Meanwhile, not only Bootle, but the whole city was constantly showered by the ash of the records of hundreds of offices, their burning files drawn upwards by the draught of the fires to make a dismal pall for a considerable time, until finally it was washed out of the air by rain, and the residue dusted up by housewives and street cleaning crews.

On the seventh day, I was so quiet as I prepared my payroll that one of the male clerks asked me what was the matter.

I was near to tears, as I responded heavily, 'I feel I've left Bootle when they needed people like me the most. They'll be in an awful mess after this. I should never have left.'

Although I must have sounded a little pompous, he was sympathetic. 'You might be able to get leave from here for a week or two,' he suggested, and after a second's thought, he added, 'without pay.'

'You think I could? I'll ask Miss Hughes at lunchtime.'

Like everyone else, I was so tired simply from lack of sleep that all I wanted to do was put my head down on the desk and nap off. Everybody tried to keep going, however, and, for myself, I often felt that if for one moment I let go of my usual routine, I would collapse, simply fall apart mentally with fear and fatigue.

By lunchtime, my courage began to fail. The old fear of being dismissed for absence engulfed me, of being without a job and kept at home by a triumphant Mother. I thought with growing dread of asking a favour of the rude man in the bowler hat, of his wandering gaze and coarse speech, or, even worse, having to go to see the manager of the entire Installation, a vague authoritarian figure, of whom the girls spoke in whispers, a personage who in five years I saw only once.

After eating my bread and margarine, I went for a little walk along the single paved road of the Installation. The smell of petrol spoiled the lovely day, and I could understand why many of the older employees suffered from ulcers.

Near the main gate guarded by the police, I met the Head Stenographer, Miss Hughes, a lady who, like the regular staff in my little office, usually kept a little apart from the wartime temporary employees. She stopped, however, and beamed and asked if everything was all right.

I replied with genuine feeling, 'Oh, yes. Everybody is very nice.' I wanted to say to her that, to me, it was like having a new, extra family to love and admire. But she would have thought I was mad. It was unlikely that she had ever been quite so lonely, so isolated, torn from her natural roots, as I had been.

She seemed in no hurry to leave me, so I asked her what she thought about my taking leave of absence for a couple of weeks, to work among the bombed-out in Bootle.

She pursed her lips while she considered the question. Then she said in a doubtful voice, 'You might get it – as long as you don't expect to be paid – I can't imagine them paying you while you were away. Do you *really* want to go?'

I sighed. 'Well, I know Bootle so well, and they wouldn't have to teach me anything – as they would an inexperienced person. I could get on with a lot of work for them.'

She looked me up and down, and cleared her throat. Then she said decisively, 'I don't think you should worry about it. Somebody will have taken over your job, I expect – and there's a lot of outside help coming into the town now. For the moment, they'll need brawn rather than brains out there – to clear it up.'

I smiled at the implied compliment – I had already discovered that approbation from Miss Hughes was unusual.

'Do you really think so?'

'Yes, I do.' She looked round her as if to encompass the whole Installation; and, though there was a hint of disparagement in her voice, she sounded convincing when she went on, 'We're working hard enough here – we've got to have petrol, after all.'

My smile became a grin. I could not say to her that I had never in my life done so little for so much money. After my loaded desk in Bootle, and the earlier five years of ruthless hounding I had endured in the Head Office of the same charity, it took me some time to realise that most people did not work themselves to a standstill in their jobs, that many employers were thankful if they got a fair day's work for a fair day's pay.

I thanked her, and then added brusquely, 'I can't afford not to be paid at all – and I doubt if the charity in Bootle could pay me, in addition to my successor.'

'All the more reason to stay here – and stop worrying about it.'

# Chapter seventeen

The premises of the chemical company for which Sylvia Poole worked had been totally destroyed during the Christmas blitz. The staff was lucky that the raid occurred at night when the building was empty. As Sylvia told me, 'The only perpendicular object in a devastated landscape was the strongroom – where the cash and ledgers were kept.'

Sylvia was my oldest friend, my theatre-going companion, a fountain of common sense which, through many discussions, sobered my passionate, idealistic interpretations of life. I was very concerned about her. Her company, however, continued to employ her for some weeks, while they reorganised. But her future seemed uncertain. When an opening occurred for a clerk in another department of the Petroleum Board, I recommended her and, since she had excellent references, she got the position. Though she worked there for the duration of the war, I saw little of her during the day. She was quick-witted and cheerful and became very popular.

She was always a little late for work, and I can remember her flashing past the policeman at the gate, blue skirts lifted in the breeze, short, blonde curls glinting in the sunlight. She would rush up the steps of the main office as fast as her high heels would allow, in order to sign the attendance book before the clock struck nine. At the stroke of nine, the Senior Clerk drew a red line across the page. If her signature was below that line, the manager would demand to see her, and she would have to give him a good reason for her tardiness.

If the Senior Clerk happened to hear her rapid steps on the stairs, he would wait with pen dripping red ink, ruler at the ready. As she shot up to him, blue eyes wide with impish hope, he would slowly lower the pen to the paper.

'Oh, no,' she would shriek, much to the glee of the watching staff. 'I'm not *really* late, am I?'

The Senior Clerk would grin, look at her slyly, and slip the ruler one line down the page, so that she could sign above the red mark.

Sylvia would thankfully scribble her signature, fling off her coat and, still puffing, slip into her seat.

Though Sylvia did not seem to care about being late, I was always very scared of not being on time. The old scars, the old fears of unemployment, were always with me. In this respect, living within a mile of my workplace was very comforting; I was not dependent upon the hard-pressed bus and tram services, of which every air raid took its toll.

On the eighth of May, the whole city was prepared for further destruction. So that Father and Tony could sleep, I helped Mother drag a double mattress downstairs again, and lay it on the cellar floor.

The underground railway stations were packed with people lying on the platforms as tightly as sausages in a frying-pan. Others walked out of the city and into surrounding fields, their bedding and younger children piled into prams. Many children were put to bed in damp Anderson shelters buried in back gardens, and some curled up in the chicken-wire bunks of street shelters, regardless of the foul smell of them. Though used in the daytime by most families as dining-room tables, cagelike Morrison shelters were crammed. Many families, like us, dragged a mattress down to the cellar, to lie beside the fine slack left over from last winter's coal.

Father and Tony, both completely worn out, slept as soon as they lay down, and only wakened when Brian returned from his messenger service at the end of the raid. Brian had had a quiet night. The raid was short and scattered, though Bootle had been bombed again, a final eradication of slums built in the nineteenth century. The gasworks of the suffering little town had also blown up.

Father went off to work on his bicycle, looking much better after practically a full night's sleep.

At the office, I heard that it had been confirmed officially that thousands of workmen had been drafted into the city, to help to repair the damage. The bad news was that much of dockland lay in ruins and huge fires still blazed. The city centre was a smouldering pyre. Rescue workers were still moling their way into acres of rubble that had once been houses. In the river and docks, fifty-seven ships lay sunk. Out at Bootle, a huge communal grave was being dug in which were laid together the remains of Roman Catholic and Protestant victims, united in death after a lifetime of communal strife.

Grimly the people – and a city is nothing but a mass of individuals – struggled to rebuild, repair, tidy up. Wrecked homes were combed for prized possessions, the dead were buried and the injured doctored. Somehow, shelter was found for the homeless. Companies, too, rescued safes, filing cabinets and precious machinery from the rubble and performed miracles of reorganisation. The government did well in keeping up the flow of food and repair material into the ravaged port. Marvellously inventive, skilled workmen – the types with whom I had danced at the club in Toxteth – found ways to hook up telephones, lay water pipes and electric cables and mend the huge sewers. Truckloads of rubble were removed from the streets, to be used as landfill, wherever possible, and as ballast in empty ships going to the United States.

The lives of survivors were not so easily repaired. In many cases, they had literally to start life anew; they had no possessions, no work, no money, no family, and no home.

As I walked home from work that Saturday afternoon, I remember being humbly thankful that, up to then at least, our house had lost only a few slates, its gutters and down-spouts and a kitchen window blown out. If the water supply was still functioning, Mother and I would soon clear the house of dust and soot, during the weekend. Probably the agent of the Earl of Sefton, who was our landlord, would be able to arrange the replacement of the missing window and the slates. All this, of course, provided we were not faced with another raid that night.

The terror of the concentrated raids had pushed my own sorrows to the back of my mind. Like everyone else, I dreaded further bombing.

As I approached our front door, crunching across the pavement through a mass of small detritus, my eyes felt like burning coals from lack of sleep. I put my fingers through the letterbox and pulled the piece of string which activated the latch. The door swung open.

Mother and Brian were in the hallway putting on their jackets. Mother looked like a small thundercloud. I could almost smell her suppressed anger.

'Don't bother to take your things off,' she ordered huffily. 'We're leaving.'

I stood in the narrow hall, my zipper bag dangling in my hand, and gaped at her. To move was the last thing I expected.

'What do you mean?'

'We're going over the water.'

'Over the Mersey? Why?'

Mother jabbed a hatpin into her pink straw hat and glared at me from under its brim. 'I told you that we are moving. Do you want to face another raid?'

'Of course not. But – but I think you might have told me, talked it over with me. Where are we going?' I glanced through the open doors of our tiny sitting-room and living-room. The furniture still sat there, filmed with soot. 'What about the furniture?'

I was indignant at being so unceremoniously uprooted again, as if I was of no consequence. It was a repeat performance of the unconsidered, ill-advised move which had catapulted us into a Liverpool slum ten years earlier, and I wondered what kind of hell we might be heading for this time.

Mother jabbed another pin into her hat, and ignored my questions. 'Come along,' she ordered, as she picked up her handbag. 'We'll take a tram to Central station. Come along, Brian.'

Brian, who probably did not remember much of our earlier life or the panic which had brought us originally to Liverpool, had stood grinning at me, enjoying my mystification. Now he buttoned his blazer and made ready to go.

I stood my ground. 'Where's Father?' I asked, trying to keep a tremor out of my voice. 'And where *are* we going?' What had Mother done?

Mother, who could not get out of the front door until I moved, looked as if she would explode at any moment, so Brian hastily interjected, 'Mum's found a house out at Moreton. It's an army officer's house, and it's furnished – he's in Scotland. And Daddy and Tony have already gone there.'

I was reminded of Father's set face during the attacks; he had looked on Thursday as if he had reached the end of his endurance. At breakfast time, however, after managing to snatch a night's sleep, he had looked much better.

'O.K.,' I acceded reluctantly. 'Give me a minute to put my clothes into my zipper.' I had so few clothes that they would easily fit into the small bag. 'I'll be quick.'

I eased past Brian and started up the stairs.

'For goodness' sake,' shouted Mother angrily. 'Never mind about packing. Hurry up and come. We don't want to be caught in another raid.'

As if I were still six years old, I felt frightened by the loudness of her voice and her intimidating expression – I guessed that she had already had a fight with Father, a fight he must have lost.

'Five minutes won't make any difference, Mother,' I managed to say.

She stamped her foot, and began to shout again, 'I insist . . .' when Brian announced suddenly, 'I've got to go to the bathroom.' He turned and trotted through the living-room, to go to the lavatory at the far end of the back yard.

'Oh, really, Brian!' Mother spat at him exasperatedly. Then she said more soberly, 'Perhaps I should go myself.' She looked up at me poised on the third stair. 'You just come downstairs, girl, and let's have no nonsense about clothes. There isn't time.'

As she followed Brian out, I flew upstairs. I was once more a child bent on thwarting her. In the bedroom, I tore off my coat and slipped over the dress I was wearing the two other dresses given me by Harry, heaved a skirt over that, and put my coat back on again; it fitted very snugly! Into the zipper bag, I shoved two blouses and my other set of underwear, a spare pair of stockings and a pair of old shoes I wore at home. My night school books, which I prized and still sometimes studied, together with a diary I had begun to keep in an old account book, had to be left on the shelf. They were too big to hide in the bag. Make-up and newly bought comb – my only other possessions – were carried at all times in my handbag. I was thankful that I had transferred Harry's few letters from my desk in the Bootle office to the back of the bottom drawer of my current desk. They were as safe as I could keep them.

When Mother and Brian returned from the back yard, I was sitting quietly on the bottom stair, seething with resentment.

It was fortunate, perhaps, that the family still had some clothing in pawn, because, when the removers collected the furniture, there was no clothing, crockery or utensils left in the house. A looter must have climbed through the broken kitchen window and removed them. The thief must have been very poor, or perhaps bombed out himself, to have been interested in such a shabby collection.

During the following week, Mother crossly retrieved some bundles from the pawnbroker's loft, which had miraculously remained undamaged.

# Chapter eighteen

In the dim electric light of Central underground station, we picked our way carefully through families sitting or lying on the dusty platform – people were easily incensed at passengers who brushed them when passing, or who trod on the blankets they had spread to mark their space. The reek of urine, of babies who needed their nappies changing, of old sweat, and musty clothing, was mixed with the peculiar, clammy odour of underground railways, and the sound of a myriad conversations rose and fell around us like the sea washing up on a shore. I thought with misgiving of the disease and vermin which could run through such a tightly packed crowd sleeping together, with inadequate lavatories and no water supply. It was only a very few years since we had ourselves finally got rid of body vermin, and I remembered how body lice could carry typhus, and how quickly influenza and typhoid could plague such a gathering.

Two feet from the edge of the platform had been kept clear by the station staff, for the use of passengers, and we waited there.

On the tram bringing us to the station, Mother had maintained a forbidding silence, and she continued frigidly silent as we sat in the unlighted train, surrounded by an Air Force contingent. For servicemen, they were unusually quiet. They clutched bumpy-sided kitbags and seemed to be festooned with other canvas bags hanging from their shoulders. I did not know then that close to Moreton was a Royal Air Force transit camp where men were collected prior to being sent overseas, and that the thought of being overseas was not always greeted with excited anticipation.

Looking down at my hands tightly clasped in my lap, I began to worry about how I was to get to work each day. There would be train fares from Moreton to Liverpool, I fretted, and then tram fares out to the Installation. I remembered the unbearable effort I had made to reach my work in Bootle. Would I have the same difficulties all over again?

There had been a time when I had looked out over the Mersey river and prayed to God to send me twopence, so that I could take the ferryboat across it and escape to my grandmother's house. Now, it seemed a cruel joke that I should be passing underneath the river and was worrying about getting back into Liverpool.

With eyes cast shyly down I sat tightly wedged between two tall servicemen carrying on a desultory conversation over my head. I began to tremble, and one of them looked down at me and asked if I was all right. Mother scowled at him from the opposite seat, and, after a sheepish grin at me, he resumed his conversation with the other airman.

The little train rattled out of the tunnel into fading daylight. Birkenhead Park and Birkenhead North. Memories of childhood journeys to Grandma's house overwhelmed me for a moment. Then Bidston, a country station, and Leasowe, a clean waste of fields. Moreton was the next red brick station, eight miles from the Birkenhead ferry. The airmen began to stir and haul their kitbags closer.

I had never been to Moreton. I had merely passed through it on the train. I knew that much of it was twenty feet below sea level and was, in those days, protected by a sea wall which was much admired by Dutch experts when they visited the village. As a child, I had viewed with disgust the shanty town built between the railway and the sea wall, just after the First World War, by people who could find no other cheap place to live. I had been told that there was only one source of water there, to serve several hundred people, and I had seen that when there was heavy rain or a very high tide these miserable shelters were flooded.

Immediately adjacent to the station a neat village of council housing had been built, but some people still lived in the old shanties. The original village of Moreton was clustered round Moreton Cross about a quarter of a mile away.

As we trudged silently towards the Cross that mild May evening, a familiar odour was borne on the clean breeze. I could smell the sea!

How wonderful it would be to run along the shore, dance in and out of the oncoming waves, and look for seashells again. Despite my worries, I took a big breath to savour the familiar odour, and my spirits rose.

We turned into a road lined with fairly new houses. Each had a front garden. In some there were more weeds than flowers – those would be the houses where the menfolk had gone to war – but in others, spring flowers were in full bloom. I could not remember when I had last seen tulips growing in a front garden.

We turned into a garden where the weeds were beginning to choke out the smaller plants. We crowded on to the porch. Before Mother could get the key out of her handbag, the door was opened by a stout, white-haired lady. I stared at her, utterly confused.

In a soft Irish accent, she welcomed me effusively. 'Come in, come in.' Then she realised my surprise, as I stepped over the doorstep, and said, with a note of puzzlement in her voice, 'Your mam must've told you? I'm going to share the house with you. I was bombed out.' She ushered me into the modern little hallway.

'I didn't know,' I replied, as I shook her hand, and Mother, wearing her best society smile, followed me in.

'Well, I'm Mrs Callaghan,' she told me. 'I met your mam in the butcher's queue the other day, and we got talkin'.'

As we took off our hats, and Mother hung her coat up, all kinds of unwelcome thoughts spun in my head. How long would these two ladies get along together? I wondered bitterly. Mrs Callaghan appeared to be a very kind and charming woman, however, so I swallowed my growing sense of panic, and said, 'I'll put my coat in whichever bedroom I am to be in.' I was anxious that Mother should not see how I had transported my small wardrobe, in spite of her instructions.

'You'll share the hall bedroom with me,' Mother told me.

'Brian, Tony and your father will have the back bedroom, and Mrs Callaghan will have the front bedroom.'

Apparently the living-rooms, kitchen and bathroom would be held in common, and, as I went up the well-carpeted staircase, I thought of the clashes of personality that would indubitably occur as a result of this.

It was a very pleasant house, newly decorated, and furnished with modern, shiny pieces. The owner was a childless army officer, and his wife was currently staying near to his camp. I guessed that they had not been long married.

Down in the white-tiled kitchen, I helped Mother cut bread and spread it with margarine, while Mrs Callaghan got out six plates and put a slice of cold meat on each. When she carried some of these into the dining-room, I asked Mother in a whisper why we were sharing the house.

'We have to share the rent. We can't afford it alone.'

As I went to help Mrs Callaghan find the knives and forks, my thoughts turned to Father. Perhaps the move would truly benefit him and thus be worthwhile.

'We're all going to eat together,' Mrs Callaghan explained to me, as I took cups and saucers out of a sideboard and set them on the table. 'And I might as well do the shopping, being as I don't have to go to work as early as your mam has to.'

It took about forty-eight hours for a sharp difference of opinion to arise between Mother and Mrs Callaghan. Mrs Callaghan had a much more generous idea of how much food to buy for six people than Mother had, and she was discovering that she was paying in part to feed us, as well as herself. As well as doing all the standing in queues, she seemed to do most of the cooking.

Aggrieved, she protested politely.

Mother told her icily that she could cater separately.

Our furniture arrived and was stowed in the attached garage, except for one or two pieces for which room was found in the house.

Ten days later, while everybody was still at work, except for Mrs Callaghan, a woman friend of our new landlord called, on his behalf, to complain that no rent had been paid, though it was due every Friday.

Mrs Callaghan asked the lady into the sitting-room, and assured her that she had paid her half of the rent to Mother. She insisted that the rent must have been sent by Mother, by post, to the landlord.

'What about the first week's?' inquired the visitor coldly. 'That was promised for the day you came in. It has not arrived.'

Mrs Callaghan, as she told me later, was so worried that she was stricken with palpitations in her heart. 'I was sure your mam must have the receipt for it stowed away somewhere,' she said. 'And I cast about as to where it could be. Then I realised that your Father's bureau had been moved into the sitting-room, and I thought it was sure to be in that. In the circumstances, I didn't think your mam would mind if I had a look.'

Apparently, she opened the unlocked bureau and began to sift through the papers in it, and, at that moment, Mother, having returned early from Liverpool, heard a stranger's voice and walked into the room, to see who it was.

'What are you doing in there?' she shot at the hapless Mrs Callaghan.

'And then, my dear,' Mrs Callaghan told me, 'there was a dreadful row, and the lady who came went away nearly crying. When your mam come in I was that flustered I didn't know what to say.'

On returning from work, I had found the poor woman standing on the front garden path, surrounded by her luggage, while the next-door neighbour's young son went to the village to get a taxi for her. She answered my inquiries as to what had happened by saying, with a hint of awe in her voice, 'Your mam was that angry she was nearly in hysterics. I couldn't believe it. I explained that I was just looking for the rent receipt – but she just went for me. There was naught I could say except that I would leave immediately. I reckoned she must have paid something in advance. But she hadn't paid nothin'. Just talked her way into the house.'

'I'm so sorry, Mrs Callaghan. Where will you go?'

'I'll go to me son in Liverpool. I'll be all right, luv.' She patted my shoulder. 'It's not your fault.'

As far as I know, Father went blithely on, glad to be out of the raids, and never questioned the sudden departure of our sub-tenant. The next morning, Mother simply announced to him that, now she was rid of 'that woman', she would go down to Shropshire that very day and bring the children back home. 'It's safe enough here,' she added.

Father gave a vague nod of his head, and I wondered if he cared. Without being asked, I gave Mother a pound note towards the fares, and, when I returned that evening, Avril and Baby Edward, both looking thin and wan, were back with us for good. They were pitifully thankful, and, rent or no rent, I was very glad that they did not have to continue as evacuees.

We survived more than a month in that house without paying a cent of rent, though Mother collected the usual contributions from Father and me. The poor owners, not being used to dealing with recalcitrant tenants, never did manage to collect the money owing. Twice, Mother managed to squeeze money out of me to pay it, until my little savings account had nothing more in it, but, as usual, the money was largely frittered. The rent was never paid.

Finally, the young, pink-cheeked Captain came down to Moreton, on his first leave, and simply ordered us out within a week. He said, 'Get out, or I'll have you thrown into the street.' As a silent and saddened spectator of the scene, I felt he was much too kind, though I was glad, for the sake of the children, that he gave us another week.

Father had begun to look much better. His hands had stopped shaking and regular sleep had eased the strain on his face. In the fresh air of Moreton, his smoker's cough had also lessened.

After the Captain had swept out of the house, Father said nervously that we should remain in Moreton. For once, Mother agreed with him. She took a day off and went house-hunting. She found, in a small back road, a jerry-built bungalow of incredible shabbiness. It looked as if only the brambles hugging its walls kept it upright. It was, however, to my mind much better than our Liverpool house. It stood in a garden, if a rough piece of fenced field could be called that. Someone, years before, must have planted roses round it, because we had hardly been in it a week when its thorny thicket became a great cascade of creamy rosebuds.

It had a dark kitchen, thick with grime, but big enough to hold a table for eating, and an even darker sitting-room. There were two tiny bedrooms and an indoor bathroom – which seemed a wonderful luxury to me, after years of washing at the kitchen sink. Moreover, the kitchen fireplace also heated a hot water boiler behind it, so, whenever we had coal, we could have baths. It was partially furnished with the poorest and grubbiest of pieces, but when our furniture was added to it, it looked quite full. We were, however, chronically short of bedding and towels and china until long after the war was finished.

Because the cottage was so damp, it had lain empty for many years and had been badly neglected. Not even a refugee from bombed Merseyside had been willing to rent it. We soon discovered that clothes left in a cupboard for more than a week or two became covered with mould. But it did have two advantages – the rent was extremely low, and it was only a mile from the sea. So modest were my ideas that I thought it was paradise.

# Chapter nineteen

Though Moreton provided a wonderful escape from the slums of Liverpool, residence there engendered the horrendous financial problem which I had anticipated. How were we going to pay the heavy train and bus fares to Liverpool?

Father paid his own without comment. Mother had to find money for her own and Tony's fares, and part of Brian's, and the housekeeping money had to provide these. Though Mother complained bitterly about this, she still seemed to be able to smoke and go to the cinema two or three times a week.

The drain on my own pocket left me with almost nothing. I was back again to working simply for food and roof.

Mother's magpie habits were much enhanced by her own dire need, and I had the utmost difficulty protecting from her my handbag containing the precious fares. Living in Moreton, there was no hope of my being able to walk to a job across the river at the south end of Liverpool, though many times I walked from Central station to the Dingle Bank Installation.

One morning, while running along the cinder track that followed the railway lines to Moreton station, a girl of my own age came panting up behind me. She was very smartly dressed, and smiled at me as we ran together for the train, already signalled.

She fumbled in her handbag and produced a season ticket to show the porter at the entrance, while I went to buy a day ticket and, consequently, missed the train.

A season ticket, that was it! I felt like Paul enlightened on the road to Damascus. Every time I was paid thereafter, I bought a season ticket before I went home. This ensured that I could, at least, get as far as Liverpool.

The hike which I so often did out to the Installation was not a pleasant one. The way lay through badly bombed slum districts, and I must, in some way, have looked peculiar to the inhabitants, because whey-faced women in black shawls would stare after me and snigger; and men, hanging around the street corners with as little to do as they had had in the 1930s, would eye me curiously. Perhaps, with my extreme neatness and old-fashioned spectacles, I looked too prim.

Mother used to borrow the season ticket in the evening, so that she could go to the cinemas in the city. Although this was illegal, I did not mind. She would often, however, try to hold on to it for use herself the next day, and on several occasions the fight to get it returned to me was so bitter that I nearly came to blows with her. She still had the fixed idea that she owned not only her daughters, but everything they had as well.

Shedding hot, angry tears, I would threaten to leave home immediately, but since I had no money, even for a night's lodging, and could not go to join Fiona without the season ticket, it was an empty threat. She knew it, and once or twice I missed a day at the office, simply because she would not part with my train ticket. When Father once intervened, she said calmly that her work was more important to the war effort than mine was. I could have the ticket the next day because I could then collect my wages, it being pay day. Once, when I was particularly distraught, after Mother had left, he lent me the day's fare, and I arrived late at work, to sign my name below the red line.

I was so used to being bullied that even at twenty-two years of age, I could be crushed. A lifetime of giving in to a strong and ruthless personality is not easily shaken off, as any beaten wife will testify.

I wondered frantically if I could be transferred to a job in Moreton, and I inquired at the Employment Exchange, but they would not even consider it. I was lucky to be where I was, I was told, and I agreed with them. Though the work was the most boring I was ever to do in my life, I truly loved each one of my colleagues in the office. The good nature which prevailed there was a revelation to me.

I had been to see Fiona, and had spent a happy evening with her. I considered asking her if I could share her flatlet.

I was quite worried about her. Although she liked her little apartment and the money she was earning, she hated the factory and the merciless sexual harassment which she was enduring. She was also not popular with the other women on her assembly line, because she worked so fast. Her output had drawn the attention of the management, because she produced two and a half times as many components as the other women did. Their game was to idle as much as possible during the day, aided and abetted by their immediate male supervisors, so that overtime became necessary. Overtime was payable at one and a half times the daily wage, double time on Sundays and public holidays. Fiona felt that this was cheating, and said so.

She soon found her overalls torn, her tools stolen, and she was verbally threatened. One day, she sat down on her chair and it collapsed under her, bruising her badly; the bolts holding it together had been loosened. She ate alone in the canteen, because nobody would sit with her.

When she went to the office to ask to be moved to another line, the manager fondled her and told her she could work in his office if she became his mistress.

She took a day off and went to the Employment Exchange to ask to be transferred to other employment.

The male clerk who interviewed her asked, 'Don't you know there's a war on?' Then he looked her over insolently, and added, 'You probably brought it on yourself – painting your face and showing yourself off.'

The idea of the wicked painted woman still lingered in the lower middle class, but poor Fiona was speechless. She burst into tears and stormed out of the building.

A couple of days later, before I could ask her if she would like to share her flatlet, Father received an urgent telephone call at his office.

Fiona's young watchmaker had plucked up courage to telephone him, because he was so concerned about her.

'She's at home with the flu. And the people she's working with aren't human – she's having a dreadful time,' he told him. 'She'd be better in the Forces – but she'd never pass the medical.'

He gave Father Fiona's address, and Father took leave from his office and went straight over to see her. She answered the door in her nightgown, and it was obvious that she had been weeping. When she saw him she burst into tears again and threw herself into his arms. He told me she was burning with temperature, so he got her back into the bed, and then collected a set of clothes for her and brought them to the bedside.

While she lay and sobbed, he packed everything he could find, and then persuaded her to get dressed while he went to see the landlady. She demanded a week's rent in lieu of notice, but he told her flatly that he could not pay it and that his daughter was so sick that he must take her home. Reluctantly, she allowed him to take out her luggage and agreed to forgo the extra rent.

He had hardly exchanged a word with Fiona, except to tell her that he was taking her home, and she sat passively, occasionally sobbing, while he went to the nearest telephone box to call a taxi, and, afterwards, they waited in the hall of the building for it to arrive.

By the time Mother and I returned from work, they were both at home. Father had put a hot water bottle into my bed and persuaded his distraught daughter to get undressed and get into it. He had then left her, to go to the telephone box nearby to phone for the doctor.

'Fi, darling, whatever happened?' I asked, as I rushed into the bedroom, followed closely by Mother. Father pattered after us in his carpet slippers, explaining what he had done.

We might, as a family, quarrel like caged cats, but we all loved Fiona, and we grouped round her to protect her like a solid phalanx of Roman soldiers.

She lay with eyes closed in exhaustion, and did not answer me. Instead, tears welled again from under the sweeping black lashes.

So, on either side of the bed, Mother and I patted and cooed comfortingly that the doctor was coming. 'And Daddy will make some tea and bring the aspirins, in the meantime,' Mother said pointedly, glancing at Father, who was himself beginning to look rather haggard.

The doctor arrived in his usual rush. He was already halfway across the living-room, having let himself in, before Father had eased himself out of the tiny bedroom in order to answer the bell.

'Now, what's to do?' he asked, as he charged into the wrong bedroom, did a fast reverse and came out into the living-room again. 'Where is she?' he barked.

He was hastily ushered to Fiona's bedside. 'Now, young leddy,' he addressed her, as he snapped open his black bag and took out a thermometer. 'Let's have your temperature first.' She opened half-glazed eyes, as in the poor light he leaned forward and thrust the thermomcter between her lips. Then he leaned closer and ran a finger gently over one eyelid. 'My goodness!' he exclaimed. 'That's going to be quite a black eye. Have you had an accident?' He turned to Mother and inquired, 'What happened?'

Mother looked at him, quite shocked. 'We don't know – that is, she has been living on her own. I thought that swelling was from crying too much.'

'No. That's a blow.' He took the thermometer from Fiona's lips, and she gave a huge, shuddering sigh.

'One hundred and two,' he announced, and then pursed his lips. 'I want to listen to your chest, and then you can tell me about the black eye,' he said very gently to Fiona.

Mother undid the buttons of the ancient Victorian nightgown, culled from a second-hand shop, to expose, as she thought, the creamy whiteness of Fiona's breasts. 'My God, whatever happened?' she exclaimed in horror. I gasped.

Most of Fiona's chest was scarlet and purple.

The doctor's eyes widened. He whipped a pair of scissors out of his bag, and without asking permission flipped the bedding off Fiona and cut down the length of her nightgown and of its sleeves. Her arms matched her chest. Very carefully, the doctor rolled her on to her side. Her back and buttocks were likewise covered with bruises.

He eased her legs apart. There was no sign of bleeding, but he sat down on the bed by her and, with extraordinary gentleness for such a belligerent little man, he took her hand and stroked it. 'Fiona,' and when she did not reply, he said again, more urgently, 'Fiona, listen. You must tell me what happened, so that I can help you. Did someone try to rape you?'

'No.'

We could hardly hear the whisper.

'Well, what happened to you?'

'They caught me in the lavatory – and beat me – the women did. And when I ran out the men were laughing outside, and one tripped me up and I fell.' Sobs burst from her, as Mother and I gasped at her explanation. 'Then the women caught me again and kicked me and hit me with a broom.'

She was weeping loudly now, and could not go on. The doctor, obviously as shocked as we were, let her cry for a minute, and then asked, 'What did you do?'

'Well, one of the men protested that they were going too far, so they let me crawl away. Then I got up and ran to the assembly line, took my handbag, and ran out of the factory. The man at the gate shouted after me, but I just ran. Then I got the bus home to my flat.'

She began to shiver, and the doctor hastily lifted the blanket over her. 'You shouldn't have gone to work, anyway,' he said almost crossly. 'You've got influenza.'

Fiona moved restlessly on the bed, and then winced with the pain of it. 'I thought I ought to go if I could. They need aeroplanes,' she said simply. 'But I did try to persuade the Employment Exchange to transfer me.' She gave a deep shuddering sigh, and then went on, haltingly, to describe to the doctor what the counter clerk had said to her.

'Humph,' the doctor grunted. 'Well, it'll be a few weeks before you're fit for anything, young leddy. I'm going to check that no bones are broken, and then I'll give you something for the bruises and the temperature. Aspirin should help the pain for a few days.'

Father got up from the old settee as we came out of the tiny bedroom. The doctor was furious at Fiona's state, and Father was horrified when he was told. 'We must tell the police,' he said. 'She can't go back there.'

'If you are agreeable,' replied the doctor, 'she certainly shall not. I'm outraged that the Employment Exchange wouldn't do anything to help her. Wartime restrictions – Registration for Employment Orders – or whatever – don't mean that an Employment Exchange clerk can behave like a little tin god.' He handed Mother a prescription form which he had scribbled out, and a second form saying that Fiona was unfit for work.

'What shall we do?' asked Father.

'Oh, I'll just keep signing her off, until you can get the Employment Exchange to transfer her. I'll talk to them if you like. I'd like to raise hell for that clerk.'

'Thank you,' Father replied. 'It would help if you could talk to them. It would carry more weight.'

Neither Fiona nor I ever knew if the doctor's complaint ever got back to the factory. We consulted our local policeman, who said Fiona could certainly lay a charge of assault. But she would need a lawyer – and lawyers cost money and we had none. The policeman recommended leaving it to the doctor and the Employment Exchange, unless Fiona wanted to claim damages.

Fiona was terrified at the idea of laying charges. 'They were shouting after me that if I told anyone, they'd murder me,' she shuddered. 'No! No charges.'

The doctor kept Fiona on the sick list for six weeks. She sat in our wilderness of garden, when she was a little better, and enjoyed the fresh air and sunshine, while occasional fighter planes zoomed overhead. Then, one day, a letter came for her from the Employment Exchange, saying that as soon as she was fit, she was to report for an interview, to the Income Tax Department, recently evacuated from Liverpool to a Moreton hotel.

Fiona's recovery was immediate, and she served as a tax clerk for the duration of the war. Her mathematics were even worse than mine, and she would often say, with a gale of laughter, that the Department of National Revenue never quite recovered from her ministrations.

# Chapter twenty

It was customary during the war, particularly amongst middle-class people, to volunteer one's services to organisations connected with the war effort. Because of the long hours of work and the difficulties of travel to Bootle, I had never done this. Sylvia Poole had, however, undertaken to do the secretarial work for a unit of the Air Training Corps, and she now asked me to share these duties with her, partly because she was not a shorthand typist.

Before I went to live in Moreton, I had been filled with delight at my new-found freedom in the first six weeks of my time with the Petroleum Board, so I had agreed. For the first time, I could afford extra tram fares, and I had a little leisure during the early hours of the evening to do something useful towards winning the war.

I had no idea what the Air Training Corps was, but during a lunch hour Sylvia gave me a fast course on the subject.

The Corps had been formed to upgrade the education of boys who hoped to join the Royal Air Force when they were called up at the age of seventeen. All the uniformed officers were themselves volunteers. Many of them had served in the Air Force during World War I; others were middle-aged schoolteachers, not yet called up.

Amongst young boys, to be in the Royal Air Force carried considerable prestige, so all of them strove to improve the mathematics and English which they had neglected during their school days. They learned the theory of flight and the mechanical make-up of the planes of the day. A considerable time was spent learning to recognise, under all conditions, the silhouettes of both the Allies' planes and those of the enemy; if the boys became air crew, their lives could depend upon this acquired knowledge. They learned from flash cards, some of them cigarette cards, to recognise in an instant the make of a plane from any angle. To test their skill, they constantly played games with each other or made up contests between teams. When finally they were called up, most of them could guarantee a perfect score.

Another skill many of them acquired, with much practice, was how to read and signal in Morse code.

So that they would be able to navigate a plane from the positions of the stars, they studied the basics of astronomy. On clear nights a lot of time was spent in the school yard, gazing at the heavens, which were much clearer in the blackout than they had been in peacetime. They made small telescopes out of cardboard cylinders, and drew star maps. Small groups tried to lose themselves in the city, so that they could find their way home again by the stars. They had a lot of fun. It is saddening to recall that most of them were dead before the war ended.

A dentist voluntarily examined the boys' teeth and encouraged them to use a toothbrush and to have fillings attended to. Many of the youngsters had rotten teeth from poor diet or plain neglect; people did not usually go to the dentist unless toothache became unbearable.

Civilian doctors were extremely hard-pressed, because all their younger colleagues had been called into the Forces. But one of them managed to find the time to help by examining the boys physically. He taught them to keep themselves clean and other simple rules to improve their health. I can remember the boys' skinny white chests glistening under the dim electric light, as they took off their shirts and jackets to have their heart and lungs listened to. There was not a fat boy amongst them.

The boys were issued with a uniform, which often did not fit very well. More than one mother whom I met was persuaded to unpick the garments and restitch them, so that they looked smarter. Then the boys would parade themselves before the local girls, like young cockerels in a barnyard.

Dressed in their uniforms, they drilled in the school yard, sometimes bumping into each other because in the long winter evenings it was almost too dark to see. They also went in a long ragged procession on route marches about the city. When it was too cold outside, they doffed their shirts and jackets, and did physical exercises inside. Many of them had never done such exercises in their lives, and there was a lot of good-natured jostling and joking, as they fell off climbing ropes or balked at vaulting the old wooden horse in the gym. Perhaps, because they were instinctively aware that they *must* learn to bear pain, they endured their bumps and bruises very stoically.

I was painfully shy amongst these youngsters and their sober, middle-aged instructors. I do not remember opening my mouth there, except to say, 'Yes, sir' or 'No, sir'. Yet I would have dearly loved, on evenings when I had not too many letters to type, to have asked if I might sit in on the mathematics and astronomy lessons. But I could not bring myself to own up to my own ignorance. I was surprised and touched when, absent with my usual dose of winter flu, the officers sent me a wonderful box of chocolates, which must have used up all their rations for at least a month. The box had a ribbon bow across one corner and a bright picture of an Elizabethan cottage. I shared the contents with the family. Then I pierced two holes in the lid, threaded them with string and hung it up over the tiny, empty fireplace in the bedroom I shared with Fiona and Avril. It was the first ornament we had had in our room, and we all thought it was very pretty.

The officers were, of course, in close touch with their counterparts in the Royal Air Force, and so I heard at second hand some of the gossip of the men who had fought the Battle of Britain and were now defending our cities, or going out to bomb German cities. According to the gossip, an alarming number of men lost their lives not from enemy action but from well-known faults in the construction or design of the aircraft they had to fly. No wonder R.A.F. men referred to planes as crates. It was expensive to lose an aircraft's crew, but it was much more expensive to abandon the production or design of a particular aircraft, or to inspire the kind of people Fiona worked with in the aircraft factory to greater care in manufacture. So young men, in the prime of life, became expendable.

This realisation appalled me. I could accept that people died in wars, but not that they should be sent to their deaths because of considerations of money.

Though moving to Moreton made it a little more difficult, I continued with the voluntary work at the Air Training Corps.

I was always a little heavy-hearted that I was assisting in sending the youngsters surging round me out to die unnecessarily. The idea weighed on me – and yet we had to have an air force. Perhaps these ideas increased my normal reserve, and, in consequence, I did not make a single new friend. I thought my plainness and dullness, as compared to Sylvia's sparkling personality and bright blondeness, were the causes. But looking back, I realise that the longer the war went on, the more sickened I became by the decimation of my generation, and I began to understand how my parents must have felt, when they remembered their friends lost unnecessarily in the ghastly trench warfare of the First World War. This attitude of mine was, I realised, not a popular one, and so I never spoke about it.

# Chapter twenty-one

Moreton and Leasowe were famous for their market gardens. Huge crops of cabbage, kale, carrots, potatoes, onions and brussels sprouts had, for a century, been raised to feed the cities of Liverpool and Birkenhead. During the war, all this produce had to pass through the wholesale market, so that the cities were plentifully supplied. It was not difficult, however, to buy a single cabbage or a few potatoes straight from the field, if one knew the owner, and, as we became acquainted with our new neighbours, we sometimes did this, to augment what we could buy in the greengrocery shops.

Though, like many people of that period, we did not cook our vegetables very well, they did help to put the roses back into little Avril's cheeks. Edward was always pale, but he grew like a weed. Both of them trotted off each morning to the village school, a small stone building in the centre of the village.

The children in the school were quite as tough as those in the Toxteth school, in Liverpool, that they had attended. Since their numbers were small, however, they were better supervised, and in due course, Edward won a scholarship to Wallasey Grammar School. Avril, equally bright and with the same sticking power as Edward, did not win one. She certainly received no encouragement from her parents, and unless a girl was absolutely outstanding teachers tended to push the boys rather than the girls. In any case, girls were not supposed to be brainy – men did not like brainy women.

Tony continued his education at the Liverpool Institute. When he matriculated, he got a job in the Mercantile Marine Office in the old Customs House, to fill in time until he was seventeen and a quarter and would be called up. His hilarious stories of the seamen he met there often enlivened our evenings at home.

Living out at Moreton meant that it was difficult for me to visit several old friends, like the Spanish lady, who, long ago, had given me the Chariot, an ancient pram, in which I had trundled Baby Edward through Liverpool's Depression-ridden streets. The pram was still with us in our first days at Moreton. As coal became scarce, we used it to carry our small ration from the railway depot to our home. Under such harsh treatment, it finally fell apart and was sold for scrap.

At the Petroleum Board, our little staff in the Wages and Personnel Department occasionally lost a member. The girl so like my childhood nanny married a farmer in the south of England and left to help him run the farm. Her place was taken by a quiet, grief-stricken young widow with ulcers. She had to eat frequently, to assuage the pain of the ulcers, and was rather unfeelingly teased by some members of the staff. She soon left, and I hoped that she found more gentle and understanding companions elsewhere. Another girl, transferred to us, became pregnant with an illegitimate child. It was her second illegitimate child, and she was dismissed because of this; one child could be forgiven, but not two.

About this time, our whole department was moved from the isolated building by the gate of the Herculaneum Dock, to the main office opposite the policeman's hut at the entrance to the Installation. We were now all in one big room. One of the men went upstairs to another department, and an elderly gentleman joined us. This man sat silently through the days of the war at a desk facing a wall, with his back to the rest of us, and I often wondered how he endured the wall and our noisy, vulgar gossip. I liked him very much, and sometimes when the room was otherwise empty, we would talk about the war together. Like Father, he had a map on which he would pinpoint our retreating front lines.

Because offices of management were now immediately above our heads, we were rather more prone to unexpected managerial invasions, despite the Purple Warning system. In consequence, it was our department which took the first blows of the Stocking War.

In June, 1941, all clothes were rationed, and with our usual ration books we were given a number of 'points'. The ration was not generous – it took six months of these tiny coupons to buy a coat, and to be shabby became fashionable. Hats were replaced by headscarves and stockings by slacks. Before the war the wearing of slacks marked a woman as fast, and, though women doing men's jobs in factories had been encouraged to wear them, most women still regarded them as not quite nice.

Many people had at the beginning of the war a good wardrobe which could be mended or renovated, but our family had nothing to fall back upon, nor could we afford to buy with our coupons quality clothing which would last.

Very, very few women owned enough stockings to last for the duration, and it became apparent to all of us that we would rarely have enough clothing points to buy them. There was a brisk trade in clothing coupons at the rate of two shillings and sixpence per point, many of these coming from the rations of working men, who had ten points more than the ordinary citizen. But to buy these black market points would make stockings so expensive that they would be reserved for special occasions only.

Over several lunches, the girls in the office discussed the situation, and agreed that stockings were out.

We shaved our legs and went barelegged. Our skin looked horribly white, and all wrong with heavy shoes. So we experimented with painting the part that showed. Liquid make-up was the most effective. But cosmetics were expensive and increasingly difficult to obtain; it took nearly a bottle of liquid make-up to paint two legs. One girl swore by gravy browning, and even went as far as drawing a careful line up the backs of her legs with her eyebrow pencil, to give a resemblance to a stocking seam. But most mothers objected to losing their carefully hoarded gravy browning!

This problem was solved by enterprising firms who made up large bottles of what felt like tinted whitewash. It was difficult to get it on smoothly, but the general effect satisfied us, and we all went to work triumphantly, with painted legs.

I was particularly thankful for this piece of entrepreneurship, because Mother, as housewife, held my ration book and, consequently, the clothing coupons in it. I suspected I would be lucky if I ever saw one of them, and, indeed, this proved to be the case. No amount of cajoling would make her part with one.

'The children must come first,' she told me loftily. But she herself never went outside the door without stockings. Throughout the war, I continued to buy second-hand clothing and shoes.

Bare, well-shaven white legs called forth many ribald remarks from the male staff, and, sometimes, from men in the street. I remember a group of aged Chinese, waiting with me at a tram stop, being convulsed with giggles and pointing at my bare legs. Nobody had any sympathy for the cold that we suffered once the winter came. The skin of my legs was ruined for ever by being constantly chapped.

Because the Installation Manager's secretary, Miss Hughes, wore strong, old-fashioned lisle stockings, she was still able to cover her legs. He was, therefore, unaware for some time that the younger females on his staff were stockingless. It was the man in the bowler hat who first told us loudly and coarsely to cover ourselves decently.

We bowed our heads and remained silent. What were we to do?

The next morning, two enterprising girls arrived neatly clad in slacks. The man in the bowler hat regarded this as an impertinent affront. The girls were subsequently sent for by the Installation Manager, who must have been informed of their impudence. They returned from the interview in tears. Either they dressed decently or they would be dismissed. Since they were young, dismissal implied that they would be either called up for the Forces or be transferred to another part of the country, possibly to a factory.

While they bemoaned the unreasonableness of the edict and wondered how they were going to tell their fathers that they faced dismissal, great waves of indignation rose up in me. This was the kind of unreasonable bullying that I had been subjected to all my life at home, and here it was again surfacing in the workplace.

'We should all go to see him together,' I said. 'He must have *some* common sense and should be able to see the point, if it's explained carefully to him.' I turned to the girls, and asked, 'What did you say to him?'

The girls looked at me bewilderedly through watery eyes, and answered, 'We didn't say anything!' They shrugged their shoulders slightly and looked helplessly round at us, and we all understood. People simply did not answer an employer back, if they wanted to keep their jobs.

The men in the offices thought it was tremendously funny, and came up with some more vulgar jokes about our naked legs. Behind my spectacles, behind my quiet mien, I was furious.

'Let's talk to Miss Hughes,' I suggested, and the girls began to gather round me, as if I were their leader. This frightened me, and yet the situation was so difficult that I felt that we had to do something about it.

At lunchtime, four of us asked the advice of Miss Hughes. Could she speak for us?

Middle-aged and with a pensionable job at stake, Miss Hughes was flustered. She suggested that we should buy thick stockings like her own.

'But they don't last *that* long, and they do cost coupons,' I protested, painfully aware of Mother having my ration book in her handbag.

The other girls looked at each other, and I could read their agreement that bare legs were better than lisle stockings, even if one could afford them.

'Could we see the Manager?' I asked Miss Hughes. 'Could you arrange it?'

'I'll speak to him,' she promised bravely.

Written in stone, the edict came down once more. All ladies on the staff would in future wear stockings.

Those girls with brothers talked uneasily of begging a few of their coupons from them. 'After all, men's clothes last a lot longer,' they argued. This did not help me; Mother held *all* the family's coupons.

In company with two other girls, I went to Miss Hughes and told her that it was impossible for the girls to comply with the order.

'I've already told him that,' she said. 'But he can't see it – he said you should learn to darn.'

'It looks as if every one of us will have to resign,' I suggested, stammering with nerves.

'You can't do that,' Miss Hughes responded, unexpectedly sharply. 'You'll disrupt the whole Installation.'

My stance hardened. 'It won't be our fault,' I retorted.

'Don't forget that you're frozen into your jobs. You can't move that easily.'

'We can volunteer,' responded one of my companions, overcoming her timidity at last.

'At least we'll get stockings in the A.T.S., even if they're awful woolly ones,' the other girl chimed in.

The first girl added, a little smugly, 'As an officer in the Wrens, I'd get nice silky ones.'

Lucky girl, I thought. She had been at a private girls' school until she was eighteen, and would stand a good chance of becoming an officer.

Miss Hughes turned a little more towards us on her swivel chair, and looked down at our pretty, neatly painted legs. She sighed, and said glumly, 'I'll try again – but it's difficult to shift a Yorkshireman!'

We all smiled at each other, a secret society of women. Yorkshire was going to have to have his mind changed.

At lunchtime, Miss Hughes announced that the Manager would see the female employees, for five minutes, the next morning at eleven o'clock. 'You can't all go,' she told us. 'You won't be able to get into his office. There are too many of you.'

A few of the older women and one or two of the younger ones refused to go. Most of them had had the foresight and the money to buy four or five dozen pairs of stockings when first the rumour of clothes rationing was circulating. Judging by the dresses they wore to the office, some of them had so great a variety of other clothing that they could have lasted through five or six years before having to buy anything but the more perishable stockings.

One of the younger, more desperate ones said, 'If, say, five of us went, and Helen did the talking . . .'

Helen was immediately petrified with fear. The reputation of our Yorkshire Purple Warning Manager was enough to strike fear into the heart of the toughest barge deckhand, never mind a crushed coward like me.

'I'm not very clever . . .' I wavered.

'Oh, come on, Helen, you know how to put things nicely. I'll come and back you up – only, if I do the talking, I'll lose my temper, and that'll put us in the soup.' This from one of my colleagues in the Wages Department, and she looked rather contemptuously round our nervous little group.

I smiled at her. And then something of the courage which had sustained me in Bootle came back to me. There, we had done nothing else but battle against the stupidities and the neglect of government, the rapacity of business, or the cruelty or bigotry of individuals. Many times, when my sweet, overworked colleague out there had been away, I had had to cope with all kinds of threats.

And here I was now, caught between male pigheadedness and dire necessity. Except possibly on the black market, which I could not afford, there was no way in which I could obtain stockings. If I lost my job for impudence, I could not help it. I mentally resigned myself to scrubbing saucepans in army kitchens, and agreed to be the leader.

The next morning, five frightened shrimps were washed into a very bare office, where sat a stout, elderly Yorkshireman, blinking at us over heavy horn-rimmed spectacles. His slightly grubby beige suit was creased across him, as if he had put on weight since he bought it. The expression on his face made me cringe.

'Well?' Scorn was in that single word and in the glance he gave us, as he looked up from a pile of papers.

'Sir, we have come to see you, because we cannot afford to buy stockings now that they are rationed,' I squeaked. Miss Hughes stood quietly by her employer, her facial expression a carefully controlled blank. She had done her best for us. She would do no more.

The small eyes seemed smaller behind the thick glasses.

'Why not? Are you telling me that you are not paid enough? You get coupons for them. Bare legs are not respectable, you know that.'

I swallowed. My throat was so dry that I thought I would not be able to reply. Then I said rather hoarsely, 'It would take all our coupons to keep us in stockings. There would be none left for anything else.'

'You'll 'ave to learn to darn, won't you?'

I thought of my carefully mended stockings, the ladders rehooked with the aid of a fine crochet hook, an eye-destroying task. I forgot my fear in a burst of anger.

'Sir, none of us wastes our stockings. We can't afford to.'

'And are you telling me you're not paid enough?' He leaned back in his chair and tapped its wooden arm with the end of a pencil. 'When I were in 'ull, the female staff was paid the same rates, and I never 'ad one complaint.' He looked us over with such an air of self-satisfied complacency that I wanted to kick his shins. Mercifully, his desk lay between us.

'No, sir. None of us is complaining about our wages.'

One of the other girls interjected, 'Sir, we could wear slacks, like the women labourers on the Installation.'

His mouth fell open. He was genuinely shocked 'Not in my office,' he replied frigidly.

'It seems to be the only alternative, sir,' I added. 'Slacks would last, they would be neat, and they would be warm in winter.'

Another girl, who had not up to then said a single word, suddenly spoke up. 'If you insist about stockings, we shall all have to find other jobs,' she said baldly.

I could have clapped my hands in relief that I had not had to make this threat. The man in front of us had had all his fit male staff under the age of thirty called up. He had just got his offices nicely reorganised with female staff; he would not want to start the whole operation again.

Encouraged by the Manager's silence, the girl went on, 'Our legs don't look too bad.' She stepped round his desk and lifted her calf-length skirt slightly and stretched out a pretty foot. Her legs were evenly stained a light brown, giving the effect of a fine silk stocking. 'Oxo,' she announced simply.

He glanced embarrassedly at the proffered leg, took off his glasses and began to polish them furiously with a crumpled handkerchief. Angry frustration was written all over his plump, pasty face.

'I'll talk to the Office Manager. You can go,' he almost snarled, as he clapped his glasses back on again and scowled at us.

'Thank you, sir,' I replied for the group.

Herded by Miss Hughes, we shuffled out of the room.

As soon as Miss Hughes had gone back to her own desk, we all began to giggle helplessly, holding on to the stair rail so that we should not fall. One of the girls who wore glasses pushed them down to the tip of her nose, and blinked at us.

'I'll send you all to 'ull to work, if you're not good,' she announced, and we broke into helpless laughter, and fled back to our respective offices.

After I had regaled the Wages Department with the story of our adventures, I asked, 'What does he mean by, when I was in 'ull?'

'He means Hull, you idiot. That's where he came from. Everybody was perfect there, didn't you know?'

After that, 'when I was in 'ull' became a catch phrase on the Installation, guaranteed to make even the most solemn person break into a grin.

I spent a whole week worrying myself sick that I, at least, would be dismissed because I had led the delegation.

Nothing happened. Not a word came down from on high.

Gradually, we all began to breathe more easily. None of us wanted to wear slacks – they were too daring – and common. So we continued to paint our legs. In the winter, our legs sometimes bled, because they were so chapped, and cold cream, to put on them at nights, was so scarce.

Though we had won our little war, I had an uneasy feeling that the Purple Warning Manager had not forgotten the name of the leader of the malcontents, and in this I was right.

Later on, the Minister of Labour decided that the young women employed by the oil companies could easily be replaced by older women. The indignant oil companies, faced with training yet another new office staff, fought back. I became the test case, a most uncomfortable position to be in.

# Chapter twenty-two

Moreton with its clean, sea air, combined with a much less demanding job and regular hours, improved my health. Despite the long journey to work, the help I gave in the house and the endless queueing for the basic materials of life, I also had more time.

As with everyone else, at the back of my mind the war was a continuous, scarifying threat to me and mine. Alan was still in Kent, an area constantly threatened by German air raids. At the age of seventeen and a quarter, Brian was called up into the Navy, which was a great disappointment to him; he had hoped to follow his brother into the Air Force. Once he was at sea, we worried constantly about him.

The news was dreadful. In North Africa, the siege of Tobruk was an ongoing litany of losses. In East Africa, there was bitter fighting – a facet of the war that not many remember now.

In Greece, an infantryman, together with his unit, slowly retreated through its harsh mountains, to Crete, only to be bombed and attacked there, and to arrive eventually, with bare and damaged feet, in threatened Egypt. His unit was regrouped and he fought his way across North Africa. He still goes each year to the El Alamein reunion, where the survivors of this bloody battle meet to touch hands and relive for a moment their shared trauma. During those dreadful days, he might have felt a little better if he had known that the most beautiful girl in his native Moreton would one day be his wife. But Fiona's future husband, a gentle, peaceful person, was a very long march away from home.

The Battle of the Atlantic was a continuous running sore, and an even more destructive battle for the Mediterranean, including the besieged and battered little island of Malta, G.C., took a frightful toll of both the Royal Navy and the Merchant Navy. I was no longer dealing with the relations of the men lost, but through the gossip of the port I heard the names of innumerable sunken ships. I cried in sympathy with more than one acquaintance who lost husband, son or lover.

As I tried to build a new life for myself, like a willowherb precariously rooted in the ruins of a bombsite, I clung to a rigid routine of daily catching the same train, concentrating on the boring payrolls, cooking, standing in queues on Saturdays, cleaning and mending for the family, and, of course, doing my voluntary work for the Air Training Corps, a welcome change. Occasionally, late in the evening, I went to a village dance. My partners were the men from the Royal Air Force transit camp or from the nearby gun sites. I sometimes accepted a date, but there was not much time to get to know any of them before they were sent overseas. One or two of them wrote to me for several years, and I always replied. I hoped that my letters were comforting, and fun to read.

To the astonishment of many who had not had time to read in the newspapers the reports of the preliminary build-up, on the 22nd June, 1941, the Germans attacked Russia. Three million German soldiers rolled like floodwater into an ill-prepared country.

Though the famous German Panzer divisions must have seemed terrifying in their immensity, the Germans themselves had certain weaknesses in other areas, to which they had not given sufficient attention. They lacked general transport. Also, they had not fully appreciated the problems raised by the fact that Soviet railways are of a different gauge from the rest of Europe, and this complicated the use of German rolling stock in occupied Russian territory. To help to shift the vast number of men and the amount of materials they needed, they employed 625,000 horses in the invasion. Horses do not need petrol, but they do have to be fed.

As they followed the retreating Russians deeper and deeper into their huge country, the Russians' scorched-earth policy, that is, burning everything in the path of the enemy, must have made the feeding of the animals progressively more difficult.

Suddenly, we all became knowledgeable about Russian cities and rivers. The names of Russian generals, at first tongue-twisters to the British, became fashionable as the names of household cats. The voyage from Britain to Murmansk in northern Russia created another graveyard for our seamen, as the Allies sent aid to a nation which had suddenly become one of us, instead of one of them. Hot water bottles and fur coats, already hard to get, vanished from the market-place; and we were told that they had been sent to Russia.

Father did not need a map of Russia to follow this latest invasion. He leaned back in his greasy easy chair and said with quiet satisfaction, 'The Germans have lost the war.'

Considering that the Germans were rolling up the Russian Army as if it were a carpet about to be discarded, this seemed a very optimistic remark. But Father knew at first hand something of Russia, of its tough peasantry, its horrendous winter, and when I demurred at his remark, he merely said, with a grin, 'Remember Napoleon.'

Particularly amongst the working class, there was considerable sympathy for the Russian people. As goods from factories began to arrive in Liverpool for shipping to Russia, it was common to see boxes, tanks and planes scrawled with messages, like, 'Another for Stalin' or 'Long live Russia'.

I simply hoped that Father was right.

At this period of the war, although I had such endearing colleagues at the office, once out at Moreton I was quite lonely. Edward and Avril soon made friends at school. Brian and Tony began to put down roots in their new village. Before being called up, Brian joined the Home Guard, and spent Saturday and Sunday, and occasional nights, guarding the coast, or practising repelling imaginary invaders amid the grass-tufted sandhills of our seashore. Fiona forgot her watchmaker and enjoyed herself at local church dances. I always went to different dances, because I felt overshadowed by her. Besides, I was shy and abrupt and, until I established myself as a very good dancer, I frequently sat depressedly watching the other couples jitterbugging to the big band music.

The shoulder flashes of the airmen on the floor were those of a myriad countries, from Australia to Czechoslovakia. A sailor of any kind was a rarity – seamen were more common in Liverpool and Birkenhead, where lay the docks.

Many of these young men wanted to meet a girl who would take them home. There, by a civilian fireplace, at no cost to themselves, they could be warmer than in the freezing camp sites and could share what there was of home-cooked food. They also often got their socks darned and buttons stitched on.

The rank and file of the Forces were paid only twenty-one shillings per week. If they wished their wife or mother to receive a family allowance from the government, they were obliged to make an allotment for her of seven shillings a week from their pay. The remaining fourteen shillings bought them very little, though I came across one or two men in Bootle who, out of this miserable pittance, sent their wives additional money, because the wife's allowance was only twenty-five shillings a week, including their allotment. As they often said, 'She's got to pay the rent *and* the hire purchase man.'

Bearing in mind that a man in a reserved occupation in a factory could earn a basic wage of one pound per day, plus boundless overtime at one and a half times or double that rate, British servicemen were ridiculously badly paid. It was no wonder that, when American servicemen arrived with their much better pay, uniforms and food, there was considerable jealousy. However, many a mother with sons in the Forces did welcome into her home someone else's boy, particularly for short leaves of twenty-four or forty-eight hours. Occasionally, the language barriers were formidable and yet friendships were cemented that lasted a lifetime, and many a girl married and went to Europe, after the war, to share the hardships of a continent which had been wrecked by the conflict. There were even a few brave souls who married German and Italian prisoners of war.

Many of the Polish, French, Dutch and Czech dancers whom I watched had already lost home and family to the Germans. Some of them were bags of rattling nerves, who should have been allowed to leave the Forces to become civilians in Britain. Instead, they had yet to face the great and bloody battles of North Africa, Sicily, Italy, and the Normandy invasion.

Mother discovered the cinema in Hoylake, and she went there frequently. Later in the war, she complained sourly, 'It's simply packed with American soldiers, and they are with the most utterly vulgar blondes. I don't know where they pick them up – I really don't.'

Though many of the girls were perfectly respectable local residents, army camps, especially American ones, drew to them professional prostitutes from all quarters; and, despite work orders and the general regimentation of civilian life, these ladies flourished mightily.

As long as the beer allocation lasted, Father found the village pubs, also full of servicemen, lively and interesting. He spent most of his evenings in them.

At times, I could find myself sitting in the evening with a cat on my lap to keep me warm, because the coal ration had run out, and wondering once more what I was living for. Sometimes, I would try to make plans about what I should do after the war, or I would toy afresh with the idea of going into the Forces and would shrink yet again from it, because I dreaded more physical hardship – I felt I had had enough.

Even worse than being alone, I could find myself sitting opposite an extremely irritable mother who had run out of money for the cinema or cigarettes and had finished her library book. If she happened to be in a good mood, however, and if I were careful to tread my way gingerly through all the verbal minefields, we were able to talk about books that we had read or about our old home of so very long ago, a whole lifestyle which I suspect Mother never really appreciated until she lost it. I was the only child who really remembered much detail of that more affluent life and could share in her recollection of it.

In the early days of her marriage, she had collected Georgian silver, and she was still interested in antiques. We would tell each other of pretty examples of silver still occasionally displayed, at usurious prices, in antique shops.

She had been brought up in a Roman Catholic convent school, and she would occasionally recount experiences she had had in this rarefied environment. She had retained her Anglican denomination, though she carried with her, from the First World War and its senseless carnage, the same doubts and bitterness that Father did. While the Second World War whirled around us, we would sit in our cold, still very comfortless sitting room under a dim, single electric light bulb which flickered occasionally, and stir our colourless tea, while we discussed whether the Body and Blood of Christ was, indeed, made real in the bread and wine of the Communion Service. Mother tended to believe, and also discussed, the idea that it was probably all right to address prayers to the Virgin Mary. I once responded that, to me, she always seemed to be only a plaster statue. This irreverent remark brought a storm down about my ears, and she was only placated by a promise to take her to the cinema the following evening.

Of course, any leisure which any of us had was quite late in the evening. Even if I had the necessary fares, I had to allow an hour and a half to get to work and an hour and a half to return, because the transport timings were uncertain, and, to begin with, I had a twenty-minute walk to Moreton station each day. Some buses ran from the end of the road to an intermediary station, but to take one would have added to my already expensive fares. Nobody in the family travelled as far as I did to work. Apparently, many of the neighbours never knew I existed, until nearly the end of the war, because I left home so early and returned so late – and yet it was an improvement upon the struggle I had had to get to and from Bootle. As buses and trains grew older and were not replaced or properly serviced, the whole nation suffered from difficulty in getting about, and the government's slogan, 'Is your journey really necessary?' became a joke. Few would want to travel for pleasure in dark, close-packed vehicles whose timing was uncertain; except those with a little leave, who battled to get home to their families for a brief reunion.

Sometimes it is the small irritations of a war which irk the most: the blackout, the inability to fight one's way down the packed corridor of a long-distance train, simply to get off or go to the lavatory; the problem of obtaining even a cup of tea on a long journey; trying to find a cobbler to mend shoes; or an electrician, or a plumber; or a washer or a switch in order to do a repair oneself. But gradually we got so used to people looking grey, shabby and unmended, to buildings left unpainted, to taps that dripped and appliances which did not work, to furniture with seats worn thin, to shopkeepers like bullyboys, that we did not even notice them.

# Chapter twenty-three

The coming of clothes rationing on 1st June, 1941, laid the foundation of a huge black market. Everybody knew somebody who knew somebody who could obtain articles of clothing, particularly dress lengths. In order to serve this market, theft must have been wholesale.

Women who had never owned a decent dress in their lives except, perhaps, their wedding dress, were now earning good wages. Naturally, after buying food, their first desire was for pretty clothes – at any price.

A very handsome girl, Betty, who lived not far from our quaint mustard pot of a bungalow, heard from her mother that I could sew. She arrived on our doorstep one evening with a fine length of blue woollen material in her arms.

I did not know her, but without preamble, she said, 'Me mam says you can sew – she saw a frock you made for your sister. Could you sew this for me? I got a pattern.'

Flattered by her trust, I invited her in. I fingered the beautiful material wistfully. Then I said, 'I'd be afraid to cut it. I'm not a professional dressmaker.'

She laughed. 'Go on with you. All the dressmakers is in factories and things. Me mam says you can do a nice enough job.' She eyed me hopefully, and then carefully laid the bundle of cloth down on the kitchen table. I hastily moved an abandoned pot of tea out of the way, and carefully eased the material away from the ring of cold tea it had left on the table's battered surface. 'Go on. Take a chance,' she urged. 'I can't sew for toffee.'

'Well.' I paused. 'If you like, I'll cut it and I can tack it up. But I don't have time to stitch it. I sewed Fiona's frock by hand, and it took me ages – we don't have a sewing machine.'

Betty's face fell, her full red lips pouting. 'Oh, blow! Me mam's got a machine she mends on. But she won't tackle a dress for me.' She giggled unexpectedly. 'Says I'm too hard to please!'

I took a big breath. Mentally I saw the girl, with her exquisite figure shown to its best advantage in a completely plain blue dress with, perhaps, a string of pearls as the only ornament. She would look lovely.

'Show me the pattern,' I commanded. 'And let's cut it. I'll tack the darts which have to be machined first. Perhaps your mother could then machine them. You could bring the pieces back to me, and I'll continue the tacking. Bit by bit, we could do it. And, finally, I'll fit it very carefully on you.' My voice gained in confidence, as I outlined the plan.

Happily she drew the pattern out from the folds of the cloth. It was not at all suitable for the material, and my heart sank. 'I thought we could trim it with blue satin ribbon, if I can find some,' she said eagerly. 'And I'd like a proper low sweetheart neckline, if you know what I mean. Do you think you could make panties to match? Like, when you jitterbug, they whirl you round so much your panties show, don't they?'

I persuaded her that the material would not be suitable for frills, as shown in the pattern, and that blue ribbon to match would be hard to find. We compromised on a full, gathered skirt and a tightly fitting bodice with a sweetheart neckline. I sighed. It seemed sacrilege to make such a vulgar dress out of such fine stuff, and I suggested that she might dye an existing pair of knickers blue – wool ones would be too warm, wouldn't they?

It was her turn to sigh, as she reluctantly agreed that they would be too warm.

When I took some pieces to her mother to show her how to machine them, I asked idly, 'Where did Betty get such lovely material?'

Her stout mother laughed. 'A lad in the village had it. And our Betty's got money to spend. She asked no questions and she got told no lies.'

Betty was delighted with her dress and went gaily to show it off at the next village dance. I thought no more about it.

About a week later, in the evening, an elderly man in crumpled work clothes came to the door and asked to see me. Mother allowed him to step into the living-room, but did not offer him a chair. She hovered in the background, while I came hastily out of the kitchen, wiping my hands on my apron.

He said gruffly, 'I'm Betty's grandpa. Her ma sent this for you. Our Betty's that pleased with the frock.' He handed me an envelope.

I took the envelope, thanked him, and, then as he seemed in no hurry to depart, I invited him to sit down.

He slowly lowered himself into an easy chair, and said, 'You'd better open t' envelope. I told 'em it weren't enough.'

Standing in front of him in my damp apron, I did as I was bidden. Inside was a clean pound note. I looked at it in amazement.

'For me? For the dress?' I exclaimed.

'Yes, you worked hard on it, Betty's mam said.'

'It was a pleasure. Betty's mother did practically all the sewing. Betty was very welcome to the help.' I made to hand the money back to him, but he waved it away. He had been looking round our dreadfully shabby living-room, its walls darkened by years of coal fires, its upholstered furniture threadbare and grey with age, the carpet with but a shadow left of its original pattern. He said stolidly, 'Don't be foolish, love. You keep it – you earned it.'

He stared past me at my mother, still fidgeting by the kitchen door. Then the bloodshot blue eyes came back to me. He twiddled the ends of his big grey moustache. It was evident that he had more to say, and I waited politely, the opened envelope still in my hand.

He cleared his throat. 'Our Betty told me you couldn't sew her frock 'cos you haven't got no sewing machine?'

I nodded. 'That's true, unfortunately. And to sew it by hand seemed too much work.'

'Well, you know, I've got a second-hand shop, and I got a good Singer sewing machine in it. I oiled it and tried it this morning, and it runs well. You could have it for five pounds, if you like.'

Five pounds was a lot of money – it seemed excessive, even bearing in mind that new machines were almost impossible to get. Yet suddenly I longed for it. There was always mending to be done, and I could sew so much better with a machine.

'I couldn't pay it all at once,' I burst out. In the background, Mother exclaimed, 'Tush!' in a derogatory way.

'That's all right. You could pay me two shillings a week.' He smiled at me, watchful old eyes nearly vanishing amid wrinkles.

I guessed that he had probably bought the machine for a few shillings years before and had forgotten about it until Betty reminded him.

I was not sure how I would find even two shillings a week, but I did have a pound note in my hand that very minute.

'I could put Betty's pound down on it, if that would be all right, and I could drop two shillings into your letterbox every Friday.'

He got up from the chair quite briskly, took the proffered pound and slipped it into his trouser pocket. 'Done,' he agreed. 'I'll bring it over tomorrow night.'

As soon as the door closed behind him, Mother berated me for giving him the pound note. 'He would have let you have it without a deposit,' she stormed. 'I could have used that money, even if you're so well off that you could part with it.'

I refused to answer.

The machine paid for itself dozens of times over. All of Betty's friends seemed to have dress lengths obtained from anonymous sources, and not one of the girls could sew. Betty was right that local seamstresses had all got wartime jobs, so I had the field to myself.

Though the work was hard – I sewed far into the night and most of the weekends – it solved my financial worries. I often made the wildest-looking dresses, especially when the country was flooded with American soldiers, fond of overdressed blondes. The décolletages sank ever lower, the waists became breathtakingly tight, the panties ever more gorgeously frilled or embroidered; I collected second-hand clothes with lace and ribbons on them, and recycled the trimmings. Buttons, too, became something to be ardently sought for. And I remember pouncing on a packet of hooks and eyes in a haberdashery department, as if I had found a gold sovereign.

Periodically I made dresses for Fiona, Avril and myself, though the material we had was either paid for with coupons or culled from second-hand garments, like old evening gowns or men's evening shirts. A frilled evening shirt was soon adapted into a pretty blouse.

A sailor sold me a uniform he did not want. The material was rough navy serge, but it made a fine warm skirt and jacket for me. I bought an almost unworn blue georgette evening gown from a neighbour, and made two blouses to wear with the serge suit.

Clothes rationing unexpectedly changed my whole existence, but the foundation for my sudden success had been laid years before. Sylvia's mother was a dressmaker and she had shown me how to cut out and fit ladies' clothes, though I was not able, of course, to emulate her fine finishing techniques.

Mother put her usual pressure upon me to share in my hard-earned monies. I refused. I was already paying her more for my keep than I would have paid a landlady. A number of times, however, when she was threatened with court proceedings by local shopkeepers, I paid the bills. I was always afraid that she might pawn or even sell the machine. Fortunately for me, there were no pawnbrokers nearby, and the machine was too heavy to carry far. Every night, when I returned home, my first thought was to look to see that it was still on its kitchen shelf.

With the money I earned I was able to buy a good lunch, because the Installation unexpectedly acquired an excellent canteen.

During the May blitz of 1941, the Germans had not only destroyed ships, docks, warehouses, homes and the core of the city, they had burned out most of the frowsy little dockside cafés in which the dockers customarily ate. These minute eating places were usually run by one woman. They had provided good plain breakfasts and snacks for a few pennies. I remember seeing a pencilled cardboard notice in a steamy window which announced that for twopence the café would provide a large bowl of porridge with sugar and milk and buttered toast to follow. Now, the ever-recalcitrant dockers began to complain bitterly that they had nowhere to eat.

Strikes were, and still are, endemic in the Liverpool docks. With remarkable alacrity, the government built subsidised canteens, to placate this vital work force. The petrol installation at which I worked counted as a dock, so a canteen was established there.

Though the canteen was allowed a certain amount of rationed food, we would have fared poorly had the Manageress not been such a good cook. She produced large plates of good, plain food every lunchtime, by using much-despised and unrationed offal, and cooking it well. The office staff and the outside workers paid a small sum for these meals, and lamented loudly about how awful the food was.

I ate everything put in front of me. I rejoiced at the sight of roast heart, fried cow's udders, devilled kidneys, and liver in a thick gravy. Steamed puddings, lacking both eggs and sugar, vanished from my plate. I thanked God heartily that my dressmaking money had come along just in time to enable me to pay for these meals. I thought all morning about the joys of lunch.

Despite the long hours of work and travel, I put on weight and my figure rounded out a little. At work, I began to laugh and sometimes to be happy, though the terrors of the war lay over all of us.

The Wages Department was responsible, through the payrolls, for collecting employees' contributions towards War Savings Bonds. Through all kinds of special promotions, such as Buy a Spitfire, the government encouraged this siphoning off of the increased earnings of the civilian population – money saved was money not spent on the few consumer goods available, which otherwise would have increased in price even more than they did. It also raised much-needed revenue.

One of my colleagues, with all a Yorkshireman's care of money, suggested that I too should save a little each week in this way. Feeling very daring, and hoping that my dressmaking would continue, I committed five shillings a week to this. I wanted to buy for Mother a set of artificial teeth. She had lost every tooth, as a result of the hunger we had endured when first we came to Liverpool, and I really pitied her. It was quite common in those days for people to manage without teeth. But Mother had been a very beautiful woman and I felt for her. Though I had lost several teeth from the same cause, the devastation had not been so great, perhaps because I was so much younger.

I knew that I would need at least twelve pounds, and thought I should save thirteen, to be certain that I could meet the Dental Hospital's bill. If I did not do this for her, I knew that nobody would.

I have always been grateful to my colleague for this suggestion, because it taught me to save methodically. He also talked one coffee time, when all of us were discussing money, about the idea of keeping a personal account of our spending.

Father's favourite complaint to Mother had always been, 'I don't know what you do with the money!' So I took my colleague's advice, and have all my life kept an account of my spending.

# Chapter twenty-four

Autumn rain was thrashing across the office windowpanes when one of the payroll clerks said, 'Eddie Parry's on leave. Saw him just now.' She slipped into her seat and began to spread out a paysheet, similar to the one that I had laid out on my desk.

We were much busier nowadays than we had been, and I sighed, as I looked down at the neatly ruled columns. What a boring job it was, to fill it in, week in and week out. I was always thankful when it was done, and I could revert to shorthand and typing. Figures never obeyed me; they seemed to jump about on the page and they never added up to the same total twice. Being a shorthand typist was not exactly mind-stretching, but it did offer a little more variety.

The regular employees of the oil companies often spoke of their male colleagues now serving in the Forces, and, gradually, mental pictures grew up in my mind of these absent friends. When one was killed or taken prisoner, I felt almost as sad as the other girls did, and, like them, I contributed to a fund to provide the prisoners with parcels of food. The virtues of the dead were extolled; the stories of the living, like those of Eddie Parry and his brother, had a tendency to become legends.

'Eddie Parry and his brother – they're both in the same regiment – are as tough as old Nick,' I was assured by one of the girls, who had worked with Eddie. 'They go on pub crawls and they get wildly drunk.'

Eddie had been seen with a known prostitute.

Bully for him, I thought. A decent business deal, rather than the importuning for favours that went on amongst the staff. Most of the girls were able, with a laugh, to brush the men off, but a few were indignant and upset. Nobody ever bothered me – I suppose I was too prim.

Eddie's father had died when the boys were young, and their mother, so went the story, had never been able to control them.

'Never been to church since they were christened,' I was informed. 'If there's a fight anywhere, they'll be at the bottom of the scrum.'

I smiled to myself. Quite a reputation.

About mid-morning, a tall, red-faced man passed rapidly through our office, without any greeting to the girls and – dreadful sin in those days – without removing his cap. He went straight into the little room occupied by the male staff members, and shut the door behind him. There was a rumble of hearty greetings from behind the partition.

I was left with an impression of a man without an ounce of spare fat on him, a man who walked lightly and swiftly, despite clumsy army boots. An infantry private's battledress certainly did nothing for him, with its ridiculous forage cap perched on top of fair hair cut extremely short. To me, he seemed too old to be wearing a Forces cap.

'How old is he?' I whispered idly to my nearest neighbour.

She grimaced. 'All of thirty, I should think.'

'Humph.' That made him younger than Harry had been.

I laboriously filled out my payroll, while, through the partition, we could hear Eddie discussing the problems of military life. Though many of the incidents sounded very funny, the stories were couched in language so bad that even I, exposed to every kind of humanity in the streets of the slums of Liverpool, was not sure of the meaning of some of the words. We made faces of disgust at each other, as we listened.

We went out for lunch and, when wc returned, he had gone.

A few days later on in his leave, he came again, and had afternoon tea with his male friends. I happened to be typing at a table right up against the partition beyond which he was sitting, and I became very annoyed at having to endure listening to such bad language.

I stopped typing, and for five minutes I kept on a piece of paper a running count of the words of which I disapproved. Then, seething with indignation, I marched into the other room.

The three men had their heads together, as they leaned over the same desk. At my entry, they looked up in surprise.

I addressed Eddie.

'Excuse me,' I said firmly. 'I'm working on the other side of the partition, and I want to ask you that, when you are speaking, you remember that there are ladies present.' I put down my list in front of him.

A subdued hurrah came from the girls in the other room.

Eddie looked at it, and then slowly rose from his chair. I found myself looking up at hazel-green eyes, astonishingly like my own. He was silent for a moment as he looked first at the paper in his hand and then at me. His red face went a deep plum colour, and then he said in a mildly Liverpool accent, 'I'm very sorry.'

'That's all right,' I responded, feeling suddenly shy. 'You probably forgot we were here.'

As I went out of the door, the other men sniggered. I felt that they were sniggering at him and not at me, and I was suddenly sorry for him.

Half an hour later, when I had moved over to my payroll desk, he came out, this time cap in hand. He asked one of the girls, who knew him, how she was, and after a minute or two's polite talk, she introduced him to the newcomers.

I was the last one to be made known to him, and he paused to look down at the payroll. 'Hm,' he grunted. He looked along the lines of crabbed figures, and then remarked, 'You know, this is a very slow way of doing it. Didn't anybody show you how to do these payrolls?'

'No,' I replied with a small shrug, 'except for the headings of the various columns – they told me what those should be.'

'Good gracious,' he exclaimed, with a grin. 'What's this office coming to?' He turned, and pulled a chair close to mine. 'Move over. I'll show you how to do it in half the time.'

He did the entire payroll for me in a very short time.

I was very grateful. His instruction improved my accuracy a little, as well as my speed.

He leaned back in his chair, letting it rock perilously on its two back legs, and began to talk as if we had been co-workers for years. He was amusing, as he told tales of when he was himself a very ignorant junior clerk and had been the butt of the jokes of the other men on the Installation. He made all of us laugh at his youthful predicaments, and not much work got done.

I began to put away the papers on my desk, and the other girls slipped on their coats and took out their powder compacts to powder their noses, before going home.

'Is it that time already?' he asked, and looked at his watch.

'Yes,' I said. 'Time to go home.'

'Where do you live?'

'Across the water.'

He got up from his complaining chair and helped me on with my coat. 'I have to go down town, to get a tram for Orrell Park,' he announced, 'I'll take you down.'

Behind his back, our two male clerks pulled wondering clown faces at me, and I hastily looked away from them. A spurt of anger went through me. They were his *friends*, weren't they?

Blow them, I thought. I looked up at Eddie and said, 'Thanks. It will be nice to have company.'

In a steady drizzle of rain, I was most politely shepherded on and off the tram. He insisted on paying my fare, and chatted away about nothing in particular. Then, after a little while, he slowly drew out of me how I came to be working at the Installation.

At the station, he inquired, 'Have you got a ticket?'

'Yes, thank you.'

'Wait here a minute, then. I have to buy one.'

'But you said you lived in Orrell Park,' I protested. 'That's this side of the river.'

'Oh, I'll see you home,' he announced airily, 'I've nothing on this evening.'

594

'Our house is quite a long walk from Moreton station,' I warned him.

His eyes twinkled. 'Do me good,' he assured me. 'Need exercise.'

I was embarrassed, and fell silent as we approached Moreton. Since he had come so far, I would have to ask him in, give him tea at least. I hoped fervently that we had some tea in the caddy – and some milk and sugar.

It had rained most of the day, and as we walked out of the station it was pelting down. The darkness was almost absolute once we had left the dim lights of the railway. I had on a coat and hat, but Eddie had only his battledress and his absurd little forage cap.

I expressed concern for him. 'It's nothing,' he said cheerfully. 'I won't melt.'

To make the walk short, I started down a muddy back lane. We had not gone far before we were splashing through deep, unseen puddles. I apologised. 'There's only one house in this whole lane, and we've passed it,' I added gloomily. 'There's absolutely nowhere to shelter.'

'Press on regardless,' he shouted over the pummelling rain.

The water was up to my ankles, and I wondered how much deeper it would become. If the tide were in, the water would not drain until it turned and the little River Birket and its tributary, the Arrowe Brook, could once more flow seaward. I stopped, and said to my almost invisible companion, 'Look, I can't drag you through this. You must go back. I'll be all right.'

'Good God! I'm not leaving you in this. I'm glad I came.' A comforting arm came round my waist.

I was sneakingly thankful that he was there. I was quite frightened.

'I'm going to carry you,' he announced, and before I could protest, I was swung up into his arms. 'Put your arms round my neck,' he ordered.

I obeyed, and suddenly the world became less scary, though wind and rain lashed us. I did not weigh much, but I was surprised that he could carry me so easily. I had not then heard of Commando training; after a course of that a man was either nearly dead or could carry anything.

He made a joke of the whole episode, as he struggled along in the water, which rapidly became knee-deep before we reached the rise on which our decrepit bungalow was built. He slid me down on to the doorstep, and I could hear him breathing deeply in the darkness, while I fumbled for my key.

It was obvious that nobody else had arrived home yet, and I was trembling a little. I shivered, not so much with the cold, but with feelings that I thought I had conquered in the long dark days after Harry's death. I did not dare look up at Eddie, as I ushered him over the doorstep into our sitting-room, and switched on the light. We had forgotten to draw back the blackout curtains before leaving in the morning, and I was thankful that I did not have to switch the light off again and pad round in the pitch black to draw them.

The bungalow was clammy and unwelcoming. Eddie took his forage cap off and shook it. Like his jacket, it was sodden, as were his trousers up to the knees. His feet squelched in his boots when he moved. I kicked off my own ruined shoes, and took off my coat and hat and shook them, regardless of our aged carpet.

'Take off your jacket and boots, and I'll get a towel for you,' I told him.

Though our single towel was not very clean, it was dry. I took his socks from him and wrung them out over the kitchen sink, and wiped his huge boots inside and out with the floor cloth. I put the kitchen bowl on the floor and he wrung his trouser ends out in that.

I persuaded him to go back into the sitting-room and sit in an easy chair, while he rubbed some life back into his feet.

The coal was kept in a lean-to hut outside, and I snatched up the coal bucket and plunged through the back door. My dress was damp already, and it was thoroughly wet by the time I had felt through our small store of fuel for some decent-sized lumps. Back in the kitchen, I was thankful to see a bundle of wood chips under the sink; at least, for once, we had kindling. I snatched up yesterday's newspaper from the table where it had been abandoned, and went back to my unexpected guest.

For all his size, Eddie looked strangely young and vulnerable, sitting by the empty hearth, in a khaki shirt with dark, wet patches across the shoulders and army braces keeping up his ill-cut trousers, from under which peeped large red toes.

I knelt down by the fireplace and began to rake out the ashes.

'Here, I'll do that,' he said quite gently. 'You go and change your frock, and put your hair back up.' My hair was straggling down my back because I had lost half my precious hairpins in the wind.

I protested. 'I can't let you.'

'Oh, go on now. Don't be silly.'

I went. On my way to the bedroom, which led off the kitchen, I stopped to fill the kettle and put it on the gas stove.

When Mother, equally wet, burst in through the front door, railing against the weather, bringing with her gusts of wind and a dripping dog, who had, somehow, got left out all day, we were kneeling close together on the rug, steaming gently.

I was shaking out my hair, to dry it, while Eddie slowly added coal to the blaze, piece by piece, to obtain the maximum heat quickly. Beside each of us, on the rug, lay half-drunk cups of tea.

The dog shook himself and then ran across the room, to nose in between us, accepting Eddie as if he were part of the family.

As we turned to look at Mother, she stopped halfway across the room, her coat slipping off one arm.

She ignored me. 'Who are you?' she asked rudely of Eddie.

In one movement, Eddie unfolded his six feet of height from the rug and looked down at her warily. Then he turned to me. I pushed back the hair from my face and scrambled to my feet. I introduced him as a colleague now called up.

'Oh,' said Mother. She neither offered her hand nor smiled, but turned and shook out her coat.

I flushed crimson. 'Do sit down again,' I begged Eddie, as he watched Mother vanish into the front bedroom, which led off the room we were in. 'You must get dry; otherwise you'll get a chill.'

His face suddenly had a hard, guarded look.

'I think I should be going,' he said. 'I told Mother I'd be back before eight.'

My mother came back into the room. She had changed her dress and shoes and combed her hair.

'Will you stay to tea?' she inquired of Eddie.

It was polite, but most unwelcoming, as if some strange aura exuded from both of them, to clash and form an instant dislike of each other.

'No, thank you. Mother is expecting me.'

He reached for his steaming socks on the fender, sat down and put them on without looking at Mother again. Nickie, the dog, climbed over the fender and into the hearth. He was shivering and his wet coat smelled strongly.

Mother said stiffly, 'Since your trousers are so wet, I presume you came through the lane. The front road and the main road are clear of water. It was foolish of Helen to bring you out here on such a night.'

'I was happy to see her home.' He slipped on the sopping jacket, which I handed to him, took his cap and boots from beside Nickie in the hearth, and moved to the front door. He put the still muddy boots on the tiny doormat and carefully laced them up without stepping on to the threadbare carpet. As I watched him, I was near to tears. Yet I was afraid that if I said anything Mother would be ruder still.

'You can get a bus at the end of the road, straight to Birkenhead Park,' I whispered, as I opened the front door for him. 'Turn left at the gate and then left again.'

He must have seen my distress, because, unseen by Mother, he gave me a careful wink. Then he said good night to Mother, and she nodded acknowledgment.

As he went out into the continuing storm, I said, 'I am so sorry.' I felt his humiliation as much as my own. To send anyone out into such weather was unforgivable, but I knew Mother. If once she lost her temper, she could be unprintable.

'Don't worry, luv,' he muttered, 'I'll be all right.'

The storm inside the bungalow broke immediately. Picking up a strange soldier and bringing him home, without first asking, was shocking. Such a common man, too.

The tirade was still going strong when Father and Fiona came home, complaining that Moreton Cross, the centre of the village, was also flooded. They were so wet and miserable, however, that they could not have cared less if the entire British Army had surrounded the house. They were followed by Avril and Edward who had been playing in the homes of friends down the road.

As I lay sleepless in bed that night, with Avril and Fiona tucked in beside me, I burned with shame that anyone could be so discourteously treated. I was thankful that I had kept all knowledge of Harry, my lost fiancé, from Mother; I could not have endured such a good man being insulted by her.

In the office the next day, I was the object of many jokes and inquiries about Eddie. I replied shortly that he had very kindly seen me to the station.

That made matters worse. The male clerks looked knowingly at each other and suggested, with gusts of laughter, that I had probably had to fight the man off. I was so depressed that I did not answer them.

# Chapter twenty-five

The next day, my Yorkshire colleague announced, 'I'm having a few people in on Sunday, mostly from the Installation, and you're invited.'

My second grown-up party! After much thought, I chose to wear a black dirndl dress which Harry had brought me. Though its black material was becoming a little shiny with wear, it had a pretty gathered waistline emphasised by lines of tiny embroidery stitches, a pattern repeated round the little collar and the edges of its puffed sleeves.

I was tremendously excited as I entered my friend's beautifully kept home and was greeted by him and by his quiet, friendly parents. I think I envied him his father and mother more than I have ever envied anybody anything.

They seemed so calm and stable.

As I went into the crowded sitting-room, I glimpsed on the other side of it a familiar red face. A scarlet blush suffused my own face and neck. Eddie nodded, and grinned at me, so I summoned up a smile, while the other guests swarmed between us.

My busy host pushed a chair forward for me, so I sat down between two girls I did not know and whose names I did not catch when I was introduced, and tried to join in their conversation. But I had little small talk, and was soon lost. They blithely continued their conversation across me. I offered to change places with one of them and the girl accepted effusively. This put me in a corner, where I sat dumbly, except to thank my host when he proffered food and tea. I was a most hopeless guest.

People were standing talking between Eddie and me, but I caught an occasional glimpse of him. He too seemed rather quiet. On his best behaviour, I thought, and wanted to giggle at the idea. He was being amiable to the many people he obviously knew.

He slipped away early, I was told by my host, because he had to return to barracks the next morning.

I must learn how to gossip, make light conversation, I thought in despair, as I went home in the train. Perhaps if I could find some film reviews and read them, it would be possible to talk about films and film stars with reasonable intelligence. And I must listen to the radio – a lot of the conversation had been about programmes I did not hear. I listened only late at night when everyone had gone to bed, a time when one could pick up all kinds of strange radio stations – one of my favourites was Schenectady in the United States – and to this day I do not know by what quirk of the air waves I was able to hear them.

Despite my lacklustre performance as a guest, I had, nevertheless, enjoyed being asked to the party. I compared the hospitable welcome to Mother's snubbing of Eddie – and felt sad, because Mother could be a very good hostess when she pleased to be. She was, for example, very pleasant to Sylvia whenever she visited me. I wondered if, perhaps, Eddie really was an incorrigible rogue, and she sensed it.

I was most surprised, a week later, to receive a letter from Dover Castle.

From behind the thick walls of the castle, Eddie wrote, he was supposed to be guarding the White Cliffs of England. In fact, he felt that he was the centre of the bullseye for target practice by the Germans, twenty-one miles away on the other side of the English Channel. The boredom, he assured me, was excruciating, relieved only by the occasional hits and misses of the enemy. He was sure he would be drawing his old age pension by the time the British got down to tackling the German Army.

Though pets were strictly forbidden in the Castle, two friends and he had, to alleviate the dreariness of their days, adopted a family of three kittens born in a local pub.

Most armies have an enormous capacity for collecting pets of every kind, and Dover Castle would indubitably have resembled a zoo, had the ban not been in force.

The problem, wrote Eddie gravely, was to smuggle their newly adopted family into the Castle. This required careful study.

The three soldiers went to town to shop. They returned with a paper bag and two boxes from the bakery – a uniform usually beguiled under-the-counter goods from a shopkeeper, and they had been successful. As they went through the guard room, a lovely smell of newly baked buns issued from the bag, and a mild scuffling from the baker's cake boxes went unnoticed by the bored guards.

It was the first time, said Eddie, that he had ever owned a mewing spongecake!

Feeding the little family had its own difficulties.

'It is not easy to smuggle rice pudding – or fish,' he informed me. 'Even if you can find a piece of greaseproof paper to wrap it in. My pockets are a disgrace to the British Army. However, Timoshenko and Voroshilov are both gaining weight. We are a little worried about Zhukov.'

There were, of course, inspections to be avoided. The Corporals or the Sergeant would roar through the damp, stone rooms, swearing that the whole place smelled as if every randy tom in Dover was prowling the place. The kittens, hastily deposited in a long-forgotten dungeon, howled unheard.

Once, when he had gone down to retrieve the little prisoners, he found only two. Trying to find them by the light of matches was not easy, because they scampered about so fast, and one had apparently escaped when he opened the door.

After a frantic hunt, it was eventually found in the kitchen, the centre of a circle of admirers, as it cleaned up a saucer of food.

Eddie and his friends decided against demanding the cat back, because they did not want to draw attention to themselves or to the other two members of the family. He justified their desertion of their small friend by saying, 'The cooks could always say that they needed a cat down there, because of the rats and mice. He's found himself a job!'

I had never before received such an amusing letter. In a quiet spell in the office, I concocted as lively a reply as I could, and thus a sporadic correspondence grew up between us. At first, so low an opinion did I have of myself, that I assumed the letters were not for me alone, but to be shared with his friends in the office. Then, though still very light-hearted, the letters became more personal and I kept them to myself. The adventures and narrow escapes of the kittens and their owners kept us going through most of the winter of 1941-42, and helped to divert me during the hardships of coal shortages, failing electricity, autumn air raids, illness in the family, and very depressing war news.

By spring, Eddie was voicing in his letters the general frustration felt by the British Army at the lack of action. He wrote about the frayed nerves and irritability of his friends, and, as the Germans continued to use the Castle as a target, their depression at being holed up in such a cold, damp place.

I knew what cold, damp and frustration could do to a person, and I was able to commiserate.

In the early spring, he came, unheralded, to see me while on leave. We spent several hours drinking half-cold coffee in an unheated café in Hoylake, while I listened sympathetically to his woes.

At one point, he said, 'I'm worried about my mother. She's not very strong, and she's living alone. Our house is fairly large and it needs more heating than the coal ration will stretch to. I'm trying to get a new electric fire for her.'

This was very different from the man who strode round the Installation, swearing like an infuriated Arab or even the soldier who kept cats and, at the same time, wanted to cut the throats of German gunners.

Afterwards, when I had seen him off on the train, a little comforted, I hoped, I walked slowly home.

I thought of two little boys being brought up fatherless, by a mother trying to keep some sense of discipline in them. As they grew up, I ruminated, they would assert their independence, endeavour to untie themselves from her apron strings. And they might easily do it by over-emphasising their masculinity. Put one of those boys into the world of oil companies, where toughness is all, and you would have Eddie, determined to show that nobody was going to kick him about. I wondered suddenly what his mother was like.

# Chapter twenty-six

Late in the same autumn that I became acquainted with Eddie, I arrived home one evening in time to hear Edward, now a tall, thin ten-year-old, complaining of a sore throat.

'You're probably getting a cold,' replied Mother, and then added, with some exasperation, 'If you *will* go out in the rain without a macintosh, you can expect to get a chill.'

The next morning the throat seemed worse, and, over breakfast, he complained of weakness and said he did not want to go to school. He was, however, bustled off by Mother, with the assurance that it was indeed only a cold.

She had to get to work.

By the next day it was obvious that he was ill. He was feverish, and when Mother thrust a spoon handle down his throat to see if his tonsils were swollen, white patches were clearly visible. 'Tonsillitis,' announced Mother. 'Perhaps we should go to the doctor.'

He was, however, too weak to walk and was near to tears. Mother put him back to bed, and walked down to the telephone box at the corner to call our explosive, overworked general practitioner.

According to Mother the doctor, after examining Edward, was very rude.

'Good God, woman!' he shouted. 'Why didn't you call me before? The child has diphtheria – and badly, too.'

The ambulance arrived within half an hour, and a very scared youngster was whisked off to the isolation hospital.

'Who would think of diphtheria?' Mother asked me plaintively. She had not been allowed to accompany Edward to the isolation hospital, and she was naturally upset. I had made her a cup of tea, Merseyside's cure-all, and was feeling very sorry for her.

'Well, I must say that I didn't,' I assured her. Frail, underfed Edward! I was sick with fear.

When he heard the news, Father, too, was genuinely distressed and, armed with a new subject of conversation, he went down to the local hotel for his usual rounds of beer.

When he mentioned diphtheria to his fellow gossips nodding over their glasses of thin wartime beer, he was surprised to be told, 'Aye, there's quite a lot of it around. Three kids in a family by us have got it. They've started to vaccinate them in the schools.'

From house to house the infection spread. Deaths began to be reported. In the next road to us a family of six died, and we felt the same helpless fear that Londoners must have suffered when visited by the plague.

'There's a carrier somewhere in the village,' people whispered, and they eyed each other speculatively.

All the teachers and children in the local schools had their throats swabbed, and by this method several cases were caught in their early stages.

The headmaster of one school worked unceasingly amongst his stricken charges and their families. He hardly slept while he supervised the examination and swabbing of every child in his school, and then had the school specially cleaned, in case the infection lay there. The only person in the school whose throat was not swabbed in the frantic haste was his own, until very late in the epidemic.

He proved to be a carrier of the disease, and it was heartbreaking to see the man's distress. Friends and parents and family, fearing that he might commit suicide, closed around him to comfort him. But I think it was a long time before he stopped blaming himself for the death of some of his pupils.

Mother took days off in order to visit poor Edward, who was, of course, kept isolated. As I remember, she was allowed to look at him through a pane of glass, so that she did not pick up the dreaded disease.

About ten days later, Father came home from work unusually silent. Instead of standing his umbrella in the kitchen sink to drip, he propped it in a corner by the door, where the water slowly ran down its shiny blackness to form a puddle. He took off his mac and draped it over the kitchen door to dry. Then he said heavily to Mother, who was herself still arranging her wet coat over the back of a chair, having only just come in, 'My throat feels very odd. I think I'd better see the doctor when his surgery opens.'

By the time I got home, he had already gone, and Mother was optimistically assuring Avril and Tony that it was nothing serious.

I had hardly washed the dishes stacked up on the kitchen draining-board after tea, when he was back.

He sank down on a kitchen chair, his face drained of its usual redness, to the point where he looked yellow. 'The ambulance will be here shortly. Have I got any clean pyjamas?'

We looked at him appalled, while something akin to terror ran through us. Fear for him, fear for ourselves.

'Doctor said I probably caught it from a dirty glass in the pub,' he told us.

With his bad heart and his generally undernourished condition, we knew and he knew that he had received a death warrant.

As with Edward, no one was allowed to go with him in the ambulance, and it seemed so cruel to me that he was going away to die alone, without family round him. We dared not even kiss him. Even Mother was silent and deflated.

Mother usually took a bus from Moreton to Birkenhead Park, and then caught a train to Liverpool. While she was waiting at the bus stop the following morning, the doctor passed her as he hurried from his car to a patient's house. She ran after him and asked him, in despair, if there was anything she could do to save the rest of her family from infection. 'Where does the germ come from? Is it only from other people?'

'It could be anywhere,' she was told. 'In the drains, in the dust in the house, the curtains. You could try boiling all your dishes and linen – all the clothing. Wash down the entire interior of the house with strong disinfectant. Sluice every drain with more disinfectant. Wash down the furniture.'

'Thank you.'

'And don't forget to have all your throats swabbed,' he called after her, as she got on the bus.

The next day, a Saturday, was clear and warm. A flawless blue sky looked so peaceful that it seemed impossible that it could ever be the stage of ruthless aerial combat. But Mother and I were bent on another battle. Neither of us now worked on Saturdays, so, with the aid of Tony, we moved every stick of furniture, except the bedframes, out of the tiny bungalow. Avril went back and forth with small items.

On the aged gas stove we boiled all the dishes. Into a gas boiler, which Mother had recently bought on the hire purchase system, went our scant supply of clothing and bedding, to bubble like some ancient cauldron until everything looked cleaner than it had ever done before.

We brushed the mattresses and then wiped them with cloths steeped in undiluted pine disinfectant. The settee and easy chairs, which belonged to the landlord, got the same treatment. Then we scrubbed them with soapsuds and a scrubbing brush, removing years of grime. A week later, when they were thoroughly dry, they looked very much nicer, though very frayed around the arms, and very sunken of seat. Standing on the yellow grass of autumn, we washed down all the wooden furniture and left it to dry in the sun.

Then we started on the bungalow itself. Disinfectant, followed by kettles and saucepans full of boiling water, went down every drain. The revoltingly clogged outside drains, still a feature of most English homes, were prised clean with the aid of a stick from the garden, and were then given a dose of undiluted disinfectant.

Standing on wooden chairs brought back in from the garden, we attacked the walls and ceilings, and with swollen red hands we scoured them with hot water, Vim and more disinfectant. The result, while wet, was grey and streaked, but by the time they had dried something of the original colours of paint and wallpaper had emerged.

Every so often, Tony was dispatched to the tiny shop at the bottom of the road for yet another bottle of pine disinfectant, for which I had to produce the money, since Mother did not have any.

We washed door handles and tap handles and the lavatory chain with particular care. We wiped picture frames and the wires and shades of the single light in the centre of the ceiling of each room, and we scrubbed the front and back doorsteps and a couple of feet of concrete in front of each. We cleaned the shoes and washed their soles.

By late afternoon we were exhausted. Everything that we could think of had been washed, except the clothes we stood up in, and as soon as a change of garment was dry, we would wash those, too.

While I pegged the clothes and linen out on the line or spread them to bleach on bushes, Mother went indoors and made tea and brought it into the garden, with bread and cheese and the newly boiled cups and jam jars we used for drinking purposes.

We sat down thankfully on the grass, still damp from the downpours earlier in the week. The back garden looked as if an auction were in progress. The front garden was almost covered by the sitting-room rug, which had been beaten and then scrubbed on both sides. It belonged to the landlord, and I was surprised to find, as it dried, that a faded flower pattern had emerged and that it looked quite presentable, except in the middle where it was worn through to the backing.

'Heavens,' Mother groaned. 'We've still got to lift everything back into the house.' Her hands, like mine, were scarlet and wrinkled from hot water and the strong cleansers we had used, her face was haggard, and her hair, damp with perspiration, straggled round her face. The front of her cotton dress was soaked where it had been splashed. I was in no better state of repair.

I sipped my tea gratefully. 'Where's Fiona?' I asked suddenly. I had seen her at breakfast. I had not thought of her since. She worked in the morning on a Saturday, but she should have been home soon after noon.

'She had a date this afternoon, straight after work.'

Smart Fiona, I thought unkindly, as I stretched my aching back and arms.

Mother looked as if she would collapse if she did much more, so I suggested to her, 'What about lying on the grass for a bit, to rest, while I do these dishes. They can go straight back into the kitchen cupboard now.'

Without demur, Mother lay down on the warm, rough grass, regardless of its inherent dampness, and I took the dishes into the kitchen. Despite their poor, white china, our cups were very precious. Mother had found them in a shop in Hoylake, and I washed them carefully. With a bit of luck, we might acquire one or two more second-hand, and thus be able to discard the rest of the jam jars.

I put the dishes into the cupboard and closed its doors slowly. Like every other door in the house, it was warped, and liable to spring open again. I leaned my head against it. God, how I ached.

From the direction of the front door came a cheery inquiry, 'Anybody home?'

'Eddie,' I yelled, fatigue forgotten, as I flew to the open door. 'Come in. Come in. How are you?'

As he entered and took off his forage cap, he grinned down at me. Then he looked round the empty room. 'What's happened? First time I've ever seen a carpeted front garden. Are you moving?'

I was suddenly sobered. 'Eddie, you must turn round and go straight home. All Moreton is rotten with diphtheria, and that includes us. We've been disinfecting everything.' I went on to explain about Edward and Father. 'And we might give it to you,' I finished up, realising that I cared very much that he should not be endangered, though all of us in going to work or to school probably endangered others.

'You O.K?'

'Yes, I think so.'

'Humph, I've never been sick in my life, to speak of.' He moved further into the room, swinging his cap between his fingers, as he looked up at the streaked ceiling.

'It's dangerous, Eddie. I wouldn't like you to catch it.'

His ruddy face broke into a grin again, the hazel eyes dancing. 'Not to worry. I doubt I'll catch it.'

'Come through then. Mother's in the back garden, taking a little rest. We've been on this job since seven this morning.'

'I'll give you a hand,' he offered, as he strode after me, through the little bungalow. 'Got nothing to do for several hours.'

'How did you get leave?' I asked.

'I'm not on leave. I brought a prisoner up. Got to go back at first light tomorrow.'

It was clear, as Mother rose gracefully from her grassy couch, that she still did not like this big, ugly man. But he was over six feet tall and well built, so he was the best sight she had seen all day, and she shook his hand as he offered to help us.

'Sit down,' she ordered, gesturing vaguely towards the grass. 'I'm sorry we are in such a state. Helen, go and put the kettle on again. Let's have some more tea.'

Tony and Avril had wandered off to play somewhere, so we drank our way through another pot of tea. The sun seemed brighter to me, as Eddie's witty tongue soon made a joke of our predicament and made us both laugh.

607

'They know how to deal with diphtheria nowadays,' he assured us. 'You'll soon have your husband and son home.'

He put down his cup on the grass and heaved himself to his feet. 'Now, where do we start?' he asked.

While Mother went to call Tony and Avril from their game of catch in the front street, Eddie and I folded the carpet up and hauled it indoors. Like the rest of the house it reeked of disinfectant and it had no little mud on its underside. We surveyed the untidy pile of it, after we had dumped it on to the living-room floor.

'Out here, the damp is so great it'll take weeks to dry properly,' I said, with a sigh.

'Once you get a fire going in here, it won't take so long,' Eddie comforted, and then gave his attention to heaving it into place.

While Mother put back the contents of the kitchen cupboard, Eddie, Tony and I brought in the mattresses and laid them on the beds, which we had not attempted to move out on to the grass before washing. I was ashamed of the grubby, stained striped covers of the thin palliasse-type mattresses, and was relieved that the bed linen was still drying on the bushes, so that he would not see that at close range.

When we went back into the living-room, the sun was streaming in through the curtainless windows. The windowpanes glittered with new-found cleanliness and the papered walls and whitewashed ceiling looked quite spruce, now that they were dry. Feeling more cheerful, I helped Eddie and Tony bring in the settee and easy chairs and place them on the damp carpet. Then we moved in the remainder of the furniture.

Mother looked up from poking the living-room fire, which she had just persuaded to burn. 'Would you like to stay to tea?' she inquired. The invitation was much more civil than on the first occasion.

'No, thanks. Promised my mam I'd be back for tea.'

I said, 'Take a seat for a moment, and I'll just tidy myself and walk with you down to the bus stop.' He turned, with a nod, to one of the easy chairs, and I shrieked, 'Not on one of those – you'll be wet through!' I lifted a wooden chair towards him, and he laughed and plonked himself on to the scratched bentwood chair that I gave him. I hurriedly washed my face and hands and put on a clean dress, thankful that Fiona had not borrowed it – Saturday was a great borrowing day, as far as she was concerned, because she usually had a date and wanted to look nice. I hastily rubbed vanishing cream into my face, from a little silver-grey tin labelled Snowfire, and then powdered it, combed my long hair carefully and tied it up, rolled over a shoestring round my head. I was ready to further my acquaintance with Eddie, and I felt elated that he and Mother had got on together a little better.

We wandered slowly down to the bus stop. The sun was warm on our backs and we were so relaxed that it did not seem necessary to talk much.

As we waited for the bus and watched the sparse traffic pass – mostly women going home on bicycles, with a shopping basket on the front piled perilously with groceries – I apologised for putting him to work during his visit.

'It was nothin'. First useful thing I've done for weeks.'

The bus came in. It was early and the driver and conductor got down and stood in the sunshine to smoke, while we looked at each other shyly.

'Hope your dad and your brother get better,' he said.

I sighed. 'Yes. We're really worried about Daddy.'

'Goddamned awful thing to happen.'

The driver, fat and red-faced, was slowly climbing into his seat again. The conductor threw away his cigarette end, swung on to the platform and up the stairs to the upper deck.

I held out my hand and he took it and held it for a moment, looking down at me with piercingly shrewd eyes. I smiled at him, and the rather forbidding face became quite gentle. 'Take care of yourself,' he said. 'See you next leave.'

I watched the bus out of sight, and then turned homeward.

A very washed-out Edward was returned to us by the isolation hospital. Physically, he recovered from his ordeal quickly, though I often wondered what scars this narrow escape from death must have left upon his mind. The isolation itself must have been terrifying to a youngest child used to being petted by a large family.

The fear of Father's dying lay heavy upon us all. Though we were far from being a happy family, faced with death we tended to huddle together. Unlike most families, we had no real circle of friends who knew us all and who would support us with their presence and sympathy, and the loss of Father would leave a frightening gap in our small ranks. I do not know if any of the younger children truly loved their father. He was kinder to them than he had been to Alan and me when we were little, though he never played with them and he lived a social life completely separate from all of us. There was, however, genuine relief when Mother announced that Father had passed the crisis point and would return home in a week's time.

After a few days at home, he was strong enough to walk slowly down to see our doctor to have his sick note renewed so that he could send it to his office to justify his absence.

When he entered the surgery, the doughty Scottish doctor gazed at him in astonishment, and then rushed round his desk, to wring his hand and say, 'Good God, old man! I never hoped to see you again.'

Poor Father did not get much care at home, but he went to bed early and walked by the sea, and gradually he was restored to his old self.

Eddie wrote to inquire how he was, and this pleased both Father and me. At the sight of the familiar handwriting, I remember thinking wistfully that I seemed to be quite rich in men friends – as a good dancer, I met quite a number of pleasant men – and yet the emptiness in my heart was often hard to bear. As I lay in bed, I would still occasionally burst into tears, and have to swallow the grief, because I might wake Fiona or Avril.

I had begun to be great friends with the girl who ran along the cinder track beside the railway, bent on catching the same train to town as me. This fast sprint together every morning, often through fog or rain, the pair of us panting rueful jokes about seven-league boots being a necessity in Moreton, or better still, a skiff to take us over the floods, formed the basis of a lifelong friendship. She had a great zest for life and I enjoyed listening to her eager chatter. She was engaged, so she did not often accompany me to dances – despite all the stories to the contrary, most women stayed faithful to husband or fiancé to a touching degree. Her daily company was, however, something to which I looked forward.

# Chapter twenty-seven

One early June evening, in 1942, I was alone in the bungalow. I washed up the dishes left from the evening meal, and then stood in the middle of the shabby little kitchen, wondering what to do. I was restless, and though there was always cleaning or mending to be attended to, I revolted at getting out either buckets or brooms or sewing needles and cotton. For once, I did not have a dress on hand to be finished.

I put on a cardigan and went out for a walk with the dog, who bounded along ahead of me, sniffing hopefully at every pig bin we passed. I thought ruefully, as I went by, that the sickly smell of the area's collection of potato peelings and other kitchen waste in these bins would have put off even the pigs it was intended for!

I took the main road to the next village, Meols. Though it was a fine summer evening, there was little traffic, except for a few army lorries. Petrol rationing made people nervous of taking their cars out in the evening, when they might be accused of using petrol for unnecessary journeys. If stopped by the police, they would be asked the source of their petrol, and if they had bought it on the black market they could be in serious trouble.

On either side of the road lay fields of young vegetables or pastureland, and the air smelled salty and fresh. Hedge birds chirruped sleepily, while gulls shrieked in a pearly sky.

At Meols, I turned down a deserted side road, lined by ancient stone walls. It led to the sand dunes on which I had, as a child, often played hide-and-seek with a patient maiden aunt, who later took care of Tony and Edward when they were first evacuated.

Beyond the grass-spiked dunes, the tide was out and wet sand stretched to the horizon. I took off my sandals and splashed through the water left by the tide, going towards Hoylake. In the distance the coast of North Wales was a purple line on the horizon.

At Hoylake, I passed the tall red brick house where I had been born. All its windows reflected the great whirls of colour from the setting sun; no wonder Turner sometimes came here to paint sunsets. I trod lightly and cautiously through slippery seaweed at the foot of the gardens of the prestigious houses of Meols Drive. Many of the houses had recently been requisitioned, and were now used as convalescent homes for the Services or as government offices. I had often played in those houses when, as a child, I had come to visit Grandma in Hoylake, and I wondered if their fine furnishings had been removed before the onslaught of careless servicemen and civil servants spoiled them.

As the dog and I splashed along, the sound of our squelching feet was the only noise; even the gulls were quiet. I wondered idly if the beach was really mined. I had not noticed any sign warning of it, though, with a fine carelessness, I had walked over the flattened barbed wire protecting the sand dunes from invasion by sea.

I was getting tired. I'll go through to the Red Rocks, and then I'll be extravagant and take the bus back to Moreton, I promised myself.

As I clambered up the familiar sandstone rocks, the sun was slipping below the horizon, but despite the lateness of the hour, I sat down contentedly on the topmost rock. The afterglow made the damp sand shine like a dance floor and cast deep shadows in the hollows between the great humps of stone. A shadowy Nickie lay panting at my feet, his pink tongue lolling out, his bright eyes glittering up at me.

The peace was so great that I was suddenly truly thankful that Mother had moved us out of Liverpool. My dressmaking had solved the problem of how to pay the fares to work, though the long evenings of sewing were very confining. This huge beach was home to me. On this high chunk of sandstone I had sat so often as a child. It was a refuge, when I had been naughty, on which I could sit and cry. Here, I had sat and wept out many small disappointments, had come and cried again when I knew my beloved Grandma was coming to the end of her life. It had always been, to me, my crying rock.

Despite my name for the lonely rock, I was not prepared for the sound of muffled sobbing which rose suddenly from the darkness below me. Nickie bristled and gave a warning bark.

I had believed myself alone and the sound was uncanny.

The sobs came again.

I stood up. 'Hello,' I called nervously. 'Hello.'

Had someone slipped down between the treacherous seaweed-covered rocks? Too hurt, perhaps, to get up?

I peered downwards, trying to see into the shadowy corners below me. Yes, someone was there. I could see what looked like a humped back. Was it blue? I squinted behind my new spectacles. It was.

Air Force blue. How odd.

I moved lightly and carefully downwards from rock to rock. Below me, a nose was blown very forcefully.

I paused uncertainly. 'Are you all right down there?'

A very weepy male voice replied that he was all right, thank you.

A male voice? Men did not cry easily, I thought, as I picked my way more slowly towards the blue back. Something must be badly wrong.

As I stood poised on a patch of sand accumulated between the rocks, my shoes swinging from my fingertips, and looked down at a crouched figure, a tear-sodden face was turned towards me. It would have been a handsome face if it had not carried such a desolate expression. A very long handlebar moustache, such as the Royal Air Force pilots often cultivated, drooped sadly. Wavy, golden hair caught the light of the after rays of the sunset. A handkerchief was being hastily stuffed into a breast pocket.

The man began to rise, winced, and then straightened himself. He was very tall with wide shoulders and slender waist. In his finely cut uniform, he was good-looking enough to be a film star.

He looked up at me, as I inquired, 'You're hurt? Did you fall? These rocks are awfully treacherous.'

'No. I'm all right, thank you.'

The voice had the polish of a good public school, the dignified dismissal was that of a trained officer. The lips had clamped tightly. The breath came in short, small gasps, like someone trying to stifle pain. Nickie whined and then scrambled down to him, to snuffle round his feet. The airman ignored him, and the dog trotted off to sniff at some interesting bits of seaweed.

I hesitated. The airman did not attempt to move. He stood rigidly, politely, staring seaward, like a bored guest waiting for a lady to say her goodbyes from a tea-party.

Then I remembered the convalescent home for airmen, on Meols Drive; it was full of flight crews with leg injuries. One often saw shoals of them gravely cycling along the drive, to exercise damaged legs and get them to work again. Some of the men could cycle before they could walk. They would laugh and joke with each other as they glided along, but none of them seemed to whistle after the local girls, like the men from the transit camp did. They seemed like a secret brotherhood, bound together by their shared experiences and their pain.

'You *are* hurt,' I said impetuously. 'You're from the Convalescent Home, aren't you?'

Wells of pity for him rose in me. But go carefully, I warned myself; many of these men are close to nervous breakdowns, too. Don't show too much pity. He'll resent it.

He had turned his face upwards, to look at me. But it was as if he did not actually see me, rather that he had turned inward mentally and cut himself off from his surroundings.

'I'm coming down,' I told him very softly. 'Do sit down again on the rock, for a minute; and then we'll help each other climb the whole pile. I have rheumatism in my knees; I can get down these rocks quite well, but it's awfully difficult for me to get up them again. I shall need to rest myself for a little while. I'll be glad of help.'

My knees, which had pained me greatly after a series of throat infections had caused rheumatism in them, were now nearly well, but, to save his pride, perhaps he could be persuaded to help me.

The blank face came slowly back to life. 'Really? Let me help you down.' He held up a hand to me, and I grasped it, and jumped the couple of feet on to the patch of sand between the rocks, where he had been sitting. The jump hurt me unexpectedly, and I groaned.

'I say!' he exclaimed in a surprisingly concerned voice.

I took in a quick breath. 'I'll be all right in a minute,' I assured him.

I sat down on a rock. He picked up a walking stick propped up by him, and with its aid, eased himself down beside me.

We sat soberly looking at each other, and then he smiled slightly under the drooping moustache. I grinned back, trying not to give any further hint of the throbbing in my outraged knees.

He was easily the most handsome man I had ever met. Yet, as we sat quietly sizing each other up, it was like looking at some beautiful gift of nature, a perfect Arab pony, for example. No jump of desire suggested a sexual attraction.

I wanted to break the silence.

'Convalescent Home?' I inquired again.

He nodded. 'Yes.'

I could clearly see his insignia on his tunic, but to open up communication, I asked, 'Air crew?'

'Bomber pilot.' He was young enough to be unable to conceal his pride, as he touched the wings on his uniform with one finger.

'What kind of aeroplane?'

'Lancaster.'

'Really? I've never heard of them. Are they something new?'

'Yes. They are.' A hint of enthusiasm entered his voice, as he added, 'They're great.'

'Did you get shot up during a raid?'

'Not exactly. The old lady was beginning to look like a colander; and Alf, the rear gunner, had bought it. I managed to nurse her back home but the landing gear was jammed. Had to crash-land – pancaked her. And I broke my thigh.'

'How about the rest of your crew?'

'Well ... Alf was killed, as I mentioned.' He paused, and then said, 'We'd been together a long time ...' He rubbed his hand over his face, and I feared he would begin to weep again.

'You must be feeling dreadful about it ...' I began.

'He was dead before I landed. One of the others was badly wounded, and he got pretty shaken up, but he'll be all right. The others were bruised. I think I made the best landing I could.' Though his lips were trembling, there was a defiant pride in his voice as he spoke of his good landing.

'I'm sure you did. It must be absolutely terrifying to have to land like that, particularly after a raid. No wonder you were cry ...' I stopped.

'Crying? Sorry about that. They say my nerves are shot, but it's nothing a good holiday wouldn't put right.' He stared moodily out to sea, a view that was practically invisible now, except for the faint glint of the afterglow on stray puddles left by the tide. 'I get fed up at times, and it's been a bad day. The everlasting orders – the quacks are worse than the regular C.O.s – and the everlasting company milling round you – never any peace.' The quiet, cultivated voice trailed off.

'It must be very difficult,' I sympathised.

'I'm fine when I'm with the Squadron, but when you're stuck in a place like this ...'

I bristled immediately. What was wrong with my favourite rocks?

He was close enough to me to have felt me stiffen, because he added quickly, 'It is a nice district, but it seems miles away from the war I'm supposed to be doing something about.'

'About eight miles,' I said. 'Have you seen Liverpool and Birkenhead?'

'No.'

'I'll take you one day, if you like. Believe me, you are very close to the war.'

I saw his teeth flash in the darkness, as he smiled. 'Really?' He sounded irritatingly supercilious.

'Yes, you are. You should see what is happening to civilians. It's no joke.'

Though he had regained his self-control, he did not answer me. Instead, he again pulled out his handkerchief and wiped his face.

The handkerchief brought with it a folded piece of paper, which fell on to my sandy feet. I bent and picked it up. It was obviously a letter. 'You've dropped this,' I said, and handed it to him.

'Oh! Thanks.'

He took it from me and looked down at the well-thumbed, folded sheets, and suddenly I sensed by his expression that the missive was the basic cause of his grief.

'Bad news?' I asked impertinently.

'Just a last straw,' he admitted, after a moment's silence. He sighed, as he returned the letter to his pocket. 'My best friend has been posted to Egypt. We've been together ever since our first day in the R.A.F. – always managed to manoeuvre our postings – somehow or other. We went to the same school, actually.'

The news from Egypt was daily getting worse. I said gently, 'The Allies may have managed to turn the tide by the time he arrives.'

He said without hope, 'Humph. He has to get there first.'

The news regarding sinkings and downed aircraft in the Mediterranean was even worse than the news from North Africa, so I did not try to counter his pessimism.

We sat for a little while longer and talked about the Convalescent Home and what a long time it took to mend a bone. I inquired where he came from and discovered he was a Yorkshireman, something not apparent from his accent. 'I'm hoping for a spot of leave soon,' he remarked wistfully.

Finally, I said I had to catch a bus back to Moreton, and pointed out that the same bus would pass his convalescent home. He immediately got to his feet. His face contorted with pain. Then he said, when his face had acquired again its curious blankness, 'I am sorry to have taken your time like this.'

'It's been my pleasure,' I assured him. 'Now, I'm going to guide you up the easiest path to the road, because it seems to me that we have both walked too far this evening. Just give me your arm.' He took my proffered arm without demur, which surprised me. The walk to the main road and the bus stop seemed very long. I was tired and he was in obvious pain.

'When your leg is better,' I said, as we crawled along, 'you must let me show you Liverpool and especially Bootle. People forget that London isn't the only target.'

My continued indignation at his not appreciating that the war was on his doorstep amused him, and he smiled faintly. He did not reply immediately, and then he said, 'I am not sure that it is a good idea for me to know precisely what bombs do to civilians.'

This remark stopped the conversation in its tracks. It had not occurred to me that our bomber pilots might not get much satisfaction from wreaking havoc in German cities. I did not care if German cities were reduced to ashes. Yet here was a modern knight, popularly regarded as nearly as much a hero as a Spitfire pilot, who questioned it – or did he?

I was hooked. I was interested. One could have a lively debate with a man like this.

He broke into my thoughts by asking suddenly what my name was.

We solemnly exchanged names. His was Derek Hampson.

As we waited for the bus, he asked me diffidently if I would like to go to the cinema with him the next evening. 'That is, if you're not engaged?' he added.

I misunderstood. 'My fiancé died at sea,' I replied stiffly.

'I am so sorry. I did not mean that. I only meant if you had nothing else arranged for tomorrow evening.' He looked at me carefully, much more searchingly than he had done up till then. 'Tough luck,' he said.

'Yes.'

'Do you feel all right about going to the cinema?'

I smiled. 'Yes,' I said. 'I do.'

And so began what proved to be a most unusual friendship, which lasted a good many months, while doctors and physiotherapists argued about how to treat his poorly healed thigh.

# Chapter twenty-eight

As Derek Hampson's leg began, at last, to respond to the efforts of the doctors and physiotherapists, he was encouraged to try to dance. We had been to the local cinema together a couple of times and to a concert in Liverpool. It was, therefore, natural that we should begin to go to the local Red Cross dances together.

He proved to be great fun, as his spirits improved and his pain became less.

One day I refused to go to a dance because I had promised to finish a dress for a girl.

'Really?' he queried in a sudden interest. 'Do you often make clothes?'

I told him about my dressmaking efforts, and it was obvious from his responses that he knew a great deal about women's clothes, particularly dresses.

'Some of the patterns the girls bring me are awful,' I confided. 'They can't get the right size – and I have to adapt them.'

'Don't you know how to make a pattern?'

'No.'

We had been for a walk and were sitting in a shelter on Hoylake Promenade, watching the tide come in, while he rested his leg. He continued to watch the whitecaps breaking over the sandbar. Then he said, 'I could show you.'

'Could you?' I queried in surprise.

His face went pink, and he turned towards me, as he said, 'You see, I'm in the rag trade.'

'What's that?' I immediately thought of rag-and-bone men. But an educated man like Derek could not really deal in rags and bones, could he?

'I sell clothes – ladies' dresses, mostly.'

'Oh!' I laughed.

He went even pinker. 'Look, you absolutely must not tell anybody, particularly the R.A.F. types. I would be ribbed to death, if they knew.'

'Of course I won't, if you don't want me to,' I promised. 'I had thought, when you told me that you were a shop manager, that perhaps you were a factory shop manager – working for your father, or something. I didn't like to inquire exactly what you did.'

'No. You never ask personal questions, do you? That's why I like you – you're not in the least nosey. You never seem to pry.' He grinned at me.

'Thanks, friend. I try not to invade people's privacy.'

He looked back at the foaming tide, and sighed. 'Well, I'll teach you how to make a pattern,' he promised. 'I own eight dress shops scattered around Yorkshire under different names. Normally I do my own buying. And I was beginning to do a bit of designing. I've an elderly woman who can cut and sew very well.

'Father left me two biggish shops when I was only twenty. I'd been working with him since I was eighteen, and in the holidays long before that, and I really enjoyed it. Mother hates anything to do with the business, though she is holding the fort at the moment. Fortunately, I've got excellent management – older women who were with Father for years.'

'How did you come by the other six shops?'

'Looked for well-placed little shops that were out of fashion or going out of business, and put a smart woman in charge of each. Nearly drove Mother mad by saving every cent I could and reinvesting it. Most of the shops I got for a song – times were so bad.'

'How exciting,' I exclaimed.

He smiled shyly. 'It's a kind of game,' he said. 'I'm doing a roaring trade now – can never get enough stock. The hat departments are dead, of course. But dresses and suits go like hot cakes, because we alter and fit the garments properly – not many department stores do a good job of that.' He turned back again to me. 'You won't tell anybody, will you?'

'Silly boy. Of course I won't.'

I began to think a great deal more about this extraordinarily handsome young man, as we discussed the history of fashion, its craziness, the present government interference in the trade, and its future. Occasionally, he talked about his bombers, the eccentricities of his crew or the pranks and wild games of the mess.

He would also talk sometimes about his friend and fellow pilot who had gone to Egypt. He heard from him quite regularly, and it was as if he pined for his company. As he grew more sure of my friendship, it became obvious that he loved the man. And then I understood why Derek presented no physical temptation to me and why he never touched me – it was not that he was being forbearing because, not too long before, I had lost a fiancé. It was that he was not sexually interested in women. He was truly and faithfully in love with a man he had known since boyhood.

Anybody who has lived in a port, at least in my day and earlier, tended to accept tacitly that sailors away from home on long voyages often turned to their own sex for consolation, and the women left alone certainly frequently had good women friends, whom they referred to as 'me mate'. Publicly such goings-on were condemned; they were illegal and punishment could be heavy. But I was not so shocked as I might have been. Derek was a charming, comfortable person to know and I enjoyed his company. It was pleasant to dance with a well-educated and cultivated man, who offered no threat to me whatever.

A trust rose up between us, as he got to know me better. Finally, he realised that I knew *why* I did not get so much as a good-night kiss from him.

He was frightened.

We were, as usual, walking to exercise his leg, and I cannot remember how it dawned on him that I knew. But he stopped and turned to look at me. He was so tense that I thought he might take flight like a hare from a furrow.

'It's all right, Derek. I can keep my mouth shut. I've kept secrets before and kept them well.'

I heard him swallow in the gloom of the blackout.

'Yes,' he replied slowly. 'Yes, I believe you.'

Later, I found that his greatest fear was of blackmail, if he were ever betrayed.

'Don't be daft, Derek,' I said roundly. 'I wouldn't harm a friend like you. I think we're true friends, aren't we?'

And he said, with feeling, 'Yes, I think you are the best *friend* I've ever had.'

On my way home, I thought about this beautiful person with considerable pity. With what mental agility he would have to face the close life he led amongst the air crews. Or did they know, and not care? I wondered what Eddie would think of him if he knew what he was; and decided that *his* language on the subject would not be fit to print.

# Chapter twenty-nine

The fact that I never asked personal questions did not stop Derek slowly worming out of me the history of my family and myself, and he became very curious about my parents.

When he was feeling stronger and it was apparent that his stay at the Convalescent Home was coming to an end, he offered to call for me at our bungalow, one Sunday afternoon, and take me for a walk.

Though I was ashamed of our intolerably shabby home, I agreed. I was also very nervous about the kind of reception he might get, so I began to prepare Mother for his arrival.

I was ironing Father's handkerchiefs when I announced to Mother, sitting reading by the fire, 'If it's fine, a friend of mine is calling for me about three o'clock.' I licked my dry lips, as she looked up from her book. 'I've been dancing with him quite a lot.'

Mother put down her novel on her knee, and asked mildly, 'Who is he?'

'He's an R.A.F. officer – a bomber pilot.'

'Humph.'

'He's a public school man,' I told her, seizing on one point which might give him standing in her eyes.

'Really?' I had captured Mother's interest. 'What does he do as a civilian?'

'He owns eight dress shops. He's interested in dress design – he hopes to expand this part of his business when the war's over.' I felt it would not hurt Derek if Mother knew this; a solid financial background might endear him to her.

'He must be too young to own such a large business.'

'He's about twenty-eight or twenty-nine. The first two shops were left him by his father when he was twenty. He still helps to run them – he's always writing to his manageresses and to his mother – she's helping out at present. When he's on leave he rushes round checking stocks and books.' I folded a handkerchief neatly, and then continued, 'It's surprising, actually, how many men I've met, who are in the Forces and who are still trying to keep a hold on businesses they have had to leave to others. There's an old chap I see on the trains. I'm told he is past ninety, and yet he's managing a law practice for his two sons, who were called up from the Naval Reserve. I bet *his* sons worry at times that he won't last the war out!'

Mother smiled, and, encouraged, I said, 'The other morning he was trotting steadily up the steps of Central Station, singing. "Put another penny in, in the nickelodeon. All I want is loving you and music, music, music."'

This made Mother really laugh, an unusual thing for her, and she asked, quite good-naturedly, 'Would you like to ask this young man of yours to tea?' She closed her book.

'If we could manage it, Mum.'

'All right. I'll make some scones.'

Hooray for a public school education, I thought a little cynically, as I swept the iron round the corners of Father's hankies. Old school ties, and all that.

As soon as I had put away the ironing, I went into our wild, unkempt back garden, where flowers continued to spring unexpectedly from amid the brambles and the knee-high grass, a reminder of another time when there was no war. I returned to the house with a huge bunch of creamy roses, and some long spurs of blue lupins.

Later, in one of his letters, Derek told me that one of the happiest memories of his life was that of sitting in our sitting-room, with the sun pouring in, and seeing vase after vase of flowers, and bright, interested faces. Perhaps, as a homosexual, he had avoided contact with families. Immersed in his business, he would, anyway, not have time for much social life.

He understood how to please older women, probably from dealing with his customers, and Mother fell in love with him immediately, as he bowed and shook her hand, and then waited for her to be seated before taking the chair indicated to him. My still convalescent father was delighted to talk about the exploits of the Air Force, and the boys were visibly impressed by his uniform and his limp, which made him something of a hero to them. In bed that night, Fiona and Avril both said, with a sigh, 'He's gorgeous!'

Derek was quite smart enough to know the impression he was making. His twinkling eyes, for a second, met mine across the tea table, and I ached to laugh.

This was the first social event I could remember in our family, in which everything seemed to go well, and in which I was not tied up with fear that Mother would be rude or Father would be patronising.

I could just imagine Derek, as he pinned and tucked and fitted in his fitting rooms, soothing, flattering valued customers, customers like my mother might have been in her heyday. While he concentrated on getting the best effect for slightly bulging figures, his handsome face would pucker up earnestly, just as it was doing as he explained to Father the tactics of night bombing. They would love him. No wonder he had been so successful so fast.

We were launched on our walk by the waving hands of the family. Though it was a beautiful day, we did not get very far because Derek's leg was aching savagely. To rest him, we sat on top of the sea wall which protected Moreton from the inroads of the tide.

We ignored the barbed wire which was supposed to protect us from invasion, and talked longingly about what would happen to us after the war was over.

Derek did most of the talking, as he lazily picked loose pebbles out of the concrete of the wall and threw them into the waves gnawing restlessly at the foot of the dike. I said simply that I had no idea what I would do when the war ended.

After a while, Derek fell silent. He smoked steadily, taking the cigarettes from a beautifully chased gold cigarette case, which I knew his lover in Egypt had given him. That man must have money, too, I had thought, when first I had learned of its origins.

With his cigarette held between his fingers, he rubbed the case gently with his thumb, as he looked down at it.

'What does your friend do for a living – in Civvie Street?' I inquired.

'He's in the Foreign Office.'

'In London?'

'Yes.' He put the case back into his inside pocket. 'I was planning to open a shop in London and he was going to put up some of the capital, when the war came. We thought we might share a house or a flat – have a real home. But it's difficult. People gossip.'

He did not need to tell me that. The neighbours would be biting about them, even in a good district.

He turned to me. 'I wondered, Helen . . .'

'Yes?'

'Helen, you've never given any indication of wanting to marry, now your fiancé is dead.' He paused awkwardly, then he said, 'And we get along very well together. What I'm trying to say is that, well, what about marrying me? My friend is as pleasant a person as you're likely to meet,' he rushed on, 'and, you know, we'd make a good family together. And, Helen, it would offer some protection to my friend and me – having a woman in the house.'

'Derek!' I was more surprised than shocked.

He put his hand on my arm. 'Now, wait a minute, and listen to what I have in mind. I would take you into the business with me, as an equal partner. Mother has a third share, so we would be about equal in that respect. She'll be thankful not to have to do anything in regard to the business. And you're good with clothes, and it's an interesting thing for a woman to be in ... I'll show you the books and you could have an accountant check everything.' The wide blue eyes looked at me hopefully.

I was lost for words. I gaped at him. This was where drifting along without thought had landed me.

He shook my arm. 'Helen, think about it. You'll have a good house, I promise you, and a lifetime career in the rag trade – between us we could make it flourish like the old green bay tree.' He was as red as a McIntosh apple by this time, as he struggled to express his need. 'It could suit you very well, Helen. And we'd never question your comings and goings – I mean, if you found, well – a lover.'

After a moment, I found my voice. If the suggestion had come from anyone else, he would have had his face sharply slapped for the impertinence. But Derek *was* good, as honest a man as a critical world allowed him to be. And he was trying to make an honest deal which would benefit both of us, while getting some cover for a proclivity which, though it harmed no one, was illegal and heavily punishable.

'I couldn't, Derek. I just could not do it. I am a normal woman with a normal set of desires and hopes. I am just very, very tired at present; yet, some time, I hope to marry.' His face had fallen, the stubby golden eyelashes covered the eyes, and I felt very sorry for him. I put one arm round his shoulder. 'Thanks for being so frank with me, Derek, and for such a generous offer in its way. Believe me, I understand your predicament. But I could not live such a lie. I just couldn't.'

The huge, waxed moustache quivered, as he grinned slyly at me. 'I was afraid you'd say that – no harm in asking, though.' He stopped, picked up another stone and shot it straight out over the sea. 'Are we still friends?'

'Of course, you idiot.'

Just before he returned to his unit, he asked me if I would like to reconsider his offer. Again, I refused.

He bent, and kissed me goodbye.

# Chapter thirty

With her usual lack of preparation, Mother announced a few days later that we would be moving to another bungalow, the following week. The rent was double that which we were at present paying.

I was filled with alarm. 'Where is it?' I asked.

'Just down the road.'

'Phew, I thought we were going to be faced with more travelling costs.'

'I shall expect half the increase in rent from you. It's useless trying to get any more out of your father or Fiona. We shall have to share the extra rent between us.' Thus Mother, laying down the law of the Medes and Persians, which cannot be altered.

I argued that we were better off to keep our overheads low and spend any extra money on food.

It was a waste of time.

With the aid of a handcart, we moved into a decent three-bedroom brick bungalow. Appearances were, however, deceptive. The back garden, we soon discovered, had never been cultivated because it was so frequently under water. The Arrowe Brook, a tributary of the River Birket from which Birkenhead got its name, formed the boundary of the back of the lot. Every time there was a high tide, the little river backed up and spilled over its banks. The house was, consequently, just as damp as the one we had left and was certainly the coldest house I have ever lived in. As far as chill was concerned, I was back in the attic rooms of our first home in Liverpool. When we could get coal, we burned only one tiny fire and this never dispelled the damp. As in our previous bungalow, shoes and clothes left in a cupboard for more than a few days gathered mildew. Bones ached, as I shivered with my sisters under inadequate bedcovers. It seemed as if we always had colds or influenza.

There was an air raid warning during the first night we spent in our new abode. A lone enemy plane, chased by the Air Force from its dockside target, jettisoned its bombs over the countryside around us. One demolished a nearby farm and one shot aslant our roof, taking slates and beams with it, and exploded in the marshy garden, shattering the back windows.

We tumbled out of bed, and huddled together in the centre hall, there being no stairs or cellar in which to shelter. We were petrified at the unexpected attack.

After a few moments of frightened uncertainty, Father tried the electric light.

It worked, and we surveyed cracked ceilings and walls. Not much plaster had fallen. We assumed, quite wrongly, that the roof had just lost a few tiles, and, when silence reigned, we went back to bed.

Early the next morning, a Saturday, we all tiptoed through the back door to look at the rough piece of field which constituted the garden.

Looming through the mist we could see a large hump of earth, and as we approached it, we found our feet crunching on a litter of broken slates. I tripped and nearly fell over a big chunk of clay thrown up by the explosion.

'Be careful,' warned Father, suddenly uneasy. 'It could be an unexploded mine.' He gestured to us to keep back, while he slowly clambered up the heap of muddy earth. Steadying himself with his hands, he stretched himself near the top and peered over the top.

He shouted quite cheerfully, 'That hole's from an explosion all right.'

We were covered with mud by the time we had all scrambled up to have a look, and exclaimed over our lucky escape. We were less cheerful when we turned back towards the bungalow and saw that a large piece of the back roof was missing.

After breakfast, Mother went to see our landlady who lived next door. She, too, of course, had been shaken by the blast and had already been into our garden to assess the damage. She asked us to send someone up into the attic to make sure that the water tank and its attendant pipes had not been cracked, while she found someone in the village to bring a tarpaulin to cover the gaping roof.

One of the advantages of living all one's life in a small village is that one knows everybody. Our landlady was no exception. That same day a withered old man with a large white moustache arrived, with his ladder on a handcart. By night, he had replaced a couple of beams and covered the hole with tarpaulin. The next day he rehung the slates. When I asked him how he managed to get new slates, his face wrinkled up in a knowing smile. 'Never you mind, young lady,' he said. 'Be thankful.'

While the boys had a great time scrambling round the attic and exclaiming over piles of old sheet music scattered in it, Fiona and I went to have another look at our bomb crater.

'Look, Helen.' Fiona held up what looked like a ball of mud. 'It's china. How extraordinary.'

She ran her hands round the object and cleared the mud, to reveal a Crown Derby egg cup without a single chip.

Eagerly we prodded around with sticks and came up with another one. A further search unearthed a metal plate, but nothing else, except dead worms.

Very intrigued with our finds, we took them indoors and washed them under the kitchen tap.

Since it was the weekend, Mother had decided to paint the sitting-room of the house, and she was levering the lid off a tin of paint, while we examined the plate we had found.

'This isn't tin,' I said. 'I think it's silver.'

Mother glanced at it. 'Rubbish.'

'But look, Mum. It has such pretty fretwork, and I'm sure this is a silver mark on the bottom.' I held out the blackened dish for her to see. 'I'd like to keep it, if you don't want it.'

'I do want it. I can put it under the paint tin to catch the drips.'

'But it would be so pretty if it were polished,' I protested. In a world where anything dainty or charming had long since vanished, I really wanted to keep my find.

'Well, I'm going to keep the egg cups,' Fiona said firmly, as she gave them a final rub with the teacloth, and she marched out of the room with them.

'Come along. Give me that.' Mother held out her hand, and she laid the paint lid down on a piece of newspaper.

'It's a shame, Mum.' I held on to the plate.

Mother snatched it off me, put it on the draining-board and heaved the heavy tin of paint on to it.

'Really, Mother. We could put the paint on a wad of newspaper.'

All that afternoon, as I painted, I simmered with rage, and the drips plopped slowly down the sides of the paint tin to form a thick encrustation cementing the tin to the plate. In the middle of my resentment, I wondered suddenly where Mother had raised the money to buy the paint, and as soon as the room was finished and my hands washed – a washing which left great scabs of dried paint all over them – I ran into the bedroom I shared with Fiona and Avril and checked my handbag, which I had tucked under the side of the bed against the wall. It was inviolate, and I heaved a sigh of relief. I guessed that she had got the paint on credit, and I was right. Later, I helped to pay the bill.

On Monday, instead of staying on the Installation during the lunch hour, I walked briskly up to Mill Street, where despite the bombing, there were still some shops. There, after a very fast hunt, I managed to buy an enamel kitchen plate.

That evening I passed it over the table to Mother and asked if the paint tin, with its dregs of paint, could be set on it and I could have the little plate I had found. 'I really would like to have it, just as a memento of the bomb coming down.'

I thought Mother would burst with rage. She lifted the enamel plate and threw it straight at me. It skimmed past my face and crashed against the wall.

'I'll decide what happens in this house,' she screamed, 'get on with the sewing you're so keen about, and mind your own business.' She jumped up and began to collect the dishes off the table. She dumped them on the draining-board, and they rattled in protest. She was shaking with anger, and muttered under her breath.

I had been familiar, since childhood, with Mother's irrational rages, and I became afraid that she might throw some of the crockery at me, so I quickly left my cup of tea on the table and went into the bedroom. Fiona was there, contentedly rooting through the contents of a battered suitcase, in which she kept her small treasures. I wanted to cry.

'Why does she blow up like that?' I asked Fiona helplessly.

Fiona clicked the suitcase shut and locked it, then pushed it under the bed. Still kneeling on the cold linoleumed floor, she looked up at me. 'I don't know. She only does it with you and Father – most of the time.' She must have seen the tears in my eyes, because she got up and put her arms round me, and said, 'Don't take it to heart. Perhaps it's because you look so like Father.'

It was no compliment to say I looked like my father. He was a plain, large-nosed man with red-rimmed blue eyes. His nose was made more prominent because it was plum red. According to Mother this was because he drank so much, but he actually suffered from a form of acne.

I sighed, and smiled waterily down at my classically beautiful sister. She was right. To look at, I was like my father. And I, too, suffered from the scourge of acne, except that in my case it took the form of septic spots on my chin.

Later on, when Mother had gone to the cinema, I rescued the enamel plate, which now had a large chip in its rim, and hid it under the mattress of the bed I shared with Fiona and Avril.

Some weeks later, when the painting of our new sitting-room had long been finished and forgotten and the residual paint had been stored in the lean-to shed at the back of the bungalow, I came across the plate while making the bed.

I stood for a moment with the ugly utilitarian dish in my hand. Then, since Mother was out shopping, I took it out to the shed.

The paint tin, well bonded to the silver platter by its drips of paint, still stood on the shelf. The paint in the tin had dried out.

With the aid of a screwdriver, I prised the tin off its stand, and put it on the enamel plate. I dipped my fingers in the dust on the shelves and rubbed them over the shiny whiteness of the new plate. It dulled its newness very satisfactorily, and, years later, it was still sitting there, undisturbed.

I spent a very satisfying hour scraping the heavy ring of paint off the old plate, and then scouring it with a newspaper dipped in earth. A silver-plated serving dish was revealed. I dried it and put it under the mattress.

I have it still and use it often. It is a reminder of an extraordinary escape from injury or death during the war – and of a mother with a temper sufficient to supply a whole opera company.

The enamel plate was not the only dish thrown by Mother that summer, but she threw the second one with much more justification.

# Chapter thirty-one

Derek wrote to me once a month quite regularly, and I replied. It was easy to write to him, because we had much in common.

'Killing off civilians is not much joy,' he wrote bitterly in one letter.

'You go for military targets,' I reminded him in my reply.

'We often miss,' he responded dryly. 'This game of tit-for-tat won't solve anything.'

It was evident that government propaganda was not getting through to everybody. The horrors of Nazi genocide had not yet burst upon us; our collective rage had not yet peaked.

Suddenly, he missed writing. I sent extra letters, feeling that he might be going through a bad attack of conscience.

No response. I was worried about this charming, gentle person who had been washed up at my feet by accident of war.

Came a letter from Yorkshire in a strange hand. I opened it with unaccountable nervousness. His mother had found a letter from me in the papers returned to her after her son's death. She said she was happy to discover that he had found a girl friend. He had been too lonely in civilian life.

Killed in action. Those awful words every mother and wife dreaded.

I took a long time to write the most comforting letter I could, and I grieved myself, not only for Derek, but for the slaughter of my generation. And this, I knew, even when added to the losses at sea, was only the beginning.

Life can deal out other kinds of grief, and, for once, I was sorry for my mother. Feeling pity for Mother was like pitying the scorpion which has bitten you. A fair amount of personal pain has to be overcome first.

Father had a long convalescence after his battle with diphtheria, partly because our doctor was concerned about the strain on his heart. For several weeks, he took little walks and stayed late in bed and had an afternoon nap.

The City continued to pay him. Each week his wages were delivered in cash to the house by one of his colleagues, with whom, normally, he went to the theatre or on pub crawls in Liverpool. Mother was delighted to have for her own use the money Father normally spent on fares and lunches. Poor Father got no pocket money, though he still seemed to be able to stand a round at the village pub.

Father's colleague himself fell ill, and another employee, who lived in the next village, kindly undertook the delivery.

The man came for the first time in the early evening, when Father had gone down to the village for a drink.

According to Mother, he was a sober, quiet person, obviously ill at ease, who sat making small talk, before he produced Father's wages in a sealed wages envelope. This surprised Mother because the earlier messenger had always counted the cash into her hand.

As he handed the envelope to her, he said, 'Your husband telephoned me, to ask me to open the envelope and put half the money on one side for him. I reluctantly agreed. Then, I felt so conscience-stricken that I talked the matter over with my wife. We both feel that your *husband* should divide the money – it is dishonest for me to open the envelope containing another employee's wages.' It was obvious to Mother that he was very embarrassed.

Mother said she looked at the amount of the net salary written on the outside of the envelope. It was over double what Father had told her he was earning, and she did not know how to reply. She felt both angry and bewildered.

The man went on, 'I know it is not really any of my business, but my wife says that you bear much of the financial burden, that you go to work in spite of having three children still at home. Forrester earns enough to make this unnecessary – I wouldn't treat my wife like that,' he finished roundly.

He had voiced his disapproval very honestly, and now he paused for breath. She thanked him for coming and then showed him out.

In the days when few homes had any labour-saving devices, there was plenty of work for a housewife to do, and added to the normal load were all the problems of the war, of queueing, trying to cook with little fuel, and making meals out of very few ingredients. It was still the custom for the husband to be the breadwinner, and many men objected strongly to their wives working outside the home.

I was always home much later than the rest of the family. On this night, Mother sat down on the other side of the table, as I began my solitary dinner, which was always kept for me in the oven at the side of the kitchen fireplace – whether it was dried out with heat or absolutely cold depended on whether or not we had any coal.

Suddenly, she put her head down on the table and began to weep, sobbing hopelessly as if she would never stop.

I put down my knife and fork with a clatter, and shot from my chair.

'Oh, Mum! Whatever is the matter? Please don't cry.' I put my arm round her heaving shoulders. 'What happened?'

Resting her head against me, she told me.

'Every word hit me like a blow,' she sobbed. 'I was so mortified that all I could think of to say was that it was a heavy load. He must have seen I was upset, because he repeated that it wasn't honest to open someone else's pay packet, and I agreed.'

I could not think how to reply. I stroked her ruffled hair and made soothing noises, and mentally cursed Father.

Finally, I said, 'I thought you enjoyed going to work, having money of your own.' I thought of all the cigarettes, the cinema seats, the Marks and Spencer's clothes that she was able to buy. Surely she was doing what she liked.

She did not reply, so I added, 'Of course, the strain on you is great, I know that. And I do try to help you, Mum.'

Totally unexpectedly, she agreed. 'Yes, you do. You are the only one I can depend upon.' And she sobbed on.

Though it was scant reward for my going without things Mother took for granted herself, it was nice to know that she had at least noted that, of all her sons and daughters, I was the one who had helped her.

She sobbed on. 'I'm so tired. And if your father paid me proper housekeeping, I could stay at home. There is no real need any more for me to go out to work.'

The crumpled pay packet on the table told me that what she said was true.

There was also the fact that there were no longer young children in the home – even Baby Edward was old enough to be studying for a scholarship to Wallasey Grammar School. The house, peacefully empty from half past seven in the morning until half past four in the afternoon, when Edward and Avril returned from school, must have appeared a much more attractive place to Mother than in years gone by. And Mother herself had aged. The line of hair along her parting, where the dye had grown out, was grey, with silver threads in it.

'It's been harder for me since we came to live in Moreton,' she said, her words muffled against my side. 'Travelling is so tiring, and it takes so long.'

She did not need to tell me that. Strap-hanging in packed, overworked trains and trams for a couple of hours a day was wearing. One was often surrounded by troops travelling with kitbags, suitcases and bulging haversacks, enveloped in a cloud of cigarette smoke, and one could end a journey to and from work bruised and exhausted. Father fared better than most of us. He had been transferred to an office in Birkenhead, and the bus from the end of the road delivered him to its door.

It had always mystified me that Father could go out so often and come home nearly drunk, on what I had assumed was a very limited amount of pocket money. I had imagined that he earned a little more than he divulged, and I had hoped that he saved some for his old age. Though men gave little enough to their wives for maintaining the home, they did sometimes save, so that if they were unemployed or on strike, they could still keep up the amount of housekeeping. Father once said flatly that he had never saved a penny in his life – money was meant to be spent.

I held my mother until she stopped weeping. I was nearly in tears myself.

'Don't go to work tomorrow, Mum. Have it out with Father. He must realise his responsibilities – Tony, Avril, Edward, yourself, *are* his responsibilities.'

'I've already had it out with him,' Mother replied sulkily, as she blew her nose.

'Where is he?'

'In bed.'

That was reasonable. If he had had a fight with Mother, the resultant constrictions in his chest would have sent him to lie down.

I sighed heavily. I did not know what, if anything, I could say to him that would make matters any better.

While I scraped my cold dinner into the rubbish bin and washed up the dishes, Mother went into long, haranguing detail about wanting to stay at home.

'I'm over forty,' she said, 'and I've still got three children under fourteen, so they won't call me up.'

I agreed that she was not likely to be bothered by the Ministry of Labour.

Mother had opened her handbag and taken out her powder compact. In between lingering sobs, she powdered her nose. I dried my hands and went over to her. I put my arm round her shoulders and kissed her for the first time for years. I pitied her.

'I'm going down to visit Mrs Brown,' she said in a shaky voice, 'I *must* get out of the house.'

Mrs Brown was a gossipy elderly lady, a widow, who lived in the same road as we did. Mother would, I knew, pour out the whole story to her, and the next day the entire village would know about it. Nevertheless, she was the nearest thing Mother had to a friend, and a sympathetic listener might diffuse the strain in the family which this upset would cause. So I helped Mother into her coat and saw her out of the back door. Then, with a heavy heart, I went to see Father in my parents' bedroom. The bed was empty.

I found him lying on top of Edward's bed. Though the curtains were closed across the window, I could see in the dim light from the hall that his eyes were shut. Along the line of his chin was a dark mark. My heart jumped in apprehension. I quickly switched on the light.

Against the pallor of his face, a long weal oozed blood. His nose also had been bleeding. There was more blood on the pillow under his head. Despite the light, he had not opened his eyes.

I was shocked.

'Daddy! Whatever happened?'

He made a deprecating gesture with one hand, and then let it drop.

I went close to him and smoothed the pillow back, so that I could see better the cut along his jaw. Beneath the shadow of the day's growth of beard, there were signs of heavy bruising, as if from more than one blow.

'Good heavens, Daddy! Whatever did you do? I'll get some water and a compress. Just a minute.'

I fled to the bathroom. Where the devil were the children? Why was Fiona never there when help was needed?

I ran the tap until the water was ice-cold. Then I wrung the family face flannel out under it. It was an old piece of towelling, but probably as clean as anything else I could find.

Back in the bedroom, I saw that Father had not moved or opened his eyes. I gently took off his spectacles and laid them on the bed. Then I looked closely at the cut and at the bruises. I pressed the flannel hard against the bleeding cut. He winced, and turned his head slightly. When I realised how white he was, apart from the bruises, I asked anxiously, 'Shall I get the doctor, Daddy?'

'No,' he whispered from between swollen lips.

'Well, this will stop the bleeding,' I assured him.

Though he was certainly conscious, he did not answer.

After a minute or two, I turned the bloody flannel over, took one of his icy hands, and told him to press the rag over the cut himself. He did so.

'I'm going to get a blanket to put over you,' I told him. In my bedroom, I tore one from the bed I shared with my sisters, and hurried back to him.

'How's it doing?' I asked, as I tucked the blanket round him. Gingerly he loosed the pressure, and I peeled back the cloth. 'I think it's stopped,' I told him. 'I'll wipe round your nose.'

When his face was cleansed, I asked him, 'Can you lift your head a bit, if I help you; and I'll turn the pillow clean side up?' I slipped a hand under his neck and eased the pillow over.

'I'll wring the flannel out under the tap again. The cold may stop the bruise from spreading. Whatever did you do?'

Still he did not answer, and after I had replaced the flannel over the bruises, I straightened up, and sighed. 'I'll make a cup of tea with lots of sugar.' I went back to the deserted kitchen to boil a couple of cups of water for tea. Why had not Mother helped him? I thought angrily. They certainly had had a row, but that was no excuse for not helping a man who was so hurt.

The gas pressure suddenly failed, and I ran into the hall to get my handbag, to find a shilling to put in the gas meter.

I brought the scalding tea and put it on the chair by the bed, to give it time to cool a little.

Father had discarded the flannel. It lay on the chair by the teacup. His eyes were open and he looked dully at me.

'Daddy, tell me, please, what happened?'

At first he would not reply. Then he said bitterly, 'She threw a plate at me, and I fell, and then she came at me with another and hit me across the chin with it.' He closed his eyes again, and muttered, 'She might have killed me, if I hadn't rolled over.'

She might indeed have killed him. He could have had a heart attack.

He was continuing. 'I think I've got bruises on my back where she kicked me.'

'Good God!' I looked down at this wreck of a man, and then I asked, 'Did you hit her back?'

'One does not strike a woman,' he said primly.

Father's sense of honour sometimes surfaced in curious ways, and suddenly I wanted to smile. Instead, I sighed again. 'I'm going to get the pillows from my bed, to prop you up, so that you can drink your tea more comfortably.' I had been shocked at Father's lack of financial concern for the family. I was far more shocked at what Mother had done. I wondered if she was insane.

Propped up comfortably, Father took his tea in short nervous sips. His hands were trembling.

I sat down on the edge of the bed. It had been bought second-hand and it creaked under our combined weights.

'Is your chin feeling better?' I inquired.

'Yes, thank you.'

'Mother told me what happened about your wages.'

'Yes?'

'I am sorry, Daddy. Sorry for you and sorry for Mother.'

He did not reply.

I plunged in. 'I don't know how you and Mother are going to make it up. But it's like a boil which has burst and has drained. Perhaps things might heal a bit now.'

'I'm sorry, Helen. Your mother fritters money so. There seems no point in giving her any more.' Despite the apology, he sounded defensive.

Frittering money away was something both my parents were good at, I thought sadly. Aloud, I said, 'She's very tired, Daddy, because really in the final analysis everything falls on her shoulders. And she's had seven children – and a very severe illness after Edward was born.'

'I'm tired, too.'

'I know,' I soothed. 'You must be exhausted. You've been dreadfully ill. You have both had a very bad time.'

I took the empty cup from him and put it on the side chair. I picked up one of his limp, cold hands and began to rub the circulation back into it. 'You know, you and Mother really need each other. There's a tremendous shared experience between you – and you've somehow stuck it out all these years, despite the fights.' I laughed softly, and he managed a rather grim smile.

In the glare of the unshaded bulb hanging from the middle of the ceiling, I sat talking with him for about an hour, reminiscing about the nicer things that had happened in his life before he went bankrupt. I pointed out that our lives were slowly improving now, and that if Mother stayed at home, she would be less tired and consequently less testy. 'You could find some interests in common and could have a little social life together.'

'I doubt it,' he said, in response to my last remark.

'Well, after all the frightful things that have happened to you, you have probably not given it much thought,' I suggested.

On I went, driven by pity for my mother and my drifter of a father. It spurred me to cajole, to mend his shattered pride, to give him ideas of how to bridge the gap between him and his wife.

Finally, I said fairly briskly, 'Edward will be in soon, I expect. I think I should put the hot water bottle in your bed, to warm it up for you, and then tidy up this bed for Edward, so that he does not know anything is wrong. I'll help you move.'

Before he could protest, I picked up the cup and whipped out of the room. I was, after all, going to put him firmly back into the bed he shared with Mother, and he probably would not be very happy about it.

He did, however, move without comment. Since we had no extra bed linen, I took the pillowcase off my own pillow to replace the bloody one on Edward's, and by the time he and Tony and Avril came breezing in from the houses of their respective friends, all was in order. I made cups of cocoa for them and sent them to bed.

I then sat down to my sewing machine, to fill in the time until Mother should arrive.

She arrived, around midnight, with Fiona, whom she had met at the end of our road. Fiona was, for once, walking back from a village dance by herself, and Mother did not hesitate to pour out her troubles to her, being bent on enlisting her on her side. This was an unpleasant custom both parents had, of making the children take sides in their quarrels.

At their entrance, I stopped turning the machine handle and looked up. Fiona gave me the faintest wink, and I nodded back. It was enough to indicate trouble, to each other.

Mother was still talking to Fiona, as she took off her coat, expressing her bitterness. Yet it seemed to me that some of the steam had gone out of it.

I had earlier made up the fire, and both women went to warm themselves by it, while I made more cocoa.

We sat round the fire for hours, drinking the sugarless, almost milkless, concoction, while Fiona reiterated to Mother much that I had already said to Father. I chimed in occasionally.

Both Fiona and I had the same instinct, to try to hold the family together. Poor as we were, together we had certain strengths; separated, we were puny individuals who could be individually crushed, and, after her experiences in the aircraft factory, nobody knew this better than Fiona.

# Chapter thirty-two

How the months of the war dragged! Like many other women I was waiting it out. Servicemen were shipped abroad to threatened India and to Singapore, in the latter case, to man guns which had been fixed facing the sea, the traditional source of danger to the little island, while the Japanese came through the jungles behind them. So many men went to North Africa that it seemed like a bottomless pit swallowing human lives.

Stories of horrifying Japanese atrocities were, at first, only half believed, and tales of military bungling came from all directions, to add to the restlessness of troops like Eddie and his friends, still cooped up in England.

With our minds filled with nightmares of what would happen to us if Britain were invaded, it was difficult to sustain hopes of what we would all do when the war was finished. We felt that, on the other side of the English Channel, the German troops were drooling over what they would do to us, once they got a footing on our shores.

I was tied, by government decree, to an organisation which would be dissolved when the war ended; the men recruited from the oil companies would want their positions back, and the droves of young women at present doing their jobs would be out of work.

I felt that I ought to be studying to prepare myself for a better future. Yet where was the time? To eat, to have travelling expenses, to clothe myself, to help with the high rent of our bungalow, I had to sew in my spare time. By the end of the evening, my eyes were red-rimmed, my body stiff from sitting all day in front of a desk, and, later, in front of the sewing machine. No wonder I walked or danced so late in the evenings. Both were very necessary exercises, and could be done after ten o'clock at night.

We missed Brian's lively presence very much. For a long time, he sailed with a crew made up largely of Newfoundland fishermen, few of whom could write, though they were superb sailors. He wrote their letters home for them, and became known throughout the ship as The Professor. He was trained as a gunner AA2, to defend the ship from aerial attack, and it still makes my flesh creep to know that, during action, he was chained to his gun. He used to wear a crucifix and a tiny glass black cat, on a chain round his neck, perhaps to beguile the powers of both light and darkness into protecting him. Something did protect him. He was in almost every major theatre of the war, including the invasion of Normandy, and came out unhurt.

I do not know how Father and Mother made up after their dreadful quarrel, nor what explanation Father gave to the younger members of his family, to explain away his bruised and cut face. But, after a period of sullen silence, they began to treat each other more normally – for them. There were many small spats between them and occasional shouting matches. Mother, however, never went to work again, and there is no doubt that Father began to be more careful about how much he drank. He stayed at home more and found solace in a steady stream of library books about other wars. Mother continued to go to the cinema.

We began to have family jokes, incomprehensible to others, yet guaranteed to make us all laugh.

Tony and Father were masters of the absurd, Tony verbally and Father of mimicry and wild improvisations.

With a towel wrapped round his head, Father could instantly transform himself into, say, an Indian prince being received by the King. The prince, with the utmost gravity and with a drawling Oxford accent, invariably got the better of our stuttering King. The same towel tied round his waist and a kitchen knife in his hand, made him into two surgeons trying to remember which leg they were supposed to amputate. Hands clasped together, as if in prayer, eyes half closed and with the indignant expression of a camel ordered to get up, he was an Egyptian queen ordering a breakfast of fried asps – hot. He was quite capable of mentally climbing inside an indignant camel and answering his camel driver back. It was as if he had, in some part, regained a boyish sense of fun. Even Mother managed to smile at his antics.

Eddie continued to write to me, sometimes from the heights of optimism, occasionally from the depths of despair, as he realised that he was well into his thirties, which could have been his best years, and was stuck in a castle feeding rice pudding to two cats.

When he had only a short leave, he would arrange to meet me under the clock in Lime Street station, and we would go out to tea at some nearby restaurant, to eat baked beans on toast or sausage and mash, followed by sponge cake which tasted exactly like sawdust. The cafés were always stuffy and underheated, filled with men in damp uniforms and women in clumping utility shoes and too much lipstick.

He had undergone training as a Commando, part of a group specially trained in silent, hand-to-hand fighting, to carry out small but devastating raids on particularly sensitive enemy positions. He was pleased at being considered tough enough to belong to such an elite group. In a dark corner, on the way to Central station to see me on to my train, a corner which a more enterprising man might have used to press for favours, he obligingly taught me how to kill a man, bare-handed, from behind. 'Could be useful if we're invaded,' he told me gravely, as I ruefully rubbed my sore throat.

'I sometimes think I should do more for the war effort – join the A.T.S.,' I told him once, over a cup of limpid liquid which was supposed to be coffee.

'You? You're mad! You stay right where you are. You're doing part of my job, aren't you?' He was quite angry and his face went even redder than usual.

'I'm much fitter than I was, Eddie.'

He replied indignantly, 'A little thing like you? Those bloody lesbian N.C.O.s! They'd make your life a hell. You'd be lucky if all they did was walk all over you. What on earth am I holed up in a bloody castle, keeping cats for, if it isn't to save you from things like that?'

'Eddie!' I protested, suppressing a desire to laugh.

He scowled. 'You don't know what you'd be up against. You stay here like a good girl, and leave the war to me.'

A chuckle burst from me. 'Eddie, there are a few other people fighting the war,' I gurgled.

The grimness left his face and the pair of us began to laugh immoderately. Two elderly ladies, sitting almost touching shoulders with us, frowned, and tried to redistribute the margarine on their toast, with loudly scraping knives.

At the back of my mind, I thought with some wonderment, he cares, he really does. And yet he's never even kissed me, even as a friend might kiss me.

At another meeting, he said savagely, 'I wish they'd start the Second Front and get it over with. It's sitting doing nothing that gets me. It's like waiting to be guillotined.'

Such a pang went through me, because I knew his unit was not made up of men who had seen much fighting, despite its fearsome training. They could easily be killed by more seasoned German troops. Though Eddie was known at the Installation as a hard-fisted brawler, he had yet to kill a man.

'Perhaps the Russians will be able to put paid to the Germans, without there ever being a Second Front,' I suggested.

He replied gloomily, 'The Russians'll be lucky if they're not ploughed under themselves.'

He became obviously quite troubled about me when, at one point, I became a test case between the Petroleum Board and the Employment Exchange. The argument of the government was that older women could do the jobs of the younger women employed by the Board, and that all the girls working on the Installation could then be redirected, either to factories or to the Forces. The Petroleum Board responded by saying that they had already lost most of their male staff to the Forces, and had had to train their current female staff to take over. It would disrupt their organisation to an intolerable extent, if they had to train a fresh female staff. The fact that I was the rabbit thrown to the governmental hounds to be chewed over made me wonder if our almost invisible General Manager on the Installation had remembered the impertinent young woman who would not wear stockings and had caused him to have to back down.

While the government's tribunal tried to make up its mind, I spent two uncomfortable days in the cold, smelly waiting-room of the Employment Exchange with another fellow sufferer, from a sugar company. This girl had been directed to a sugar manufacturer and had found that the sugar penetrated her shoes, causing her feet to swell abnormally. Her doctor had recommended that she seek different employment. The Employment Exchange clerks had refused to permit this. So she sat beside me, clad in her father's carpet slippers, to be judged by as supercilious, self-righteous a group of people as I have ever met in a chequered life.

If they are so keen on factory work, why aren't they doing it themselves? I wondered crossly.

Acutely aware of my lack of education and, therefore, the certainty that wherever I was sent I would be at the bottom of the pile, I sat, wooden-faced, in front of the tribunal and let them talk at me. The more caustic the tribunal became, the more I silently raged within. It was obvious that if they could not make the oil companies yield up their young women, they were determined to make as many as possible volunteer for factory work. But I had seen what had happened to Fiona. It was not going to happen to me.

Eddie had heard the news of the impending call-up, and nestling in my handbag was a hastily scribbled note to me.

'Let the oil companies fight it. You are not to volunteer. They'll probably try to shame you into joining the A.T.S. or some bloody factory. It will kill you. Be shameless, little lady, be shameless. You are doing as good a job as anybody, already.'

I clutched my handbag in my lap, and answered the patronising tribunal in monosyllables. After two wasted work-days, I was allowed to return to the office, while the oil companies consulted their legal representatives. The unfortunate girl with swollen feet was told that there was a war on, and was sent, weeping, back to the sugar company.

As we went out together, I said to her, 'Get your doctor to sign you off until they change their minds. That's what my sister did. You don't have to suffer so.'

She stopped crying, and a big grin dawned across her wet face. 'Thanks, pal,' she said. 'I'll do it.'

The oil companies talked to higher echelons of government, bypassing the local tribunal. They simply said that they could not guarantee their distribution system, if the girls were removed, and the whole war effort would, in consequence, come to a slow stop.

Ernest Bevin's administration knew when it was wise to give a little, so I went back to my desk, and hundreds of other girls in other parts of the country stayed in front of theirs, for the duration.

The experience had tired me immeasurably, and I realised that, despite canteen lunches and a more bearable situation at home, I did not have as much endurance as many girls did.

Civilians bore their own particular difficulties without a great deal of complaint. Perhaps the lack of fuel was the greatest hardship. We queued for coal at the railway stations, gas jets flickered down to a tiny, almost useless flame; and, despite dropping shillings into the electric meter, the lights often went off. Nothing lay between our bungalow and the sea, except windswept marshes and the dike, and the gale howled through the uninsulated structure, while every wave hitting the dike made the bungalow shudder on its cement raft.

The smallness of the soap ration also bothered us. There never seemed to be enough to wash clothes properly, and we would use the water from the wash to scour the floors.

The question on the billboards, 'Is your journey really necessary?' became rhetorical. If they did not have to do so, few would put up with the acute discomfort of cold, slow, packed trains and buses.

In the winter winds, our bare legs got increasingly chapped and sore, and we had to admit that one of the very few advantages of being in the Forces would be to have thick woollen bloomers and woollen stockings. Our Wizard-of-Oz-type manager continued to forbid us to wear trousers in the office, and we, fools that we were, obeyed him.

I continued my habit of buying bits of old, hand-knitted garments from second-hand shops and unravelling them. Whether sitting or standing during my train journeys to Liverpool, if I had enough elbow room, I knitted gloves, cardigans and jumpers, either for myself or for various members of the family. Considering how the trains shook, it was surprising that I never impaled a fellow passenger on a knitting needle!

Since I had no clothing coupons, I watched the small advertisements pinned up in the window of the village tobacconist, in order to buy second-hand shoes. Because shoes were often trodden out of shape by their original owners, it meant that to find a reasonably comfortable pair, I had to follow up several advertisements. I was plagued by chilblains on my heels and toes, caused by exposure to the winter weather. To get a blister from an ill-fitting shoe, on top of a chilblain, and have it turn septic, which it usually did, was very painful.

All through the war, late at night, I danced. I danced with men from every nation in Europe, and they had one attitude in common: they never talked about what they would do after the war. Perhaps they accepted, what I feared, that they would be killed.

# Chapter thirty-three

Civilians were not the only people who fell ill and had their sickness made worse by overcrowded conditions and poor food. Alan, travelling home on leave, was stuck in a train which became mired in an enormous snowdrift in Derbyshire. There were many children on the train who became fractious with cold and hunger. Alan volunteered, with some other servicemen, to walk through the waist-high snow covering the bare fields surrounding the train, in the hope of finding help. They came upon an isolated farm, which provided milk, bread and candles. Unfortunately, it did not have a telephone, though they promised to send out a messenger to the nearest phone, some miles off, to try to hasten help to the stricken train. Back in the freezing train, Alan and the other men were unable to dry their sodden uniforms, and when he arrived home, forty-eight hours later, he had pneumonia.

Because of the tremendous snowfall, we were unable to get him to the transit camp hospital. Their telephone lines were down and the lanes leading to the camp were choked. Our local doctor was out at a confinement, and by the time he saw poor Alan, the crisis was approaching and the family was nearly beside itself with worry. The doctor examined the tossing young man, who was extremely thin from overwork and poor food, and said flatly that he doubted if he would live. When Mother burst into tears, he said uneasily that he had a sample of some new tablets put out by May and Baker, which might help, though he was not sure. A powder with the same base had been used by the Russians, to pack wounds before removing their men from the battlefield, and they had had great success in lowering the rate of infection in the wounds.

Unanimously, we pressed him to give Alan the tablets.

Within two days, Alan was nearly free of fever, though weak; and we were the first family in our village to bless the names of Fleming and Florey, the discoverers of penicillin.

A long-distance telephone call at the office brought me into touch with another group which was sometimes sick.

'Could you get over to Doncaster tonight?' asked Eddie, without preamble. 'I've got to bring another P.O.W. up for treatment, and I could spend all day there . . .'

644

'But Doncaster's in Yorkshire. I'd have to travel right across country overnight.'

'I know, but I won't get any leave for months.'

The ears of my colleagues had pricked up, and grins of amusement spread from face to face.

I blushed with annoyance. Then I asked, 'Where shall I meet you?'

'If we arrive first, we'll be in the general waiting room, provided some blasted M.P. doesn't get over-fussy. If you arrive first, wait in the ladies' waiting room.'

I hesitated, and a very humble voice at the other end of the phone pleaded, 'Please, Helen.'

When the office manager had received the call, he had, of course, recognised the voice, and had actually said, 'Hold the line, Eddie.' So everybody knew that I felt strongly enough about the man to make one of the more difficult train journeys in the north, overnight, to see him. Gleefully, they spent the day telling me horror stories about him and his unknown brother.

I escaped at lunchtime and went to the post office to withdraw all I had saved, and to telephone Fiona to say that I would be away overnight.

'You haven't got any night clothes, and Mother will think you are spending the night with him.'

'I won't be staying anywhere. I'll be travelling both nights. And I've got make-up with me.'

'Well, I'll tell Mother,' Fiona promised. 'But I think you're dotty.'

In the early hours of the morning, a disconsolate German prisoner of war, so young and so drawn of face that pity immediately welled up within me, and a sleepy Eddie with a chin frosted with golden beard, his uniform crumpled, sat on a bench outside the general waiting room, both of them slouched forward, arms resting on knees.

Even the prisoner seemed glad to see me, because both their faces lit up, as I was carried towards them by a surge of luggage-carrying passengers. They both sprang up, and Eddie clasped my hand and put an arm round my waist as he turned to introduce me to his companion, who clicked his heels politely and bowed. The prisoner was muffled up in pullovers and, with his greenish-coloured trousers, could have passed as an Englishman in a reserved occupation.

'The porter says there's a little café across the road which serves breakfast,' announced Eddie, and hustled the pair of us through the station barrier.

Except for a cup of tea on a Manchester railway station, while I waited for a connection, I had had nothing to eat since the previous day's lunch, and I went happily with my odd companions into the steamy little café.

In good English, the prisoner said that, to give us a little privacy, he would sit at the next table, where Eddie could see him. He smiled at me, and added, 'I only wish my girl were here, too.'

I laughed, and said thank you, and thought that, judging by his emaciated frame, it would be a miracle if he ever saw his fräulein again.

'T.B.,' Eddie told me, as he seated me in a worn wooden chair. 'In the lungs. I've brought him for treatment.'

Sick or not, even the prisoner ate a hearty breakfast of porridge without milk or sugar, scrambled dried egg on cardboard-like toast, and two pots of weak tea. I doubt if the fat, languid woman who waited on us realised she was dealing with an enemy prisoner.

It was a memorable meal. Eddie cheered up immensely, once he had been fed, and, while he drank his last cup of tea, he held my hand under the table, and talked about a film he had seen.

I omitted to tell him of my struggle to get there, of being faced with having to change stations in Manchester in the blackout, and being unable to find a taxi.

A kindly Flight Sergeant in charge of some eighty men had realised my predicament and inquired which station I wanted. When I told him, he bundled me into the double-decker bus waiting for his contingent, and up the stairs. 'Hey, you,' he ordered an aircraftsman, 'you look after her.' The aircraftsman got me a seat and stood hanging from a strap by me, as if he were afraid the rest of the grinning, teasing gang with us would rape me.

At the other end of the bus trip, the Flight Sergeant came up the stairs and said that he would be handing over the men to another Flight Sergeant. 'So you wait while everybody gets off and he's real busy. Then you slip off quietly.'

This I did and passed unnoticed into the station.

I eased myself on to the train for Sheffield, where I expected to change again. This train was filled with troops being moved overnight, presumably because they were less visible at night. The less the enemy knew about troop movements the better it was. The only light on the blacked-out train was given by miserable blue bulbs which made it impossible to read. The soldiers seemed tired, too.

Just outside Sheffield, the train stopped, because the city was being bombed. The passengers, at first, did not know where they were, and we sat uneasily listening to the roar of planes. The lights went out. Planes swept along the railway track and, between the scream of the bombs coming down and their explosion, came the sharp rat-tat of machine-gun fire. I sat, terrified, with my face pressed into my lap, between two soldiers cursing softly into their own laps, while machine-gun bullets whipped along the side of the train, and somewhere further in front of us glass shattered as a windowpane was broken.

I thought the men might panic and try to get out of the train, since the railway line was an obvious target.

In no other raid had I ever felt so helpless. Confined in the non-corridor train, with blinds drawn over painted windows, the dim blue lights turned off, the heavy breathing and muttering of the men round me, and the smell of the sweat of fear, I felt trapped. Every minute seemed hours long, every bullet seemed destined for our crowded little compartment.

Very slowly, the train began to back, its wheels squealing. After a little while, it stopped. The noise outside was more distant, and within, a collective sigh of relief went up, as we slowly straightened ourselves.

A pair of army boots was vaguely outlined in front of my face, as the man travelling in the luggage rack above me also sat up. ''Ave a dekko, Joe, and see where we are,' a disembodied voice urged.

The soldier next to me heaved himself up, brushing my face with coarse khaki. He wound down the window and looked out. Immediately, there was a rush of fresh air into the tiny compartment and a glimmer of light, probably from the moon.

Feet crunched along the track outside, and Joe shouted down, 'Where are we?'

'Near Sheffield.'

'Are we going in?'

'Na. They'll reroute us.'

Panic struck me. Where would I end up? The man outside had stopped by the door, to answer Joe, so I tugged at the overcoat in front of me, and whispered, 'Ask him how I'll get to Doncaster.'

'Lady here wants to know how to get to Doncaster.'

'Tell her to stay on train. That's where you're going.'

It seemed as if we spent hours backing and shunting and then slowly making our way to Doncaster. The ten or so men in our compartment grumbled steadily about being hungry and thirsty; and I was thankful when a faint light through the painted windows told us it was morning, and I heard the women porters shouting, 'Doncaster, Doncaster, all change.'

I wondered what had happened to the train I was supposed to have changed on to in Sheffield. Perhaps it lay burning, amid twisted railway lines and shattered glass from the railway station roof.

I shivered. It was comforting to hold Eddie's warm hand, and see the light of mischief dancing in his greenish eyes. His attitude was different at this meeting, more easily friendly. I caught the prisoner viewing us with amusement, and felt shy and reticent. With a sudden pang, I remembered Harry's remark about my being as distrustful as the ship's cat. And yet, I reminded myself, I had come on a long and difficult journey, very much on trust, just to spend a few hours with the soldier holding my hand.

He was saying casually, 'I must have been nuts to ask you to come – but I'm glad you did.'

I waited at the gate of the hospital, while Eddie delivered his prisoner. The man had faltered, as we marched him between us through the streets crowded with people going to work. I said impulsively to Eddie, 'He's very sick. Let's go more slowly.'

Eddie had stopped immediately, and the prisoner had leaned thankfully against a soot-encrusted stone wall, to get his breath. After that, we proceeded at a gentle amble. I did not talk to the prisoner and neither did Eddie. At the gate, however, I had said, 'Auf wiedersehen.'

He gave a small mocking salute, and trailed up the path, beside Eddie.

Eddie and I spent the morning in a windswept park, with last winter's leaves whirling round our feet as we walked. He talked and I listened. After the usual groans about the High Command keeping the Army penned up in Britain for years, he began to talk about his childhood and his home. 'My dad died when I was twelve,' he said. 'Lucky for Mum, we owned the house, and there was a little money and her widow's pension.' He grinned. 'She's had her hands full with my brother and me. But once we were both earning, she didn't have to worry so much about money.'

'Is your brother married?'

'No.' He was quiet for a moment, and then he said, 'Neither of us will get married while the war is on – wartime marriages never seem to work.'

I thought of my parents' unhappy wartime union, and replied, 'I think you're right.'

He looked at me in surprise, the heavy, fair eyebrows nearly shooting up to touch the cowlick of golden hair sticking out from under his forage cap.

'I thought all girls wanted to get married, regardless.'

'Not this one,' I replied, feeling a glint of amusement. I had told him long ago that I had lost a fiancé in the Atlantic, so after glancing at me, he said dryly, 'I suppose not.'

It began to rain, so we scuttled back to the little café where we had had breakfast, and ate a mysterious stew with mashed potatoes for lunch. Then we inquired about a return train for me. There was one at 4.30 p.m., which meant that, barring air raids, I would be home by bedtime. The train Eddie would catch went in the early evening.

As we wandered out into the light rain, I realised that Eddie's army greatcoat was getting very wet. I was better clad, in a macintosh, though my feet were wet. Nevertheless, we walked on for a little while, until I saw, peeping above a row of shops, a church spire. I caught Eddie's arm, and asked, 'Do you mind sitting in a church?'

'No.' He laughed.

'Well, it would be dry, and we could talk if we are very quiet.'

The small Anglican church was open. A fat woman in a big black apron was placidly polishing the pews at the front.

We slipped into the cold gloom of the back pew. While Eddie put his arm round me, the fat woman surveyed us unsmilingly, and then went back to her polishing.

Behind the thick stone walls, it was incredibly quiet, and as we sat cuddled together, the peace of it washed over us, two tired people stepping out of the hurly-burly of the war for a few minutes. We did not talk much, yet there was no sense of boredom. Occasionally, he would shift himself and hold me more tightly. I wondered if he felt the rising sense of passion that I did, and the unspoken question was answered when I looked up, because he bent over me and kissed me.

The polishing lady had reached the matching pew to ours on the other side of the aisle, and Eddie said heavily, 'I suppose we'd better get over to the station. We might get you a seat, if we're there early.'

I nodded, and he kissed me again, and this time I kissed him back. The polishing lady clucked, presumably at the length of the silent kiss.

I slowly slipped from his encircling arm on to the faded embroidered hassock in front of me. I closed my eyes and prayed intensely for the safety of one Private Edward Parry.

A small thud beside me. To my utter astonishment, Eddie knelt beside me, put his arm round me again and closed his eyes. Perhaps this tough, hard-headed man realised that, once the Second Front was opened, the odds for him were not very favourable. And like many another unbeliever, he turned to the faith and hope his mother had taught him as a child. I put my arm round him.

He did not kiss me goodbye. But a new relationship had been established. I was bewildered by it, uncertain that anything would come of it. And was not even sure that I wanted it to flower.

# Chapter thirty-four

In a wooden hut, which stood apart from other buildings on the Installation, dwelt two laboratory assistants, fondly known to the Payroll Department as the lab assists. They checked the quality of the oil and petrols being imported. They also obligingly filled our cigarette lighters with some of their samples. The petrol was of such poor quality that we used to lay bets on how many strikes our lighters would need before they flared. At all times of day, these technicians made tea on their bunsen burners, and anybody was welcome to a cup.

They swore soulfully that they were both dying of loneliness, because the wife of one and the fiancée of the other were in the Forces.

In despair, they began to plot how to get their womenfolk home on leave, so that infants might be fathered and the mothers discharged into civilian life. They had long conversations on the efficacy of everything from garlic to ginseng to increase the chance of a pregnancy, and offers of help from the other male members of the staff were plentiful.

The female staff asked if anyone had inquired of the ladies concerned whether they wanted a family – or the concomitant discharge.

Our inquiries were met with deep scowls.

The ladies were shipped abroad for the duration, and, despite embarkation leave, their husbands' efforts came to nought.

One fine spring day there was a sharp explosion. We all leapt to our feet wondering which way to run; an explosion in a petrol installation is not an event which one stops to watch.

A girl ran to the window. 'It's the lab,' she shrieked.

Flames engulfed the only entrance, and two tattered figures flew through them, to roll on the ground outside, to put out their burning clothes.

The men in our department tore out to help the technicians, and the fire alarm went.

The Installation had its own auxiliary fire brigade and the flames were soon put out. The poor scorched young men were rushed to hospital.

The burns were fortunately light, but they were extensive, over their faces, heads, necks and hands. Though painful, their injuries were not serious, and they returned to work swathed in bandages, looking rather like a couple of Air Force pilots caught in the flames of their shot-down plane.

That was it. They had a wonderful time. The general public thought they were, indeed, injured air crew, and nothing was too good for them. No tram conductor would take a fare from them. They rode free. They had only to go into a pub and, with pitying glances, the barmaids would shove full pints of the best ale across the counter to them, and refuse payment. Cigarettes rolled out from under shop counters. Cinemas? Theatres? The best seats at no charge.

'We tried to explain to everybody,' they assured us, in chorus. 'But it was no good. Everybody thought we were being modest. So what could we do?'

Even when the bandages were off, it was some time before their hair, eyelashes and eyebrows grew again and their skin looked normal, so they enjoyed several weeks as heroes, while we teased them unmercifully.

When they looked quite well again, they returned to making cups of tea and trying to seduce us into visits to drink it.

When repairs to their hut were made, nobody considered the wisdom of supplying them with two exits; employee safety was not high on the list of wartime priorities. So short were we of timber and spare parts that it was always averred that, apart from the personal ingenuity of our invisible manager, the Installation was held together by bits of string and chewing gum.

Unlike the lab assists, office boys were called up at seventeen and a quarter. They were usually grammar school boys, who came to us at sixteen. They were not quite so knowing or so worldly-wise as the overalled products of the elementary schools, who formed the outside staff.

We had one amiable roly-poly of an office boy whose innocence was so great that he became a target for the workmen. One man said to him, pointing out of the window, 'You see that big crane on the dock? Well, it isn't a crane. It's the new fog lifter.'

The boy looked at his instructor open-mouthed. 'You don't say?'

'Yes. Invented by a chap who works in the docks. When they get a bad fog, they attach the hook to it and simply roll it up. Works like a charm, I tell you. Super magnetic, that hook – that's the secret of it.'

'Well, I never!'

Another day, the foreman borrowed his services and sent him speeding from workshop to workshop on the Installation to borrow a left-handed spanner. Another time, they sent him to the garage where the big Scammell lorries were repaired, for a long stand.

'Mr Jones wants a long stand,' he told the foreman there.

'All right. You just wait here.'

A wearisome hour later, he was told he could go back to Mr Jones.

'Where's the stand?'

'You've had it.' Very forlornly he returned to our yard, to be received with laughter by the hands, and to be consoled, with sweet biscuits with his tea, by the girls in the office.

One favourite youngster, who was called up, returned, six months later, to visit us. His khaki uniform was loose on him and he looked years older.

'The rumour is that we're going to Palestine,' he said unhappily.

'But you're so young,' I said.

'I'm not. I'm eighteen.'

To cheer him up, we opened up the office safe and carefully poulticed off its door, with the aid of the washroom towels, our favourite centrefold from a men's magazine, a voluptuous blonde in a transparent black nightgown, lying in a languorous pose on a fur-covered settee. We dried her out on the radiator, folded her carefully and put her in an envelope, for him to carry her.

Laughing, he went back to his unit.

We were left with a sad sinking feeling that we would never see him again.

The permanent staff welcomed back a colleague whose health had broken and who had been demobbed.

I shall never forget my dumb amazement when I saw him seated at his desk on the first morning of his return. He wore a beautifully cut beige suit, perfectly pressed, with a blue tie and blue socks, and from his jacket pocket peeped a pale blue silk handkerchief. His fair hair shone with brilliantine and his shaven face was as smooth as pink icing.

We had totally forgotten the high standards of dress required by employers before the war. This man had got ready for work with the same care that he must have exercised in 1939, before he was called up. He had taken out one of his suits from his pre-war wardrobe, unaware that few civilians had anything left that was remotely comparable.

We looked at the other men in their shabby sports jackets, frayed collars, crumpled, mended trousers, and shrunken pullovers. We girls suddenly saw ourselves through his eyes – our shiny skirts, yellowed blouses, and our truly awful collection of cardigans, mostly a musty grey. We were neat, and one girl had a better collection of dresses than many, also from a large pre-war wardrobe, but this vision of sartorial perfection left us low and dispirited. We realised how far we had slipped.

He was a very pleasant person and never complained of his ill-health. We watched with glee his frequent changes of suits and ties.

'The only way he could get a shave like that,' remarked one irate man, 'is by having a girl friend in a chemist's shop, to get him razor blades.'

The crews of the American tankers which brought the oil and petrol to our installation were great smugglers and continued to provide us with such luxuries. But their prices were very high – some girls would give a week's pay to get a pair of nylon stockings.

Our contact was still the dipper. He was the man who climbed the narrow metal steps to the tops of the great storage tanks to dip the contents of the tank, so that the quantity of petrol or oil could be checked. He carried his dipstick in a box slung on his shoulder. Like the policeman guarding the gate, he was part of the landscape and nobody noticed him particularly.

But when a tanker was in, we would corral him in a quiet corner of the grounds and happily rifle his dipstick box, which looked to us like a pirate's treasure trove.

Another small treasure came our way, when a freighter in the river jettisoned its deck cargo of oranges. They had either been ruined by the ship being driven off-course by the Germans and consequently taking too long to get home, or by machine-gun fire. It did not pay to sort through them, to retrieve the fruit which might be still good.

Leaving our shoes and stockings on the river bank, we spent a merry lunch hour, paddling in the shallows, gathering the oranges as they floated in. Many were, indeed, bad, but I was able to take several home.

'Eat fruit which has been in the river? You must be mad. Throw them out at once,' Mother ordered. But the rest of the staff washed theirs and ate them, and nobody was sick.

A cook on one of the tankers brought a whole frozen sheep, but was defeated in his smuggling efforts when the tanker was redirected to the Herculaneum Dock next door, where the Customs officers were much more in evidence.

The story of the sheep flew round the office. Our mouths watered. Real mutton! Consultations were held between the tanker crew and our representatives who went aboard.

'I'll cook it!' announced the frustrated smuggler. 'And you can all come down and eat it for lunch.'

A price was settled, and the number of Installation officials who felt it necessary to inspect the cargo, talk to the ship's master, or take samples, was innumerable.

'When can we go down?' the girls demanded.

The men, sleek from lovely mutton stew, said in shocked tones, '*Girls* can't go! You'd have to eat in the crew's quarters – and they eat from communal dishes. It wouldn't do at all for a girl.'

'We don't care.'

'You forget. They're Americans. They're not like us!'

'They won't touch us.'

'You never know!'

So we sulked, and at teatime we made sure that the men's cups of tea were stone cold.

Wartime rations did not allow for much breakfast, and in the mornings, with canteen lunches still hours away, we were often hungry. One sunny summer day, the whole staff was complaining about empty tummies. In desperation, one of the male clerks went to the nearest corner grocery shop, and came back triumphantly with a newly baked white loaf and a tiny pat of tightly rationed margarine.

'Sweet talk,' he explained.

We did not ask him what he had had to pay for such a nice treat. We joyfully tore the loaf into fair shares and dipped our hunks into the fishy-tasting margarine.

In his spare time, this man was a well-known watercolour artist, and I often saw his delicate landscapes in a city art store. I would dearly have loved to own one, but, like the watercolour paints that I longed for for myself, they were too expensive. My artistic attempts were limited to drawing tiny pencilled cartoons to amuse the staff.

One spring, the same man went down to Shropshire to visit his evacuated wife and children. When he returned, he brought with him, for each girl, a large bouquet of primroses centred with a knot of violets and edged with the big, green primrose leaves. We were all so moved that we did not know what to say. Our world was such a depressingly grey place that we had forgotten that spring comes each year, no matter what men do.

As I carried the precious gift home in the train, I nearly cried with longing for the primrose woods, the sweeps of bluebells, the masses of wild anemones, amid which I had walked as a small child – another world which had gone for ever.

Civilians and servicemen in the train exclaimed at the flowers, and leaned over me to smell them. Mother was entranced by them, and nursed the little yellow and mauve flowers carefully in a soup bowl until they faded, and the last one or two violets were put in an egg cup until they, too, died.

# Chapter thirty-five

One wet and windy day, the Installation fire brigade decided that, since it would be on duty overnight, anyway, it would give a New Year's party in the basement of one of the offices. All firewatchers and all the girls in our department were invited.

After eating our evening meal in the canteen, the girls streamed back to the office, to monopolise the little sink and badly distorted mirror, while they washed and made up their faces, and redid their elaborate hairstyles.

In a time of great shabbiness, beautiful hair was of prime importance. I now wore mine in sweeps combed upwards from my face, with an arrangement of soft waves and curls on top, all secured with hair grips from the dipstick man. The back hair was shoulder length, curled and gathered into the nape of my neck by a fine tortoiseshell hairslide. A friend had found the slide in a tiny shop in a Cornish village, where she had been for a holiday, and had brought it home to me as a gift. It was my most prized possession.

We crowded down the narrow stairs into the small basement room encumbered by old desks, a table and odd chairs. The ceiling was a web of pipes, heavy with dust, and, to one side, the furnace loomed darkly.

The firemen had lit the room with a few candles. Dressed in their navy blue uniforms, peaked caps pushed to the back of their heads, they handed us each a drink. Mine tasted of lemonade powder, and I did not ask what else was in it, but sipped it slowly. The cigarette smokers lit up and soon the room was a sea of smoke. I sat gravely on the corner of a desk, sticking shyly close to the firewatchers from our department. From darker corners came an occasional protesting squeak, from girls less nervous than me.

Unexpectedly, the chief fireman produced a violin and began to play. He went through popular songs, bits of *Carmen* and some light, classical pieces which I did not know.

The bow flicked up and down in the soft light of the candles, and I sat spellbound, so happy to hear live music instead of the tinniness of the radio. Occasionally the guests would hum the chorus of a song, but for the most part they sat quietly in a rare moment of relaxation. The music seemed a special New Year's gift.

At five minutes to twelve, the fireman put down his magic bow, and we broke into applause, which sounded thunderous in the confined space. Then we all stumbled up the dark staircase and out of the office, towards the postern gate, normally kept locked, which led into Grafton Street above the Herculaneum Dock.

The weather had cleared up, though the sky was still overcast, and it was extremely dark. The river was invisible, except for an occasional glint of a wave. Below us, in the dock, there was the sound of voices; a ship was in.

Men peered at their wrist watches, trying to see the time.

'Don't worry, every hooter and siren on the river'll go off when it's time,' a fireman assured them. Then he nudged me. 'Keep your eyes on the river. You're in for a surprise.'

Not quite in unison, the hooters and ships' sirens did go off. We all laughed and shouted Happy New Year to each other and to the invisible ships.

And then the miracle occurred. From end to end of our line of sight, all the ships switched on their lights, giving a glimpse of a peacetime river lasting about five seconds. Then they all went out, and we were left shivering in the dark.

Bemused, we clasped each other's hands and formed a circle.

'Should auld acquaintance be forgot and never brought to mind . . .'

We swung our hands up and down as we sang and I was happy, with friends whom I loved dearly, and yet, in the back of my mind, there was a silence as if part of me could not join in. There lay a memory of someone who was not there and never would be.

I missed the last train from Liverpool, and had to cross the river on the ferry boat to the Birkenhead terminal. From there, I walked home through the sleeping town, past fields and villages where nothing stirred. There was no traffic and it was absolutely dark. Only the grey macadamed road showed as a faint line ahead of me. It was a curious beginning to a new year.

'How did they manage it – the lights, I mean?' I asked one of my colleagues at the office the next morning.

'It wouldn't be too difficult. Messages go up and down the river all the time between ships and shore. The sparks talk to each other.'

'It was so quick. I don't suppose the wardens would have had more than time to blink before it was over.'

'Nor the ships' masters, either.'

I could almost hear the protests, if the authorities inquired amongst the ships' crews. The rumpled, bleary faces of the morning after New Year would protest, 'Me, sir? Never touch a light switch. Not my job.' Or, 'No, sir. Nobody come in and switch 'em on. I were here meself. I'd know.' Or, 'I never saw nothin' unusual. Anyway, I were too busy.' The flow of

Liverpudlian denials would be so uniform that any self-respecting officer would retire in honourable defeat.

The switching-on of the lights was a lovely joke, a schoolboy cocking of a snook at authority, and for weeks afterwards we would occasionally refer to it.

Soon after the New Year, I frightened my colleagues by fainting at my desk, as a result of a particularly painful menstrual stomach ache. I was put to bed on one of the firewatchers' beds, and, when I came round, one of the girls offered me two tablets, which I gratefully swallowed.

They were Codeine, and she told me where to buy them. They released me from a great deal of regular suffering.

None of the girls realised that the tablets were a derivative of morphine and sometimes addictive. They could be bought at any chemist's, though one sometimes had to sign the Poison Book when purchasing them.

I gave some of the tablets to my father, when he had salmonella poisoning, from eating improperly processed American dried egg. Our doctor was out on another case, and Father was rolling on the bed, clutching his stomach. He was covered with perspiration, and a further pain in his chest threatened another heart attack. He had been vomiting, but he managed to keep three tablets down, and the pain vanished.

Stomach upsets were very common during the war and for some years afterwards. Standards of hygiene were very low in cafés, restaurants and canteens, and more people were eating away from home, partly because of the long hours of work and partly to augment inadequate rations.

As men were called up and fourteen-year-olds found they could earn more in factories, the innumerable small shops and cafés had difficulty in getting help. Complicated by a sea of government regulations, it was difficult to find time to keep such places properly clean and food adequately stored. Anyone selling sweets, for instance, had to count, and thread together with a needle and cotton, coupons about a quarter of the size of a postage stamp, before sending them to the Ministry of Food. It must have driven shopkeepers, mostly women, nearly mad. Concentrated bombing, with its subsequent heavy dust fall and its disorganisation, did not help.

In the spring of 1943, the first marriage in our family took place. Alan was to be posted to North Africa and decided to marry his sweetheart, an A.T.S. girl serving on a gun post, before he left. Like many wartime marriages, the arrangements were made so quickly that our family could not get to the ceremony, held in the south of the country. He did, however, bring her to stay with us for a few days' honeymoon.

There was a hasty doubling up in an already overcrowded house, so that we could give them a bedroom where the roses were growing right across the window, the only pretty thing we could offer in our shabby home.

Though we three sisters were delighted by the new bride, it took very little time for her to become the victim of Mother's vicious temper; and Father was by no means nice to her. He seemed to think she was just a housemaid.

This sickening situation was the beginning of a clear separation between my family and myself. I had always kept my own counsel, but now I intensified my independence. When the war was over and life in Britain had settled down, I would try to build a home of my own – it was as well that I did not realise that it would be many years before life in Britain returned to normal! All I knew was that I could not stomach such unkindness towards a stranger, and it brought home to me what my future life would be, if I stayed with my parents. Occasionally, I would tell myself that I might marry, anyway, and that would take me away – but I was not going to count on it.

# Chapter thirty-six

After Christmas 1943, London became the target of a new German weapon, an extremely fast and destructive pilotless plane, which the British named the Doodlebug. A number of Londoners fled to the north, amongst them the sister of Alan's wife, and her little daughter. It was decided that they should stay with us.

It took only a week or two for this terrified woman to decide that the Doodlebugs were preferable to Mother, and she returned to London.

Eddie came on leave, and I waited for him under the clock in Lime Street station. I wondered how he would behave, after our last meeting.

It was as if nothing had changed. He took me to our usual café, and we gossiped about everything under the sun, except what lay between us.

'The invasion won't be long now,' he told me jubilantly.

'How can you be so cheerful about it?'

'Well, if you know you're going to be hanged, it's a relief to have some idea when!' He then went on to tell me that he had been returned to his own unit, halfway through some advanced Commando training. 'I'm too heavy. Every time I climb a tree, for sniping, the bally tree bends and tells the world that I'm there!'

From later conversation, however, I gathered that probably the main reason the Commandos did not want him was that he was older and, consequently, not as quick and agile as a youngster would be. He said flatly, 'If I'm killed, it will be because I can't move fast enough.'

With the aid of the greasy menu, a teaspoon and a piece of string, he instructed me in how to climb a quarry wall or the side of a cliff, or even a building. At first I laughed at him. But then I sobered, as I saw, mentally, men struggling through surf, to reach a sandy shore overshadowed by well-defended cliffs. The invasion, I thought, could be another Dardanelles, another botched effort, like Dieppe, where under-trained men had been simply butchered by the Germans. He must have seen it, too, because he put the spoon down quietly and shoved the menu to one side.

Seeing his expression suddenly harden, I asked quickly, 'How are the kittens?'

He grinned. 'They've got great-great-grandchildren. The ruddy castle's rotten with them – they all hunt for themselves. Our sergeant found one on his bed last week, and he was properly put out. Told us we could get some practice wringing the little tykes' necks. Says the Old Man himself is saying there are too many pets, and that they've got to be cleaned out.'

'Never mind,' I comforted. 'There's probably not a mouse in the place. If you're right about the invasion, it'll soon be over, and you can come home. What are you going to do then?'

'Go back to Shell, I suppose, if I've any sense. The way they pay, it would be beer money at least.' He grinned wickedly at me, and I was again reminded how alike we were – he could have been my brother, with his greenish eyes, his big nose and thin, reddish skin. We shared an underlying endurance, too, a particular inner strength. His young life had not been easy either. We shared, also, an inner reserve; his covered by a humorous defiance of life, mine by a high-pitched chattiness or a nervous silence. I liked immensely the man behind the facade, his interest in everything going on around him, his care for his mother, his general exuberance.

Two evenings later, he came over to our bungalow, and spent the evening talking with Father and me. The old soldier and the new one got on surprisingly well. He stayed so late that he missed the last train to Liverpool, and had to walk to the ferry.

He continued to write to me in an ordinary, friendly way. And it seemed as if the invasion of Europe was as far away as ever.

While Eddie's unit continued to climb up and down quarries, and I worked and sewed and danced, Alan toiled up the leg of Italy and spent the bitter winter of 1943–44 in the Apennine Mountains.

Brian was at sea, and went to the United States to be part of the crew of a minesweeper being built in Seattle. They had a rough passage bringing the little tub back to British waters, where, for a while, he swept mines.

On 5th June, 1944, he was minesweeping along the coast of France, a ready target for German guns. He saw the British invasion at Arromanches, and helped to pull the dead and dying out of the water. A day or two after the landing was assured, he went ashore, found a post office still in business, and sent Mother a picture postcard.

Mother nearly collapsed, when she saw that the card was from France, but she kept it for years.

After seeing the hideous results of the attack on France, to send a post-card, as if on holiday, seemed to me to be the epitome of the British stiff upper lip. The sallow-skinned little boy who suffered from nightmares grew up to live them through his youth. He fought in the Atlantic and the Pacific, walked through Tokyo, after it was burned to the ground by one of the biggest fire storms ever created by man, and afterwards walked through the cold ashes of Hiroshima. Later, he served in a ship cleaning out pirates from Chinese waterways. There, the starvation was so intense that the women porters, loading the ship's coal in baskets on their heads,

fell in their tracks from hunger, and the sorely distressed British crew had
to be forbidden to hand over their rations to them. He saw slain or burned
servicemen and civilians under almost every possible situation, and found
that, all over a desperate, ruined world, a few cigarettes from his ration
would buy anything.

Eddie was not under any illusion about *his* near future. He said, while
on one leave, 'The poor bloody infantry are going to get it, as usual.'

I felt sick. Despite his tough reputation, I could not imagine Eddie
killing anybody; yet he would have to, if he was not to die himself.

On his final leave before the invasion of France, he again missed the
last train to Liverpool, so I walked down to the bus stop with him. We
were just in time to see the bus vanish into the gloom.

'Never mind,' he said comfortably, 'I'll walk to the ferry.'

'Then I'm going to walk some of the way with you.'

I had not anticipated going more than a mile or two, but we were so
quietly companionable and the starry night was so pleasant that we swung
along together, regardless of the distance.

At the foot of Bidston Hill, Eddie paused and looked around the quiet
fields and the empty road. Satisfied, he looked down at me. 'Helen,' he
said, 'I want to ask you something.'

'Yes?'

'Helen, after the war – when I've got started again, Helen, would you
marry me then?' he blurted out.

I was astonished. After all the tales I had heard, I had expected that
some time or other he would proposition me. I never thought he would
ask me to marry him. I stared doubtfully up at him.

'I know I'm no catch, Helen.' He sounded anxious when I still did not
reply, and went on, 'I can earn a living for you, though. And I want to
settle down.'

No word of love?

I took a big breath and smiled at his confusion. 'I didn't think you had
holy matrimony in mind,' I finally responded lightly.

'Holy or unholy, I've got it in mind.' He put his arms round my
shoulders and eased himself close to me. 'I want to come back to you,
Helen. Nobody else.'

He bent and kissed me tentatively, and such desire shot through me that
the rigidly maintained self-control I had learned in my sorrow threatened
to crumple. With a great effort, I drew myself back, though he still held
me loosely. In the faint light, I could see the wicked grin on his face, and
the knowledge that he would probably win. I blushed scarlet.

It was my turn to be confused. Here was a man who would never
remember birthdays, take for granted much that a wife would do for him,
sire children without a thought.

Yet, and yet, perhaps I was being too hard. When times got rough, I thought, he was not the kind to desert me, and he was a great deal more civilised than he liked to make out.

'Yes,' I said, and put my arms round his neck. He kissed me again, and, though I knew it would be different from all my young girl's hopes, I felt it would be all right.

I expected him to whoop his satisfaction to the shivering trees in the churchyard nearby. But he kissed me long and soberly and then let me go. 'I'll take you home to see my mother next time I'm on leave. And we can buy a ring, if you'd like one.'

Slowly we turned and walked on until the wind rose and it became cold. He insisted that I turn back, so we kissed again, and I watched him jog steadily down the long straight road until he was out of sight. He did not look back.

With a heavy heart, I began the long walk home. I feared to lose what I had just gained.

I never saw him again. His next leave was cancelled, as everyone was confined to barracks or to training grounds, preparatory to the invasion of France. Letters there were, oddly loving and funny. 'We'll get married next leave. Be ready.'

He survived the invasion itself. I got letters scribbled in haste, so funny it was hard to believe that they were written on the battlefield. Then a very sad one telling me how one of his old friends had been hit by a sniper's bullet and had died in his arms. Fortunately for his mother, Eddie's brother was still in England.

Life at home went on as usual, but we all waited for the B.B.C.'s Nine O'Clock News every night, with nervous intensity. The news reader reported the give-and-take of the invasion battles as if it had nothing to do with killing or dying. Not a hint was there of the further horrifying suffering inflicted on both German and Allied troops, all men of my generation, who died slowly, went mad under misdirected shelling or bombing, or to this day lie in hospital beds or are confined to wheelchairs. Not a word of those unseasoned conscripts who faced battle for the first time, civilians who had never killed before.

In July, British and Canadian troops bled the Germans, by drawing their reserves into the battles of Falaise and Caen. This enabled the Americans to sweep through the Germans' weakened defences, into the heart of France.

The British then got bogged down.

There were only four bridges across the River Orne on which Caen stood, and there is a limit, even under the best of circumstances, to the amount of traffic which can pass over a bridge in a given time, a point which was apparently mislaid in the group military mind. When the bridges became choked, the Germans saw their chance amid the all-enveloping dust and mix-up of vehicles. Many, many British and

Canadians died in the resultant chaos before the city of Caen fell to the Allies.

After the war, I saw the city before it had been rebuilt. It must have been a dreadful battle. Looking out over the rubble, from the top of a hill, stood, almost undamaged, the twin churches built by William the Conqueror and Matilda, his wife, in gratitude for his winning the Battle of Hastings and for the subsequent conquest of Britain. The British, I thought forlornly, had paid a terrible price to liberate the Conqueror's city.

I had caught, at the time of the invasion, a bad dose of flu and was subsequently confined to bed. An infection in my throat and ears followed and, without the help of sulpha drugs, took a long time to get better. It left me with more rheumatism in my legs. The doctor ordered a slow convalescence, while I gained strength.

I had got to the point where I was taking little walks up and down the road and then getting into bed immediately after tea, when, one evening, Father kindly brought the *Liverpool Echo* in to me, to read. He then retired to the sitting-room, which he regarded as his own particular room.

It was quite late and I first lit my bedside candle, then leisurely turned the pages of the paper.

Finally, I came to the section referred to by Liverpudlians as the Hatches, Matches and Dispatches. The Dispatches section was frighteningly long. Almost without thinking, I ran my finger down the names.

And there it was.

'No,' I whispered. 'No! Not him!'

Mother must have heard my cry, because she came running from the kitchen, her hands dripping.

'What is it?'

I lifted the paper towards her. 'It's Eddie.'

Then I turned my head into the pillow, so full of anguish that I could not speak, could not cry. I just wanted to die myself.

Mother was incredibly kind. She had never held me in her life and she did not now, but she stroked my head and whispered, rather helplessly, that everything would be all right after a little while.

In such a situation, words have no meaning, but one sometimes remembers them later on and is grateful for them. I was vaguely aware of other members of the family milling around the bedroom. But it was Mother who was left with the task of helping me.

With frantic, unleashed energy, I began to thrash around in the bed, like a butterfly skewered on a pin. Finally, I sat up, and said, 'I have to get up.'

I stumbled into my clothes, vests, pullovers, cardigan, the layers with which people in those days sustained themselves in icy homes.

While Mother watched me anxiously, I looked wildly round the confining room. 'I think I must go out, Mum – into the fresh air.'

'I'll come, too.'

'No, Mummy,' I told her gently, between gasps for air. 'I need to be by myself – very badly. I'll be all right.'

Mother did not try to deter me, though the rain was lashing the bedroom windowpanes, bubbling from the down-spouts, flooding our waterlogged district.

More clothes were pressed upon me, a second cardigan, a macintosh, rubber boots, gloves, an umbrella.

'Don't worry, Mum. I'll just walk for a little while. I'll be home soon.'

Putting up the umbrella, I dived out of the house, with no idea where I was going, only the desperate need to run away from my pain.

Despite the torrent of rain, it was better outside. Like an Indian about to die, I wanted to lie on the ground, to gain comfort from the feel of earth and grass. But deep puddles already glistened on our little lawn, and I sloshed down to the gate, pulled it open and went out.

Though weak from illness, the same weird energy carried me mile upon frantic mile. Through dear, familiar Meols, Hoylake and West Kirby, I strode without meeting a single other pedestrian – only a couple of shadowy vehicles with shaded lights.

'Eddie,' I cried, to the slashing, unheeding rain, 'Eddie, darling.'

At Caldy Hill, I faltered, and then slowly began to climb. At the top, there is a sandstone pillar, a marker for sailors using the Dee Estuary. Panting, I leaned on a wall nearby, to look out at an invisible sea. Any tiny glowing of the coming summer dawn was masked by the weeping clouds.

What was I going to do? How was I to assuage the tearing grief inside me? With one arm clutched across my stomach, the other holding the dripping umbrella, it was as if I had stumbled into a torturing, wet hell.

What instinct turned me homeward, I do not know, but back I went, some mechanical ability keeping me from tripping over the usual pedestrian hazards, as I stumbled through the dark.

As I entered the unlocked back door into the kitchen, Mother in her dressing-gown rose from her chair by the kitchen fire, which she had kept unusually high for my return. She looked old and haggard.

'You poor girl,' she said, and took the sheathed umbrella from me and put it to drip in the sink. I took off my macintosh, shook it in the lean-to shed which lay against the back door and then hung it, mechanically, over the door to dry. I was wet to the skin, like a bedraggled dog.

'Take your shoes off,' Mother ordered.

I did as I was told.

She helped me undress in front of the blazing fire and put on my nightgown. 'Now,' she said, 'I'm going to make you a really strong cup of tea and give you three aspirins, and you'll feel a little better in the morning.'

I could not speak. I felt that if I once opened my mouth, I would have hysterics. But it was as if she truly understood what was happening to me. This strange, bitter, violent woman was, for the first time in my memory, mothering me. Of course, I did not consider this at the time – I was immersed in shock. But I remembered it afterwards and forgave her much, in consequence of it.

Three cups of tea and three aspirins later, warmed by the fire, I said to Mother, 'I'll go to work tomorrow. Perhaps they'll have more news of him.'

She accepted this decision with a quiet nod, and drained the contents of the teapot into her cup.

Except for my dry sobs, we sat silently together, looking into the hot coals in the fire-grate.

Mother cleared her throat, and began to speak, at first hesitatingly, and then, when she saw she had caught my interest, with more confidence.

'You know, before the war, long before I met your father, I was engaged. He was the youngest of seven sons of a widowed lady, who had been left a cotton mill by her husband. In the first two years of the war, she lost all her sons in battle, except him. He was allowed to stay at home and run the business. His mother was an Indian lady, whom his father had met in India and brought home with him, so you can imagine he was very handsome. I loved him very much.

'One day, he was walking through the mill, when the floor above him collapsed under the weight of the machinery – and he was crushed to death.'

For a moment I was shaken out of my own suffering. 'Oh, Mum,' I cried in horror. 'How dreadful! How awful for you. And his poor mother?'

'She lived out the rest of her life in complete seclusion – cut herself off completely, except for a couple of old servants.'

'Oh, God!'

On Mother's face I glimpsed a dreadful look of abject despair, and then it was gone.

'I'm so sorry, Mum. I had no idea.'

She smiled slightly, and got up and collected the teacups and put them in the washing-up bowl, for attention in the morning.

After a couple of hours of deep sleep and an inadequate toilet, I was running along the cinder track beside the railway. Though it had stopped raining, my leg make-up and shoes were mired as I ran through the puddles, past the abandoned quarry and the market gardens. On the station, I piled into a crowded carriage with my girl friend, who had arrived earlier.

'Are you feeling quite well again?' she asked.

I jumped. Had she read the *Echo*, too? Then I realised that she was referring to my influenza bout, and that I would have to tell her about Eddie.

But not today, I thought, not today. I replied simply, 'Yes, thanks.'

'You look awful.'

'I feel weak.'

I hung on to a strap and swayed with other standing passengers, and let her talk, while I looked in my mind at the shattered pieces of my hopes. And, ever burning in the forefront of my mind, was the prayer that Eddie had died instantly.

# Chapter thirty-seven

That morning, I wept openly in the office, when Eddie's name was sadly mentioned. And, later, when I was seated in the steamy canteen with two of my colleagues, and faced a lunch I was sure would choke me, I asked my companions bitterly, 'Why did it have to be him? He was so bright and intelligent. Why didn't God take a fool like me, instead?'

In the ensuing silence, I played around with my meal. Then one of the men, a Methodist, said cautiously, 'Perhaps God has something special for you to do yet.'

It pulled me up short. I never forgot it. If I believed in Almighty God, then I must accept that He knew when my use in this world was ended, and would take me then, not before.

I held the speaker in great affection, and through sleepless, tossing nights and long, dreary days, his remark stayed with me.

He also mentioned that he had been to see Eddie's mother.

Eddie's mother? She probably did not even know I existed.

What should I do? What could I do?

For some days the matter was settled for me. My throat flared up with a new infection, and I took once more to my bed. A week later, however, though still weak, I returned to work and to the problem of Eddie's mother.

My mother had, seeing my grief, drawn up a truce regarding Eddie's character, but it was her opinion, she said, that Eddie's mother was probably not a very refined woman. I should stay away from her.

Refined or not, she was probably going through hell. So, armed with a bouquet of summer flowers begged from a neighbour's garden, I set out for the north end of Liverpool.

Eddie's home was much bigger than I had expected, a fine Victorian house set back from a quiet road. I walked up and down the pavement several times, before working up enough courage to open the handsome cast-iron gate, go slowly up the path, and ring the old-fashioned bell.

A tall, slender, elderly lady answered the door. Her face was pink-flushed as Eddie's had been, and Eddie's eyes stared down at me. She wore a black dress and a fine necklace of grey natural pearls.

'I'm Eddie's girl friend,' I said, in a trembling voice. Suppose he had had other girl friends besides the one he had asked to marry him.

She put out a welcoming hand. 'Oh, my dear,' she exclaimed. 'I'm so glad you've come. Come in.' She opened the door wide, and I stepped into a house not unlike the home I had left so precipitately when Father had gone bankrupt.

Wordlessly, I handed her the bouquet, and she buried her nose in it. When she looked up, there were tears running down her face.

I was led into a large drawing-room, furnished in good Edwardian taste, with Japanese flower-patterned wallpaper, unchanged, I guessed, since Mrs Parry had first moved into the house. Everything was extraordinarily well kept.

I must not cry, I warned myself. I have come to help.

Mrs Parry bent down to plug in an electric fire, though the day was far from cold. 'I'm so glad you've come,' she repeated. 'We didn't know how to find you, you know. Fred – that's Eddie's elder brother – told me about you, and we were nearly frantic with worry. You see, Eddie's things haven't been sent home yet, so we had no address.' Her voice broke, and for a moment she remained bent over the glowing electric fire. Then she laughed softly. 'Officially, I didn't know anything, of course, but I guessed from odd things Eddie let slip before he went back last time that something was in the wind. All Fred knew was that he had a girl he was very keen on, living in the Wirral.' She smiled up at me, and then straightened herself, and took a hanky from the sleeve of her dress and wiped away her tears.

'Well, now. Do sit down. I'll put the kettle on and we'll have a cup of tea.'

I sat down and smiled up at her, confidence returning. 'That would be lovely,' I assured her.

A dragon? A tartar? Really, Eddie! She was a fine, well-bred, northern lady, and she was being heart-warmingly kind. I loved her on sight, and continued to love her until her death. She provided for me a warmth and affection that Mother, even at her best, had been unable to give me.

'You're so like Eddie,' she would sometimes say. 'I can't get over it. I wish I had had a daughter like you.'

I think that in a vague way, she hoped that her burly elder son would take a fancy to me. Though we did become quite friendly, there was none of the natural attraction that there had been between Eddie and me. He did, however, eventually bring her a very sweet daughter-in-law.

She showed me Eddie's room and his books. She had the same ready sense of the ridiculous that Eddie had had, and she told me lots of funny stories about his various escapades.

When Eddie proposed to me, I accepted him on chance. But he knew what he was doing. I would have fitted into his life very well. Though he might swear like a docker and play tough, I knew now who had taught him the attitudes which had endeared him to me.

'Losing their father so young had a profound effect on both the boys,' Mrs Parry told me. 'I knew it but I could not do much about it. Without a father, it is harder to learn how a man should behave, and they were quite wild, and I was very worried about both of them. I used to lay down the law like a High Court judge! But it's surprising. In the last few years, they both settled down quite well. And then, of course, the war came . . .' She fell silent after such confidences, and I would hold her hand until she felt better. I did not know what else to do.

# Chapter thirty-eight

As the Allies advanced in Europe and Asia, we became impatient, and asked each other, 'Will it never end?' And when faced with a task we did not want to undertake, we would say, 'I'll do it after the war,' as if, by saying that, we would never actually have to do it.

Our family worried that, during this last lap of the conflict, we might lose either Alan or Brian. And we simply prayed that neither of them were sent to the East, because of the tales of Japanese atrocities.

The son of a friend of mine died of beating and starvation while doing forced labour for the Japanese, on the Burma Road. She was so stricken, when a scarred survivor came to tell her what had actually happened to her boy, that she was unable to speak or eat for several weeks, and lay in hospital being artificially fed like some poor suffragette.

Pictures of the death camps in Germany and Poland, taken as the Allies released the survivors, raised the hatred of the Germans, in Britain, to new heights.

Despite the feeling of the general public that the war would never end, government and business were planning for that happy day. A civil servant called William Beveridge had designed a plan to overhaul the entire health and welfare system of the country, and when, after the war, it was implemented, it changed the lives of almost every man, woman and child in the country. The Petroleum Board was preparing to dismember itself, and I was told, at the end of the Japanese war, that there would be a post for me with one of the companies.

I remember laughing, when I was told that the post was a pensionable one. After the atomic destruction of Hiroshima and Nagasaki, nobody expected to survive long enough to draw a pension. Long before that, another war would obliterate us.

Our tight little group in the Wages Department was restless. Some of the camaraderie began to wane, as faces new to many of us began to appear. Unfit men were being demobbed and returned to civilian life.

On 8th May, Churchill announced that the war in Europe was over, and someone took a picture of the girls in our department. We still looked young; yet in many ways we were old, just as our parents had been after World War I.

While the war still raged in the East against the Japanese, many people began to get married, to househunt without much hope – to look for peacetime employment.

I was twenty-five years old and, once again, my life was going to change. Like everybody else, I was tired to my very bones, and almost any effort seemed too much. I sat in the train, amid a very merrily drunk group of Air Force men who had been celebrating the victory, and wondered what to do with my life.

Though Mother had been very kind in helping me when Eddie was killed, like the leopard she still had her spots, and when I arrived home she was very cross at being left alone on a day of rejoicing. As I sat down to two shrivelled sausages and a small mound of potatoes, she asked fretfully, 'And what are you going to do?'

'Do you mean this evening?'

'Yes.'

'I thought I'd finish the dress for Mary.'

'Well, I hope she pays you for it. She'll be out of work soon – they won't want any munitions.'

I looked up quickly. She was right. My dressmaking business could shrink, even vanish, once properly trained dressmakers returned to their peacetime occupation. The girls for whom I had made so many dresses would never again earn such high wages as they had enjoyed in the war.

My salary had increased slowly during my time with the Petroleum Board, but I had not realised until recently how really low it was. I had tried to save a little by contributing to war savings bonds through payroll deductions, and had long ago given Mother the money for a set of artificial teeth. I do not know what she spent it on, but she never had any false teeth, and, once she had discovered that I could save, she had been merciless – and often successful – in squeezing extra money out of me.

Mother poured herself another cup of tea out of the pot I had made. She was nearly fifty, yet she looked like a very old woman. Her dyed, black hair contrasted strangely with a heavily lined face and toothless mouth. Her hands, like mine, were ruined by too much scrubbing of floors and rubbing of washing. She was running to fat, and her shoulders stooped. She did not seem to care much what happened to her, as long as she had cigarettes and cinema money.

As I listened to her monotonous, nagging voice, I thought, My God, I *must* pull myself together. I must try for a real career. Otherwise, in a few years' time, I'll be just like her.

It was a salutary idea. And at that moment, in quiet despair, afraid of being hurt again, I gave up all hope of marriage as an escape route. I would work and save for a home of my own.

In Liverpool, 8th May – V. E. Day – had been celebrated with street parties and dances, and it became a custom to give a street party for returning servicemen.

Kitchen tables were put end to end along the centre of the road, followed by almost every chair in the neighbourhood. Children had a great time making fancy dresses, while their mothers used precious rations to bake rock buns and scones. Hoarded tins of Spam and sardines were sacrificed to make sandwiches, and anything green was tossed into a salad. If anybody owned a piano, it was dragged on to the pavement, so that there could be music for singing and dancing. Otherwise, they made do with accordions or mouth organs. The local publicans were under great pressure to produce a barrel of beer. For years afterwards, one would come across brick walls with *Welcome home Joey* or *George* or *Henry*, splashed across it, in drippy, faded whitewash.

I never saw such a message painted for the Marys, Margarets, Dorothys and Ellens, who also served. It was still a popular idea that women did not need things. They could make do. They could manage without, even without welcomes. But these were the women who would give impetus to the feminist movement. At the time of demobilisation they did not realise it, but they were going to do a lot more marching.

The 15th August, 1945, was declared V. J. Day, the end of the war with Japan. The same six girls in our office had their photograph taken, this time with a returned soldier in the centre of the picture. How quaint we look, in our heavy utility shoes and our ill-fitting dresses. One of the six had been widowed and, like me, must begin again, one had a merchant seaman for a fiancé, mercifully spared, one was engaged to a civilian, and two were still fancy free. I smiled for the photographer, but I remember that I wanted to scream at the unfairness of life.

That night, I sat down at the kitchen table and wrote replies to every advertisement in the *Liverpool Echo* for secretaries.

Firms that had closed for the duration, or who had gone over to war work, now reopened, like crocuses in the sun. I had several replies, and accepted a post as personal secretary to an electrical engineer, at double my previous salary. It was the first step in a long climb which led me, eventually, into the packaging industry, a fascinating world for a woman to be in.

When I left the warm companionship of my friends in the Petroleum Board, I was stepping out blindly into a rapidly changing world.

I felt dreadfully alone.